Basics of Research Methods for Criminal Justice and Criminology

FOURTH EDITION

MICHAEL G. MAXFIELD
John Jay College of Criminal Justice, City University of New York

EARL R. BABBIE
Chapman University

CENGAGE
Learning®

Australia • Brazil • Mexico • Singapore • United Kingdom • United States

CENGAGE
Learning·

Basics of Research Methods for Criminal Justice and Criminology, **Fourth Edition**

Michael G. Maxfield and Earl R. Babbie

Product Director: Marta Lee-Perriard

Senior Product Manager: Carolyn Henderson Meier

Content Developer: Wendy Langerud, S4Carlisle Publishing Services

Product Assistant: Julia Catalano

Media Developer: Ting Jian Yap

Senior Marketing Manager: Kara Kindstrom

Senior Content Project Manager: Christy Frame

Managing Art Director: Andrei Pasternak

Senior Manufacturing Planner: Judy Inouye

Production Service: Anne Talvacchio, Cenveo Publisher Services

Text Researcher: Dharanivel Baskar, Lumina Datamatics

Copy Editor: Caroline Define

Text Designer: Brenda Carmichael, Lumina Datamatics

Cover Designer: Michael Cook

Cover Image: muratart/Shutterstock.com

Composition: Cenveo Publisher Services

Library of Congress Control Number: 2014955937

Student Edition:
ISBN: 978-1-305-26110-5

Cengage Learning
20 Channel Center Street
Boston, MA 02210
USA

Cengage Learning is a leading provider of customized learning solutions with office locations around the globe, including Singapore, the United Kingdom, Australia, Mexico, Brazil, and Japan. Locate your local office at **www.cengage.com/global**.

Cengage Learning products are represented in Canada by Nelson Education, Ltd.

To learn more about Cengage Learning Solutions, visit **www.cengage.com**.
Purchase any of our products at your local college store or at our preferred online store **www.cengagebrain.com**.

Printed in the United States of America
Print Number: 01   Print Year: 2015

About the Authors

Michael G. Maxfield is Professor of Criminal Justice at John Jay College, City University of New York. He is the author of numerous articles and books on a variety of topics, including victimization, policing, homicide, community corrections, and long-term consequences of child abuse and neglect. Working with students and colleagues at the John Jay College Research and Evaluation Center, Prof. Maxfield developed the evidence generation approach to applied justice research. He is editor of the *Journal of Research in Crime and Delinquency*.

Earl R. Babbie graduated from Harvard University before enlisting in the U.S. Marine Corps. He received his PhD from the University of California–Berkeley, and began teaching shortly thereafter. Credited with defining research methods for the social sciences, Dr. Babbie has written several texts, including the bestselling *The Practice of Social Research*.

To Max Jacob Fauth and Laine Ellen Fauth
To Suzanne Babbie

Contents

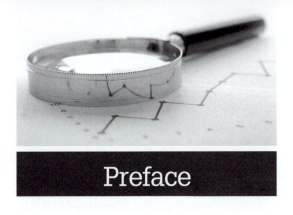

Preface

S ince the first edition of *Research Methods for Criminal Justice and Criminology* (RMCJC) was published in 1995, we have been delighted to hear comments from instructors who have used the text—and from a few who do not use it! Although it is always gratifying to learn of positive reactions, we have also listened to suggestions for revising the book through its seven editions. Some colleagues suggested trimming the text substantially to focus on the most important principles of research methods in criminal justice. Students and instructors are also increasingly sensitive to the cost of college texts.

As a result, we introduced *Basics of Research Methods for Criminal Justice and Criminology* about eight years ago. Our objective in producing that text was fivefold: (1) retain the key elements of the parent text; (2) concentrate on fundamental principles of research design; (3) appeal to a broad variety of teaching and learning styles; (4) retain salient examples that illustrate various methods; and (5) reduce less-central points of elaboration and the examples used to illustrate them. That proved to be more challenging than we initially thought. At one point, we were tempted to do something simple like drop two chapters, wrap the result in a soft cover, and declare what was left to be the basics. Fortunately that sentiment was reined in, and we pursued a more deliberate approach that involved planning from the ground up.

Basics is shorter, more concise, and focused on what we believe is the most central material for introductory courses in research methods. Rather than simply offering a truncated version of the full text, *Basics* has been crafted to appeal to those seeking a more economical alternative while retaining the big book's highly successful formula. Many instructors teaching shorter courses, or courses where students are better served by concentrating on basic principles of criminal justice research, have used the *Basics* edition. Others, especially instructors teaching introductory graduate courses, prefer the more extensive coverage offered in *RMCJC*.

Goals and Objectives

Criminal justice has always been a fascinating topic for students, partly because it is the stuff of news stories, fiction, and much popular entertainment. Criminal justice research goes behind and beyond the headlines to address important questions of *who, what, why,* and *how. Who* is involved as offender, victim, and justice professional? *What* are the nature and frequency of different kinds of crime and disorder problems, and what new problems are emerging? *Why* are incidents happening in particular places, and why are offenders involved in particular patterns of behavior? *How* are different kinds of offenses committed? *How* should justice agencies prevent and respond to problems of crime and safety?

Our primary goal in writing this edition is unchanged: to help students learn how to conduct research to answer these and related questions. Toward that end, certain principles have guided our revision of each edition of the text. Our intent is to:

- provide a careful description of the varied options for doing research in criminal justice.
- clarify and demystify what is traditionally a difficult subject for students at all levels.
- illustrate research methods with examples that are informative and interesting.
- incorporate new approaches that reflect methodological developments in the field.
- emphasize the application of criminal justice research to real-world problems and justice policy examples.
- bridge the gap between authors, instructors, and students by drawing on examples of our own research, especially research conducted with student colleagues.

Organization of the Text

The fourth edition of *Basics of Research Methods for Criminal Justice and Criminology* has 11 chapters, although chapter topics have changed slightly:

- Chapter 1, "An Introduction to Criminal Justice Inquiry," introduces research methods. Material in this chapter describes how social scientific inquiry differs from other ways of learning things. This chapter also advises students on how to select research topics, conduct a literature review, evaluate different kinds of Internet resources, and write a research proposal.
- Chapter 2, "Ethics and Criminal Justice Research," examines how research has the potential to harm subjects and the obligations of researchers to minimize the risk of such harm. Examples illustrate the range of ethical issues in justice research and the steps researchers take to address them.
- Chapter 3, "General Issues in Research Design," describes basic features of all research studies that have to be considered when planning a research project. These include causation, the time dimension, and different fundamental avenues for criminal justice inquiry.
- Chapter 4, "Concepts, Operationalization, and Measurement," considers these central topics. All research requires some sort of measurement, and this chapter examines its key elements. As an in-depth example of measurement, we describe different approaches to measuring crime—a fundamental dependent and independent variable in criminal justice research.
- Chapter 5, "Experimental and Quasi-Experimental Designs," examines how to plan research that has explanatory purposes. Research design involves a collection of building blocks that can be combined in different ways. We emphasize the flexibility of research designs, drawing on interesting and creative examples.

- Chapter 6, "Sampling," describes approaches to selecting subjects for research. We cover the two general categories of probability and nonprobability sampling, describing different subtypes in each category. The basics of probability theory are introduced as key principles underlying sampling and statistical significance.
- Chapter 7, "Survey Research," explores traditional survey research and other types of interviewing. Changes in technology continue to affect how surveys are conducted.
- Chapter 8, "Qualitative Interviewing," is new to this edition. The chapter describes different applications of qualitative and specialized interviewing. Earl and I are pleased that Amber Horning has joined us in writing this chapter, drawing on her own work and research by others to examine this family of data-gathering techniques.
- Chapter 9, "Field Observation," includes discussion of traditional approaches as well as more structured environmental surveys and related techniques. Examples illustrate the use of different approaches.
- Chapter 10, "Agency Records, Content Analysis, and Secondary Data," covers data extracted from administrative records as well as data series regularly collected by researchers and government agencies. Examples illustrate the wide range of research opportunities supported by data from different secondary sources.
- Chapter 11, "Evaluation Research and Problem Analysis," focuses on applied research that aims to improve criminal justice policy and practice. The chapter describes how problem analysis is increasingly used in justice agencies to reduce crime and related problems.

What's New in This Edition

In preparing this fourth edition, we stayed with what has proved to be a popular formula. But we have also responded to suggestions from several people—reviewers, colleagues, and instructors—who used earlier editions.

Qualitative Research

Many reviewers and instructors who use the book have suggested expanding coverage of qualitative research techniques. Although we have always included qualitative methods in our discussion of how to do research, a new chapter offers more depth in specialized interviewing and related field techniques. With contributions from Amber Horning, a PhD student at John Jay College of Criminal Justice, we present a new chapter on qualitative interviewing. Amber draws heavily on her own research studying pimps and other sex workers, mostly in New York City. Her work is fascinating and creative, offering excellent examples of how to do field work on sensitive topics with elusive subjects.

Amber's contributions also supplement our discussion of focus groups in criminological research, a topic Earl and I previously included in the chapter on survey research. What results is a new chapter that provides especially useful insights in doing field research on people engaged in illegal activities. Amber Horning's work also illustrates creative approaches to sampling and learning about hidden populations.

We are pleased that Amber Horning has joined us for this edition for many reasons. Among these is our continuing effort to include examples of student research. Amber's work involves extensive field presence in an urban environment; we feel she has conveyed much of that experience very nicely.

Opening Vignettes

A reviewer noted that the opening box, "Home Detention," in Chapter 1 was especially helpful in framing topics to be covered in the chapter. We agreed and have added similar boxes as chapter-opening vignettes. Some of these draw on recent research by former colleague Ronald Clarke and me, collaborating with graduate students at Rutgers University. Other opening vignettes describe research by former students or research on topics of recent popular interest. We have linked these with chapter themes and tried to add timely topics that will interest students.

The vignettes can be points of departure for class discussion. For example, the opening vignette in Chapter 3 applies criminal justice theory to the important applied topic of serial sex offenders. We especially like this example because it shows the very practical application of *theory*, something students sometimes assume is irrelevant, to an issue that receives much media attention at the expense of analytic thinking.

Expanded Examples of Student Research

Reviewers and colleagues have often commented on the use of examples from student research in earlier editions and in the larger text. We have included more of these throughout the book, many in featured boxes.

Highlighting student research serves different purposes. First, it amplifies what some colleagues call the "over-the-shoulder" tone of the text, in which readers feel they are experiencing more than just words on a printed page. Second, student research examples embody the kind of collaborative supervision that exists between students and faculty. Third, we have great familiarity with the details of work by our students. Such details are rarely described in published articles, and being able to report them adds behind-the-scenes information not readily available elsewhere. Finally, Earl and I believe the examples presented here are topical and inherently interesting to readers. Among the new examples in this edition are projects that address pimps and other sex workers, terrorism, sex offenders, auto theft, and an evaluation of a Cure Violence project in New York City.

Interpreting Data

Previous editions included a chapter on data analysis. The chapter's focus was always conceptual, introducing students to descriptive and inferential statistics, but focusing on the logic of data analysis. We have since learned that many instructors did not assign the chapter, largely because the requirements for criminal justice majors at most colleges and universities include separate courses on research design and statistics. As a result, and to make room for the new chapter on qualitative techniques, the chapter on interpreting data was dropped from this edition.

We have also made a variety of changes in each chapter:

- **Chapter 1** was extensively revised in the previous edition to provide an overview of criminal justice research the way it is commonly taught. This has been well received. On the advice of reviewers, we added material on how to evaluate the quality of information presented on different kinds of web pages.

- **Chapter 2** includes some new examples and updated material on working with offenders. Amber Horning's research on the ethical challenges of studying active pimps offers an excellent example of the special problems that criminal justice researchers sometimes face.

- **Chapter 3** expands discussion of qualitative and quantitative data. Following a reviewer's suggestion, we added material on units of analysis and the ecological fallacy. We also added a figure to illustrate inductive and deductive reasoning.

- **Chapter 4** adds a figure to illustrate levels of measurement, in response to a reviewer's suggestion. Discussion of the National Incident-Based Reporting System (NIBRS) is updated. We also offer a new example to illustrate criterion validity.

- **Chapter 5** begins with a vignette describing an experimental study of phishing. This experiment has generated quite a lot of interest in the ethics of online research. We've added a new example of a double-blind experiment in a correctional setting.

- **Chapter 6** expands discussion of snowball sampling, stemming from the new qualitative interviewing chapter.

- **Chapter 7** adds new examples, and updates information on the diminished use of telephone surveys. Other material was reorganized or deleted to reflect the revised treatment of qualitative interviews.

- **Chapter 8**, "Qualitative Interviewing," is new to this edition.

- **Chapter 9** includes several new examples of field observation and field research. Two of these, counting homeless and studying neighborhood conditions, illustrate ways to enhance the reliability of field observations. A box by former John Jay student Sheyla Delgado, writing with colleague Jeffrey Butts, describes creative approaches to sampling street populations and conducting field interviews.

- **Chapter 10** presents a new example of online data analysis using secondary data. We also followed suggestions from reviewers to expand discussion of the advantages of secondary data. The introductory vignette describes content analysis of terrorist recruitment materials seized by police in Turkey.

- **Chapter 11** briefly introduces evidence generation as a new type of applied research. This reflects my work with community-based organizations in New York City. Tinus Kruger contributes a fascinating new box on community-based crime analysis in South Africa. This illustrates how analytic techniques and mapping can be used in large undocumented settlements.

Learning Tools
Online Instructor's Manual

The instructor's manual contains a variety of resources to aid instructors in preparing and presenting text material in a manner that meets their personal preferences and course needs. It presents chapter-by-chapter suggestions and resources to enhance and facilitate learning.

Online Test Bank

The Test Bank contains multiple-choice and essay questions to challenge your students and assess their learning.

Cengage Learning Testing Powered by Cognero

The Test Bank also is available through Cognero, a flexible, online system that allows you to author, edit, and manage test bank content as well as create multiple test versions in an instant. You can deliver tests from your school's learning management system, your classroom, or wherever you want.

Online PowerPoints

These vibrant, Microsoft PowerPoint lecture slides for each chapter assist you with your lecture by providing concept coverage using images, figures, and tables directly from the textbook!

Acknowledgments

A number of students at the Rutgers University School of Criminal Justice offered advice, feedback, and contributions for this and earlier editions. Most have now moved on to their own academic careers as faculty or other researchers. I thank: Dr. Carsten Andresen (Travis County Department of Community Corrections and Supervision); Dr. Gisela Bichler (California State University–San Bernardino); Dr. Stephen Block (Central Connecticut State University); Dr. Sharon Chamard (University of Alaska); Dr. Niyazi Ekici (Turkish National Police); Dr. Shuryo Fujita (Farmingdale State College); Dr. Galma Jahic (Istanbul Bilgi University, Turkey); Dr. Jarret Lovell (California State University–Fullerton); Dr. Nerea Marteache (California State University–San Bernardino); Dr. Marie Mele; Dr. Nancy Merritt (National Institute of Justice); Dr. Melanie-Angela Neuilly (Washington State University); Dr. Dina Perrone (California State University–Long Beach); Dr. Gohar Petrossian (John Jay College of Criminal Justice); Dr. Stephen Pires (Florida International University); Dr. James Roberts (University of Scranton); Dr. William Sousa (University of Nevada–Las Vegas); Dr. Christopher Sullivan (University of Cincinnati); and Dr. Sung-suk Violet Yu (John Jay College of Criminal Justice).

With my move to John Jay College in 2010, I have enjoyed contributions and suggestions from new students: Amber Horning, Michelle Cubellis, Sheyla Delgado, Dr. Brittany Hayes (Sam Houston State University), Alana Henninger, Leonid Lantsman (U.S. Department of State), Cynthia-Lee Maragh, Dr. Bryce Peterson (Urban Institute), and Julie Viollaz. Special thanks to Dr. Jeffrey Butts, Director of the Research and Evaluation Center at John Jay College, for being a gracious colleague and host.

Finally, Earl and I are very grateful for the patient, professional assistance from developmental editor Wendy Langerud (S4Carlisle Publishing Services), production manager Anne Talvacchio (Cenveo Publisher Services), and the professionals at Cengage: Carolyn Henderson Meier, Christy Frame, and the entire book team.

Mike Maxfield

An Introduction to Criminal Justice Inquiry

What comes to mind when you encounter the word *science*? What do you think of when we describe criminal justice as a social science? For some people, science is mathematics; for others, it is white coats and laboratories. Some confuse it with technology or equate it with difficult courses in high school or college.

Science is, of course, none of these things per se, but it is difficult to specify exactly what science is. Scientists, in fact, disagree on the proper definition. Some object to the whole idea of social science; others question more specifically whether criminal justice can be a social science.

For the purposes of this book, we view science as a method of inquiry—a way of learning and knowing things about the world around us. Like other ways of learning and knowing about the world, science has some special characteristics. We'll examine these traits in this opening set of chapters. We'll also see how the scientific method of inquiry can be applied to the study of crime and criminal justice.

Part 1 lays the groundwork for the rest of the book by examining the fundamental characteristics and issues that make science different from other ways of knowing things. Chapter 1 begins with a look at native human inquiry, the sort of thing all of us have been doing all our lives. We'll also consider research purposes and the basics of how to design a research project.

Chapter 2 considers the ethics of social science research. The study of crime and criminal justice often presents special challenges with regard to ethics. We'll see that most ethical questions are rooted in two fundamental principles: (1) research subjects should not be harmed, and (2) their participation must be voluntary.

The overall purpose of Part One, therefore, is to construct a backdrop against which to view more specific aspects of research design and execution. By the time you complete the chapters in Part One, you will be ready to look at some of the more concrete aspects of criminal justice research.

CHAPTER 1

Criminal Justice and Scientific Inquiry

People learn about their world through a variety of methods, and they often make mistakes along the way. Science is different from other ways of learning and knowing. We'll consider errors people commonly make and how science tries to avoid them, different purposes of research, and principles for designing a research project.

Sexual Assault in Jails and Prisons

Responding to reports of sexual assault in prisons and jails, the Prison Rape Elimination Act became law in 2003. The act enhanced penalties for sexual violence in most detention facilities and required the Department of Justice to collect systematic data on the problem. The newspaper article, "County Misreports Data about Sexual Violence in Juvenile Jails," is an example of how sexual assault continues to be a problem in San Diego, California (Maass 2012). Researchers have conducted studies to better understand the problem and assess ways to reduce sexual violence.

Allen Beck and associates (2013) describe data collected from a sample of prisons and jails by the Bureau of Justice Statistics. They report that 4 percent of prison inmates and 3.2 percent of jail inmates were victims of sexual assault in the previous 12 months or since being admitted to the facility. Projecting those percentages to all prisons and jails nationwide produces an estimate of 88,500 adult victims. In addition, the researchers report that about 2.4 percent of prison inmates and 1.8 percent of those in jail had sexual contact with facility staff, often willingly.

Nancy La Vigne and other researchers from the Urban Institute (2011) describe their research on how to prevent sexual assault in jails. Working with three facilities, they described efforts to improve supervision of inmates and corrections officers, install surveillance cameras, and train corrections officers in crisis intervention. Based on their evaluation, La Vigne and associates recommended that jail administrators use a systematic process to assess problems in specific facilities, design changes that address those problems, and collect data to assess the effects of the new actions.

This example illustrates how researchers take steps to better understand the scope of a problem and then try different approaches to reduce it. The Urban Institute analysts went one step further in their efforts to train corrections officials to do their own applied research. Jail managers were consumers of research produced by La Vigne and associates and gained some of the skills needed to become producers of applied studies in their own facilities.

Introduction

Criminal justice professionals are both consumers and producers of research.

Spending a semester studying criminal justice research methodology may not be high on your list of "Fun Things to Do." Perhaps you are, or plan to be, a criminal justice professional, and you are thinking, "Why do I have to study research methods? When I graduate, I'll be working in probation (or law enforcement, or corrections, or court services), not conducting research! I would benefit more from learning about probation counseling (or police management, or corrections policy, or youth counseling)." Fair enough. But as a criminal justice professional or service provider, you will need to be a consumer of research. One objective of this book is to help you become an informed consumer of research.

For example, in the section "Two Realities," we will see how findings from one of the first experimental studies of policing appeared to contradict a traditional tenet of law enforcement—that a visible patrol force prevents crime. Acting as a consumer of research findings, a police officer, supervisor, or executive should be able to understand how that research was conducted and how the study's findings might apply in his or her department.

Most criminal justice professionals, especially those in supervisory roles, routinely review various performance reports and statistical tabulations. Countless research reports may now be found on the Internet. For example, the National Criminal Justice Reference Service (NCJRS) was established to archive and distribute research reports to criminal justice professionals and researchers around the world. Many such reports are prepared specifically to keep the criminal justice community informed about new research developments and may be downloaded from the NCJRS website (http://www.ncjrs.gov). An understanding of research methods can help decision makers critically evaluate such reports and recognize when methods are properly and improperly applied. The box titled "Home Detention" describes an example of how knowledge of research methods can help policy makers avoid mistakes.

Another objective of this book is to help you produce research. In other courses you take or in your job, you may become a producer of research. Probation officers sometimes test new approaches to supervising or counseling clients, and police officers try new methods of dealing with recurring problems. Many cities and states have a compelling need to evaluate services provided to offenders released from prison or jail. New York State, for example, began an initiative in 2012 to reform juvenile justice by closing secure detention centers in remote areas. Determining whether changes or existing programs are effective is an example of applied research. Police and other justice agencies are increasing pursuing evidence-based practice rooted in systematic research. As a result, justice professionals need to know not only how to interpret research accurately, but also how to produce accurate research.

What Is This Book About?

This book focuses on how we know what we know.

This book focuses on how we learn. Although you will come away from the book knowing many things you don't know right now, our primary purpose is to help you look at how you know things, not what you know.

HOME DETENTION

Home detention with electronic monitoring (ELMO) was widely adopted as an alternative punishment in the United States in the 1980s. The technology for this new sanction was made possible by advances in telecommunications and computer systems. Prompted by growing prison and jail populations, not to mention sales pitches by equipment manufacturers, criminal justice officials embraced ELMO. Questions about the effectiveness of these programs quickly emerged, however, and led to research to determine whether the technology worked. Comprehensive evaluations were conducted in Marion County (Indianapolis), Indiana. Selected findings from these studies illustrate the importance of understanding research methods in

general and the meaning of various ways to measure program success in particular.

ELMO programs directed at three groups of people were studied: (1) convicted adult offenders, (2) adults charged with a crime and awaiting trial, and (3) juveniles convicted of burglary or theft. People in each of the three groups were assigned to home detention for a specified time. They could complete the program in one of three ways: (1) successful release after serving their term, (2) removal due to rule violations, such as being arrested again or violating program rules, or (3) running away or absconding. The agencies that administered each program were required to submit regular reports to county officials on how many

(continued)

individuals in each category completed their home detention terms. The accompanying table summarizes the program-completion types during the evaluation study.

	Convicted Adults (%)	Pretrial Adults (%)	Juveniles (%)
Success	81	73	99
Rule violation	14	13	1
Abscond	5	14	0

These percentages, reported by agencies to county officials, indicate that the juvenile program was a big success; virtually all juveniles were successfully released.

Now consider some additional information on each program collected by the evaluation team. Data were gathered on new arrests of program participants and on the number of successful computerized telephone calls to participants' homes.

	Convicted Adults (%)	Pretrial Adults (%)	Juveniles (%)
New arrest	5	1	11
Successful calls	53	52	17

As the table shows, many more juveniles were arrested, and juveniles successfully answered a much lower percentage of telephone calls to their homes. What happened?

The simple answer is that the staff responsible for administering the juvenile program were not keeping track of offenders. The ELMO equipment was not maintained properly, and police were not visiting the homes of juveniles as planned. Because staff were not keeping track of program participants, they were not aware that many juveniles were violating the conditions of home detention. And because they did not detect violations, they naturally reported that the vast majority of young burglars and thieves completed their home detention successfully.

A county official who relied on only agency reports of program success would have made a big mistake in judging the juvenile program to be 99 percent successful. In contrast, an informed consumer of such reports would have been skeptical of a 99 percent success rate and searched for more information.

Source: Adapted from Maxfield and Baumer (1991) and Baumer, Maxfield, and Mendelsohn (1993).

Two Realities

Ultimately, we live in a world of two realities. Part of what we know could be called our *experiential reality*—the things we know from direct experience. If you dive into a glacial stream flowing down through the Canadian Rockies, you don't need anyone to tell you the water is cold; you notice that all by yourself. And if you step on a piece of broken glass, you know it hurts without anyone telling you. These are things you experience.

The other part of what we know could be called our *agreement reality*—the things we consider real because we've been told they're real, and everyone else seems to agree they are real. A big part of growing up in any society, in fact, is learning to accept what everybody around us "knows" to be true. If we don't know those same things, we can't really be a part of society. Ideas about gender, race, religion, and different nations that you learned

as you were growing up would fit in this category. We may test a few of these truths on our own, but we simply accept the great majority of them. These are the things that "everybody knows."

To illustrate the difference between agreement and experiential realities, consider preventive police patrol. The term *preventive* implies that when police patrol their assigned beats they prevent crime. Police do not prevent all crime, of course, but it is a commonsense belief that a visible, mobile police force will prevent some crimes. In fact, the value of patrol in preventing crime was a fundamental principle of police operations for many years. A 1967 report on policing for President Lyndon Johnson by the President's Commission on Law Enforcement and Administration of Justice (page 1) stated that "the heart of the police effort against crime is patrol.... The object of patrol is to disperse policemen in a way that will eliminate or reduce the opportunity for misconduct and to increase the probability that a criminal will be apprehended while he is committing a crime or immediately thereafter." This statement was not based on research, but on traditions that had been embraced by police departments for many years (National Research Council 2004, 20).

Seven years after the President's Commission repot, the Police Foundation, a private research organization, published results from an experimental study that presented a dramatic challenge to the conventional wisdom on police patrol. Known as the Kansas City Preventive Patrol Experiment, this study compared police beats with three levels of preventive patrol: (1) control beats, with one car per beat; (2) proactive beats, with two or three cars per beat; and (3) reactive beats, with no routine preventive patrol. After almost one year, researchers examined data from the three types of beats and found no differences in crime rates, citizen satisfaction with police, fear of crime, or other measures of police performance (Kelling et al. 1974).

Researchers and law enforcement professionals alike were surprised by these findings. For the record, the Kansas City researchers never claimed to have proved that preventive patrol had no impact on crime. Instead, they argued that police should work more closely with community members and that routine patrol might be more effective if combined with other strategies that used police resources in a more thoughtful way. Subsequent research has supported that last statement. An experimental study of foot patrol in Philadelphia found that assigning foot patrol officers based on analytically identified "hot spots" of crime produced a 23 percent reduction in violent crime after 12 weeks (Ratcliffe et al. 2011).

Additional studies conducted in the 1970s cast doubt on other fundamental assumptions about police practices. A quick response to crime reports made no difference in arrests, according to a research study in Kansas City (Van Kirk 1977). And criminal investigation by police detectives rarely resulted in an arrest (Greenwood 1975).

We mention these examples not to attack routine law enforcement practices but to show that systematic research on policing has illustrated how traditional beliefs—as examples of agreement reality—can be misleading. Simply increasing the number of police officers on patrol does not reduce crime because police patrol often lacks direction. Faster response time to calls for police assistance does not increase arrests because there is often a long delay between the time when a crime occurs and when it is reported to police. Clever detective work seldom solves crimes: investigators get most of their information from reports prepared by patrol officers, who, in turn, get their information from victims and witnesses.

Traditional beliefs about patrol effectiveness and other routine practices are examples of agreement reality, a "reality" that a number of people still embrace. In contrast, the research projects that produced alternative views about each enforcement practice represent experiential reality. These studies are examples of **empirical**[1] research, the production of knowledge based on experience or observation. In each case, researchers conducted studies of police practices and based their conclusions on observations and experience. Empirical research is a way of learning about crime and criminal justice, and explaining how to conduct empirical research is the purpose of this book.

The Role of Science

Science offers an approach to both agreement reality and experiential reality. Scientists have certain criteria that must be met before they will agree on the reality of something they haven't personally experienced. In general, an assertion must have both *logical* and *empirical* support: it must make sense, and it must agree with actual observations. For example, why do earthbound scientists accept the assertion that it's cold on the dark side of the moon? First, it makes sense because the surface heat of the moon comes from the sun's rays. Second, scientific measurements made on the moon's dark

---

1. Words set in boldface are in the glossary at the end of the book.

side confirm this logical explanation. So scientists accept the reality of things they don't personally experience—they accept an agreement reality—but they have special standards for doing so.

More to the point of this book, however, is that science offers a special approach to the discovery of reality through personal experience. Epistemology is the science of knowing; methodology (a subfield of epistemology) might be called the *science of finding out*. This book focuses on criminal justice **methodology**—how social scientific methods can be used to better understand crime and criminal justice policy. To understand scientific inquiry, let's first look at the kinds of inquiry we all do each day.

Personal Human Inquiry

Everyday human inquiry draws on personal experience and secondhand authority.

Most of us would like to be able to predict how things are going to be for us in the future. We seem quite willing, moreover, to undertake this task using causal and probabilistic reasoning. First, we generally recognize that future circumstances are somehow caused or conditioned by present ones. For example, we learn that getting an education will affect what kind of job we have later in life, and that running stoplights may result in an unhappy encounter with an alert traffic officer. As students, we learn that studying hard will result in better examination grades.

Second, we recognize that such patterns of cause and effect are *probabilistic* in nature: the effects occur more often when the causes occur than when the causes are absent—but not always. Thus, as students, we learn that studying hard produces good grades in most instances, but not every time. We recognize the danger of ignoring stoplights without believing that every such violation will produce a traffic ticket.

The concepts of causality and probability play a prominent role in this book. Science makes causality and probability more explicit, providing techniques for dealing with them more rigorously than does casual human inquiry.

However, our attempts to learn about the world are only partly linked to personal inquiry and direct experience. Another, much larger, part comes from the agreed-on knowledge that others give us. This agreement reality both assists and hinders our attempts to find out things for ourselves. Two important sources of agreement reality—tradition and authority—deserve brief consideration here.

Tradition

Each of us is born into and inherits a culture made up, in part, of firmly accepted knowledge about the workings of the world and the values that guide our participation in it. We may learn from others that planting corn in the spring will result in the greatest assistance from the gods, that the circumference of a circle is approximately 3.14 times its diameter, or that driving on the left side of the road (in the United States) is dangerous.

Tradition, in this sense, has some clear advantages for human inquiry. By accepting what everybody knows, we are spared the overwhelming task of starting from scratch in our search for regularities and understanding. Knowledge is cumulative, and an inherited body of information and understanding is the jumping-off point for the development of more knowledge.

Authority

Despite the power of tradition, new knowledge appears every day. Throughout life, we learn about new discoveries and understandings from others. However, our acceptance of this new knowledge often depends on the status of the discoverer. For example, you are more likely to believe a judge who declares that your next traffic violation will result in a suspension of your driver's license than your parents when they say the same thing.

Like tradition, authority can both help and hinder human inquiry. We do well to trust the judgment of individuals who have special training, expertise, and credentials in a matter, especially in the face of contradictory arguments on a given question. At the same time, inquiry can be greatly hindered by the legitimate authorities who err within their own special province. Biologists, after all, do make mistakes in the field of biology, and biological knowledge changes over time. Criminal justice research sometimes yields mistaken results, and we are wise to accept research findings with caution even if they come from experts. The box titled "Arrest and Domestic Violence" illustrates the problems that can result when criminal justice policy makers accept too quickly the results from criminal justice research.

Inquiry is also hindered when we depend on the authority of experts speaking outside their realm of expertise. Consider a political or religious leader, lacking any biochemical expertise, who declares climate change to be a myth. The advertising industry plays heavily on this misleading use of authority by having popular athletes discuss the value of various sports drinks and having movie stars evaluate the performance of automobiles.

ARREST AND DOMESTIC VIOLENCE

In 1983, preliminary results were released from a study on the deterrent effects of arrest in cases of domestic violence. The study reported that male abusers who were arrested were less likely to commit future assaults than offenders who were not arrested. Conducted by researchers from the Police Foundation, the study used rigorous experimental methods adapted from the natural sciences. Criminal justice scholars generally agreed that the research was well designed and executed. Public officials were quick to embrace the study's findings that arresting domestic violence offenders deterred them from future violence.

Here, at last, was empirical evidence to support an effective policy in combating domestic assaults. Results of the Minneapolis Domestic Violence Experiment were widely disseminated, in part because of aggressive efforts by the researchers to publicize their findings (Sherman and Cohn 1989). The attorney general of the United States recommended that police departments make arrests in all cases of misdemeanor domestic violence. Within five years, more than 80 percent of law enforcement agencies in U.S. cities adopted arrest as the preferred way of responding to domestic assaults (Sherman 1992a, 2).

Several things contributed to the rapid adoption of arrest policies to deter domestic violence. First, the experimental study was conducted carefully by highly respected researchers. Second, results were widely publicized in newspapers, in professional journals, and on television programs. Third, officials could understand the study, and most believed that its findings made sense. Finally, mandating arrest in less serious cases of domestic violence was a straightforward and politically attractive approach to a growing problem.

Sherman and Berk (1984), however, urged caution in uncritically embracing the results of their study. Others urged that similar research be conducted in other cities to check on the Minneapolis findings (Lempert 1984). Recognizing the need for more research, the U.S. National Institute of Justice sponsored more experiments—known as replications—in six other cities. Not everyone was happy about the new studies. For example, a feminist group in Milwaukee opposed the replication in that city because it believed that the effectiveness of arrest had already been proved (Sherman and Cohn 1989, 138).

Results from the replication studies brought into question the effectiveness of arrest policies. In three cities, no deterrent effect was found in police records of domestic violence. In other cities, there was no evidence of deterrence for longer periods (6 to 12 months), and in three cities, researchers found that violence actually escalated when offenders were arrested (Sherman 1992a, 30). For example, Sherman and associates (1992, 167) report that in Milwaukee "the initial deterrent effects observed for up to thirty days quickly disappear. By one year later [arrests] produce an escalation effect." Arrest works in some cases but not in others. In responding to domestic assaults, as in many other cases, it's important to carefully consider the characteristics of offenders and the nature of the relationship between offender and victim.

After police departments throughout the country embraced arrest policies following the Minneapolis study, researchers were faced with the difficult task of explaining why initial results must be qualified. Arrest seemed to make sense; officials and the general public believed what they read in the papers and saw on television. Changing their minds by reporting complex findings was more difficult.

Both tradition and authority, then, are double-edged swords in the search for knowledge about the world. Simply put, they provide us with a starting point for our own inquiry, but they may lead us to start at the wrong point or push us in the wrong direction.

Errors in Personal Human Inquiry

Everyday personal human inquiry reveals a number of potential biases.

Aside from the potential dangers of relying on tradition and authority, we often stumble when we set out to learn for ourselves. Let's consider some of the common errors we make in our own casual inquiries and then look at the ways science provides safeguards against those errors.

Inaccurate Observation

The keystone of inquiry is observation. But quite frequently we fail to observe things right in front of us or mistakenly observe things that aren't so. Do you recall what your instructor was wearing on the first day of this class? If you had to guess now, what are the chances you would be right?

In contrast to casual human inquiry, scientific observation is a conscious activity. Simply making observations in a more deliberate way helps to reduce error. If you had gone to the first class meeting with a conscious plan to observe and record what your instructor was wearing, you would have increased your chances of accuracy.

In many cases, using both simple and complex measurement devices helps to guard against inaccurate observations. Suppose that you had taken photographs of your instructor on the first day. The photos would have added a degree of precision well beyond that provided by unassisted human memory.

Overgeneralization

When we look for patterns among the specific things we observe around us, we often assume that a few similar events are evidence of a general pattern.

The tendency to overgeneralize is probably greatest when there is pressure to reach a general understanding, yet overgeneralization also occurs in the absence of pressure. Whenever overgeneralization does occur, it can misdirect or impede inquiry.

Imagine you are a rookie police officer newly assigned to foot patrol in an urban neighborhood. Your sergeant wants to meet with you at the end of your shift to discuss what you think are the major law enforcement problems on the beat. Eager to earn favor with your supervisor, you interview the manager of a convenience store in a small shopping area. If the manager mentions vandalism as the biggest concern, you might report that vandalism is the main problem on your beat, even though other business owners and area residents believe that drug dealing contributes to the neighborhood problems of burglary, street robbery, and vandalism. Overgeneralization leads to misrepresentation and simplification of the problems on your beat.

Criminal justice researchers guard against overgeneralization by committing themselves in advance to a sufficiently large sample of observations and by being attentive to how representative those observations are. The **replication** of inquiry provides another safeguard. Replication means repeating a study, checking to see whether similar results are obtained each time. The study may also be repeated under slightly different conditions or in different locations. The box titled "Arrest and Domestic Violence" describes an example of why replication can be especially important in applied research.

Selective Observation

Another danger of overgeneralization is that it may lead to selective observation. Once we have concluded that a particular pattern exists and have developed a general understanding of why, we will be tempted to pay attention to future events and situations that correspond with the pattern and to ignore those that do not. Racial, ethnic, and other prejudices are reinforced by selective observation.

Research plans often specify in advance the number and kind of observations to be made as a basis for reaching a conclusion. For example, if we wanted to learn whether women are more likely than men to support long prison sentences for sex offenders, we would plan to make a specified number of observations on that question. We might select a thousand people to be interviewed. Even if the first 10 women supported long sentences and the first 10 men opposed them, we would continue to interview everyone selected for the study and record each observation. We would base our conclusion on an analysis of all the observations, not just those first 20 respondents.

Illogical Reasoning

People have various ways of handling observations that contradict their judgments about the way things are. Surely one of the most remarkable creations of the human mind is the maxim about the exception that proves the rule, an idea that makes no sense at all. An exception can draw attention to a rule or to a supposed rule, but in no system of logic can it prove the rule it contradicts. Yet we often use this pithy saying to brush away contradictions with a simple stroke of illogic.

What statisticians call the *gambler's fallacy* is another illustration of illogic in day-to-day reasoning. According to this fallacy, a consistent run of good or bad luck is presumed to foreshadow its opposite. An evening of bad luck at poker may kindle the belief that a winning hand is just around the corner; many a poker player has stayed in a game too long because of that mistaken belief. Conversely, an extended period of good weather may lead us to worry that it is certain to rain on our weekend picnic.

Ideology and Politics

Crime is, of course, an important social problem, and a great deal of controversy surrounds policies for dealing with crime. Many people feel strongly one way or another about the death penalty, gun control, and long prison terms as approaches to reducing crime. There is ongoing concern about racial bias in police practices and sentencing policies. Being tougher on sex offenders has become a favorite topic of state legislatures. Ideological or political views on such issues can undermine objectivity in the research process. Criminal justice professionals may have particular difficulty separating ideology and politics from a more detached, scientific study of crime.

Criminologist Samuel Walker (1994, 16) compares ideological bias in criminal justice research to theology: "The basic problem … is that faith triumphs over facts. For both liberals and conservatives, certain ideas are unchallenged articles of faith, almost like religious beliefs that remain unshaken by empirical facts."

Most of us have our own beliefs about public policy, including policies for dealing with crime. The danger lies in allowing such beliefs to distort how research problems are defined and how research results are interpreted. The scientific approach to the study of crime and criminal justice policy guards against, but does not prevent, ideology and theology from coloring the research process. In empirical research, so-called articles of faith are compared with experience.

Purposes of Research

We conduct criminal justice research to serve various purposes.

Criminal justice research serves many purposes. Explaining associations between things such as police patrol and crime levels is one of those purposes; others include exploration, description, and application. Although a given study can have several purposes, it is useful to examine them separately because each has different implications for how we structure research.

Exploration

Much research in criminal justice is conducted to explore a specific problem, known as **exploratory research**. A researcher or official may be interested in a crime or criminal justice policy issue about which little is known. Or perhaps an innovative approach to mentoring in juvenile justice has been tried in some jurisdiction, and the researcher wishes to determine how common such practices are in other cities or states. An exploratory project might collect data on a measure to establish a baseline with which future changes will be compared.

For example, heightened concern with bullying might prompt efforts to estimate the level of bullying in high schools. How many reports are made to high school teachers? Do parents complain that their children have been subject to intimidation at school? Does bullying take different forms when the targets are male or female? Are gay, lesbian, and bisexual students particular targets? Are students suspected of bullying involved in delinquency? Does bullying have an effect on school attendance? These are examples of research questions intended to explore different aspects of the problem of bullying. Exploratory questions may also be formulated in connection with how parents and schools respond to the problem. How many schools have created special anti-bullying education programs? Are services available to victims? Can cyber-bullying be reduced by installing special applications on smart phones?

Description

A key purpose of many criminal justice studies is to describe the scope of the crime problem or policy responses to the problem. In **descriptive research**, a researcher or public official observes and then describes what was observed. Criminal justice observation and description, methods grounded in the social sciences, tend to be more accurate than the casual observations people may make about how much crime there is or how violent teenagers are today. Descriptive studies are often concerned with counting or documenting observations; exploratory studies focus more on developing a preliminary understanding about a new or unusual problem.

Descriptive studies are frequently conducted in criminal justice. The Federal Bureau of Investigation has compiled Uniform Crime Reports (UCR) since 1930. UCR data are routinely reported in newspapers and widely interpreted as accurately describing crime in the United States. For example,

2012 UCR figures (Federal Bureau of Investigation 2013a) showed that California had the highest rate of auto theft (443.2 thefts per 100,000 residents) in the nation and Vermont had the lowest (69.5 per 100,000 residents).

Descriptive studies in criminal justice have other uses. A researcher may attend meetings of neighborhood anticrime groups and observe their efforts to organize block watch committees. These observations form the basis for a case study that describes the activities of neighborhood anticrime groups. Such a descriptive study might present information that officials and residents of other cities can use to promote such organizations themselves. Or consider research by Copes, Hochstetler, and Cherbonneau (2012) in which they describe how carjackers use different techniques to overcome victim resistance.

Explanation

A third general purpose of criminal justice research is to explain things. Reporting that urban residents have generally favorable attitudes toward police is a descriptive activity, but reporting *why* some people believe that police are doing a good job while other people do not is an example of **explanatory research**. Similarly, reporting why California has the highest auto-theft rate in the nation is explanation; simply reporting auto-theft rates for different states is description. A researcher has an explanatory purpose if he or she wishes to know why the number of 14-year-olds involved in gangs has increased, as opposed to simply describing changes in gang membership.

Application

Researchers also conduct criminal justice studies of an applied nature. **Applied research** stems from a need for facts and findings with specific policy implications. Another purpose of criminal justice research, therefore, is its application to public policy. We can distinguish two types of applied research: evaluation and policy/problem analysis.

Applied research is often used to evaluate the effects of specific criminal justice programs. Determining whether a program designed to reduce burglary actually had the intended effect is an example of evaluation. In its most basic form, evaluation involves comparing the goals of a program with the results. If one goal of increased police foot patrol is to reduce fear of crime, then an evaluation of foot patrol might compare levels of fear before and after increasing the number of police officers on the beat on foot. In most cases, evaluation research uses social scientific methods to test the results of a program or policy change.

The second type of applied research is the analysis of general justice policies and more specific problems. What would happen to court backlogs if we designated a judge and prosecutor who would handle only drug-dealing cases? How many new police officers would have to be hired if a department shifted to community policing? These are examples of *what-if* questions addressed by policy analysis. Policy analysis is different from other forms of criminal justice research primarily in its focus on future events. Rather than observing and analyzing current or past behavior, policy analysis tries to anticipate the future consequences of alternative actions.

Similarly, justice organizations are increasingly using techniques of problem analysis to study patterns of cases and devise appropriate responses. Problem-oriented policing is perhaps the best-known example, in which crime analysts work with police and other organizations to examine recurring problems. Ron Clarke and John Eck (2005) have prepared a comprehensive guide for this type of applied research.

Our brief discussion of distinct research purposes is not intended to imply that research purposes are mutually exclusive. Many criminal justice studies have elements of more than one purpose. Suppose you want to examine the problem of bicycle theft at your university. First, you need some information that describes the problem of bicycle theft on campus. Let's assume your research finds that thefts from some campus locations have declined but that there was an increase in bikes stolen from racks outside dormitories. You might explain these findings by noting that bicycles parked outside dorms tend to be unused for longer periods of time and that there is more coming and going among bikes parked near classrooms. One

option to further reduce thefts would be to purchase more secure bicycle racks. A policy analysis might compare the costs of installing the racks with the predicted savings resulting from a reduction in bike theft.

Incidentally, the Center for Problem-Oriented Policing has published an extremely useful guide on the problem of bicycle theft (Johnson, Sidebottom, and Thorpe 2008). In addition to its substantive value, this guide is an example of applied research that can be conducted and used by justice professionals. Visit the website http://www.popcenter.org for more information and examples.

How to Design a Research Project

Designing research requires planning several stages, but the stages do not always occur in the same sequence.

We've now seen how casual human inquiry can set us up for making mistakes, and we have summarized basic research purposes. But what if you were to undertake a research project yourself? Where would you start? Then where would you go? How would you begin planning your research? College courses on research methods in criminal justice often require students to design a research project. The rest of this chapter covers the basics of planning research and writing a proposal.

Every project has a starting point, but it is important to think through later stages, even at the beginning. Figure 1.1 presents a schematic view of the social scientific research process. Think of this as a sort of map that provides an overview of the whole process before we launch into the details of particular components of research.

The Research Process

At the top of the diagram in Figure 1.1 are interests, ideas, theories, and new programs—the possible beginning points for a line of research. The letters (*A, B, X, Y,* and so forth) represent concepts such as deterrence or burglary. Thus, you might

FIGURE 1.1 The Research Process

have a general interest in finding out why the threat of punishment deters some but not all people from committing crimes, or you might want to investigate how burglars select their targets. Question marks in the diagram indicate that you aren't sure things are the way you suspect they are. We have represented a theory as a complex set of relationships among several concepts (*A, B, E,* and *F*).

The research process might also begin with an idea for a new program. Imagine that you are the director of a community-based organization that provides tutoring for students of incarcerated parents and want to see how writing skills develop as a result. Because you have taken a course on criminal justice research methods, you decide to design an evaluation of the new program before trying it out. The research process begins with your idea for the tutoring program.

Notice the movement back and forth among these several possible beginnings, represented by the arrows between the top boxes. An initial interest may lead to the formulation of an idea, which may fit into a larger theory, and the theory may produce new ideas and create new interests. Or your understanding of some theory may encourage you to consider new policies.

To make this discussion more concrete, let's take a specific research example. Suppose you are concerned about the problem of sexual assault on your campus and you have a special interest in learning more about how other students view the issue and what they think should be done about it. Going a step further, let's say you have the impression that students are especially concerned about the problem and how college officials are addressing it. Further, given the passage of the Campus Sexual Violence Elimination Act in 2013, you recognize that the scope and nature of sexual assault are not well understood, in general as well as on college campuses (National Research Council 2013). The source of this idea might be your own interest after being a student for a couple of years. You might develop the idea while reading about violent crime in a course you are taking. Perhaps you recently read stories about sexual violence and alleged cover-up attempts (Steinhauer 2014). Or maybe some combination of factors makes you want to learn more about campus crime.

Considering the research purposes discussed earlier in this chapter, your research will be mainly exploratory. You probably have descriptive and explanatory interests as well: How much of a problem is sexual violence crime on campus? Are students especially concerned about sexual assault in certain settings? Are some students more worried about the problem than others? Why? What do students think would be effective ways to address sexual assault on campus?

Getting Started

To begin pursuing your interest in student concerns about violent crime, you undoubtedly will want to read something about the issue. You might begin by finding out what research has been done on sexual assault and campus crime generally. Items posted on a campus website might provide information about crimes that occurred recently. In addition, you will probably want to talk to people, such as other students, college officials, or campus police officers. These activities will prepare you to handle various decisions about research design. As you review the research literature, you should make note of how other researchers approached the problem and consider whether the same designs will meet your research objective.

What is your objective, by the way? It's important that you are clear about that before you design your study. Do you plan to write a paper based on your research to satisfy a course requirement or as an honors thesis? Is your purpose to gain information that will support an argument for improvements in efforts to protect students from sexual assault? Do you want to write an article for the campus newspaper or blog?

Usually, your objective for undertaking research can be expressed in a report. The website for this book includes information that will help you with the organization of research reports. We recommend that you make an outline of such a report as the first step in the design of any project. You should be clear about the kinds of statements you will want to make when the research is complete. Here are two examples of such statements: "X percentage of State U students believe that sexual assault is a big problem on campus," and "Female students living off campus are more likely than females living in dorms to feel that emergency phones should be installed near buildings where evening classes are held." Although your final report may not look much like your initial image of it, outlining the planned report will help you make better decisions about research design.

Conceptualization

We often talk casually about criminal justice concepts such as deterrence, recidivism, crime prevention, community policing, and child abuse, but it is necessary to specify what we mean by these concepts to do research on them. Chapter 4 will examine this process of **conceptualization** in depth. For now, let's see what it might involve in our hypothetical example.

If you are going to study student concerns about violent crime, you must first specify what you mean by *concern about sexual assault*. This ambiguous phrase can mean different things to different people. Campus police officers are concerned about sexual assault because that is part of their job. Students may have two kinds of concerns. On the one hand, they might be concerned about sexual assault in much the same way they are concerned about other social problems, such as immigration, health care, and the global economy. They recognize these issues as problems society must deal with, but they don't feel that the issues affect them directly; we could specify this concept as *general concern about sexual assault*. On the other hand, students, especially women, may feel that sexual assault does affect them directly, and they express some fear about the possibility of being a victim; let's call this *fear for personal safety*.

Of course, you need to specify all the concepts you wish to study. If you want to study the possible effect of concern about sexual assault on student behavior, you'll have to decide whether you want to limit your focus to specific precautionary behavior, such as keeping doors locked, or general behavior, such as going to classes and parties or dating.

Choice of Research Method

A variety of methods are available to the criminal justice researcher. Each method has strengths and weaknesses, and certain concepts are more appropriately studied by some methods than by others.

A survey is the most appropriate method for studying both general concern and fear of personal sexual assault victimization. You might interview students directly or ask them to fill out an online questionnaire. As we'll see in Chapter 7, surveys are especially well suited to the study of individuals' attitudes and opinions. Thus, if you wish to examine whether students who are concerned about sexual assault are more likely to believe that college officials are not doing enough about the problem compared to students who are not concerned, then a survey is a good method.

Other methods described later in this book may be appropriate. Through content analysis (discussed in Chapter 10), you might examine postings on a campus blog and analyze what the writers believe should be done to reduce sexual assault. Field research (see Chapter 9), in which you observe behavior at parties, will help you understand social contexts that are believed to heighten risk of sexual violence. Or you might study official complaints made to police and college administrators. This may be difficult given the profoundly sensitive topic of sexual attacks. As you read Part Three, you'll see how other research methods might be used to study this topic. Often the best study design is one that uses more than one research method, taking advantage of their different strengths.

Operationalization

Having specified the concepts to be studied and chosen the research method, you now must develop specific measurement procedures. **Operationalization**, discussed in Chapter 4, refers to the concrete steps, or operations, used to measure specific concepts.

If you decide to use a survey to study concern about sexual assault, your operationalization will take the form of questionnaire items. You might operationalize concern about sexual assault with the question: "How worried are you about the risk of being sexually attacked while on campus or at college-related social events?" This could be followed by boxes indicating the possible answers "Worried" and "Not worried." Student attitudes about ways of responding to reported cases of assault could be operationalized with the item "Listed below are different actions that might be taken in response to a report of sexual assault. Beside each description, indicate whether you favor or oppose the action described." This could be followed by several different actions, with "Favor" and "Oppose" boxes beside each.

Population and Sampling

In addition to refining concepts and measurements, decisions must be made about whom or what to study. The population for a study is that group about whom we want to be able to draw conclusions. Groups are usually made up of people, but we may wish to study a group of drug rehabilitation clinics. We are almost never able to study all the members of the population that interests us, so we often sample subjects for study. Chapter 6 describes methods for selecting samples that adequately reflect the whole population that interests us. Notice in Figure 1.1 that decisions about population and sampling are related to decisions about the research method to be used.

In the study of concern about sexual assault, the relevant population is the student population of your college. As you'll discover in Chapter 6, however, selecting a sample requires you to be more specific than that. Will you include part-time as well as full-time students? Students who live on campus, off campus, or both? Many such questions must be answered in terms of your research purpose. In a study of concern about sexual assault, you might consider limiting your population to female students. If you're more interested in attitudes about preventing sexual violence, you will want to be sure that your study population includes faculty, campus officials, and others who are thought to be possible resources for prevention.

Observations

Having decided what to study, among whom, and by what method, you are ready to make observations—to collect empirical data. The chapters of Part Three, which describe various research methods, discuss the different observation methods appropriate to each.

For a survey of concern about sexual violence, you would probably prepare an electronic questionnaire and e-mail a link to the questionnaire to a sample selected from the student body. You might also have a team of interviewers conduct the survey over the telephone. The relative advantages and disadvantages of these and other possibilities are discussed in Chapter 7.

Analysis

We manipulate the collected data for the purpose of drawing conclusions that reflect on the interests, ideas, and theories that initiated the inquiry. Notice in Figure 1.1 that the results of your analyses feed back into your initial interests, ideas, and theories. In practice, this feedback may initiate another cycle of inquiry. In the study of student concern about sexual violence, the analysis phase will have both descriptive and explanatory purposes. You might begin by calculating the percentage of students who are very concerned about the problem.

Moving beyond simple description, you might examine the opinions of different subsets of the student body: men versus women; freshmen, sophomores, juniors, seniors, and graduate students; and students who live in dorms versus off-campus apartments. You might then conduct some explanatory analysis to make the point that students who live in off-campus apartments are least satisfied with how college officials respond to reports of sexual assault.

Application

The final stage of the research process involves using the research you've conducted and the conclusions you've reached. To start, you will probably want to communicate your findings so that others will know what you've learned. You will usually prepare some kind of written report. Perhaps you will make oral presentations in class or at a professional meeting. Or you might create a web page that presents your results. Other students will be interested in hearing what you have learned about sexual assault on campus.

Your study might also be used to actually do something about campus safety. Drawing on a summary of prevention strategies prepared by the Centers for Disease Control and Prevention, you might recommend hot-spot mapping of reported incidents and creating bystander intervention programs (Centers for Disease Control and Prevention 2014, 4). Prevention programs might be launched in dormitories if residents are more concerned about sexual violence than students who live in other types of housing.

Thinking About Research Problems

One of the most important, yet surprisingly difficult, parts of the research process is specifying and framing your interest in a particular problem or question.

What are you interested in understanding? Surely you have several questions about crime and possible policy responses. Why do some juvenile gangs sell drugs whereas others steal cars? Why do particular neighborhoods near campus seem to have higher rates of burglary? How often are guns found in stop-and-frisk operations? Do sentencing policies discriminate against minorities? Do cities with gun control laws have lower murder rates? Is burglary more common in single-family homes or apartment buildings? Are sentences for rape more severe in some states than in others? Are mandatory jail sentences more effective than license suspension in reducing repeat drunk-driving offenses? Think for a while about the kinds of questions that interest and concern you.

To give you ideas about the many possible subjects for research, here are topics of papers written by students in the first class Michael Maxfield taught at John Jay College in fall 2010:

- Risk assessment in juvenile parole hearings★
- The effect of religion and culture on attitudes about suicide
- Determining the extent to which arrest frequency is associated with substance addiction and mental illness

- Links between domestic violence and indirect spouse abuse after separation★★
- An exploratory study of pimps in Atlantic City, New Jersey★
- An experimental study of attitudes toward sex offenders in Spain★★★
- Whether sexual abuse by Catholic priests is a product of sexual preference or situational factors
- Community disorganization and crime on Native American lands[2]

In most cases, researchers find themselves reworking or clarifying research problems as they learn more about a topic. That was the case for students in Maxfield's class. The student studying pimps was surprised to learn that only a minority of prostitutes in Atlantic City had anything like the classic worker/manager relationship with a pimp. That led to reframing the research to begin by classifying the different ways prostitutes worked with pimps and others playing pimplike roles.

You're advised to begin with your own interests and experiences and then learn more about what research has been done. For example, the third topic listed above was examined by a student with considerable experience in correctional settings. She began with her observation that people arrested frequently for minor offenses often seem driven more by substance abuse and mental health problems than by any overt criminal intent. The student then conducted research to learn more about existing research on jail populations, and she revised her topic as she read more of the research literature.

Students sometimes have difficulty narrowing interests to researchable questions. We are all concerned about crime and justice problems to some degree, but our casual interests can be misleading. Reading research about crime and justice problems is a good way to get ideas about research topics and to see how social science addresses problems that are treated more casually in popular literature. The box "Getting Ideas about Research Questions" offers more advice in this regard.

2. Those topics marked with ★ led to completed dissertations; ★★ signals completed dissertations and published articles; and ★★★ marks a completed dissertation, published articles, and the winner of the European Society of Criminology Young Criminologist Award.

GETTING IDEAS ABOUT RESEARCH TOPICS

Many people will have some idea what sort of research question they're interested in, no matter how general the idea may be. Even so, it can be difficult for beginning researchers to get started. Here are some tips for finding and fleshing out preliminary ideas about research topics.

Do an Internet Search, but Use Specialized Tools

For example, type this phrase into a Google search panel: "sex offender residency restrictions." In May 2014 this entry produced an estimated 146,000 results that included mass media stories, links to legislation, and many other types of sites. Then type the same phrase into a Google Scholar search panel (go to http://scholar.google.com). In May 2014 this yielded about 280 results of scholarly books and articles on the topic. Reading examples of these, or mass media stories for that matter, will give you ideas about how to begin research on sex offender residency restrictions.

Replicate an Existing Study

Berenson and Appelbaum (2011) examined where sex offenders lived in two New York counties. They were interested in laws that required sex offenders to live a minimum distance from places like schools and other public facilities, as well as the effects that such laws have on housing choices for sex offenders. Two findings were noteworthy. First, 73 to 97 percent of existing housing units in the two counties were off-limits to sex offenders because they were too close to specified facilities. Second, and a consequence of the first finding, most sex offenders living in the two counties were in violation of the restrictions. What about in your city or county? Since data on where sex offenders live is widely available, you could conduct a similar kind of study in a different place.

Follow Up on Recommendations for Further Research

Many research articles and books conclude by describing how subsequent research can add to knowledge. So if you find an article interesting, you might get an idea from the authors' suggestions for further research. For example, White and Loeber (2008) examined links between bullying in school, placement in special education programs, and later involvement in serious delinquency. They found that later delinquency often followed bullying, regardless of placement in special education programs. Their research was based on interviews over a period of years with students in Pittsburgh, Pennsylvania schools. Near the end of their article, they recommend that future research use systematic observations of behavior in different types of school activity (page 393). If you were interested in the problem of bullying or violence in middle schools, reading articles that report research on the topic could give you ideas about designing your own study.

Ask Your Professor

If one of the requirements for your research methods course is to write a research proposal or actually do some research, you should find out what topics are of special interest to your instructor. This does not mean you should engage in idle flattery. Instead, think of your instructor as both an expert and a professional scholar, someone who is probably doing research for a book, scholarly article, or dissertation. Your professor is an expert in what research might need to be done in a particular area. So don't hesitate to ask for ideas. Be sure use focused questions, such as: "What sorts of topics are you interested in?" That's better than asking something like: "Can you give me some ideas? I don't know where to begin."

Reviewing the Literature

Researchers begin a research project with a review of the literature.

Research should be seen as an extension of what has previously been learned about a particular topic. A review of the literature will tell you what's already known and not known. In most cases, you should organize your search of the literature around the key concepts you wish to study. Alternatively, you may want to study a certain population: corrections officers, sex offenders, drug counselors, computer hackers, and so forth. In any case, you'll identify a set of terms that represent your core interests.

Conducting a literature review has become both much easier and much more challenging with the expansion of information and search tools on the Internet. It's easier in the sense that much information can be accessed through the Internet without having to visit bricks-and-mortar libraries. Most colleges and universities now have online access to academic journals. Reports by government agencies and private organizations are readily available to anyone with access to the web.

Reviewing what others have found about a problem has become more difficult largely for the same reason: it's easy to access a seemingly endless supply of documents. This has produced a related problem of how to sort through all the information, separating research findings from the demented ramblings of ideologues and everything in between. After providing guidelines on how to find relevant literature, we'll suggest some cautionary strategies.

General Strategies

Doing a literature review is basically a process of accumulating, sorting through, and synthesizing information. We all do this every day in different, usually informal ways. Doing a literature review for research is more systematic and deliberate, just like the research process in general. It's best to keep notes of articles, books, websites, or other things as you review them. Also keep in mind that research literature accumulates; research studies usually build on previous studies, as we noted in the box "Getting Ideas about Research Topics."

Getting Started Start with a book or an article that deals with your topic and expand from there. We'll call this your source document. Expanding can mean going both backward, consulting readings cited in your source document, and forward, in which you find later research that is based on your source document. For example, if you're interested in terrorism, you might read the book *Outsmarting the Terrorists* by Ronald Clarke and Graeme Newman (2006). In conducting your literature review, you would read the selected references shown in the book's bibliography.

But you would also be interested in later research that expands on what Clarke and Newman wrote in 2006. One of the best ways to do this is to use the website Google Scholar (http://scholar.google.com).

Type "clarke newman outsmarting" in the search box, and one of the first references that pops up should be their book. In May 2014 this search showed that 170 subsequent publications had cited the book. Clicking on "cited by 170" produces a list of these publications, together with links to further information about the books or journals that cite Clarke and Newman. In this way, you can find out about more current research that's been published since your source document. For example, Cynthia Lum and colleagues (2013) apply some of the "outsmarting principles" to their study of fairness in passenger screening at airports.

Being Selective Sources like Google Scholar offer a built-in quality control by limiting your search to academic journals and related publications. However, you may want to find other types of materials, such as government reports, or studies published by other types of organizations. Ronald Clarke and Phyllis Schultze offer a useful warning and guideline: "Unlike scholarly books and journal articles, websites are seldom reviewed or refereed. You need to be critical of the information you use when it comes to the Web, because anyone can make a website that looks expert. In general, rely more heavily on those sites sponsored by colleges and universities, government agencies, and professional organizations" (Clarke and Schultze 2005, 24).

Some college or university libraries provide more detailed suggestions on how to evaluate information you discover in your research. For example, the Meriam Library at California State University Chico (2010) describes evaluation criteria referred to as the "CRAAP Test":

- Currency: Information timeliness
- Relevance: Does the information apply to your specific topic?
- Authority: The source of the information
- Accuracy: Is the information based on fact or opinion?
- Purpose: Why does the information exist? Why is it presented?

Another useful guide is an online tutorial prepared by the teaching library at the University of

California Berkeley (University of California Berkeley Library 2014). See especially the advice on how to sort out different domains and how to check out the authenticity of a named author.

Even the fabled National Security Agency (NSA) has gotten into the act, with their publication, *Untangling the Web: A Guide to Internet Research* (National Security Agency 2007). Approved for public release six years after the 12th edition had been completed, this 600+ page guide lists general-purpose and specialized tools. Much has changed since the guide's publication, but the NSA authors offer timeless advice on how to think about search strategies and combine terms in productive ways.

Using a Library Although it is no longer necessary to visit a physical library to access many published research materials, libraries and librarians remain critical resources for research. Librarians can help you develop strategies for searching the literature and evaluating the different sources you find. Clarke and Schultze offer excellent advice on how to use different types of libraries. For research on crime and justice, the Don M. Gottfredson Library of Criminal Justice at Rutgers University, under the direction of Phyllis Schultze, is the best single resource available anywhere in the world, with unmatched physical and online resources. Visit the library through the World Criminal Justice Library Electronic Network at http://andromeda.rutgers.edu/~wcjlen/WCJ/.

How to Read Scholarly Research

You don't read a social research report the same way you'd read a novel. You can, of course, but it's not the most effective approach. Journal articles and books are laid out somewhat differently, so here are some initial guidelines for reading each.

Reading a Journal Article In most journals, each article begins with an abstract. Read it first. It should tell you the purpose of the research, the methods used, and the major findings. The abstract serves two major functions. First, it gives you a good idea as to whether you'll want to read the rest of the article. If you're reviewing the literature for a paper you're writing, the abstract tells you whether that particular article is relevant. Second, the abstract establishes a framework within which to read the rest of the article. It may raise questions in your mind regarding method or conclusions, thereby creating an agenda to pursue in your reading.

After you've read the abstract, you might go directly to the summary and/or conclusions at the end of the article. That will give you a more detailed picture of what the article is all about. Jot down any new questions or observations that occur to you.

Next, skim the article, noting the section headings and any tables or graphs. You don't need to study any of these things in your skimming, though it's fine to review anything that catches your attention. By the end of this step, you should start feeling familiar with the article. You should be pretty clear on the researcher's conclusions and have a general idea of the methods used in reaching them.

If you decide to carefully read the whole article, you'll have a good idea of where it's heading and how each section fits into the logic of the whole article. Keep taking notes. Mark any passages you think you might like to quote later on. After carefully reading the article, it's a good idea to skim it quickly one more time. This way you get back in touch with the forest after having focused on the trees.

If you want to fully grasp what you've just read, find someone else to explain it to. If you're doing the reading in connection with a course, you should have no trouble finding someone willing to listen. However, if you can explain it coherently to someone who has no prior contact with the subject matter, you'll know you have an absolute lock on the material.

Reading a Book-Length Report The approach for articles can be adapted to reading a book-length report, sometimes also called a research monograph. These longer research reports cover the same basic terrain and roughly the same structure. Instead of an abstract, the preface and opening chapter of the book lay out the purpose, method, and main findings of the study. The preface is usually written more informally and so may be easier to understand than an abstract.

As with an article, it's useful to skim through the book, getting a sense of its organization, its use of tables and graphs, and its main findings. You should come away from this step feeling somewhat familiar with the book. Take notes as you go along, writing down things you observe and questions that are raised.

As you settle in to read the book more carefully, you should repeat this same process with each chapter. Read the opening paragraphs to get a sense of what's to come and then skip to the concluding paragraphs for the summary. Skim the chapter to increase your familiarity with it, and then read more deliberately, taking notes as you go.

It's sometimes okay to skip portions of a scholarly book, but this depends on your purpose in reading it in the first place. Perhaps only a few portions of the book are relevant to your research. However, if you are interested in the researcher's findings, you must pay some attention to the methods used (e.g., who was studied, how, and when?) to be able to judge the quality of the conclusions offered by the author.

The Research Proposal

Research proposals describe planned activities and include a budget and time line.

If you undertake a research project—an assignment for this course, perhaps, or even a major study funded by the government or a research foundation—you will probably have to provide a research proposal describing what you intend to accomplish and how. We'll conclude this chapter with advice on how you might prepare such a proposal. As we do this, think of the research proposal as another way to get an overview of the research process.

Elements of a Research Proposal

Some funding agencies have specific requirements for a proposal's elements, structure, or both. For example, the National Institute of Justice (NIJ) describes a range of funding opportunities together with what should be included in research proposals (http://www.nij.gov/funding/Pages/current.aspx? status=current). Your instructor may also have certain requirements for a research proposal you are to prepare in this course. Here are some basic elements that should be included in almost any research proposal.

Problem or Objective What exactly do you want to study? Why is it worth studying? Does the proposed study contribute to our general understanding of crime or policy responses to crime? Does it have practical significance? If your proposal describes an evaluation study, then the problem, objective, or research questions may already be specified for you. For example, in its request for research on violent victimization in Native American communities, the NIJ asked that proposals describe how they would address certain topics (National Institute of Justice 2014, 5):

- Provide tested measures of violence and victimization among tribal youth.
- Develop improved collection procedures for self-report data from tribal youth.

In most cases, however, you will specify the research problem or objective.

Literature Review As we described in the previous section, research begins by reviewing what others have said about your topic.

Research Questions What specific questions will your research try to answer? Given what others have found, as stated in your literature review, what new information do you expect to find? It's useful to view research questions as a more specific version of the problem or objective described earlier. Then, of course, your specific questions should be framed in the context of what other research has found.

Subjects for Study Whom or what will you study in order to collect data? Identify the subjects in general terms, and then specifically identify who (or what) are available for study and how you will reach them. Is it appropriate to select a sample? If so, how will you do that? If there is any possibility that your research will have an impact on those you study, how will you ensure that they are not harmed by the research? Finally, if you will be interacting directly with human subjects, you will probably have to include a consent form, as we describe in Chapter 2.

Measurement What are the key variables in your study? How will you define and measure them? Do your definitions and measurement methods duplicate (which is okay, incidentally) or differ from those of previous research on this topic?

Data Collection Methods How will you actually collect the data for your study? Will you observe behavior directly or conduct a survey? Will you undertake field research, or will you focus on the reanalysis of data already collected by others? Criminal justice research often includes more than one such method.

Analysis Briefly describe the kind of analysis you plan to conduct. Spell out the purpose and logic of your analysis. Are you interested in precise description? Do you intend to explain why things are the way they are? Will you analyze the impact of a new program? What possible explanatory variables will your analysis consider, and how will you know whether you've explained the program impact adequately?

References Be sure to include a list of all materials you consulted and cited in your proposal. Formats for citations vary. Your instructor may specify certain formats or may refer you to specific style manuals for guidelines on how to cite books, articles, and web-based resources.

Schedule It is often appropriate to provide a schedule for the various stages of research. Even if you don't do this for the proposal, do it for yourself. If you don't have a time line for accomplishing the stages of research and keeping track of how you're doing, you may end up in trouble.

Budget If you are asking someone to give you money to pay the costs of your research, you will need to provide a budget that specifies where the money will go. Large, expensive projects include budgetary categories such as personnel, equipment, supplies, and expenses (such as travel, copying, and printing). Even for a more modest project you will pay for yourself, it's a good idea to spend some time anticipating any expenses involved: office supplies, photocopying, computer disks, telephone calls, transportation, and so on.

As you can see, if you are interested in conducting a criminal justice research project, it is a good idea to prepare a research proposal for your own purposes, even if you aren't required to do so by your instructor or a funding agency. If you are going to invest your time and energy in such a project, you should do what you can to ensure a return on that investment.

Knowing Through Experience: Summing Up and Looking Ahead

Empirical research involves measurement and interpretation.

This chapter introduced the foundation of criminal justice research: empirical research, or learning through experience. Doing scientific research in criminal justice is different from the ordinary ways we learn about things because ordinary modes of inquiry have some built-in limits. The coming chapters describe how science tries to overcome such limits and biases.

We also considered the different purposes we may have in mind for conducting criminal justice research, ranging from exploration to examining links between policy action and justice problems.

Our advice on how to design a research project will be useful in two respects. First, it can serve as an annotated outline of what a typical research report would include, a guide for preparing a research report or proposal for this course. Second, Figure 1.1 and our discussion of how to design a research project offer an introduction and overview to later chapters.

Finally, it is helpful to think of criminal justice research as organized around two basic activities: measurement and interpretation. Researchers measure aspects of reality and then draw conclusions about what their measurements mean. All of us are observing all the time, but *scientific measurement* refers to something more deliberate and rigorous. Parts Two and Three of this book describe ways of structuring observations to produce more deliberate, rigorous measures.

The other key to criminal justice research is interpretation. Much of interpretation is based on data analysis, which is introduced in Part Four. More generally, however, interpretation very much depends on how observations are structured, a point we will encounter repeatedly.

As we put the pieces together—measurement and interpretation—we are in a position to describe, explain, or predict something. And that is what social science is all about.

SUMMARY

- Knowledge of research methods is valuable to criminal justice professionals as consumers and producers of research.

- The study of research methods is the study of how we know what we know.

- Inquiry is a natural human activity for gaining an understanding of the world around us.

- Much of our knowledge is based on agreement rather than direct experience.

- Tradition and authority are important sources of knowledge.

- Empirical research is based on experience and produces knowledge through systematic observation.

- In day-to-day inquiry, we often make mistakes. Science offers protection against such mistakes.

- Whereas people often observe inaccurately, science avoids such errors by making observation a careful and deliberate activity.

- Sometimes we jump to general conclusions on the basis of only a few observations. Scientists avoid overgeneralization through replication.

- Scientists avoid illogical reasoning by being as careful and deliberate in their thinking as in their observations.

- The scientific study of crime guards against, but does not prevent, ideological and political beliefs influencing research findings.

- Different research purposes are exploratory, descriptive, explanatory, and applied.

- The research process is flexible, involving different steps that are best considered together. The process usually begins with some general interest or idea.

- A careful review of previous literature is an essential part of the research process.

- A research proposal provides an overview of why a study will be undertaken and how it will be conducted. It is a useful device for planning and is required in some circumstances.

KEY TERMS

These terms are defined in the chapter where they are set in boldface and can also be found in the glossary at the end of the book.

applied research, p. 11	empirical, p. 6	methodology, p. 7
conceptualization, p. 15	explanatory research, p. 11	operationalization, p. 15
descriptive research, p. 11	exploratory research, p. 10	replication, p. 9

REVIEW QUESTIONS AND EXERCISES

1. Review the common errors of personal inquiry discussed in this chapter. Find a mass media or blog article about crime that illustrates one or more of those errors. Discuss how methods of social science might be applied to avoid these errors.

2. Briefly describe examples of descriptive research and applied research about bullying in public schools. What sorts of things would be measured in descriptive and applied research on bullying?

3. Often things we think are true and supported by considerable experience and evidence turn out not to be true, or at least not true with the certainty we expected. Criminal justice seems especially vulnerable to this phenomenon, perhaps because crime and criminal justice policy are so often the subjects of mass and popular media attention. If news stories, movies, and TV shows all point to growing sex trafficking, cyber-crime, or gang-related violence, it is easy to assume that these are real problems identified by systematic study. Choose a criminal justice topic or claim that is currently prominent in news stories or entertainment. Then visit the Bureau of Justice Statistics website (http://www.bjs.gov). Search the website for publications or data that provide information about the problem.

CHAPTER 2

Ethics and Criminal Justice Research

We'll examine some of the ethical considerations that must be taken into account, along with the scientific ones, in the design and execution of research. We'll consider different types of ethical issues and ways of handling them.

Ethics and Research with Pimps

by Amber Horning

Human trafficking of women for sex work is a criminal justice topic that has attracted considerable attention in news reports and popular culture. It is also widely reported that young American-born children, often runaways, are coerced into sex work by predatory pimps. Here's an example from a Cleveland newspaper:

> Eric Turnstone warned the buyer that the next time he made a sale to her, he'd charge a lot more. But that day in 2010 he settled for $300, saying it would at least give him some pocket change. What Turnstone sold, inside a Starbucks in Cleveland's Warehouse District, was a 16-year old girl. Yes, that's correct. He *sold* a girl—to a madam in the commercial sex industry…. [I]ncreasingly, pimps are coercing vulnerable teens into the sex trade. They flatter the girls by telling them they're pretty, develop their trust and entice them to leave their families. (Bernstein 2012, emphasis in original)

Mass media accounts typically describe exploitation and sexual slavery. The problem is real of course, but criminal justice research has revealed that the situation is more complex. In their study of sex trafficking in Asia, researchers Ko-Lin Chin and James Finckenauer (2012) interviewed female sex workers in 10 cities in Asian counties and the United States. Among other things, they found that women generally knew they would be sex workers in other countries, and as many as 40 percent of women interviewed

in China had worked in prostitution before leaving the country.

The image of pimps as exploiters who use violence and threats to coerce sex workers is similarly oversimplified. A paper that I wrote with Anthony Marcus and colleagues (2012) describes some of our findings in two years of ethnographic research in New York City and Atlantic City, New Jersey. Among other things, we learned that adolescents become involved in sex work for many reasons, and relationships between females and pimps acting as "market facilitators" can be complex. Also, I recently completed a year-long project that involved interviewing former and current sex-market facilitators or pimps in Harlem. I'll have more to say about this work in later chapters. Here I note some of the ethical questions that come up in conducting research on the commercial sex market.

When recruiting and interviewing people from hard-to-reach populations, the first issue was assuring them that the interview was confidential. Those currently pimping were particularly cautious, and in a few cases, they were even worried that I was an undercover police officer. Besides the actual assurance of confidentiality, subjects may also be assured of this based on how they are recruited, whether they are asked to give oral versus written consent, and where the interviews take place.

For the pimp project in Harlem, I drew on a few contacts in the community to identify people to interview. One contact grew up in the area, and another was a regular fixture in the community.

(continued)

They endorsed us as legitimate researchers to their friends, acquaintances, and sometimes even strangers. Our contacts hung around during the interviews, which assured potential subjects that the situation was safe. Contacts were essential for establishing the kind of trust necessary for this type of research.

The ethical principle of voluntary participation can be tricky in research on criminal behaviors or lifestyles. We had to work carefully with our institutional review board. For example, it's customary to have subjects sign a document indicating that they agree to participate in the research. Because the people we interviewed were hesitant to sign anything, we used a type of verbal consent.

Location played a role in establishing trust. I conducted a number of interviews outside around housing projects in Harlem, and inside two nonprofit organizations. I used empty office space in one of the nonprofits, and there wasn't yet any furniture in these offices, with the exception of a few chairs. Further, there were tangled wires sticking out of the ceiling and a phone that occasionally rang. One subject asked us outright if this was a sting operation; questions like this never arose when the interviews were outdoors (which is where most of the interviews took place).

We asked our subjects to use fake names when discussing their sex workers, their friends, and themselves. I told them that if a question made them uncomfortable that they could skip it. For the pimp project, none of the subjects asked to skip a question, but they sometimes edited their own stories, especially when prior arrests/convictions or gang affiliations came up in conversation, saying things like, "I am in a gang, but I don't wanna say which one."

Interviews with sex workers and pimps may reveal sensitive information about trauma, violence, other crime, and prior arrests/convictions. It can also be difficult to verify whether someone is an adult or juvenile. Interviewees may lie about their age, and you cannot ask hard-to-reach populations for identification; you have to trust them. This can be tricky, because research on juveniles requires special protections.

Interviewees can also be enticed by monetary incentives, especially if they are in need of money. We paid subjects $20 to $30 per interview. Despite popular images of pimps living the high life, this was rare among those we encountered; many of them were struggling financially. Interviewees from disenfranchised communities may not qualify as vulnerable by institutional review board standards, but may be essentially vulnerable, and researchers should keep this in mind.

Finally, many ethical issues in criminal justice research are concerned with protecting vulnerable populations. Our subjects were vulnerable in multiple, complex ways. Working in the commercial sex market, they engaged in illegal behavior that was often intertwined with other illegal markets. We suspect that some were juveniles, but could not verify ages. Many subjects lived and worked in communities troubled by violence and drug markets.

As you read about research ethics in this chapter, think about how my research with pimps and sex workers raises questions about ethics. Also consider how research should be structured to comply with basic principles of ethics. What sorts of protection should be provided to subjects? Who should determine whether those protections are adequate? How should they do that?

Introduction

Despite our best intentions, we don't always recognize ethical issues in research.

Most of this book focuses on scientific procedures and constraints. We'll see that the logic of science suggests certain research procedures, but we'll also see that some scientifically "perfect" study designs are not feasible, because they would be too expensive or take too long to execute. Throughout the book, we'll deal with workable compromises.

Before we get to scientific and practical constraints on research, it's important to explore another essential consideration in doing criminal justice research in the real world—ethics. Just as certain designs or measurement procedures are impractical, others are constrained by ethical problems.

All of us consider ourselves ethical—not perfect perhaps, but more ethical than most of humanity. The problem in criminal justice research—and probably in life—is that ethical considerations are not always apparent to us. As a result, we often plunge into things without seeing ethical issues that may be obvious to others and even to ourselves when they are pointed out. Our excitement at the prospect of a new research project may blind us to obstacles that ethical considerations present.

Any of us can immediately see that a study that requires juvenile gang members to demonstrate how they steal cars is unethical. You'd speak out immediately if we suggested interviewing people about drug use and then publishing what they said in the local newspaper. But, as ethical as we think we are, we are likely to miss the ethical issues in other situations—not because we're bad, but because we're human.

Ethical Issues in Criminal Justice Research

A few basic principles encompass the variety of ethical issues in criminal justice research.

In most dictionaries and in common usage, ethics is typically associated with morality, and both deal with matters of right and wrong. But what is right and what is wrong? What is the source of the distinction? Depending on the individual, sources vary from religion to political ideology to pragmatic observations of what seems to work and what doesn't.

Webster's New World Dictionary (4th ed.) is typical among dictionaries in defining **ethical** as "conforming to the standards of conduct of a given profession or group." Although the relativity embedded in this definition may frustrate those in search of moral absolutes, what we regard as moral and ethical in day-to-day life is no more than a matter of agreement among members of a group. And, not surprisingly, different groups have agreed on different ethical codes of conduct. If someone is going to live in a particular society, it is extremely useful to know what that society considers ethical and unethical. The same holds true for the criminal justice research "community."

Anyone preparing to do criminal justice research should be aware of the general agreements shared by researchers about what's proper and improper in the conduct of scientific inquiry. Ethical issues in criminal justice can be especially challenging because our research questions frequently address illegal behavior that people are anxious to conceal. This is true of offenders and, sometimes, people who work in criminal justice agencies.

The sections that follow explore some of the more important ethical issues and agreements in criminal justice research. Our discussion is restricted to ethical issues in research, not in policy or practice. Thus, we will not consider such issues as the morality of the death penalty, acceptable police practices, the ethics of punishment, or codes of conduct for attorneys and judges. If you are interested in substantive ethical issues in criminal justice policy, consult Jocelyn Pollock (2012) for an introduction.

No Harm to Participants

Weighing the potential benefits from doing research against the possibility of harm to the people being studied—or harm to other people—is a fundamental ethical dilemma in all research. For example, biomedical research can involve potential physical harm to people or animals. Social research may cause psychological harm or embarrassment in people who are asked to reveal information about themselves. Criminal justice research has the potential to produce both physical and psychological harm, as well as embarrassment. Although the likelihood of physical harm may seem remote, it is worthwhile to consider possible ways it might occur.

Harm to subjects, researchers, or third parties is possible in field studies that collect information from or about persons engaged in criminal activity; this is especially true for field research. For example, studies of drug crimes may involve locating and interviewing active users and dealers. Scott Jacques and Richard Wright (2008) studied active drug sellers in Atlanta and St. Louis, recruiting subjects by spreading the word through various means. Collecting such information from active criminals presents at least the possibility of violence against research subjects by other drug dealers.

Potential danger to field researchers should also be considered. For instance, Peter Reuter and associates (1990) selected their drug-dealer subjects by consulting probation department records. The researchers recognized that sampling persons from different Washington, D.C., neighborhoods would have produced a more generalizable group of subjects, but they rejected that approach because mass media reports of widespread drug-related violence generated concern about the safety of research staff (Reuter, MacCoun, and Murphy 1990, 119). Whether such fears were warranted is unclear, but this example does illustrate how safety issues can affect criminal justice research. More generally, Paterson, Gregory, and Thorne (1999) describe guidelines for assessing possible threats to researcher safety in qualitative field research.

Other researchers acknowledge the potential for harm in the context of respect for ethical principles. The box titled "Ethics and Extreme Field Research" gives examples of subtle and not-so-subtle ethical dilemmas encountered by a Rutgers University graduate in her study of drug use in rave clubs. For more information on this research, see Dina Perrone's book, *The High Life* (Perrone 2009).

More generally, John Monahan and associates (1993) distinguish three different groups at potential risk of physical harm in their research on violence. First are research subjects themselves. Women at risk of domestic violence may be exposed to greater danger if assailants learn they have disclosed past victimizations to researchers. Second, researchers might trigger attacks on themselves when they interview subjects who have a history of violent offending. Third, and most problematic, is the possibility that collecting information from unstable individuals might increase the risk of harm to third parties. The last category presents a new dilemma if researchers learn that subjects intend to attack some third party. Should researchers honor a promise of confidentiality to subjects or intervene to prevent the harm?

The potential for psychological harm to subjects exists when interviews are used to collect information. Crime surveys that ask respondents about their experiences as victims of crime may remind them of a traumatic, or at least an unpleasant, experience. Surveys may also ask respondents about illegal behaviors such as drug use or crimes they have committed. Talking about such actions with interviewers can be embarrassing.

Researchers have taken special steps to reduce the potential for emotional trauma in interviews of domestic violence victims (Black et al. 2011). One of the most interesting examples involves the use of self-completed computer questionnaires in the British Crime Survey (Mirrlees-Black 1999). Rather than verbally respond to questions from interviewers, respondents read and answer questions on a laptop computer. This procedure affords a greater degree of privacy for research subjects.

Recent developments in the use of crime mapping software have raised concerns about the privacy of crime victims. Many police departments now use some type of computer-driven crime map, and some have made maps of small areas available to the public on the web. Researchers and police alike must recognize the potential for such problems before publishing or otherwise displaying detailed crime maps. Kounadi, Bowers, and Leitner (2014) discuss how the increased availability of online crime maps produces concerns for privacy by making it possible for people to identify where crime victims live.

Crime maps for many cities can be found on the following website: http://www.crimemapping.com.

By now, it should be apparent that virtually all research runs some risk of harming other people somehow. A researcher can never completely guard against all possible injuries, yet some study designs make harm more likely than others. If a particular research procedure seems likely to produce unpleasant effects for subjects, such as asking survey respondents to report deviant behavior, the researcher should have firm scientific grounds for using that procedure. If researchers pursue a design that is essential and also likely to be unpleasant for subjects, they will find themselves in an ethical netherworld, forced to do some personal agonizing.

ETHICS AND EXTREME FIELD RESEARCH

by Dina Perrone
California State University, Long Beach

As a female ethnographer studying active drug use in a New York dance club, I have encountered awkward and difficult situations. The main purpose of my research was to study the use of ecstasy and other drugs in rave club settings. I became a participant observer in an all-night dance club (The Plant) where the use of club drugs was common. I covertly observed activities in the club, partly masking my role as a researcher by assuming the role of club-goer.

Though I was required to comply with university institutional review board guidelines, published codes and regulations offered limited guidance for many of the situations I experienced. As a result, I had to use my best judgment, learning from past experiences to make immediate decisions regarding ethical issues. I was forced to make decisions about how to handle drug episodes, so as not to place my research or my informants in any danger. Because my research was conducted in a dance club that is also a place for men to pick up women, I faced problems in getting information from subjects while watching out for my physical safety.

Drug Episodes and Subject Safety

I witnessed many drug episodes—adverse reactions to various club drugs—in my visits to The Plant. I watched groups trying to get their friends out of K-holes resulting from ketamine, or Special K. I even aided a subject throwing up. Being a covert observer made it difficult to handle these episodes. There were times in the club when I felt as though I was the only person not under the influence of a mind-altering substance. This led me to believe that I had better judgment than the other patrons. Getting involved in these episodes, however, risked jeopardizing my research.

During my first observation, I tried to intervene in what appeared to be a serious drug episode but was warned off by an informant. I was new to the club and unsure what would happen if I got involved. If I sought help from club staff or outsiders in dealing with acute drug reactions, patrons as well as the bouncers would begin to question why I kept coming there. I needed to gain the trust of the patrons to enlist participants in my research. Furthermore, the bouncers could throw me out of the club, fearing I was a troublemaker who would summon authorities.

As a researcher, I have an ethical responsibility to my participants, and as a human being, I have an ethical responsibility to my conscience. I decided to be extra cautious during my research and to pay close attention to how drug episodes are handled. I would first consult my informants and follow their suggestions. But if I ever thought a person suffering a drug episode was at risk while other patrons were neither able nor inclined to help, I would intervene to the best of my ability.

Sexual Advances in the Dance Club

The Plant is also partly a "meat market." Unlike most bars and dance clubs, the patrons' attire and the dance club entertainment are highly erotic. Most of the males inside the club are shirtless, and the majority of females wear extremely revealing clothes. In staged performances, males and females perform dances with sexual overtones, and clothing is partly shed. This atmosphere promotes sexual encounters; men frequently approach single women in search of a mate. Men had a tendency to approach me—I appeared to be unattached, and because of my research role, I made it a point to talk to as many people as possible. It's not difficult to imagine how this behavior could be misinterpreted.

There were times when men became sexually aggressive and persistent. In most instances, I walked

(continued)

away, and the men usually got the hint. However, some men are more persistent than others, especially when they are on ecstasy. In situations in which men make sexual advances, Terry Williams and colleagues (1992) suggest developing a trusting relationship with key individuals who can play a protective role. Throughout my research, I established a good rapport with my informants, who assumed that protective role. Unfortunately, acting in this role had the potential to place my informants in physically dangerous circumstances.

During one observation, "Tom" grabbed me after I declined his invitation to dance. Tom persisted, grabbed me again, and then began to argue with "Jerry," one of my regular informants, who came to my aid. This escalated to a fistfight broken up only after two bouncers ejected Tom from the club.

I had placed my informant and myself in a dangerous situation. Although I tried to convince myself that I really had no control over Jerry's actions, I felt responsible for the fight. A basic principle of field research is to not invite harm to participants. In most criminal justice research, harm is associated mainly with the possibility of arrest or psychological harm from discussing private issues. Afterward, I tried to think about how the incident escalated and how I could prevent similar problems in the future.

Ethical Decision Rules Evolving from Experience

Academic associations have formulated codes of ethics and professional conduct, but limited guidance is available for handling issues that arise in some types of ethnographic research. Instead, like criminal justice practitioners, those researchers have to make immediate decisions based on experience and training, without knowing how a situation will unfold. Throughout my research, I found myself in situations that I would normally avoid and would probably never confront. Should I help the woman over there get through a drug episode? If I don't, will she be okay? If I walk away from this aggressive guy, will he follow me? Does he understand that I wanted to talk to him just for research?

The approach I developed to tackle these issues was mostly gained by consulting with colleagues and reading other studies. An overarching theme regarding all codes of ethics is that ethnographers must put the safety and interests of their participants first, and they must recognize that their informants are more knowledgeable about many situations than they are. Throughout the research, I used my judgment to make the best decisions possible when handling these situations. To decide when to intervene during drug episodes, I followed the lead of my informants. Telling men that my informant was my boyfriend and walking away were successful tactics in turning away sexual advances.

As a general principle, possible harm to subjects may be justified if the potential benefits of the study outweigh the harm. Of course, this raises a further question of how to determine whether possible benefits offset possible harms. There is no simple answer, but as we will see, the research community has adopted certain safeguards that help subjects to make such determinations themselves.

Not harming people is an easy norm to accept in theory, but it is often difficult to ensure in practice. Sensitivity to the issue and experience in research methodology, however, should improve researchers' efforts in delicate areas of inquiry. Review Dina Perrone's observations in the box "Ethics and Extreme Field Research" for examples.

Voluntary Participation

Criminal justice research often intrudes into people's lives. The interviewer's telephone call or the arrival of a questionnaire via e-mail signals the beginning of an activity that respondents have not requested and that may require a significant portion of their time and energy. Being selected to participate in any sort of research study disrupts subjects' regular activities.

A major tenet of medical research ethics is that experimental participation must be voluntary. The same norm applies to research in criminal justice. No one should be forced to participate. But this norm is far easier to accept in theory than to apply in practice.

For example, prisoners are sometimes used as subjects in experimental studies. In the most rigorously ethical cases, prisoners are told the nature—and the possible dangers—of the experiment; they are told that participation is completely voluntary; and they are further instructed that they can expect no special rewards (such as early parole) for participation. Even under these conditions, volunteers often are motivated by the belief that they will personally benefit from their cooperation. In other cases, prisoners—or other subjects—may be offered small cash payments in exchange for participation. To people with very low incomes, small payments may be an incentive to participate in a study they would not otherwise endure. Amber Horning notes this point in the opening vignette in her discussion of research on pimps.

When an instructor in an introductory criminal justice class asks students to fill out a questionnaire that she or he plans to analyze and publish, students should always be told that their participation in the survey is completely voluntary. Even so, students might fear that nonparticipation will somehow affect their grade. The instructor should therefore be especially sensitive to the implied sanctions and make provisions to obviate them, such as allowing students to drop the questionnaires in a box near the door prior to the next class.

Notice how this norm of voluntary participation works against a number of scientific concerns or goals. In the most general terms, the goal of generalizability is threatened if experimental subjects or survey respondents are only the people who willingly participate. The same is true when subjects' participation can be bought with small payments. Research results may not be generalizable to all kinds of people. Most clearly, in the case of a descriptive study, a researcher cannot generalize the study findings to an entire population unless a substantial majority of a scientifically selected sample actually participates—both the willing respondents and the somewhat unwilling.

Qualitative interviewing and field research (Chapters 8 and 9) face ethical dilemmas in this regard. Often, a researcher who conducts observations in the field cannot even reveal that a study is being done, for fear that this revelation might significantly affect what is being studied. Imagine that you are interested in whether the way stereo headphones are displayed in a discount store affects rates of shoplifting. Therefore, you plan a field study in which you will make observations of store displays and shoplifting. You cannot very well ask all shoppers whether they agree to participate in your study.

The norm of voluntary participation is an important one, but it is sometimes impossible to follow. In cases in which researchers ultimately feel justified in violating it, it is all the more important to observe the other ethical norms of scientific research.

Anonymity and Confidentiality

The clearest concern in the protection of the subjects' interests and well-being is the protection of their identity. If revealing their behavior or responses would injure them in any way, adherence to this norm becomes crucial. Two techniques—anonymity and confidentiality—assist researchers in this regard, although the two are often confused.

Anonymity A research subject is considered anonymous when the researcher cannot associate a given piece of information with the person. **Anonymity** addresses many potential ethical difficulties. Studies that use field observation techniques are often able to ensure that research subjects cannot be identified. Researchers may also gain access to nonpublic records from courts, corrections departments, or other criminal justice agencies in which the names of persons have been removed.

One example of anonymity is a web-based survey where no login or other identifying information is required. Respondents anonymously complete online questionnaires that are then tabulated. Likewise, a telephone survey is anonymous if residential phone numbers are selected at random and respondents are not asked for identifying information. Interviews with subjects in the field are anonymous if the researchers neither ask for nor record the names of subjects.

Assuring anonymity makes it difficult to keep track of which sampled respondents have been interviewed, because researchers did not record their names. Nevertheless, in some situations, the price of anonymity is worth paying. In a survey of drug use, for example, we may decide that the likelihood and accuracy of responses will be enhanced by guaranteeing anonymity. A useful compromise is to record street names for subjects, as Amber Horning describes in the opening vignette, "Ethics and Research with Pimps."

Respondents in many surveys cannot be considered anonymous because an interviewer collects the information from individuals whose names and addresses are known. Other means of data collection may similarly make it impossible to guarantee anonymity for subjects. If we wished to examine juvenile arrest records for a sample of ninth-grade students, we would need to know their names even though we might not be interviewing them or having them fill out a questionnaire.

Confidentiality A researcher who is able to link information with a given person's identity but promises not to is providing **confidentiality**. In a survey of self-reported drug use, the researcher is in a position to make public the use of illegal drugs by a given respondent, but the respondent is assured that this will not be done. Similarly, if field interviews are conducted with juvenile gang members, researchers can certify that information will not be disclosed to police or other officials. Studies using court or police records that include individuals' names may protect confidentiality by not including any identifying information.

Some techniques ensure better performance on this guarantee. To begin, field or survey interviewers who have access to respondent identifications should be trained in their ethical responsibilities. As soon as possible, all names and addresses should be removed from data collection forms and replaced by identification numbers. A master identification file should be created linking numbers to names to permit the later correction of missing or contradictory information.

Whenever a survey is confidential rather than anonymous, it is the researcher's responsibility to make that fact clear to respondents. He or she must never use the term *anonymous* to mean *confidential*. Note, however, that research subjects and others may not understand the difference. For example, a former assistant attorney general in New Jersey once demanded that Michael Maxfield disclose the identities of police officers who participated in an anonymous study. It required repeated explanations of the difference between *anonymous* and *confidential* before the lawyer finally understood that it was not possible to identify participants who were anonymous. In any event, subjects should be assured that the information they provide will be used for research purposes only and not be disclosed to third parties.

Deceiving Subjects

We've seen that the handling of subjects' identities is an important ethical consideration. Handling our own identity as researchers can be tricky, too. Sometimes it's useful and even necessary to identify ourselves as researchers to those we want to study. It would take a master con artist to get people to participate in a laboratory experiment or complete a lengthy questionnaire without letting on that research was being conducted. We should also keep in mind that deceiving people is unethical; in criminal justice research, deception needs to be justified by compelling scientific or administrative concerns.

Sometimes, researchers admit that they are doing research but fudge about why they are doing it or for whom. Cathy Spatz Widom and associates interviewed victims of child abuse some 15 years after their cases had been heard in criminal or juvenile courts (Widom, Weiler, and Cotler 1999). Widom was interested in whether child abuse victims were more likely than a comparison group of nonvictims to have used illegal drugs. Interviewers could not explain the purpose of the study without potentially biasing responses. Still, it was necessary to provide a plausible explanation for asking detailed questions about personal and family experiences. Widom's solution was to inform subjects that they had been selected to participate in a study of human development. She also prepared a brochure describing her research on human development that was distributed to respondents.

Deception is sometimes used in experimental studies, but subjects usually eventually learn they were deceived. For example, Raymond Paternoster and associates (2013) studied whether students who witnessed staged cheating on a course assignment were more likely to cheat themselves compared to students who were not exposed to staged cheating. After the experiment was completed, participants were "debriefed" and informed about the deception:

If you were a participant in the memory/recall study that took place in the computer labs of LeFrak Hall, the experiment involved an element of deception. You were recruited under the idea that the study was about your ability to remember and recall words. The actual purpose of the study was to examine the effect of peers on cheating behavior. There was a confederate of the researcher in the sessions, who was a professional actor hired by the researcher. (Paternoster et al. 2013, 496)

Although we might initially think that concealing our research purpose by deception would be particularly useful in studying active offenders, James Inciardi (1993), in describing methods for studying "crack houses," makes a convincing case that this is inadvisable. First, concealing our research role when investigating drug dealers and users implies that we are associating with them for the purpose of obtaining illegal drugs. Faced with this situation, a researcher would have the choice of engaging in illegal behavior or offering a convincing explanation for declining to do so. Second, masquerading as a crack-house patron would expose the researcher to the considerable danger of violence that was found to be common in such places. Because the choice of committing illegal acts or becoming a victim of violence is really no choice at all, Inciardi (1993, 152) advises researchers who study active offenders in field settings: "Don't go undercover."

Analysis and Reporting

As criminal justice researchers, we have ethical obligations to our subjects of study. At the same time, we have ethical obligations to our colleagues in the scientific community; a few comments on those obligations are in order. In any rigorous study, the researcher should be more familiar than anyone else with the technical shortcomings and failures of the study. Researchers have an obligation to make those shortcomings known to readers. Even though it's natural to feel foolish admitting mistakes, researchers are ethically obligated to do so.

Any negative findings should be reported. There is an unfortunate myth in social scientific reporting that only positive discoveries are worth reporting. As editor of the *Journal of Research in Crime and Delinquency*, Michael Maxfield confesses to being sometimes guilty of believing that as well. This is not restricted to social science. Helle Krogh Johansen and Peter Gotzsche (1999) describe how published research on new drugs tends to focus on successful experiments. Unsuccessful research on new formulations is less often published, which leads pharmaceutical researchers to repeat studies of drugs already shown to be ineffective. Largely because of this bias, researchers at the Harvard University School of Dental Medicine have established the *Journal of Negative Observations in Biomedicine*, dedicated to publishing negative findings from biomedical research (http://www.jnrbm.com). In social science, as in medical research, it is often as important to know that two things are not related as to know that they are.

In general, science progresses through honesty and openness, and is retarded by ego defenses and deception. We can serve our fellow researchers—and the scientific community as a whole—by telling the truth about all the pitfalls and problems experienced in a particular line of inquiry. With luck, this will save others from the same problems.

Legal Liability

Two types of ethical problems expose researchers to potential legal liability. To illustrate the first, assume you are making field observations of criminal activity, such as street prostitution, that is not reported to police. Under criminal law in many states, you might be arrested for obstructing justice or being an accessory to a crime. Potentially more troublesome is the situation in which participant observation of crime or deviance draws researchers into criminal or deviant roles themselves, such as smuggling cigarettes into a lockup in order to obtain the cooperation of detainees.

The second and more common potential source of legal problems involves knowledge that research subjects have committed illegal acts. Self-report surveys or field interviews may ask subjects about crimes they have committed. If respondents report committing offenses they have never been arrested for or charged with, the researcher's knowledge of them might be construed as obstruction of justice. Or research data may be subject to subpoena by a criminal court. Because disclosure of research data that could be traced to individual subjects violates the ethical principle of confidentiality, a new dilemma emerges.

Fortunately, federal law protects researchers from legal action in most circumstances, provided that appropriate safeguards are used to protect research data. Research plans for 2002 published by organizations in the Office of Justice Programs summarized this protection: "[Research] information and copies thereof shall be immune from legal process, and shall not, without the consent of the person furnishing such information, be admitted as evidence or used for any purpose in any action, suit, or other judicial, legislative, or administrative proceedings" (42 U.S. Code §22.28a). This not only protects researchers from legal action but also can be valuable in assuring subjects that they cannot be prosecuted for crimes they describe to an interviewer or field worker. Note that such immunity requires confidential information to be protected. We have already discussed the principle of confidentiality, so this bargain should be an easy one to keep.

Somewhere between legal liability and physical danger lies the potential risk to field researchers from law enforcement. Despite being upfront with crack users about his role as a researcher, Inciardi (1993) points out that police could not be expected to distinguish him from his subjects. Visibly associating with offenders in natural settings brings some risk of being arrested or inadvertently being an accessory to crime. On one occasion, Inciardi fled the scene of a robbery and on another was caught up in a crack-house raid. Another example is the account Bruce Jacobs (1996) gives of his contacts with police while he was studying street drug dealers.

Special Problems

Certain types of criminal justice studies present special ethical problems in addition to those we have mentioned. Applied research, for example, may evaluate some existing or new program. Evaluations frequently have the potential to disrupt the routine operations of agencies being studied. Obviously, it is best to minimize such interferences whenever possible.

Staff Misbehavior While conducting applied research, researchers may become aware of irregular or illegal practices by staff in public agencies. They are then faced with the ethical question of whether to report such information. For example, investigators conducting an evaluation of an innovative probation program learned that police visits to the residences of probationers were not taking place as planned. Instead, police assigned to the program had been submitting falsified log sheets and had not actually checked on probationers.

What is the ethical dilemma in this case? On the one hand, researchers were evaluating the probation program and so were obliged to report reasons it did or did not operate as planned. Failure to deliver program treatments (home visits) is an example of a program not operating as planned. Investigators had guaranteed confidentiality to program clients—the offenders assigned to probation—but no such agreement had been struck with program staff. On the other hand, researchers had assured agency personnel that their purpose was to evaluate the probation program, not individuals' job performance. If researchers disclosed their knowledge that police were falsifying reports, they would violate this implied trust.

What would you have done in this situation? We will tell you what the researchers decided at the end of this chapter (see page 45). You should recognize, however, how applied research in criminal justice agencies can involve a variety of ethical issues.

Research Causes Crime Because criminal acts and their circumstances are complex and imperfectly understood, some research projects have the potential to produce crime or influence its location or target. Certainly, this is a potentially serious ethical issue for researchers.

Most people agree that it is unethical to encourage someone to commit an offense solely for the purpose of a research project. What's more problematic is recognizing situations in which research might indirectly promote offending. Scott Decker and Barrik Van Winkle (1996) discuss such a possibility in their research on gang members. Some gang members offered to illustrate their willingness to use violence by inviting researchers to witness a drive-by shooting. Researchers declined all such invitations (1996, 46). Another ethical issue was the question of how subjects used the $20 cash payments they received in exchange for being interviewed (1996, 51):

> We set the fee low enough that we were confident that it would not have a criminogenic effect. While twenty dollars is not a small amount of money, it is not sufficient to purchase a gun or bankroll a large drug buy. We are sure that some of our subjects used the money for illegal purposes. But, after all, these were individuals who were regularly engaged in delinquent and criminal acts.

You may or may not agree with the authors' reasoning in the last sentence. But their consideration of how cash payments would be used by active offenders represents an unusually careful recognition of the ethical dilemmas that emerge in studying active offenders.

A different type of ethical problem is the possibility of crime displacement in studies of crime prevention programs. Consider an experimental program to reduce street prostitution in one area of a city. Researchers studying such a program might designate experimental target areas for enhanced enforcement, as well as nearby comparison areas that will not receive an intervention. If prostitution is displaced from target areas to adjacent neighborhoods, the evaluation study contributes to an increase in prostitution in the comparison areas.

In a review of more than 200 evaluations of crime prevention projects, Rob Guerette and Kate Bowers (2009) report that the scope of displacement is limited. An earlier study by Rene Hesseling (1994) shows that the type of crime prevention action makes a difference, with displacement more common for target-hardening programs. For example, installing security screens on ground-floor windows in some buildings seemed to displace burglary to less protected structures.

In any event, when it does occur, displacement tends to follow major policy changes that are not connected with criminal justice research. Researchers cannot be expected to control actions by criminal justice officials that may benefit some people at the expense of others. However, it is reasonable to expect researchers involved in planning an evaluation study to anticipate the possibility of such things as displacement and bring them to the attention of program staff.

Withholding of Desirable Treatments Certain kinds of research designs in criminal justice can lead to different kinds of ethical questions. Suppose researchers believe that diverting domestic violence offenders from prosecution to counseling reduces the possibility of repeat violence. Is it ethical to conduct an experiment in which some offenders are prosecuted but others are not?

You may recognize the similarity between this question and those faced by medical researchers who test the effectiveness of experimental drugs. Physicians typically respond to such questions by pointing out that the effectiveness of a drug cannot be demonstrated without such experiments. Failure to conduct research, even at the potential expense of subjects not receiving the trial drugs, would therefore make it impossible to develop new drugs or distinguish beneficial treatments from those that are ineffective and even harmful.

One solution to this dilemma is to interrupt an experiment if preliminary results indicate that a new policy, or drug, does in fact produce improvements in a treatment group. Michael Dennis (1990) describes how such plans were incorporated into a long-term evaluation of enhanced drug treatment counseling. If preliminary results had indicated that the new counseling program reduced drug use, researchers and program staff were prepared to provide enhanced counseling to subjects in the control group. Dennis recognized this potential ethical issue and planned his elaborate research design to accommodate such midstream changes. Similarly, Martin Killias and associates (2000) planned to interrupt their experimental study of heroin prescription in Switzerland if compelling evidence pointed to benefits from that approach to treating drug dependency.

Research in criminal justice, especially applied research, can pose a variety of ethical dilemmas, only some of which we have mentioned here.

Promoting Compliance with Ethical Principles

Codes of ethics and institutional review boards are two main ways of promoting compliance with ethical principles.

No matter how sensitive they might be to the rights of individuals and possible ways subjects might be harmed, researchers are not always the best judges of whether or not adequate safeguards are used. In 1974, the National Research Act was signed into law after a few highly publicized examples of unethical practices in medical and social science research.[1] A few years later, what has become known as the **Belmont Report** prescribed a brief but comprehensive set of ethical principles for protecting human subjects (National Commission for the Protection of Human Subjects of Biomedical and Behavioral Research 1979). In only six pages, three principles were presented:

1. *Respect for persons*: Individuals must be allowed to make their own decisions about participation in research, and those with limited capacity to make such decisions should have special protection.
2. *Beneficence*: Research should do no harm to participants, and seek to produce benefits.

3. *Justice*: The benefits and burdens of participating in research should be distributed fairly.

Copious federal regulations have stemmed from these three principles. But in most cases, the research community has adopted two general mechanisms for promoting ethical research practices: codes of professional ethics and institutional review boards.

Codes of Professional Ethics

If the professionals who design and conduct research projects can fail to recognize ethical problems, how can such problems be avoided? One approach is for researchers to consult one of the codes of ethics produced by professional associations. Formal codes of conduct describe what is considered acceptable and unacceptable professional behavior. The American Psychological Association's (2010) amended code of ethics is quite detailed, reflecting the different professional roles of psychologists in research, clinical treatment, and educational contexts.

Many of the ethical questions criminal justice researchers are likely to encounter are addressed in the ethics code of the American Sociological Association (1999). Paul Reynolds (1979, 442–449) has created a composite code for the use of human subjects in research, drawing on 24 codes of ethics published by national associations of social scientists. The National Academy of Sciences publishes a very useful booklet on a variety of ethical issues, including the problem of fraud and other forms of scientific misconduct (Committee on Science, Engineering, and Public Policy 2009).

The two national associations representing criminology and criminal justice researchers have one code of ethics between them. The Academy of Criminal Justice Sciences (ACJS) based its code of ethics on that developed by the American Sociological Association. ACJS members are bound by a very general code that reflects the diversity of its membership: "Most of the ethical standards are written

1. We'll consider one of these examples near the end of this chapter.

broadly, to provide applications in varied roles and varied contexts. The Ethical Standards are not exhaustive—conduct that is not included in the Ethical Standards is not necessarily ethical or unethical" (Academy of Criminal Justice Sciences 2000, 1).

A committee of the American Society of Criminology (ASC) proposed a draft code of ethics in 1998, which drew extensively on the code for sociology. But no ethics code had been adopted as of June 2014, and the ASC withdrew its draft code from circulation in 1999. The ASC website includes the following statement on a page titled "Code of Ethics":

> The American Society of Criminology has not formally adopted a code of ethics. We would suggest that persons interested in this general topic examine the various codes of ethics adopted by other professional associations. (http://asc41.com/ethicspg.html)

Links to a number of ethics codes for social science associations are listed, including those listed above and the British Society of Criminology.

What can we make of the inability of the largest professional association of criminologists to agree on a code of ethics? The wide variety of approaches to doing research in this area probably has something to do with it. Criminologists also encounter a range of ethical issues and have diverging views on how those issues should be addressed. Finally, we have seen examples of the special problems criminologists face in balancing ethics and research. Not all of these problems have easy solutions that can be embodied in a code.

Even when they exist, professional codes of ethics for social scientists cannot be expected to prevent unethical practices in criminal justice research any more than the American Bar Association's Code of Professional Responsibility eliminates breaches of ethics by lawyers. For this reason, and in reaction to some controversial medical and social science research, the U.S. Department of Health and Human Services (HHS) has established regulations protecting human research subjects. These regulations do not apply to all social science or criminal justice research. It is, however, worthwhile to understand some of

their general provisions. Material in the following section is based on the Code of Federal Regulations, Title 45, Chapter 4.6. Those regulations are themselves rooted in the *Belmont Report*.

Institutional Review Boards

Government agencies and nongovernment organizations (including universities) that conduct research involving human subjects must establish review committees, known as institutional review boards (IRBs). These IRBs have two general purposes. First, board members make judgments about the overall risks to human subjects and whether these risks are acceptable, given the expected benefits from actually doing the research. Second, they determine whether the procedures to be used include adequate safeguards regarding the safety, confidentiality, and general welfare of human subjects.

Under HHS regulations, virtually all research that uses human subjects in any way, including simply asking people questions, is subject to IRB review. The few exceptions potentially include research conducted for educational purposes and studies that collect anonymous information only. However, even those studies may be subject to review if they use certain special populations (discussed later) or procedures that might conceivably harm participants. In other words, it's safe to assume that most research is subject to IRB review if original data will be collected from individuals whose identities will be known. If you think about the various ways subjects might be harmed and the difficulty of conducting anonymous studies, you can understand why this is the case.

Federal regulations and IRB guidelines address other potential ethical issues in social research. Foremost among these is the typical IRB requirement for dealing with the ethical principle of voluntary participation.

Informed Consent The norm of voluntary participation is usually satisfied through **informed consent**—informing subjects about research procedures and then obtaining their consent to participate. Although this may seem like a simple requirement, obtaining informed consent can present several practical difficulties. It requires that subjects understand the purpose of the research, possible risks and side effects, possible benefits to subjects, and the procedures that will be used.

If you accept that deception may sometimes be necessary, you will realize how the requirement to inform subjects about research procedures can present something of a dilemma. Researchers usually address this problem by telling subjects at least part of the truth or offering a slightly revised version of why the research is being conducted. In Widom's study of child abuse, subjects were partially informed about the purpose of the research—human development—one component of which is being a victim of child abuse, which the subjects were not told.

Another potential problem with obtaining informed consent is ensuring that subjects have the capacity to understand the descriptions of risks, benefits, procedures, and so forth. Researchers may have to provide oral descriptions to participants who are unable to read. For subjects who do not speak English, researchers should be prepared to describe procedures in the subjects' native language. And if researchers use specialized terms or language common in criminal justice research, participants may not understand the meaning and thus be unable to grant informed consent. Consider this statement: "The purpose of this study is to determine whether less restrictive sanctions such as restitution produce heightened sensitivity to social responsibility among persistent juvenile offenders and a decline in long-term recidivism." Can you think of a better way to describe this study to delinquent 14-year-olds? Figure 2.1 presents a good example of an informed consent statement that was used in a study of juvenile burglars. Notice how the statement clearly describes research procedures and also unambiguously tells subjects that participation is voluntary.

Other guidelines for obtaining informed consent include explicitly telling people that their participation is voluntary and assuring them of confidentiality. However, it is more important to understand how informed consent addresses key ethical issues in conducting criminal justice research. First, it ensures that participation is voluntary. Second, by informing subjects of procedures,

risks, and benefits, researchers are empowering them to resolve the fundamental ethical dilemma of whether the possible benefits of the research offset the possible risks of participation.

Special Populations Federal regulations on human subjects include special provisions for certain types of subjects, called **special populations**, and two of these are particularly important in criminal justice research—juveniles and prisoners. Juveniles, of course, are treated differently from adults in most aspects of the law. Their status as a special population of human subjects reflects the legal status of juveniles, as well as their capacity to grant informed consent. In most studies that involve juveniles, consent must be obtained both from parents or guardians and from the juvenile subjects themselves.

In some studies, however, such as those that focus on abused children, it is obviously not desirable to obtain parental consent. Decker and Van Winkle faced this problem in their study of St. Louis gang members. See the box "Ethics and Juvenile Gang Members" for a discussion of how they reconciled the conflict between two ethical principles and satisfied the concerns of their university's IRB.

Prisoners are treated as a special population for somewhat different reasons. Because of their ready accessibility for experiments and interviews, prisoners have frequently been used in biomedical experiments that produced serious harm (Mitford 1973). Recognizing this, HHS regulations specify that prisoner subjects may not be exposed to risks that would be considered excessive for nonprisoner subjects. Furthermore, undue influence or coercion cannot be used in recruiting prisoner subjects. Informed consent statements presented to prospective subjects must indicate that a decision not to participate in a study will have no influence on work assignments, privileges, or parole decisions. To help ensure that these ethical issues are recognized, if an IRB reviews a project in which prisoners will be subjects, at least one member of that IRB must be either a prisoner or someone specifically designated to represent the interests of prisoners. Figure 2.2 presents a checklist required by the

You and your parents or guardian are invited to participate in a research study of the monitoring program that you were assigned to by the Juvenile Court. The purpose of this research is to study the program and your reactions to it. In order to do this a member of the research team will need to interview you and your parents/guardians when you complete the monitoring program. These interviews will take about 15 minutes and will focus on your experiences with the court and monitoring program, the things you do, things that have happened to you, and what you think. In addition, we will record from the court records information about the case for which you were placed in the monitoring program, prior cases, and other information that is put in the records after you are released from the monitoring program.

Anything you or your parents or guardian tell us will be strictly confidential. This means that only the researchers will have your answers. They will not under any conditions (except at your request) be given to the court, the police, probation officers, your parents, or your child!

Your participation in this research is voluntary. If you don't want to take part, you don't have to! If you decide to participate, you can change your mind at any time. Whether you participate or not will have no effect on the program, probation, or your relationship with the court.

The research is being directed by Dr. Terry Baumer and Dr. Robert Mendelsohn from the Indiana University School of Public and Environmental Affairs here in Indianapolis. If you ever have any questions about the research or comments about the monitoring program that you think we should know about, please call one of us at 274-0531.

Consent Statement

We agree to participate in this study of the Marion County Juvenile Monitoring Program. We have read the above statement and understand what will be required and that all information will be confidential. We also understand that we can withdraw from the study at any time without penalty.

Juvenile _____ Date: _____

Parent/Guardian _____

Parent/Guardian _____

Researcher _____

FIGURE 2.1   Informed Consent Statement for Evaluation of Marion County Juvenile Monitoring Program

ETHICS AND JUVENILE GANG MEMBERS

Scott Decker and Barrik Van Winkle faced a range of ethical issues in their study of gang members. Many of these should be obvious given what has been said so far in this chapter. Violence was common among subjects and presented a real risk to researchers. Decker and Van Winkle (1996, 252) reported that 11 of the 99 members of the original sample had been killed since the project began in 1990. There was also the obvious need to assure confidentiality to subjects.

Their project was supported by a federal agency and administered through a university, so Decker and Van Winkle had to comply with federal human subjects guidelines as administered by the university institutional review board (IRB). And because many of the subjects were juveniles, they had to address federal regulations concerning that special population. Foremost among these was the normal requirement that informed consent for juveniles include parental notification and approval.

You may immediately recognize the conflicting ethical principles at work here, together with the potential for conflict. The promise of confidentiality to

(continued)

gang members is one such principle that was essential for the researchers to obtain candid reports of violence and other law-breaking behavior. But the need for confidentiality conflicted with initial IRB requirements to obtain parental consent for their children to participate in the research:

> This would have violated our commitment to maintain the confidentiality of each subject, not to mention the ethical and practical difficulties of finding and informing each parent. We told the Human Subjects Committee that we would not, in effect, tell parents that their child was being interviewed because they were an active gang member, knowledge that the parents may not have had. (Decker and Van Winkle 1996, 52)

You might think deception would be a possibility—informing parents that their child was selected for a youth development study, for example. This would not, however, solve the logistical difficulty of locating parents or guardians, some of whom had lost contact with their children. Furthermore, it was likely that even if parents or guardians could be located, suspicions about the research project and the reasons their children were selected would prevent many parents from granting consent. Loss of juvenile subjects in this way would compromise the norm of generality as we have described it in this chapter and elsewhere.

Finally, waiving the requirement for parental consent would have undermined the legal principle that the interests of juveniles must be protected by a supervising adult. Remember that researchers are not always the best judges of whether sufficient precautions have been taken to protect subjects. Here is how Decker and Van Winkle (1996, 52) resolved the issue with their IRB:

> We reached a compromise in which we found an advocate for each juvenile member of our sample; this person—a university employee—was responsible for making sure that the subject understood (1) their rights to refuse or quit the interview at any time without penalty and (2) the confidential nature of the project. All subjects signed the consent form.

Source: Adapted from Decker and Van Winkle (1996).

Rutgers University IRB for proposed research involving prisoners.

Regarding the last item in Figure 2.2, random selection is generally recognized as an ethical procedure for selecting subjects or deciding which subjects will receive an experimental treatment. HHS regulations emphasize this in describing special provisions for using prison subjects: "Unless the principal investigator provides to the [IRB] justification in writing for following some other procedures, control subjects must be selected randomly from the group of available prisoners who meet the characteristics needed for that particular research project" (45 CFR 46.305[4]).

Institutional Review Board Requirements and Researcher Rights

Federal regulations contain many more provisions for IRBs and other protections for human subjects. Some researchers believe that such regulations actually create problems by setting constraints on their freedom and professional judgments in conducting research. Recall that potential conflict between the rights of researchers to discover new knowledge and the rights of subjects to be free from unnecessary harm is a fundamental ethical dilemma. It is at least inconvenient to have outsiders review a research proposal. Or a researcher may feel insulted by the implication that the potential benefits of research will not outweigh the potential harm or inconvenience to human subjects.

Many university IRBs have become extremely cautious in reviewing research proposals. See Richard Shweder's (2006) discussion for examples of problems resulting from this. Professional associations and research-oriented federal agencies have tried to offer guidance on what is and is not subject to various levels of IRB approval. Joan Sieber (2001) prepared an analysis of human subject issues associated with large surveys for the Bureau of Justice Statistics. Always alert for possible restrictions on academic freedom, the American Association of University Professors (2006) published a useful summary of how IRBs have come to regulate social science research.

- Does the research entail any possible advantages accrued to the prisoner through their participation in the research that impairs their ability to weigh the risk/benefits of the participation in the limited choice environment that exists in a prison? This comparison is to be made with respect to the general living conditions, medical care, amenities, and earning opportunities that exist in a prison.

- Are the risks of the research commensurate with those that would be accepted by nonprisoner participants? Provide rationale below.

- Is the information presented to the prisoners in the consent form or oral consent script done so in a language understandable by the participants?

- Does the consent form explicitly state to the subject that "Do not tell us any information about past or future crimes that are unknown to the authorities as we cannot guarantee confidentiality of that information. Additionally, I [the researcher] must report to the authorities information you tell me about harming yourself or other people, or any plans you have to escape."

- Does adequate assurance exist that parole boards will not take into account participation in the research when determining parole and that the prisoners were clearly informed of this prior to participation in the research?

- Describe what specific steps were taken to ensure that the informed consent form includes information specific to the prisoner subject population. This is not necessary if the research is limited to data analysis.

- Is the selection of prisoner research participants fair and equitable and immune from arbitrary intervention by prisoner authorities? If not, has the principal investigator provided sufficient justification for the implementation of alternative procedures?

Source: Adapted from Office for Human Research Protections, Department of Health & Human Services, Guidance on the Involvement of Prisoners in Research. http://www.hhs.gov/ohrp/policy/prisoner.html

FIGURE 2.2   Excerpts from Checklist for Research Involving Prisoners

There is some merit in such concerns; however, we should not lose sight of the reasons IRB requirements and other regulations were created. Researchers are not always the best judges of the potential for their work to harm individuals. In designing and conducting criminal justice research, they may become excited about learning how to better prevent crime or more effectively treat cocaine addiction. That excitement and commitment to scientific advancement may lead researchers to overlook possible harms to individual rights or well-being. You may recognize this as another way of asking whether the ends justify the means. Because researchers are not always disinterested parties in answering such questions, IRBs are established to provide outside judgments. Also recognize that IRBs can be sources of expert advice on how to resolve ethical dilemmas. Decker and Van Winkle shared their university's concern about balancing confidentiality against the need to obtain informed consent from juvenile subjects; together, they were able to fashion a workable compromise.

All colleges and universities have IRBs. Consult the City University of New York website (http://www.cuny.edu/research/compliance.html) for an example, or visit the IRB website at your institution.

Ethical Controversies

Examples illustrate how ethics is a problem in justice research.

By way of illustrating the importance of ethics principles, together with problems that may be encountered in applying those principles, we now describe a research project that provoked widespread ethical controversy and discussion. This is followed by further examples of ethical questions for discussion.

The Stanford Prison Experiment

Few people would disagree that prisons are dehumanizing. Inmates forfeit freedom, of course, but their incarceration also results in a loss of privacy and individual identity. Violence is among the realities of prison life that people point to as evidence of the failure of prisons to rehabilitate inmates.

Although the problems of prisons have many sources, psychologists Craig Haney, Curtis Banks, and Philip Zimbardo (1973) were interested in two general explanations. The first was the dispositional hypothesis—prisons are brutal and dehumanizing because of the types of people who run them and are incarcerated in them. Inmates have demonstrated their disrespect for legal order and their willingness to use deceit and violence; persons who work as prison guards may be disproportionately authoritarian and sadistic. The second was the situational hypothesis—the prison environment itself creates brutal, dehumanizing conditions independent of the kinds of people who live and work in the institutions.

Haney and associates set out to test the situational hypothesis by creating a functional prison simulation in which healthy, psychologically normal male college students were assigned to roles as prisoners and guards. The "prison" was constructed in the basement of a psychology department building: three 6 × 9-foot "cells" furnished with only a cot, a prison "yard" in a corridor, and a 2 × 7-foot "solitary confinement cell." Twenty-one subjects were selected from 75 volunteers after screening to eliminate those with physical or psychological problems. Offered $15 per day for their participation, the 21 subjects were randomly assigned to be either guards or prisoners.

All subjects signed contracts that included instructions about prisoner and guard roles for the planned two-week experiment. "Prisoners" were told that they would be confined and under surveillance throughout the experiment, and their civil rights would be suspended; they were, however, guaranteed that they would not be physically abused.

"Guards" were given minimal instructions, most notably that physical aggression or physical punishment of "prisoners" was prohibited. Together with a "warden," however, they were generally free to develop prison rules and procedures.

The researchers planned to study how both guards and prisoners reacted to their roles, but guards were led to believe that the purpose of the experiment was to study prisoners.

If you had been a prisoner in this experiment, you would have experienced something like the following after signing your contract: First, you would have been arrested without notice at your home by a real police officer, perhaps with neighbors looking on. After being searched and taken to the police station in handcuffs, you would have been booked, fingerprinted, and placed in a police detention facility. Next, you would have been blindfolded and driven to "prison," where you would have been stripped, sprayed with a delousing solution, and left to stand naked for a period of time in the "prison yard." Eventually, you would have been issued a prison uniform (a loose overshirt stamped with your ID number), fitted with an ankle chain, led to your cell, and ordered to remain silent. Your prison term would then have been totally controlled by the guards.

Wearing mirrored sunglasses, khaki uniforms, and badges, and carrying nightsticks, guards supervised prisoner work assignments and held lineups three times per day. Although lineups initially lasted only a few minutes, guards later extended them to several hours. Prisoners were fed bland meals and accompanied by guards on three authorized toilet visits per day.

The behavior of all subjects in the prison yard and other open areas was videotaped; audiotapes were made continuously while prisoners were in their cells. Researchers administered brief questionnaires throughout the experiment to assess emotional changes in prisoners and guards. About 4 weeks after the experiment concluded, researchers conducted interviews with all subjects to assess their reactions.

Haney and associates (1973, 88) had planned to run the prison experiment for two weeks, but they halted the study after six days because subjects displayed "unexpectedly intense reactions." Five prisoners had to be released even before that time because they showed signs of acute depression or anxiety.

Subjects in each group accepted their roles all too readily. Prisoners and guards could interact with each other in friendly ways because guards had the power to make prison rules. But interactions turned out to be overwhelmingly hostile and negative. Guards became aggressive, and prisoners became passive. When the experiment ended prematurely, prisoners were happy about their early "parole," but guards were disappointed that the study would not continue.

Haney and colleagues justify the prison simulation study in part by claiming that the dispositional/situational hypotheses could not be evaluated using other research designs. Clearly, the researchers were sensitive to ethical issues. They obtained subjects' consent to the experiment through signed contracts. Prisoners who showed signs of acute distress were released early. The entire study was terminated after less than half of the planned two weeks had elapsed when its unexpectedly harsh impact on subjects became evident. Finally, researchers conducted group therapy debriefing sessions with prisoners and guards and maintained follow-up contacts for a year to ensure that subjects' negative experiences were temporary.

Two related features of this experiment raise ethical questions. First, subjects were not fully informed of the procedures. Although we have seen that deception, including something less than full disclosure, can often be justified, in this case deception was partially due to the researchers' uncertainty about how the prison simulation would unfold. This relates to the second and more important ethical problem: guards were granted the power to make up and modify rules as the study progressed, and their behavior became increasingly authoritarian. Comments by guards illustrate their reactions as the experiment unfolded (Haney, Banks, and Zimbardo 1973, 88):

> "They [the prisoners] didn't see it as an experiment. It was real and they were fighting to keep their identity. But we were always there to show them just who was boss."

> "During the inspection, I went to cell 2 to mess up a bed which the prisoner had made and he grabbed me, screaming that he had just made it.... He grabbed my throat, and although he was laughing, I was pretty scared. I lashed out with my stick and hit him in the chin (although not very hard), and when I freed myself I became angry."

> "Acting authoritatively can be fun. Power can be a great pleasure."

You can get a good impression of what guards and prisoners experienced by viewing videos of "arrest" and "prison" scenes available on the Internet. Search for "video Stanford prison experiment" or visit the Stanford Prison Experiment website (www.prisonexp.org) for more information.

How do you feel about this experiment? On the one hand, it provided valuable insights into how otherwise normal people react in a simulated prison environment. Subjects appeared to suffer no long-term harm, in part because of precautions taken by researchers. Paul Reynolds (1979, 139) found a certain irony in the short-term discomforts endured by the college student subjects: "There is evidence that the major burdens were borne by individuals from advantaged social categories and that the major benefactors would be individuals from less advantaged social categories [actual prisoners], an uneven distribution of costs and benefits that many nevertheless consider equitable." On the other hand, researchers did not anticipate how much and how quickly subjects would accept their roles. In discussing their findings, Haney and associates (1973, 90) note: "Our results are ... congruent with those of Milgram[2] who most convincingly demonstrated the proposition that evil acts are not necessarily the deeds of evil men, but may be attributable to the operation of powerful social forces." This quote illustrates the fundamental dilemma—balancing the right to conduct research against the rights of subjects. Is it ethical for researchers to create powerful social forces that lead to evil acts?

2. Here the authors refer to controversial research on obedience to authority by Lester Milgram (1965).

Discussion Examples

Research ethics is an important and ambiguous topic. The difficulty of resolving ethical issues cannot be an excuse for ignoring them. You need to keep ethics in mind as you read other chapters in this book and whenever you plan a research project.

To further sensitize you to the ethical component of criminal justice and other social research, we've prepared brief descriptions of real and hypothetical research situations. Can you see the ethical issue in each? How do you feel about it? Are the procedures described ultimately acceptable or unacceptable? It would be very useful to discuss these examples with other students in your class.

1. In a study of "phishing," researchers obtain university e-mail addresses from a sample of undergraduate students. Bogus social networking messages are sent to participants to determine which features of messages are more likely to lure recipients to click on web links. The university computing services center has supplied the e-mail addresses, and the university IRB has approved the study.

2. In a federally funded study of a probation program, a researcher discovers that one participant was involved in a murder while on probation. Public disclosure of this incident might threaten the program, which the researcher believes, from all evidence, is beneficial. Judging the murder to be an anomaly, the researcher does not disclose it to federal sponsors or describe it in published reports.

3. While studying aggression in bars and nightclubs, a researcher records observations of a savage fight in which three people are seriously injured. Ignoring pleas for help from one of the victims, the researcher retreats to a restroom to write up notes from these observations.

4. In a study of state police, researchers learn that officers have been instructed by superiors to "not sign anything." Fearing that asking officers to sign informed consent statements will sharply reduce participation, researchers seek some other way to satisfy their university IRB. What should they do?

5. In the example mentioned in the section "Staff Misbehavior" (page 35), the researchers disclosed to public officials that police were not making visits to probationers as called for in the program intervention. Published reports describe the problem as "irregularities in program delivery."

SUMMARY

- In addition to technical and scientific considerations, criminal justice research projects are shaped by ethical considerations.

- What's ethically "right" and "wrong" in research is ultimately a matter of what people agree is right and wrong.

- Researchers tend not to be the best judges of whether their own work adequately addresses ethical issues.

- Most ethical questions involve weighing the possible benefits of research against the potential for harm to research subjects.

- Criminal justice research may generate special ethical questions, including the potential for legal liability and physical harm.

- Scientists agree that participation in research should, in general, be voluntary. This norm, however, can conflict with the scientific need for generalizability.

- Most scientists agree that research should not harm subjects unless they willingly and knowingly accept the risks of harm.

- Anonymity and confidentiality are two ways to protect the privacy of research subjects.

- Compliance with ethical principles is promoted by professional associations and by regulations issued by the Department of Health and Human Services (HHS).

- HHS regulations include special provisions for two types of subjects of particular interest to many criminal justice researchers: prisoners and juveniles.

- Institutional review boards (IRBs) play an important role in ensuring that the rights and interests of human subjects are protected. But some social science researchers believe that IRBs are becoming too restrictive.

KEY TERMS

anonymity, p. 32

Belmont Report, p. 37

confidentiality, p. 33

ethical, p. 28

informed consent, p. 38

special populations, p. 39

REVIEW QUESTIONS AND EXERCISES

1. Obtain a copy of the Academy of Criminal Justice Sciences' (2000) code of ethics at this website: http://acjs.org/pubs/167_671_2922.cfm. Read the document carefully. How would the code apply to the Stanford prison simulation?

2. As mentioned earlier in the chapter, Ko-Lin Chin and James Finckenauer (2012) conducted research on sex trafficking of Chinese women. As you might imagine, this research required that they consider a number of ethical questions on protecting human subjects, including researcher safety. As the authors describe, their work was guided by principles developed by the World

Health Organization (2003). Download a copy of the World Health Organization report (http://www.who.int/gender/documents/women_and_girls/9789242595499/en/) and discuss how it illustrates our discussion of ethics in criminal justice research.

3. Review the box "Ethics and Juvenile Gang Members" on page 40. Although it is not shown in the box, Decker and Van Winkle developed an informed consent form for their subjects. Keeping in mind the various ethical principles discussed in this chapter, try your hand at preparing an informed consent statement that Decker and Van Winkle might have used.

PART 2

Structuring Criminal Justice Inquiry

At its base, scientific research is a process for achieving generalized understanding through observation. Part 3 will describe some of the specific methods of observation for criminal justice research. But first, Part 2 deals with the development of proper questions, which is the structuring of inquiry. Developing questions properly is often more difficult than answering them. Indeed, a properly phrased question often seems to answer itself.

Chapter 3 addresses some of the fundamental issues that must be considered in planning a research project. We start by considering some basic foundations of social science, beginning with the role of theory. Then we'll introduce different general approaches to doing research in criminal justice. Chapter 3 also examines questions of causation, the units of analysis in a research project, and the important role of time.

Chapter 4 deals with the specification of what it is we want to study—a process known as conceptualization—and the measurement of the concepts we specify. We'll look at some of the terms that we use casually in everyday life, and we'll see how essential it is to be clear about what we really mean by such terms when we do research. Once we are clear on what we mean when we use certain terms, we are in a position to create measurements of what those terms refer to. The process of devising steps or operations for measuring what we want to study is known as operationalization. By way of illustrating this process, Chapter 4 includes an extended discussion of different approaches to measuring crime.

Chapter 5 concentrates on the overall design of a criminal justice research project. A criminal justice research design specifies a strategy for finding out something, for structuring a research project. Chapter 5 describes commonly used strategies for experimental and quasi-experimental research. Each is adapted in some way from the classical scientific experiment.

CHAPTER 3

General Issues in Research Design

Here we'll examine some fundamental principles about conducting empirical research, from the foundations of social science through causation, validity, the different units on which we conduct research, and the time dimension.

Theory and Serial Sex Offenders

Criminologist Eric Beauregard and colleagues (Beauregard, Rossmo, and Proulx 2007) studied 69 incarcerated serial sex offenders in Canada. The research had two objectives. First, the researchers developed a descriptive model of how sex offenders "hunted" for victims. Drawing on lengthy interviews with subjects, they systematically classified the different search methods and places where offenders looked for victims. Rational choice and routine activity theories of crime helped Beauregard and colleagues classify sex offender actions into summary categories for their descriptive model:

Victim Search Methods

- Offender's routine activities
- Victim's routine activities
- Choice of a hunting field
- Victim selection preferences

Offender Attack Methods

- Attack location choice
- Method to bring victim to crime location
- Crime location choice

The second objective was to see if this descriptive model was potentially useful in *profiling* serial sex offenders. If the researchers could identify patterns of behavior based on what they learned from convicted sex offenders, then it might be possible to profile the actions of active offenders at large. Profiling is a form of prediction based on observed regularities. Results showed clear patterns and sequences of offense stages. Sex offenders' behavior was limited to certain situations where they encountered victims. For example, 57 percent of offenders chose public areas such as parks or shopping malls as their "hunting field"—where the searched for possible victims. These serial sex offenders were quite different in this regard than sex offenders generally, who tend to limit their search to family members and acquaintances (Leclerc, Wortley, and Smallbone 2011).

This example illustrates three ways in which theory is involved in criminal justice research. First, Beauregard and associates drew on existing theories to frame their analysis of serial sex offender behavior. We will see further examples of this *deductive* use of theory. Second, findings from the preliminary model: "also make a contribution to the theoretical assumptions regarding offender profiling" (Beauregard, Rossmo, and Proulx 2007, 461). This is *inductive* theory building, pulling together research findings to make more general statements and predictions. Third, criminal justice theory and policy have much in common. Each depends on general explanations and patterns of behavior.

Also notice how this example examines aggregates of sex offenders, not individuals. Finally, the researchers are interested in relationships between types of places and sex offender behavior.

Introduction

Certain principles guide all the different approaches to scientific research in criminal justice.

Science is an enterprise dedicated to "finding out." No matter what we want to find out, though, there are likely to be a great many ways of going about it. Topics examined in this chapter address the foundations of social science, different general approaches to doing research in criminal justice, and elements of causation and time.

In practice, all aspects of research design are interrelated. They are separated here and in subsequent chapters so that we can explore particular topics in detail. We start by discussing basic principles of social science, those that apply to different broad approaches to conducting scientific inquiry.

Next, we examine causation in social science, the foundation of explanatory research, and the validity of statements about cause. We then consider units of analysis—the what or whom we want to study. Deciding on units of analysis is an important part of all research, partly because people sometimes inappropriately use data measuring one type of unit to say something about a different type of unit.

The chapter concludes with a discussion of alternative ways of handling time in criminal justice research. It is sometimes appropriate to examine a static cross section of social life, but other studies follow social processes over time. In this regard, researchers must consider the time order of events and processes in making statements about cause.

Foundations of Social Science

Social scientific inquiry generates knowledge through logic and observation.

The two pillars of science are logic, or rationality, and observation. A scientific understanding of the world must make sense and must agree with what we observe. Both of these elements are essential to social science and relate to three key aspects of the overall scientific enterprise: theory, data collection, and data analysis.

As a broad generalization, scientific theory deals with the logical aspect of science, data collection deals with the observational aspect, and data analysis looks for patterns in what is observed. This book focuses mainly on issues related to data collection—demonstrating how to conduct empirical research—but social science involves all three elements. Figure 3.1 offers a schematic view of these three aspects of social science.

Let's now consider some of the fundamental things that distinguish social science from other ways of looking at social phenomena.

Theory, Not Philosophy or Belief

Social scientific theory has to do with what *is*, not what *should be*. A **theory** is a systematic explanation for the observed facts and laws that relate to a particular aspect of life—juvenile delinquency, for example, or perhaps social stratification or political revolution. Joseph Maxwell (2005, 42) defines theory as "a set of concepts and the proposed relationships among these, a structure that is intended to represent or model something about the world."

Often, social scientists begin constructing a theory by observing aspects of social life, seeking to discover patterns that may point to more or less universal principles. Barney Glaser and Anselm Strauss (1967) coined the term *grounded theory* to describe this method of theory construction. Field research—the direct observation of events in progress—is frequently used to develop theories, or survey research may reveal patterns of attitudes that suggest particular theoretical explanations.

Once developed, theories provide general statements about social life that are used to guide research. For example, routine activity theory states that crimes are more likely to occur when a motivated offender encounters a suitable victim in the absence of a capable guardian (Cohen and Felson 1979). Mike Townsley and associates used routine activity theory to guide their research on "contagious" burglaries (Townsley, Homel, and Chaseling 2003). They argued that once burglars struck one house in a neighborhood, they were more likely to break into nearby houses because

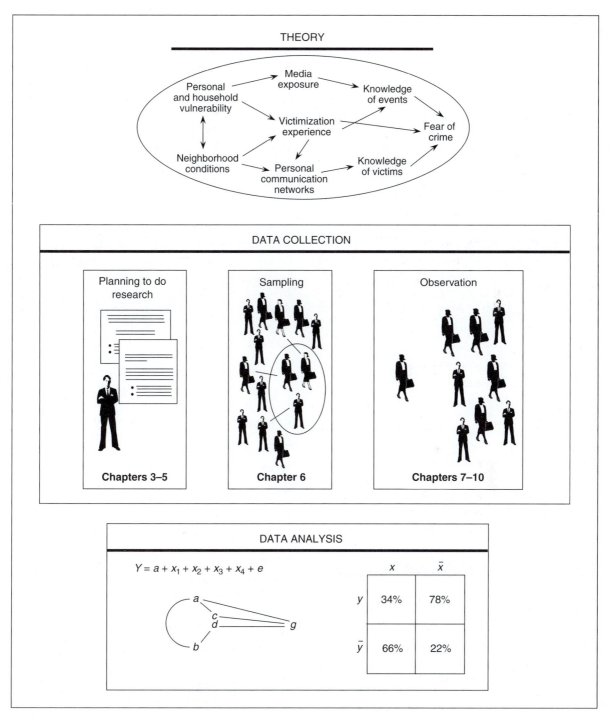

FIGURE 3.1   Social Science = Theory + Data Collection + Data Analysis

they had become more familiar with an area and its potential targets. The research results were generally consistent with these expectations—burglaries tended to cluster around houses of similar type in a neighborhood.

Townsley and associates used routine activity theory to generate a **hypothesis** about patterns of burglary. A hypothesis is an expectation about the nature of things derived from a theory. Taking a different example, a theory might contain the hypothesis "high school dropouts will have higher delinquency rates compared with youths enrolled in high school." Such a hypothesis could then be tested through research.

Drawing on theories to generate hypotheses that are tested through research is the traditional image of science, illustrated in Figure 3.2. Here we see the researcher beginning with an interest in something or an idea about it. Next comes the

development of a theoretical understanding of how a number of concepts, represented by the letters A, B, C, and so on, may be related to each other. The theoretical considerations result in a hypothesis, or an expectation about the way things would be in the world if the theoretical expectations were correct. The notation $Y = f(X)$ is a conventional way of saying that Y (for example, auto-theft rate) is a function of or is in some way caused by X (for example, availability of off-street parking). At that level, however, X and Y have general rather than specific meanings.

In the operationalization process, general concepts are translated into specific indicators. Thus, the lowercase x is a concrete indicator of capital X. As an example, census data on the number of housing units that have garages (x) are a concrete indicator of off-street parking (X). This operationalization process results in the formation of a

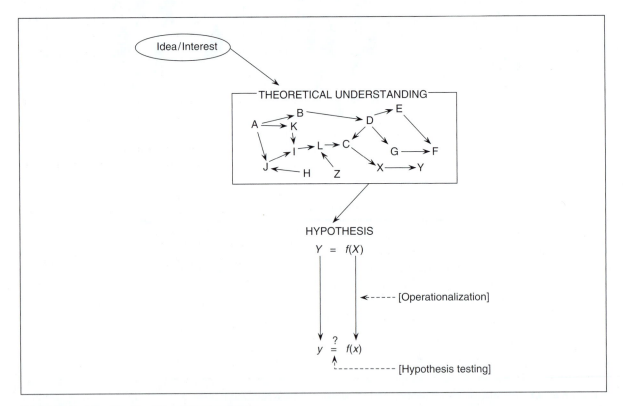

FIGURE 3.2 The Traditional Image of Science

testable hypothesis: is the rate of auto theft higher in areas where fewer housing units have garages? Observations aimed at finding out are part of what is typically called **hypothesis testing**.

Regularities

Ultimately, social scientific theory aims to find patterns of regularity in social life. This assumes, of course, that life is regular, not chaotic or random. That assumption applies to all science, but it is sometimes a barrier for people when they first approach social science.

A vast number of norms and rules in society create regularity. Only persons who have reached a certain age may obtain a driver's license. In the U.S. Supreme Court, only lawyers sit on the bench. Such informal and formal prescriptions regulate, or regularize, social behavior.

In addition to regularities produced by norms and rules, social science is able to identify other types of regularities. For example, teenagers commit more crimes than middle-aged people. When males commit murder, they usually kill another male, but female murderers more often kill a male. On average, white urban residents view police more favorably than nonwhites do. Judges receive higher salaries than social workers. Probation officers have more empathy for the people they supervise than prison guards do.

What About Exceptions?

The objection that there are always exceptions to any social regularity misses the point. The existence of exceptions does not invalidate the existence of regularities. Thus, it is not important that a particular social worker earns more money than a particular judge if, overall, judges earn more than social workers. The pattern still exists. Social regularities represent **probabilistic** patterns, and a general pattern does not have to be reflected in 100 percent of the observable cases to be a pattern.

This rule applies in the physical as well as the social sciences. In genetics, the mating of a blue-eyed person with a brown-eyed person will probably result in brown-eyed offspring. The birth of a blue-eyed child does not challenge the observed regularity, however. Rather, the geneticist states only that brown-eyed offspring are more likely and, furthermore, that a brown-eyed offspring will be born in only a certain percentage of cases. The social scientist makes a similar, probabilistic prediction, that women overall are less likely to murder anybody, but when they do, their victims are most often males.

Aggregates, Not Individuals

Social scientists primarily study social patterns rather than individual ones. All regular patterns reflect the aggregate, or combined, actions and situations of many individuals. Although social scientists study motivations that affect individuals, **aggregates** are more often the subject of social scientific research.

A focus on aggregate patterns rather than on individuals distinguishes the activities of criminal justice researchers from the daily routines of many criminal justice practitioners. Consider the task of processing and classifying individuals newly admitted to a correctional facility. Prison staff administer psychological tests and review the prior record of each new inmate to determine security risks, program needs, and job options. A researcher who is studying whether white inmates tend to be assigned to more desirable jobs than nonwhite inmates would be more interested in patterns of job assignment. The focus would be on aggregates of white and nonwhite persons rather than the assignment for any particular individual.

Social scientific theories, then, typically deal with aggregate, not individual, behavior. Their purpose is to explain why aggregate patterns of behavior are so regular even when the individuals who perform them change over time. In fact, social science is not so much interested in people but rather variables.

A Variable Language

Suppose someone says to you, "Women are too soft-hearted and weak to be police officers." You are likely to hear that comment in terms of what you know about the speaker. If it's your old Uncle Albert, who, you recall, is also strongly opposed to daylight saving time, cell phones, and computers, you are likely to think his latest pronouncement simply fits into his dated views about things in general. If the statement comes from a candidate for sheriff who is trailing a female challenger and who has begun making other statements about women being unfit for public office, you may hear his latest comment in the context of this political challenge.

In both of these examples, you are trying to understand the thoughts of a particular, concrete individual. In social science, however, we go beyond that level of understanding to seek insights into classes or types of individuals. In the two preceding examples, we might use terms like *old-fashioned* or *bigoted* to describe the person who made the comment. In other words, we try to identify the actual individual with some set of similar individuals, and that identification operates on the basis of abstract concepts.

One implication of this approach is that it enables us to make sense out of more than one person. In understanding what makes the bigoted candidate think the way he does, we can also learn about other people who are like him. This is possible because we have not been studying bigots as much as we have been studying bigotry.

Bigotry is considered a variable in this case because the level of bigotry varies; that is, some people in an observed group are more bigoted than others. Social scientists may be interested in understanding the system of variables that causes bigotry to be high in one instance and low in another. However, bigotry is not the only variable here. Gender, age, and economic status also vary among members of the observed group.

Here's another example. Consider the problem of whether police should make arrests in cases of domestic violence. The object of a police officer's attention in handling a domestic assault is the individual case. Of course, each case includes a victim and an offender, and police are concerned with preventing further harm to the victim. The officer must decide whether to arrest one or both parties, or to take some other action. The criminal justice researcher's subject matter is different: does arrest as a general policy prevent future assaults? The researcher may study an individual case (victim and offender), but that case is relevant only as a situation in which an arrest policy might be invoked, which is what the researcher is really studying.

Variables and Attributes

Social scientists study variables and the attributes that compose them. Social scientific theories are written in a variable language, and people get involved mostly as the carriers of those variables.

Attributes are characteristics or qualities that describe some object, such as a person. Examples are *bigoted, old-fashioned, married, unemployed,* and *intoxicated.* Any quality we might use to describe ourselves or someone else is an attribute.

Variables are logical groupings of attributes. *Male* and *female* are attributes, and *gender* is the variable composed of the logical grouping of those two attributes. The variable *occupation* is composed of attributes such as *dentist, professor,* and *truck driver. Prior record* is a variable composed of a set of attributes such as *prior convictions, prior arrests without convictions,* and *no prior arrests.* It's helpful to think of attributes as the categories that make up a variable. See Figure 3.3 for a schematic view of what social scientists mean by variables and attributes. Panel A lists both variables and attributes, mixing them together. Panel B separates these concepts to distinguish variables from attributes. Panel C presents variables together with the attributes they carry.

The relationship between attributes and variables lies at the heart of both description and explanation in science. We might describe a prosecutor's office in terms of the variable *gender* by reporting the observed frequencies of the attributes *male* and *female*: "The office staff is 60 percent men and 40 percent women." An incarceration rate can be thought of as a description of the variable *incarceration status* of a state's population in terms of the attributes *incarcerated* and *not incarcerated.* Even the report of family income for a city is a summary of attributes composing the *income* variable: *$23,210, $57,124, $74,980, $96,000,* and so forth.

The relationship between attributes and variables becomes more complicated as we try to

A.

Some Common Criminal Justice Concepts
Female
Probation
Thief
Gender
Sentence
Property crime
Middle-aged
Age
Auto theft
Occupation

B.

Two Different Kinds of Concepts	
Variables	Attributes
Gender	Female
Sentence	Probation
Property crime	Auto theft
Age	Middle-aged
Occupation	Thief

C.

The Relationship Between Variables and Attributes	
Variables	Attributes
Gender	Female, male
Age	Young, middle-aged, old
Sentence	Fine, prison, probation
Property crime	Auto theft, burglary, larceny
Occupation	Judge, lawyer, thief

FIGURE 3.3 Variables and Attributes

explain how concepts are related to each other. Here's a simple example involving two variables: type of defense attorney and sentence. For the sake of simplicity, let's assume that the variable *defense attorney* has only two attributes: *private attorney* and *public defender*. Similarly, let's give the variable *sentence* two attributes: *probation* and *prison*.

Now let's suppose that 90 percent of people represented by public defenders are sentenced to prison and the other 10 percent are sentenced to probation. And let's suppose that 30 percent of people with private attorneys go to prison and the other 70 percent receive probation. This is shown visually in Figure 3.4A.

Figure 3.4A illustrates a relationship between the variables *defense attorney* and *sentence*. This relationship can be seen by the pairings of attributes on the two variables. There are two predominant pairings: (1) persons represented by private attorneys who are sentenced to probation and (2) persons represented by public defenders who are sentenced to prison. But there are two other useful ways of viewing that relationship.

First, imagine that we play a game in which we bet on your ability to guess whether a person is sentenced to prison or probation. We'll pick the people one at a time (not telling you which ones we've picked), and you have to guess which

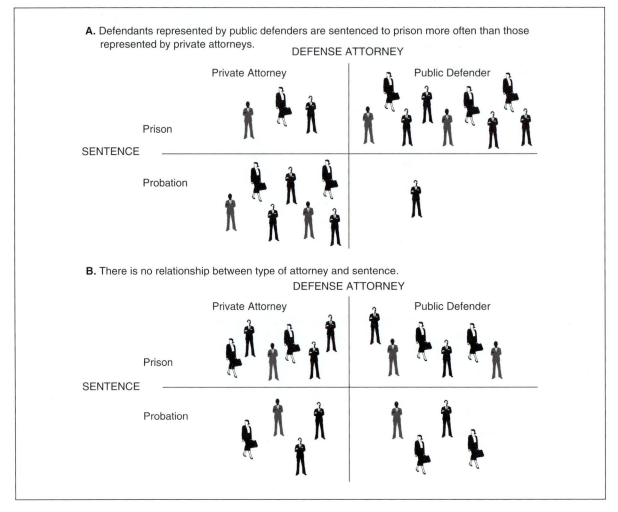

A. Defendants represented by public defenders are sentenced to prison more often than those represented by private attorneys.

B. There is no relationship between type of attorney and sentence.

FIGURE 3.4   Illustration of Relationships Between Two Variables

sentence each person receives. We'll do it for all 20 people in Figure 3.4A. Your best strategy in this case is to always guess prison because 12 out of the 20 people are categorized that way. You'll get 12 right and 8 wrong, for a net success score of 4.

Now suppose that we pick a person from Figure 3.4A and we have to tell you whether the person has a private attorney or a public defender. Your best strategy now is to guess prison for each person with a public defender and probation for each person represented by a private attorney. If you follow that strategy, you will get 16 right and 4 wrong.

Your improvement in guessing the sentence on the basis of knowing the type of defense attorney illustrates what it means to say that the variables are related. You would have made a probabilistic statement on the basis of some empirical observations about the relationship between type of lawyer and type of sentence.

Second, let's consider how the 20 people would be distributed if type of defense attorney and sentence were unrelated. This is illustrated in Figure 3.4B. Notice that half the people have private attorneys and half have public defenders.

Also notice that 12 of the 20 (60 percent) are sentenced to prison—6 who have private attorneys and 6 who have public defenders. The equal distribution of those sentenced to probation and those sentenced to prison, no matter what type of defense attorney each person had, allows us to conclude that the two variables are unrelated. Here, knowing what type of attorney a person had would not be of any value to you in guessing whether that person was sentenced to prison or probation.

Variables and Relationships

Theories describe relationships that might logically be expected among variables. This expectation often involves the notion of *causation*: a person's attributes on one variable are expected to *cause* or encourage a particular attribute on another variable. In the example just given, having a private attorney or a public defender seemed to cause a person to be sentenced to probation or prison, respectively. Apparently there is something about having a public defender that leads people to be sentenced to prison more often than if they are represented by a private attorney.

Type of defense attorney and sentence are examples of independent and dependent variables, respectively. In this example, we assume that criminal sentences are determined or caused by something; the type of sentence depends on something and so is called the **dependent variable**. The dependent variable depends on an **independent variable**; in this case, sentence depends on type of defense attorney.

Notice, at the same time, that type of defense attorney might be found to depend on something else—our subjects' employment status, for example. People who have full-time jobs are more likely to be represented by private attorneys than those who are unemployed. In this latter relationship, the type of attorney is the dependent variable, and the subject's employment status is the independent variable. In cause-and-effect terms, the independent variable is the cause and the dependent variable is the effect.

How does this relate to theory? Our discussion of Figure 3.4 involved the interpretation of data. We looked at the distribution of the 20 people in terms of the two variables. In constructing a theory, we

form an expectation about the relationship between the two variables based on what we know about each. For example, we know that private attorneys tend to be more experienced than public defenders. Many law school graduates gain a few years of experience as public defenders before they enter private practice. Logically, then, we would expect the more experienced private attorneys to be better able to get more lenient sentences for their clients. We might explore this question directly by examining the relationship between attorney experience and sentence, perhaps comparing inexperienced public defenders with public defenders who have been working for a few years. Pursuing this line of reasoning, we could also compare experienced private attorneys with private attorneys fresh out of law school.

Notice that the theory has to do with the variables *defense attorney, sentence,* and *years of experience,* not with individual people per se. People are the carriers of those variables. We study the relationship between the variables by observing people. Ultimately, however, the theory is constructed in terms of variables. It describes the associations that might logically be expected to exist between particular attributes of different variables.

Differing Avenues for Inquiry

Social scientific research is conducted in a variety of ways.

Three broad and interrelated distinctions underlie many of the variations of social scientific research: (1) idiographic and nomothetic explanations, (2) inductive and deductive reasoning, and (3) quantitative and qualitative data. Sometimes these distinctions are described as alternative ways to conduct research. That's misleading, because criminal justice researchers often use all variations of social science research.

Idiographic and Nomothetic Explanations

All of us go through life explaining things; we do it every day. In our everyday explanations, we engage in two distinct forms of causal reasoning—idiographic and nomothetic explanation—although we do not ordinarily think about the difference, or even distinguish them.

Sometimes we attempt to explain a single situation exhaustively. You might have done poorly on an exam because (1) you had forgotten there was an exam that day, (2) it was in your worst subject, (3) a traffic jam caused you to be late to class, and (4) your roommate kept you up the night before by hosting a party. Given all these circumstances, it is no wonder that you did poorly on the exam.

This type of causal reasoning is **idiographic** explanation. *Idio* in this context means "unique, separate, peculiar, or distinct," as in the word *idiosyncrasy*. When we complete an idiographic explanation, we feel that we fully understand the many causes of what happened in a particular instance. At the same time, the scope of our explanation is limited to the case at hand. Although parts of the idiographic explanation might apply to other situations, our intention is to explain one case fully.

Now consider a different kind of explanation. For example, every time you study with a group, you do better on an exam than if you study alone. Your favorite team does better at home than on the road. You get more speeding tickets on weekends than during the week. This type of explanation—called **nomothetic**—seeks to explain a class of situations or events rather than a single one. Moreover, it seeks to explain efficiently, using only one or just a few explanatory factors. Finally, it settles for a partial rather than a full explanation of a type of situation.

In each of the preceding nomothetic examples, you might qualify your causal statements with phrases such as "on the whole" or "usually." You usually do better on exams when you've studied in a group, but there have been exceptions. Your team has won some games on the road and lost some at home. And last week you got a speeding ticket on the way to Tuesday's chemistry class, but you did not get one over the weekend. Such exceptions are an acceptable price to pay for a broader range of overall explanation.

Both idiographic and nomothetic approaches to understanding can be useful in daily life. They are also powerful tools for criminal justice research. The researcher who seeks an exhaustive understanding of the inner workings of a particular juvenile gang or the rulings of a specific judge is engaging in idiographic research. The aim is to understand that particular group or individual as fully as possible.

Rick Brown and Ron Clarke (2004) sought to understand thefts of a particular model of Nissan trucks in the south of England. Most stolen trucks were never recovered. Their research led Brown and Clarke to a shipping yard where trucks were taken apart and shipped to ports in France and Nigeria as scrap metal. They later learned that trucks were reassembled and sold to individuals and small companies. In the course of their research, they linked most thieves in England and most resellers abroad to legitimate shipping and scrap metal businesses. Even though Brown and Clarke sought answers to the idiosyncratic problem of stolen trucks in one region of England, they came to some tentative conclusions about loosely organized international theft rings.

In contrast to the idiographic study of Nissan truck theft, Pierre Tremblay and associates (Tremblay, Talon, and Hurley 2001) explored how a theory of offending helped explain different types of offender networks. After examining auto thefts over 25 years in Quebec, the authors concluded that different types of relationships were involved in different types of professional car theft. However, Tremblay and associates found that persons involved in legitimate car sales and repair businesses were key members in all networks. The researchers showed how complex relationships among people involved in legitimate and illegitimate activities helped explain patterns of car theft over a quarter century. This is an illustration of the nomothetic approach to understanding.

Thus, social scientists have access to two distinct logics of explanation. We can alternate between searching for broad, albeit less detailed, universals (nomothetic) and probing more deeply into more specific cases (idiographic).

Inductive and Deductive Reasoning

The distinction between inductive and deductive reasoning exists in daily life as well as in criminal justice research. As an example, let's assume we are interested in the relationship between the number of hours spent studying for an exam and the grade earned on that exam. Figure 3.5 shows a graphic comparison of the deductive and inductive approaches to reasoning. Using **deductive reasoning**, we begin by

examining the matter logically. Doing well on an exam reflects a student's ability to recall and to manipulate information. Both of these abilities should be increased by exposure to the information before the exam. In this fashion, we arrive at a hypothesis suggesting a positive relationship between the number of

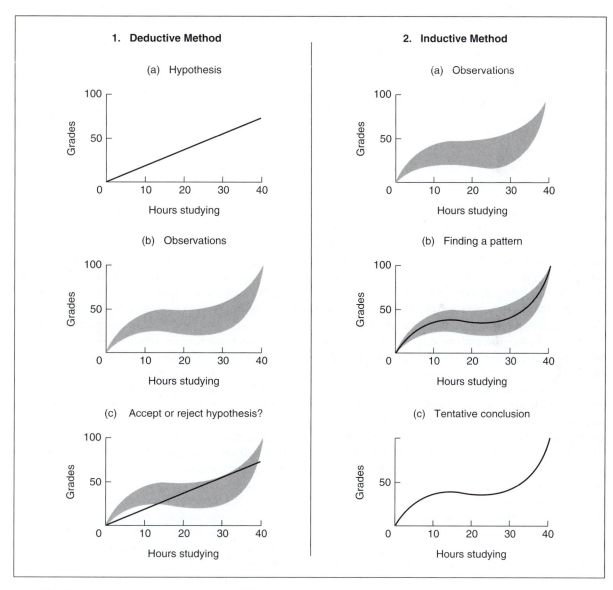

F I G U R E 3.5   Deductive and Inductive Methods

hours spent studying and the grade earned on the exam. We say *positive* because we expect grades to increase as the hours of studying increase. If increased hours produced lower grades, that would be called a *negative* relationship. The hypothesis is represented by the graph in part 1(a) of Figure 3.5.

Our next step, using deductive reasoning, is to make observations relevant to testing our hypothesis. The shaded area in part 1(b) of Figure 3.5 represents perhaps hundreds of observations of different students, noting how many hours they studied and what grades they got. Finally, in part 1(c) of the figure, we compare the hypothesis and the observations. Because observations in the real world seldom (if ever) match our expectations perfectly, we must decide whether the match is close enough to consider the hypothesis confirmed. Put differently, can we conclude that the hypothesis, represented by the straight line in part 1(c), describes the general pattern illustrated by the shaded pattern, granting some variations in real life?

Now let's address the same research question using **inductive reasoning**. In this case, we begin—as in part 2(a) of Figure 3.5—with a set of observations, shown in the shaded pattern. Curious about the relationship between hours spent studying and grades earned, we arrange to collect some relevant data. Then we look for a pattern that best represents or summarizes our observations. In part 2(b) of the figure, the pattern is shown as a curved line running through the center of the curving mass of points.

The pattern found among the points in this case—and shown in part 2(c) of Figure 3.5—suggests that with 1 to 15 hours of studying, each additional hour generally produces a higher grade on the exam. Studying 15 to 25 hours actually seems to slightly lower the grade. Studying more than 25 hours, however, results in a return to the initial pattern: more hours produce higher grades. Using the inductive method, then, we end up with a tentative conclusion about the pattern of the relationship between the two variables. The conclusion is tentative because the observations we have made cannot be taken as a test of the pattern; those observations are the source of the pattern we've created.

In summary, the scientific norm of logical reasoning provides a bridge between theory and research—a two-way bridge. Scientific inquiry in practice typically involves an alternation between deductive and inductive reasoning. Using the deductive approach, we reason from general statements *toward* observations. The inductive approach reasons *from* observations to general statements. Both logic and observation are essential. Both inductive and deductive reasoning are valid avenues for criminal justice and other social scientific research. Moreover, they work together to provide ever more powerful and complete understandings.

Quantitative and Qualitative Data

Simply put, the distinction between quantitative and qualitative data is the distinction between numerical and nonnumerical data. When we say that someone is witty, we are making a qualitative assertion. When we say that that person has appeared three times in a local comedy club, we are attempting to quantify our assessment.

Most observations are qualitative at the outset, whether it is our experience of someone's sense of humor, the location of a pointer on a measuring scale, or a check mark entered in a questionnaire. None of these things is inherently numerical, but it is often useful to convert observations to a numerical form. Quantification often makes our observations more explicit, makes it easier to aggregate and summarize data, and opens up the possibility of statistical analyses, ranging from simple descriptions to more complex testing of relationships between variables.

Quantification requires focusing our attention and specifying meaning. Suppose someone asks whether your friends tend to be older or younger than you. A quantitative answer seems easy. You think about how old each of your friends is, calculate an average, and see whether it is higher or lower than your own age. Case closed.

Or is it? Although we focused our attention on "older or younger" in terms of the number of years people have been alive, we might mean something different with that idea—for example, "maturity" or "worldliness." Your friends may tend to be a little younger than you in age but may act more mature. Or we might have been thinking of how young or old your friends look or of the variation in their life experiences, their worldliness. All these other meanings are lost in the numerical calculation of average age.

In addition to greater detail, nonnumerical observations seem to convey a greater richness of meaning than do quantified data. Think of the cliché "he is older than his years." The meaning of that expression is lost in attempts to specify how much older. In this sense, the richness of meaning is partly a function of ambiguity. If the expression meant something to you when you read it, that meaning came from your own experiences, from people you have known who might fit the description of being older than their years.

This concept can be quantified to a certain extent, however. For example, we could make a list of life experiences that contribute to what we mean by worldliness:

Getting married

Getting divorced

Having a parent die

Being fired from a job

Moving to another country

We could quantify people's worldliness by counting how many of these experiences they have had: the more such experiences, the more worldly we say they are. If we think that some experiences are more powerful than others, we can give those experiences more points than others. Once we decide on the specific experiences to be considered and the number of points each warrants, scoring people and comparing their worldliness is fairly straightforward.

To quantify a concept like worldliness, we must be explicit about what we mean. By focusing specifically on what we will include in our measurement of the concept, as we did here, we also exclude the other possible meanings. Inevitably, then, quantitative measures will be more superficial than qualitative descriptions. This is the trade-off.

What a dilemma! Which approach should we choose? Which is better? Which is more appropriate to criminal justice research?

The good news is that we don't have to choose. In fact, by choosing to undertake a qualitative or quantitative study, researchers run the risk of artificially limiting the scope of their inquiry. Both qualitative and quantitative methods are useful and legitimate. Some research situations and topics require elements of both approaches.

Chapters 7 and 8 illustrate the complementary nature of qualitative and quantitative interviewing. Interviews are fundamental tools in all social science research and can be especially important in criminal justice research. To paraphrase our discussion so far, qualitative interviewing can convey a greater richness of meaning compared to closed-ended questions in structured interviews.

Similarly, field observation, covered in Chapter 9, can be structured quantitatively, to systematically record and tabulate observations of behavior and settings, or qualitatively, in an effort to understand patterns of behavior and its contexts. For example, we might map and count the locations of street drug arrests or observe a street drug market for several hours and describe how transactions occurred. Counting street drug arrests and different locations would give us a quantitative measure of drug markets, while field observation would provide more detail on how sellers and buyers found each other and completed transactions. Using both approaches would give us a better understanding of street drug markets.

Causation in the Social Sciences

Causation is the focus of explanatory and evaluation research.

One of the chief goals of social scientific researchers is to explain why things are the way they are. Typically, we do that by specifying the *causes* for the way things are: some things are caused by other things.

At the outset, it's important to keep in mind that cause in social science is inherently probabilistic, as we noted earlier in this chapter. We say, for example, that certain factors make delinquency more or less *likely*. Thus, victims of childhood abuse or neglect are *more likely* to report alcohol abuse as adults (Schuck and Widom 2001). Recidivism is less *likely* among offenders who receive more careful assessment and classification at institutional intake (Cullen and Gendreau 2000).

Criteria for Causality

We begin our consideration of cause by examining what criteria must be satisfied before we can infer that something causes something else. Joseph Maxwell (2013, 122–123) writes that criteria for assessing an idiographic explanation are (1) how credible and believable it is and (2) whether alternative explanations ("rival hypotheses") were seriously considered and found wanting. The first criterion relates to logic as one of the foundations of science. We demand that our explanations make sense, even if the logic is sometimes complex. The second criterion reminds us of Sherlock Holmes's dictum that when all other possibilities have been eliminated the remaining explanation, however improbable, must be the truth.

Regarding nomothetic explanation, we examine three specific criteria for causality, as described by William Shadish, Thomas Cook, and Donald Campbell (2002). The first requirement in a causal relationship between two variables is that the cause must precede the effect in time. It makes no sense to imagine something being caused by something else that happened later on. A bullet leaving the muzzle of a gun does not cause the gunpowder to explode; it works the other way around. As simple and obvious as this criterion may seem, criminal justice research suffers many problems in this regard. Often the time order connecting two variables is simply unclear. Which comes first: drug use or crime? Even when the time order seems clear, exceptions may be found. For example, we normally assume that obtaining a master's degree in management is a cause of more rapid advancement in a state department of corrections. Yet corrections executives might pursue graduate education after they have been promoted and recognize that

advanced training in management skills will help them do their job better.

The second requirement in a causal relationship is that the two variables must be empirically correlated with each other—they must occur together. It makes no sense to say that exploding gunpowder causes a bullet to leave the muzzle of a gun if, in observed reality, a bullet does not come out after the gunpowder explodes.

Again, criminal justice research has difficulties with this requirement. In the probabilistic world of nomothetic models of explanation, at least, we encounter few perfect correlations. Most judges sentence repeat drug dealers to prison, but some don't. We are forced to ask, therefore, how strong the empirical relationship must be for that relationship to be considered causal.

The third requirement for a causal relationship is that the observed empirical correlation between two variables cannot be explained away as being due to the influence of some other variable that causes both of them. For example, we may observe that drug markets are often found near bus stops, but this does not mean that bus stops encourage drug markets. A third variable is at work here: groups of people naturally congregate near bus stops, and street drug markets are often found where people naturally congregate.

To sum up, most social researchers consider two variables to be causally related—one causes the other—if (1) the cause precedes the effect in time, (2) there is an empirical correlation between them, and (3) the relationship is not found to result from the effects of some third variable on each of the two initially observed. Any relationship that satisfies all these criteria is causal, and these are the only criteria that need to be satisfied.

Validity and Causal Inference

Paying careful attention to cause-and-effect relationships is crucial in criminal justice research. Cause and effect are also key elements of applied studies, in which a researcher may be interested in whether, for example, a new mandatory sentencing law actually causes an increase in the prison population.

When we are concerned with whether we are correct in inferring that a cause produced an effect, we are concerned with the **validity** of causal inference. In the words of Shadish, Cook, and Campbell (2002, 34), validity is "the approximate truth of an inference…. When we say something is valid, we make a judgment about the extent to which relevant evidence supports that inference as being true or correct." They emphasize that *approximate* is an important word because one can never be absolutely certain about cause.

Researchers are mostly concerned with different **validity threats** in causal inference—reasons we might be incorrect in stating that some cause produced some effect. As Maxwell (2013, 123) puts it, "A key concept for validity is thus the *validity threat*: a way you might be wrong" (emphasis in original). Chapter 5 discusses different types of validity threats in detail, linking the issue of validity to different ways of designing research. Here we will describe how validity threats might emerge in examining possible relationships between drug use and crime.

Does Drug Use Cause Crime?

Understanding causal statements about drug use and crime requires carefully specifying two key concepts—drug use and crime—and considering the different ways these concepts might be related. Jan Chaiken and Marcia Chaiken (1990) provide unusually careful and well-reasoned insights that will guide our consideration of links between drugs and crime. The three criteria for inferring cause—time order, empirical relationship, and eliminating alternative explanations—will guide our discussion.

First is the question of temporal order: which comes first, drug use or crime? Research summarized by Chaiken and Chaiken provides no conclusive answer. In an earlier study of prison inmates, Chaiken and Chaiken (1982) found that 12 percent of their adult subjects committed crimes after using drugs for at least two years, whereas 15 percent committed predatory crimes two or more years before using drugs. Studies of juveniles revealed similar findings: "About 50 percent of delinquent youngsters are delinquent before they start using drugs; about 50 percent start concurrently or after" (Chaiken and Chaiken 1990, 235).

Regarding an empirical relationship, many studies have found that some drug users commit crimes and that some criminals use drugs. Trevor Bennett and associates (Bennett, Holloway, and Farrington 2008) conducted summary analysis of 30 research studies on drug use and crime. They found that drug users were over three times more likely to be involved in crime than nonusers. So a statistical association between drug use and crime clearly exists.

What about the possible influence of other factors, things that might be related to both drug use and crime? Chaiken and Chaiken (1990, 234) conclude that "drug use and crime participation are weakly related as contemporaneous products of factors generally antithetical to traditional United States lifestyles." Stated somewhat differently, drug use and crime (as well as delinquency) are each deviant activities produced by other underlying causes. The presence of other factors suggests the relationship is not directly causal. Drug use and crime are linked, but each appears to be related to other variables.

To further consider the threats to the validity of links between drugs and crime, let's think for a moment about different patterns of each behavior, rather than assume that drug use and crime are uniform behaviors. Many adolescents in the United States experiment with drugs; just as many commit delinquent acts or petty crimes. A large number of adults may be occasional users of illegal drugs as well. Many different patterns of drug use, delinquency, and adult criminality have been found in research in other countries. Stephen Pudney (2002) and Trevor Bennett and Katy Holloway (2005) report on varying patterns of drug use in England and Wales, ranging from experimentation with marijuana to chronic heroin addiction. Because both drug use and crime take different forms, searching for a single cause-and-effect relationship misrepresents a complex process.

In further analysis, Bennett and colleagues compared offending by type of drug use, finding that users of crack cocaine were more likely to be offenders than users of any other drug. They also found that the relationship between occasional marijuana use and delinquency among teenagers is different from that between occasional cocaine use and adult crime; each relationship, in turn, varies from that between crack cocaine addiction and persistent criminal behavior among adults.

Basic and applied research on the relationships among drug use and crime readily illustrates threats to the validity of causal inference. It is often difficult to find a relationship because there is so much variation in drug use and crime participation. A large number of studies have demonstrated that, when statistical relationships are found, both drug use and crime can be attributed to other, often

multiple, causes. Different patterns among different population groups mean there are no readily identifiable cause-and-effect constructs. Because of these differences, policies developed to counter drug use among the population as a whole cannot be expected to have much of an impact on serious crime. For example, Bennett and associates argue that government antidrug policy should distinguish more carefully between types of drug use (2008, 117–118).

None of the above is to say that there is no cause-and-effect relationship between drug use and crime. However, research has clearly shown that there is no simple causal connection. For more on how questions of cause and effect emerge, see the box "Causation and Declining Crime in New York City."

CAUSATION AND DECLINING CRIME IN NEW YORK CITY

Did changes in police strategy and tactics in New York City cause a decline in crime? That question is central to what became quite a spirited debate, a debate that centers our attention on causation. In fact, former police commissioner William Bratton (1999, 17) used language strikingly similar to what you will find in this chapter to argue that crime dropped in New York because of police action:

> As a basic tenet of epistemology … we cannot conclude that a causal relationship exists between two variables unless … three necessary conditions occur: one variable must precede the other in time, an empirically measured relationship must be demonstrated between the variables, and the relationship must not be better explained by any third intervening variable. Although contemporary criminology's explanations for the decline in New York City meet the first two conditions, they don't explain it better than a third intervening variable.

With these words, Bratton challenged researchers to propose some empirical measure of a variable that better accounted for the crime reduction. A number of researchers have advanced alternative explanations. Let's now consider what some of those variables might be.

Changing Drug Markets

After falling from 1980 through 1984, homicide rates in larger U.S. cities rose sharply through the early 1990s. This corresponded with the emergence of crack cocaine, a low-cost drug sold by loosely organized gangs that settled business disputes with guns instead of lawyers. The decline in crack use in the mid-1990s corresponded with the beginning of decreasing homicide rates. Alfred Blumstein and Richard Rosenfeld (1998) point to changes in crack markets as a plausible explanation—gun homicides and crack markets both increased and decreased together. Other researchers claim that changes in crack markets had some effect on violence (Johnson, Golub, and Dunlap 2000; Karmen 2000).

Regression

A common threat to validity in research on crime trends is regression to the mean. This refers to a phenomenon whereby social indicators move up and down over time, and abnormally high or low values are eventually followed by a return (regression) to more normal levels. Jeffrey Fagan and associates (Fagan, Zimring, and Kim 1998) present evidence to suggest that rates of gun homicide in New York were relatively stable from 1969 through the mid-1980s, when they began to increase sharply. Around 1991,

(continued)

rates began to decline, returning to approximate previous levels.

Homicides Declined Everywhere

Fagan and associates (1998) point out that although New York's decline was considerable, it was not unprecedented. Many large cities saw sharp reductions in homicide during the same period, and a few cities had even greater declines. Blumstein and Rosenfeld (1998) cite similar data, pointing out that sharp reductions in homicide rates occurred in cities where no major changes in policing were evident. This suggests that declining crime in New York was simply part of a national trend.

Incapacitation

The decline of homicide rates in the 1990s followed more than a decade of growth in incarceration rates in state and federal correctional facilities. According to the incapacitation argument, rates of homicide and other violent crimes declined because growing numbers of violent criminals were locked up. Some researchers have presented evidence to challenge that claim (Rosenfeld 2000; Spelman 2000).

Economic Opportunity

The early 1990s marked the beginning of a sustained period of economic growth in the United States. With greater job opportunities, crime naturally declined. A number of authors have cited this example of how change in one of the "root causes" of crime might have caused changes in rates of homicide and other serious crimes (for example, Karmen 2000; Silverman 1999), but none have offered any evidence to support it.

Demographic Change

Because violent and other offenses tend to be committed more by younger people, especially young males, a decline in the number of members in those demographic groups may be responsible for New York's reduced crime rate. Fagan and associates (1998) present data that show relatively stable numbers of 15- to 19-year-old males in New York, so it seems unlikely that demographic factors account for changes in crime rates. Additional analysis of demographic change has been conducted by Rosenfeld (2000) and James Alan Fox (2000).

Continuation of a Trend

George Kelling and William Bratton (1998) claim that crime declined in New York immediately following the implementation of major changes in policing. But other analysts argue that the beginning of the shift preceded these changes. Notice that this brings into question another of the three criteria for inferring cause by claiming that the effect—declining crime—occurred before the cause—changes in policing. Even more possible explanations have been offered, but those presented here are the most plausible and are most often cited by researchers. Andrew Karmen (2000, 263) offers a good summary of different explanations for New York's crime drop.

Introducing Scientific Realism

In our final consideration of cause and effect in this chapter, we revisit the distinction between idiographic and nomothetic ways of explanation. Doing research to find what causes what reflects nomothetic concerns more often than not. We wish to find causal explanations that apply generally to situations beyond those we actually study in our research. At the same time, researchers and public officials are often interested in understanding specific causal mechanisms in more narrowly defined situations—what we have described as the idiographic mode of explanation.

Scientific realism bridges idiographic and nomothetic approaches to explanation by seeking to understand how causal *mechanisms* operate in specific *contexts*. Traditional approaches to finding cause and effect usually try to isolate causal mechanisms from other possible influences, something you should now recognize as trying to control threats to validity. The scientific realist approach views these other possible influences as contexts in which causal mechanisms operate. Rather than try to exclude or otherwise control possible outside influences, scientific realism studies how such influences are involved in cause-and-effect relationships.

For example, we reviewed at some length the cause-and-effect conundrum surrounding drug use and crime. That review was framed by traditional nomothetic research to establish cause and effect. A scientific realism approach to the question would recognize that drug use and crime co-occur in some contexts but not in others.

We say that scientific realism bridges idiographic and nomothetic modes of explanation because it exhibits elements of both. Because it focuses our attention on very specific questions, scientific realism seems idiographic. Here's an example: "Will redesigning the Interstate 78 exit in Newark, New Jersey, cause a reduction in the number of suburban residents seeking to buy heroin in this neighborhood?" But this specific question is compatible with more general questions of causation: "Can the design of streets and intersections be modified to make it more difficult for street drug markets to operate?" Changing an expressway exit ramp to reduce drug sales in Newark is a specific example of cause and effect that is rooted in the more general causal relationship between traffic patterns and drug markets. Research by Nicholas Zanin and colleagues (Zanin, Shane, and Clarke 2004) addresses both the idiographic explanation in Newark and the potential for broader applications elsewhere.

These illustrations of the scientific realist approach to cause and effect are examples of research for the purpose of application, a topic treated at length by British researchers Ray Pawson and Nick Tilley (1997). Application is a type of explanatory research, as we indicated in Chapter 1. In later chapters, we call on scientific realism as a strategy for designing explanatory research (Chapter 5) and conducting evaluations (Chapter 11).

Sorting out causes and effects is one of the most difficult challenges of explanatory research. Our attention now turns to two other important considerations that emerge in research for explanation and other purposes: units of analysis and the time dimension.

Units of Analysis

To avoid mistaken inferences, researchers must carefully specify the people or phenomena that will be studied.

In criminal justice research, there is a great deal of variation in what or who is studied—what are technically called **units of analysis**. Individual people are often units of analysis. Researchers may make observations describing certain characteristics of offenders or crime victims, such as age, gender, or race. The descriptions of many individuals are then combined to provide a picture of the population that comprises those individuals.

For example, we may note the age and gender of persons convicted of drunk driving in Fort Lauderdale over a certain period. Aggregating these observations, we might characterize drunk-driving offenders as 72 percent men and 28 percent women, with an average age of 26.4 years. This is a descriptive analysis of convicted drunk drivers in Fort Lauderdale. Although the description applies to the group of drunk drivers as a whole, it is based on the characteristics of individual people convicted of drunk driving.

Units of analysis in a study are typically also the units of observation. Thus, to study what steps people take to protect their homes from burglary, we might observe individual household residents, perhaps through interviews. Sometimes, however, we observe units of analysis indirectly. We might ask individuals about crime prevention measures for the purpose of describing households. We might want to find out whether homes with double-cylinder deadbolt locks are burglarized less often than homes with less substantial protection. In this case, our units of analysis are households, but the units of observation are individual household members who are asked to describe burglaries and home protection to interviewers.

Some studies try to describe or explain more than one unit of analysis. In these cases, the researcher must anticipate what conclusions she or he wishes to draw with regard to which units of analysis. For example, we may want to discover what kinds of college students (individuals) are most successful in their careers; we may also want to learn what kinds of colleges (organizations) produce the most successful graduates.

Here's an example that illustrates the potential complexity of units of analysis. Murders usually involve one individual who kills another individual. However, when Charis Kubrin and Ronald Weitzer (2003, 157) ask, "Why do these neighborhoods generate high homicide rates?" the unit of analysis in that phrase is neighborhood. You can probably imagine some kinds of neighborhoods (e.g., poor, urban) that would have high homicide rates and some (e.g., wealthy, suburban) that would have low rates. In this particular conversation, the unit of analysis (neighborhood) would be categorized in terms of variables such as economic level, locale, and homicide rate.

Individuals

Any variety of individual people may be the units of analysis in criminal justice research. Individual people may be partly defined by their roles in our research—as victims, judges, drug sellers, sex offenders, or general population. Individuals in the general population are units in surveys like the National Crime Victimization Survey (NCVS), where nationally representative samples of individuals are interviewed about the experiences with crime. Beauregard and colleagues (2007), as described in the beginning of this chapter, examined individual sex offenders. Or we might study inmates of a correctional institution. In each of these cases, our units would be individual people. Other examples of units of analysis at the individual level are police, defendants in criminal court, gang members, and active burglars. Note that each of these terms implies some population of individual persons.

Groups

Social groups may also be the units of analysis for criminal justice research. This is not the same as studying the individuals within a group. If we study the members of a juvenile gang to learn about teenagers who join gangs, the individual (teen gang member) is the unit of analysis. But if we study all the juvenile gangs in a city to learn the differences between big gangs and small ones, between gangs selling drugs and gangs stealing cars, and so forth, the unit of analysis is the social group (gang).

Police beats or patrol districts might be the units of analysis in a study. A police beat can be described in terms of the total number of people who live within its boundaries, total street mileage, annual crime reports, and whether the beat includes a special facility such as a park or high school. We can then determine, for example, whether beats that include a park report more assaults than beats without such facilities or whether auto thefts are more common in beats with more street mileage. Here, the individual police beat is the unit of analysis.

Other examples of units at the group level are *households, city blocks, census tracts, cities, counties*, and *other geographic regions*. Each of these terms also implies some population of groups. *Street gang* implies some population that includes all street gangs. The population of street gangs could be described, say, in terms of its geographic distribution throughout a city. An explanatory study of street gangs might discover, for example, whether large gangs are more likely than small ones to engage in intergang warfare.

Organizations

Formal political or social organizations may also be the units of analysis in criminal justice research. An example is correctional facilities, which implies, of course, a population of all correctional facilities. Individual facilities might be characterized in terms of their number of employees, status as state or federal prisons, security classification, percentage of inmates who are from racial or ethnic minority groups, types of offenses for which inmates are sentenced to each facility, average length of sentence served, and so forth. We might determine whether federal prisons house a larger or smaller percentage of offenders sentenced for white-collar crimes than do state prisons. Other examples of formal organizations suitable as units of analysis are police departments, courtrooms, probation offices, drug treatment facilities, and the Fortune Society, a nonprofit organization that helps returning prisoners.

When social groups or formal organizations are the units of analysis, their characteristics are often derived from the characteristics of their individual members. Thus, a correctional facility might be described in terms of the inmates it houses—gender distribution, average sentence length, ethnicity, and so on. In a descriptive study, we might be interested in the percentage of institutions housing only females. Or, in an explanatory study, we might determine whether institutions housing both males and females report, on the average, fewer or more assaults by inmates on staff compared with male-only institutions. In each example, the correctional facility is the unit of analysis. In contrast, if we ask whether male or female inmates are more often involved in assaults on staff, then the individual inmate is the unit of analysis.

Some studies involve descriptions or explanations of more than one unit of analysis. Consider an evaluation of community policing programs in selected neighborhoods of a large city. In such an evaluation, we might be interested in how citizens feel about the program (individuals), whether arrests increased in neighborhoods with the new program compared with those without it (groups), and whether the police department's budget increased more than the budget in a similar city (organizations). In such cases, it is imperative that researchers focus their analysis and interpretations on appropriate units.

Social Artifacts

Yet another potential unit of analysis may be referred to as *social artifacts*, or the products of social behavior. One class of social artifacts is stories about crime in newspapers or online videos that shown actual crimes being committed. A newspaper story might be characterized by its length, placement on front or interior pages, size of headlines, and presence of photographs. A researcher could analyze whether videos are actual recordings of crimes in progress or reports of crimes from media sources.

Social interactions are also examples of social artifacts suitable for criminal justice research. Police crime reports are an example. We might analyze assault reports to find how many involved three or more people, whether assaults involved strangers or people with some prior acquaintance, or whether they more often occurred in public or private locations.

At first, crime reports may not seem to be social artifacts, but consider for a moment what they represent. When a crime is reported to the police, officers usually record what happened from descriptions by victims or witnesses. For instance, an assault victim may describe how he suffered an unprovoked attack when he was innocently enjoying a cold beer after work. However, witnesses to the incident might claim that the "victim" started the fight by insulting the "offender." The responding police officer must interpret who is telling the truth in trying to sort out the circumstances of a violent social interaction. The officer's report becomes a social artifact that represents one among the population of all assaults.

Records of different types of social interactions are common units of analysis in criminal justice research. Criminal history records, meetings of community anticrime groups, pre-sentence investigations, and interactions between police and citizens are examples. Notice that each example requires information about individuals but that social interactions between people are the units of analysis.

The Ecological Fallacy

We now briefly consider one category of problems commonly encountered with respect to units of analysis. The **ecological fallacy** refers to the danger of making assertions about individuals as the unit of analysis based on the examination of groups or other aggregations.

As an example, suppose we are interested in learning about robbery in different police precincts of a large city. Let's assume that we have information on how many robberies were committed in 2014 in each police precinct of Chicago. Assume also that we have census data describing some of the characteristics of those precincts. Our analysis of such data might show that a large number of robberies in 2014 occurred in the downtown precinct and that the average family income of persons who live in downtown Chicago (the Loop) was substantially higher than in other precincts in the city. We might be tempted to conclude that high-income downtown residents are more likely to be robbed than are people who live in other parts of the city—that robbers select richer victims. In reaching such a conclusion, we run the risk of committing an ecological fallacy, because lower-income people who did not live in the downtown area were also being robbed there in 2014. Victims might be commuters to jobs in the Loop, people visiting downtown theaters or restaurants, passengers on subway or elevated train platforms, or homeless persons who are not counted by the census. Our problem is that we examined police precincts as our unit of analysis, but we wish to draw conclusions about individual people who were robbery victims.

The same problem will arise if we discover a state-level relationship between incarceration rates and the average age of the state's population. We could say: "Incarceration rates are higher in states where the average population age is older, compared to states where the average population age is younger." However, we could not say something like: "Older people are more likely to be incarcerated than younger people." That's an example of the ecological fallacy—using aggregate data at the state level to make inferences about individuals.

Don't let these warnings against ecological fallacy lead you to commit what is called an *individualistic fallacy*. Some students approaching criminal justice research for the first time have trouble reconciling general patterns of attitudes and actions with individual exceptions they know of. If you read a newspaper story about a Utah resident visiting New York who is murdered on a subway platform, the fact remains that most visitors to New York and most subway riders are not at risk of murder. Similarly, mass media stories and popular films about drug problems in U.S. cities frequently focus on drug use and dealing among African Americans. But that does not mean that most African Americans are drug users or that drugs are not a problem among whites.

The individualistic fallacy can be especially troublesome for beginning students of criminal justice. Newspapers, local television news, and television police dramas often present unusual or highly dramatized versions of crime problems and criminal justice policy. These messages may distort the way many people initially approach research problems in criminal justice.

Units of Analysis in Review

The purpose of this section has been to specify what is sometimes a confusing topic, in part because criminal justice researchers use a variety of different units of analysis. Although individual people are often the units of analysis, that is not always the case. Many research questions can more appropriately be answered through the examination of other units of analysis.

Understanding the logic of units of analysis is more important than memorizing a list of the units. It is irrelevant what we call a given unit of analysis—a group, a formal organization, or a social artifact. It is essential, however, that we be able to identify our unit of analysis. We must decide whether we are studying assaults or assault victims, police departments or police officers, courtrooms or judges, and prisons or prison inmates. Without keeping this point in mind, we run the risk of making assertions about one unit of analysis based on the examination of another. The box titled "Units of Analysis in the National Youth Gang Survey" offers examples of using inappropriate units of analysis. It also illustrates that lack of clarity about units of analysis in criminal justice results in part from difficulties in directly measuring the concepts we want to study.

UNITS OF ANALYSIS IN THE NATIONAL YOUTH GANG SURVEY

In 1997, the third annual National Youth Gang Survey was completed for the federal Office of Juvenile Justice and Delinquency Prevention (OJJDP). This survey reflects keen interest in developing better information about the scope of youth gangs and their activities in different types of communities around the country. As important and useful as this effort is, the National Youth Gang Survey—especially reports of its results—illustrates how some ambiguities can emerge with respect to units of analysis.

(continued)

A variety of methods, often creative, are used to gather information from or about active offenders. Partly this is because it is difficult to systematically identify offenders for research. Studying youth gangs presents more than the usual share of problems with units of analysis. Are we interested in gangs (groups), gang members (individuals), or offenses (social artifacts) committed by gangs?

Following methods developed in earlier years, the 1997 National Youth Gang Survey was based on a sample of law enforcement agencies. The sample was designed to represent different types of communities: rural areas, suburban counties, small cities, and large cities. Questionnaires were mailed to the police chief for municipalities and to the sheriff for counties (National Youth Gang Center 1999, 3). Questions asked respondents to report on gangs and gang activity in their jurisdiction—municipality for police departments, and unincorporated service area for sheriffs' departments.

Here are examples of the types of questions included in the survey:

1. How many youth gangs were active in your jurisdiction?
2. How many active youth gang members were in your jurisdiction?
3. In your jurisdiction, what percentage of street sales of drugs were made by youth gang members? (followed by list: powder cocaine, crack cocaine, marijuana, heroin, methamphetamine, other)
4. Does your agency have the following? (list of special youth gang units)

Notice the different units of analysis embedded in these questions. Seven are stated or implied:

1. Gangs: item 1
2. Gang members: items 2, 3
3. Jurisdiction (city or part of county area): items 1, 2, 3
4. Street sales of drugs: item 3
5. Drug types: item 3
6. Agency: item 4
7. Special unit: item 4

Now consider some quotes from a summary report on the 1997 survey (National Youth Gang Center 1999). Which ones do or do not reasonably reflect the actual units of analysis from the survey?

- "Fifty-one percent of survey respondents indicated that they had active youth gangs in their jurisdictions in 1997." (page 7)
- "Thirty-eight percent of jurisdictions in the Northeast, and 26 percent of jurisdictions in the Middle Atlantic regions reported active youth gangs in 1997." (extracted from Table 3, page 10)
- "Results of the 1997 survey revealed that there were an estimated 30,533 youth gangs and 815,986 gang members active in the United States in 1997." (page 13)
- "The percentage of street sales of crack cocaine, heroin, and methamphetamine conducted by youth gang members varied substantially by region.... Crack cocaine sales involving youth gang members were most prevalent in the Midwest (38 percent), heroin sales were most prevalent in the Northeast (15 percent), and methamphetamine sales were most prevalent in the West (21 percent)." (page 27)
- "The majority (66 percent) of respondents indicated that they had some type of specialized unit to address the gang problem." (page 33)

The youth gang survey report includes a number of statements and tables that inaccurately describe units of analysis. You probably detected examples of this in some of the statements shown here. Other statements accurately reflect units of analysis measured in the survey.

If you read the 1997 survey report and keep in mind our discussion of units of analysis, you will find more misleading statements and tables. This will enhance your understanding of units of analysis.

Source: Information drawn from National Youth Gang Center (1999).

To test your grasp of the concept of units of analysis, here are some examples of real research topics. See if you can determine the unit of analysis in each. (The answers are given later in the chapter, on page 77.)

1. "Taking into account preexisting traffic fatality trends and several other relevant factors, the implementation of the emergency cellular telephone program resulted in a substantial and permanent reduction in the monthly percentage of alcohol-related fatal crashes." (D'Alessio, Stolzenberg, and Terry 1999, 463–464)

2. "The survey robbery rate was highest in Canada and the Netherlands, and lowest in Scotland.... In

1999 the survey robbery rate was lowest in the United States." (Farrington et al. 2004, xii)

3. "On average, probationers were 31 years old, African American, male, and convicted of drug or property offenses. Most lived with family, and although they were not married, many were in exclusive relationships (44 percent) and had children (47 percent)." (MacKenzie et al. 1999, 433)

4. "Seventy-five percent (n = 158) of the cases were disposed at district courts, and 3 percent (n = 6) remained pending. One percent of the control and 4 percent of the experimental cases were referred to drug treatment court." (Taxman and Elis 1999, 42)

5. "The department's eight Field Operations Command substations (encompassing 20 police districts and 100 patrol beats) comprised the study's cross-sectional units. From January 1986 through July 1989, a period of 43 months, data were collected monthly from each substation for a total of 344 cases." (Kessler 1999, 346)

The Time Dimension

Because time order is a requirement for causal inferences, the time dimension of research requires careful planning.

We saw earlier in this chapter how the time sequence of events and situations is a critical element in determining causation. In general, observations may be made more or less at one time point or they may be deliberately stretched over a longer period. Observations made at more than one time point can look forward or backward.

Cross-Sectional Studies

Many criminal justice research projects are designed to study a phenomenon by taking a cross section of it at one time and analyzing that cross section carefully. Exploratory and descriptive studies are often **cross-sectional studies**. A single U.S. census, for instance, is a study aimed at describing the U.S. population at a given time. A single wave of the NCVS is a descriptive cross-sectional study that estimates how many people have been victims of crime in a given time.

A cross-sectional exploratory study might be conducted by a police department in the form of a survey that examines what residents believe to be the sources of crime problems in their neighborhood. In all likelihood, the study will ask about crime problems in a single time frame, with the findings used to help the department explore various methods of introducing community policing.

Cross-sectional studies for explanatory or evaluation purposes have an inherent problem. Typically their aim is to understand causal processes that occur over time, but their conclusions are based on observations made at only one time. For example, a survey might ask respondents whether their home has been burglarized and whether they have any special locks on their doors, hoping to explain whether special locks prevent burglary. Because the questions about burglary victimization and door locks are asked at only one time, it is not possible to determine whether burglary victims installed locks after a burglary or whether special locks were already in place but did not prevent the crime. Some of the ways we can deal with the difficult problem of determining time order will be discussed in the section on approximating longitudinal studies.

Longitudinal Studies

Research projects known as **longitudinal studies** are designed to permit observations over an extended period. An example is a researcher who observes the activities of a neighborhood anticrime organization from the time of its inception until its demise. Analyses of the numbers of prison inmates over time or of monthly drug arrests for one year are other examples. In many cases, it is irrelevant whether the researcher's observations are made over the course of the actual events under study or at one time by examining 10 years of annual reports on correctional populations. For example, visiting the Bureau of Justice Statistics website (bjs.gov) and searching for "capital punishment" produces a list of annual reports on the numbers of people facing death sentences. The series runs from the 1970s through the present.

Three types of longitudinal studies are common in criminal justice research: *trend, cohort,* and *panel studies. Trend studies* look at changes within some general population over time. An example is a comparison of Uniform Crime Report figures over time, showing an increase in reported crime from 1960 through 1993 and then a general pattern of decline through 2012. Or a researcher might want to know whether changes in sentences for certain offenses were followed by increases in the number of people imprisoned in state institutions. In this case, a trend study might examine annual figures for prison population over time, comparing totals for the years before and after new sentencing laws took effect.

Cohort studies examine more specific populations (cohorts) as they change over time. Typically, a cohort is an age group, such as those people born in 1983, but it can also be based on some other time grouping. Cohorts are often defined as a group of people who enter or leave an institution at the same time, such as persons entering a drug treatment center during July, offenders released from custody in 2009, or high school seniors in March 2010.

In one of the most well-known cohort studies, Marvin Wolfgang and associates (Wolfgang, Figlio, and Sellin 1972) studied all males born in 1945 who lived in the city of Philadelphia from their 10th birthday through age 18 or older. The researchers examined records from police agencies and public schools to determine how many boys in the cohort had been charged with delinquency or arrested, how old they were when first arrested, and what differences there were in school performance between delinquents and nondelinquents.

Panel studies are similar to trend and cohort studies except that observations are made on the same set of people on two or more occasions. The NCVS is a good example of a descriptive panel study. A member of each household selected for inclusion in the survey is interviewed seven times at six-month intervals. The NCVS serves many purposes, but it was developed initially to estimate how many people were victims of various types of crimes each year. It is designed as a panel study so that persons can be asked about crimes that occurred in the previous six months, and two waves of panel data are combined to estimate the nationwide frequency of victimization over a one-year period.

Approximating Longitudinal Studies

It is sometimes possible to draw conclusions about processes that take place over time even when only cross-sectional data are available. It is worth noting some of the ways to do that.

Logical Inferences Cross-sectional data sometimes imply processes that occur over time on the basis of simple logic. Consider a study of gun ownership and violence by Swiss researcher Martin Killias (1993). Killias compared rates of gun ownership as reported in an international crime survey to rates of homicide and suicide committed with guns. He was interested in the possible effects of gun availability on violence: do nations with higher rates of gun ownership also have higher rates of gun violence?

Killias reasoned that inferring causation from a cross-sectional comparison of gun ownership and homicides committed with guns would be ambiguous. Gun homicide rates could be high in countries with high gun-ownership rates because the availability of guns was higher. Or people in countries with high gun-ownership rates could have bought guns to protect themselves, in response to rates of homicide. Cross-sectional analysis would not make it possible to sort out the time order of gun ownership and gun homicides.

But does that reasoning hold for gun suicides? Killias argued that the time order in a relationship between gun ownership and gun suicides is less ambiguous. It makes much more sense to infer that suicides involving guns are at least partly a result of gun availability. But it is not reasonable to assume that people might buy guns in response to high gun-suicide rates.

Logical inferences may also be made whenever the time order of variables is clear. If we discover in a cross-sectional study of high school students that males are more likely than females to smoke marijuana, we can conclude that gender affects the propensity to use marijuana, not the other way around. Thus, even though our observations are made at only one time, we are justified in drawing conclusions about processes that take place across time.

Retrospective Studies Research that asks people to recall their pasts, called retrospective research, is a common way of approximating observations over time. In a study of recidivism, for example, we might select a group of prison inmates and analyze their history of delinquency or crime. Or suppose we are interested in whether college students convicted of drunk driving are more likely to have parents with drinking problems than college students with no drunk-driving record. Such a study is retrospective because it focuses on the histories of college students who have or have not been convicted of drunk driving.

The danger in this technique is evident. Sometimes people have faulty memories; sometimes they lie. Retrospective recall is one way of approximating observations across time, but it must be used with caution. Retrospective studies that analyze records of past arrests or convictions suffer from different problems: records may be unavailable, incomplete, or inaccurate.

A more fundamental issue in retrospective research hinges on how subjects are selected and how subject selection affects the kinds of questions such studies can address.

Imagine that you are a juvenile court judge and you're troubled by what appears to be a large number of child abuse cases in your court. Talking with a juvenile caseworker, you wonder whether the parents of these children were abused or neglected during their own childhood. Together, you formulate a hypothesis about the intergenerational transmission of violence: victims of childhood abuse later abuse their own children. How might you go about investigating that hypothesis?

Given your position as a judge who regularly sees abuse victims, you will probably consider a retrospective approach that examines the backgrounds of families appearing in your court. Let's say you

and the caseworker plan to investigate the family backgrounds of 20 abuse victims who appear in your court during the next three months. The caseworker consults with a clinical psychologist from the local university and obtains copies of a questionnaire, or protocol, that has been used by researchers to study the families of child abuse victims. After interviewing the families of 20 victims, the caseworker reports to you that 18 of the 20 child victims have a mother or father who was abused as a child. It seems safe to conclude that your hypothesis about the intergenerational transmission of violence is strongly supported, because 90 percent (18 out of 20) of abuse or neglect victims brought before your court come from families with a history of child abuse.

Think for a moment about how you approached the question of whether child abuse breeds child abuse. You began with abuse victims and retrospectively established that many of their parents had been abused. However, this is different from the question of how many victims of childhood abuse later abuse their own children. That question requires a prospective approach, in which you begin with childhood victims and then determine how many of them later abuse their own children.

To clarify this point, let's shift from the hypothetical study to actual research that illustrates the difference between prospective and retrospective approaches to the same question. Rosemary Hunter and Nancy Kilstrom (1979) conducted a study of 255 infants and their parents. The researchers began by selecting families of premature infants in a newborn intensive care unit. Interviews with the parents of 255 infants revealed that either the mother or the father in 49 of the families had been the victim of abuse or neglect; 206 families revealed no history of abuse. In a prospective follow-up study, Hunter and Kilstrom found that within one year 10 of the 255 infants had been abused. Nine of those 10 infant victims were from the 49 families with a history of abuse, and 1 abused infant was from the 206 families with no background of abuse.

Figure 3.6 illustrates these prospective results graphically. Infants in 18 percent (9 out of 49) of

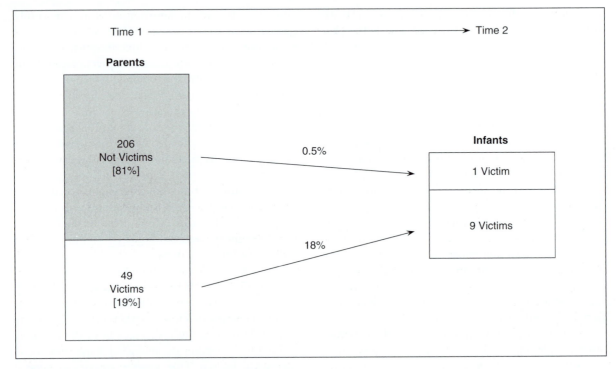

FIGURE 3.6   Prospective Approach to a Subject
Source: Adapted from Hunter and Kilstrom (1979), as suggested by Widom (1989).

families with a history of abuse showed signs of abuse within one year of birth, whereas less than 1 percent of infants born to parents with no history of abuse were abused within one year. Although that is a sizable difference, notice that the 18 percent figure for continuity of abuse is very similar to the 19 percent rate of abuse discovered in the histories of all 255 families.

Now consider what Hunter and Kilstrom would have found if they had begun with the 10 abused infants at Time 2 and then checked their family backgrounds. Figure 3.7 illustrates this

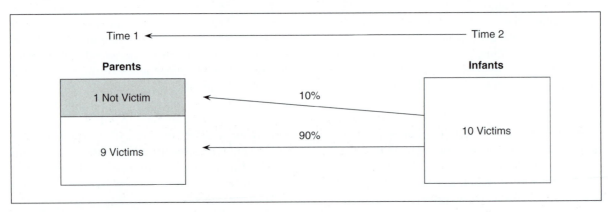

FIGURE 3.7   Retrospective Approach to a Subject
Source: Adapted from Hunter and Kilstrom (1979), as suggested by Widom (1989).

retrospective approach. A large majority of the 10 infant victims (90 percent) had parents with a history of abuse.

You probably realize by now that the prospective and retrospective approaches address fundamentally different questions, even though the questions may appear similar on the surface:

Prospective: What percentage of abuse victims later abuse their children? (18 percent; Figure 3.6)

Retrospective: What percentage of abuse victims have parents who were abused? (90 percent; Figure 3.7)

In a study of how child abuse and neglect affect drug use, Cathy Spatz Widom and associates (Widom, Weiler, and Cotler 1999) present a similar contrast of prospective and retrospective analysis. Looking backward, 75 percent of subjects with a drug abuse diagnosis in semi-clinical interviews were victims of childhood abuse or neglect. Looking forward, 35 percent of childhood victims and 34 percent of nonvictims had a drug abuse diagnosis.

More generally, Robert Sampson and John Laub (1993, 14) comment on how retrospective and prospective views yield different interpretations about patterns of criminal offending over time:

Looking *back* over the careers of adult criminals exaggerates the prevalence of stability. Looking *forward* from youth reveals the success and failures, including adolescent delinquents who go on to be normal functioning adults [emphasis in original]. This is the paradox noted [by Lee Robins] earlier: adult criminality seems to be always preceded by childhood misconduct, but most conduct-disordered children do not become antisocial or criminal adults.

Notice how the time dimension is linked to how research questions are framed. A retrospective approach is limited in its ability to reveal how causal processes unfold over time. A retrospective approach is therefore not well suited to answer questions such as how many childhood victims of abuse or neglect later abuse their own children. A retrospective study can be used, however, to compare whether childhood victims are more likely than nonvictims to have a history of abuse in their family background.

The Time Dimension Summarized

Joel Devine and James Wright (1993, 19) offer a clever metaphor that distinguishes longitudinal studies from cross-sectional ones. Think of a cross-sectional study as a snapshot, a trend study as a slide show, and a panel study as a motion picture. A cross-sectional study, like a snapshot, produces an image at one point in time. This can provide useful information about crime—burglary, for example—at a single time, perhaps in a single place. A trend study is akin to a slide show—a series of snapshots in sequence over time. By viewing a slide show, we can tell how some indicator—change in burglary rates—varies over time. But a trend study is usually based on aggregate information. It can tell us something about aggregations of burglary over time, but not, for instance, whether the same people are committing burglaries at an increasing or decreasing rate or whether there are more or fewer burglars with a relatively constant rate of crime commission. A panel study, like a motion picture, can capture moving images of the same individuals and give us information about individual rates of offending over time.

SUMMARY

- Social science involves three fundamental aspects: theory, data collection, and data analysis.

- Social scientific theory addresses what is, not what should be.

- Theory guides research. In grounded theory, observations contribute to theory development.

- Social scientists are interested in explaining aggregates, not individuals.

- Although social scientists observe people, they are primarily interested in discovering relationships that connect variables.

- Explanations may be idiographic or nomothetic.

- Theories may be inductive or deductive.

- Data may be quantitative or qualitative.

- Explanatory scientific research centers on the notion of cause and effect.

- Most explanatory social research uses a probabilistic model of causation. X may be said to cause Y if it is seen to have some influence on Y.

- Three basic requirements determine a causal relationship in scientific research: (1) the independent variable must occur before the dependent variable, (2) the independent and dependent variables must be empirically related to each other, and (3) the observed relationship cannot be explained away as the effect of another variable.

- When scientists consider whether causal statements are true or false, they are concerned with the validity of causal inference.

- A scientific realist approach to examining mechanisms in context bridges idiographic and nomothetic approaches to causation.

- Units of analysis are the people or things whose characteristics researchers observe, describe, and explain. The unit of analysis in criminal justice research is often the individual person, but it may also be a group, organization, or social artifact.

- Researchers sometimes confuse units of analysis, resulting in the ecological fallacy or the individualistic fallacy.

- Cross-sectional studies are those based on observations made at one time. Although such studies are limited by this characteristic, inferences can often be made about processes that occur over time.

- Longitudinal studies are those in which observations are made at many times. Such observations may be made of samples drawn from general populations (trend studies), samples drawn from more specific subpopulations (cohort studies), or the same sample of people each time (panel studies).

- Retrospective studies can sometimes approximate longitudinal studies, but retrospective approaches must be used with care.

KEY TERMS

REVIEW QUESTIONS AND EXERCISES

1. Discuss one of the following statements in terms of what you have learned about the criteria of causation and threats to the validity of causal inference. What cause-and-effect relationships are implied? What are some alternative explanations?

   a. Guns don't kill people; people kill people.

   b. Capital punishment prevents murder.

   c. Marijuana is a gateway drug that leads to the use of other drugs.

2. Go to the Bureau of Justice Statistics website (bjs.gov). Type "arrest-related deaths" in the search window, and find the publication *Arrest-Related Deaths, 2003-2009–Statistical Tables* (Burch 2011). Download the publication and examine the graphs and tables. You will find data on deaths that occur shortly after someone is arrested. Briefly describe an example of a cross-sectional question that the data address and an example of a longitudinal question. Think of it this way: a cross-sectional question asks about differences, whereas a longitudinal question asks about change (Sherman 1995).

3. William Julius Wilson (1996, 167) cites the following example of why it's important to think carefully about units and time. Imagine a 13-bed hospital, in which 12 beds are occupied by the same 12 people for one year. The other hospital bed is occupied by 52 people, each staying one week. At any given time, 92 percent of beds are occupied by long-term patients (12 out of 13), but over the entire year, 81 percent of patients are short-term patients (52 out of 64). Discuss the implications of a similar example, using jail cells instead of hospital beds.

ANSWERS TO UNITS-OF-ANALYSIS EXERCISE

1. Social artifacts (alcohol-related fatal crashes)
2. Groups (countries)
3. Individuals (probationers)
4. Social artifacts (court cases)
5. Organizations (police substations)

CHAPTER 4

Concepts, Operationalization, and Measurement

It's essential to specify exactly what we mean (and don't mean) by the terms we use. This is the first step in the measurement process, and we'll cover it in depth.

Measuring Neighborhood Characteristics

Criminologists have always been interested in how features of neighborhoods might be linked to crime problems. Researchers have traditionally used measures of social and economic characteristics, such as those collected every 10 years in the U.S. Census. Census tracts and blocks are small areas into which measures of demographic, social, and economic characteristics are aggregated. Much criminological research has used census data to examine what kinds of neighborhood characteristics are related to crime.

Another way to measure neighborhood characteristics is to observe them. While census data are collected through questionnaires completed by neighborhood residents, more recent research has sent researchers into the field to observe things such as housing conditions, the presence of graffiti and litter, and the types of buildings in an area. However, such measures are difficult and costly to obtain. Field observers (more on this in Chapter 9) must be trained and sent to walk or drive streets. Sampson and Raudenbush (1999) describe an example where observers drove around Chicago neighborhoods, making video recordings of people and conditions on sampled streets.

An alternative is to view the existing images of city streets available on the web through Google Street View (GSV). If you have not used GSV on the Google Maps site, you may have seen such images through some other application on a smart phone or other mobile device. Try it now, by going to http://www.google.com/maps.

The most complete coverage is available for major cities in the United States, but GSV also covers many smaller cities and places in other countries. For example, you can see a couple of buildings at John Jay College of Criminal Justice by typing the following address into the search window: 899 Tenth Ave, New York, NY. You'll see a map or satellite image depending on how your browser is set up. You should also see a photo in a separate panel that shows the intersection of Tenth Avenue and 59th Street in New York City. You can pan the image with your mouse to look around the area. You can also virtually travel up or down New York City streets, seeing continual images along the way.

What results for New York and most other major cities is a photo archive of everything that can be seen from a car (Google's camera-equipped vehicles) traveling down the street. This has tremendous potential for researchers by offering a low-cost method for making observations of large areas.

But what about the quality of measures developed through such images? More fundamentally, what concepts can be measured by GSV images? As you read this chapter, the first of two on measurement, think about GSV as a source of measures for different concepts. For example, images might produce measures for housing conditions, but they cannot be very useful for measuring other things, such as household income or family size. Much of this chapter describes how to create measures that are valid and reliable. How might you determine the reliability and validity of such measures? It would be very helpful to try out GSV while reading this chapter. One of the compelling features of GSV is that you can make observations of streets in Moscow, Russia, while sitting at a computer in Moscow, Idaho.

Introduction

Because measurement is difficult and imprecise, researchers try to describe the measurement process explicitly.

This chapter describes the progression from having a vague idea about what we want to study to being able to recognize it and measure it in the real world. We begin with the general issue of conceptualization, which sets up a foundation for our examination of operationalization and measurement. We then turn to different approaches to assessing measurement quality. The chapter concludes with an overview of strategies for combining individual measures into more complex indicators.

As you read this chapter, keep in mind a central theme: communication. Ultimately, criminal justice and social scientific research seek to communicate findings to an audience, such as professors, classmates, journal readers, or coworkers in a probation services agency. Moving from vague ideas and interests to a completed research report involves communication at every step—from general ideas to more precise definitions of critical terms. With more precise definitions, we can begin to develop measures to apply in the real world.

Conceptions and Concepts

Clarifying abstract mental images is an essential first step in measurement.

If you hear the word *recidivism*, what image comes to mind? You might think of someone who has served time for burglary and who breaks into a house soon after being released from prison. Or, in contrast to that rather specific image, you might have a more general image of a habitual criminal. Someone who works in a criminal justice agency might have a different mental image. Police officers might think of a specific individual they have arrested repeatedly for a variety of offenses, and a judge might think of a defendant who has three prior convictions for theft.

Ultimately, *recidivism* is simply a term we use in communication—a word representing a collection of related phenomena that we have either observed or heard about somewhere. It's as though we have file drawers in our minds containing thousands of sheets of paper, and each sheet has a label in the upper right-hand corner. One sheet of paper in your file drawer has the term *recidivism* on it, and the person who sits next to you in class has one, too.

The technical name for those mental images, those sheets of paper in our file drawers, is **conception**. Each sheet of paper is a conception—a subjective thought about things that we encounter in daily life. But those mental images cannot be communicated directly. There is no way we can directly reveal what is written on our mental images. Therefore, we use the terms written in the upper right-hand corners as a way of communicating about our conceptions and the things we observe that are related to those conceptions.

For example, the word *crime* represents our conception about certain kinds of behavior. But individuals have different conceptions; they may think of different kinds of behavior when they hear the word *crime*. Police officers in most states would include possession of marijuana among their conceptions of crime, whereas residents of Colorado and Washington would not. Recent burglary victims might recall their own experiences in their conceptions of crime, whereas more fortunate neighbors might think about the murder story in yesterday's newspaper.

Because conceptions are subjective and cannot be communicated directly, we use the words and symbols of language as a way of communicating about our conceptions and the things we observe that are related to those conceptions.

Concepts are the words or symbols in language that we use to represent these mental images. We use concepts to communicate with one another, to share our mental images. Although a common language enables us to communicate, it is important to recognize that the words and phrases we use represent abstractions. Concepts are abstract because they are independent of the labels we assign to them. Crime as a concept is abstract, meaning that in the English language this label represents mental images of illegal acts. Of course, actual crimes are real events, and our mental images of crime may be based on real events (or the stuff of TV drama). However, when we talk about crime, without being more specific, we are talking about an abstraction. Thus, for example, the concept of crime proposed by Michael Gottfredson and Travis Hirschi (1990, 15)—using force or fraud in pursuit of self-interest—is abstract. Crime is the symbol, or label, they have assigned to this concept.

Let's discuss a specific example. What is your conception of *serious crime*? What mental images come to mind? Most people agree that airplane hijacking, rape, bank robbery, and murder are serious crimes. What about a fist fight that results in a concussion and facial injuries? Many of us would classify it as a serious crime but not if the incident took place in a boxing ring. Is burglary a serious crime? It doesn't rank up there with drive-by shooting, but we would probably agree that it is more serious than shoplifting. What about drug use or drug dealing?

Our mental images of serious crime may vary depending on our backgrounds and experiences. If your home has ever been burglarized, you might be more inclined than someone who has not suffered that experience to rate it as a serious crime. If you have been both burglarized and robbed at gunpoint, you would probably think the burglary was less serious than the robbery.

Disagreement over the seriousness of drug use continues. Younger people, whether or not they have used drugs, may be less inclined to view drug use as a serious crime, whereas police and other public officials might rank drug use as very serious. California, Michigan, New Jersey, and Oregon are among states that have legalized the use of marijuana for medical purposes. However, during the administration of George Bush, the U.S. Department of Justice viewed all marijuana use as a crime, challenging state laws and raiding San Francisco medical marijuana dispensaries (Murphy 2005).

Serious crime is an abstraction, a label we use to represent a concept. However, we must be careful to distinguish the label we use for a concept from the reality that the concept represents. There are real robberies, and robbery is a serious crime, but the concept of crime seriousness is not real.

The concept of serious crime, then, is a construct created from your conception of it, our conception of it, and the conceptions of all those who have ever used the term. The concept of serious crime cannot be observed directly or indirectly. We can, however, meaningfully discuss the concept, observe examples of serious crime, and measure it indirectly.

Conceptualization

Day-to-day communication is made possible through general but often vague and unspoken agreements about the use of terms. Often other people do not understand exactly what we wish to communicate, but they get the general drift of our meaning. Although we may not fully agree about the meaning of the term *serious crime*, it's safe to assume that the crime of bank robbery is more serious than the crime of bicycle theft. A wide range of misunderstandings is the price we pay for our imprecision, but somehow we muddle through. Science, however, aims at more than muddling, and it cannot operate in a context of such imprecision.

Conceptualization is the process by which we specify precisely what we mean when we use particular terms. Suppose we want to find out whether violent crime is more serious than nonviolent crime. Most of us would probably assume that is true, but it might be interesting to find out whether it's really so. Notice that we can't meaningfully study the issue, let alone agree on the answer, without some precise working agreements about the meanings of the terms we are using. They are working agreements in the sense that they allow us to work on the question.

We begin by clearly differentiating violent and nonviolent crime. In violent crimes, an offender uses force or threats of force against a victim. Nonviolent crimes either do not involve any direct contact between a victim and an offender or involve contact but no force. For example, pickpockets have direct contact with their victims but use no force. In contrast, robbery involves at least the threat to use force on victims. Burglary, auto theft, shoplifting, and the theft of unattended personal property such as bicycles are examples of nonviolent crimes. Assault, rape, robbery, and murder are violent crimes.

Indicators and Dimensions

The end product of the conceptualization process is the specification of a set of indicators of what we have in mind, indicating the presence or absence of the concept we are studying. To illustrate this process, let's discuss the more general concept of *crime seriousness*. This concept is more general than *serious crime* because it implies that some crimes are more serious than others.

One good indicator of crime seriousness is harm to the crime victim. Physical injury is an example of harm, and physical injury is certainly more likely to result from violent crime than from nonviolent crime. What about other kinds of harm? Burglary victims suffer economic harm from property loss and perhaps damage to their homes. Is the loss of $800 in a burglary an indicator of more serious crime than a $10 loss in a robbery in which the victim was not injured? Victims of both violent crime and nonviolent crime may suffer psychological harm. Or people might feel a sense of personal violation after discovering that their home has been burglarized. Other types of victim harm can be combined into groups and subgroups as well.

The technical term for such groupings is **dimension**—some specifiable aspect of a concept. Thus, we might speak of the "victim harm dimension" of crime seriousness. This dimension could include indicators of physical injury, economic loss, or psychological consequences. We can easily think of other indicators and dimensions related to the general concept of crime seriousness. If we consider the theft of $20 from an unemployed person to be more serious than the theft of $20,000 from a wealthy hedge fund manager, victim wealth might be another dimension. Also consider a victim identity dimension. Killing a burglar in self-defense would not be as serious as threatening to kill the president of the United States.

It is possible to subdivide the concept of crime seriousness into several dimensions. Specifying

dimensions and identifying the various indicators for each of those dimensions are both parts of conceptualization.

Specifying the different dimensions of a concept often paves the way for a better understanding of what we are studying. We might observe that fist fights among high school students result in thousands of injuries per year but that the annual costs of auto theft cause direct economic harm to hundreds of insurance companies and millions of auto insurance policyholders. Recognizing the many dimensions of crime seriousness, we cannot say that violent crime is more serious than nonviolent crime in all cases.

Creating Conceptual Order

The design and execution of criminal justice research require that we clear away the confusion over concepts and reality. To this end, logicians and scientists have found it useful to distinguish three kinds of definitions: real, conceptual, and operational. With respect to the first of these, Carl G. Hempel (1952, 6) cautioned:

> A "real" definition, according to traditional logic, is not a stipulation determining the meaning of some expression but a statement of the "essential nature" or the "essential attributes" of some entity. The notion of essential nature, however, is so vague as to render this characterization useless for the purposes of rigorous inquiry.

A *real* or *essential nature* definition is inherently subjective. The specification of concepts in scientific inquiry depends instead on conceptual and operational definitions. A **conceptual definition** is a working definition specifically assigned to a term. In the midst of disagreement and confusion over what a term really means, the scientist specifies a working definition for the purposes of the inquiry. Wishing to examine socioeconomic status (SES), we may simply specify that we are going to treat it as a combination of income and educational attainment. With that definitional decision, we rule out many other possible aspects of SES:

occupational status, money in the bank, property, lifestyle, and so forth.

The specification of conceptual definitions does two important things. First, it serves as a specific working definition we present so that readers will understand exactly what we mean by a concept. Second, it focuses our observational strategy. Notice that a conceptual definition does not directly produce observations; rather, it channels our efforts to develop actual measures.

As a next step, we must specify exactly what we will observe, how we will do it, and what interpretations we will place on various possible observations. These further specifications make up the **operational definition** of the concept—a definition that spells out precisely how the concept will be measured. Strictly speaking, an operational definition is a description of the operations undertaken in measuring a concept.

Pursuing the definition of SES, we might decide to ask the people we are studying three questions:

1. What was your total household income during the past 12 months?
2. How many persons are in your household?
3. What is the highest level of school you have completed?

Next, we need to specify a system for categorizing the answers people give us. For income, we might use the categories "under $25,000" and "$25,000–$35,000." Educational attainment might be similarly grouped into categories, and we might

simply count the number of people in each household. Finally, we need to specify a way to combine each person's responses to these three questions to create a measure of SES.

The end result is a working and workable definition of SES. Others might disagree with our conceptualization and operationalization, but the definition has one essential scientific virtue: it is absolutely specific and unambiguous. Even if someone disagrees with our definition, that person will have a good idea of how to interpret our research results because what we mean by SES—reflected in our analyses and conclusions—is clear.

Here is a diagram showing the progression of measurement steps from our vague sense of what a term means to specific measurements in a scientific study:

Conceptualization

↓

Conceptual definition

↓

Operational definition

↓

Measurements in the real world

To test your understanding of these measurement steps, return to the beginning of the chapter, where we asked you what image comes to mind in connection with the word *recidivism*. Recall your own mental image, and compare it with Tony Fabelo's discussion in the box titled "What Is Recidivism?"

 WHAT IS RECIDIVISM?

by Tony Fabelo

The Senate Criminal Justice Committee will be studying the record of the corrections system and the use of recidivism rates as a measure of performance for the system. The first task for the committee should be to clearly define recidivism, understand how it is measured, and determine the implications of adopting recidivism rates as measures of performance.

Defining Recidivism

Recidivism is the recurrence of criminal behavior. The rate of recidivism refers to the proportion of a specific group of offenders (for example, those released on parole) who engage in criminal behavior within a given period of time. Indicators of criminal behavior are rearrests, reconvictions, or reincarcerations.

(continued)

Each of these indicators depends on contact with criminal justice officials and will therefore underestimate the recurrence of criminal behavior. However, criminal behavior that is unreported and not otherwise known to officials in justice agencies is difficult to measure in a consistent and economically feasible fashion.

In 1991, the Criminal Justice Policy Council recommended to the Texas legislature and state criminal justice agencies that recidivism be measured in the following way:

Recidivism rates should be calculated by counting the number of prison releases or number of offenders placed under community supervision who are reincarcerated for a technical violation or new offense within a uniform period of at-risk street time.

The at-risk street time can be one, two, or three years, but it must be uniform for the group being tracked so that results are not distorted by uneven at-risk periods.

Reincarceration should be measured using data from the "rap sheets" collected by the Texas Department of Public Safety in their Computerized Criminal History system. A centralized source of information reduces reporting errors.

Systemwide Recidivism Rates

Recidivism rates can be reported for all offenders in the system—for all offenders released from prison or for all offenders placed on probation. This I call systemwide recidivism rates. Approximately 48 percent of offenders released from prison on parole or mandatory supervision, or released from county jails on parole, in 1991 were reincarcerated by 1994 for a new offense or a parole violation.

For offenders released from prison in 1991, the reincarceration recidivism rates three years after release from prison by offense of conviction are as follows:

Burglary	56%	Assault	44%
Robbery	54%	Homicide	40%
Theft	52%	Sexual assault	39%
Drugs	43%	Sex offense	34%

For the same group, the reincarceration recidivism rate three years after release by age group is listed below:

17–25	56%
26–30	52%
31–35	48%
36–40	46%
41 or older	35%

The Meaning of Systemwide Recidivism Rates

The systemwide recidivism rate of prison releases should not be used to measure the performance of institutional programs. There are many socioeconomic factors that can affect systemwide recidivism rates.

For example, the systemwide recidivism rate of offenders released from prison in 1995 declined because of changes in the characteristics of the population released from prison. Offenders are receiving and serving longer sentences, which will raise the average age at release. Therefore, performance in terms of systemwide recidivism will improve but not necessarily because of improvements in the delivery of services within the prison system.

On the other hand, the systemwide recidivism rate of felons released from state jail facilities should be expected to be relatively high, because state jail felons are property and drug offenders who tend to have high recidivism rates.

Source: Adapted from Fabelo (1995).

Operationalization Choices

Describing how to obtain empirical measures begins with operationalization.

Recall from Chapter 1 that the research process is not usually a set of steps that proceed in order from first to last. This is especially true of operationalization, the process of developing operational definitions. Although we begin by conceptualizing what we wish to study, once we start to consider operationalization, we may revise our conceptual definition. Developing an operational definition also moves us closer to measurement, which requires that we think about selecting a data collection method as well. In other words, operationalization does not proceed according to a systematic checklist.

To illustrate this fluid process, let's return to the issue of crime seriousness. Suppose we want to conduct a descriptive study that shows which crimes are more serious and which crimes are less serious.

One obvious dimension of crime seriousness is the penalties that are assigned to different crimes by law. Let's begin with this conceptualization. Our conceptual definition of crime seriousness is therefore the level of punishment that a state criminal code authorizes for different crimes. Notice that this definition has the distinct advantage of being unambiguous, which leads us to an operational definition something like this:

> Consult the Texas Criminal Code. (1) Those crimes that may be punished by death will be judged most serious. (2) Next will be crimes that may be punished by a prison sentence of more than one year. (3) The least serious crimes are those with jail sentences of less than a year, fines, or both.

The operations undertaken to measure crime seriousness are specific. Our data collection strategy is also clear: go to the library, make a list of crimes described in the Texas Code, and classify each crime into one of the three groups.

Note that we have produced rather narrow conceptual and operational definitions of crime seriousness. We might presume that penalties in the Texas Code take into account additional dimensions such as victim harm, offender motivation, and other circumstances of individual crimes. However, the three groups of crimes include very different types of incidents and so do not tell us much about crime seriousness.

An alternative conceptualization of crime seriousness might center on what people think of as serious crime. In this view, crime seriousness is based on people's beliefs, which may reflect their perceptions of harm to victims, offender motivation, or other dimensions. Conceptualizing crime seriousness in this way suggests a different approach to operationalization: you will present descriptions of various crimes to other students in your class and ask them to indicate how serious they believe the crimes are. If crime seriousness is operationalized in this way, a questionnaire is the most appropriate data collection method.

Think of some examples of the process. Your instructor assigns number or letter grades to exams and papers to represent your mastery of course material. You count the number of pages in this week's history assignment to represent how much time you will have to spend studying. The American Bar Association rates nominees to the U.S. Supreme Court as qualified, highly qualified, or not qualified. You might rank last night's date on the proverbial scale of 1 to 10, reflecting whatever conceptual properties are important to you.

Measurement as Scoring

Another way to think of measurement is in terms of scoring. Your instructor scores exams by counting the right answers and assigning some point value to each answer. Referees keep score at basketball games by counting the number of one-point free throws and two- and three-point field goals for each team. Judges or juries score persons charged with crime by pronouncing "guilty" or "not guilty." City murder rates are scored by counting the number of murder victims and dividing by the number of city residents.

Many people consider measurement to be the most important and difficult phase of criminal justice research. It is difficult, in part, because so many basic concepts in criminal justice are not easy to define as specifically as we would like. Without being able to settle on a conceptual definition, we find operationalizing and measuring things challenging. This is illustrated by the box titled "Jail Stay."

 JAIL STAY

Recall from Chapter 1 that two of the general purposes of research are description and explanation. The distinction between them has important implications for the process of definition and measurement.

If you have formed the opinion that description is a simpler task than explanation, you may be surprised to learn that definitions can be more problematic for descriptive research than for explanatory research.

(continued)

To illustrate this, we present an example based on an attempt by one of the authors to describe what he thought was a simple concept.

In the course of an evaluation project, Maxfield wished to learn the average number of days people stayed in the Marion County (Indiana) jail. This concept was labeled *jail stay*. People can be in the county jail for three reasons: (1) They are serving a sentence of one year or less. (2) They are awaiting trial. (3) They are being held temporarily while awaiting transfer to another county or state, or to prison. The third category includes people who have been sentenced to prison and are waiting for space to open up, or those who have been arrested and are wanted for some reason in another jurisdiction.

Maxfield vaguely knew these things but did not recognize how they complicated the task of defining and ultimately measuring jail stay. So the original question—"What is the average jail stay?"—was revised to "What is the average jail stay for persons serving sentences and for persons awaiting trial?"

Just as people can be in jail for different reasons, an individual can be in jail for more than one reason. Let's consider a hypothetical jail resident we'll call Allan. He was convicted of burglary in July 2002 and sentenced to a year in jail. All but 30 days of his sentence were suspended, meaning that he was freed but could be required to serve the remaining 11 months if he got into trouble again. It did not take long. Two months after being released, Allan was arrested for robbery and returned to jail.

Now it gets complicated. A judge imposes the remaining 11 months of Allan's suspended sentence. Allan is denied bail and must wait for his trial in jail. It is soon learned that Allan is wanted by police in Illinois for passing bad checks. Many people would be delighted to send Allan to Illinois; they tell officials in that state they can have him, pending resolution of the situation in Marion County.

Allan is now in jail for three reasons: (1) serving his sentence for the original burglary, (2) awaiting trial on a robbery charge, and (3) waiting for transfer to Illinois.

Is this one jail stay or three? In a sense, it is one jail stay because one person, Allan, is occupying a jail cell. But let's say Allan's trial on the robbery charge is delayed until after he completes his sentence for the burglary. He stays in jail and begins a new jail stay. When he comes up for trial, the prosecutor asks to waive the robbery charges against Allan in hopes of exporting him to the neighboring state, and a new jail stay begins as Allan awaits his free trip to Illinois.

You may recognize this as a problem with units of analysis. Is the unit the person who stays in jail? Or are the separate reasons Allan is in jail—which are social artifacts—the units of analysis? After some thought, Maxfield decided that the social artifact was the more appropriate unit because he was interested in whether jail cells are more often occupied by people serving sentences or people awaiting trial. But that produced a new question of how to deal with people like Allan. Do we double-count the overlap in Allan's jail stays, so that he accounts for two jail stays while serving his suspended sentence for burglary and waiting for the robbery trial? This seemed to make sense, but then Allan's two jail stays would count the same as two other people with one jail stay each. In other words, Allan would appear to occupy two jail beds at the same time. This was neither true nor helpful in describing how long people stay in jail for different reasons.

In addition to being challenging, different operationalization choices can produce different results. In the box titled "What Is Recidivism?" Tony Fabelo argues that the at-risk period for comparing recidivism for different groups of offenders should be uniform. It's possible to examine one-, two-, or three-year rates, but comparisons should use standard at-risk periods. Varying the at-risk period produces, as we might expect, differences in recidivism rates. Evaluating a Texas program that provided drug abuse treatment, Michael Eisenberg (1999, 8) reports rates for different at-risk periods:

	1-Year	2-Year	3-Year
All participants	14%	37%	42%

Note that the difference between one- and two-year rates is much larger than that between two- and three-year rates. Operationalizing "recidivism" as a one-year failure rate would be much less accurate than operationalizing the concept as a two-year rate, because recidivism rates seem to stabilize at the two-year point.

Exhaustive and Exclusive Measurement

Briefly revisiting terms introduced in Chapter 3, an attribute is a characteristic or quality of something. *Female* is an example, as are *old* and *student*. Variables, in contrast, are logical sets of attributes.

Thus, *gender* is a variable traditionally composed of the attributes *female* and *male*. The conceptualization and operationalization processes can be seen as the specification of variables and the attributes composing them. Thus, *employment status* is a variable that has the attributes *employed* and *unemployed*, or the list of attributes could be expanded to include other possibilities such as *employed part time, employed full time*, and *retired*.

Every variable should have two important qualities. First, the attributes composing it should be *exhaustive*. If the variable is to have any utility in research, researchers must be able to classify every observation in terms of one of the attributes composing the variable. We will run into trouble if we conceptualize the variable *sentence* in terms of the attributes *prison* and *fine*. After all, some convicted persons are assigned to probation, some have a portion of their prison sentence suspended, and others may receive a mix of prison term, probation, suspended sentence, or perhaps community service. Notice that we could make the list of attributes exhaustive by adding *other* and *combination*. Whatever approach we take, we must be able to classify every observation.

At the same time, attributes composing a variable must be *mutually exclusive*. Researchers must be able to classify every observation in terms of one and only one attribute. Thus, for example, we need to define *prison* and *fine* in such a way that nobody can possess both attributes at the same time. That means we must be able to handle the variables for a person whose sentence includes both a prison term and a fine. In this case, attributes could be defined more precisely by specifying *prison only, fine only*, and *both prison and fine*.

Levels of Measurement

Attributes composing any variable must be mutually exclusive and exhaustive. Attributes may be related in other ways as well. Of particular interest is that variables may represent different levels of measurement: nominal, ordinal, interval, and ratio. Levels of measurement tell us what sorts of information we can gain from the scores assigned to the values of a variable.

Nominal Measures Variables whose attributes have only the characteristics of exhaustiveness and mutual exclusiveness are **nominal measures**. Examples are gender, city of residence, college major, Social Security number, and marital status. The attributes composing each of these variables—male and female for the variable gender—are distinct from one another and pretty much cover the traditional possibilities among people. Nominal measures merely offer names or labels for characteristics.

Imagine a group of people being characterized in terms of a nominal variable and physically grouped by the appropriate attributes. Suppose we are at a convention attended by hundreds of state court judges. At a social function, we ask them to stand together in groups according to the states in which they live: all those from Vermont in one group, those from California in another, and so forth. The variable is *state of residence*; the attributes are *live in Vermont, live in California*, and so on. All the people standing in a given group have at least one thing in common; the people in any one group differ from the people in all other groups in that same regard. Where the individual groups are formed, how close they are to one another, and how they are arranged in the room are irrelevant. All that matters is that all the members of a given group share the same state of residence and that each group has a different shared state of residence.

Ordinal Measures Variables whose attributes may be logically rank ordered are **ordinal measures**. The different attributes represent relatively more or less of the variable. Examples of variables that can be ordered in some way are opinion of police, occupational status, crime seriousness, and fear of crime.

Let's pursue the earlier example of grouping state court judges at a social gathering and imagine that we ask all those who have sat on appellate courts to stand in one group, all those serving felony trial courts to stand in another group, and all those who sit on misdemeanor trial courts to stand in a third group. This manner of grouping people satisfies the requirements for exhaustiveness and mutual exclusiveness. In addition, however, we might logically arrange the three groups in terms of the level of court where they serve (the shared attribute). We might arrange the three groups in a row, ranging from highest court to lowest court. This arrangement provides a physical representation of an ordinal measure. If we know which groups two individuals are in, we can determine what level of court they sit on.

Note that in this example it is irrelevant how close or far apart the court groups are from one another. They might stand 5 feet apart or 500 feet apart; the appellate and felony trial court groups could be 5 feet apart, and the misdemeanor trial court group might be 500 feet farther down the line. These physical distances have no meaning. The felony group, however, should be between the misdemeanor group and the appellate group, or else the rank order is incorrect.

Interval Measures When the actual distance that separates the attributes composing some variables does have meaning, the variables are **interval measures**. The logical distance between attributes can then be expressed in meaningful standard intervals.

For example, in the Fahrenheit temperature scale, the difference, or distance, between 80 degrees and 90 degrees is the same as that between 40 degrees and 50 degrees. However, 80 degrees Fahrenheit is not twice as hot as 40 degrees, because the zero point in the Fahrenheit scale is arbitrary; zero degrees does not really mean lack of heat. Similarly, minus 30 degrees on this scale doesn't represent 30 degrees less than no heat. This is true for the Celsius scale as well. In contrast, the Kelvin scale is based on an absolute zero, which *does* mean a complete lack of heat.

Ratio Measures Most of the social scientific variables that meet the minimum requirements for interval measures also meet the requirements for **ratio measures**. In ratio measures, the attributes that compose a variable, besides having all the structural characteristics mentioned previously, are based on a true zero point. Examples from criminal justice research are age, dollar value of property loss from burglary, number of prior arrests, blood alcohol content, and length of incarceration.

Returning to the example of various ways to classify judges, we might ask them to group themselves according to years of experience in their present position. All those new to their job would stand together, as would those with one year of experience, those with two years on the job, and so forth. The facts that members of each group share the same years of experience and that each group has a different shared length of time satisfy the minimum requirements for a nominal measure. Arranging the several groups in a line from those with the least to those with the most experience meets the additional requirements for an ordinal measure and permits us to determine whether one person is more experienced, is less experienced, or has the same level of experience as another. If we arrange the groups so that there is the same distance between each pair of adjacent groups, we satisfy the additional requirements of an interval measure and can say how much more experience one chief has than another. Finally, because one of the attributes included—experience—has a true zero point (judges just appointed or elected to their job), the phalanx of judges also meets the requirements for a ratio measure, permitting us to say that one person is twice as experienced as another.

Comparing two people in terms of a ratio variable, then, allows us to conclude (1) whether they are different (or the same), (2) whether one is more than the other, (3) how much they differ, and (4) what the ratio of one to another is. Figure 4.1 summarizes this discussion by presenting a graphic illustration of the four levels of measurement.

Implications of Levels of Measurement

To review this discussion and to illustrate why the level of measurement may make a difference, consider Table 4.1. It presents information on crime seriousness adapted from a survey of crime severity conducted for the Bureau of Justice Statistics (Wolfgang et al. 1985). The survey presented brief descriptions of more than 200 different crimes to a sample of 60,000 people. Respondents were asked to assign a score to each crime based on how serious they thought the crime was compared with bicycle theft (scored at 10).

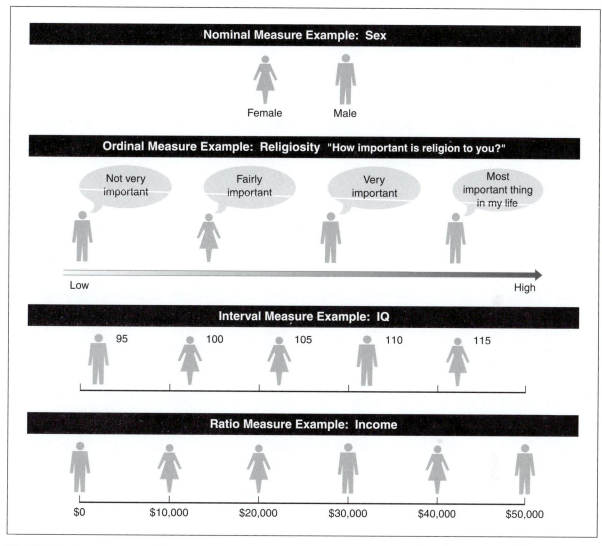

FIGURE 4.1   Levels of Measurement

The first column in Table 4.1 lists some of the crimes described. The second column shows a nominal measure that identifies the victim in the crime: home, person, business, or society. Type of victim is an attribute of each crime. The third column lists seriousness scores computed from survey results, ranging from 0.6 for trespassing to 35.7 for murder. These seriousness scores are interval measures because the distance between, for example, auto theft (at 8.0) and accepting a bribe (at 9.0) is

the same as that between accepting a bribe (at 9.0) and obstructing justice (at 10.0). Seriousness scores are not ratio measures; there is no absolute zero point, and three instances of obstructing justice (at 10.0) do not equal one rape with injury (at 30.0).

The fourth column shows the ranking for each of the 17 crimes in the table; the most serious crime, murder, is ranked 1, followed by rape with injury, and so on. The rankings express only the order of seriousness, however, because the

TABLE 4.1   Crime Seriousness and Levels of Measurement

Crime	Victim	Seriousness Score	Rank	Value of Property Loss
Accepting a bribe	Society	9.0	9	0
Arson	Business	12.7	6	$ 10,000
Auto theft	Home	8.0	10	$ 12,000
Burglary	Business	15.5	5	$100,000
Burglary	Home	9.6	8	$ 1,000
Buying stolen property	Society	5.0	12	0
Heroin sales	Society	20.6	4	0
Heroin use	Society	6.5	11	0
Murder	Person	35.7	1	0
Obstructing justice	Society	10.0	7	0
Public intoxication	Society	0.8	15	0
Rape and injury	Person	30.0	2	0
Robbery and injury	Person	21.0	3	$ 1,000
Robbery attempt	Person	3.3	13	0
Robbery, no injury	Person	8.0	10	$ 1,000
Shoplifting	Business	2.2	14	$ 10
Trespassing	Home	0.6	16	0

Source: Adapted from Wolfgang et al. (1985).

difference between murder (ranked 1) and rape (ranked 2) is smaller than the distance between rape and robbery with injury (ranked 3).

Finally, the crime descriptions presented to respondents indicated the value of property loss for each offense. This is a ratio measure with a true zero point, so that 10 burglaries with a loss of $1,000 each have the same property value as one arson offense with a loss of $10,000.

Specific analytic techniques require variables that meet certain minimum levels of measurement. For example, we could compute the average property loss from the crimes listed in Table 4.1 by adding up the individual numbers in the fifth column and dividing by the number of crimes listed (17). However, we would not be able to compute the average victim type because that is a nominal variable. In that case, we could report the modal—the most common—victim type, which is society in Table 4.1.

Researchers may treat some variables as representing different levels of measurement. Ratio measures are the highest level, followed by interval, ordinal, and nominal. A variable that represents a given level of measurement—say, ratio—may also be treated as representing a lower level of measurement—say, ordinal. For example, age is a ratio measure. If we wish to examine only the relationship between age and some ordinal-level variable, such as delinquency involvement (high, medium, or low), we might choose to treat age as an ordinal-level variable as well. We might characterize the subjects of our study as being young, middle age, or old, specifying the age range for each of those groupings. Finally, age might be used as a nominal-level variable for certain research purposes. Thus, people might be grouped as baby boomers if they were born between 1945 and 1955.

The analytic uses planned for a given variable, then, should determine the level of measurement to be sought, with the realization that some variables are inherently limited to a certain level. If a variable is to be used in a variety of ways that require different levels of measurement, the study should be designed to achieve the highest level possible. Although ratio measures such as number of arrests can later be reduced to ordinal or nominal ones, it is not possible to convert a nominal or ordinal measure to a ratio one. More generally, you cannot convert a lower-level measure to a higher-level one. That is a one-way street worth remembering.

Criteria for Measurement Quality

The key standards for measurement quality are reliability and validity.

Measurements can be made with varying degrees of precision, which refers to the fineness of the distinctions made between the attributes that compose a variable. Saying that a woman is 43 years old is more precise than saying that she is in her forties. Describing a felony sentence as 18 months is more precise than describing it as more than one year.

As a general rule, precise measurements are superior to imprecise ones, as common sense would suggest. Precision is not always necessary or desirable, however. If knowing that a felony sentence is more than one year is sufficient for your research purpose, then any additional effort invested in learning the precise sentence would be wasted. The operationalization of concepts, then, must be guided partly by an understanding of the degree of precision required. If your needs are not clear, be more precise rather than less.

However, don't confuse precision with accuracy. Describing someone as "born in Stowe, Vermont" is more precise than "born in New England," but suppose the person in question was actually born in Boston? The less precise description, in this instance, is more accurate; it's a better reflection of the real world. This is a point worth keeping in mind. Many criminal justice measures are imprecise, so reporting approximate values is often more accurate.

Precision and accuracy are obviously important qualities in research measurement, and they probably need no further explanation. When criminal justice researchers construct and evaluate measurements,

they pay special attention to two technical considerations: reliability and validity.

Reliability

Fundamentally, **reliability** is a matter of whether a particular measurement technique, applied repeatedly to the same thing, will yield the same result each time. In other words, measurement reliability is roughly the same as measurement consistency or stability. Imagine a police officer standing on the street, guessing the speed of cars that pass by and issuing speeding tickets based on that judgment. If you received a ticket from this officer and went to court to contest it, you would almost certainly win your case. The judge would no doubt reject this way of measuring speed, regardless of the police officer's experience. The reliability or consistency of this method of measuring vehicle speed is questionable at best. If the same police officer used a laser speed detector, however, it is doubtful that you would be able to beat the ticket. The laser device is judged a much more reliable way of measuring speed.

Reliability, though, does not ensure accuracy any more than precision does. The speedometer in your car may be a reliable instrument for measuring speed, but it is common for speedometers to be off by a few miles per hour, especially at higher speeds. If your speedometer shows 55 miles per hour when you are actually traveling at 60, it gives you a consistent but inaccurate reading that might attract the attention of police officers with more accurate laser guns.

Measurement reliability is often a problem with indicators used in criminal justice research. For example, forensic DNA evidence is increasingly being used in violent crime cases. National Research Council studies (1996; 2009) found a variety of errors in laboratory procedures, including sample mishandling, evidence contamination, and analyst bias. These are measurement reliability problems that can lead to unwarranted exclusion of evidence or to the conviction of innocent people (Roth 2010).

Reliability problems crop up in many forms. Reliability is a concern every time a single observer is the source of data because we have no way to guard against that observer's subjectivity. We can't tell for sure how much of what's reported represents true variation and how much is due to the observer's unique perceptions.

Reliability can also be an issue when more than one observer makes measurements. Survey researchers have long known that different interviewers get different answers from respondents as a result of their own attitudes and demeanor. Suppose we want to classify different types of right-wing extremist organizations in terms of some standard coding scheme, such as a set of categories created by the National Institute of Justice. However, a supporter of Mayors against Illegal Guns and a member of the National Rifle Association would be unlikely to code all groups into the same categories.

How do we create reliable measures? Because the problem of reliability is a basic one in criminal justice measurement, researchers have developed a number of techniques for dealing with it.

The Test–Retest Method   Sometimes it is appropriate to make the same measurement more than once. If there is no reason to expect the information to change, we should expect the same response every time. If answers vary, however, then the measurement method is, to the extent of that variation, unreliable. Here's an illustration.

In their classic research on delinquency in England, Donald West and David Farrington (1977) interviewed a sample of 411 males from a working-class area of London at age 16 and again at age 18. The subjects were asked to describe a variety of aspects of their lives, including educational and work history, leisure pursuits, drinking and smoking habits, delinquent activities, and experience with police and courts.

West and Farrington assessed reliability in several ways. One was to compare responses from the interview at age 18 with those from the interview at age 16. For example, in each interview, the youths were asked at what age they left school. In most cases, there were few discrepancies in stated age from one interview to the next, which led the authors to conclude, "There was therefore no

systematic tendency for youths either to increase or lessen their claimed period of school attendance as they grew older, as might have occurred if they had wanted either to exaggerate or to underplay their educational attainments" (1977, 76–77). If West and Farrington had found less consistency in answers to this and other items, they would have had good reason to doubt the truthfulness of responses to more sensitive questions. The test–retest method suggested to the authors that memory lapses were the most common source of minor differences.

Although this method can be a useful reliability check, it is limited in some respects. Faulty memory may produce inconsistent responses if there is a lengthy gap between the initial interview and the retest. In their study of childhood victimization, Christine Walsh et al. (2008) addressed this problem by asking their respondents about experiences of violence and then retesting by repeating the questions to their sample only four weeks later. A different problem can arise in trying to use the test–retest method to check the reliability of attitude or opinion measures. If the test–retest interval is short, then answers given in the second interview may be affected by earlier responses if subjects try to be consistent.

Interrater Reliability   It is also possible for measurement unreliability to be generated by research workers—for example, interviewers and coders. To guard against interviewer unreliability, it is common practice in surveys to have a supervisor call a subsample of the respondents on the telephone and verify selected information. West and Farrington (1977, 173) checked interrater reliability in their study of London youths and found few significant differences in results obtained from different interviewers.

Comparing measurements from different raters works in other situations as well. Michael Geerken (1994) presents an important discussion of reliability problems that researchers are likely to encounter in measuring prior arrests through police rap sheets. Duplicate entries, the use of aliases, and the need to transform official crime categories into a smaller number of categories for analysis are among the problems Geerken cites. One way to increase consistency in translating official records into research measures—a process often referred to as coding—is to have more than one person code a sample of records and then compare the consistency of coding decisions made by each person. This approach was used by Michael Maxfield and Cathy Spatz Widom (1996) in their analysis of adult arrests of child abuse victims.

In general, whenever researchers are concerned that measures obtained through coding may not be classified reliably, they should have each independently coded by different people. A great deal of disagreement among coders would most likely be due to ambiguity in operational definitions.

The reliability of measurements is a fundamental issue in criminal justice research, and we'll return to it in the chapters to come. For now, however, we hasten to point out that even total reliability doesn't ensure that our measures actually measure what we think they measure. That brings us to the issue of validity.

Validity

In Chapter 3, we discussed validity in connection with the accuracy of causal inference. We are also interested in validity as a criterion for measurement quality—whether an empirical measure adequately reflects the meaning of the concept under consideration. Put another way, measurement validity involves whether you are really measuring what you say you are measuring. Recall that an operational definition specifies the operations you will perform to measure a concept. Does your operational definition accurately reflect the concept you are interested in? If the answer is yes, you have a valid measure. A radar gun is a valid measure of vehicle speed, but a wind velocity indicator is not because it measures total wind speed, not vehicle speed with respect to the ground.

Although methods for assessing reliability are relatively straightforward, it is more difficult to demonstrate that individual measures are valid. Because concepts are not real, but abstract, we cannot

directly demonstrate that measures, which are real, are actually measuring an abstract concept. Nevertheless, researchers have some ways of dealing with the issue of validity.

Face Validity First, there's something called **face validity**. Particular empirical measures may or may not jibe with our common agreements and our individual mental images about a particular concept. We might debate the adequacy of measuring satisfaction with police services by counting the number of citizen complaints registered by the mayor's office, but we'd surely agree that the number of citizen complaints has something to do with levels of satisfaction. If someone suggested that we measure satisfaction with police by finding out whether people like to watch police dramas on TV, we would probably agree that the measure has no face validity; it simply does not make sense.

Second, there are many concrete agreements among researchers about how to measure certain basic concepts. The Census Bureau, for example, has created operational definitions of such concepts as family, household, and employment status that seem to have a workable validity in most studies using those concepts.

Criterion-Related Validity A more formal way to assess validity is to compare a measure with some external criterion, known as **criterion-related validity**. A measure can be validated by showing that it predicts scores on another measure that is generally accepted as valid; this is sometimes referred to as *convergent validity*. The validity of College Board exams, for example, is shown in their ability to predict the success of students in college.

Robert Voas and associates (Voas, Romano, and Peck 2009) offer a good example of criterion-related validity in their efforts to validate a measure of alcohol-related auto accidents. Of course, conducting a blood alcohol laboratory test on everyone involved in auto accidents would be a valid measure. But this is not routinely done, so Voas and colleagues tested an alternate measure adapted from one used to estimate alcohol-related *fatal* accidents: single-vehicle accidents occurring between midnight and 3:00 a.m. The validity of this measure was shown by comparing it with the blood alcohol test results obtained from samples of drivers involved in nonfatal accidents in two test sites— Long Beach, California, and Fort Lauderdale, Florida. Because the two measures agreed closely, Voas and associates claimed that the proxy or surrogate measure would be valid in other sites.

Another approach to criterion-related validity is to show that our measure of a concept is different from measures of similar but distinct concepts. This is called *discriminant validity*, meaning that measures can discriminate between different concepts.

Sometimes it is difficult to find behavioral criteria that can be used to validate measures as directly as described here. In those instances, however, we can often approximate such criteria by considering how the variable in question ought, theoretically, to relate to other variables.

Construct Validity Another way to think about validity is to consider logical relationships among variables, known as **construct validity**. Let's suppose that we are interested in studying fear of crime—its sources and consequences. As part of our research, we develop a measure of fear of crime, and we want to assess its validity.

In addition to our measure, we will also develop certain theoretical expectations about the way the variable fear of crime relates to other variables. For instance, it's reasonable to conclude that people who are afraid of crime are less likely to leave their homes at night for entertainment than people who are not afraid of crime. If our measure of fear of crime relates to how often people go out at night in the expected fashion, that constitutes evidence of our measure's construct validity. However, if people who are afraid of crime are just as likely to go out at night as people who are not afraid, that challenges the validity of our measure. This and related points about measures of fear are nicely illustrated by Jason Ditton and Stephen Farrall in their analysis of data from England (2007).

Tests of construct validity, then, can offer a weight of evidence that our measure either does or does not tap the quality we want it to measure, without providing definitive proof.

Multiple Measures Another approach to validation of an individual measure is to compare it with alternative measures of the same concept. The use of multiple measures is similar to establishing criterion validity. However, the use of multiple measures does not necessarily assume that the criterion measure is always more accurate. For example, many crimes never result in an arrest, so arrests are not good measures of how many crimes are committed by individuals. Self-report surveys have often been used to measure delinquency and criminality. But how valid are survey questions that ask people how many crimes they have committed?

The approach used by West and Farrington (and by others) is to ask people, for example, how many times they have committed robbery and how many times they have been arrested for that crime. Those who admit to having been arrested for robbery are asked when and where the arrest occurred. Self-reports can then be validated by checking police arrest records. This works two ways: (1) it is possible to validate individual reports of being arrested for robbery, and (2) researchers can check police records for all persons interviewed to see if there are any records of robbery arrests that subjects do not disclose to interviewers.

Figure 4.2 illustrates the difference between validity and reliability. Think of measurement as analogous to hitting the bull's-eye on a target. A reliable measure produces a tight pattern, regardless of where it hits, because reliability is a function of consistency. Validity, in contrast, relates to the arrangement of shots around the bull's-eye. The failure of reliability in the figure can be seen as a random error; the failure of validity is a systematic error. Notice that neither an unreliable nor an invalid measure is likely to be very useful.

Measuring Crime

Different approaches to measuring crime illustrate basic principles in conceptualization and measurement.

By way of illustrating basic principles in measurement, we now focus more specifically on different

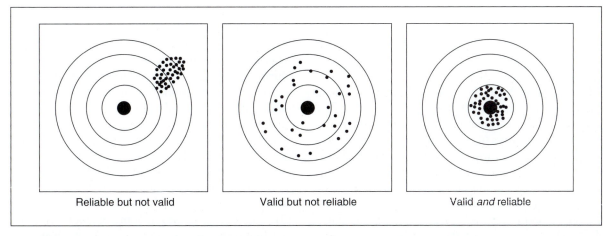

FIGURE 4.2   Analogy to Validity and Reliability

ways of measuring crime. Crime is a fundamental dependent variable in criminal justice and criminology. Explanatory studies frequently seek to learn what causes crime, whereas applied studies often focus on what actions might be effective in reducing crime. Descriptive and exploratory studies may simply wish to count how much crime there is in a specific area, a question of obvious concern to criminal justice officials as well as researchers.

Crime can also be an independent variable—for example, in a study of how crime affects fear or other attitudes, or of whether people who live in high-crime areas are more likely than others to favor long prison sentences for drug dealers. Sometimes crime can be both an independent and a dependent variable, as in a study about the relationship between drug use and other offenses.

General Issues in Measuring Crime

At the outset, we must consider two general questions that influence whatever approach we might take to measuring crime: (1) How will we conceptualize *crime*? and (2) What units of analysis should be used?

Conceptualization   Let's begin by proposing a conceptual definition of crime—one that will enable us to decide what specific types of crime we'll measure. Recall a definition from Gottfredson and

Hirschi (1990, 15), mentioned earlier: "acts of force or fraud undertaken in pursuit of self-interest." This is an interesting definition, but it is better suited to an extended discussion of theories of crime than to our purposes in this chapter. For example, we would have to clarify what was meant by *self-interest*, a term that has engaged philosophers and social scientists for centuries.

James Q. Wilson and Richard Herrnstein (1985, 22) propose a different definition that should get us started: "A crime is any act committed in violation of a law that prohibits it and authorizes punishment for its commission." Although other criminologists (such as Gottfredson and Hirschi) might not agree with this conceptual definition, it has the advantage of being reasonably specific. We could be even more specific by consulting a state or federal code and listing the types of acts for which the law provides punishment.

Our list would be very long. In fact, one of the principal difficulties we encounter when we try to measure crime is that many different types of behaviors and actions are included in our conceptualization of crime as an *act committed in violation of a law that prohibits it and authorizes punishment for its commission*, but we may be interested in only a small subset of things included under such a broad definition. Different measures tend to focus on different types of crime, primarily because not all crimes can be measured the same way with any degree of reliability or validity. Therefore, one important step in selecting a measure is deciding what crimes will be included.

What Units of Analysis? Recall that units of analysis are the specific entities researchers collect information about. Chapter 3 considered individuals, groups, social artifacts, and other units of analysis. Deciding how to measure crime requires that we once again think about these units.

Crimes involve four elements that are often easier to recognize in the abstract than they are to actually measure: offender, victim, offense, and incident. The most basic of these elements is the offender. Without an offender, there's no crime, so a crime must, at a minimum, involve an offender. The offender is therefore one possible unit of analysis. We might decide to study burglars, auto thieves, bank robbers, child molesters, drug dealers, or people who have committed many different types of offenses.

Crimes also require some sort of victim, the second possible unit of analysis. We could study victims of burglary, auto theft, bank robbery, or assault. Notice that this list of victims includes different types of units: households or businesses for burglary, car owners for auto theft, banks for bank robbery, and individuals for assault. Some of these units are organizations (banks, businesses), some are individual people, some are abstractions (households), and some are ambiguous (individuals or organizations can own automobiles).

What about so-called victimless crimes like drug use or prostitution? In a legal sense, victimless crimes do not exist because crimes are acts that injure society, organizations, or individuals. But studying crimes in which only society is the victim—prostitution, for example—presents special challenges, and specialized techniques have been developed to measure certain types of victimless crimes.

The final two elements of crimes—offense and incident—are closely intertwined and so will be discussed together. An offense is defined as an individual act of burglary, auto theft, bank robbery, and so on. The Federal Bureau of Investigation (FBI) defines incident as "one or more offenses committed by the same offender, or group of offenders acting in concert, at the same time and place" (Federal Bureau of Investigation 2013b, 9).

Think about the difference between offense and incident for a moment. A single incident can include multiple offenses, but it's not possible to have one offense and multiple incidents.

To illustrate the different units of analysis—offenders, victims, offenses, and incidents—consider the examples in the box titled "Units of Analysis and Measuring Crime." These examples help distinguish units from each other and illustrate the links among different units. Notice that we have said nothing about aggregate units of analysis, a topic we examined in Chapter 3. We have considered only individual units, even though measures of crime are often based on aggregate units of analysis—neighborhoods, cities, counties, states, and so on.

 UNITS OF ANALYSIS AND MEASURING CRIME

Figuring out the different units of analysis in counting crimes can be difficult and confusing at first. Much of the problem comes from the possibility of what database designers call one-to-many and many-to-many relationships. The same incident can have multiple offenses, offenders, and victims or just one of each. Fortunately, thinking through some examples usually clarifies the matter. Our two examples are adapted from an FBI publication (2000, 18).

Example 1

Two males entered a bar. The bartender was forced at gunpoint to hand over all money from the cash register. The offenders also took money and jewelry

(continued)

from three customers. One of the offenders used his handgun to beat one of the customers, thereby causing serious injury. Both offenders fled on foot.

> One incident
>> One robbery offense
>> Two offenders
>> Four victims (bar owner, three patrons)
>
> One aggravated assault offense
>> Two offenders
>> One victim

Even though only one offender actually assaulted the bar patron, the other offender would be charged with assisting in the offense because he prevented others from coming to the aid of the assault victim.

Example 2

Two males entered a bar. The bartender was forced at gunpoint to hand over all the money from the cash register. The offenders also took money and jewelry from two customers. One of the offenders, in searching for more people to rob, found a customer in a back room and raped her there, outside the view of the other offender. When the rapist returned, both offenders fled on foot.

This example includes two incidents because the rape occurred in a different place and the offenders were not acting in concert. And because they were not acting in concert in the same place, only one offender was associated with the rape incident.

> Incident 1
>> One robbery offense
>>> Two offenders
>>> Three victims (bar owner, two patrons)
>
> Incident 2
>> One rape offense
>> One offender
>> One victim

We cover units at some length because they play a critical, and often overlooked, role in developing operational definitions, to which our attention now turns.

Measures Based on Crimes Known to Police

The most widely used measures of crime are based on police records and are commonly referred to as *crimes known to police*. This phrase is at the core of police-based operational definitions and has important implications for understanding what police records do and do not measure. The most obvious implication is that crimes not known to police cannot be measured by consulting police records. Other features of measures based on police records can best be understood by considering specific examples.

Uniform Crime Reports Police measures of crime form the basis for the FBI's Uniform Crime Reports (UCR), a data series that has been collected since 1930 and has been widely used by criminal justice researchers. But certain characteristics and procedures related to the UCR affect its suitability as a measure of crime. Most of our comments highlight shortcomings in this regard, but keep in mind that the UCR is and will continue to be a very useful measure for researchers and public officials.

The UCR does not even try to count all crimes reported to police. Eight offense types are recorded if these offenses are reported to police (and recorded by police). These eight types include four violent offenses (murder and nonnegligent manslaughter, forcible rape, robbery, and aggravated assault) and four property crime offenses (burglary, larceny-theft, motor vehicle theft, and arson) (Federal Bureau of Investigation 2012). An additional 20 offenses are counted only if a person has been arrested and charged with a crime. The UCR therefore does not include such offenses as drug sale or use, fraud, prostitution, simple assault, vandalism, receiving stolen property, and all other nontraffic offenses unless someone is arrested. This means that a large number of crimes reported to police are not measured in the UCR.

Another source of measurement error in the UCR is produced by the hierarchy rule used by police agencies and the FBI to classify crimes. Under the hierarchy rule, if multiple crimes are committed in a single incident, only the most serious is counted in the UCR. For example, if a burglar breaks into a home, stabs one of the occupants, and flees in the homeowner's car, at least three crimes are committed—burglary, aggravated assault, and vehicle theft. Under the FBI hierarchy rule, however, only the most serious crime, aggravated assault, is counted in the UCR, even though the offender could be charged with all three offenses. In the examples described in the box "Units of Analysis and Measuring Crime," the UCR would count one offense in each incident: a single robbery in the first example and rape in the second.

Before we move on to other approaches to measuring crime, consider another important way units of analysis figure into UCR data. The UCR system produces what is referred to as a **summary-based measure** of crime. This means that UCR data include summary, or total, crime counts from reporting agencies—cities or counties. UCR summary data, therefore, represent groups as units of analysis. Crime reports are available for cities or counties, and these may be aggregated upward to measure crime for states or regions of the United States. But UCR data available from the FBI cannot represent individual crimes, offenders, or victims as units.

Recall that it is possible to aggregate units of analysis to higher levels, but it is not possible to disaggregate grouped data to the individual level. Because UCR data are aggregates, they cannot be used in descriptive or explanatory studies that focus on individual crimes, offenders, or victims. UCR data are therefore restricted to the analysis of such units as cities, counties, states, or regions.

Incident-Based Police Records The U.S. Department of Justice sponsors two series of crime measures that are based on incidents as units of analysis. The first of these **incident-based measures**, Supplementary Homicide Reports (SHR), was begun in 1961 and is part of the UCR program, as implied by *supplementary*.

Local law enforcement agencies submit detailed information about individual homicide incidents under the SHR program. This includes information about victims and, if known, offenders (age, gender, race); the relationship between victim and offender; the weapon used; the location of the incident; and the circumstances surrounding the killing.

Notice how the SHR relates to our discussion of units of analysis. Incidents are the basic unit and can include one or more victims and offenders; because the series is restricted to homicides, offense is held constant.

Because the SHR is an incident-based system, investigators can use SHR data to conduct descriptive and explanatory studies of individual events. For example, it's possible to compare the relationship between victim and offender for male victims and female victims or to compare the types of weapons used in killings by strangers and killings by nonstrangers. Such analyses are not possible if we are studying homicide using UCR summary data.

Crime measures based on incidents as units of analysis therefore have several advantages over summary measures. It's important to keep in mind, however, that SHR data still represent crimes known to police and recorded by police.

The National Incident-Based Reporting System A relatively new development in police-based measures at the national level is the ongoing effort by the FBI and the Bureau of Justice Statistics (BJS) to convert the UCR to a National Incident-Based Reporting System (NIBRS, pronounced "nybers"). Planning for replacement of the UCR began in the mid-1980s, but because NIBRS represents major changes, law enforcement agencies have shifted only gradually to the new system.

About 17,000 law enforcement agencies report UCR summary data each year; that's 17,000 annual observations, one for each reporting agency. In 2012, 108 agencies in Idaho reported UCR data, so Idaho submitted a maximum of 108 observations for 2012. Under NIBRS, Idaho reported over 81,000 incidents in 2012. So, for Idaho, shifting from the summary UCR system for measuring crime to the incident-based NIBRS system meant shifting from 108 units (UCR reporting jurisdictions) to more than 81,000 units. In other words, rather than reporting 108 summary crime counts for eight UCR Part I offenses, Idaho reported detailed information on 81,147 individual incidents—and this is only Idaho, which ranked 39th among the states in 2012 resident population (Idaho State Police 2013)!

In addition, NIBRS guidelines call for gathering information about a much broader array of offenses. Whereas the UCR reports information about 8 Part I offenses, NIBRS is designed to collect detailed information on 46 "Group A" offenses. Table 4.2 shows what kinds of information are collected for offenses, victims, and offenders under NIBRS. Table 4.3 shows NIBRS crime data for Idaho in 2012. Compare the top part of the table, reporting crime counts for UCR summary offenses, to the bottom part. Additional NIBRS Group A offenses more than double the number of crimes "known to police" in Idaho (34,909 UCR summary offenses plus 46,238 additional Group A offenses). Simple assault and destruction of property (vandalism) are by far the most common of these additional offenses, but drug violations accounted for almost 15,000 offenses in 2012 (drug violations plus drug equipment violations).

TABLE 4.2   Selected Information in National Incident-Based Reporting System Records

Administrative Segment	Offense Segment
Incident date and time	Offense type
Reporting agency ID	Attempted or completed
Other ID numbers	Offender drug/alcohol use
	Location type
	Weapon use
Victim Segment	**Offender Segment**
Victim ID number	Offender ID number
Offense type	Offender age, gender, race
Victim age, gender, race	
Resident of jurisdiction?	
Type of injury	
Relationship to offender	
Victim type:	
Individual person	
Business	
Government	
Society/public	

Source: Adapted from Federal Bureau of Investigation (2000, 6–8, 90).

TABLE 4.3   Crime in Idaho, 2012

UCR Summary Offenses	
Murder, non-negligent manslaughter	30
Rape	466
Robbery	239
Aggravated assault	2,510
Burglary	6,732
Larceny	23,330
Motor vehicle theft	1,363
Arson	239
Subtotal	34,909
Additional NIBRS Group A Offenses	
Simple assault	11,771
Intimidation	1,272
Bribery	2
Counterfeit/forgery	759
Destruction of property	10,667
Drug violations	8,039
Drug equipment violations	6,938
Embezzlement	116
Extortion/blackmail	13
Fraud	3,604
Gambling	3
Kidnapping/abduction	212
Pornography/obscene material	130
Prostitution	35
Forcible sex offenses	1,119
Nonforcible sex offenses	143
Stolen property	382
Weapons violations	1,033
Subtotal	46,238
Group A Total	81,147

Source: Adapted from Idaho State Police, "Crime in Idaho, 2012," http://www.isp.idaho.gov/BCI/ucr/crimeinidaho2012.html

Collecting detailed information on each incident for each offense, victim, and offender, and doing so for a large number of offense types, represent the most significant changes in NIBRS compared with the UCR. Dropping the hierarchy rule is also a major change, but that is a consequence of incident-based reporting.

Victim Surveys

Conducting a **victim survey** that asks people whether they have been the victim of a crime is an alternative approach to operationalization. In principle, measuring crime through surveys has several advantages. Surveys can obtain information on crimes that were not reported to police. Asking people about victimizations can also measure incidents that police may not have officially recorded as crimes. Finally, asking people about crimes that may have happened to them provides data on victims and offenders (individuals) and on the incidents themselves (social artifacts). Like an incident-based reporting system, a survey can therefore provide more disaggregated units of analysis.

The National Crime Victimization Survey The U.S. Census Bureau has conducted the National Crime Victimization Survey (NCVS) since 1972, the longest continuous crime survey in the world. The NCVS is based on a nationally representative sample of households and uses uniform procedures to select and interview respondents, which enhances the reliability of crime measures. Because individual people living in households are interviewed, the NCVS can be used in studies in which individuals or households are the unit of analysis. And the NCVS uses a panel design, interviewing respondents from the same household seven times at six-month intervals.

The NCVS cannot measure all crimes, however, in part because of the procedures used to select victims. Because the survey is based on a sample of households, it cannot count crimes in which businesses or commercial establishments are the victims. Bank robberies, gas station holdups, shoplifting, embezzlement, and securities fraud are examples of crimes that cannot be systematically counted by interviewing household members. Samples of banks, gas stations, retail stores, business establishments, or stockbrokers would be needed to measure those crimes. In much the same fashion, crimes directed at homeless victims cannot be counted by surveys of households such as the NCVS.

What about victimless crimes? For example, think about how you would respond to a Census Bureau interviewer who asked whether you had been the victim of a drug sale. If you have bought illegal drugs, you might think of yourself as a customer rather than as a victim. Or if you lived near a park where drug sales were common, you might think of yourself as a victim even though you did not participate in a drug transaction. The point is that victim surveys are not good measures of victimless crimes because the respondents can't easily be conceived as victims.

Measuring certain forms of delinquency through victim surveys presents similar problems. Status offenses such as truancy and curfew violations do not have identifiable victims who can be included in samples based on households. Homicide and manslaughter are other crimes that are not well measured by victim surveys, for obvious reasons.

Since its inception, the NCVS has served as a measure to monitor the volume of crime, including crimes not reported to police. In a regular series of publications, the BJS reports annual victimization data together with analysis of victimization for special topics such as hate crimes (Wilson 2014), intimate partner violence (Truman and Morgan 2014), and contacts between individuals and the police (Langton and Durose 2013). In addition, the NCVS is a valuable tool for researchers who take advantage of detailed information about individual victimizations to examine such topics as victimization in public schools (Dinkes et al. 2007), identity theft (Langton and Planty 2010), and why domestic violence victimizations may or may not be reported to police (Felson et al. 2002).

Community Victimization Surveys Following the initial development of victim survey methods in the late 1960s, the Census Bureau completed a series of city-level surveys. These were discontinued for a variety of reasons, but researchers and officials in the BJS occasionally conducted city-level victim surveys in specific communities. In 1998, the BJS and the Office of Community Oriented Policing Services (COPS) launched pilot surveys in 12 large- and medium-sized cities (Smith et al. 1999).

The city-level initiative underscores one of the chief advantages of measuring crime through victim surveys—obtaining counts of incidents not reported to police. In large part, city-level surveys were promoted by BJS and COPS to enable local law enforcement agencies to better understand the scope of crime—reported and unreported—in their communities. Notice also the title of the first report: "Criminal Victimization and *Perceptions* of Community Safety in 12 Cities, 1998." We emphasize perceptions to illustrate that city-level surveys can be valuable tools for implementing community policing, a key component of the 1994 Crime Bill that provided billions of dollars to hire new police officers nationwide. It is significant that the Department of Justice recognized the potential value of survey measures of crime and perceptions of community safety to develop and evaluate community policing.

The initial BJS/COPS effort was a pilot test of new methods for conducting city-level surveys. In 2010, the BJS began new efforts to develop local-level estimates of victimization for selected areas through a redesign of the NCVS (Cantor et al. 2010).

Surveys of Offending

Just as survey techniques can measure crime by asking people to describe their experiences as victims, **self-report surveys** ask people about crimes they may have committed. We might initially be skeptical of this technique: how truthful are people when asked about crimes they may have committed? Our concern is justified in one sense. Many people do not wish to disclose illegal behavior to interviewers, even if they are assured of confidentiality. Others might deliberately lie to interviewers and exaggerate the number of offenses they have committed.

Self-report surveys are the best method available for trying to measure certain crimes that are poorly represented by other techniques. Thinking about the other methods we have discussed—crimes known to police and victimization surveys—suggests several examples. Crimes such as prostitution and drug abuse are excluded from victimization surveys and underestimated by police records of people arrested for these offenses. Public order crimes and

delinquency are other examples. A third class of offenses that might be better counted by self-report surveys is crimes that are rarely reported to or observed by police—shoplifting and drunk driving are examples.

Think of it this way: As we saw earlier, all crimes require an offender. Not all crimes have clearly identifiable victims who can be interviewed, however, and not all crimes are readily observed by police, victims, or witnesses. If we can't observe the offense and can't interview a victim, what's the next logical step?

There are no nationwide efforts to systematically collect self-report measures on a variety of offenses, as is the case with the UCR and NCVS. Instead, periodic surveys yield information either on specific types of crime or on crimes committed by a specific target population. We will briefly consider two ongoing self-report surveys here.

National Survey on Drug Use and Health Like the NCVS, the National Survey on Drug Use and Health (NSDUH) is based on a national sample of households. Currently sponsored by the Substance Abuse and Mental Health Services Administration in the U.S. Department of Health and Human Services, the NSDUH samples households and household residents ages 12 and older. In the 2012 sample, about 67,500 individuals responded to questions regarding their use of illegal drugs, alcohol, and tobacco (Substance Abuse and Mental Health Services Administration 2013). Because it has been conducted for more than three decades, the NSDUH provides information on trends and changes in drug use among respondents. The 2013 survey was designed to obtain statistically reliable samples from the eight largest states in addition to the overall national sample.

Think for a moment about what sorts of questions we would ask to learn about people's experience in using illegal drugs. Among other things, we would probably want to distinguish someone who tried marijuana once from daily users. The drug use survey does this by including questions to distinguish lifetime use (ever used) of different drugs from current use (used within the past month). You may or may not agree that use in the past month represents current use, but it is the standard used in regular reports on NSDUH results. That's the operational definition of current use.

Monitoring the Future Our second example is different in two respects: (1) it targets a specific population, and (2) it asks sampled respondents a broader variety of questions.

Since 1975, the National Institute on Drug Abuse has sponsored an annual survey of high school seniors, "Monitoring the Future: A Continuing Study of the Lifestyles and Values of Youth," or the MTF for short. As its long title implies, the MTF survey is intended to monitor the behaviors, attitudes, and values of young people. The MTF includes several samples of high school students and other groups, totaling about 41,700 respondents in 2012 (Johnston et al. 2014).

Each spring almost 400 secondary schools are sampled within particular geographic areas. In larger high schools, samples of up to 350 seniors are selected; in smaller schools, all seniors may participate. Students fill out computer scan sheets containing batteries of questions that include self-reported use of alcohol, tobacco, and prescription and illegal drugs. In most cases, students record their answers in classrooms during normal school hours.

The core sample of the MTF—surveys of high school seniors—thus provides a cross section for measuring annual drug use and other illegal acts. Now recall our discussion of the time dimension in Chapter 3. Each year, both the MTF and the NSDUH survey drug use for a cross section of high school seniors and adults in households, thus providing a snapshot of annual rates of self-reported drug use. Examining annual results from the MTF and the NSDUH over time provides a time series, or trend study, that enables researchers and policy makers to detect changes in drug use among high school seniors and adults. Finally, a series of follow-up samples of MTF respondents constitute a series of panel studies whereby changes in drug use among individual respondents can be studied over time.

Measuring Crime Summary

Table 4.4 summarizes the strengths and weaknesses of different measures of crime. The UCR and SHR provide the best counts for murder and crimes in which the victim is a business or a commercial

TABLE 4.4   Measuring Crime Summary

	Units	Target Population	Crime Coverage	Best Count for
Known to police				
UCR	Aggregate: reporting agency	All law enforcement agencies; 98% reporting	Limited number reported and recorded crimes	Commercial and business victims
SHR	Incident	All law enforcement agencies; 98% reporting	Homicides only	Homicides
NIBRS	Incident	All law enforcement agencies; limited reporting	Extensive	Details on local incidents; victims under age 12
Surveys				
NCVS	Victimization, individuals and households	Individuals in households	Household and personal crimes	Household and personal crimes not reported to police
NSDUH	Individual respondent, offender	Individuals in households	Drug use	Drug use by adults in households
MTF	Individual respondent, offender	High school seniors; follow-up on sample	Substance use, delinquency, offending	Drug use by high school seniors

establishment. Crimes against persons or households that are not reported to police are best counted by the NCVS. Usually these are less serious crimes that are counted only if a suspect is arrested. Recent changes in NCVS procedures have improved counts of sexual assault and other violent victimizations. Compared with the UCR, NIBRS potentially provides much greater detail for a broader range of offenses. NIBRS complements the NCVS by including disaggregated incident-based reports for state and local areas and by recording detailed information on crimes against children younger than age 12.

Self-report surveys are best at measuring crimes that do not have readily identifiable victims and that are less often observed by or reported to police. The two self-report surveys listed in Table 4.4 sample different populations and use different interview procedures.

Don't forget that all crime measures are selective, so it's important to understand the selection process. Despite their various flaws, the measures of crime available to you can serve many research purposes. Researchers are best advised to be critical and careful users of whatever measure of crime best suits their research purpose.

Composite Measures

Combining individual measures often produces more valid and reliable indicators.

Sometimes it is possible to construct a single measure that captures the variable of interest. For example, asking auto owners whether their car has been stolen in the previous six months is a straightforward way to measure auto-theft victimization. But other variables may be better measured by more than one indicator. A "property crime" index might combine burglary, larceny, and motor vehicle theft; a "violent crime" index would be a composite of murder, rape, robbery, and assault.

Composite measures are frequently used in criminal justice research for three reasons. First, despite carefully designing studies to provide valid and reliable measurements of variables, the researcher is often unable to develop single indicators of complex concepts. That is especially true with regard to attitudes and opinions that are measured through surveys. For example, measuring fear of crime through a question that asks about feelings of safety on neighborhood streets measures some dimensions of fear but certainly not all of them. This leads us to question the validity of using that single question to measure fear of crime.

Second, we may wish to use a rather refined ordinal measure of a variable, arranging cases in several ordinal categories from very low to very high according to a variable, such as degree of parental supervision. A single data item might not have enough categories to provide the desired range of variation, but an index or scale formed from several items would.

Finally, indexes and scales are *efficient* devices for data analysis. If a single data item gives only a rough indication of a given variable, considering several data items may give us a more comprehensive and more accurate indication. For example, the results of a single drug test would give us some

---

 THEORY AND MEASUREMENT

Opportunity-based theories of crime argue that offenders will evaluate specific situations before selecting crime targets. Thus, theory suggests that auto thieves will search for unlocked cars, and burglars try to find properties that are unoccupied. What about parrot poachers—people who steal parrots to sell on illegal markets? Finding little previous research on parrot poaching, Stephen Pires and Ronald Clarke (2011) reasoned that parrot thieves in Mexico would target birds that nested close to ground level. So nesting location was an important variable for assessing the vulnerability of different species to poaching. Nesting location was a measure derived from opportunity-based theory.

indication of drug use by a probationer. Examining results from several drug tests would give us a better indication, but the manipulation of several data items simultaneously can be very complicated. In contrast, composite measures are efficient data reduction devices. Several indicators may be summarized in a single numerical score, even while very nearly maintaining the specific details of all the individual indicators.

Typologies

Researchers combine variables in different ways to produce different composite measures. The simplest of these is a **typology**, sometimes called a taxonomy. Typologies are produced by the intersection of two or more variables to create a set of categories or types. We may, for example, wish to classify people according to the range of their experience in criminal court. Assume we have asked a sample of people whether they have ever served as a juror and whether they have ever testified as a witness in criminal court. Table 4.5 shows how the yes and no responses to these two questions can be combined into a typology of experience in court.

Typologies can be more complex—combining scores on three or more measures or combining scores on two measures that take many different values. For an example of a complex typology, consider research by Rolf Loeber and associates (1991) on patterns of delinquency over time. The researchers used a longitudinal design in which a sample of boys was selected from Pittsburgh public schools and interviewed many times. Some questions asked about their involvement in delinquency and criminal offending. This approach made it possible to distinguish boys who reported different types of offending at different times.

Loeber and associates first classified delinquent and criminal acts into the following ordinal seriousness categories (1991, 44):

None: No self-reported delinquency
Minor: Theft of items worth less than $5, vandalism, fare evasion
Moderate: Theft of more than $5, gang fighting, carrying weapon
Serious: Car theft, breaking and entering, forced sex, selling drugs

Next, to measure changes in delinquency over time, the researchers compared reports of delinquency from the first screening interview with reports from follow-up interviews. These two measures—delinquency at time 1 and delinquency at time 2—formed the typology, which they referred to as a "dynamic classification of offenders" (1991, 44). Table 4.6 summarizes this typology.

The first category in the table, nondelinquent, includes those boys who reported committing no offenses at both the screening and follow-up interviews. Starters reported no offenses at screening and then minor, moderate, or serious delinquency at follow-up, whereas desistors were just the opposite. Those who committed the same types of offenses at both times were labeled stable; deescalators reported committing less serious offenses at follow-up; and escalators moved on to more serious offenses.

Notice the efficiency of this typology. Two variables (delinquency at screening and follow-up) with four categories each are reduced to a single variable with six categories. Furthermore, the two measures of delinquency are themselves composite measures, produced by summarizing self-reports of a large number of individual offenses. Finally, notice also how this efficiency is reflected in the clear meaning of the new composite measure. This dynamic typology summarizes information about time, offending, and offense seriousness in a single measure.

TABLE 4.5 Typology of Court Experience

| | | Serve on Jury? | |
		No	Yes
Testify as Witness?	**No**	A	B
	Yes	C	D

Typology

A: No experience with court

B: Experience as juror only

C: Experience as witness only

D: Experience as juror and witness

Typology	Juvenile Offending	
	Screening (Time 1)	Follow-Up (Time 2)
A. Nondelinquent	0	0
B. Starter	0	1, 2, or 3
C. Desistor	1, 2, or 3	0
D. Stable	1	1
D. Stable	2	2
D. Stable	3	3
E. Deescalator	3	2
E. Deescalator	2 or 3	1
F. Escalator	1	2 or 3
F. Escalator	2	3

TABLE 4.6   Typology of Change in Juvenile Offending

Juvenile Offending Typology

  0: None

  1: Minor

  2: Moderate

  3: Serious

Source: Adapted from Loeber and associates (1991, 43–46).

An Index of Disorder

"What is disorder, and what isn't?" asks Wesley Skogan (1990a) in his book on the links between crime, fear, and social problems such as public drinking, drug use, litter, prostitution, panhandling, dilapidated buildings, and groups of boisterous youths. In an influential article titled "Broken Windows," James Q. Wilson and George Kelling (1982) describe disorder as a sign of crime that may contribute independently to fear and crime itself. The argument goes something like this: Disorder is a symbol of urban decay that people associate with crime. Signs of disorder can produce two related problems. First, disorder may contribute to fear of crime, as urban residents believe that physical decay and undesirables are symbols of crime. Second, potential offenders may interpret evidence of disorder as a signal that informal social control mechanisms in a neighborhood have broken down and that the area is fair game for mayhem and predation.

We all have some sort of mental image (conception) of disorder, but, to paraphrase Skogan's question: how do we measure it? Let's begin by distinguishing two conceptions of disorder. First, we can focus on the physical presence of disorder—whether litter, public drinking, public drug use, and the like are evident in an urban neighborhood. We might measure the physical presence of disorder through a series of systematic observations. This is the approach used by Robert Sampson and Stephen Raudenbush (1999) in their study of links between disorder and crime in Chicago. Unfortunately, these authors observed very few examples of disorder and altogether ignored the question of whether such behaviors were perceived as problematic by residents of Chicago neighborhoods.

That brings us to the second conception, one focusing on the perception of disorder. Thus, some people might view public drinking as disorderly, whereas others (New Orleans residents, for example) consider public drinking to be perfectly acceptable. Questionnaires and survey methods are best suited for measuring perceived disorder.

Skogan used questions about nine different examples of disorder and classified them into two groups representing what he calls social and physical disorder (Skogan 1990a, 51, 191):

Social Disorder	Physical Disorder
Groups of loiterers	Abandoned buildings
Drug use and sales	Garbage and litter
Vandalism	Junk in vacant lots
Gang activity	
Public drinking	
Street harassment	

Questions corresponding to each of these examples of disorder asked respondents to rate them as a big problem (scored 2), some problem (scored 1), or almost no problem (scored 0) in their neighborhood. Together, these nine items measure different types of disorder and appear to have reasonable face validity. However, examining the relationship between each individual item and respondents' fear of crime or experience as a crime victim would be unwieldy at best. So Skogan created two indexes, one for social disorder and one for physical disorder, by adding up the scores for each item and dividing by the number of items in each group. Figure 4.3 shows a hypothetical sample questionnaire for these nine items, together with the scores that would be produced for each index.

This example illustrates how several related variables can be combined to produce an index that has three desirable properties. First, a composite index is a more valid measure of disorder than is a single question. Second, computing and averaging across all items in a category create more variation in the index than we could obtain in any single item. Finally, two indexes are more parsimonious than nine individual variables; data analysis and interpretation can be more efficient.

Measurement Summary

We have covered substantial ground in this chapter, introducing the important and often complex issue of measurement in criminal justice research. More than a step in the research process, measurement involves continuous thinking about what conceptual properties we wish to study, how we will operationalize those properties, and how we will develop measures that are reliable and valid. Often some type of composite measure better represents underlying concepts and thus enhances validity.

Subsequent chapters will pursue issues of measurement further. Part 3 of this book will describe data collection—how we go about making actual measurements. The next chapter will focus on different approaches to measuring crime.

Introduction:

Now I'm going to read you a list of crime-related problems that may be found in some parts of the city. For each one, please tell me how much of a problem it is in your neighborhood. Is it a big problem, some problem, or almost no problem?

	Big problem	Some problem	No problem
(S) Groups of people loitering	②	1	0
(S) People using or selling drugs	2	①	0
(P) Abandoned buildings	2	1	⓪
(S) Vandalism	2	①	0
(P) Garbage and litter on street	②	1	0
(S) Gangs and gang activity	2	1	⓪
(S) People drinking in public	②	1	0
(P) Junk in vacant lots	2	1	⓪
(S) People making rude or insulting remarks	2	①	0

(S) Social = 2 + 1 + 1 + 0 + 2 + 1 = 7

Index score = 7/6 = 1.16

(P) Physical = 0 + 2 + 0 = 2

Index score = 2=3 = 0.67

F I G U R E 4.3   Index of Disorder

SUMMARY

- Concepts are mental images we use as summary devices for bringing together observations and experiences that seem to have something in common.

- Our concepts do not exist in the real world, so they can't be measured directly.

- In operationalization, we specify concrete empirical procedures that will result in measurements of variables.

- Operationalization begins in study design and continues throughout the research project, including the analysis of data.

- Categories in a measure must be mutually exclusive and exhaustive.

- Higher levels of measurements specify categories that have ranked order or more complex numerical properties.

- Precision refers to the exactness of the measure used in an observation or description of an attribute.

- Reliability and validity are criteria for measurement quality. Valid measures are true indicators of underlying concepts. A reliable measure is consistent.

- Crime is a fundamental concept in criminal justice research. Different approaches to measuring crime illustrate general principles of conceptualization, operationalization, and measurement. We have different measures of crime because each measure has its strengths and weaknesses.

- Different measures of crime are based on different units of analysis. Uniform Crime Reports (UCRs) are summary measures that report totals for individual agencies. Other measures use offenders, victims, incidents, or offenses as the units of analysis.

- Crimes known to police have been the most widely used measures. UCR data are available for most of the twentieth century through the present; more detailed information about homicides was added to the UCR in 1961. Summary UCR data are gradually being shifted to data on individual incidents.

- Surveys of victims reveal information about crimes that are not reported to police. The National Crime Victimization Survey (NCVS) includes detailed information about personal and household incidents, but it does not count crimes against businesses or individual victims under age 12.

- Self-report surveys were developed to measure crimes with unclear victims that are less often detected by police. Two surveys estimate drug use among high school seniors and adults.

- The creation of specific, reliable measures often seems to diminish the richness of meaning our general concepts have. A good solution is to use multiple measures, each of which taps different aspects of the concept.

- Composite measures, formed by combining two or more variables, are often more valid measures of complex criminal justice concepts.

KEY TERMS

conception, p. 80

concepts, p. 80

conceptual definition, p. 82

conceptualization, p. 81

construct validity, p. 94

criterion-related validity, p. 93

REVIEW QUESTIONS AND EXERCISES

1. Review the box titled "What Is Recidivism?" on page 83. From that discussion, write conceptual and operational definitions for recidivism. Summarize how Fabelo proposes to measure the concept. Finally, discuss possible reliability and validity issues associated with Fabelo's proposed measure.

2. On its web page, "Definitions of Terrorism in the U.S. Code" (http://www.fbi.gov/about-us/investigate/terrorism/terrorism-definition), the FBI lists the following definition:
   "Domestic terrorism" means activities with the following three characteristics:

   ■ Involve acts dangerous to human life that violate federal or state law;

   ■ Appear intended (i) to intimidate or coerce a civilian population; (ii) to influence the policy of a government by intimidation or coercion; or (iii) to affect the conduct of a government by mass destruction, assassination, or kidnapping; and

   ■ Occur primarily within the territorial jurisdiction of the U.S.

   This is a conceptual definition. Write an operational definition, and then see how it applies to stories about terrorism in a local newspaper or news feed.

3. Measuring gang-related crime is an example of trying to measure a particular dimension of crime: motive. Other examples are hate crimes, terrorism, and drug-related crimes. Specify conceptual and operational definitions for at least one of these types. Find one newspaper story and one research report that present an example.

CHAPTER 5

Experimental and Quasi-Experimental Designs

We'll learn about the experimental approach to social scientific research. We'll consider a wide variety of experimental and other designs available to criminal justice researchers.

An Experiment in Spear Phishing

We're willing to bet that any person reading this book has received many offers of riches to be bestowed by bankers and oil ministers from England, Nigeria, Ukraine, and just about everywhere else. Maybe you've wondered how anyone could be so gullible to be taken in by this form of "phishing." Or maybe you, like many people, have responded to or wondered about more sophisticated e-mail phishing attempts. Maxfield was temporarily taken in by the following message: "Your new computer has shipped and will arrive in two days! Click here to review or change payment and delivery information."

Computer scientists at Indiana University conducted an experiment to learn something about what influences people to respond to phishing. Their basic research question was "How easily and effectively can a phisher exploit social networking data found on the Internet to increase the yield of a phishing attack?" (Jagatic et al. 2007).

Tom Jagatic and colleagues searched for publicly available information about 23,000 Indiana students, seeking students who participated in social networking sites such as Facebook. About 1,700 students met the researchers' criteria, which included having several friends or circles of friends on the sites.

They then sent two versions of phishing e-mails to different groups of students. One group received a *treatment* condition message that mimicked someone in the student's circle of friends; this is sometimes known as "spear phishing." The other group received a *control* message that contained no information suggesting the sender was part of the receiver's network. For example, assume Maxfield was selected as a treatment subject, and Babbie was among his circle of friends on Facebook. The researchers might have sent Maxfield a message that appeared to be from Babbie, something like: "Hi Mike! I just found this great new website that has copies of hundreds of survey questionnaires. Check it out at: megasurveys.com. Take care, Earl." Or, if Maxfield was a control subject in this experiment, the message might have read: "Dear Professor: Please click on the link below to learn more about our collection of survey questionnaires." In either case, the message would have redirected Maxfield to some other site—harmless, but clearly not a compilation of survey questionnaires. Which message—treatment or control—do you think would be more likely to prompt recipients to click on the enclosed link?

Jagatic and associates found that a whopping 72 percent of people receiving the treatment message followed the link, compared to 16 percent of those who got the control message. In addition, spear phishing was more effective in cross-gender messages. Females more often clicked on links they believed were from their male friends than on links from female friends; male recipients were similarly duped when they thought messages came from female friends.

This is an excellent example of an experiment. It involved an unambiguous intervention that could be easily controlled: applied to a

(continued)

treatment group, but not to a control group. Researchers could readily determine which subjects were in each group and assign them in a random, unbiased way. As you read this chapter, compare this example to our general discussion of designs and to other examples. What features of the setting for this study facilitated an experimental approach? How is the setting different from the environment in which criminal justice agencies routinely work?

Introduction

Experimentation is an approach to research best suited for explanation and evaluation.

Research design in the most general sense involves devising a strategy for finding out something. We'll first discuss the experiment as a mode of scientific observation in criminal justice research. At base, experiments involve (1) taking action, and (2) observing the consequences of that action. Social scientific researchers typically select a group of subjects, do something to them, and observe the effect of what was done.

It is worth noting at the outset that experiments are often used in nonscientific human inquiry as well. We experiment copiously in our attempts to develop a more generalized understanding about the world we live in. We learn many skills through experimentation: riding a bicycle, driving a car, swimming, and so forth. Students discover how much studying is required for academic success through experimentation. Professors experiment to learn how much preparation is required for successful lectures.

Experimentation is especially appropriate for hypothesis testing and evaluation. Suppose we are interested in studying alcohol abuse among college students and in discovering ways to reduce it. We might hypothesize that acquiring an understanding about the health consequences of binge drinking and long-term alcohol use will have the effect of reducing alcohol abuse. We can test this hypothesis experimentally. To begin, we might ask a group of experimental subjects how much beer, wine, or spirits they drank on the previous day and how

frequently, in an average week, they consume alcohol for the specific purpose of getting drunk. Next, we might show these subjects a video depicting the various physiological effects of chronic drinking and scenes of a horrific auto crash involving a drunk driver that killed four people. Finally—say, one month later—we might again ask the subjects about their use of alcohol in the previous week to determine whether watching the video reduced alcohol use.

You might typically think of experiments as being conducted in laboratories under carefully controlled conditions. Although this may be true in the natural sciences, few social scientific experiments take place in laboratory settings. The most notable exception to this occurs in the discipline of psychology, in which laboratory experiments are common. Criminal justice experiments are almost always conducted in field settings outside the laboratory.

The Classical Experiment

Variables, time order, measures, and groups are the central features of the classical experiment.

Like much of the vocabulary of research, the word *experiment* has acquired both a general and a specialized meaning. So far, we have referred to the general meaning, defined by David Farrington, Lloyd Ohlin, and James Q. Wilson (1986, 65) as "a systematic attempt to test a causal hypothesis about the effect of variations in one factor (the independent variable) on another (the dependent variable).... The defining feature of an experiment lies in the control of the independent variable by the experimenter." In a narrower sense, the term *experiment* refers to a specific way of structuring research, usually called the **classical experiment**. In this section, we examine the requirements and components of the classical experiment. Later in the chapter, we will consider designs that can be used when some of the requirements for classical experiments cannot be met.

The most conventional type of experiment in the natural and the social sciences involves three major pairs of components: (1) independent and dependent variables, (2) pretesting and posttesting, and (3) experimental and control groups. We will now consider each of those components and the way they are put together in the execution of an experiment.

Independent and Dependent Variables

Essentially, an experiment examines the effect of an **independent variable** on a **dependent variable**. Typically the independent variable takes the form of an experimental stimulus that is either present or absent—that is, having two attributes. In the example concerning alcohol abuse, how often subjects used alcohol is the dependent variable and exposure to a video about alcohol's effects is the independent variable. The researcher's hypothesis suggests that levels of alcohol use depend, in part, on understanding its physiological and health effects. The purpose of the experiment is to test the validity of this hypothesis.

The independent and dependent variables appropriate to experimentation are nearly limitless. It should be noted, moreover, that a given variable might serve as an independent variable in one experiment and as a dependent variable in another. Alcohol use is the dependent variable in our example, but it might be the independent variable in an experiment that examines the effects of alcohol abuse on academic performance.

Recalling our discussion of cause and effect in Chapter 3, the independent variable is the cause and the dependent variable is the effect. Thus, we might say that watching the video causes a change in alcohol use or that reduced alcohol use is an effect of watching the video.

It is essential that both independent and dependent variables be operationally defined for the purposes of experimentation. Such operational definitions might involve a variety of observation methods. Responses to a questionnaire, for example, might be the basis for defining self-reported alcohol use on the previous day. Alternatively, alcohol use by subjects could be measured with a Breathalyzer® or other blood alcohol test.

Pretesting and Posttesting

In the simplest experimental design, subjects are measured on a dependent variable (pretested), exposed to a stimulus that represents an independent variable, and then remeasured on the dependent variable (posttested). Differences noted between the first and second measurements on the dependent variable are then attributed to the influence of the independent variable.

In our example of alcohol use, we might begin by pretesting the extent of alcohol use among our experimental subjects. Using a questionnaire, we measure the extent of alcohol use reported by each individual and the average level of alcohol use for the whole group. After showing subjects the video on some of the effects of alcohol, we administer the same questionnaire again. Responses given in this posttest permit us to measure the subsequent extent of alcohol use by each subject and the average level of alcohol use of the group as a whole. If we discover a lower level of alcohol use on the second administration of the questionnaire, we might conclude that the video indeed reduced the use of alcohol among the subjects.

In the experimental examination of behaviors such as alcohol use, we face a special practical problem relating to validity. As you can imagine, the subjects might respond differently to the questionnaires the second time, even if their level of drinking remained unchanged. During the first administration of the questionnaire, the subjects might have been unaware of its purpose. By the time of the second measurement, however, they might have figured out the purpose of the experiment, become sensitized to the questions about drinking, and changed their answers. Thus the video might *seem* to have reduced alcohol abuse, although, in fact, it did not.

This is an example of a more general problem that plagues many forms of criminal justice research: the very act of studying something may change it. Techniques for dealing with this problem in the context of experimentation are covered throughout the chapter.

Experimental and Control Groups

The traditional way to offset the effects of the experiment itself is to use a **control group**. Social scientific experiments seldom involve only the observation of an **experimental group**, to which a stimulus has been administered. Researchers also observe a control group, to which the experimental stimulus has not been administered.

In our example of alcohol abuse, two groups of subjects are examined. To begin, each group is administered a questionnaire designed to measure their alcohol use in general and binge drinking in particular. Then only one of the groups—the experimental group—is shown the video. Later, the researcher administers a posttest of alcohol use to both groups. Figure 5.1 illustrates this basic experimental design.

Using a control group allows the researcher to control for the effects of the experiment itself. If participation in the experiment itself, rather than the treatment, leads the subjects to report less alcohol use, then the effects of participation should occur in both the experimental and the control groups. If, on the one hand, the overall level of drinking exhibited by the control group decreases between the pretest and posttest as much as for the experimental group, then the apparent reduction in alcohol use must be a function of some external factor, not a function of watching the video specifically. In this situation, we can conclude that the video did not cause any change in alcohol use.

If, on the other hand, drinking decreases only in the experimental group, then we can be more confident in saying that the reduction is a consequence of exposure to the video (because that's the only difference between the two groups). Alternatively, if drinking decreases more in the experimental group than in the control group, then that too is grounds for assuming that watching the video reduced alcohol use.

The need for control groups in experimentation has been most evident in medical research. Patients who participate in medical experiments appear to improve, but it can be unclear how much of the improvement came from the experimental treatment and how much from the experiment. Now, in testing the effects of new drugs, medical researchers frequently administer a placebo (for example, sugar pills) to a control group. Thus, the control group

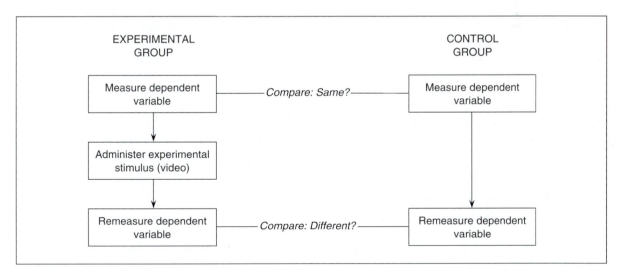

FIGURE 5.1 Basic Experimental Design

patients believe that they, like members of the experimental group, are receiving an experimental drug—and they often improve. If the new drug is effective, however, those who receive that drug will improve more than those who receive the placebo.

In criminal justice experiments, control groups are important as a guard against the effects of not only the experiments themselves but also events that may occur outside the laboratory during the course of experiments. Suppose the alcohol use experiment was being conducted on your campus and at that time a popular athlete was hospitalized for acute alcohol poisoning after he and a chum drank a bottle of rum. This event might shock the experimental subjects and thereby decrease their reported drinking. Because such an effect should happen about equally for members of the control and experimental groups, lower levels of reported alcohol use in the experimental group than in the control group would again demonstrate the impact of the experimental stimulus: watching the video that describes the health effects of alcohol abuse.

Sometimes an experimental design requires more than one experimental or control group. In the case of the alcohol video, we might also want to examine the impact of participating in group discussions about why college students drink alcohol, with the intent of demonstrating that peer pressure may promote drinking by people who would otherwise abstain. We might design our experiment around three experimental groups and one control group. One experimental group would see the video and participate in the group discussions, another would only see the video, and still another would only participate in group discussions; the control group would do neither. With this kind of design, we could determine the impact of each stimulus separately, as well as their combined effect.

Double-Blind Experiments

As we saw with medical experimentation, patients sometimes improve when they think they are receiving a new drug; thus, it is often necessary to administer a placebo to a control group.

Sometimes experimenters have this same tendency to prejudge results. In medical research, the experimenters may be more likely to "observe" improvements among patients who receive the experimental drug than among those receiving the placebo. That would be most likely, perhaps, for the researcher who developed the drug. A double-blind experiment eliminates this possibility because neither the subjects nor the experimenters know which is the experimental group and which is the control. In medical experiments, those researchers who are responsible for administering the drug and for noting improvements are not told which subjects receive the drug. Thus, both researchers and subjects are blind with respect to who is receiving the experimental drug and who is getting the placebo. Another researcher knows which subjects are in which group, but that person is not responsible for administering the experiment.

An experimental study of prison inmate classification offers a good example. Lawrence Bench and Terry Allen (2003) were interested in how security classification might affect the way prison guards view inmates and levels of disciplinary action against inmates. You probably have a general understanding of security classification. Persons sentenced to prison are rated on a security risk scale, usually low, middle, and high risk, or something like that. As you might expect, inmates classified as high risk are treated differently than their low-risk counterparts. But Bench and Allen were interested in whether prison discipline reflected inmate behavior or the security risk labels applied to inmates. For example, did guards write up high-risk inmates for disciplinary actions because of their behavior or because they were labeled high risk?

The researchers selected a sample of 200 inmates admitted to prison in Utah and classified at the highest security level. Half of these inmates were randomly assigned to treatment and control groups. Those in the treatment group were placed in medium-security facilities, while control group subjects were assigned to maximum-security sites. In addition, the researchers examined a second control group of prisoners who had been classified as medium security and placed in medium-security facilities.

Analyzing disciplinary actions for one year after prison placement, Bench and Allen (2003, 377) found that: "Overall, inmates receive about the same number of average weighted disciplinaries regardless of security classification." Interpreting their findings, the researchers argue that classification of inmates as maximum security is costly and often unnecessary.

The study was double-blinded so that neither prisoners nor guards knew that the treatment group inmates (placed in medium-security facilities) had been classified as maximum security. Double-blinding allowed researchers to separate the effects of labeling and classification.

Selecting Subjects

Before beginning an experiment, we must make two basic decisions about who will participate. First, we must decide on the target population—the group to which the results of our experiment will apply. If our experiment is designed to determine, for example, whether restitution is more effective than probation in reducing recidivism, our target population is some group of persons convicted of crimes. In our hypothetical experiment about the effects of watching a video on the health consequences of alcohol abuse, the target population might be college students.

Second, we must decide how particular members of the target population will be selected for the experiment. In most cases, the methods used to select subjects must meet the scientific norm of generalizability; it should be possible to generalize from the sample of subjects studied to the population those subjects represent.

Aside from the question of generalizability, the cardinal rule of subject selection and experimentation is the comparability of the experimental and control groups. Ideally, the control group represents what the experimental group would have been like if it had not been exposed to the experimental stimulus. It is essential, therefore, that the experimental and control groups be as similar as possible.

Randomization

Having recruited, by whatever means, a group of subjects, we randomly assign those subjects to either the experimental or the control group. This might be accomplished by numbering all the subjects serially and selecting numbers by means of a random-number table. Or we might assign the odd-numbered subjects to the experimental group and the even-numbered subjects to the control group.

Randomization is a central feature of the classical experiment. The most important characteristic of randomization is that it produces experimental and control groups that are statistically equivalent. Put another way, randomization reduces possible sources of systematic bias in assigning subjects to groups. The basic principle is simple: if subjects are assigned to experimental and control groups through a random process such as flipping a coin, the assignment process is said to be unbiased and the resultant groups are equivalent.

Although the rationale underlying this principle is a bit complex, understanding how randomization produces equivalent groups is a key point. David Farrington and associates (Farrington, Ohlin, and Wilson 1986, 66) compare randomization in criminal justice research to laboratory controls in the natural sciences:

> The control of extraneous variables by randomization is similar to the control of extraneous variables in the physical sciences by holding physical conditions (e.g., temperature, pressure) constant. Randomization insures that the average unit in [the] treatment group is approximately equivalent to the average unit in another [group] before the treatment is applied.

You've surely heard the expression "All other things being equal." Randomization makes it possible to assume that all other things are equal.

Experiments and Causal Inference

Experiments potentially control for many threats to the validity of causal inference, but researchers must remain aware of these threats.

The central features of the classical experiment are independent and dependent variables, pretesting and posttesting, and experimental and control groups created through random assignment. Think of these features as building blocks of a research design to demonstrate a cause-and-effect relationship. This point will become clearer by comparing the criteria for causality, discussed in Chapter 3, to the features of the classical experiment, as shown in Figure 5.2.

The experimental design ensures that the cause precedes the effect in time by taking posttest measurements of the dependent variable after introducing the experimental stimulus. The second criterion for causation—an empirical correlation between the cause-and-effect variables—is determined by comparing the pretest (in which the experimental stimulus is not present) to the posttest for the experimental group (after the experimental stimulus is administered). A change in pretest to posttest measures demonstrates correlation.

The final requirement is to show that the observed correlation between cause and effect is not due to the influence of a third variable. The classical experiment makes it possible to satisfy this criterion for cause in two ways. First, the posttest measures for the experimental group (stimulus present) are compared with those for the control group (stimulus not present). If the observed correlation between the stimulus and the dependent variable is due to some other factor, then the two posttest scores will be similar. Second, random assignment produces experimental and control groups that are equivalent and will not differ on some other variable that could account for the empirical correlation between cause and effect.

Experiments and Threats to Validity

The classical experiment is designed to satisfy the three requirements for demonstrating cause-and-effect relationships. But what about threats to the validity of causal inference? We mentioned validity threats in Chapter 3. Here, we consider different types of validity threats and describe how the classical experiment reduces many of them. Our discussion draws mostly on the book by William Shadish, Thomas Cook, and Donald Campbell (2002). We present these threats in a slightly different order than those authors, beginning with threats to internal validity.

Threats to Internal Validity

The problem of threats to **internal validity** refers to the possibility that conclusions drawn from experimental results may not accurately reflect what went on in the experiment itself. Put differently, conclusions about cause and effect may be biased in some systematic way. Shadish, Cook, and Campbell (2002, 54–60) pointed to several sources of the problem. As you read about these different threats to internal validity, keep in mind that each is an example of a simple point: possible ways researchers might be wrong in inferring causation.

History Historical events may occur during the course of the experiment that confound the experimental results. The hospitalization of a popular

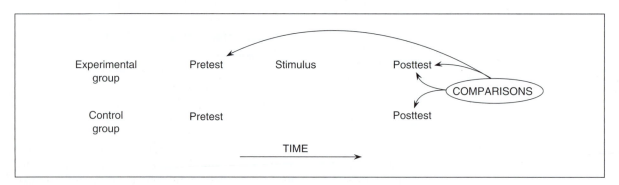

F I G U R E 5.2 Another Look at the Classical Experiment

athlete for acute alcohol poisoning during an experiment on reducing alcohol use is an example.

Maturation People are continually growing and changing, whether in an experiment or not, and those changes affect the results of the experiment. In a long-term experiment, the fact that the subjects grow older may have an effect. In shorter experiments, they may become tired, sleepy, bored, or hungry, or change in other ways that affect their behavior in the experiment. A long-term study of alcohol abuse might reveal a decline in binge drinking as the subjects mature.

History and maturation are similar in that they represent a correlation between cause and effect that is due to something other than the independent variable. They're different in that history represents something that's outside the experiment altogether, whereas maturation refers to change within the subjects themselves.

Testing Often, the process of testing and retesting influences people's behavior and thereby confounds the experimental results. Suppose we administer a questionnaire to a group as a way of measuring their alcohol use, then we administer an experimental stimulus and remeasure their alcohol use. By the time we conduct the posttest, the subjects may have gotten more sensitive to the issue of alcohol use and so provide different answers. In fact, they may believe we are trying to determine whether they drink too much. Because excessive drinking is frowned on by university authorities, our subjects will be on their best behavior and give answers that they think we want or that will make them look good.

Instrumentation Thus far we haven't said much about the process of measurement in pretesting and posttesting, and it's appropriate to keep in mind the problems of conceptualization and operationalization discussed in Chapter 4. If we use different measures of the dependent variable (say, different questionnaires about alcohol use), how can we be sure that they are comparable? Perhaps alcohol use seems to have decreased simply because the pretest measure was more sensitive than the posttest measure.

If the measurements are being made by the experimenters, their procedures may change over the course of the experiment. You probably recognize this as a problem with reliability. Instrumentation is always a potential problem in criminal justice research that uses secondary sources of information, such as police records about crime or court records about probation violations. There may be changes in how probation violations are defined or changes in the record-keeping practices of police departments.

In general, testing refers to changes in how subjects respond to measurement, whereas instrumentation is concerned with changes in the measurement process itself. If police officers respond differently to pretest and posttest questionnaires about prejudice, for example, that is a testing problem. However, if different questionnaires about prejudice are used in pretest and posttest measurements, instrumentation is a potential threat.

Statistical Regression Sometimes it's appropriate to conduct experiments on subjects who start out with extreme scores on the dependent variable. Many sentencing policies, for example, target chronic offenders. Commonly referred to as *regression to the mean*, this threat to validity can emerge whenever researchers are interested in extreme cases. As a simple example, statisticians often point out that extremely tall people as a group are likely to have children shorter than themselves, and extremely short people as a group are likely to have children taller than themselves. The danger, then, is that changes occurring by virtue of subjects starting out in extreme positions will be attributed erroneously to the effects of the experimental stimulus.

Statistical regression can also be at work in aggregate analysis of changes in crime rates. For example, some researchers initially viewed declines in crime rates throughout U.S. cities in the 1990s as a return to more normal levels of crime after abnormally high rates in the 1980s.

Selection Biases Randomization eliminates the potential for systematic bias in selecting subjects, but subjects may be chosen in other ways that threaten validity. Volunteers are often solicited for experiments conducted on college campuses. Students who volunteer for an experiment may not be typical of students as a whole, however. Volunteers may be more interested in the subject of the experiment and more likely to respond to a stimulus.

A common type of selection bias in applied criminal justice studies results from the natural caution of public officials. Let's say you are a bail commissioner in a large city, and the mayor wants to try a new program to increase the number of arrested persons who are released on bail. The mayor asks you to decide what kinds of defendants should be eligible for release and informs you that staff from the city's criminal justice services agency will be evaluating the program. In establishing eligibility criteria, you will probably try to select defendants who will not be arrested again while on bail and defendants who will most likely show up for scheduled court appearances. In other words, you will try to select participants who are least likely to fail. This is a threat to validity because the low-risk persons selected for release, although most likely to succeed, do not represent the jail population as a whole.

Experimental Mortality Experimental subjects often drop out of an experiment before it is completed, and that can affect statistical comparisons and conclusions. This is termed *experimental mortality*, also known as *attrition*. In the classical experiment involving an experimental and a control group, each with a pretest and a posttest, suppose that the heavy drinkers in the experimental group are so turned off by the video on the health effects of binge drinking that they tell the experimenter to forget it and leave. Those subjects who stick around for the posttest were less heavy drinkers to start with, and the group results will thus reflect a substantial "decrease" in alcohol use.

Mortality may also be a problem in experiments that take place over a long period (people may move away) or in experiments that require a substantial commitment of effort or time by subjects; they may become bored with the study or simply decide it's not worth the effort.

Ambiguous Causal Time Order In criminal justice research, there may be ambiguity about the time order of the experimental stimulus and the dependent variable. Whenever this occurs, the research conclusion that the stimulus caused the dependent variable can be challenged with the explanation that the "dependent" variable actually caused changes in the stimulus. Many early studies of the relationship between different types of punishments and rates of offending exhibited this threat to validity by relying on single interviews with subjects who were asked how they viewed alternative punishments and whether they had committed any crimes.

Ruling Out Threats to Internal Validity

The classical experiment, coupled with proper subject selection and assignment, can *potentially* handle each of these threats to internal validity. Let's look again at the classical experiment, presented graphically in Figure 5.2.

Pursuing the example of the educational video as an attempt to reduce alcohol abuse, if we use the experimental design shown in Figure 5.2, we should expect two findings. For the experimental group, the frequency of drinking measured in their posttest should be less than in their pretest. In addition, when the two posttests are compared, the experimental group should have less drinking than the control group.

This design guards against the problem of history because anything occurring outside the experiment that might affect the experimental group should also affect the control group. There should still be a difference in the two posttest results. The same comparison guards against problems of maturation as long as the subjects have been randomly assigned to the two groups. Testing and instrumentation should not be problems because both the experimental and the control groups are subject to the same tests and experimenter effects. If the subjects have been assigned to the two groups randomly, statistical regression should affect both equally, even if people with extreme scores on drinking (or whatever the dependent variable is) are being studied. Selection bias is ruled out by the random assignment of subjects.

Experimental mortality can be more complicated to handle because dropout rates may be different between the experimental and control groups. The experimental treatment itself may increase mortality in the group exposed to the video. As a result, the group of experimental subjects that received the posttest will differ from the group that received the pretest. In our example of the alcohol video, it would probably not be possible to handle this problem by administering a placebo, for instance. In general, however, the potential for mortality can be reduced by shortening the time between pretest and posttest, by emphasizing to subjects the importance of completing the posttest, or perhaps by offering cash payments for participating in all phases of the experiment.

The remaining problems of internal invalidity can be avoided through the careful administration of a controlled experimental design. We emphasize *careful administration*. Random assignment, pretest and posttest measures, and use of control and experimental groups do not automatically rule out threats to validity. This caution is especially true in field studies and evaluation research, in which subjects participate in natural settings and uncontrolled variation in the experimental stimulus may be present. Control over experimental conditions is the hallmark of this approach, but conditions in field settings are usually more difficult to control.

For example, Richard Berk and associates (2003) randomly assigned several thousand inmates entering California prisons to an experimental or traditional (control) procedure for classifying inmate risk. That was a straightforward intervention that was easily administered and unlikely to vary much; classification also took place over a short period of time. In contrast, Denise Gottfredson and colleagues (2006) conducted a classical experiment to assess the effects of drug courts in reducing recidivism. Drug courts involve a range of interventions that are more difficult to standardize. The treatment—drug-court participation—can take place over a long period of time. Researchers examined how long individuals stayed in drug-court treatment, but they acknowledged that the quality of treatment was more difficult to control and could have varied quite a lot.

Generalizability and Threats to Validity

Potential threats to internal validity are only some of the complications faced by experimenters. They also have the problem of generalizing from experimental findings to the real world. Even if the results of an experiment are an accurate gauge of what happened during that experiment, do they really tell us anything about life in the wilds of society? With our examination of cause and effect in Chapter 3 in mind, we consider two dimensions of **generalizability**: construct validity and external validity.

Threats to Construct Validity In the language of experimentation, **construct validity** is the correspondence between the empirical test of a hypothesis and the underlying causal process that the experiment is intended to represent. This parallels construct validity as discussed in Chapter 4: Do measures correspond with the underlying construct we wish to measure? Construct validity is thus concerned with generalizing from our observations in an experiment to causal processes in the real world. In our hypothetical example, the educational video is how we operationalize the construct of understanding the health effects of alcohol abuse. Our questionnaire represents the dependent construct of actual alcohol use.

Are these reasonable ways to represent the underlying causal process in which understanding the effects of alcohol use causes people to reduce excessive or abusive drinking? It's a reasonable representation but also one that is certainly incomplete. People develop an understanding of the health effects of alcohol use in many ways. Watching an educational video is one way; having personal experience, talking to friends and parents, taking other courses, and reading books and articles are others. Our video may do a good job of representing the health effects of alcohol use, but it is an incomplete representation of that construct. Alternatively, the video may be poorly produced, too technical, or incomplete. Then the experimental stimulus may not adequately represent the construct we are interested in—educating students about the health effects of alcohol use. There may also be problems with our measure of the dependent variable: questionnaire items on self-reported alcohol use.

By this time, you should recognize a similarity between construct validity and some of the measurement issues discussed in Chapter 4. Almost any empirical example or measure of a construct is incomplete. Much of construct validity involves how completely an empirical measure can represent a construct or how well we can generalize from a measure to a construct.

A related issue in construct validity is whether a given level of treatment is sufficient. Perhaps showing a single video to a group of subjects would have little effect on alcohol use, but administering a series of videos over several weeks would have a greater impact. We could test this experimentally by having more than one experimental group and varying the number of videos seen by different groups.

Threats to External Validity Will an experimental study, conducted with the kind of control we have emphasized here, produce results that would also be found in more natural settings? Can an intensive probation program shown to be successful in Minneapolis achieve similar results in Miami? **External validity** represents a slightly different form of generalizability, one in which the question is whether results from experiments in one setting (time and place) will be obtained in other settings or whether a treatment found to be effective for one population will have similar effects on a different group.

Threats to external validity are greater for experiments conducted under carefully controlled conditions. If the alcohol education experiment reveals that drinking decreased among students in the experimental group, then we can be confident that viewing the video led to reduced alcohol use among our experimental subjects. But will the video have the same effect on high school students or adults if it is broadcast on television? We cannot be certain because the carefully controlled conditions of the experiment might have had something to do with the video's effectiveness.

In contrast, criminal justice field experiments are conducted in more natural settings. Real probation officers in different local jurisdictions deliver intensive supervision to real probationers. This is not to say that external validity is never a problem in field experiments. However, one of the advantages of field experiments in criminal justice is that, because they take place under real-world conditions, results are more likely to be valid in other real-world settings as well.

You may have detected a fundamental conflict between internal and external validity. Threats to internal validity are reduced by conducting experiments under carefully controlled conditions. But such conditions do not reflect real-world settings, and this restricts our ability to generalize results. Field experiments generally have greater external validity, but their internal validity may suffer because such studies are more difficult to monitor than those taking place in more controlled settings. John Eck describes this trade-off as a diabolical dilemma (Eck 2002, 104).

Shadish, Cook, and Campbell (2002, 98–101) offer some useful advice for resolving the potential for conflict between internal and external validity. Explanatory studies that test cause-and-effect theories should place greater emphasis on internal validity, whereas applied studies should be more concerned with external validity. This is not a hard and fast rule because internal validity must be established before external validity becomes an issue. That is, applied researchers must have confidence in the internal validity of their cause-and-effect relationships before they ask whether similar relationships would be found in other settings.

Threats to Statistical Conclusion Validity

Statistical conclusion validity refers to whether we are able to determine if two variables are related. Statistical conclusion validity most often becomes an issue when findings are based on small samples of cases. Because experiments can be costly and time consuming, they are frequently conducted with relatively small numbers of subjects. In such cases, only large differences between experimental and control groups on posttest measures can be detected with any degree of confidence.

In practice, this means that finding cause-and-effect relationships through experiments depends on two related factors: (1) the number of subjects, and (2) the magnitude of posttest differences between the experimental and control groups. Experiments with large numbers of cases may be able to reliably detect small differences, but experiments with smaller numbers can detect only large differences.

Threats to statistical conclusion validity can be magnified by other difficulties in field experiments. Unreliable measurement is one such problem that is often encountered in criminal justice research. More generally, David Weisburd and associates (Weisburd, Petrosino, and Mason 1993) concluded, after reviewing a large number of criminal justice experiments, that failure to maintain control over experimental conditions reduces statistical conclusion validity even for studies with large numbers of subjects.

Variations on the Classical Experimental Design

The basic experimental design is adapted to meet different research applications.

We now turn to a more systematic consideration of variations on the classical experiment that can be produced by manipulating the building blocks of experiments.

Slightly restating our earlier remarks, four basic building blocks are present in experimental designs: (1) the number of experimental and control groups, (2) the number and variation of experimental stimuli, (3) the number of pretest and posttest measurements, and (4) the procedures used to select subjects and assign them to groups. By way of illustrating these building blocks and the ways they are used to produce different designs, we adopt the widely used system of notation introduced by Donald Campbell and Julian Stanley (1966). Figure 5.3 presents this notation and shows how it is used to represent the classical experiment and examples of variations on this design.

In Figure 5.3, the letter O represents observations or measurements, and X represents an experimental stimulus or treatment. Different time points are displayed as t, with a subscript number to represent time order. Thus, for the classical experiment

		Classical Experiment	
Experimental group	O	X	O
Control group	O		O
	t_1	t_2	t_3
		Time	

O = observation or measurement
X = experimental stimulus
t = time point

		Posttest Only	
Experimental group		X	O
Control group			O
		t_1	t_2

		Factorial	
Experimental treatment 1	O	X_1	O
Experimental treatment 2	O	X_2	O
Control	O		O
	t_1	t_2	t_3

FIGURE 5.3 Variations in the Experimental Design

shown in Figure 5.3, O at t_1 is the pretest, O at t_3 is the posttest, and the experimental stimulus, X, is administered to the experimental group at t_2, between the pretest and posttest. Measures are taken for the control group at times t_1 and t_3, but the experimental stimulus is not administered to the control group.

Now consider the design labeled "Posttest Only." As implied by its name, no pretest measures are made on either the experimental or the control group. Thinking for a moment about the threats to internal validity, we can imagine situations in which a posttest-only design is appropriate. Testing and retesting might especially influence subjects' behavior if measurements are made by administering a questionnaire, with subjects' responses to the posttest potentially affected by their experience in the pretest. A posttest-only design can reduce the possibility of testing being a threat to validity by eliminating the pretest.

Without a pretest, it is obviously not possible to detect change in measures of the dependent variable, but we can still test the effects of the experimental stimulus by comparing posttest measures for the experimental group with posttest measures for the control group. For example, if we are concerned about the possibility of sensitizing subjects in a study of an alcohol education video, we might eliminate the pretest and examine the posttest differences between the experimental and control groups. Randomization is the key to the posttest-only design. If subjects are randomly assigned to experimental and control groups, we expect them to be equivalent. Any posttest differences between the two groups on the dependent variable can then be attributed to the influence of the video.

In general, posttest-only designs are appropriate when researchers suspect that the process of measurement may bias subjects' responses to a questionnaire or other instrument. This is more likely when only a short time elapses between pretest and posttest measurements. The number of observations made on subjects is a design building block that can be varied as needed. We emphasize here that random assignment is essential in a posttest-only design.

Figure 5.3 also shows a factorial design, which has two experimental groups that receive different treatments, or different levels of a single treatment, and one control group. This design is useful for comparing the effects of different interventions or different amounts of a single treatment. In evaluating a probation program, we might wish to compare how different levels of contact between probation officers and probation clients affect recidivism. In this case, subjects in one experimental group might receive weekly contact (X_1), the other experimental group is seen by probation officers twice each week (X_2), and control-group subjects have normal contact (say, monthly) with probation officers. Because more contact is more expensive than less contact, we would be interested in seeing how much difference in recidivism was produced by monthly, weekly, and twice-weekly contacts.

Thus, an experimental design may have more than one group receiving different versions or levels of experimental treatment. We can also vary the number of measurements made on dependent variables. No hard and fast rules exist for using these building blocks to design a given experiment. A useful rule of thumb, however, is to keep the design as simple as possible to control for potential threats to validity. The specific design for any particular study depends on the research purpose, available resources, and unavoidable constraints in designing and actually carrying out the experiment.

One very common constraint is how subjects or units of analysis are selected and assigned to experimental or control groups. This building block brings us to the subject of quasi-experimental designs.

Quasi-Experimental Designs

When randomization is not possible, researchers can use different types of quasi-experimental designs.

By now, the value of random assignment in controlling threats to validity should be apparent. However, it is often impossible to randomly select subjects for experimental and control groups and satisfy other requirements. Most often, there may be practical or administrative obstacles. There may also be legal or ethical reasons that randomization cannot be used in criminal justice experiments.

When randomization is not possible, the next best choice is often a **quasi-experiment**. The prefix *quasi-*, meaning "to a certain degree," is significant— a quasi-experiment is, to a certain degree, an experiment. In most cases, quasi-experiments do not randomly assign subjects and therefore may suffer from the internal validity threats that are so well controlled in true experiments. Without random assignment, the other building blocks of experimental design must be used creatively to reduce validity threats. We group quasi-experimental designs into two categories: (1) nonequivalent-groups designs, and (2) time-series designs. Each can be represented with the same *O*, *X*, and *t* notation used to depict experimental designs.

Nonequivalent-Groups Designs

The name for this family of designs is also meaningful. The main strength of random assignment is that it allows us to assume equivalence in experimental and control groups. When it is not possible to create groups through randomization, we must use some other procedure, one that is not random. If we construct groups through a nonrandom procedure, however, we cannot assume that the groups are equivalent—hence the label *nonequivalent-groups design.*

Whenever experimental and control groups are not equivalent, we should select subjects in a way that makes the two groups as comparable as possible. Often the best way to achieve comparability is through a matching process in which subjects in the experimental group are matched with subjects in a comparison group. The term *comparison group* is commonly used, rather than *control group*, to highlight the nonequivalence of groups in quasi-experimental designs. A comparison group does, however, serve the same function as a control group.

Some examples of research that use nonequivalent-groups designs illustrate various approaches to matching and the creative use of experimental design building blocks. Examples include studies of child abuse (Widom 1989), obscene phone calls (Clarke 1997a), and video cameras for crime prevention (Gill and Spriggs 2005). Figure 5.4 shows a diagram of each design using the X, O, and t notation. The solid line that separates treatment and comparison groups in the figure signifies that subjects have been placed in groups through some nonrandom procedure.

Child Abuse and Later Arrest Cathy Spatz Widom (1989) studied the long-term effects of child abuse—whether abused children are more likely to be charged with delinquent or adult criminal offenses than children who were not abused. Child abuse was the experimental stimulus, and the number of subsequent arrests was the dependent variable.

Of course, it is not possible to assign children randomly to groups in which some are abused and others are not. Widom's design called for selecting a sample of children who, according to court records, had been abused. She then matched each abused subject with a comparison subject—of the

Widom (1989)

Treatment group		X	O
Comparison group			O
		t_1	t_2

X = official record of child abuse
O = counts of juvenile or adult arrest

Clarke (1997a)

Treatment group	O	X	O
Comparison group	O		O
	t_1	t_2	t_3

X = caller identification and call tracing
O = customer complaints of obscene calls

Gill and Spriggs (2005)

Target area 1	O	X_1	O
Comparison area 1	O		O
Target area 2	O	X_2	O
Comparison area 2	O		O
Target area 13	O	X_{13}	O
Comparison area 13	O		O
	t_1	t_2	t_3

X_i = CCTV installation in area i
O = Police crime data, survey data on fear of crime

FIGURE 5.4 Quasi-Experimental Design Examples

same gender, race, age, and approximate socioeconomic status (SES)—who had not been abused. The assumption with these matching criteria was that age at the time of abuse, gender, race, and SES differences might confound any observed relationship between abuse and subsequent arrests.

You may be wondering how a researcher selects important variables to use in matching experimental and comparison subjects. We cannot provide a definitive answer to that question, any more than we can specify what particular variables should be used in a given experiment. The answer ultimately depends on the nature and purpose of the experiment. As a general rule, however, the two groups should be comparable in terms of variables that are likely to be related to the dependent variable under study. Widom matched on gender, race, and SES because these variables are correlated with juvenile and adult arrest rates. Age at the time of reported abuse was also an important variable because children abused at a younger age had a longer "at-risk" period for delinquent arrests.

Widom produced experimental and comparison groups matching individual subjects. It is also possible to construct experimental and comparison groups through aggregate matching, in which the average characteristics of each group are comparable. This is illustrated in our next example.

Deterring Obscene Phone Calls In 1988, the New Jersey Bell telephone company introduced caller identification (ID) and instant call tracing in a small number of telephone exchange areas. Now ubiquitous in mobile phones, caller ID was a new technology in 1988. Instant call tracing allows the recipient of an obscene or threatening call to automatically initiate a procedure to trace the source of the call.

Ronald Clarke (1997a) studied the effects of these new technologies in deterring obscene phone calls. Clarke expected that obscene calls would decrease in areas where the new services were available. To test this, he compared records of formal customer complaints about annoying calls in the New Jersey areas that had the new services to formal complaints in other New Jersey areas where caller ID and call tracing were not available. One year later, the number of formal complaints had dropped sharply in areas serviced by the new technology; no decline was found in other New Jersey Bell areas.

In this study, telephone service areas with new services were the treatment group, and areas without the services were the comparison group. Clarke's matching criterion was a simple one: telephone service by New Jersey Bell, assuming the volume of obscene phone calls was relatively constant within a single phone service area. Of course, matching on

telephone service area cannot eliminate the possibility that the volume of obscene phone calls varies from one part of New Jersey to another, but Clarke's choice of a comparison group was straightforward and certainly more plausible than comparing New Jersey to, say, New Mexico.

Clarke's study is a good example of a natural field experiment. The experimental stimulus—caller ID and call tracing—was not specifically introduced by Clarke, but he was able to obtain measures for the dependent variable before and after the experimental stimulus was introduced. This design made it possible for Clarke to infer with reasonable confidence that caller ID and call tracing reduced the number of formal complaints about obscene phone calls.

Cameras and Crime Prevention U.S. residents have probably become accustomed to seeing closed-circuit television (CCTV) cameras in stores and at ATMs, but this technology is less used in public spaces such as streets and parking lots. With an estimated 4 million cameras deployed, CCTV is widely used as a crime prevention and surveillance tool in the United Kingdom (McCahill and Norris 2003). CCTV enabled the London Metropolitan Police to quickly identify suspects in the Underground bombing attacks that took place in 2005. Cameras are increasingly used to monitor traffic and even to record license plates of cars running traffic lights. But does CCTV have any effect in reducing crime?

Martin Gill and associates (Gill and Spriggs 2005; Gill et al. 2005) conducted an evaluation of 13 CCTV projects installed in a variety of residential and commercial settings in England. These were a mix of smaller and large-scale CCTV projects involving multiple cameras. One area on the outskirts of London included more than 500 cameras installed to reduce thefts of and from vehicles in parking facilities. Five projects in London and other urban areas placed 10 to 15 cameras in low-income housing areas, seeking to reduce burglary and robbery. Researchers examined two types of dependent variables before and after cameras were installed: crimes reported to police and fear of crime.

Fear was measured through surveys of people living in residential areas and interviews with people on local streets for commercial areas and parking facilities.

Measuring police data and fear of crime before and after cameras were installed made it possible for Gill and associates to satisfy two criteria for cause—time order and covariation between the independent variable (CCTV) and dependent variables. However, they were not able to randomly assign some areas to receive the CCTV intervention while other areas did not. This was because the intervention was planned for only a small number of locations of each type (residential, commercial, parking) and also because CCTV was carefully tailored to each site. Instead, the researchers created two types of comparison areas. First, comparison areas were similar on sociodemographic and geographical characteristics, together with types of crime problems. The second type of comparison was "buffer zones," defined as an area in a one-mile radius from the edge of the target area where CCTV cameras were installed; buffer zones were defined only for CCTV areas.

The rationale for comparison areas is clear. If CCTV is effective in reducing crime, we should expect declines in target areas, but not in comparison areas. Alternatively, if post-treatment measures of crime went down in both treatment and comparison areas, we might expect greater declines in the CCTV sites. But what about buffer areas? After defining buffer areas, researchers then subdivided them into concentric rings around a target area, shown as T in Figure 5.5. The stated purpose was to assess any movement of crime around the target area. If CCTV was effective in reducing crime, any reduction should be greatest in the target area; the size of the reduction should decline moving outward from the target area.

Short-term results found some reduction of some types of crime in some CCTV areas. In other treatment areas, some crimes increased more than in comparison areas. In particular, Gill and Spriggs found that public order offenses such as drunkenness tended to *increase* more in CCTV target areas. Overall, significant drops in crime were found in

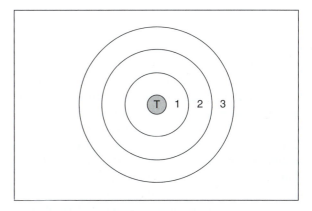

FIGURE 5.5   Buffer Zones in CCTV Quasi-Experiment
Source: Adapted from Gill and Spriggs (2005, 40).

just 2 of 13 target areas. Fear and related attitudes declined in all target and comparison areas, but the authors believed this was largely due to declining crime in all areas.

This example illustrates why nonequivalent comparison groups are important. Because crime declined in most areas and fear declined in all, a simple comparison of pre- and postintervention measures would have been misleading. That strategy would have suggested that CCTV was responsible for reduced crime and fear. Only by adding the comparison and buffer areas to their research were Gill and Spriggs able to learn that CCTV was probably not the cause of declines, since similar patterns were found in many areas where CCTV systems were not installed.

Together, these three studies illustrate different approaches to research design when it is not possible to randomly assign subjects to treatment and control groups. Lacking random assignment, researchers must use creative procedures for selecting subjects, constructing treatment and comparison groups, measuring dependent variables, and exercising other controls to reduce possible threats to validity.

Cohort Designs

Chapter 3 mentioned cohort studies as examples of longitudinal designs. We can also view cohort studies as a type of nonequivalent-groups design.

Recall from Chapter 3 that a cohort may be defined as a group of subjects who enter or leave an institution at the same time. For example, a class of police officers who graduate from a training academy at the same time could be considered a cohort. Or we might view all persons who were sentenced to probation in May as a cohort.

Now think of a cohort that is exposed to some experimental stimulus. The May probation cohort might be required to complete 100 hours of community service in addition to meeting other conditions of probation. If we are interested in whether probationers who receive community service sentences are charged with fewer probation violations, we can compare the performance of the May cohort with that of the April cohort, or the June cohort, or some other cohort not sentenced to community service.

Cohorts that do not receive community service sentences serve as comparison groups. The groups are not equivalent because they were not created by random assignment. But if we assume that a comparison cohort does not systematically differ from a treatment cohort on important variables, we can use this design to determine whether community service sentences reduce probation violations.

That last assumption is very important, but it may not be viable. Perhaps a criminal court docket is organized to schedule certain types of cases at the same time, so a May cohort would be systematically different from a June cohort. But if the assumption of comparability can be met, cohorts may be used to construct nonequivalent comparison and experimental groups by taking advantage of the natural flow of cases through an institutional process.

Time-Series Designs

Time-series designs are common examples of longitudinal studies in criminal justice research. As the name implies, a time-series design involves examining a series of observations on some variable over time. A simple example is examining trends in arrests for drunk driving over time to see whether the number of arrests is increasing, decreasing, or staying constant. A state police supervisor might be interested in keeping track of arrests for texting while driving, or for other traffic violations, as a way of monitoring the performance of patrol officers. Or state corrections officials might want to study trends in prison admissions as a way of predicting the future need for correctional facilities.

An interrupted time series is a special type of time-series design that can be used in cause-and-effect studies. A series of observations is compared before and after an intervention is introduced. For example, a researcher might want to know whether roadside sobriety checkpoints cause a decrease in fatal automobile accidents. Trends in accidents could be compared before and after the roadside checkpoints are established.

Interrupted time-series designs can be very useful in criminal justice research, especially in applied studies. They do have some limitations, however, just like other ways of structuring research. Shadish, Cook, and Campbell (2002) describe the strengths and limitations of different approaches to time-series designs. We will introduce these approaches with a hypothetical example and then describe some specific criminal justice applications.

Continuing with the example of sobriety checkpoints, Figure 5.6 presents four possible patterns of alcohol-related automobile accidents. The vertical line in each pattern shows the time when the roadside checkpoint program was introduced. Which of these patterns indicates that the new program caused a reduction in car accidents?

If the time-series results looked like Pattern 1 in Figure 5.6, we might think initially that the checkpoints caused a reduction in alcohol-related accidents, but there seems to be a general downward trend in accidents that continues after the intervention. It's safer to conclude that the decline would have continued even without the roadside checkpoints.

Pattern 2 shows that an increasing trend in auto accidents has been reversed after the intervention, but this appears to be due to a regular pattern in which accidents have been bouncing up and down. The intervention was introduced at the peak of an upward trend, and the later decline may be an artifact of the underlying pattern rather than of the new program.

Patterns 1 and 2 exhibit some outside trend, rather than an intervention, that may account for a pattern observed over time. We may recognize this as an example of history as a validity threat to the inference that the new checkpoint program caused a change in auto accidents. The general decline in Pattern 1 may be due to reduced drunk driving that has nothing to do with sobriety checkpoints. Pattern 2 illustrates what is referred to as *seasonality* in a time series—a regular pattern of change over time.

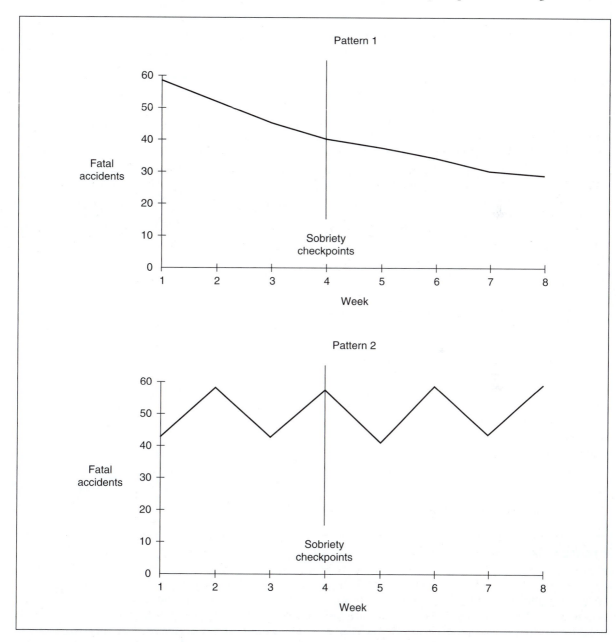

FIGURE 5.6   Four Patterns of Change in Fatal Automobile Accidents (Hypothetical Data)

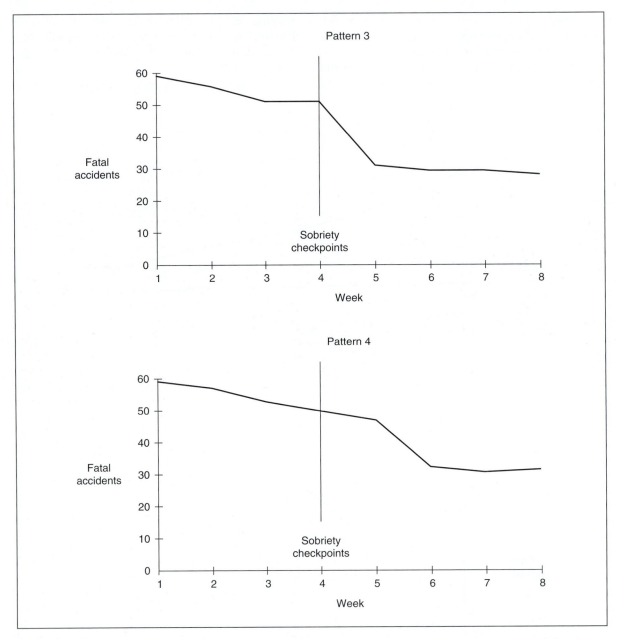

FIGURE 5.6 *(Continued)*

In our example, the data might reflect seasonal variation in alcohol-related accidents that occurs around holidays or maybe on football weekends near a college campus.

Patterns 3 and 4 lend more support to the inference that sobriety checkpoints caused a decline in alcohol-related accidents, but the two patterns are different in a subtle way. In Pattern 3, accidents decline more sharply from a general downward trend immediately after the checkpoint program was introduced, whereas Pattern 4 displays a sharper decline sometime after the new program was established. Which pattern provides stronger support for the inference?

In framing your answer, recall what we have said about construct validity. Think about the underlying causal process these two patterns represent, or consider possible mechanisms that might be at work. Pattern 3 suggests that the program was immediately effective and supports what we might call an incapacitation mechanism: roadside checkpoints enabled police to identify and arrest drunk drivers, thereby getting them off the road and reducing accidents. Pattern 4 suggests a deterrent mechanism: as drivers learned about the checkpoints, they less often drove after drinking, and accidents eventually declined. Either explanation is possible given the evidence presented. This illustrates an important limitation of interrupted time-series designs: they operationalize complex causal constructs in simple ways. Our interpretation depends in large part on how we understand this causal process.

The classic study by Richard McCleary and associates (McCleary, Nienstedt, and Erven 1982) illustrates the need to think carefully about how well time-series results reflect underlying causal patterns. McCleary and colleagues reported a sharp decline in burglaries immediately after a special burglary investigation unit was established in a large city. This finding was at odds with their understanding of how police investigations could reasonably be expected to reduce burglary. A special unit might eventually be able to reduce the number of burglaries after investigating incidents over a period of time and making arrests. However, it is highly unlikely that changing investigative procedures would have an immediate impact. This discrepancy prompted McCleary and associates to look more closely at the policy change and led to their conclusion that the apparent decline in burglaries was produced by changes in record-keeping practices. No evidence existed of any decline in the actual number of burglaries.

This example illustrates our discussion of instrumentation earlier in this chapter. Changes in

the way police counted burglaries produced what appeared to be a reduction in burglary. Instrumentation can be a particular problem in time-series designs for two reasons. First, observations are usually made over a relatively long time period, which increases the likelihood of changes in measurement instruments. Second, time-series designs often use measures that are produced by an organization such as a police department, criminal court, probation office, or corrections department. There may be changes or irregularities in the way data are collected by these agencies that are not readily apparent to researchers and that are, in any case, not subject to their control.

Variations in Time-Series Designs

If we view the basic interrupted time-series design as an adaptation of basic design building blocks, we can consider how modifications can help control for many validity problems. The simplest time-series design studies one group—the treatment group—over time. Rather than making one pretest and one posttest observation, the interrupted time-series design makes a longer series of observations before and after introducing an experimental treatment.

What if we considered the other building blocks of experimental design? Figure 5.7 presents the basic design and some variations using the familiar O, X, and t notation. In the basic design, shown at the top of Figure 5.7, many pretest and posttest observations are made on a single group that receives some type of treatment.

We could strengthen this design by adding a comparison series of observations on a group that does not receive the treatment. If, for example, roadside sobriety checkpoints were introduced all over the state of Ohio but were not used at all in Michigan, then we could compare auto accidents in Ohio (the treatment series) with auto accidents in Michigan (the comparison series). If checkpoints caused a reduction in alcohol-related accidents, we would expect to see a decline in Ohio following the intervention, but there should be no change or a lesser decline in Michigan over the same time period. The second part of Figure 5.7 shows this

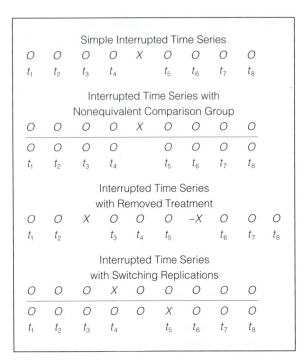

FIGURE 5.7 Interrupted Times-Series Designs

design—an interrupted time series with a nonequivalent comparison group. The two series are not equivalent because we did not randomly assign drivers to Ohio or Michigan. Wesley Skogan and associates (2008) present a good example of this design in their analysis of police problem solving in Chicago. They compared changes in crime for police beats where specific problems were identified and addressed to comparison beats where no crime-specific interventions were developed.

A single-series design may be modified by introducing and then removing the intervention, as shown in the third part of Figure 5.7. We might test sobriety checkpoints by setting them up every weekend for a month and then not setting them up for the next few months. If the checkpoints caused a reduction in alcohol-related accidents, we might expect an increase after they were removed. Or the effects of weekend checkpoints might persist even after we removed them.

Because different states or cities sometimes introduce new drunk-driving programs at different times, we might be able to use what Shadish, Cook, and Campbell (2002, 192) called a "time-series design with switching replications." The bottom of Figure 5.7 illustrates this design. For example, assume that Ohio begins using checkpoints in May 2009 and Michigan introduces them in July of the same year. A switching-replications design could strengthen our conclusion that checkpoints reduce accidents if we saw that a decline in Ohio began in June and a similar pattern was found in Michigan beginning in August. The fact that similar changes occurred in the dependent variable in different states at different times, corresponding to when the program was introduced, would add to our confidence in stating that sobriety checkpoints reduced auto accidents.

Variable-Oriented Research, Case Studies, and Scientific Realism

Case studies measure many variables for a small number of cases.

Another way to think about a time-series design is as a study of one or a few cases with many observations. If we design a time-series study of roadside checkpoints in Ohio, we will be examining one case (Ohio) with many observations of auto accidents. Or a design that compares Ohio and Michigan will examine many observations for two cases. Thinking once again about design building blocks, notice how we have slightly restated one of those building blocks. Instead of considering the number of experimental and control *groups*, our attention centers on the number of subjects or *cases* in our study. In Figure 5.7, the first and third time-series designs have one case each, while the second and fourth designs examine two cases each.

Classical experiments and quasi-experiments with large numbers of subjects are examples of what Charles Ragin (2000) terms **case-oriented research**, in which many cases are examined to understand a small number of variables. Time-series designs and case studies are examples of **variable-oriented research**, in which a large number of variables are studied for a small number of cases or subjects. Suppose we wish to study inmate-on-inmate assaults in correctional facilities. With a case-oriented approach, we might send a questionnaire to a sample of 500 correctional facilities, asking facility staff to provide information about assaults, facility design, inmate characteristics, and housing conditions. Here, we are gathering information on a few variables from a large number of correctional facilities. Using a variable-oriented approach, we might visit one or a few facilities to conduct in-depth interviews with staff, observe the condition of facilities, and gather information from institutional records. Here, we are collecting information on a wide range of variables from a small number of institutions.

Case studies are examples of variable-oriented research. Here, the researcher's attention centers on an in-depth examination of one or a few cases on many dimensions. Robert Yin (2008) points out that the terms *case* and *case study* are used broadly. Cases can be individual people, neighborhoods, correctional facilities, courtrooms, or other aggregations.

Robert Yin cautions that the case-study design is often misunderstood as representing "qualitative" research or participant observation study. Instead,

Yin advises that the case study is a design strategy and that the labels *qualitative* and *quantitative* are not useful ways to distinguish design strategies. Case studies might appear qualitative because they focus on one or a small number of units. But many case studies employ sophisticated statistical techniques to examine many variables for those units. An example illustrates how misleading it can be to associate case studies with qualitative research.

In what has come to be known as the "Boston Gun Project," Anthony Braga and associates (2001) studied violence by youth gangs in Boston neighborhoods. Theirs was an applied explanatory study. They worked with local officials to better understand gang violence, develop ways to reduce it, and eventually assess the effects of their interventions. Neither a classical experiment nor a nonequivalent-groups design was possible. Researchers sought to understand and reduce violence by all gangs in the city. Their research centered on gangs, not individuals, although some interventions targeted particular gang members.

Researchers collected a large amount of information about gangs and gang violence from several sources. They used network analysis to examine relationships between gangs in different neighborhoods

---

THEORY AND DESIGN

Robert Yin (2008) describes the key role of theory in designing case studies, whether for descriptive or explanatory research. Theory describes what researchers think is going on, and *rival* theories provide alternative explanations. For example, Ronald Clarke and associates (Clarke, Contre, and Petrossian 2010) structured their evaluation of fare evasion in a mass transit system to assess alternative theories of how modifying penalties and enforcement would affect rates of violation. Much of their thinking and design drew on classical theories of deterrence.

Even more generally, Alex Hirschfield (2005, 634) summarizes how different theories of crime distribution offer different implications for analysis. Routine activity theory, for example, requires designing research to assess guardianship and the locations of

potential victims and offenders. In crime pattern theory, the movement of victims and offenders in time and space plays a central role. Accordingly, designs that compare different areas are most appropriate.

Finally, consider our description of time-series design with nonequivalent variable comparison groups as a type of theory, something Shadish, Cook, and Campbell (2002) describe as *pattern matching.* When Wesley Skogan and associates (2008) compared change in crime rates within areas where specific police problem solving was introduced to areas where there was no such police action, they specified a theory-based pattern of effects that was supported by their analysis. Their expectations and analysis were based on a theory of action that described expected impacts of police deployment.

and conflicts over turf within neighborhoods. Police records of homicides, assaults, and shootings were studied. Based on extensive data on a small number of gangs, researchers collaborated with public officials, neighborhood organizations, and a coalition of religious leaders—the "faith community." A variety of interventions were devised, but most were crafted from a detailed understanding of the specific nature of gangs and gang violence as they existed in Boston neighborhoods. David Kennedy (1998) summarizes these using the label "pulling levers," signifying that key gang members were vulnerable to intensive monitoring via probation or parole. The package of strategies was markedly successful: youth homicides were reduced from about 35 to 40 each year in the 20 years preceding the program to about 15 per year in the first 5 postintervention years (Braga 2008b).

The Boston research is also a good example of the scientific realist approach of Ray Pawson and Nick Tilley (1997). Researchers examined a small number of subjects—gangs and gang members—in a single city and in the context of specific neighborhoods where gangs were active. Extensive data were gathered on the mechanisms of gang violence. Interventions were tailored to those mechanisms in their context.

Braga and associates (2001) emphasize that the success of the Boston efforts was due to the *process* by which researchers, public officials, and community members collaboratively studied gang violence and then developed appropriate policy actions based on their analyses. Other jurisdictions mistakenly tried to reproduce Boston's interventions, with limited or no success, failing to recognize that the interventions were developed specifically for Boston. In case-study language, researchers examined many variables for one site and based policy decisions on that analysis. In the words of scientific realism, researchers studied the gang violence mechanism in the Boston context. In other contexts (Baltimore or Minneapolis, for example), gang violence operated as a different mechanism; the "levers" pulled in Boston did not work elsewhere. Braga and associates emphasize that the problem-solving process is exportable to other

settings but that the interventions used in Boston are not (2001, 220).

How do case studies address threats to validity? In the most general sense, case studies attempt to isolate causal mechanisms from possible confounding influences by studying very precisely defined subjects. Donald Campbell (2003, ix–x) likened this to laboratory experiments in the natural sciences, in which researchers try to isolate causal variables from outside influences. Case-study research takes place in natural field settings, not in laboratories. But the logic of trying to isolate causal mechanisms by focusing on one or a few cases is a direct descendant of the rationale for experimental isolation in laboratories.

Figure 5.8 summarizes advice from Yin (2008, 40–41) on how to judge the quality of case-study designs in language that should now be familiar. Construct validity is established through multiple sources of evidence, the establishment of chains of causation that connect independent and dependent variables, and what are termed *member checks*—asking key informants to review tentative conclusions about causation. Examples of techniques for strengthening internal validity are theory-based pattern matching and time-series analysis. The first technique follows Shadish, Cook, and Campbell (2002), calling on researchers to make specific theory-based predictions about what pattern of

Construct validity	Multiple sources of evidence
	Establishment of chains of causation
	Member checks
Internal validity	Pattern matching
	Time-series analysis
External validity	Replication through multiple case studies

FIGURE 5.8   Case Studies and Validity
Source: Adapted from Yin (2008, 40–41).

results will support hypothesized causal relationships. Alternative explanations, also termed *rival hypotheses*, are less persuasive when specific predictions of results are actually obtained.

For example, Braga and associates (2001) predicted that gun killings among male Boston residents under age 25 would decline following implementation of the package of interventions in the Boston gun strategy. Although other explanations are possible for the sharp observed declines, the specific focus of the researchers' interventions and the concomitant results undermine the credibility of rival hypotheses. Having many measures of variables over time strengthens internal validity if observations support our predicted expectations about cause. We saw earlier how nonequivalent time-series comparisons and switching replications can enhance findings. This is also consistent with pattern matching—we make specific statements about what patterns of results we expect in our observations over time.

Finally, a single case study is vulnerable to external validity threats because it is rooted in the context of a specific site. Conducting multiple case studies in different sites illustrates the principle of replication. By replicating research findings, we accumulate evidence. We may also find that causal relationships are different in different settings, as did researchers who tried to transplant specific interventions from the Boston Gun Project. Although such findings can undermine the generalizability of causality, they also help us understand how causal mechanisms can operate differently in different settings.

Time-series designs and case studies are examples of variable-oriented research. A case study with many observations over time can be an example of a time-series design. Adding one or more other cases offers opportunities to create nonequivalent comparisons. Time-series designs, case studies, and nonequivalent comparisons are quasi-experimental designs—they are conducted in the manner of experiments, using design building blocks in different ways.

Experimental and Quasi-Experimental Designs Summarized

Understanding the building blocks of research design and adapting them accordingly works better than trying to apply the same design to all research questions.

By now it should be clear that there are no simple formulas or recipes for designing an experimental or quasi-experimental study. Researchers have an almost infinite variety of ways of varying the number and composition of groups of subjects, selecting subjects, determining how many observations to make, and deciding what types of experimental stimuli to introduce or study.

Variations on experimental and quasi-experimental designs are constructed for basic and applied explanatory studies. As we stated earlier in this chapter, experiments are best suited to topics that involve well-defined concepts and propositions. Experiments and quasi-experiments also require that researchers be able to exercise, or at least approximate, some degree of control over an experimental stimulus. Finally, these designs depend on the ability to unambiguously establish the time order of experimental treatments and observations on the dependent variable. Often, it is not possible to achieve the necessary degree of control.

In designing research projects, researchers should be alert to opportunities for using experimental designs. Researchers should also be aware of how quasi-experimental designs can be developed when randomization is not possible. Experiments and quasi-experiments lend themselves to a logical rigor that is often much more difficult to achieve in other modes of observation. The building blocks of research design can be used in creative ways to address a variety of criminal justice research questions. Careful attention to design issues, and to how design elements can reduce validity threats, is essential to the research process.

SUMMARY

- Experiments are excellent vehicles for the controlled testing of causal processes. Experiments may also be appropriate for evaluation studies.

- The classical experiment tests the effect of an experimental stimulus on some dependent variable through the pretesting and posttesting of experimental and control groups.

- It is less important that a group of experimental subjects be representative of some larger population than that experimental and control groups be similar to each other.

- Randomization is the best way to achieve comparability in the experimental and control groups.

- The classical experiment with random assignment of subjects guards against most of the threats to internal invalidity.

- Because experiments often take place under controlled conditions, results may not be generalizable to real-world constructs. Or findings from an experiment in one setting may not apply to other settings.

- The classical experiment may be modified to suit specific research purposes by changing the number of experimental and control groups, the number and types of experimental stimuli, and the number of pretest or posttest measurements.

- Quasi-experiments may be conducted when it is not possible or desirable to use an experimental design.

- Nonequivalent-groups and time-series designs are two general types of quasi-experiments.

- Time-series designs and case studies are examples of variable-oriented research, in which a large number of variables are examined for one or a few cases.

- Not all research purposes and questions are amenable to experimental or quasi-experimental designs because researchers may not be able to exercise the required degree of control.

- Both experiments and quasi-experiments may be customized by using design building blocks to suit particular research purposes.

KEY TERMS

case-oriented research, p. 130
case studies, p. 131
classical experiment, p. 112
construct validity, p. 119
control group, p. 113
dependent variable, p. 112

experimental group, p. 113
external validity, p. 120
generalizability, p. 119
independent variable, p. 112
internal validity, p. 116
quasi-experiment, p. 122

randomization, p. 115
statistical conclusion validity, p. 120
variable-oriented research, p. 130

REVIEW QUESTIONS AND EXERCISES

1. Review the definition of an experiment by Farrington and associates presented in the first part of this chapter, especially: "The defining feature of an experiment lies in the control of the independent variable by the experimenter" (Farrington, Ohlin, and Wilson 1986, 65). Think of one example where controlling the independent variable is not possible; explain why that's not possible. Then briefly describe a quasi-experimental design for studying that example.

2. Experiments are often conducted in public health research where a distinction is made between an efficacy experiment and an effectiveness experiment. Efficacy experiments focus on whether a new health program works under ideal conditions; effectiveness experiments test the program under typical conditions that health professionals encounter in their day-to-day work. Discuss how efficacy experiments and effectiveness experiments reflect concerns about internal validity threats on the one hand and generalizability on the other.

3. Crime hot spots are areas where crime reports, calls for police service, or other measures of crime are especially common. Police in departments with a good analytic capability routinely identify hot spots and launch special tactics to reduce crime in these areas. What kinds of validity threats should researchers be especially attentive to in studying the effects of police interventions on hot spots?

PART 3

Modes of Observation

Having covered the basics of structuring research, from general issues to research design, let's dive into the various observational techniques available for criminal justice research.

Chapter 6 examines how social scientists go about selecting people or things for observation. Our discussion of sampling addresses the fundamental scientific issue of generalizability. As we'll see, it is possible for us to select a few people or things for observation and then apply what we observe to a much larger group of people or things than we actually observed. It is possible, for example, to ask a thousand people how they feel about "three strikes and you're out" laws and then accurately predict how tens of millions of people feel about it.

Chapter 7 describes survey research and other techniques for collecting data by asking people questions. We'll cover different ways of asking questions and discuss the various uses of surveys and related techniques in criminal justice research.

Chapter 8 describes additional ways to gather information by asking questions. Here we learn how to design different types of qualitative interviews, including focus groups.

Chapter 9, on field research, examines what is perhaps the most natural form of data collection: the direct observation of phenomena in natural settings. As we will see, observations can be highly structured and systematic (such as counting pedestrians who walk by a specified point) or less structured and more flexible.

Chapter 10 discusses ways to take advantage of some of the data available all around us. Researchers often examine data collected by criminal justice and other public agencies. Content analysis is a method of collecting data through carefully specifying and counting communications such as news stories, court opinions, or even recorded visual images. Criminal justice researchers may also conduct secondary analysis of data collected by others.

CHAPTER 6

Sampling

Sampling makes it possible to select a few hundred or thousand people for study and discover things that apply to many more people who are not studied.

Sampling and Election Polls

One of the many interesting features of the 2012 presidential election was the large number of polls that tracked public opinion for several months. Some polls reported just a few days before the election predicted victory by Obama by a razor-thin margin, while others showed a slight edge for Romney. The small differences in predictions by individual polls illustrate a couple of important principles of sampling. Here's a summary from the Huffington Post web page published November 3, 2012:

	Obama (%)	Romney (%)
Ipsos/Reuters	49	48
ABC/Post	48	49
Rasmussen	48	48
National Journal	50	45
Gallup	46	51
Final election results	51	49

Sources: http://www.huffingtonpost.com/2012/11/03/presidential-polls-2012_n_2068889.html?utm_hp_ref_@pollster; http://elections.nytimes.com/2012/results/president.

Notice two things about the poll estimates and final election results. First, three poll estimates are very close or tied. Second, two of them show differences of 5 percentage points between the two candidates, but in opposite directions. All polls were completed within two weeks before the election. What accounts for these differences?

Two things affect the accuracy of poll estimates: sampling and how accurately questions reflect the underlying construct being measured. We examined measurement generally in earlier chapters; Chapter 9 centers on survey research.

For now, you should recognize that asking someone how they intend to vote is a pretty simple measurement task that does not vary much across polls: "If the presidential election were being held today and the candidates were Obama and Biden and Romney and Ryan, for whom would you vote?"

Most of the variation in the election poll estimates shown in the previous table is due to differences in sampling, the topic of this chapter. The five polls shown above used different sampling techniques. For example, the Rasmussen poll used automated "robo-call" techniques that produced a large number of hang-ups. Further, the Rasmussen and Gallup polls called landline phones only, thus missing the growing proportion of people who use only cell phones (Shepard 2012; Silver 2012). These tend to be younger people and urban residents, both more likely to vote for Obama in the 2012 election.

As we'll see in this chapter, the accuracy of sampling depends on reducing bias in selection of subjects. Changes in the technology of communications have increased bias in traditional approaches to sampling people by telephone numbers. At the same time, increased use of cell phones and the Internet, the growth of social networks, and mobile computing offer new opportunities to sample and interview people. Later in this chapter, we present some recent data on telephone coverage in households. How many people in your class have landline telephone service?

Introduction

How we collect representative data is fundamental to criminal justice research.

Much of the value of research depends on how data are collected. A critical part of criminal justice research is deciding what will be observed and what won't. If you want to study drug users, for example, which drug users should you study? This chapter discusses the logic and fundamental principles of sampling and then describes different general approaches for selecting subjects or other units.

Sampling is the process of selecting observations. Sampling is ordinarily used to select observations for one of two related reasons. First, it is often not possible to collect information from all persons or other units we wish to study. We may wish to know what proportion of all persons arrested in U.S. cities have recently used drugs, but collecting all that data would be virtually impossible. Thus, we have to look at a sample of observations.

The second reason for sampling is that it is often not necessary to collect data from all persons or other units. Probability sampling techniques enable us to make relatively few observations and then generalize from those observations to a much wider population. If we are interested in what proportion of high school students have used marijuana, collecting data from a probability sample of a few thousand students will serve just as well as trying to study every high school student in the country.

Although probability sampling is central to criminal justice research, it cannot be used in many situations of interest. A variety of nonprobability sampling techniques are available in such cases. Nonprobability sampling has its own logic and can provide useful samples for criminal justice inquiry. In this chapter, we examine both the advantages and the shortcomings of such methods, and we discuss where they fit in the larger picture of sampling and collecting data. Keep in mind one important goal of all sampling: to reduce, or at least understand, the potential biases that may be at work in selecting subjects.

The Logic of Probability Sampling

Probability sampling helps researchers generalize from observed cases to unobserved ones.

In selecting a group of subjects for study, social science researchers often use some type of sampling. Sampling in general refers to selecting part of a population. In selecting **samples**, we want to do two related things. First, we select samples to represent some larger population of people or other things. If we are interested in attitudes about a prisoner reentry facility, we might draw a sample of neighborhood residents, ask them some questions, and use their responses to represent the attitudes of all neighborhood residents. Or, in studying cases in a criminal court, we may not be able to examine all cases, so we select a sample to represent that population of all cases processed through some court.

Second, we may want to generalize from a sample to an unobserved population the sample is intended to represent. If we interview a sample of community residents, we may want to generalize our findings to all community residents—those we interviewed and those we did not. We might similarly expect that our sample of criminal court cases can be generalized to the population of all criminal court cases.

A special type of sampling that enables us to generalize to a larger population is known as **probability sampling**, a method of selection in which each member of a population has a known chance or probability of being selected. Knowing the probability that any individual member of a population could be selected makes it possible for us to make predictions that our sample accurately represents the larger population.

If all members of a population are identical in all respects—demographic characteristics, attitudes, experiences, behaviors, and so on—there is no need for careful sampling procedures. Any sample will be sufficient. In this extreme case of homogeneity, in fact, a single case will be sufficient as a sample to study characteristics of the whole

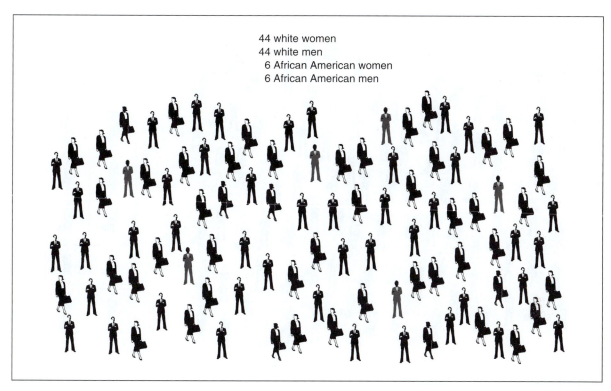

44 white women
44 white men
6 African American women
6 African American men

FIGURE 6.1 A Population of 100 People

population. Or, as George Gallup put it, "One spoonful can reflect the taste of the whole pot if the soup is well-stirred" (Best and Radcliff 2005, 716).

In reality, of course, the human beings who make up any real population are heterogeneous, varying in many ways. Figure 6.1 offers a simplified illustration of a heterogeneous population: the 100 members of this small population differ by gender and race. We'll use this hypothetical micropopulation to illustrate various aspects of sampling.

A sample of individuals from a population, if it is to provide useful descriptions of the total population, must contain essentially the same variations that exist in the population. This is not as simple as it might seem. Let's look at some of the possible biases in selection or ways researchers might go astray. Then we will see how probability sampling provides an efficient method for selecting a sample

that should adequately reflect variations that exist in the population.

Conscious and Unconscious Sampling Bias

At first glance, it may seem as if sampling is a rather straightforward matter. To select a sample of 100 lawyers, a researcher might simply go to a courthouse and interview the first 100 lawyers who walk through the door. This kind of sampling method is often used by untrained researchers, but it is subject to serious biases. In connection with sampling, *bias* simply means that those selected are not "typical" or "representative" of the larger populations they have been chosen from. This kind of bias is virtually inevitable when a researcher picks subjects casually.

Figure 6.2 illustrates what can happen when we simply select people who are convenient for

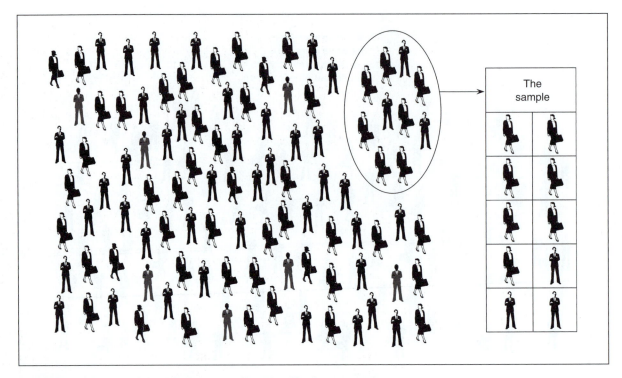

FIGURE 6.2   A Sample of Convenience: Easy, but Not Representative

study. Although women make up only 50 percent of our micropopulation, those closest to the researcher (people in the upper right-hand corner of Figure 6.2) happen to be 70 percent women. Although the population is 12 percent African American, none were selected into this sample of people who happened to be conveniently situated near the researcher.

Moving beyond the risks inherent in simply studying people who are convenient, we need to consider other potential problems as well. To begin, our own personal leanings or biases may affect the sample selected in this manner; hence, the sample will not truly represent the population of lawyers. Suppose a researcher is a little intimidated by lawyers who look particularly prosperous, believing that they might ridicule his research effort. He might consciously or unconsciously avoid interviewing them. Or he might believe that the attitudes of "establishment" lawyers are irrelevant to his research purposes and avoid interviewing them.

Even if the researcher seeks to interview a "balanced" group of lawyers, he won't know the exact proportions of different types of lawyers who make up such a balance and won't always be able to identify the different types merely by watching them walk by.

The researcher might make a conscious effort to interview, say, every 10th lawyer who enters the courthouse, but he still cannot be sure of a representative sample because different types of lawyers visit the courthouse with different frequencies, and some never go to the courthouse at all. Thus, the resulting sample will overrepresent lawyers who visit the courthouse more often.

Similarly, polls linked to weblogs, text messages, or e-mail cannot be trusted to represent the general population. Blogs tend to be selective; people regularly visit blogs that present views on personal and political issues they endorse (McKenna and Pole 2008). As a result, the population of people who respond to weblog polls can only represent the population of people who regularly visit individual blogs. In the same way, most commercial e-mail services include some type of advertising, and such ads are sometimes cleverly disguised as opinion polls. As a general principle, the more self-selection is involved, the more bias will be introduced into the sample.

The possibilities for inadvertent sampling bias are endless and not always obvious. Fortunately, some techniques can help us avoid bias.

Representativeness and Probability of Selection

Although the term *representativeness* has no precise, scientific meaning, it carries a commonsense meaning that makes it useful in the discussion of sampling. As we'll use the term here, a sample is *representative* of the population from which it is selected if the aggregate characteristics of the sample closely approximate those same aggregate characteristics in the population. If the population, for example, contains 50 percent women, a representative sample will also contain "close to" 50 percent women. Later in this chapter, we'll discuss "how close" in detail. Notice that samples need not be representative in all respects; representativeness is limited to those characteristics that are relevant to the substantive interests of the study.

A basic principle of probability sampling is that a sample will be representative of the population from which it is selected if all members of the population have an equal chance of being selected in the sample. Samples that have this quality are often labeled **equal probability of selection method (EPSEM)** samples.

Even carefully selected EPSEM samples are seldom, if ever, perfectly representative of the populations from which they are drawn. Nevertheless, probability sampling offers two special advantages. First, probability samples, though never perfectly representative, are typically more representative than other types of samples because they avoid the biases discussed in the preceding section. In practice, there is a greater likelihood that a probability sample will be representative of the population from which it is drawn than that a nonprobability sample will be.

Second, and more importantly, probability sampling permits us to estimate the accuracy or representativeness of the sample. Conceivably, a researcher might wholly by chance select a sample that closely represents the larger population. The odds are against doing so, however, and we cannot estimate the likelihood that a haphazard sample will achieve representativeness. The probability sample can provide an accurate estimate of success or failure, because probability samples enable us to draw on probability theory.

Probability Theory and Sampling Distribution

Probability theory permits inferences about how sampled data are distributed around the value found in a larger population.

With a basic understanding of the logic of probability sampling in hand, we can examine how probability sampling works in practice. We will then be able to devise specific sampling techniques and assess the results of those techniques. To do so, we first need to understand four important concepts.

A **sample element** is that unit about which information is collected and that provides the basis of analysis. Typically, in survey research, elements are people or certain types of people. However, other kinds of units can be the elements for criminal justice research—correctional facilities, police beats, or court cases, for example. Elements and units of analysis are often the same in a given study, although the former refers to sample selection and the latter to data analysis.

A **population** is the theoretically specified grouping of study elements. Whereas the vague term *delinquents* might describe the target for a study, a more precise description of the population includes the definition of the element *delinquents* (for example, a person charged with a delinquent offense), the time referent for the study (charged with a delinquent offense in the previous six months), and often a particular area (in the city of Los Angeles). Translating the abstract *adult drug addicts* into a workable population requires specifying the age that defines adult and the level of drug use that constitutes an addict. Specifying *college student* includes a consideration of full- and part-time students, degree and nondegree candidates, undergraduate and graduate students, and so on.

A **population parameter** is the value for a given variable in a population. The average income of all families in a city and the age distribution of the city's population are parameters. An important portion of criminal justice research involves estimating population parameters on the basis of sample observations.

The summary description of a given variable in the sample is called a **sample statistic**. Sample statistics are used to make estimates of population parameters. Thus, the average income computed from a sample and the age distribution of that sample are statistics, and those statistics are used to estimate income and age parameters in a population.

The ultimate purpose of sampling is to select a set of elements from a population in such a way that descriptions of those elements (sample statistics) accurately portray the parameters of the total population from which the elements are selected. Probability sampling enhances the likelihood of accomplishing this aim and also provides methods for estimating the degree of probable success.

The key to this process is random selection. In random selection, each element has an equal chance of being selected independent of any other event in the selection process. Flipping a coin is the most frequently cited example: the "selection" of a head or a tail is independent of previous selections of heads or tails.

There are two reasons for using random selection methods. First, this procedure serves as a check on conscious or unconscious bias on the part of the researcher. The researcher who selects cases on an intuitive basis might choose cases that will support his or her research expectations or hypotheses. Random selection erases this danger. Second, and more importantly, with random selection we can draw on probability theory, which allows us to estimate population parameters and to estimate how accurate our statistics are likely to be.

The Sampling Distribution of 10 Cases

Suppose there are 10 people in a group, and each person has a certain amount of money in his or her pocket. To simplify, let's assume that one person has no money, another has $1, another has $2, and so forth up to the person who has $9. Figure 6.3 illustrates this population of 10 people.

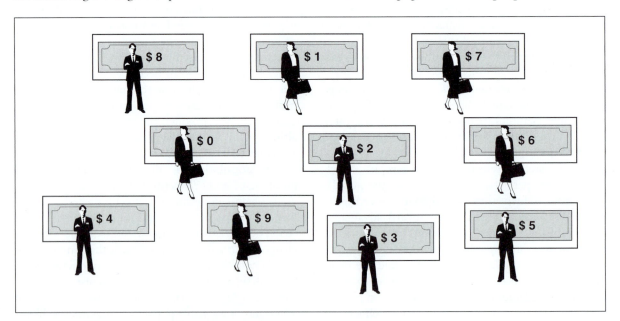

FIGURE 6.3   A Population of 10 People with $0 to $9

Our task is to determine the average amount of money one person has—specifically, the mean number of dollars. If you simply add up the money shown in Figure 6.3, the total is $45, so the mean is $4.50 (45 ÷ 10). Our purpose in the rest of this example is to estimate that mean without actually observing all 10 individuals. We'll do that by selecting random samples from the population and using the means of those samples to estimate the mean for the whole population.

To start, suppose we select—at random—a sample of only 1 person from the 10. Depending on which person we select, we will estimate the group's mean as anywhere from $0 to $9. Figure 6.4 shows a display of those 10 possible samples. The 10 dots shown on the graph represent the 10 "sample" means we will get as estimates of the population. The range of the dots on the graph is the **sampling distribution**, defined as the range of sample statistics we will obtain if we select many samples. Figure 6.4 shows how all of our possible samples of 1 are

distributed. Obviously, it is not a good idea to select a sample of only 1 because we stand a good chance of missing the true mean of $4.50 by quite a bit.

What if we take samples of 2 each? As you can see from Figure 6.5, increasing the sample size improves our estimations. Once again, each dot represents a possible sample. There are 45 possible samples of two elements: $0/$1, $0/$2, ..., $7/$8, $8/$9. Moreover, some of these samples produce the same means. For example, $0/$6, $1/$5, and $2/$4 all produce means of $3. In Figure 6.5, the three dots shown above the $3 mean represent those 3 samples.

Notice that the means we get from the 45 samples are not evenly distributed. Rather, they are somewhat clustered around the true value of $4.50. Only 2 samples deviate by as much as $4 from the true value ($0/$1 and $8/$9), whereas 5 of the samples give the true estimate of $4.50, and another 8 samples miss the mark by only $.50 (plus or minus).

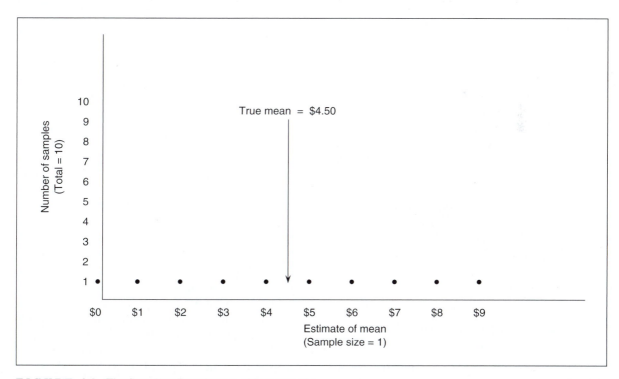

FIGURE 6.4 The Sampling Distribution of Samples of 1

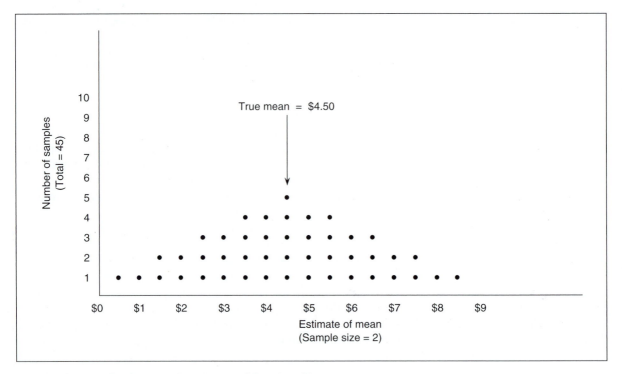

FIGURE 6.5   The Sampling Distribution of Samples of 2

Now suppose we select even larger samples. What will that do to our estimates of the mean? Figure 6.6 presents the sampling distributions of samples of 3, 4, 5, and 6. The progression of the sampling distributions is clear. Every increase in sample size improves the distribution of estimates of the mean in two related ways. First, in the distribution for samples of 5, for example, no sample means are at the extreme ends of the distribution. Why? Because it is not possible to select five elements from our population and obtain an average of less than $2 or greater than $7. The second way sampling distributions improve with larger samples is that sample means cluster more and more around the true population mean of $4.50. Figure 6.6 clearly shows this tendency.

From Sampling Distribution to Parameter Estimate

Let's turn now to a more realistic sampling situation and see how the notion of sampling distribution applies. Assume that we wish to study the population of Placid Coast, California, to assess the levels of approval or disapproval of a proposed law to ban possession of assault rifles within the city limits.

Our target population is all adult residents. In order to draw an actual sample, we need some sort of list of elements in our population; such a list is called a **sampling frame**. Assume our sampling frame is a voter registration list of, say, 20,000 registered voters in Placid Coast. The elements are the individual registered voters.

The variable under consideration is attitudes toward the proposed law: approve or disapprove. Measured in this way, attitude toward the law is a **binomial variable**; it can have only two values. We'll select a random sample of, say, 100 persons for the purpose of estimating the population parameter for approval of the proposed law.

Figure 6.7 presents all the possible values of this parameter in the population—from 0 percent approval to 100 percent approval. The midpoint of

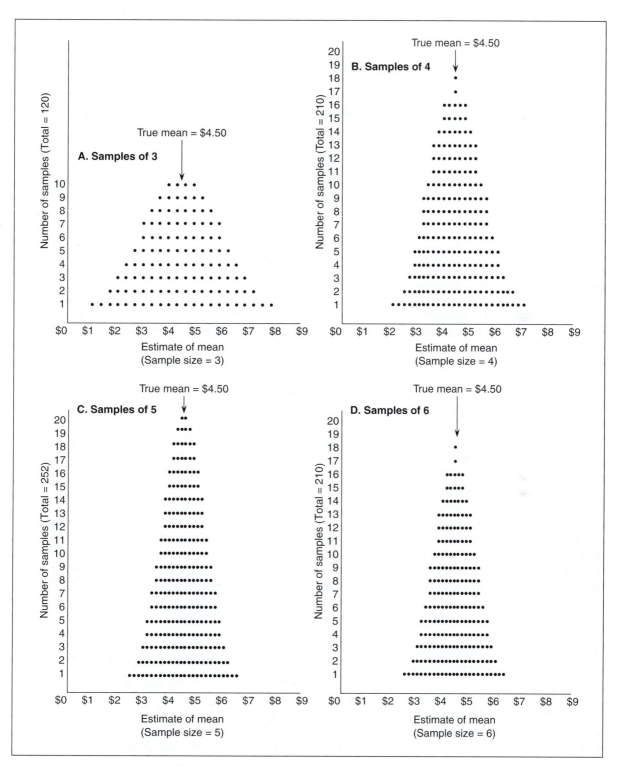

FIGURE 6.6   The Sampling Distribution of Samples of 3, 4, 5, and 6

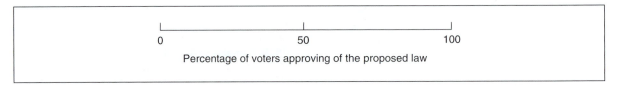

F I G U R E 6.7   The Range of Possible Sample Study Results

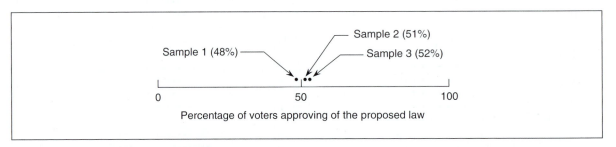

F I G U R E 6.8   Results Produced by Three Hypothetical Samples

the line—50 percent—represents half the voters approving of the assault rifle ban and the other half disapproving.

To choose our sample, we assign each person on the voter registration list a number and use a computer program to generate 100 random numbers. Then we interview the 100 people whose numbers have been selected and ask for their attitudes toward the assault rifle ban: whether they approve or disapprove. Suppose this operation gives us 48 people who approve of the law and 52 who disapprove. We present this statistic by placing a dot at the point representing 48 percent, as shown in Figure 6.8.

Now suppose we select another sample of 100 people in exactly the same fashion and measure their approval or disapproval of the proposed law. Perhaps 51 people in the second sample approve of the law. We place another dot in the appropriate place on the line in Figure 6.8. Repeating this process once more, we may discover that 52 people in the third sample approve banning assault rifles; we add a third dot to Figure 6.8.

Figure 6.8 now presents the three different sample statistics that represent the percentages of people in each of the three random samples who approved of the proposed law. Each of the random samples, then, gives us an estimate of the percentage of people in the total population of registered voters

who approve of the assault rifle law. Unfortunately, we now have three separate estimates.

To rescue ourselves from this dilemma, let's draw more and more samples of 100 registered voters each, question each of the samples concerning their approval or disapproval, and plot the new sample statistics on our summary graph. In drawing many such samples, we discover that some of the new samples provide duplicate estimates, as in our earlier illustration with 10 cases. Figure 6.9 shows the sampling distribution of hundreds of samples. This is often referred to as a normal or bell-shaped curve.

Notice that by increasing the number of samples selected and interviewed we have also increased the range of estimates provided by the sampling operation. In one sense, we have increased our dilemma in attempting to find the parameter in the population. Fortunately, probability theory provides certain important rules about the sampling distribution shown in Figure 6.9.

Estimating Sampling Error

Probability theory can help resolve our dilemma with some basic statistical concepts. First, if many independent random samples are selected from a population, then the sample statistics provided by those samples will be distributed around the population

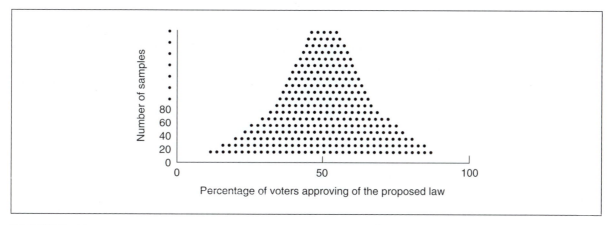

FIGURE 6.9   The Sampling Distribution

parameter in a known way. Thus, although Figure 6.9 shows a wide range of estimates, more of them are in the vicinity of 50 percent than elsewhere in the graph. Probability theory tells us, then, that the true value is in the vicinity of 50 percent.

Second, probability theory gives us a formula for estimating how closely the sample statistics are clustered around the true value:

$$s = \sqrt{\frac{P \times Q}{n}}$$

where s is the **standard error**—defined as a measure of sampling error—n is the number of cases in each sample, and p and q are the population parameters for the binomial. If 60 percent of registered voters approve of the ban on assault rifles and 40 percent disapprove, then p and q are 60 percent and 40 percent, or 0.6 and 0.4, respectively.

To see how probability theory makes it possible for us to estimate sampling error, suppose that in reality 50 percent of the people approve of the proposed law and 50 percent disapprove. These are the population parameters we are trying to estimate with our samples. Recall that we have been selecting samples of 100 cases each. When these numbers are plugged into the formula, we get:

$$s = \sqrt{\frac{0.5 \times 0.5}{100}} = 0.05$$

The standard error equals 0.05, or 5 percent.

In probability theory, the standard error is a valuable piece of information because it indicates how closely the sample estimates will be distributed around the population parameter. A larger standard error indicates that sample estimates are widely dispersed, while a smaller standard error means that estimates are more clustered around a population parameter. Probability theory tells us that approximately 34 percent (0.3413) of the sample estimates will fall within one standard error increment above the population parameter, and another 34 percent will fall within one standard error increment below the parameter. In our example, the standard error increment is 5 percent, so we know that 34 percent of our samples will give estimates of approval between 50 percent (the parameter) and 55 percent (one standard error above); another 34 percent of the samples will give estimates between 50 and 45 percent (one standard error below the parameter). Taken together, then, we know that roughly two-thirds (68 percent) of the samples will give estimates between 45 and 55 percent, which is within 5 percent of the parameter.

The standard error is also a function of the sample size—an inverse function. This means that as the sample size increases, the standard error decreases. And as the sample size increases, the several samples will be clustered nearer to the true value. Figure 6.6 illustrates this clustering. Another rule of thumb is evident in the formula for the standard error: because of the square root operation, the standard error is reduced by half if the sample size is quadrupled. In our example, samples of 100 produce a standard error of 5 percent; to reduce the standard error to 2.5 percent, we would have to increase the sample size to 400.

All of this information is provided by established probability theory in reference to the selection of large numbers of random samples. If the population parameter is known and many random samples are selected, probability theory allows us to predict how many of the samples will fall within specified intervals from the parameter.

Of course, this discussion illustrates only the *logic* of probability sampling. It does not describe the way research is actually conducted. Usually, we do not know the parameter; we conduct a sample survey precisely because we want to estimate that value. Moreover, we don't actually select large numbers of samples; we select only one sample. What probability theory does is provide the basis for making inferences about the typical research situation. Knowing what it would be like to select thousands of samples allows us to make assumptions about the one sample we do select and study.

Confidence Levels and Confidence Intervals

Probability theory specifies that 68 percent of that fictitious large number of samples will produce estimates that fall within one standard error of the parameter. As researchers, we can turn the logic around and infer that any single random sample has a 68 percent chance of falling within that range. In this regard, we speak of **confidence levels**: we are 68 percent confident that our sample estimate is within one standard error of the parameter. Or we may say that we are 95 percent confident that the sample statistic is within two standard errors of the parameter, and so forth. Quite reasonably, our confidence level increases as the margin for error is extended. We are virtually positive (99.9 percent) that our statistic is within three standard errors of the true value.

Although we may be confident (at some level) of being within a certain range of the parameter, we seldom know what the parameter is. To resolve this dilemma, we substitute our sample estimate for the parameter in the formula; lacking the true value, we substitute the best available guess.

The result of these inferences and estimations is that we are able to estimate a population parameter and also the expected degree of error on the basis of one sample drawn from a population. We begin with this question: what percentage of the registered voters in Placid Coast approve of the proposed assault rifle ban? We select a random sample of 100 registered voters and interview them. We might then report that our best estimate is that 50 percent of registered voters approve of the gun ban and that we are 95 percent confident that between 40 and 60 percent (plus or minus two standard errors) approve. The range from 40 to 60 percent is called the **confidence interval**. At the 68 percent confidence level, the confidence interval is 45 to 55 percent.

The logic of confidence levels and confidence intervals also provides the basis for determining the appropriate sample size for a study. Once we decide on the sampling error we can tolerate, we can calculate the number of cases needed in our sample.

Probability Theory and Sampling Distribution Summed Up

This, then, is the basic logic of probability sampling. Random selection permits the researcher to link findings from a sample to the body of probability theory so as to estimate the accuracy of those findings. All statements of accuracy in sampling must specify both a confidence level and a confidence interval. The researcher must report that he or she is *x* percent confident that the population parameter is between two specific values.

In this example, we have demonstrated the logic of sampling error using a binomial variable—a variable analyzed in percentages. A different statistical procedure would be required to calculate the standard error for a mean, but the overall logic is the same.

Notice that nowhere in this discussion did we consider the size of the population being studied. This is because the population size is almost always irrelevant. A sample of 2,000 respondents drawn properly to represent residents of Vermont will be no more accurate than a sample of 2,000 drawn properly to represent residents in the United States, even though the Vermont sample would be a substantially larger proportion of that small state's residents than would the same number chosen to represent the nation's residents. The reason for this counterintuitive fact is that the equations for calculating sampling error assume that the populations being sampled are infinitely large, so all samples would equal zero percent of the whole.

Two cautions are in order before we conclude this discussion of the basic logic of probability sampling. First, the survey uses of probability theory as discussed here are technically not wholly justified. The theory of sampling distribution makes assumptions that almost never apply in survey conditions. The exact proportion of samples contained within specified increments of standard errors mathematically assumes an infinitely large population, an infinite number of samples, and sampling with replacement—that is, every sampling unit selected is "thrown back into the pot" and could be selected again. Second, our discussion has greatly oversimplified the inferential jump from the distribution of several samples to the probable characteristics of one sample.

We offer these cautions to provide perspective on the uses of probability theory in sampling. Researchers in criminal justice and other social sciences often appear to overestimate the precision of estimates produced by the use of probability theory. Variations in sampling techniques and nonsampling factors may further reduce the legitimacy of such estimates. For example, those selected in a sample who fail or refuse to participate further detract from the representativeness of the sample.

Nevertheless, the calculations discussed in this section can be extremely valuable to you in understanding and evaluating your data. Being familiar with the basic logic underlying the calculations can help you react sensibly both to your own data and to those reported by others.

Probability Sampling

Different types of sampling designs can be used alone or in combination for different research purposes.

As researchers and as consumers of research, we need to understand the theoretical foundations of sampling. It is no less important to appreciate the less-than-perfect conditions that exist in the field. Most of what we have considered so far assumes we are using simple random sampling. In reality, researchers have a number of options in choosing their sampling method, each with its own advantages and disadvantages.

Populations and Sampling Frames

Our discussion begins with a more practical consideration of one key feature of all probability sampling designs: the relationship between populations and sampling frames.

A sampling frame is the list or quasi-list of elements from which a probability sample is selected. Put another way, a sampling frame is a list or quasi-list of our target population. We say "quasi-list" because, even though an actual list might not exist, we can draw samples as if there were a list. Properly drawn samples provide information appropriate for describing the population of elements that compose the sampling frame—nothing more. This point is important in view of the common tendency for researchers to select samples from a particular sampling frame and then make assertions about a population that is similar, but not identical, to the study population defined by the sampling frame.

For example, if we want to study the attitudes of corrections administrators toward determinant sentencing policies, we might select a sample by consulting the membership roster of the American Correctional Association. In this case, the membership roster is our sampling frame, and corrections administrators are the population we wish to describe. However, unless all corrections administrators are members of the American Correctional Association and all members are listed in the roster, it would be incorrect to generalize results to all corrections administrators.

This example illustrates an important general point with respect to sampling. Studies of organizations are often the simplest from a sampling standpoint because organizations typically have membership lists. In such cases, the list of members may be an acceptable sampling frame. If a random sample is selected from a membership list, then the data collected from that sample may be taken as representative of all members—if all members are included in the list. It is, however, imperative that researchers learn how complete or incomplete such lists might be and limit their generalizations to listed sample elements rather than to an entire population. The membership lists of organizations now often include e-mail addresses. In such cases, organizations are especially well suited to web-based sampling and e-mail contacts.

Other lists of individuals may be especially relevant to the research needs of a particular study. Lists of licensed drivers, automobile owners, welfare recipients, taxpayers, holders of weapons permits, and licensed professionals are just a few examples. Although it may be difficult to gain access to some of these lists, they provide excellent sampling frames for specialized research purposes.

Telephone directories are sometimes used for "quick and dirty" public opinion polls. Undeniably, they are easy and inexpensive to use, and that is no doubt the reason for their popularity. Still, they have several limitations. A given directory will not include new subscribers or those who have requested unlisted numbers. Sampling is further complicated by the inclusion of nonresidential listings in directories. Telephone companies may not publish listings for temporary residents such as

students. And persons who live in institutions or group quarters—dormitories, nursing homes, rooming houses, and the like—are not listed in phone directories. More households are served only by wireless phone service and so are not listed in directories. A national study conducted in 2011 reported that 32 percent of adults lived in households with wireless phone service only (Blumberg and Luke 2012).

Street directories and tax maps may be used as sampling frames for households, but they may also suffer from incompleteness and possible bias. For example, illegal housing units such as basement apartments are unlikely to appear on official records. As a result, such units have no chance for selection, and sample findings will not be representative of those units, which are often substandard and overcrowded.

In a more general sense, it's worth viewing sampling frames as operational definitions of a study population. Just as operational definitions of variables describe how abstract concepts will be measured, sampling frames serve as a real-world version of an abstract study population. For example, we may want to study how criminologists deal with ethical issues in their research. We don't know how many criminologists exist out there, but we could develop a general idea about the population of criminologists. We could also operationalize the concept by using the membership directory for the American Society of Criminology (ASC)—that list is our operational definition of the population of criminologists. Since most criminologists use e-mail extensively, a sample of e-mail addresses from the ASC directory would suit our purposes nicely.

Simple Random Sampling

Simple random sampling forms the basis of probability theory and the statistical tools we use to estimate population parameters, standard error, and confidence intervals. More accurately, such statistics assume unbiased sampling, and simple random sampling is the foundation of unbiased sampling.

Once a sampling frame has been established in keeping with the guidelines we presented, to use simple random sampling, the researcher assigns a single number to each element in the list, not skipping any number in the process. A table of random numbers, or a computer program for generating them, is then used to select elements for the sample.

If the sampling frame is a computerized database or some other form of electronic data, a **simple random sample** can be selected by computer. In effect, the computer program numbers the elements in the sampling frame, generates its own series of random numbers, and prints out the list of elements selected.

Systematic Sampling

Simple random sampling is seldom used in practice, primarily because it is not usually the most efficient method, and it can be tedious if done manually. It typically requires a list of elements. And when such a list is available, researchers usually use **systematic sampling** rather than simple random sampling.

In systematic sampling, the researcher chooses all elements in the list for inclusion in the sample. If a list contains 10,000 elements and we want a sample of 1,000, we select every 10th element for our sample. To ensure against any possible human bias, we should select the first element at random. Thus, to systematically select 1,000 from a list of 10,000 elements, we begin by selecting a random number between 1 and 10. The element having that number, plus every 10th element following it, is included in the sample. This method technically is referred to as a systematic sample with a random start.

In practice, systematic sampling is virtually identical to simple random sampling. If the list of elements is indeed randomized before sampling, one might argue that a systematic sample drawn from that list is, in fact, a simple random sample.

Systematic sampling has one danger. A periodic arrangement of elements in the list can make systematic sampling unwise; this arrangement is usually called *periodicity*. If the list of elements is arranged in a cyclical pattern that coincides with the sampling interval, a biased sample may be drawn. Suppose we

select a sample of apartments in an apartment building. If the sample is drawn from a list of apartments arranged in numerical order (for example, 101, 102, 103, 104, 201, 202, and so on), there is a danger of the sampling interval coinciding with the number of apartments on a floor or some multiple of it. For example, in Maxfield's apartment building in New York City, apartments ending in 01, 02, 03, and 04 have spectacular views and cost more than three times as much as apartments ending in 05, 06, 07, and 08 (Maxfield's number). If the number 02 is selected as a starting point, only the premium apartments will be sampled.

In considering a systematic sample from a list, then, we need to carefully examine the nature of that list. If the elements are arranged in any particular order, we have to figure out whether that order will bias the sample to be selected and take steps to counteract any possible bias.

In summary, systematic sampling is usually superior to simple random sampling, in terms of convenience if nothing else. Problems in the ordering of elements in the sampling frame can usually be remedied quite easily.

Stratified Sampling

We have discussed two methods of selecting a sample from a list: random and systematic. **Stratification** is not an alternative to these methods, but it represents a possible modification in their use. Simple random sampling and systematic sampling both ensure a degree of representativeness and permit an estimate of the sampling error present. Stratified sampling is a method for obtaining a greater degree of representativeness—decreasing the probable sampling error. To understand why that is the case, we must return briefly to the basic theory of sampling distribution.

Recall that sampling error is reduced by two factors in the sample design: (1) a large sample produces a smaller sampling error than a small sample does, and (2) a homogeneous population produces samples with smaller sampling errors than a heterogeneous population does. If 99 percent of the population agrees with a certain statement, it is extremely unlikely that any probability sample will greatly misrepresent the extent of agreement. If the population is split 50–50 on the statement, then the sampling error will be much greater. Recall the close vote and close opinion polls in the 2012 presidential election. Larger sampling error was a result of the almost even population split between the two candidates, making some polls "too close to call."

Stratified sampling is based on this second factor in sampling theory. Rather than selecting our sample from the total population at large, we select appropriate numbers of elements from homogeneous subsets of that population. To get a stratified sample of university students, for example, we first organize our population by college class and then draw appropriate numbers of freshmen, sophomores, juniors, and seniors. In a nonstratified sample, representation by class is subject to the same sampling error as other variables. In a sample stratified by college class, the sampling error on that variable is reduced to zero.

Even more complex stratification methods are possible. In addition to stratifying by class, we might also stratify by gender, grade point average, and so forth. In this fashion, we could ensure that our sample contains the proper numbers of freshman men with a 4.0 average, freshman women with a 4.0 average, and so forth.

The ultimate function of stratification, then, is to organize the population into homogeneous subsets (with heterogeneity between subsets) and to select the appropriate number of elements from each. To the extent that the subsets are homogeneous on the stratification variables, they may also be homogeneous on other variables. Because age is usually related to college class, a sample stratified by class will be more representative in terms of age as well.

The choice of stratification variables typically depends on what variables are available and what variables might help reduce sampling error for a particular study. Gender can often be determined in a list of names. Many local government sources of information on housing units are arranged geographically. Age, race, education, occupation, and other variables are often included on lists of persons who have had contact with criminal justice officials.

In selecting stratification variables, however, we should be concerned primarily with those that are presumably related to the variables we want to represent accurately. Because gender is related to many behavioral variables and is often available for stratification, it is frequently used. Age and race are related to many variables of interest in criminal justice research. Income is also related to many variables, but it is often not available for stratification. Geographic location within a city, state, or nation is related to many things. Within a city, stratification by geographic location usually increases representativeness in social class and ethnicity.

Stratified sampling ensures the proper representation of the stratification variables to enhance representation of other variables related to them. Taken as a whole, then, a stratified sample is likely to be more representative on a number of variables than a simple random sample is.

Disproportionate Stratified Sampling

Another use of stratification is to purposively produce samples that are not representative of a population on some variable, referred to as **disproportionate stratified sampling**. Because the purpose of sampling, as we have been discussing, is to represent a larger population, you may wonder why anyone would want to intentionally produce a sample that was not representative.

To understand the logic of disproportionate stratification, consider again the role of population homogeneity in determining sample size. If members of a population vary widely on some variable of interest, then larger samples must be drawn to adequately represent the larger sampling error in that population. Similarly, if only a small number of people in a population exhibit some attribute or characteristic of interest, then a large sample must be drawn to produce adequate numbers of elements that exhibit the uncommon condition. Disproportionate stratification is a way of obtaining sufficient numbers of these rare cases by selecting a number disproportionate to their representation in the population.

The best example of disproportionate sampling in criminal justice is a national crime survey in which one goal is to obtain some minimum number of crime victims in a sample. Because crime victimization for certain offenses—such as robbery or aggravated assault—is relatively rare on a national scale, persons who live in large urban areas, where serious crime is more common, are disproportionately sampled.

The British Crime Survey (BCS) is a nationwide survey of people ages 16 and over in England and Wales. Over its first 20 years (since 1982), the BCS selectively oversampled people or areas to yield larger numbers of designated subjects than would result from proportionate random samples of the population of England and Wales. Beginning in 2004, the BCS disproportionately oversampled areas served by smaller police forces to produce a large enough number of cases to statistically represent rural areas (Smith and Hoare 2009).

Multistage Cluster Sampling

The preceding sections have described reasonably simple procedures for sampling from lists of elements. Unfortunately, however, many interesting research problems require the selection of samples from populations that cannot easily be listed for sampling purposes—that is, sampling frames are not readily available. Examples are the population of a city, state, or nation and all police officers in the United States. In such cases, the sample design must be much more complex. Such a design typically involves the initial sampling of groups of elements—clusters—followed by the selection of elements within each of the selected clusters. This procedure yields multistage **cluster samples**.

Cluster sampling may be used when it is either impossible or impractical to compile an exhaustive list of the elements that compose the target population, such as all law enforcement officers in the United States. Often, however, population elements are already grouped into subpopulations, and

a list of those subpopulations either exists or can be created.

Population elements, or aggregations of those elements, are referred to as **sampling units**. In the simplest forms of sampling, elements and units are the same thing—usually people. But in cases in which a listing of elements is not available, we can often use some other unit that includes a grouping of elements.

Because U.S. law enforcement officers are employed by individual cities, counties, or states, it is possible to create lists of those political units. For cluster sampling, then, we could sample the list of cities, counties, and states in some manner as discussed previously (for example, a systematic sample stratified by population). Next, we could obtain lists of law enforcement officers from agencies in each of the selected jurisdictions. We could then sample each of the lists to provide samples of police officers for study.

Another typical situation concerns sampling among population areas such as a city. Although there is no single list of a city's population, citizens reside on discrete city blocks or census blocks. It is possible, therefore, to select a sample of blocks initially, create a list of persons who live on each of the selected blocks, and then sample persons from that list. In this case, blocks are treated as the primary sampling unit.

In a more complex design, we might sample blocks, list the households on each selected block, sample the households, list the persons who reside in each household, and, finally, sample persons within each selected household. This multistage sample design will lead to the ultimate selection of a sample of individuals without requiring the initial listing of all individuals in the city's population.

Multistage cluster sampling, then, involves the repetition of two basic steps: listing and sampling. The list of primary sampling units (city blocks) is compiled and perhaps stratified for sampling. Next, a sample of those units is selected. The list of secondary sampling units is then sampled, and the process continues.

Cluster sampling is highly recommended for its efficiency, but the price of that efficiency is a less accurate sample. A simple random sample drawn from a population list is subject to a single sampling error, but a two-stage cluster sample is subject to two sampling errors. First, the initial sample of clusters represents the population of clusters only within a range of sampling error. Second, the sample of elements selected within a given cluster represents all the elements in that cluster only within a range of sampling error. Thus, for example, we run a certain risk of selecting a sample of disproportionately wealthy city blocks, plus a sample of disproportionately wealthy households within those blocks. The best solution to this problem involves the number of clusters selected initially and the number of elements selected within each cluster.

A good general guideline for cluster design is to maximize the number of clusters selected while decreasing the number of elements within each cluster. But this scientific guideline must be balanced against an administrative constraint. The efficiency of cluster sampling is based on the ability to minimize the list of population elements. By initially selecting clusters, we need only list the elements that make up the selected clusters, not all elements in the entire population. Increasing the number of clusters, however, reduces this efficiency in cluster sampling. A small number of clusters may be listed more quickly and more cheaply than a large number. Remember that all the elements in a selected cluster must be listed, even if only a few are to be chosen in the sample.

The final sample design will reflect these two constraints. In effect, we will probably select as many clusters as we can afford. So as not to leave this issue too open-ended, here is a rule of thumb: population researchers conventionally aim for the selection of 5 households per census block. If a total of 2,000 households are to be interviewed, researchers select 400 blocks and interview 5 households on each. Figure 6.10 presents a graphic overview of this process.

As we turn to more detailed procedures in cluster sampling, keep in mind that this method almost inevitably involves a loss of accuracy. First, as noted earlier, a multistage sample design is subject to a sampling error at each stage. Because the sample size is necessarily smaller at each stage than the total sample size, the sampling error at each stage will be greater than would be the case for a single-stage random sample of elements. Second, sampling error is estimated on the basis of observed variance among the sample elements. When those elements are drawn from relatively homogeneous clusters, the estimated sampling error will be too optimistic and so must be corrected in light of the cluster sample design.

Multistage Cluster Sampling with Stratification

Thus far, we have looked at cluster sampling as though a simple random sample were selected at each stage of the design. In fact, we can use stratification techniques to refine and improve the sample being selected. The basic options available are essentially the same as those possible in single-stage sampling from a list. In selecting a national sample of law enforcement officers, we might initially stratify our list of agencies by type (state, county, municipal), geographic region, size, and rural or urban location.

Once the primary sampling units (law enforcement agencies) have been grouped according to the relevant, available stratification variables, either simple random or systematic sampling techniques can be used to select the sample. We might select a specified number of units from each group or stratum, or we might arrange the stratified clusters in a continuous list and systematically sample that list.

To the extent that clusters are combined into homogeneous strata, the sampling error at this stage will be reduced. The primary goal of stratification, as before, is homogeneity.

In principle, stratification can take place at each level of sampling. The elements listed within a selected cluster might be stratified before the next stage of sampling. Typically, however, that is not done because we strive for relative homogeneity within clusters. If clusters are sufficiently similar, it is not necessary to stratify again.

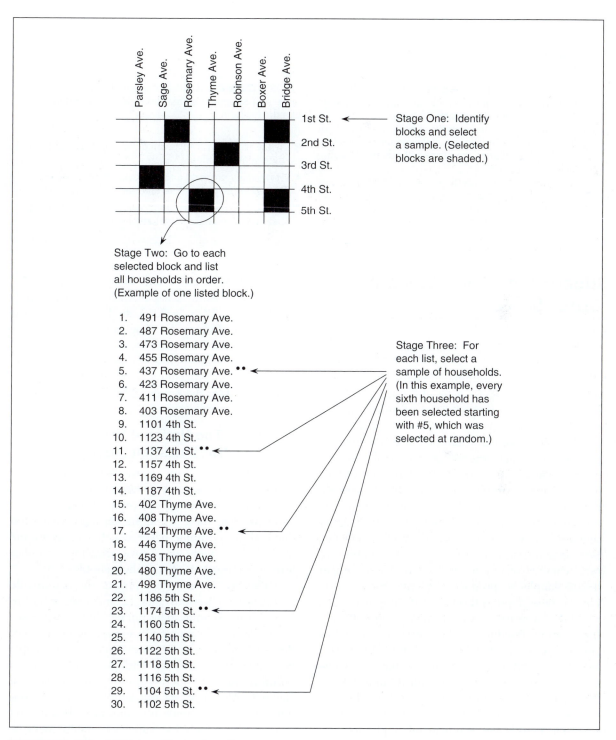

FIGURE 6.10 Multistage Cluster Sampling

THEORY AND SAMPLING

Theories of offending often describe why different types of people begin committing crimes, what sorts of paths or trajectories they follow over time, and what things might be associated with desistance, or ending criminal involvement. Collectively, this is often referred to as "crime through the life course" (Sampson and Laub 2005).

If you wanted to study people at different stages of offending, what sorts of samples would you draw? Stated somewhat differently, what are some possible sampling frames for studying crime through the life course? Think about some appropriate study populations and sampling frames for addressing questions like the following:

- What is the rate of involvement in crime among high school students?
- How many property and personal offenses are committed in the year before entering a state prison?
- Among former offenders, what is the effect of being married on criminal involvement?

Illustration: Two National Crime Surveys

Two national crime surveys show different ways of designing samples to achieve desired results.

Our discussion of sampling designs suggests that researchers can combine many different techniques of sampling and their various components in different ways to suit various needs. In fact, the different components of sampling can be tailored to specific purposes in much the same way that research design principles can be modified to suit various needs. Because sample frames suitable for simple random sampling are often unavailable, researchers use multistage cluster sampling to move from aggregate sample units to actual sample elements. We can add stratification to ensure that samples are representative of important variables. And we can design samples to produce elements that are proportionate or disproportionate to the population.

Two national crime surveys illustrate how these various building blocks may be combined in complex ways: (1) the National Crime Victimization Survey (NCVS), conducted by the U.S. Census Bureau; and (2) the British Crime Survey (BCS). Each is a multistage cluster sample, but the two surveys use different strategies for sampling to produce sufficient numbers of respondents in different categories. Our summary description is adapted from Truman and Planty (2012) for the NCVS and from Chaplin, Flatley, and Smith (2011) for the BCS. In 2012, the BCS was renamed the "Crime Survey for England and Wales" to reflect the establishment of a separate crime survey in Scotland. Our discussion draws on the innovative sampling procedures introduced and better documented for the pre-2012 BCS.

The National Crime Victimization Survey

Although various parts of the NCVS have been modified since the surveys were begun in 1972, the basic sampling strategies have remained relatively constant. The most significant changes have been fluctuations in sample size and a shift to telephone interviewing, with samples of telephone number listings eventually leading to households.

The NCVS seeks to represent the nationwide population of persons ages 12 and over who are living in households. The phrase "living in households" is significant. NCVS procedures are not designed to sample homeless persons or people who live in institutional settings such as military group housing, temporary housing, or correctional facilities. Also, because the sample targets persons who live in households, it cannot provide estimates of crimes in which a commercial establishment or business is the victim.

Because there is no national list of households in the United States, multistage cluster sampling must be used to proceed from larger units to households and their residents. The national sampling frame used in the first stage defines primary sampling units (PSUs) as large metropolitan areas, nonmetropolitan counties, or groups of contiguous counties (to represent rural areas).

The largest 93 PSUs are specified as "self-representing" and are automatically included in the first stage of sampling. The remaining PSUs are stratified by size, population density, reported crimes, and other variables. An additional 110 non-self-representing PSUs are then selected with a probability proportionate to the population of the PSU. Thus, for example, if one stratum includes Bugtussle, Texas (population 7,000), Punkinseed, Indiana (5,000), and Rancid, Missouri (3,000), the probability that each PSU will be selected is 7 in 15 for Bugtussle, 5 in 15 for Punkinseed, and 3 in 15 for Rancid.

The second stage of sampling involves designating four different sampling frames within each PSU. Each of these frames is used to select different types of subsequent units. First, the housing unit frame lists addresses of housing units from census records. Second, a group quarters frame lists group quarters such as dormitories and rooming houses from census records. Third, a building permit frame lists newly constructed housing units from local government sources. Finally, an area frame lists census blocks (physical geographic units), from which independent address lists are generated and sampled. Notice that these four frames are necessary because comprehensive, up-to-date lists of residential addresses are not available in this country.

For the 2011 NCVS, these procedures yielded completed interviews from 143,120 individuals living in 79,800 households (Truman and Planty 2012, 12). The sample design for the NCVS is an excellent illustration of the relationship between sample size and variation in the target population. Because serious crime is a relatively rare event when averaged across the entire U.S. population, very large samples must be drawn. And because no single list of the target population exists, samples are drawn in several stages.

For further information, consult NCVS documentation maintained by the Bureau of Justice Statistics (http://bjs.ojp.usdoj.gov/index.cfm?ty=dcdetail&iid=245). Also see the "National Crime Victimization Survey Resource Guide," maintained at the National Archive of Criminal Justice Data (http://www.icpsr.umich.edu/icpsrweb/NACJD/NCVS/).

The British Crime Survey

We have seen that NCVS sampling procedures begin with demographic units and work down to selection of housing units. BCS sampling is simplified by the existence of a national list of something close to addresses. The Postcode Address File (PAF) lists postal delivery points nationwide and is further subdivided to distinguish "small users," those addresses receiving less than 50 items per day. Even though 50 pieces of mail might still seem like quite a bit, this classification makes it easier to distinguish household addresses from commercial ones.

Postcode sectors, roughly corresponding to U.S. five-digit zip codes, are easily defined clusters of addresses from the PAF. Samples of addresses are then selected from within these sectors.

In addition to the core PAF sample, BCS researchers devised "booster samples" to increase the number of respondents who were ethnic minorities or ages 16 to 24. Victimization experiences of ethnic minorities were of special interest to police and other public officials. Young people were oversampled to complete a special questionnaire of self-report behavior items.

The ethnic minority booster was accomplished by first selecting respondents using formal sampling procedures. Interviewers then sought information about four housing units adjacent to the selected unit in an effort to determine if any residents were nonwhite. If adjacent units housed minority families, one was selected to be interviewed for the ethnic minority booster sample. This is an example of what Steven Thompson (1997) calls "adaptive sampling": probability samples are first selected, then those respondents are used to identify other individuals who meet some criterion. Increasing the number of respondents ages 16 to 24 was simpler—interviewers sought additional respondents in that age group within sampled households.

One final sampling dimension reflected the regional organization of police in England and Wales into 43 police areas. The BCS was further stratified to produce about 1,000 interviews in each police area to support analysis within those areas.

Apart from the young-person booster, once individual households were selected, one person age 16 or over was randomly chosen to provide information for all household members. Since 2009, children ages 10 to 15 have been sampled from some households. Sampling procedures initially produced about 60,000 addresses for the 2008–2009 BCS. Interviews were completed with 46,286 individuals for a response rate of about 76 percent.

Although sampling designs for both the BCS and the NCVS are more complex than we have represented in this discussion, the important point is how multistage cluster sampling is used in each. Notice two principal differences between the samples. First, the NCVS uses proportionate sampling to select a large number of respondents who may then represent the relatively rare attribute of victimization. The BCS samples a disproportionate number of minority and young residents, who are more likely to be victims of crime. Second, sampling procedures for the BCS are somewhat simpler than those for the NCVS, largely because a suitable sampling frame exists at the national level. Stratification and later-stage sampling are conducted to more efficiently represent each police area and to oversample minority respondents.

Probability Sampling in Review

Depending on the field situation, probability sampling can be very simple or extremely complex, time consuming, and expensive. Whatever the situation, however, it is usually the preferred method for selecting study elements. It's worth restating the two main reasons for this.

First, probability sampling avoids conscious or unconscious biases in element selection on the part of the researcher. If all elements in the population have an equal (or unequal and subsequently weighted) chance of selection, there is an excellent chance that the sample so selected will closely represent the population of all elements.

Second, probability sampling permits estimates of sampling error. Although no probability sample will be perfectly representative in all respects, controlled selection methods permit the researcher to estimate the degree of expected error.

Despite these advantages, it is sometimes impossible to use standard probability sampling methods. Sometimes, it isn't even appropriate to do so. In those cases, researchers turn to nonprobability sampling.

Nonprobability Sampling

In many research applications, nonprobability samples are necessary or advantageous.

You can no doubt envision situations in which it would be either impossible or unfeasible to select the kinds of probability samples we have described. Suppose we want to study auto thieves. There is no list of all auto thieves, nor are we likely to be able to create anything other than a partial and highly selective list. Moreover, probability sampling is sometimes inappropriate even if it is possible. In many such situations, **nonprobability sampling** procedures are called for. Recall that probability samples are defined as those in which the probability that any given sampling element will be selected is known. Conversely, in nonprobability sampling, the likelihood that any given element will be selected is not known.

We'll examine four types of nonprobability samples in this section: (1) purposive or judgmental sampling, (2) quota sampling, (3) the reliance on available subjects, and (4) snowball sampling.

Purposive Sampling

Occasionally, it may be appropriate to select a sample on the basis of our own knowledge of the population, its elements, and the nature of our research aims—in short, based on our judgment and the purpose of the study. Such a sample is called a **purposive sample**.

We may wish to study a small subset of a larger population in which many members of the subset are easily identified but the enumeration of all of them would be nearly impossible. For example, we might want to study members of community crime prevention groups; many members are easily visible, but it is not feasible to define and sample all members of community crime prevention organizations. In studying a sample of the most visible members, however, we may collect data sufficient for our purposes.

Criminal justice research often compares practices in different jurisdictions—cities or states, for example. In such cases, study elements may be selected because they exhibit some particular attribute. For example, Michael Leiber and Jayne Stairs (1999) were interested in how economic inequality combined with race to affect sentencing practices in Iowa juvenile courts. After controlling for economic status, they found that African American defendants received more restrictive sentences than white defendants did. Leiber and Stairs purposively selected three jurisdictions to obtain sample elements with adequate racial diversity in the state of Iowa. The researchers then selected over 5,000 juvenile cases processed in those three courts.

Researchers may also use purposive or judgmental sampling to represent patterns of complex variation. In their study of closed-circuit television (CCTV) systems, Martin Gill and Angela Spriggs (2005) describe how sites were sampled to reflect variation in the type of area (residential, commercial, city center, large parking facilities). Some individual CCTV projects were selected because of certain specific features—they were installed in a high-crime area, or the CCTV setup was notably expensive. One element of this study involved interviews to assess changes in fear of crime following CCTV installation. Angela Spriggs and associates (2005) sampled passersby on city-center streets. They first selected purposive samples of areas and spread their interviews across four day and time periods. This was done to reflect variation in the types of people encountered on different streets at different times. Sampling strategies were thus adapted because of an expected heterogeneity that would have been difficult to capture with random selection.

Pretesting a questionnaire is another situation in which purposive sampling is common. If, for example, we plan to study people's attitudes about court-ordered restitution for crime victims, we might want to test the questionnaire on a sample of crime victims. Instead of selecting a probability sample of the general population, we might select some number of known crime victims, perhaps from court records.

Quota Sampling

Like probability sampling, **quota sampling** addresses the issue of representativeness, although the two methods approach the issue quite differently. Quota sampling begins with a matrix or table describing the characteristics of the target population we wish to represent. To do this, we need to know, for example, what proportion of the population is male or female and what proportions fall into various age categories, education levels, ethnic groups, and so forth. In establishing a national quota sample, we need to know what proportion of the national population is, say, urban, eastern, male, under 25, white, working-class, and all the combinations of these attributes.

Once we have created such a matrix and assigned a relative proportion to each cell in the matrix, we can collect data from people who have all the characteristics of a given cell. We then assign all the persons in a given cell a weight appropriate to their portion of the total population. When all the sample elements are weighted in this way, the overall data should provide a reasonable representation of the total population.

Although quota sampling may resemble probability sampling, it has two inherent problems. First, the quota frame (the proportions that different cells represent) must be accurate, and it is often difficult to get up-to-date information for this purpose. A quota sample of auto thieves or teenage vandals would obviously suffer from this difficulty. Second, biases may exist in the selection of sample elements within a given cell—even though its proportion of the population is accurately estimated. An interviewer, instructed to interview five persons who meet a given complex set of characteristics, may still avoid people who live at the top of seven-story walk-ups, have particularly run-down homes, or own vicious dogs.

Quota and purposive sampling may be combined to produce samples that are intuitively, if not statistically, representative. For example, David Farrington, Trevor Bennett, and Brandon Welsh (2007) designed an experimental evaluation of CCTV impact on perceptions of crime and disorder in Cambridge, England. They wished to represent several characteristics of people who spent time outside in certain areas of the city. A probability sample was rejected because the authors wished to represent characteristics of city-center residents who used city streets, not necessarily people who lived in the city. So researchers selected passersby in target areas of Cambridge to meet quotas of 52 percent male, 40 percent between the ages of 16 and 29, and 92 percent white (2007, 190).

Reliance on Available Subjects

Relying on available subjects—that is, stopping people at a street corner or some other location—is sometimes misleadingly called "convenience sampling." University researchers frequently conduct surveys among the students enrolled in large lecture classes. The ease and economy of such a method explain its popularity; however, it seldom produces data of any general value. It may be useful to pretest a questionnaire, but it should not be used for a study purportedly describing students as a whole.

Reliance on available subjects can be an appropriate sampling method in some situations. It is generally best justified if the researcher wants to study the characteristics of people who are passing the sampling point at some specified time. For example, in her study of street lighting as a crime prevention strategy, Kate Painter (1996) interviewed samples of pedestrians as they walked through specified areas of London just before and 6 weeks after improvements were made in lighting conditions. Painter clearly understood the scope and limits of this sampling

technique. Her findings are described as applying to people who actually use area streets after dark, while recognizing that this population may be quite different from the population of area residents. Interviewing a sample of available evening pedestrians is an appropriate sampling technique for generalizing to the population of evening pedestrians, and the population of pedestrians will not be the same as the population of residents. Unlike Farrington and associates, Painter had no specific quotas for subjects in her sample.

In a more general sense, samples like Painter's select elements of a *process*—the process that generates evening pedestrians—rather than elements of a *population*. If we can safely assume that no systematic pattern generates elements of a process, then a sample of available elements as they happen to pass by can be considered to be representative. So, for example, if you are interested in studying crimes reported to police, then a sample of, say, every seventh crime report over a two-month period will be representative of the general population of crime reports over that two-month period.

Sometimes nonprobability and probability sampling techniques can be combined. For example, most attempts to sample homeless or street people rely on available subjects found in shelters, parks, or other locations. Salaam Semaan, Jennifer Lauby, and Jon Liebman (2002) suggest that once areas are located where homeless people congregate, individuals found there can be enumerated and then sampled. Here's a semi-hypothetical example.

In recent years, Michael Maxfield has casually observed that many people who appear to be homeless congregate at the corner of 9th Avenue and 41st Street in Manhattan. An efficient strategy for interviewing samples of homeless people would be a time-space sample where, for example, each hour individuals would be counted and some fraction sampled. Let's say we wished to interview 30 people and we spread those interviews over a six-hour period; we would try to interview five people per hour. So each hour we would count the number of people within some specific area (say, 30 at 1:00 p.m.), and then divide that number by five to

TABLE 6.1 Systematic Sampling of Available Subjects

Time	People Present	Interviews	Sampling Fraction
10:00 a.m.	15	5	1/3
11:00 a.m.	20	5	1/4
12:00 p.m.	15	5	1/3
1:00 p.m.	30	5	1/6
2:00 p.m.	20	5	1/4
3:00 p.m.	50	5	1/5
Total	135	30	1/4

obtain a sampling fraction (6 in this case). Recalling our earlier discussion of systematic probability sampling, we would then select a random starting point to identify the first person to interview. Then we would select the sixth person after that, and so on. This approach would yield an unbiased sample that represented the population of street people on one Manhattan corner over a six-hour period. Table 6.1 illustrates how we could complete our 30 interviews, selecting varying fractions of those present at different times.

As it happens, 41st Street and 9th Avenue in Manhattan is the rear entrance to the Port Authority bus terminal. Marcus Felson and associates (1996) described efforts to reduce crime and disorder in the Port Authority terminal, a place they claim is the world's busiest bus station. Among the most important objectives were to reduce perceptions of crime problems and to improve how travelers felt about the Port Authority terminal. These are research questions appropriate to some sort of survey. Because more than 170,000 passengers pass through the bus station on an average spring day, obtaining a sufficiently large sample of users presents no difficulty. The problem was how to select a sample. Felson and associates point out that stopping passengers on their way to or from a bus was out of the question. Most passengers are commuters whose journey to and from work is timed to the minute, with none to spare for interviewers' questions. Here's how Felson and associates

describe the solution and the sampling strategy it embodied (1996, 90–91):

> Response rates would have been low if the Port Authority had tried to interview rushing customers or to hand out questionnaires to be returned later. Their solution was ingenious. The Port Authority drew a sample of outgoing buses … and placed representatives aboard. After the bus had departed, he or she would hand out a questionnaire to be completed during the trip … [and] collect these questionnaires as each customer arrived at the destination. This procedure produced a very high response rate and high completion rate for each item.

Snowball Sampling

Another type of nonprobability sampling that closely resembles the available-subjects approach is called **snowball sampling**. Commonly used in field observation studies or specialized interviewing, snowball sampling begins by identifying a single subject or small number of subjects and then asking the subject(s) to identify others like him or her who might be willing to participate in a study.

Criminal justice research on active criminals or deviants frequently uses snowball sampling techniques. The researcher often makes an initial contact by consulting criminal justice agency records to identify, say, someone convicted of auto theft and placed on probation. That person is interviewed and asked to suggest other auto thieves whom researchers could contact. Stephen Baron and Timothy Hartnagel (1998) studied violence among homeless youths in Edmonton, Canada, identifying their sample through snowball techniques. Similarly, snowball sampling is often used to study drug users and dealers. Martin Bouchard (2007) began with contacts from colleagues to identify marijuana growers in Quebec, Canada, who then referred him to other active cultivators.

Contacting an initial subject or informant who will then refer the researcher to other subjects can be especially difficult in studies of active offenders. As in most aspects of criminal justice research, the various approaches to initiating contacts for snowball sampling have advantages and disadvantages. Beginning with subjects who have a previous arrest or conviction is usually the easiest method for researchers, but it suffers from potential bias by depending on offenders who are known to police or other officials (Jacobs, Topalli, and Wright 2003).

Studies by researchers at the University of Missouri–St. Louis offer good examples of snowball samples of offenders that are not dependent on contacts with criminal justice officials. Beginning with a street-savvy ex-offender, these researchers identified samples of burglars (Wright and Decker 1994), members of youth gangs (Decker and

Van Winkle 1996), armed robbers (Wright and Decker 1997), and carjackers (Jacobs 2012). It's especially difficult to identify active offenders as research subjects, but these examples illustrate notably clever uses of snowball sampling techniques.

Wright and Decker's (1994) study provides a good example. The ex-offender contacted a few active burglars and a few "streetwise noncriminals," who, in turn, referred researchers to additional subjects, and so on. This process is illustrated in Figure 6.11, which shows the chain of referrals that accumulated a snowball sample of 105 individuals.

Starting at the top of Figure 6.11, the ex-offender put researchers in contact with two subjects

FIGURE 6.11   Snowball Sample Referral Chart

Source: Reprinted from Richard T. Wright and Scott H. Decker, *Burglars on the Job: Streetlife and Residential Break-ins* (Boston: Northeastern University Press, 1994). Reprinted by permission of Northeastern University Press.

directly (001 and 003), a small-time criminal, three streetwise noncriminals, a crack addict, a youth worker, and someone serving probation. Continuing downward, the small-time criminal was especially helpful, identifying 12 subjects who participated in the study (005, 006, 008, 009, 010, 021, 022, 023, 025, 026, 030, and 032). Notice how the snowball effect continues, with subject 026 identifying subjects 028 and 029. Notice also that some subjects were themselves "nominated" by more than one source. In the middle of the bottom row in Figure 6.11, for example, subject 064 was mentioned by subjects 060 and 061.

Amber Horning describes another good example of snowball sampling in Chapter 8, based on her qualitative interviews with New York City pimps.

Nonprobability Sampling in Review

Snowball samples are essentially variations on purposive samples (we want to sample juvenile gang members) and on samples of available subjects (sample elements identify other sample elements that are available to us). Each of these is a nonprobability sampling technique. And, like other types of

nonprobability samples, snowball samples are most appropriate when it is impossible to determine the probability that any given element will be selected in a sample. Furthermore, snowball sampling and related techniques may be necessary when the target population is difficult to locate or even identify. Approaching pedestrians who happen to pass by, for example, is not an efficient way to select a sample of prostitutes or juvenile gang members. In contrast, approaching pedestrians *is* an appropriate sampling method for studying pedestrians, whereas drawing a probability sample of urban residents to identify people who walk in specific areas of the city would be costly and inefficient.

Like other elements of criminal justice research, sampling plans must be adapted to specific research applications. When it's important to make estimates of the accuracy of our samples, and when suitable sampling frames are possible, we use probability sampling techniques. When no reasonable sampling frame is available and we cannot draw a probability sample, we cannot make estimates about sample accuracy. Fortunately, in such situations, we can make use of a variety of approaches for drawing nonprobability samples.

SUMMARY

- The logic of probability sampling forms the foundation for representing large populations with small subsets of those populations.

- The chief criterion of a sample's quality is the degree to which it is representative—the extent to which the characteristics of the sample are the same as those of the population from which it was selected.

- The most carefully selected sample is almost never a perfect representation of the population from which it was selected. Some degree of sampling error always exists.

- Probability sampling methods provide one excellent way of selecting samples that will be

  quite representative. They make it possible to estimate the amount of sampling error that should be expected in a given sample.

- The chief principle of probability sampling is that every member of the total population must have some known nonzero probability of being selected in the sample.

- Our ability to estimate population parameters with sample statistics is rooted in the sampling distribution and probability theory. If we draw a large number of samples of a given size, sample statistics will cluster around the true population parameter. As sample size increases, the cluster becomes tighter.

- A variety of sampling designs can be used and combined to suit different populations and research purposes. Each type of sampling has its own advantages and disadvantages.

- Simple random sampling is logically the most fundamental technique in probability sampling, although it is seldom used in practice.

- Systematic sampling involves using a sampling frame to select units that appear at some specified interval—for example, every 8th, or 15th, or 1,023rd unit. This method is functionally equivalent to simple random sampling.

- Stratification improves the representativeness of a sample by reducing the sampling error.

- Disproportionate stratified sampling is especially useful when we want to select adequate numbers of certain types of subjects who are relatively rare in the population we are studying.

- Multistage cluster sampling is frequently used when there is no list of all the members of a population.

- The NCVS and the BCS are national crime surveys based on multistage cluster samples. Sampling methods for each survey illustrate different approaches to representing relatively rare events.

- Nonprobability sampling methods are less statistically representative and less reliable than probability sampling methods. However, they are often easier and cheaper to use.

- Purposive sampling is used when researchers wish to select specific elements of a population. This may be because the elements are believed to be representative of extreme cases or because they represent the range of variation expected in a population.

- In quota sampling, researchers begin with a detailed description of the characteristics of the total population and then select sample members in a way that includes the different composite profiles that exist in the population.

- When it is not possible to draw nonprobability samples through other means, researchers often rely on available subjects. Professors sometimes do this—students in their classes are available subjects.

- Snowball samples accumulate subjects through chains of referrals and are most commonly used in field research.

KEY TERMS

binomial variable, p. 146

cluster samples, p. 155

confidence interval, p. 150

confidence levels, p. 150

disproportionate stratified sampling, p. 154

equal probability of selection method (EPSEM), p. 143

nonprobability sampling, p. 160

population, p. 143

population parameter, p. 144

probability sampling, p. 140

purposive sample, p. 161

quota sampling, p. 161

sample element, p. 143

sample statistic, p. 144

samples, p. 140

sampling distribution, p. 145

sampling frame, p. 146

sampling units, p. 155

simple random sample, p. 153

snowball sampling, p. 163

standard error, p. 149

stratification, p. 153

systematic sampling, p. 153

REVIEW QUESTIONS AND EXERCISES

1. Discuss possible study populations, elements, sampling units, and sampling frames for drawing a sample to represent the populations listed here. You may wish to limit your discussion to populations in a specific state or other jurisdiction.

   a. Municipal police officers

   b. Felony court judges

   c. Auto thieves

   d. Licensed automobile drivers

   e. State police superintendents

   f. Persons incarcerated in county jails

2. What steps would be involved in selecting a multistage cluster sample of undergraduate students taking criminal justice research methods courses in U.S. colleges and universities?

3. Stop-and-frisk is a controversial tactic in which police approach persons on the street who appear to act suspiciously, "frisk" them for weapons or contraband, then ask some questions. Research in New York City has shown that young males of color are more often stopped than older people, females, or whites (Jones-Brown, Gill, and Trone 2010). Briefly describe two approaches to sampling subjects for a research study on people's experiences of stop-and-frisk.

CHAPTER 7

Survey Research

We'll examine how mail, interview, and telephone surveys can be used in criminal justice research.

Knowledge and Attitudes About Sex Offenders

by Nerea Marteache
California State University, San Bernardino

In my second year of graduate study at Rutgers University, I worked with Professor Michael Maxfield to do research on what people know about sex offenders and how they believe sex offenders should be punished or treated. It took a lot longer than I thought, but results were finally published in the summer of 2012 (Marteache 2012). Because it illustrates many features of research discussed in this and earlier chapters of this textbook, Professor Maxfield asked me to write a brief description of the project and how it developed.

Knowledge and attitudes about sex offenders are the kinds of topic that can only be studied by asking questions. State governments in the United States and in other countries, including my native Spain, have reacted to widely publicized stories about sex offenses by increasing penalties for sex offenders and expanding supervision of offenders after they are released from custody. My study had two main goals: (1) to provide detailed data and information about sex offenders to study participants and then assess how their knowledge and attitudes changed, and (2) to assess the stability of attitudes and knowledge after subjects viewed simulated mass media coverage of sex offenses.

My principal questions were as follows:

- Does instruction about sex offenders change knowledge about sex offenders and attitudes regarding punishment or treatment?

- Does viewing a sensationalist video about a serious sex offense change knowledge and attitudes less among those who had instruction about sex offenders?

I enlisted the aid of two colleagues in Spain, one at a university in Barcelona and the other at a university in Madrid. They distributed to students at each university questionnaires that I designed. Students completed the questionnaires at three time points over the course of the fall 2009 semester. Students in treatment groups participated in a special class that offered two hours of instruction and a debate about sex offenders and treatment. Students in control groups at each university attended a normal class session of the course. With Professor Maxfield's assistance at Rutgers, I designed the instructional materials that were presented by my colleagues in Spain. After participating in a treatment or control class, all subjects completed a second questionnaire.

In the next stage of the project, I developed an intervention to simulate mass media coverage of sex offenders. This was a sensationalist news video about a horrific sex offense case that was widely known in Spain. For the control group, I used a similarly sensationalist video about cocaine use in Spain. Students in Barcelona and Madrid were randomly assigned to view either the sex offense or drug abuse video. After viewing the videos, students completed a third questionnaire that measured their knowledge and attitudes about sex offenders.

The English version of part of the questionnaire I used is shown below. Questions are part of a battery of items developed by Wesley Church and associates (2008). The reliability of these questions has been established, so I used them rather than make up new questions. Data collection was completed by the end of the fall

(continued)

2009 semester. I returned to Rutgers after the semester break with 801 completed questionnaires.

This project went pretty much as planned. But it was a lot more work than I initially thought. This was due partly to the complex design and partly to the logistics of being in New Jersey while two colleagues were collecting the data in Spain.

Survey for University Students About Public Opinion on Sexual Offenders

Our research group is carrying out a project about public opinion on sexual offenders. To do so, we need your help. Please answer the questions below and provide the answer that most accurately expresses your opinion. If you have any doubt about the meaning of a question, just raise your hand and a member of the research group will help you. The information provided will be confidential.

Thank you for participating in this study.

Below are 18 statements about sex offenders and sex offenses. Please select the corresponding number from the rating scale given below for the answer that best describes the way you feel or what you believe.

Most of the statements below are difficult to prove or verify in an absolute sense, and many are specifically about your opinion based on what you may have heard, read, or learned; thus, we are less interested in the "right" or "wrong" answers, and more interested in your beliefs and opinions regarding sex offenders.

Even if you have no general knowledge about the issue, please provide an answer to each question.

RATING SCALE:

1 – Strongly disagree 2 – Disagree 3 – Probably disagree   4 – Probably agree   5 – Agree   6 – Strongly agree

	Rating
a. With support and therapy, someone who committed a sexual offense can learn to change their behavior.	☐
b. People who commit sex offenses should lose their civil rights (e.g., voting and privacy).	☐
c. People who commit sex offenses want to have sex more often than the average person.	☐
d. Male sex offenders should be punished more severely than female sex offenders.	☐
e. Sexual fondling (inappropriate unwarranted touch) is not as bad as rape.	☐
f. Sex offenders prefer to stay home alone rather than be around lots of people.	☐
g. Most sex offenders do not have close friends.	☐

Source: Church, Wesley T., et al. 2008. "The Community Attitudes Toward Sex Offenders Scale: The Development of a Psychometric Assessment Instrument." *Research on Social Work Practice* 18: 251–259.

Introduction

Asking people questions is the most common data collection method in social science.

A little-known survey was attempted among French workers in 1880. A German political sociologist mailed some 25,000 questionnaires to workers to determine the extent of their exploitation by employers. The rather lengthy questionnaire included items such as these:

> Does your employer or his representative resort to trickery in order to defraud you of a part of your earnings? If you are paid piece-rates, is the quality of the article made a pretext for fraudulent deductions from your wages?

The survey researcher in this case was not George Gallup but Karl Marx (1880, 208). Although 25,000 questionnaires were mailed out, there is no record of any being returned. And you need not know much about survey methods to recognize the loaded questions posed by Marx.

Survey research is perhaps the most frequently used mode of observation in sociology and political science, and surveys are often used in criminal justice research as well. You have no doubt been a respondent in a survey, and you may have conducted a **survey** yourself.

We begin this chapter by discussing the criminal justice topics that are most appropriate for survey methods. Next, we cover the basic principles of how to ask people questions for research purposes, including some of the details of questionnaire construction. We describe the three basic ways of administering questionnaires—self-administration, face-to-face interviews, and telephone interviews—and summarize the strengths and weaknesses of each method. After discussing more specialized interviewing techniques, such as focus groups, we conclude the chapter with some advice on the benefits and pitfalls of conducting your own surveys.

Topics Appropriate to Survey Research

Surveys have a wide variety of uses in basic and applied criminal justice research.

Surveys may be used for descriptive, explanatory, exploratory, and applied research. They are best suited for studies that have individual people as the units of analysis. They are often used for other units of analysis as well, such as households or organizations. Even in these cases, however, one or more individual people act as **respondent** or informant.

For example, researchers sometimes use victimization incidents as units of analysis in examining data from crime surveys. The fact that some people may be victimized more than once and others not at all means that victimization incidents are not the same units as individuals. However, a survey questionnaire must still be administered to people who provide information about victimization incidents. In a similar fashion, the National Jail Census, conducted every five or so years by the Census Bureau, collects information about local detention facilities. Jails are the units of analysis, but information about each jail is provided by individuals. The National Youth Gang Survey has been conducted for many years. Though it seeks information about gangs, the survey is sent to law enforcement agencies and the questionnaire is completed by individuals in police departments.

We now consider some broad categories of research applications in which survey methods are especially appropriate.

Counting Crime

We touched on this use of surveys in Chapter 4. Asking people about victimization is a measure of crime that adjusts for some of the limitations of data collected by police. Of course, survey measures have their own shortcomings. Most of these difficulties, such as recall error and reluctance to discuss victimization with interviewers, are inherent in survey methods. Nevertheless, victim surveys have become important sources of data about the volume of crime in the United States and in other countries.

Self-Reports

Surveys that ask people about crimes they may have committed were also discussed in Chapter 4. For research that seeks to explore or explain why people commit criminal, delinquent, or deviant acts, asking questions is the best method available.

Within the general category of self-report surveys, two different applications are distinguished by their target population and sampling methods. Studies of offenders select samples of respondents known to have committed crimes, often prisoners. Typically the focus is on the *frequency* of offending—how many crimes of various types are committed by active offenders over a period of time.

The other type of self-report survey focuses on the *prevalence* of offending—how many people commit crimes, in contrast to how many crimes are committed by a target population of offenders. Such surveys typically use samples that represent a broader population, such as U.S. households, adult males, or high school seniors. The Monitoring the Future survey, briefly described in Chapter 4, is a self-report survey that centers on measuring the prevalence of offending among high school seniors.

General-population surveys and surveys of offenders tend to present different types of difficulties in connection with the validity and reliability of self-reports. Recall error and the reporting of fabricated offenses may be problems in a survey of high-rate offenders (Roberts et al. 2005), whereas respondents in general-population self-report surveys may be reluctant to disclose illegal behavior. When we discuss questionnaire construction later in this chapter, we will present examples and suggestions for creating self-report items.

Perceptions and Attitudes

Another application of surveys in criminal justice is to learn how people feel about crime and criminal justice policy. Public views about sentencing policies,

gun control, police performance, and drug abuse are often solicited in opinion polls. Begun in 1972, the General Social Survey is an ongoing survey of social indicators in the United States. Questions about fear of crime and other perceptions of crime problems are regularly included. Since the 1970s, a growing number of explanatory studies have been conducted on public perceptions of crime and crime problems. A large body of research on fear of crime has grown, in part, from the realization that fear and its behavioral consequences are much more widespread among the population than is actual criminal victimization (Ditton and Farrall 2007).

Targeted Victim Surveys

Victim surveys that target individual cities or neighborhoods are important tools for evaluating policy innovations. Many criminal justice programs seek to prevent or reduce crime in a specific area, but crimes reported to police cannot be used to evaluate many types of programs.

To see why this is so, consider a hypothetical community policing program that encourages neighborhood residents to report all suspected crimes to the police. Results from the National Crime Victimization Survey (NCVS) have consistently shown that many minor incidents are not reported because victims believe that police will not want to be bothered. But if a new program stresses that police actually *want* to be bothered, the proportion of crimes reported may increase, resulting in what appears to be an increase in crime.

The solution is to conduct targeted victim surveys before and after introducing a policy change. Such victim surveys are especially appropriate for evaluating any policy that may increase crime reporting as a side effect.

Consider also that large-scale surveys such as the NCVS cannot be used to evaluate local crime prevention programs. This is because the NCVS is designed to represent the national population of persons who live in households. Although NCVS data for the 11 largest states and 3 largest cities can be analyzed separately (Lauritsen and Schaum 2005), the NCVS is not representative of any particular local jurisdiction. It is not possible to identify the specific location of victimizations from NCVS data.

The community victim surveys designed by the Bureau of Justice Statistics (BJS) and the Office of Community Oriented Policing Services (COPS) help with each of these needs. Local surveys can be launched specifically to evaluate local crime prevention efforts. Or innovative programs can be timed to correspond to regular cycles of local surveys. In each case, the BJS-COPS guide (Weisel 1999) presents advice on drawing samples to represent local jurisdictions.

Another type of targeted victim survey is one that focuses on particular types of incidents that might target more narrowly defined population segments. A good example is the National Intimate Partner and Sexual Violence Survey by the Centers for Disease Control and Prevention National Center for Injury Prevention and Control (Black et al. 2011). Screening questions presented explicit descriptions of sexual and other violence with the specific purpose of providing better information about these incidents that have proved difficult to measure through general-purpose crime surveys.

Other Evaluation Uses

Other types of surveys may be appropriate for applied studies. A good illustration of this is a continuing series of neighborhood surveys to evaluate community policing in Chicago. Here's an example of how the researchers link their information needs to surveys (Chicago Community Policing Evaluation Consortium 2004, 2):

> Because it is a participatory program, CAPS [Chicago's Alternative Policing Strategy] depends on the effectiveness of campaigns to bring it to the public's attention and on the success of efforts to get the public involved in beat meetings and other district projects. The surveys enable us to track the public's awareness and involvement in community policing in Chicago.

In general, surveys are well suited to evaluate policy that seeks to change attitudes, beliefs, or perceptions. Consider a program designed to promote victim and witness cooperation in criminal court by reducing case-processing time. At first, we might consider direct measures of case-processing time as indicators of program success. If the program goal is to increase cooperation, however, a survey that asks how victims and witnesses perceive case-processing time will be more appropriate.

Guidelines for Asking Questions

How questions are asked is the single most important feature of survey research.

A defining feature of survey methods is that research concepts are operationalized by asking people questions. Several general guidelines can assist in framing and asking questions that serve as excellent operationalizations of variables. It is important also to be aware of pitfalls that can result in useless and even misleading information. We'll begin with some of the options available for creating a questionnaire.

Open-Ended and Closed-Ended Questions

In asking questions, researchers have two basic options, and each can accommodate certain variations. The first is the **open-ended question**, in which the respondent is asked to provide his or her own answers. For example, the respondent may be asked, "What do you feel is the most important crime problem facing the police in your city today?" and be provided with a space to write in the answer (or be asked to report it orally to an interviewer). The other option is a **closed-ended question**, in which the respondent is asked to select an answer from among a list provided by the researcher.

Closed-ended questions are especially useful because they provide more uniform responses and are more easily processed. They often can be transferred directly into a data file. Open-ended responses, in contrast, must be coded before they can be processed for analysis. This coding process often requires that the researcher interpret the meaning of responses, which opens up the possibility of misunderstanding and researcher bias. Also, some respondents may give answers that are essentially irrelevant to the researcher's intent.

The chief shortcoming of closed-ended questions lies in the researcher's structuring of responses. When the relevant answers to a given question are relatively clear, there should be no problem. In some cases, however, the researcher's list of responses may fail to include some important answers. When we ask about "the most important crime problem facing the police in your city today," for example, our checklist might omit certain crime problems that respondents consider important. Chapter 8 on qualitative interviewing offers details on phrasing and using open-ended questions.

In constructing closed-ended questions, we are best guided by two of the requirements for operationalizing variables stated in Chapter 4. First, the response categories provided should be exhaustive: they should include all the possible responses that might be expected. Often, researchers ensure this by adding a category labeled something like "Other (Please specify: ___)." Second, the answer categories must be mutually exclusive: the respondent should not feel compelled to select more than one. In some cases, researchers solicit multiple answers, but doing so can create difficulties in subsequent data processing and analysis. To ensure that categories are mutually exclusive, we should carefully consider each combination of categories, asking whether a person could reasonably choose more than one answer. In addition, it is useful to add an instruction that respondents should select the one best answer. However, this is still not a satisfactory substitute for a carefully constructed set of responses.

Questions and Statements

The term **questionnaire** suggests a collection of questions, but a typical questionnaire probably has as many statements as questions. This is because researchers often are interested in determining the extent to which respondents hold a particular attitude or perspective. Researchers try to summarize the attitude in a fairly brief statement; then they present that statement and ask respondents whether they agree or disagree with it. Rensis Likert formalized this procedure through the creation of the Likert scale, a format in which respondents are asked whether they strongly agree, agree, disagree, or strongly disagree, or perhaps strongly approve, approve, and so forth. The sample items from Nerea Marteache's questionnaire provided at the beginning of this chapter illustrate this technique.

Both questions and statements may be used profitably. Using both in a questionnaire adds flexibility in the design of items and can make the questionnaire more interesting as well.

Make Items Clear

It should go without saying that questionnaire items must be clear and unambiguous, but the broad proliferation of unclear and ambiguous questions in surveys makes the point worth stressing here. Researchers commonly become so deeply involved in the topic that opinions and perspectives that are clear to them will not be at all clear to respondents, many of whom have given little or no thought to the topic. Or researchers may have only a superficial understanding of the topic and so may fail to specify the intent of a question sufficiently. The question "What do you think about the governor's decision concerning prison furloughs?" may evoke in the respondent some counterquestions: "Which governor's decision?" "What are prison furloughs?" "What did the governor decide?" Questionnaire items should be precise so that the respondent knows exactly what the researcher wants an answer to.

Frequently, researchers ask respondents for a single answer to a combination question. Such double-barreled questions seem to occur most often when the researcher has personally identified with a complex question. For example, the researcher might ask respondents to agree or disagree with the statement "The Department of Corrections should stop releasing inmates for weekend furloughs and concentrate on rehabilitating criminals." Although many people will unequivocally agree with the statement and others will unequivocally disagree, still others will be unable to answer. Some might want to terminate the furlough program and punish—not rehabilitate—prisoners. Others might want to expand rehabilitation efforts while maintaining weekend furloughs; they can neither agree nor disagree without misleading the researcher.

Short Items Are Best

In the interest of being unambiguous and precise and pointing to the relevance of an issue, researchers often create long, complicated items. That should be avoided. In the case of questionnaires that respondents complete themselves, they are often unwilling to study an item to understand it. The respondent should be able to read an item quickly, understand its intent, and select or provide an answer without difficulty. In general, it's safe to assume that respondents will read items quickly and give quick answers; therefore, short, clear items that will not be misinterpreted under those conditions are best. Questions read to respondents in person or over the phone should be similarly brief.

Avoid Negative Items

A negation in a questionnaire item paves the way for easy misinterpretation. Asked to agree or disagree with the statement "Drugs such as marijuana should not be legalized," many respondents will overlook the word *not* and answer on that basis. Thus, some will agree with the statement when they are in favor of legalizing marijuana and others will agree when they oppose it. And we may never know which is which.

Biased Items and Terms

Recall from the earlier discussion of conceptualization and operationalization that there are no ultimately true meanings for any of the concepts we typically study in social science. This same general principle applies to the responses we get from persons in a survey.

The meaning of a given response to a question depends in large part on the wording of the question. That is true of every question and answer. Some questions seem to encourage particular responses more than other questions. In the context of questionnaires, **bias** refers to any property of a question that encourages respondents to answer in a particular way. Most researchers recognize the likely effect of a question such as "Do you support the president's use of targeted killing by remotely controlled drone aircraft to promote the safety and security of all Americans?" and no reputable researcher would use such an item. The biasing effect of items and terms is far subtler than this example suggests, however.

The mere identification of an attitude or position with a prestigious (or unpopular) person or agency can bias responses. For example, an item that starts with "Do you agree or disagree with the recent Supreme Court decision that …" might have this effect. We are not suggesting that such wording will necessarily produce consensus or even a majority in support of the position identified with the prestigious person or agency. Rather, support will likely be greater than what would have been obtained without such identification.

Sometimes, the impact of different forms of question wording is relatively subtle. For example, Kenneth Rasinski (1989) analyzed the results of several General Social Survey studies of attitudes toward government spending. He found that the way programs were identified had an impact on the amount of public support they received. Here are some comparisons:

More Support	Less Support
"Assistance to the poor"	"Welfare"
"Halting the rising crime rate"	"Law enforcement"
"Dealing with drug addiction"	"Drug rehabilitation"
"Protecting Social Security"	"Social Security"

In 1986, for example, 63 percent of respondents said too little money was being spent on "assistance to the poor," while in a matched survey that year, only 23 percent said we were spending too little on "welfare."

The main guidance we offer for avoiding bias is that researchers imagine how they would feel giving each of the answers they offer to respondents. If they would feel embarrassed, perverted, inhumane, stupid, irresponsible, or anything like that, then they should give some serious thought to whether others will be willing to give those answers. Researchers must carefully examine the purpose of their inquiry and construct items that will be most useful to it.

We also need to be generally wary of what researchers call the *social desirability* of questions and answers. Whenever we ask people for information, they answer through a filter of what will make them look good. That is especially true if they are being interviewed in a face-to-face situation.

The Centers for Disease Control and Prevention (Choi and Pak 2005) provides an excellent analysis of both obvious and not-so-obvious ways in which your choice of terms can bias and otherwise confuse responses to questionnaires. Among other things, they warn against using ambiguous, technical, uncommon, or vague words. Their thorough analysis includes many concrete illustrations.

Designing Self-Report Items

Social desirability is one of the problems that plagues self-report crime questions in general population surveys. Adhering to the ethical principles of confidentiality and anonymity, as well as convincing respondents that we are doing so, is one way of getting more truthful responses to self-report items. Other techniques can help us avoid or reduce problems with self-report items.

One method, used in earlier versions of the British Crime Survey (BCS), is to introduce a group of self-report items with a disclaimer and to sanitize the presentation of offenses. The self-report section of the 1984 BCS began with this introduction:

> There are lots of things which are actually crimes, but which are done by lots of people, and which many people do not think of as crimes. On this card [printed card handed to respondents] are a list of eight of them. For each one, can you tell me how many people

you think do it—most people, a lot of people, or no one.

Respondents then read a card, shown in Figure 7.1, that presented descriptions of various offenses. Interviewers first asked respondents how many people they thought ever did X, where X corresponded to the letter for an offense shown in Figure 7.1. Next, respondents were asked whether they had ever done X. Interviewers then moved on down the list of letters for each offense on the card.

This procedure incorporates three techniques to guard against the socially desirable response of not admitting to having committed a crime. First, the disclaimer seeks to reassure respondents that "many people" do not really think of various acts as crimes. Second, respondents are asked how many people they think commit each offense before being asked whether they have done so themselves. This takes advantage of a common human

---

A.	Taken office supplies from work (such as stationery, envelopes, and pens) when not supposed to.
B.	Taken things other than office supplies from work (such as tools, money, or other goods) when not supposed to.
C.	Fiddled expenses [fiddled is the Queen's English equivalent of fudged].
D.	Deliberately traveled [on a train] without a ticket or paid too low a fare.
E.	Failed to declare something at customs on which duty was payable.
F.	Cheated on tax.
G.	Used cannabis (hashish, marijuana, ganga, grass).
H.	Regularly driven a car when they know they have drunk enough to be well above the legal limit.

FIGURE 7.1 Showcard for Self-Report Items, 1984 British Crime Survey

Source: Adapted from the 1984 British Crime Survey (NOP Market Research Limited 1985).

justification for engaging in certain kinds of behavior—other people do it. Third, asking whether they "have ever done X" is less confrontational than asking whether they "have ever cheated on an expense account." Again, the foibles of human behavior are at work here, in much the same way that people use euphemisms such as *restroom* for "toilet" and *sleep together* for "have sexual intercourse." It is, of course, not realistic to expect that such ploys will reassure all respondents. Furthermore, disclaimers about serious offenses such as rape or bank robbery would be ludicrous. But such techniques illustrate how thoughtful wording and introductions can be incorporated into sensitive questions.

Self-report surveys of known offenders encounter different problems. Incarcerated persons may be reluctant to admit committing crimes because of the legal consequences. High-rate offenders may have difficulty distinguishing among a number of different crimes or remembering even approximate dates. Sorting out dates and details of individual crimes among high-rate offenders requires different strategies.

One technique that is useful in surveys of active offenders is to interview subjects several times at regular intervals. Other research asks offenders to complete "crime calendars" on which they make records of weekly or monthly offenses committed. Jennifer Roberts and associates (2005) found that more frequent interviews were necessary for use by high-rate offenders and that crime calendars were best suited for tracking more serious offenses.

Obtaining valid and reliable results from self-report items is challenging, but self-report survey techniques are important tools for addressing certain types of criminal justice research questions. For this reason, researchers are constantly striving to improve self-report items. See the collection of essays by Joel Kennet and Joseph Gfroerer (2005) for a detailed discussion of issues involved in measuring self-reported drug use through the National Household Survey on Drug Abuse. A National Research Council report (2001) discusses self-report survey measures more generally.

Computer technology has made it possible to significantly improve self-reported items. David Matz (2007) describes advances in self-report items from recent surveys that supplement the British Crime Survey. We present examples later in the chapter when we focus on different modes of survey administration.

Questionnaire Construction

After settling on question content, researchers must consider the format and organization of all items in a questionnaire.

Because questionnaires are the fundamental instruments of survey research, we now turn our attention to some of the established techniques for constructing them. The following sections are best considered as a continuation of our theoretical discussions in Chapter 4 of conceptualization and measurement.

General Questionnaire Format

The format of a questionnaire is just as important as the nature and wording of the questions. An improperly laid-out questionnaire can cause respondents to miss questions, confuse them about the nature of the data desired, and even lead them to throw the questionnaire away.

As a general rule, the questionnaire should be uncluttered. Inexperienced researchers tend to fear that their questionnaire will look too long, so they squeeze several questions onto a single line, abbreviate questions, and try to use as few pages as possible. Such efforts are ill-advised and even counterproductive. Putting more than one question on a line will cause some respondents to miss the second question altogether. Some respondents will misinterpret abbreviated questions. And, more generally, respondents who have spent considerable time on the first page of what seemed a short questionnaire will be more demoralized than respondents who quickly completed the first several pages of what initially seemed a long form. Moreover, the latter will have made fewer errors and will not have been forced to reread confusing, abbreviated questions. Nor will they have been forced to write a long answer in a tiny space.

Contingency Questions

Quite often in questionnaires, certain questions are clearly relevant to only some of the respondents and irrelevant to others. A victim survey, for example, presents batteries of questions about victimization incidents that are meaningful only to crime victims.

Frequently, this situation—realizing that the topic is relevant only to some respondents—arises when we wish to ask a series of questions about a certain topic. We may want to ask whether respondents belong to a particular organization and, if so, how often they attend meetings, whether they have held office in the organization, and so forth. Or we might want to ask whether respondents have heard anything about a certain policy proposal, such as opening a youth shelter in the neighborhood, and then investigate the attitudes of those who have heard of it.

The subsequent questions in series such as these are called *contingency questions*; whether they are to be asked and answered is *contingent* on the response to the first question in the series. The proper use of contingency questions can make it easier for respondents to complete the questionnaire because they do not have to answer questions that are irrelevant to them.

Contingency questions can be presented in several formats on printed questionnaires. The one shown in Figure 7.2 is probably the clearest and most effective. Note that the questions shown in the figure could have been dealt with in a single question: "How many times, if any, have you smoked marijuana?" The response categories then would be: "Never," "Once," "2 to 5 times," and so forth. This single question would apply to all respondents, and each would find an appropriate answer category. Such a question, however, might put pressure on some respondents to report having smoked marijuana, because the main question asks how many times they have smoked it. The contingency question format illustrated in Figure 7.2 reduces the subtle pressure on respondents to report having smoked marijuana. This discussion shows how seemingly theoretical issues of validity and reliability are involved in so mundane a matter as how to format questions on a piece of paper.

Used properly, even complex sets of contingency questions can be constructed without confusing respondents. Sometimes a set of contingency questions is long enough to extend over several pages. Victim surveys typically include many contingency questions. Figure 7.3 presents a few questions from an NCVS questionnaire. All respondents are asked a series of screening questions to reveal possible victimizations. Persons who answer yes to any of the screening questions then complete a crime incident report that presents a large number of items designed to measure details of the victimization incident.

As Figure 7.3 shows, the crime incident report itself also contains contingency questions. You might notice that even this brief adaptation from the NCVS

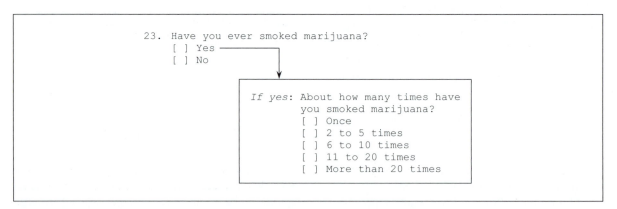

FIGURE 7.2 Contingency Question Format

Screening Question:

36a. I'm going to read you some examples that will give you an idea of the kinds of crimes this study covers. As I go through them, tell me if any of these happened to you in the last 6 months, that is, since [date].

Was something belonging to YOU stolen, such as

(a) Things that you carry, like luggage, a wallet, purse, briefcase, book

(b) Clothing, jewelry or calculator

(c) Bicycle or sports equipment

(d) Things in your home—like a TV, stereo, or tools

(e) Things outside your home, such as a garden hose or lawn furniture

(f) Things belonging to children in the household

(g) Things from a vehicle, such as a package, groceries, camera, or tapes
     OR

(h) Did anyone ATTEMPT to steal anything belonging to you?

Crime Incident Report:

20a. Were you or any other member of this household present when this incident occurred?

___ Yes [ask item 20b]

___ No [skip to 56, page 8]

20b. Which household members were present?

___ Respondent only [ask item 21]

___ Respondent and other household member(s) [ask item 21]

___ Only other household member(s) [skip to 59, page 8]

21. Did you personally see an offender?

___ Yes

___ No

....

56. Do you know or have you learned anything about the offender(s)—for instance, whether there was one or more than one offender involved, whether it was someone young or old, or male or female?

___ Yes [ask 57]

___ No [skip to 88, page 11]

FIGURE 7.3   NCVS Screening Questions and Crime Incident Report

Source: Adapted from National Crime Victimization Survey, NCVS-1 Basic Screen Questionnaire, 9/16/2004 version, http://bjs.ojp.usdoj.gov/content/pub/pdf/ncvs104.pdf, National Crime Victimization Survey, NCVS-2 Crime Incident Report, 9/16/2004 version, http://bjs.ojp.usdoj.gov/content/pub/pdf.ncvs204.pdf.

screening and crime incident report questionnaires is rather complex. NCVS questionnaires are administered primarily through computer-assisted telephone interviews in which the flow of contingency questions is more or less automated. It would be difficult to construct a self-administered victimization questionnaire with such complicated contingency questions.

Matrix Questions

Often researchers want to ask several questions that have the same set of answer categories. This happens whenever the Likert response categories are used. Then it is often possible to construct a matrix of items and answers, as illustrated in Figure 7.4.

This format has three advantages. First, it uses space efficiently. Second, respondents probably find it easier to complete a set of questions presented in this fashion. Third, this format may make it easier for the respondent as well as the researcher to compare responses given to different questions. Because respondents can quickly review their answers to earlier items in the set, they might choose between, say, "strongly agree" and "agree" on a given statement by comparing their strength of agreement with their earlier responses in the set.

Some dangers are inherent in using this format, as well. Its advantages may promote structuring an item so that the responses fit into the matrix format when a different, more idiosyncratic, set of responses might be more appropriate. Also, the matrix question format can generate a response set among some respondents. This means that respondents may develop a pattern of, say, agreeing with all the statements, without really thinking about what the statements mean. That is especially likely if the set of statements begins with several that indicate a particular orientation (for example, a conservative political perspective) and then offers only a few subsequent ones that represent the opposite orientation. Respondents might assume that all the statements represent the same orientation and, reading quickly, might misread some of them, thereby giving the wrong answers. This problem can be reduced somewhat by alternating statements that represent different orientations and by making all statements short and clear.

A more difficult problem is when responses are generated through respondent boredom or fatigue. This can be avoided by keeping matrix questions and the entire questionnaire as short as possible. Later in this chapter, in the section on comparing different methods of questionnaire administration, we will describe a useful technique for avoiding response sets generated by respondent fatigue.

Ordering Items in a Questionnaire

The order in which questions are asked can also affect the answers given. The content of one question can affect the answers given to later ones. If several questions ask about the dangers of illegal drug use and then a question (open-ended) asks respondents to volunteer what they believe to be the most serious crime problems in U.S. cities, drug use will receive more mentions than would otherwise be the case. In this situation, it is preferable to ask the open-ended question first.

If respondents are asked to rate the overall effectiveness of corrections policy, they will answer subsequent questions about specific aspects of correctional institutions in a way that is consistent with their initial assessment. The converse is true as well:

---

17. Beside each of the statements presented below, please indicate whether you Strongly Agree (SA), Agree (A), Disagree (D), Strongly Disagree (SD), or are Undecided (U).

	SA	A	D	SD	U
a. What this country needs is more law and order.	[ ]	[ ]	[ ]	[ ]	[ ]
b. Police in America should not carry guns.	[ ]	[ ]	[ ]	[ ]	[ ]
c. Repeat drug dealers should receive life sentences.	[ ]	[ ]	[ ]	[ ]	[ ]

FIGURE 7.4 Matrix Question Format

if respondents are first asked specific questions about prisons and other correctional facilities, their subsequent overall assessment will be influenced by the earlier question.

The best solution is sensitivity to the problem. Although we cannot avoid the effect of question order, we should attempt to estimate what that effect will be. Then we will be able to interpret results in a meaningful fashion. If the order of questions seems an especially important issue in a given study, we could construct several versions of the questionnaire that contain the different possible orderings of questions. We could then determine the effects of ordering. At the very least, different versions of the questionnaire should be pretested.

The desired ordering of questions differs somewhat between self-administered questionnaires and interviews. In the former, it is usually best to begin the questionnaire with the most interesting questions. Potential respondents who glance casually at the first few questions should want to answer them. Perhaps the questions involve opinions that they are aching to express. At the same time, however, the initial questions should be neither threatening nor sensitive. It might be a bad idea to begin with questions about sexual behavior or drug use. Requests for demographic data (age, gender, and the like) should generally be placed at the end of a self-administered questionnaire. Placing these questions at the beginning, as many inexperienced researchers are tempted to do, might make the questionnaire appear overly intrusive, so the person who receives it may not want to complete it.

Finally, it's common for less experienced researchers to assume that questionnaires must be newly constructed for each application. In contrast, it's almost always possible—and usually preferable—to use an existing questionnaire as a point of departure. See the box "Don't Start from Scratch!" for more on this.

DON'T START FROM SCRATCH!

It's always easier to modify an existing questionnaire for a particular research application than it is to start from scratch. It's also difficult to imagine asking questions that nobody has asked before. Here are examples of websites that present complete questionnaires or batteries of questionnaire items.

- Bureau of Justice Statistics (BJS; http://bjs.gov). In addition to administering the NCVS, the BJS collects information from a variety of justice organizations. Copies of recent questionnaires for all BJS-sponsored surveys are available on the Bureau's website. Look for a ribbon of links near the top of the page. Mouse over "Data Collections" to find a series (e.g., corrections, courts and sentencing, law enforcement, victims), and then click on one of interest. Browse through collections and follow links to find questionnaires for the series.

- California Healthy Kids Survey (http://chks.wested.org/administer/download). This set of questionnaires is useful for assessing behavior routines. Most include items on alcohol, tobacco, and other drug use; fighting; and other behaviors of potential interest for school-based interventions. English and Spanish versions are available for elementary, middle, and high school.

- Centers for Disease Control and Prevention (CDC; http://www.cdc.gov/qbank/home.aspx). Various centers within the CDC regularly collect a variety of health-related data through questionnaires and other data collection systems. Q-Bank is a CDC resource for finding and evaluating questionnaire items on a variety of topics. Try searching for a topic of interest, for example, "marijuana." Copies of complete questionnaire instruments are also available at the CDC website.

- Survey Monkey (http://www.surveymonkey.com). We're willing to bet that you've not only heard of the Survey Monkey website, but that you have also responded to a questionnaire distributed through this free service. The site also maintains a Question Bank that includes hundreds of questions developed by Survey Monkey staff or contributed by users. You can access the Question Bank by creating an account with Survey Monkey.

Self-Administered Questionnaires

Self-administered questionnaires are generally the least expensive and easiest to complete.

Although the mail survey is the typical method used in self-administered studies, several other methods are also possible. In some cases, it may be appropriate to administer the questionnaire to a group of respondents gathered at the same place at the same time, such as police officers at roll call or prison inmates at some specially arranged assembly. The Monitoring the Future survey (see Chapter 4) has high school students complete self-administered questionnaires in class.

Some experimentation has been conducted on the home delivery of questionnaires. A research worker delivers the questionnaire to the home of sample respondents and explains the study. Then the questionnaire is left for the respondent to complete, and the researcher picks it up later.

Home delivery and the mail can be used in combination as well. Questionnaires can be mailed to families, and then research workers may visit the homes to pick up the questionnaires and check them for completeness. In the opposite approach, survey packets are hand-delivered by research workers with a request that the respondents mail the completed questionnaires to the research office. In general, when a research worker delivers the questionnaire, picks it up, or both, the completion rate is higher than for straightforward mail surveys.

As the Internet has become an increasingly important part of people's lives, self-administered questionnaires are now more often completed online. Before discussing web-based questionnaires, let us turn our attention to the fundamentals of mail surveys, which might still be used for people without Internet access.

Mail Distribution and Return

The basic method for collecting data through the mail is transmittal of a questionnaire accompanied by a letter of explanation and a self-addressed, stamped envelope for returning the questionnaire. You have probably received a few. As a respondent, you are expected to complete the questionnaire, put it in the envelope, and mail it back. If, by any chance, you have received such a questionnaire and failed to return it, it would be a valuable exercise for you to recall your reasons for not returning it—and keep those in mind any time you plan to send questionnaires to others.

Timing is important to consider in the actual mailing of questionnaires. In most cases, the holiday months of November, December, and January should be avoided. Overall mail volume is greatest during those periods, which can substantially slow down the process of both distribution and return of questionnaires. And because a greater volume of mail is flowing through post offices, people receive more mail of all types. If a questionnaire arrives in the company of glossy gift catalogs, holiday greetings, bills, and assorted junk mail, respondents will be more likely to discard the survey packet.

Warning Mailings and Cover Letters

Warning mailings can be used to verify who lives at sampled addresses and to increase response rates. Warning mailings work like this: After researchers generate a sample, they send a postcard to each selected respondent, with the notation "Address correction requested" printed on the postcard. If the addressee has moved and left a forwarding address, the questionnaire is sent to the new address. When someone has moved and not left a forwarding address, or more than a year has elapsed and the post office no longer has information about a new address, the postcard is returned marked something like "Addressee unknown." Selected persons who still reside at the original listed address are warned in suitable language to expect a questionnaire in the mail. In such cases, postcards should briefly describe the purpose of the survey for which the respondent has been selected.

Warning letters can be more effective than postcards in increasing a survey's **response rate**, the percentage of people contacted who actually participate. Letters printed on letterhead stationery can present a longer description of the survey's purpose and a more reasoned explanation of why it is important for everyone to respond.

Cover letters accompanying the questionnaire offer a similar opportunity to increase response rates. Two features of cover letters warrant some attention. First, the content of the letter is obviously important. The message should communicate why a survey is being conducted, how and why the respondent was selected, and why it is important for the respondent to complete the questionnaire. In line with our discussion of the protection of human subjects in Chapter 2, the cover letter should also assure respondents that their answers will be confidential.

Second, the cover letter should identify the institutional affiliation or sponsorship of the survey. The two alternatives are (1) an institution that the respondent respects or can identify with, or (2) a neutral but impressive-sounding affiliation. For example, if we are conducting a mail survey of police chiefs, printing our cover letter on International Association of Chiefs of Police (IACP) stationery and having the letter signed by an official in the IACP might increase the response rate. Of course, we cannot adopt such a procedure unless the survey is endorsed by the IACP.

By the same token, it is important to avoid controversial affiliations or those inappropriate for the target population. The Police Misconduct Reporting Project, for instance, would not be a useful affiliation for most law enforcement target populations. A university affiliation is appropriate in many cases, unless the university is on bad terms with the target population.

Follow-Up Mailings

Follow-up mailings may be administered in a number of ways. In the simplest, nonrespondents are sent a letter of additional encouragement to participate. A better method, however, is to send a new copy of the survey questionnaire with the follow-up letter. If potential respondents have not returned their questionnaires after two or three weeks, the questionnaires probably have been lost or misplaced. In general, the longer a potential respondent delays replying, the less likely he or she is to do so at all. Properly timed follow-up mailings provide additional stimuli to respond.

The effects of follow-up mailings may be seen by monitoring the number of questionnaires received over time. Initial mailings will be followed by a rise in and subsequent subsiding of returns, and follow-up mailings will spur a resurgence of returns. In practice, three mailings (an original and two follow-ups) are most effective.

Acceptable Response Rates

A question frequently asked about mail surveys concerns the percentage return rate that should be achieved. Note that the body of inferential statistics used in connection with survey analysis assumes that *all* members of the initial sample complete and return their questionnaires. Because this almost never happens, response bias becomes a concern. Researchers must test (and hope for) the possibility that respondents look essentially like a random sample of the initial sample and thus a somewhat smaller random sample of the total population. For example, if the gender of all people in the sample is known, a researcher can compare the percentages of males and females indicated on returned questionnaires with the percentages for the entire sample.

Nevertheless, overall response rate is one guide to the representativeness of the sample respondents. If the response rate is high, there is less chance of significant response bias than if the rate is low. As a rule of thumb, a response rate of at least 50 percent is adequate for analysis and reporting. A response rate of at least 60 percent is good, and a response rate of 70 percent is very good. Bear in mind that these are only rough guides; they have no statistical basis, and a demonstrated lack of response bias is far more important than a high response rate. Response rates tend to be higher for surveys that target a narrowly defined population, whereas general population surveys yield lower response rates.

Don Dillman and associates (Dillman, Smyth, and Christian 2014) have undertaken an extensive review of the various techniques survey researchers use to increase return rates on mail surveys, and they evaluate the impact of each. More importantly, Dillman and colleagues stress the necessity of paying attention to all aspects of the study—termed the "total design method"—rather than one or two special gimmicks.

Computer-Based Self-Administration

Advances in computer and telecommunications technology over the past several decades have produced additional options for distributing and collecting self-administered questionnaires. As the Internet and web have permeated work and leisure activities, different types of computer-assisted self-administered surveys have become more common.

The most common and useful type is the web-based survey, in which respondents are asked to click on a link that eventually takes them to a questionnaire application. The advantages of this method are obvious. Responses are automatically recorded in computer files, saving time and money. Web page design tools make it possible to create attractive questionnaires that include contingency questions, matrixes, and other complex tools for presenting items to respondents.

All electronic versions of self-administered questionnaires face a couple of problems. The first concerns representativeness: will the people who can be surveyed online be representative of meaningful populations, such as all U.S. adults, all registered voters, or all residents of particular urban neighborhoods? This criticism has also been raised with regard to surveys via fax and, in the mid-twentieth century, with regard to telephone surveys.

Finding and selecting samples of Internet users can be challenging. Put in terms that should be familiar from the previous chapter, how closely do available sampling frames for electronic surveys match possible target populations? If, for example, our target population is university students, how can we obtain a list of e-mail addresses or other identifiers that will enable us to survey a representative sample? It's easy to think of other target populations of interest to criminal justice researchers that might be difficult to reach via e-mail or web-based questionnaires.

The second problem is an unfortunate consequence of the rapid growth of e-mail and related technologies. Just as junk mail clutters our physical mailboxes with all sorts of advertising, "spam" and other kinds of unwanted messages pop up all too often in our virtual mailboxes. The proliferation of junk e-mail has led to the development of antispam filters that screen out unwanted correspondence. Unfortunately, such programs can also screen out unfamiliar but well-meaning mail such as e-mail questionnaires. Similar problems with telemarketing have made it increasingly difficult to conduct surveys by telephone.

In yet another example of technology advances being accompanied by new threats, the spread of computer viruses and other "malware" has made people even more cautious about opening e-mail or attachments from unfamiliar sources. This problem, and the electronic version of junk mail, can be addressed in a manner similar to warning mailings for printed questionnaires. One solution is a version of the warning letter described above for mail surveys. In the electronic adaptation, researchers distribute e-mail messages from trusted sources to warn recipients to expect to receive a questionnaire or link in a later message.

We should keep one basic principle in mind when considering whether a self-administered questionnaire can be distributed electronically: web-based surveys depend on access to the web, which, of course, implies having a computer. The use of computers and the web continues to increase rapidly. Just as telephones eventually spread to larger numbers of households, access to the Internet continues to grow. According to estimates from a market research firm, about 78 percent of the U.S. population had access to the Internet in mid-2012 (http://www.cadsr.udel.edu/sqa/index.htm). Although access to this technology still is unequally distributed across socioeconomic classes, web-based surveys can be readily conducted for many target populations of interest to criminal justice researchers.

For example, in their recommendations for rethinking crime surveys, Michael Maxfield and associates argue that web-based surveys are well suited for learning more about victims of computer-facilitated fraud. Since only people with Internet access are possible victims, an Internet-based sample is ideal (Maxfield, Hough, and Mayhew 2007). Mike Sutton (2007) describes other examples of nontraditional crimes where Internet samples of computer users are appropriate.

Recalling our discussion in Chapter 6, the correspondence between a sampling frame and target population is a crucial feature of sampling. Most justice professionals and criminal justice organizations routinely use the web and e-mail. Lower-cost but generalizable victim surveys can use web-based samples of university students to distribute questionnaires. Or printed warning letters can be mailed, inviting respondents to complete either traditional or e-mail self-administered questionnaires. Just as e-mail, electronic bill-paying, and other transactions have replaced letters, check-writing, and other correspondence, self-administered surveys will increasingly be conducted on web-based computers. At the end of this chapter, we list a small sample of resources for conducting web-based surveys.

In-Person Interview Surveys

Face-to-face interviews are best for complex questionnaires and other specialized needs.

The in-person **interview survey** is an alternative method of collecting survey data. Rather than asking respondents to read questionnaires and enter their own answers, researchers send interviewers to ask the questions orally and record respondents' answers. Most interview surveys require more than one interviewer, although a researcher might undertake a small-scale interview survey alone.

The Role of the Interviewer

In-person interview surveys typically attain higher response rates than mail surveys. Respondents seem more reluctant to turn down an interviewer who is standing on their doorstep than to throw away a mail questionnaire. A properly designed and executed interview survey ought to achieve a completion rate of at least 80 to 85 percent.

The presence of an interviewer generally decreases the number of "don't know" and "no answer" responses. If minimizing such responses is important to the study, the interviewer can be instructed to probe for answers ("If you had to pick one of the answers, which do you think would come closest to your feelings?"). The interviewer can also help respondents with confusing questionnaire items. If the respondent clearly misunderstands the intent of a question, the interviewer can clarify matters and thereby obtain a relevant response. Such clarifications must be strictly controlled, however, through formal specifications.

Finally, the interviewer can observe as well as ask questions. For example, the interviewer can make observations about the quality of the respondent's dwelling, the presence of various possessions, the respondent's ability to speak English, or the respondent's general reactions to the study. Interviewers for the BCS routinely make observations of the physical conditions outside each respondent's home and in the surrounding area (Bolling, Grant, and Donovan 2009). Items include the physical condition of dwellings, how the sampled unit's condition compared to nearby dwelling units, and what types of locks were evident.

Survey research is, of necessity, based on an unrealistic stimulus–response theory of cognition and behavior. That is, it is based on the assumption that a questionnaire item will mean the same thing to every respondent, and every given response must mean the same thing when given by different respondents. Although this is an impossible goal, survey questions are drafted to approximate the ideal as closely as possible. The interviewer also plays a role in this ideal situation. The interviewer's presence should not affect a respondent's perception of a question or the answer given. The interviewer, then, should be a neutral medium through which questions and answers are transmitted. If this goal is met, different interviewers will obtain the same responses from a given respondent, an example of reliability in measurement (see Chapter 4).

Familiarity with the Questionnaire The interviewer must be able to read the questionnaire items to respondents without stumbling over words and phrases. A good model for interviewers is the actor reading lines in a play or film. The interviewer must read the questions as though they are part of a natural conversation, but that "conversation" must precisely follow the language set down in the question.

By the same token, the interviewer must be familiar with the specifications for administering the questionnaire. Inevitably, some questions will not exactly fit a given respondent's situation, and the interviewer must determine how those questions should be interpreted in that situation. The specifications provided to the interviewer should include adequate guidelines in such cases, but the interviewer must know the organization and content of the specifications well enough to refer to them efficiently.

Probing for Responses Probes are frequently required to elicit responses to open-ended questions. For example, to a question about neighborhood crime problems, the respondent might simply reply, "Pretty bad." The interviewer could obtain an elaboration on this response through a variety of probes. Sometimes, the best probe is silence; if the interviewer sits quietly with pencil poised, the respondent will probably fill the pause with additional comments. Appropriate verbal probes are "How is that?" and "In what ways?" Perhaps the most generally useful probe is "Anything else?"

In every case, however, it is imperative that the probe be completely neutral. The probe must not in any way affect the nature of the subsequent response. If we anticipate that a given question may require probing for appropriate responses, we should write one or more useful probes next to the item in the questionnaire. This practice has two important advantages. First, it allows for more time to devise the best, most neutral probes. Second, it ensures that all interviewers will use the same probes as needed. Thus, even if the probe is not perfectly neutral, the same stimulus is presented to all respondents. This is the same logical guideline as for question wording. Although a question should not be loaded or biased, it is essential that every respondent be presented with the same question, even if a biased one.

Coordination and Control

Whenever more than one interviewer will administer a survey, it is essential that the efforts be carefully coordinated and controlled. Two ways to ensure this control are by (1) training interviewers, and (2) supervising them after they begin work.

Whether the researchers will be administering a survey themselves or paying a professional firm to do it for them, they should be attentive to the importance of training interviewers. The interviewers usually should know what the study is all about. Even though the interviewers may be involved only in the data collection phase of the project, they should understand what will be done with the information they gather and what purpose will be served.

Obviously, training should ensure that interviewers understand the questionnaire. Interviewers should also understand procedures to select respondents from among household members. And interviewers should recognize circumstances in which substitute sample elements may be used in place of addresses that no longer exist, families who have moved, or persons who simply refuse to be interviewed.

Training should include practice sessions in which interviewers administer the questionnaire to one another. The final stage of the training should involve some real interviews conducted under conditions like those in the survey.

While interviews are being conducted, it is a good idea to review questionnaires as they are completed. This may reveal questions or groups of questions that respondents do not understand. By reviewing completed questionnaires, it is also possible to determine if interviewers are completing items accurately.

Computer-Assisted In-Person Interviews

Just as e-mail and web-based surveys apply new technology to the gathering of survey data through self-administration, laptop and hand-held computers are increasingly being used to conduct in-person interviews. Different forms of **computer-assisted interviewing (CAI)** offer major advantages in the collection of survey data. At the same time, CAI has certain disadvantages that must be considered. We'll begin by describing an example of how this technology was adopted in the BCS, one of the earliest uses of CAI in a general-purpose crime survey.

Computer-Assisted Interviewing in the BCS
Early waves of the BCS, a face-to-face interview survey, asked respondents to complete a self-administered questionnaire about drug use, printed as a small booklet that was prominently marked "Confidential." Beginning with the 1994 survey, respondents answered self-report questions on laptop computers. The BCS includes two related versions of CAI. In computer-assisted personal interviewing (CAPI), interviewers read questions from computer screens, instead of printed questionnaires, and then key in respondents' answers. For self-report items, interviewers hand the computers to subjects, who then key in the responses themselves. This approach is known as computer-assisted self-interviewing (CASI). In addition, CASI as used in the BCS is supplemented with audio instructions—respondents listen to interview prompts on headphones connected to the computer. After subjects key in their responses to self-report items, the answers are scrambled so the interviewer cannot access them. Notice how this feature of CASI enhances the researcher's ethical obligation to keep responses confidential.

Malcolm Ramsay and associates (2001) report that CASI had at least two benefits. First, respondents seemed to sense a greater degree of confidentiality when they responded to questions on a computer screen as opposed to questions on a written form. Second, the laptop computers were something of a novelty that stimulated respondents' interest; this was especially true for younger respondents.

Examining results from the BCS reveals that CASI techniques produced higher estimates of illegal drug use than those revealed in previous surveys. Table 7.1 compares self-reported drug use from the 1998 BCS (Ramsay and Partridge 1999) with results from the 1992 BCS (Mott and Mirrlees-Black 1995), in which respondents answered questions in printed booklets. We present results

TABLE 7.1   Self-Reported Drug Use, 1992 and 1998 British Crime Survey

	Percentage of Respondents Ages 16–29 Who Report Use	
	1992	1998
Marijuana or cannabis		
Ever used?	24	42
Used in previous 12 months?	12	23
Amphetamines		
Ever used?	9	20
Used in previous 12 months?	4	8
Semeron		
Ever used?	0.3	0.0
Used in previous 12 months?	0.1	0.0
Any drug		
Ever used?	28	49
Used in previous 12 months?	14	25

Source: 1992 data adapted from Mott and Mirrlees-Black (1995, 41–42); 1998 data adapted from Ramsay and Partridge (1999, 68–71).

for only three drugs here, together with tabulations about the use of any drug. For each drug, the survey measured lifetime use ("Ever used?") and use in the past 12 months.

Notice that rates of self-reported use were substantially higher in 1998 than in 1992, with the exception of "semeron" use, reported by very few respondents in 1992 and none in 1998. If you've never heard of semeron, you're not alone. It's a fictitious drug, included in the list of real drugs to detect untruthful or exaggerated responses. If someone confessed to using semeron, his or her responses to other self-reported items would be suspect. Notice in Table 7.1 that CASI use in 1998 reduced the number of respondents who admitted using a drug that doesn't exist.

CASI has also been used in the BCS since 1996 to measure domestic violence committed by partners and ex-partners of males and females age 16 to 59. Catriona Mirrlees-Black (1999) reports that CASI techniques reveal higher estimates of domestic violence victimization among both females and males.

Advantages and Disadvantages Different types of CAI offer a number of advantages for in-person interviews. The BCS and other surveys that include self-report items indicate that CAI is more productive in that self-reports of drug use and other offending tend to be higher. In 1999, the National Household Survey on Drug Abuse (now the National Household Survey on Drug Use and Health) shifted completely to CAI (Wright et al. 2002). Other advantages include the following:

- Responses can be quickly keyed in and automatically reformatted into data files for analysis.

- Complex sequences of contingency questions can be automated. Instead of printing many examples of "If answer is yes, go to question 43a; if no …," computer-based questionnaires automatically jump to the next appropriate question contingent on responses to earlier ones.

- CAI offers a way to break up the monotony of a long interview by shifting from verbal interviewer prompts to self-interviewing, with or without an audio supplement.

- Questionnaires for self-interviewing can be programmed in different languages, readily switching to the language appropriate for a particular respondent.

- Audio-supplemented CASI produces a standardized interview, avoiding any bias that might emerge from interviewer effects.

- Audio supplements, in different languages, facilitate self-interviews of respondents who cannot read.

At the same time, CAI has certain disadvantages that preclude its use in many survey applications:

- Although computers become more of a bargain each day, doing a large-scale in-person interview survey requires providing computers for each interviewer. Costs can quickly add up. CAI also requires specialized software to format and present on-screen questionnaires.

- Although CAI reduces costs in data processing, it requires more up-front investment in programming questionnaires, skip sequences, and the like.

- Automated skip sequences for contingency questions are great, but if something goes wrong with the programmed questionnaire, all sorts of subsequent problems are possible. As Emma Forster and Alison McCleery (1999) point out, such question-routing mistakes might mean that whole portions of a questionnaire are skipped. Whereas occasional random errors are possible with pen-and-paper interviews, large-scale systematic error can happen with CAI technology.

- Proofreading printed questionnaires is straightforward, but it can be difficult to audit a computerized questionnaire. Doing so might require special technical skills.

- It can be difficult to print and archive a complex questionnaire used in CAI. This was a problem with early applications of CAI technology, but improvements in software are helping to solve it.

- Batteries of laptops run down, and computers and software are more vulnerable to malfunctions and random weirdness than are stacks of printed questionnaires.

In sum, CAI can be costly and requires some specialized skills. As a result, these and related technologies are best suited for use by professional survey researchers or research centers that regularly conduct large-scale in-person interviews. We will return to this issue in the concluding section of this chapter.

Telephone Surveys

Telephone surveys are fast and relatively low cost.

Telephone surveys have many advantages that make them a popular method. Probably the greatest advantages involve money and time. In a face-to-face household interview, a researcher may drive several miles to a respondent's home, find no one there, return to the research office, and drive back the next day—possibly finding no one there again.

When interviewing by telephone, researchers can dress any way they please, and it will have no effect on the answers respondents give. Respondents may also be more honest in giving socially disapproved answers if they don't have to look the questioner in the eye. Similarly, it may be possible to probe into more sensitive areas, although that is not necessarily the case. People are, to some extent, more suspicious when they can't see the person asking them questions—perhaps a consequence of telemarketing and salespeople conducting bogus surveys before making sales pitches.

In computer-assisted telephone interviewing (CATI), interviewers wearing telephone headsets sit at computer workstations. Computer programs dial sampled phone numbers, which can be either generated through random-digit dialing (RDD) or extracted from a database of phone numbers compiled from some source. As soon as phone contact is made, the computer screen displays an introduction ("Hello, my name is … calling from the Survey Research Center at Ivory Tower University") and the first question to be asked, which is often a query about the number of residents who live in the household. As interviewers key in answers to each question, the computer program displays a new screen that presents the next question, until the end of the interview is reached. Perhaps you've occasionally marveled at newspaper stories that report the results of a nationwide opinion poll the day after some major speech or event. The speed of CATI technology makes these instant poll reports possible.

Telephone surveys can give a researcher greater control over data collection if several interviewers are engaged in the project. If all the interviewers are calling from the research office, they can get clarification from the supervisor whenever problems occur, as they inevitably do. Alone in the field, an interviewer may have to wing it between weekly visits with the interviewing supervisor.

A related advantage is rooted in the growing diversity of U.S. cities. Because many major cities have growing immigrant populations, interviews may need to be conducted in different languages. Telephone interviews are usually conducted from a central site so that one or more multilingual interviewers can be quickly summoned if an English-speaking interviewer makes contact with, say, a Spanish-speaking respondent. In-person interview surveys present much more difficult logistical problems in handling multiple languages. And mail surveys require printing and distributing questionnaires in different languages.

Telephone interviewing has its problems, however. As we described in Chapter 8, a growing number of households have only mobile phone service, and regulations restrict the use of RDD samples using mobile phone numbers. Jan van Dijk (2007) describes how this is especially troublesome in some European countries where mobile-only households are more common.

In addition, phone surveys are much less suitable for individuals not living in households. Homeless people are obvious examples; those who live in institutions are also difficult to reach out and touch via telephone.

A related sampling problem involves unlisted numbers. If the survey sample is selected from the pages of a local telephone directory, it totally omits all those people who have requested that their numbers not be published. Similarly, those who recently moved and transient residents are not well represented in published telephone directories. This potential bias has been eliminated through RDD, a technique that has advanced telephone sampling substantially.

RDD samples use computer algorithms to generate lists of random telephone numbers—usually the last four digits. This procedure gets around the sampling problem of unlisted telephone numbers but may substitute an administrative problem. Randomly generating phone numbers produces numbers that are not in operation or that serve a business establishment or pay phone. In most cases, businesses and pay phones are not included in the target population; dialing these numbers and learning that they're out of scope will take time away from producing completed interviews with the target population.

The ease with which people can hang up is, of course, another shortcoming of telephone surveys. Once a researcher is inside someone's home for an interview, that person is unlikely to order the researcher out of the house in mid-interview.

It's much easier to terminate a telephone interview abruptly, saying something like "Whoops! Someone's at the door. Gotta go" or simply hanging up.

Partly as a result of extensive telemarketing in past years, completion rates for telephone surveys have declined (Cantor and Lynch 2007). Though commercial telemarketing is sharply reduced, people still commonly receive solicitations from charitable organizations, college alumni groups, aggressive political campaigns, and other "soft" telemarketers. People who are weary of bothersome calls are less inclined to complete telephone interviews, especially those lasting longer than a couple of minutes (Tourangeau 2004).

Comparison of the Three Methods

Cost, speed, and question content are issues to consider in selecting a survey method.

We've now examined three ways of collecting survey data: self-administered questionnaires, in-person interviews, and telephone surveys. We have also considered some recent advances in each mode of administration. Although we've touched on some of the relative advantages and disadvantages of each, let's take a minute to compare them more directly.

Self-administered questionnaires are generally cheaper to use than interview surveys. Moreover, for self-administered e-mail or web-based surveys, it costs no more to conduct a national survey than a local one. Obviously, the cost difference between a local and a national in-person interview survey is considerable. The cost of telephone surveys continues to decline, as Internet-based calling services eliminate long-distance toll charges. Mail surveys typically require a small staff. One person can conduct a reasonable mail survey, although it is important not to underestimate the work involved. Web-based surveys can be very inexpensive, particularly because they combine data collection and tabulation.

Up to a point, cost and speed are inversely related. In-person interview surveys can be completed very quickly if a large pool of interviewers is available and funding is adequate to pay them. In contrast, if a small number of people are con-

ducting a larger number of face-to-face interviews, costs are generally lower, but the survey takes much longer to complete. Telephone surveys that use CATI technology are easily the fastest.

Self-administered surveys may be more appropriate to use with especially sensitive issues if the surveys offer complete anonymity. Respondents are sometimes reluctant to report controversial or deviant attitudes or behaviors in interviews, but they may be willing to respond to an anonymous self-administered questionnaire. However, the successful use of computers for self-reported items in the BCS and the National Household Survey on Drug Use and Health indicates that interacting with a machine can promote more candid responses. This is supported by experimental research comparing different modes of questionnaire administration (Kreuter, Presser, and Tourangeau 2008).

Interview surveys have advantages, too. For example, in-person or telephone surveys are more appropriate when respondent literacy may be a problem. Interview surveys also result in fewer incomplete questionnaires. Respondents may skip questions in a self-administered questionnaire, but interviewers are trained not to do so. CAI offers a further check on this in telephone and in-person surveys.

Self-administered questionnaires may be more effective in dealing with sensitive issues, but interview surveys are definitely more effective in dealing with complicated ones. Interviewers can explain complex questions to respondents and use visual aids that are not possible in mail or phone surveys.

In-person interviews, especially with computer technology, can also help reduce response sets. Respondents (like students?) eventually become bored listening to a lengthy series of similar types of questions. It's easier to maintain individuals' interest by changing the kind of stimulation they are exposed to. A mix of questions verbalized by a person, presented on a computer screen, and heard privately through earphones is more interesting for respondents and reduces fatigue.

Interviewers who question respondents face to face are also able to make important observations aside from responses to questions asked in the interview. In a household interview, they may summarize characteristics of the neighborhood, the dwelling unit, and so forth. They may also note characteristics of the respondents or the quality of their interaction with the respondents—whether the respondent had difficulty communicating, was hostile, seemed to be lying, and so on. Finally, when the safety of interviewers is an issue, a mail or phone survey may be the best option.

Ultimately, researchers must weigh all these advantages and disadvantages of the three methods against research needs and available resources.

Strengths and Weaknesses of Survey Research

Surveys tend to be high on reliability and generalizability, but validity can often be a weak point.

Like other modes of collecting data in criminal justice research, surveys have strengths and weaknesses. It is important to consider these in deciding whether the survey format is appropriate for a specific research purpose.

Surveys are particularly useful in describing the characteristics of a large population. The NCVS has become an important tool for researchers and public officials because of its ability to describe levels of crime. A carefully selected probability sample, in combination with a standardized questionnaire, allows researchers to make refined descriptive statements about a neighborhood, a city, a nation, or some other large population.

Standardized questionnaires have an important advantage in regard to measurement. Earlier chapters discussed the ambiguous nature of concepts: they ultimately have no real meanings. One person's view about, say, crime seriousness or punishment severity is quite different from another's. Although we must be able to define concepts in ways that are most relevant to research goals, it's not always easy to apply the same definitions uniformly to all subjects. Nevertheless, the survey researcher is bound to the requirement of having to ask exactly the same questions of all subjects and having to impute the same intent to all respondents giving a particular response.

At the same time, survey research has its weaknesses. First, the requirement for standardization might mean that we are trying to fit round pegs into square holes. Standardized questionnaire items often represent the least common denominator in assessing people's attitudes, orientations, circumstances, and experiences. By designing questions that are at least minimally appropriate to all respondents, we may miss what is most appropriate to many respondents. In this sense, surveys often appear superficial in their coverage of complex topics.

Using surveys to study crime and criminal justice policy presents special challenges. The target population frequently includes lower-income, transient persons who are difficult to contact through customary sampling methods. For example, homeless persons are excluded from any survey that samples households, but people who live on the street no doubt figure prominently as victims and offenders. Michael Maxfield (1999) describes how new data from the National Incident-Based Reporting System suggest that a number of "non-household-associated" persons are systematically undercounted by sampling procedures used in the NCVS. Research by Census Bureau staff has tried to document how many individuals might be missed in household-based surveys, finding that young males and minorities appear to be most undercounted (Martin 1999).

Crime surveys such as the NCVS and the BCS have been deficient in getting information about crimes of violence when the victim and offender have some prior relationship. This is particularly true for domestic violence, although Michael Rand and Callie Rennison report some advantages of large surveys in this regard (2005).

Underreporting of domestic violence appears to be due, in part, to the very general nature of large-scale crime surveys. Catriona Mirrlees-Black (1995, 8) summarizes the trade-offs of using survey techniques to learn about domestic violence:

Measuring domestic violence is difficult territory. The advantage of the BCS is that it is based on a large nationally representative sample, has a relatively high response rate, and collects information on enough incidents to provide reliable details of their nature. One disadvantage is that domestic violence is measured in the context of a crime survey, and some women may not see what happened to them as "crime," or be reluctant to do so. Also, there is little time to approach the topic "gently." A specially designed questionnaire with carefully selected interviewers may well have the edge here.

An experimental use of computer-assisted self-interviewing in the BCS produced higher estimates of victimization prevalence among women as well as the first measurable rates of domestic violence victimization for males (Mirrlees-Black 1999). The BCS now routinely uses CASI to get better estimates of violent victimization.

Survey research is generally weaker on validity and stronger on reliability. In comparison with field research, for instance, the artificiality of the survey format puts a strain on validity. As an illustration, most researchers agree that fear of crime is not well measured by the standard question "How safe do you feel, or would you feel, out alone in your neighborhood at night?" Survey responses to that question are, at best, approximate indicators of what we have in mind when we conceptualize fear of crime.

Reliability is a different matter. By presenting all subjects with a standardized stimulus, survey research goes a long way toward eliminating unreliability in observations made by the researcher.

However, even this statement is subject to qualification. Critics of survey methods argue that questionnaires for standard crime surveys and many specialized studies embody a narrow, legalistic conception of crime that cannot reflect the perceptions and experiences of minorities and women. Survey questions typically are based on male views and do not adequately tap victimization or fear of crime among women (Straus 1999; Tjaden and Thoennes 2000). Concern that survey questions might mean different things to different respondents raises important questions about reliability and about the generalizability of survey results across subgroups of a population.

Other Ways of Asking Questions

As with all methods of observation, a full awareness of the inherent or probable weaknesses of survey research may partially resolve them. Ultimately, though, we are on the safest ground when we can use several different research methods to study a given topic. For example, in-depth interviews of small numbers of people can yield rich, detailed information about such difficult problems as domestic violence and sexual assault. Similarly, focus groups are semi-structured group interviews used to develop or elaborate understanding of complex topics. Chapter 8, written by Amber Horning, provides a detailed examination of focus groups, qualitative interviews, and other ways of asking questions.

SUMMARY

- Survey research, a popular social research method, involves the administration of questionnaires to a sample of respondents selected from some population.

- Survey research is especially appropriate for descriptive or exploratory studies of large populations, but surveys have many other uses in criminal justice research.

- Surveys are the method of choice for obtaining self-reported offending data. Continuing efforts to improve self-report surveys include

using confidential computer-assisted personal interviews.

- Questions may be open-ended or closed-ended. Each technique for formulating questions has advantages and disadvantages.

- Short items in a questionnaire are usually better than long ones.

- Bias in questionnaire items encourages respondents to answer in a particular way or to support a particular point of view. It should be avoided.

- Questionnaires are administered in three basic ways: self-administered questionnaires, face-to-face interviews, and telephone interviews. Each mode of administration can be varied in a number of ways.

- Computers can be used to enhance each type of survey. Computer-assisted surveys have many advantages, but they often require special skills and equipment.

- It is generally advisable to plan follow-up mailings for self-administered questionnaires, sending new questionnaires to respondents who fail to respond to the initial appeal.

- The essential characteristic of interviewers is that they be neutral; their presence in the data collection process must not have any effect on the responses given to questionnaire items.

- Surveys conducted over the telephone are fast and flexible.

- Each method of survey administration has a variety of advantages and disadvantages.

- Survey research has the weaknesses of being somewhat artificial and potentially superficial. It is difficult to gain a full sense of social processes in their natural settings through the use of surveys.

KEY TERMS

bias, p. 175

closed-ended question, p. 173

computer-assisted interviewing (CAI), p. 186

interview survey, p. 185

open-ended question, p. 173

questionnaire, p. 174

respondent, p. 171

response rate, p. 182

survey, p. 171

REVIEW QUESTIONS AND EXERCISES

1. Locate a survey being conducted on the web. Briefly describe the survey and discuss its strengths and weaknesses.

2. For each of the open-ended questions listed, construct a closed-ended question that could be used in a questionnaire.

   a. What was your family's total income last year?

   b. How do you feel about shock incarceration or "boot camp" programs?

   c. How do people in your neighborhood feel about the police?

   d. What do you feel is the biggest problem facing this community?

   e. How do you protect your home from burglary?

3. Survey methods change as communications technology changes. The spread of telephones in the United States in the mid-twentieth century made it possible to conduct telephone interviews. The Internet and e-mail are used for different types of web-based surveys. Most recently, the spread of smart phones makes it possible to send self-administered questionnaires via text messaging or social media. Review our discussion of question types, questionnaire formatting, and mode of administration. Briefly describe how surveys by smart phone present potential challenges and advantages as a survey method. Also think about how smart phone users might be sampled.

CHAPTER 8

Qualitative Interviewing

Contributed by Amber Horning,
John Jay College of Criminal Justice

We'll learn when qualitative interviewing is appropriate, different types of in-depth interviews, how to design your questions, and how to interact with participants. Finally, we consider different ways to record and analyze data.

Gaining Access to Hard-to-Reach Groups

In 2011–2012, I conducted a study about pimps in Harlem, New York City. Pimps are considered to be a hard-to-reach group, and many people were skeptical that I would find participants. One of the reasons that I thought this study was possible was because one of my colleagues knew someone who had been pimping for over 20 years. Although the pimp agreed to a pilot interview, he was reluctant to be our contact or to give us sponsorship. He was worried about our intentions and exposing the secrets of the business. It seemed that the study would not be possible or, at the least, that we would have trouble finding participants. We considered going to nonprofit organizations dedicated to helping sex workers to see if we could find referrals to potential contacts. Sometimes, you can find sponsors by connecting to local organizations.

By a stroke of luck, I needed to have an industrial-sized air conditioner moved, and I asked the same friend if one of her clients (people on probation or parole) would be interested in the job. The person who came over to move my air conditioner turned out to be a former pimp who still had access to many members of this community. We had a nice chat, and I mentioned the study in casual conversation. He was very interested in the research and agreed to connect me with people who were actively pimping in his neighborhood.

He trusted me because of our mutual connection and the rapport that I established with him. This was a fortuitous moment for the study and

illustrates that access can be gained through friends of friends or acquaintances and that even a distant connection can be useful for finding a willing contact. In addition, finding a contact who was formerly involved in a criminal lifestyle can be beneficial because that person may have less fear about the research process.

My contact's presence during the interviews and the fact that the interviews were largely conducted in public spaces (housing project courtyards in New York City) may have allayed some participants' fears. Many of them knew or recognized him from the neighborhood. In addition, they were able to watch interviews taking place and did not witness any adverse consequences. Our presence in the housing project courtyards would have been difficult to navigate without sponsorship. Access can be about connecting with your participants, but sponsorship may also allow you access to spaces that enable participants to feel the trust required for participation.

After working with my contact for several months, he was arrested and sent back to prison. Although I had collected a lot of phone numbers of participants who were interested in the progress of the study, only one person struck me as the right person for continued access. He was one of the first people interviewed and was always hanging around watching interviews and asking questions about the progress of the study. He seemed to be a regular fixture in the community, and he knew a lot of people. I texted him to see if he was still interested in connecting us

(continued)

with participants. Through his sponsorship, we were able to interview over 60 more participants. Sometimes your initial sponsor may disappear for various reasons, so it's important to connect with other people in the same community. By connecting with other members of the group, you may be able to continue your study should something happen to your original contact.

Introduction

Qualitative interviews are frequently used in criminological research.

Sample surveys are perhaps the best-known way of asking questions in criminal justice research. However, as discussed in Chapter 7, surveys and standardized questionnaires sometimes fall short on validity. A survey would be appropriate to ask people if they have ever been the victim of a robbery, but a survey questionnaire would not be as useful to understand how robbers select victims. To learn how robbers select victims, you would want to use more specialized interviewing techniques.

To illustrate the difference, suppose you want to study robbery in the shanty settlements of South African townships. You may be interested in the percentage of robberies happening in South African townships between 8 p.m. and 8 a.m. A victim survey would be a good approach to finding that out. However, you might also want to understand the decision-making process of nighttime robbers and how they select victims in South African townships. You also may be interested in how robbers' actions are influenced by police foot patrols. In that case, it would be best to talk to robbers in person. Generally, when you find yourself wondering about the complexities of any process or the *hows* or *whys* involving human perspectives, emotions, or decisions, qualitative interviews are usually appropriate.

Unlike a survey, a **qualitative interview** is an interaction between an interviewer and a respondent where the interviewer has a general plan of inquiry, including the topics to be covered, but not necessarily a specific set of questions that have to be asked in a particular order. The qualitative interview can also be thought of as a purposeful conversation

(Patton 2002). As we have seen, survey interviews are based on the use of standardized questions. Qualitative interviews are based on a deliberate plan but are inherently flexible.

Topics Appropriate for Qualitative Interviewing

Qualitative interviews have many applications and are especially well suited for exploratory research.

Qualitative interviews are crucial to various kinds of studies. They are an important part of field research, the topic of Chapter 9. Historically, qualitative methods have been used by anthropologists and sociologists for studying other cultures and subcultures. An illustration of this approach is the study by David Brotherton and Luis Barrios (2004) of the Almighty Latin King and Queen Nation in New York City. By attending important meetings, hanging around with key informants, and interviewing gang members, Brotherton and Barrios were able to capture the process of this group's transformation from a street gang to an organized social movement. Another notable example is Lisa Maher's (1997) work on females engaged in sex work within Brooklyn drug markets. She gathered much of her information through informal conversations with these women on the streets. Each of these studies is process oriented, where the purpose is to understand human experiences holistically and in context.

Qualitative interviews can be the sole way of gathering data in criminal justice studies. If you want to understand the perspective of those who are labeled as deviant or criminal by society, your best tactic is to talk to them in person. Through interviews, you may gather firsthand accounts about their impressions of their world that is their *lived experience*. For instance, when I[1] began my studies of pimps, I found very little prior research. I wanted to understand pimps' perspectives about their use of space in urban areas and their views about social interactions with sex workers. Because so little was known about this group, the best way to capture their experiences and feelings was qualitative interviewing through purposeful conversations. Many pimps were engaged in criminal activity and therefore only accessible for conversations on the street. Through interviews with 95 pimps in Harlem, New York City, conducted in 2011 and 2012, I learned much about their experiences.

Another example of a topic appropriate for qualitative interviewing is research on how people think about their roles and/or identities. Ferdinand Sutterlüty (2007) wanted to know how young people felt about the process of adopting violent lifestyles, so he interviewed 18 repeat violent offenders in Berlin. He found that some thought of the transition to acting violently as a *turning point*. For some, there was even an identity switch from victim to perpetrator. Many had experienced violence within their families and used violence to reclaim power. He also uncovered several different kinds of *violent action schemes*, or ways these young people thought about violence. The most effective way for him to understand meanings of violence and the process of identity change was through in-depth interviews. If you are interested in role or identity construction or reconstruction, it's necessary to interview your participants.

Another reason for choosing qualitative interviewing as part of your design is if your group of interest is part of a "scene" and you want to understand their perspective in context. A scene could be a group that is united socially or politically. To illustrate, Dina Perrone (2009) wanted to get beyond stereotypes of club drug users to understand how the settings of rave clubs influenced drug experience and harm. The best way for her to understand this and get quality interviews was to go where the "dance club kids" hung out. By visiting

clubs and attending parties, she observed, made connections, and talked to people. Perrone found that unlike popular stereotypes about drug users, the people she encountered were largely middle class. Further, many were socially embedded, such as lawyers with families. Club kids who invested in their outside lives had more control over their drug use. In addition, she found the scene to be an escape into a "carnivalesque atmosphere" where lights and music afforded a sharp contrast from typical middle-class routine. This study of dance clubs revealed a social group outside their daily grind within the capitalist machine. This was only apparent because Perrone visited her participants in context.

Understanding an illicit market often requires a longer-term project and interviews with different players involved in the market. After 20 years of fieldwork in New York City, Ric Curtis and Travis Wendel (2007) published the article, "You're Always Training the Dog: Strategic Interventions to Reconfigure Drug Markets." Their research documented different types of drug markets and the types of systematic violence that were characteristic of each. A market is a complex system, and they wanted to understand its variation and changes over time. They found that changes to the market, for better or worse, were often in response to law enforcement interventions. Curtis and Wendel completed many interviews over the years with police and other people who worked in New York City drug markets.

Sometimes, the only way to obtain the information that you need is through qualitative data collection. Chris Overall, Shalendra Singh, and Bhekekhya Gcina (2008) used crime mapping and other statistical procedures to understand crime hotspots in South Africa. However, they noted that because many poorer South African townships were informal settlements interwoven with formal settlements, they could not be understood through standard crime mapping. Overall and colleagues described how these spaces develop through the interplay between sociohistoric events, people, and physical environments. Township spaces were captured through *cognitive maps* that express how

---

1. In this chapter, the first-person singular refers to Amber Horning.

people understand their environment. Obtaining these maps required qualitative interviews about residents' perceptions of these informal settlements.

I did something very similar in my study of pimps in Harlem. Pimps' work spaces have traditionally been in open-air markets, similar to lower level drug dealers (Harocopos and Hough 2005). Although some sex-market facilitation has moved off the street (Venkatesh 2011), business still occurs in outdoor public space. I gave participants in my study a pen and paper and asked them to draw their

work space. This method was not only useful for building rapport (there was much discussion about the pictures), but also a great way to understand how these marginalized men conceived of their everyday work space within the urban landscape. See the box, "Maps of an Illicit Economy: Conceptions of Masculinized Outdoor Work Space," for details on cognitive maps by pimps. While you review this box, keep in mind that it's a good illustration of the flexibility available through qualitative interviewing.

MAPS OF AN ILLICIT ECONOMY: CONCEPTIONS OF MASCULINIZED OUTDOOR WORK SPACE

Historically, geographers have used maps to understand how they help people find their way around town, cultural geographers have used maps to understand how social and culture dimensions are shaped by landscapes and vice versa (Jackson 1989; Sauer 1925), anthropologists have used maps to understand the perspectives of isolated groups (Madaleno 2010), and criminologists have used maps to understand crime patterns and decision making (Brantingham and Brantingham 1984; Canter and Hodge 2000; Cornish and Clark 1986; Lopez and Lukinbeal 2010) and perceptions of danger (Wallace 2009). Urban space claimed by lower-class males for work has been documented in Phillip Bourgois's *In Search of Respect: Selling Crack in El Barrio* (2002) on Harlem crack dealers, Mitch Duneier's *Sidewalk* (2000) on street vendors in New York City, and Sudhir Venkatesh's *Off the Books: The Underground Economy of the Urban Poor* (2006) on how residents in a Chicago housing project make ends meet. While criminologists have had offenders draw maps to understand offenders' decision-making and crime patterns, the types of offenders in these studies often seek out new targets each time. Ethnographers have photographed and described informal economies, but there is very little use of maps drawn by offenders to understand their visual conceptualization and use of their semi-permanent, everyday illicit work space.

Pimps, like drug dealers, often work in certain spots or use/claim outdoor space (semi-permanently) to conduct business. If you try to imagine claiming space in the urban environment, you may quickly realize how difficult this could be. If you are female, you may not even be able to conceive of this, because there are few documented examples of women

informally claiming outdoor space. Males engaged in the illicit economy may be what James Messerschmidt (1993) calls "doing masculinity"; that is, they are trying to prove their masculine worth through attempts at financial solvency within the capitalist social structure, albeit illicitly. In order to do this, they sometimes must carve out, or at least inhabit, public space.

Documentation describes marginalized males claiming public space, especially in the literature on gangs. For instance, William Whyte's (1993) seminal study on Boston slums distinguished between "corner boys" and "college boys." Often, in these accounts, males occupy urban space not only for business purposes, but also to display masculinity and show they have "juice" to establish and maintain street credibility, as discussed in Jack Katz's *Seductions of Crime* (1988). While publicly being involved in "the hustle" for various reasons is well researched, how these predominantly masculine spaces are conceived of and protected has less documentation.

In the maps that the pimps drew in my study, depictions of outdoor work space and conceptions of the self within the larger informal economy showed variation. There were differences in "territory" and the roles taken in order to protect it from competitors, police, and others. These blueprints for the business, including social exchanges with sex workers, were communicated through spatial depictions.

The accompanying figure is a map drawn by a former pimp. While he was currently living in Harlem, he operated his business in a smaller town in New York State (this is more apparent when you notice the post office and the pharmacy in close proximity).

(continued)

At 8 p.m., the *post office*, la *farmacia* (the pharmacy), and la *bodega* (corner store) closed. Selling sex did not begin until all of these formal businesses closed. These males, shown in front of the bodega, depicted by *me* and *pimp*, claimed this public space (one side of a block) from 8 p.m. to 6 a.m.

This participant was gifted a portion of the business by an uncle; that is, he was given some instruction, a few sex workers, and a place to house them (they all lived together in one large house). Their residence is indicated by the scribbled *ten blocks away* as this was the distance from his work space to his house. It is important to note that it was fairly common that related males taught or handed down the business to younger males in the family. Formal and illicit businesses passed down through family generations are well documented as families try to ensure that successive generations are solvent. This test of masculine worth may be more evident with businesses operating in outdoor space, with mismanagement or failure displayed quite publicly.

The sex workers stood on a small block near an abandoned building (left-hand side of the drawing). The sex workers took their clients in or behind this building. The participant, along with other pimps, stood in front of the bodega (right-hand side of the drawing). This public work space was split by gender, with females (sex workers) on one part of the block and males (pimps) on the other.

The participating pimp's presence in front of the bodega is a form of "doing masculinity." It is a masculine display showing protection of sex workers, ownership of territory/sex workers, and perhaps performativity for one another. The participant discussed his presence as being necessary to ensure that everything ran smoothly and for the safety of sex workers. It is interesting to note that he identifies sex workers primarily by their appearance (e.g., *brown hair, hazel eyes*) and age. They are categorized much like one would if selling wares. He did not have any major conflicts with other pimps despite standing in close proximity. The act of watching from afar in a group displays many different messages.

Although this was a small street-based business operation, spanning one city block, it was connected to a more elaborate business owned by his uncle. The arrangement was a trial run. Much to his dismay, this participant was unable to succeed in the business. When I asked him specifically why he couldn't continue this work, he said that he didn't like to be rough with the girls, and he hinted that this contributed to him having some trouble controlling them. He claimed that his uncle probably felt that he was a failure. Nonetheless, this illicit business operated in an outdoor public space for three years.

Another type of qualitative interview is a focus group, a directed discussion with a small group of people. Focus groups are especially useful in learning about group dynamics. Tarja Pösö, Päivi Honkatukia, and Leo Nyqvist (2008) studied violence in youth residential care facilities in Finnish reform schools. They were interested in how group dynamics affected the ways these young people spoke about violence. The study explored how this knowledge was collectively produced. A focus group with qualitative interviewing was the best approach because the group format acted as a needed stimulus to generate data. Focus groups can also be used in connection with quantitative studies. For instance, James Nolan and Yoshio Akiyama (1999) studied police routines for making records of hate crimes. In a general sense, they knew what concepts they wanted to measure but were unsure how to operationalize them. They convened five focus groups in different cities, groups that included police administrators, mid-level managers, patrol officers, and civilian employees, to learn about different perspectives on hate crime recording. Analyzing focus group results, Nolan and Akiyama prepared a self-administered questionnaire that was sent to a large number of individuals in four police departments.

Key Features of Qualitative Interviewing

All qualitative interview techniques are rooted in a few basic principles.

Qualitative interviews assume different forms depending on the type of study, but some important principles are consistent no matter what the design. Regarding studies discussed above, you may have noticed how these project descriptions were highly contextualized. This means that explorations of the complexity of human experience examine people living in specific environments.

Richness, Meaning, and Shared Cultural Views

Qualitative interviews involve hearing the richness of human experiences, sifting through layered meaning in context, and recognizing shared cultural meanings.

To illustrate this, Clifford Geertz (1973) makes an important distinction between what he called thin and thick description. In his seminal work, *The Interpretation of Cultures*, he discussed ways to interpret the wink of an eye. In a thin description, the observer would merely state that three different people winked and therefore performed the same behavior. Underscoring the importance of interpreting behaviors in context, Geertz (1973, 7–8) described the different meanings of winks.

> The first boy got dust in his eye and his behavior only looked like a wink. Another boy who noticed that it was not a real wink gave a clowning wink to another friend, thereby mocking the boy with dust in his eye. A nearby girl then gave a flirtatious wink to the clowning boy.

This is what Geertz called "thick" description because it involves not only describing actions, but also understanding meanings of behaviors in context. Qualitative interviews are important tools for producing thick description that helps reveal the richness of human experience.

Philippe Bourgois's work studying crack dealers in East Harlem is another example of research that retains the richness of human experience. Bourgois talks about his relationship with Ray, who was the leader of a local spot where crack was for sale—La Farmacia. Notice the detailed description of behaviors and context in this excerpt from *In Search of Respect: Selling Crack in El Barrio* (Bourgois 2002, 28).

> Whether Ray was a Gumby Bear, a violent pervert, or an omnipotent street don "with juice," my long-term relationship with the man ultimately uncovered a vulnerability that he kept hidden in his street persona. In his private conversations with me over his aspirations for the future, he often seemed naïve or even learning-disabled. He was completely incapable of fathoming the intricate rules and regulations of legal society despite his brilliant success

at directing a retail network for crack distribution. To borrow the French sociologist Pierre Bourdieu's analytical category, Ray lacked the "cultural capital" necessary to succeed in the middle-class or even working-class world.

As another example, Valli Rajah (2010) interviewed poor, inner-city women with a history of drug addiction and violent intimate relationships. She sought to uncover their meanings of why they secretly withheld money from their violent partners. Though they were labeled as victims, many of these women took control and exerted agency, despite their circumstances and societal roles. Rajah's description shows how a focus on meanings, in this case about one act, can reveal complex social processes.

Often, people living in similar communities or subcultures have shared cultural meanings that are transmitted through communication among people (Barth 2002). For example, the best way to understand why and how people join right-wing extremist groups would be to interact with members of these groups. Members of right-wing extremist groups may come from similar subcultures and have common values even before joining the group. You can learn something about shared meaning and sometimes subcultures through communication with people who, knowingly or unknowingly, belong to certain groups.

The Critical Realist Approach and the Qualitative Interview

It's useful to think of qualitative interviewing as an approach to learning. But it's important to keep in mind that how qualitative interviews are conducted is rooted in our perspective of reality in the social world. In my research on pimps, I obtained multiple perspectives about how they viewed their sex workers. Some viewed workers as friends/girlfriends, others viewed them as business partners, and some viewed them as employees or just a product. Even within a single interview, the participant may change perspectives. However, each of these perspectives contributes to some reality about pimping. This is known as the **critical realist perspective** (Maxwell 2012). There are two parts

to understanding this position; one involves your stance about the nature of reality and the other about the nature of knowledge (Maxwell 2012). Even though this seems heady, your eventual opinion may influence how you tackle your study.

The nature of reality, or *ontology*, is viewed in two distinct ways: (1) some people believe that a real world exists beyond our perceptions and constructions, (2) whereas others, known as radical constructivists, think that reality is a construction based on what we perceive reality to be. Critical realists believe that reality does exist, which offers a firmer and less complicated platform to begin research. A belief in reality allows you to have some faith that your findings contribute to something real.

The next part is how you view the nature and scope of knowledge. Critical realists believe that interpretations of the world are constructions derived from many individual perspectives (Maxwell 2012). There is no way to find a single, "correct" understanding of the world. Critical realists are comfortable with the idea that knowledge is constructed through multiple meanings.

The idea that the nature of knowledge is constructed from many different individual perspectives is not all that surprising if you think about it for a bit. For example, after Hurricane Katrina, two different photos circulated on Internet news sites showing people wading through the water with food or other items. When the people were white, the byline stated, "two residents wade through water after *finding* some bread." But when the photo was of a black man, the caption read, "a young man walks through chest deep flood water after *looting* groceries" (Sommers et al. 2006). These people were doing exactly the same thing, but the interpretations were quite different. Even if two people look at similar images or hear the same story, they may have very different ways of perceiving what the images or words mean. This example illustrates how peoples' understanding of the world is constructed—knowledge is based on a multiplicity of constructions.

You may be wondering how this influences your overall approach to qualitative interviewing. First, consider how interviewing involves hearing peoples' constructions of lived experiences that give meaning to their life stories. Second, perspectives of lived experience may be shared by members of a group and may be thought of as shared cultural meaning. Third, after listening and being self-aware, you interpret and transmit these meanings to others. This requires being able to admit that your interpretations are also constructions. There is power to acknowledging your subjectivity; that is, recognizing that your interpretations are influenced by your own social lenses, including biases.

Platform for Creating Questions

As a part of planning your approach, before you create questions, you want to figure out who you will interview, along with the depth of your interview questions. This is sometimes termed the *substantive frame*. Weiss (1994, 41) described the substantive frame as "a sense of the breadth and density of the material we want to collect."

For instance, since the 9/11 attacks, Muslim communities in many cities have been monitored by law enforcement. In 2012, news reports revealed that the New York City Police Department (NYPD) had been monitoring Muslim student organizations for potential ties to terrorist activities. Public outrage emerged about this potential infringement on privacy, along with lame justifications about spying in the name of public safety (Baker and Taylor 2012). Let's say you want to conduct research on Muslim students' perspectives of reported police surveillance, such as their feelings about the violation of their civil rights. You might simply interview the students. However, if you wanted a deeper understanding of the problem, you could interview New York's mayor, members of the NYPD, and students who belong to Muslim student organizations.

Next, you should familiarize yourself with studies on the same or similar topics. There may be prior research that examined the treatment of Muslim youth in the United States after 9/11. These prior works will be helpful to find the right framework for your interview questions. When you come up with a set of possible questions, you

should pilot them on someone from the group of interest. In this example, you may ask members of a Muslim student organization some basic questions about their feelings and experiences about being monitored. An earlier pilot interview might change your approach to how you frame the research and the questions, and put you on a different track.

Creating a solid platform for interview questions is essential because it will help you to decide other important steps, such as whether your questions are semi-structured or unstructured, whether your interview is one-on-one or a focus group, and how you should approach your role as the interviewer. The execution of these steps will ultimately lead to analysis that is steeped in richness, contextualized meaning, and shared cultural meanings.

Different Kinds of Qualitative Interviews

As in survey research, qualitative interviews can be conducted in different ways.

Decisions about the form (face-to-face or phone) and type of **interview schedule** influence how in-depth and interactive your interviews should be. Three general types of interview schedules are structured, semi-structured, and unstructured. Most surveys use **structured interview** schedules. Interviews become more natural, in-depth, and exploratory as you move toward unstructured interviewing. Another important point is that the type of interview schedule that you choose often hinges on whether you are testing a specific concept, being guided by existing theory, or doing an exploratory study. If you think of this as a spectrum, unstructured interviewing is the best for an exploratory study where a theory may be generated.

Let's return to the example of Muslim students' perceptions of being monitored by law enforcement. You may already have a particular idea that you want to explore. Maybe you theorized that Muslim students' feelings of being monitored by law enforcement could be explained by labeling theory, which holds that being labeled as deviant by society affects the way people view themselves (Becker 1963). You might ask students how being monitored influenced their self-image in different domains of their lives, such as at home, at work, in school, in the mosque, or in the community more generally. You may decide to use a structured interview schedule that consists of predetermined question and answer sets, where the questions and sometimes the answers are standardized. The reason for standardizing your interview is to try to give participants the same stimulus so that responses will be comparable. A structured qualitative interview can be thought of as a procedure where slivers of information are retrieved for a very particular purpose. These kinds of answers can also be quantified sometimes. The disadvantages of this approach are a lack of depth, sometimes stilted exchanges with participants, and a limited ability to explore unexpected responses.

Both structured and **semi-structured interview** schedules have standardized questions, but the semi-structured interview allows you to explore themes that emerge in the interview. Semi-structured interviews make it possible to allow for unscheduled probes, or spontaneous questions that are relevant to the dialogue. During the pilot interview of your study of Muslim students, you may realize that your study could benefit from unscheduled probes and thus opt for a semi-structured interview schedule. This style of interviewing is usually guided by a specific idea about the group but allows you to probe beyond participants' answers and your own questions.

Scheduled Question

Interviewer: After finding out about being monitored, did you feel any differently when you were at school?

Participant: I felt that people were looking at me more suspiciously.

Scheduled Probe

Interviewer: Can you give me an example of this happening?

Participant: I was buying lunch and all of a sudden, I felt that everyone was watching me. It seemed like the cashier was afraid to take my money and didn't want to interact with me. It made me feel like a suspect. There are not many Muslim students at my school, but lately I have gotten to know a few.

Unscheduled Probe

Interviewer: Did you talk with the other Muslim students about being monitored?

Participant: Yes, we were shocked when we discovered that this was going on. We kind of came together in a way. I wasn't that close with them before this.

The semi-structured interview format allows you to ask a spontaneous question and discover an emerging theme. Through the unscheduled probe, you found that the monitoring was not only negatively influencing self-concept in certain social spheres, but also that it brought some Muslim students closer together. The semi-structured interview has the benefit of producing more standardized and therefore comparable answers, while retaining a natural spontaneity where important themes may be discovered.

Unstructured Interviews

For in-depth interviews, your ideal approaches are semi-structured or unstructured. The most open style of interviewing is the **unstructured interview**. This style provides the most breadth, depth, and natural interaction with participants. Perhaps police monitoring only had a minimal or no influence on Muslim students' self-image. There were other important elements about this experience that you missed because you began with a narrow focus. When there is a lack of existing information about a group's experiences, sometimes in-depth, unstructured interviews yield the best insights. The main drawback is that your interviews are less comparable.

Unstructured interviews take different shapes. Two main approaches to unstructured interviewing are a *conversation* and an *interview guide* (Patton 2002). A conversation is an informal "chat" where participants may forget that they are being interviewed and the conversation flows organically. You might be in a local nightclub or hanging out on the street and strike up a conversation with a member of the group of interest. This type of unstructured interview can be used in exploratory studies but is traditionally used during participant observation or ethnographies. For example, Peter Moskos (2009) joined the Baltimore Police Department to understand police subculture. Moskos obtained much of his data through participant observation and on-the-job conversations with fellow police officers. An *interview guide* includes a list of topical areas that you want to cover in the conversation. Here you have a free-flowing conversation that is guided but allows for conversation that is more natural. With this style, you are free to delve deeply into topics that come up during the exchange, but you use the guide as a reference.

Semi-structured interviews are especially useful if two or more people are interviewing, but you still want to be able to explore emerging themes. For example, if you and a few other people were interviewing female street sex workers in Los Angeles, it would be best to have the same questions. If you only had a list of topics to be discussed such as *clients*, *business negotiations*, and *safety*, these all could be interpreted in multiple ways. One person may see safety and think that he or she should ask about safety from clients, whereas another may interpret this to mean safety from pimps or police. Even if this is outlined beforehand, the subtleties of language may dramatically change the meaning of a question. Standardization helps establish continuity across interviews, but open-ended questions with unscheduled probes still leave room to explore new areas.

Moreover, if you are interested in unadulterated views that center on important themes about sex work, you should choose the unstructured interview. A common misperception is that unstructured interviews lack purpose because they resemble a free-flowing conversation. Margot Ely and colleagues (1991) describe how every interview has a structure. Whether you choose a structured, semi-structured, or unstructured format, there is still preparation for interviews and modifications that you will need to make along the way.

Focus Group Interviews

Some researchers opt to interview groups of people at the same time using; this method is called a **focus group** interview. This technique originated in market research in the 1950s and is still used by companies to learn from potential customers how to the best market their products. Focus groups have come to be widely used by social scientists to gather qualitative data from groups. The group generally consists of 6 to 12 participants and is usually moderated by the researcher (Krueger and Casey 2000). Focus groups can be used to generate hypotheses. Focus groups can also be combined with other types of data gathering such as participant observation. In these scenarios, focus groups generate research ideas or add support to existing findings from other sources of data. The study by Pösö, Honkatukia, and Nyqvist (2008) on how Finnish youth in reform schools produced knowledge about violence is a good example of how focus groups can generate data about group dynamics.

Group discussions can show how opinions are produced, expressed, and exchanged in everyday life. It is important to keep in mind that the focus group is not a problem-solving session or a decision-making group, but rather an interview (Flick 2009, 196–197). The interview schedule for focus groups can also be structured, semi-structured, or unstructured depending on your purpose. Unstructured focus group interviews are used for research that is more exploratory and are often used to understand a research topic or to generate questions, whereas the more structured interviews use questions to guide the discussion.

Participant Dynamics Two basic types of focus groups are a *natural group* and an *artificial group*. Individuals in a natural group may already be acquainted or have an existing connection; they sometimes also have shared cultural meaning. Let's say that you became interested in the Muslim student who said that monitoring by law enforcement brought her closer to other Muslim students at school. You may realize that monitoring created a process of unification among Muslim students and become interested in how this process works. A natural focus group would be a great way to learn how this experience brought the group together. You could ask students if they would be interested in a focus group and then use a type of snowball sample. Although you cannot recreate the initial conversations that they had or see the initial process, you may be able to witness similar dynamics and hear how they collectively reacted to being spied on by their government.

An artificial group includes people selected according to some criteria and brought together for research purposes (Flick 2009). For instance, maybe you are interested in how men think about avoiding crime. You could create a focus group of men and have them discuss the different ways that they interpret danger and the tactics that they used to stay away from potential crime spots. The only factor that this group has in common is that they are men from urban areas, so it is an artificial group. Artificial groups are best when researchers want to avoid having discussion affected by preexisting relationships.

Designing Qualitative Interview Questions

Qualitative interview questions can assume different forms.

The different approaches to framing interviews depend on how focused and in depth you want your questions to be. One approach is to have a main topic, such as *safety* in sex work, with branching questions that you explore at the same level. One line of questioning, such as safety from clients, does not take precedence over other areas, like safety from police.

Maybe you interview sex workers to find that while discussing safe/unsafe situations some sex workers mention their leisure activities such as having lunch with their pimp. You may find that some workers talk about how these activities make them feel safe. This is where the questions return to the main topic. On the other hand, maybe they feel like their activities outside of the job are important parts of their lived experience. In this case, the topic diverges. You may decide to probe more about other activities that they do outside of work.

The way that you create your interview schedule mirrors the way you examine research questions. Think of it as deciding about how to write a short story. Is the story better told chronologically, or is it more compelling without the element of time? A *diachronic* delivery of material starts at the beginning and progresses chronologically (Weiss 1994). This approach may center on developments over time. With the example of the sex workers in Los Angeles, you may ask them to describe how they dealt with safety issues when they first started working and how these issues may have changed over time. Diachronic story lines are sometimes explanatory, such as a description about why sex workers get involved in selling sex.

The other framework is *synchronic*, where structure does not depend on the element of time. With this approach, you may move from sector to sector. You may ask how sex workers negotiate their safety in different spheres of their lives, such as at home, on the street, or with police. Synchronic story lines are also about function. You may want to understand how a process operates. If you are looking at the street-based commercial sex industry, you may try to understand how sex workers negotiate with clients, how they interact with pimps, their contacts with police, or even social networks among sex workers. Essentially, you are interested in interrelationships between actors within and peripheral to this informal economy.

Interview Schedule

Before you begin writing up your interview schedule, it is usually best to create an outline of more categories of information you want to obtain. If your main research question is about female sex workers navigating work on the streets of Los Angeles, you would create categories and nested sets of questions for each topical area. Here is an example of a topical list with questions:

1. Clients
   a. What are your typical clients like?
   b. Where do you meet clients?
   c. What happens when you have a conflict with a client?
      i. Can you tell me more about this?
2. Pimps
   a. Do you have a friend or boyfriend who helps you out with work?
   b. Do you have a pimp?
   c. What is he/she like?
   d. Where did you meet him/her?
   e. What happens when you have a conflict with him/her?
3. Business negotiations
   a. How do you find clients?
   b. When do you negotiate prices with customers?
   c. Where do you go with customers?
   d. What do you do if something goes wrong?
4. Safety measures
   a. Are there some things that you do to make sure that you are safe at work?
   b. How do you make sure that nothing bad happens while you are at work?
   c. Can you tell me about any problems that you've had while you are at work?
      i. Can you tell me a little more about this?

It is important to keep in mind that questions "frame" how the participant is going to respond. Your list will probably change as you fine-tune your questions.

In qualitative interviews, the *main questions* guide the conversation because they are directly related to your research questions. There are some things that you should ask yourself about your main questions (Rubin and Rubin 2011): (1) Do they encompass the overall subject? (2) Is there a good flow in terms of transitions from question to question? (3) Does the chronology (if synchronic) make sense?

(4) Is the language at the appropriate level for your participants? Your main questions generate answers, which are the core of your data, so it's important to think very carefully about them. Table 8.1 offers more guidelines for preparing qualitative interview questions.

How a question is worded can influence how it's answered, so framing questions with care is very important. You can add extra questions that are similar to the main questions in your schedule to check for reliability (Berg 1998). However, be careful not to overdo this because participants may become annoyed if they think that you are repeating questions; they may think that you are not listening or did not like their initial answers.

There are different approaches to placement of the main questions in the interview. You can put them all together or intersperse them with other questions. One rule of thumb is to avoid placing the main questions in the beginning of the interview. Imagine if you started an interview by asking a sex worker: "How do you make sure that nothing bad happens while you are at work?" It's customary to make sure that the first questions are not emotionally loaded. The main questions should come after some level of comfort between you and the participant is established. You can have throw away questions, which could be about demographics or less threatening topics in the beginning in order to establish this rapport (Berg 1998).

Probes

Probes are important tools for qualitative interviewing because they prompt participants to elaborate on responses by filling in more detail and, therefore, depth. Another important purpose of probes is to signal participants that you are actively listening. You may have already noticed a built in probe in one of the questions for the sex workers that you are going to interview. Notice the probe at the end of this question (italicized): Can you tell me about any problems that you've had with people while you are at work? *Can you tell me a little more about this?* The built-in probe following this question helps gently prompt participants to reveal

TABLE 8.1   The Nitty-Gritty of Writing Questions

Problems to Avoid		Elements of a Good Question	
Double-barreled questions	These questions simultaneously ask the participant two questions.	**Clear**	Your questions should be very easy to understand.
	Example: How many times have you had sex, and did you use a condom?		*Example: How many times have you had sex? How many of these times did you use a condom?*
Complex questions	Questions that are involved and long should be avoided because the participant may forget part of the question or become annoyed.	**Concise**	Your questions should be short and to the point.
			Example: After joining the gang, did you feel any differently?
	Example: Once you joined the gang, did you feel that you underwent a transformation where you felt differently from how you felt before you became a gang member?	**Appropriate language level**	Language level may vary depending on the participants. Generally, language level should be simple.
			Example: Have you ever hit, punched, or badly hurt someone during casual sex?
Difficult language	Language level should never be overly difficult.	**More neutral words**	When your questions involve sensitive subject matter, use words that are not as emotionally loaded.
	Example: Whilst engaging in trysts, did you ever use brute physical force?		*Example: Have you ever hurt someone seriously in a fight?*
Affective words	Be cautious about using emotional words.		
	Example: Have you ever beaten someone so badly they were hospitalized?		

sensitive information. On the other hand, if the respondent gives a detailed response to the question, then the probe may not be necessary. When you create your interview schedule, it is important to have built-in probes in case you have reluctant or quiet participants.

Think for a moment about how we use probes in regular conversations. If a friend starts telling you some gossip, you might use an *attention probe* such as leaning in to signal that you are interested in the information. Or maybe you use a *continuation probe*, such as a nod, that acts as another gesture to elaborate. If part of the story is not clear, you might use a *clarification probe*. We use this type of probe when we do not understand something a participant says. Probes are standard in regular everyday conversations, and they are essential tools for qualitative interviews.

Follow-up questions are a type of probe that you can use during the interview or in a second interview. You may recognize that a theme is emerging after interviews with different participants, and you may want more elaboration. Suppose that one participant in your study of sex workers is a client who regularly beats up workers. Maybe the second or third time that you hear this same story, you ask the participant if she has talked with other sex workers about keeping an eye on this client. It may not have occurred to you to ask this during the first interview or it may have occurred to you near the end of the interview. This may become an important point of inquiry about how sex workers try to protect each other against predatory clients. These follow-ups can occur spontaneously or even in a second interview. You can add follow-up questions that emerge to your interview schedule.

Such flexibility is one of the strengths of qualitative interviewing. If you have recognized an important theme, such as that some sex workers unify and help each other with specific safety issues, you may want to explore this.

Gaining Access to Participants

Arranging access to subjects depends on their role in organizations or subcultures.

Research in criminology can involve participants from a variety of formal organizations, participants who are active offenders, or people involved in a variety of subcultures. In planning qualitative interviews, it's important to think carefully about your role vis-à-vis participants.

Establishing Your Role

One of the first considerations is **insider/outsider status** relative to the group that you want to study. Your level of insiderness depends on how close you are to the group. The more connected you are to the group, then the more of an insider you are. Suppose that you want to study the subculture of drug dealers. You could credibly play more of an insider role if you used to sell drugs or had friends who are drug dealers. There are advantages and disadvantages to being an insider. Familiarity with your participants' lives allows you to delve deeply into topics without having to learn the subculture and its associated jargon (Ely et al. 1991). However, as an insider, you may be too close to participants and, therefore, the topics discussed. Biases can result because you already have rooted ideas about the subculture. No consensus exists about whether is it is better to be an insider or an outsider, but your role will undoubtedly influence your access to the group and how you conduct your research more generally.

You may already be part of the group of interest, as Dina Perrone (2009) became accepted by the "club kids." With insider status, you can exploit your own experience to gain access because you may know a few people from the group. Or you may at least know enough about some group members to gain access more easily. An example of this is what's referred to as "convict criminology," where people who were formerly incarcerated study aspects of incarceration or prisoner reentry. Other researchers insert themselves into the lives of the group of interest, as exhibited in Jeff Ferrell's (2002) work on graffiti artists, where he engaged in spray painting, drinking, and general socializing with participants. Some researchers are already insiders, whereas others insert themselves into the lives of participants to attain quasi-insider status.

Criminal justice researchers are more commonly outsiders, having no existing connection to the group of interest. In such cases, researchers have to navigate access to participants. Your group of interest influences the way that you gain access. You use formal channels to gain access if your group is affiliated with an organization/institution. For example, if they are in a treatment program, are incarcerated, or are a part of a police department, then you will probably have to gain access through the institution. On the other hand, if you are interested in people who are engaged in criminal lifestyles, you can find informal access. You find sponsorship, gaining the trust of someone on the inside who will vouch for you and introduce you to members of the group. Both formal and informal access usually involve negotiation.

Access to Formal Organizations

Suppose you decide to conduct research on a community corrections agency in a large city. Let's assume that you do not know a great deal about the agency and that you will identify yourself as an outside researcher to staff and other people you encounter. Your research interests are primarily descriptive: you want to observe the routine operations of the agency in the office and elsewhere. In addition, you want to interview agency staff and persons who are serving community corrections sentences. This section will discuss some of the ways you might prepare before you conduct your interviews and direct observations.

Any research on a criminal justice institution, or on persons who work either in or under the supervision of an institution, normally requires a formal request and approval. One of the first steps in preparing for the field, then, is to arrange access to the community corrections agency.

Obtaining initial approval can be confusing and frustrating. Many criminal justice agencies in large cities have a complex organization, combining a formal hierarchy with a bewildering variety of informal organizational cultures. Criminal courts are highly structured organizations in which a presiding judge may oversee court assignments and case scheduling for judges and many support personnel. At the same time, courts are chaotic organizations in which three constellations of professionals—prosecutors, defense attorneys, and judges—episodically interact to process large numbers of cases.

Continuing with the example of your research on community corrections, the best strategy in gaining access to virtually any other formal criminal justice organization is to use a four-step procedure: sponsor, letter, phone call, and meeting. Our discussion of these steps assumes that you will begin your field research by interviewing the agency executive director and gaining that person's approval for subsequent interviews and observations.

Sponsor The first step is to find a sponsor—a person who is personally known to and respected by the executive director. Ideally, a sponsor will be able to advise you on a person to contact, that person's formal position in the organization, and her or his informal status, including her or his relationships with other key officials. Such advice can be important in helping you initiate contact with the right person while avoiding people who have bad reputations.

Finding the right sponsor is often the most important step in gaining access. It may require a couple of extra steps, because you might first need to ask a professor whether she or he knows someone. You could then contact that person (with the sponsorship of your professor) and ask for further assistance. For purposes of illustration, we will assume that your professor is knowledgeable, well connected, and happy to act as your sponsor.

Letter Next, write a letter to the executive director. Your letter should have three parts: introduction, brief statement of your research purpose, and action request. See Figure 8.1 for an example. The introduction begins by naming your sponsor, thus immediately establishing your mutual acquaintance.

Next, you describe your research purpose succinctly. This is not the place to give a detailed description as you would in a proposal. If possible, keep the description to one or two paragraphs, as in Figure 8.1. If a longer description is necessary to explain what you will be doing, you should *still* include only a brief description in your introductory letter, referring the reader to a separate attachment in which you summarize your research.

The action request describes what immediate role you are asking the contact person to play in your research. You may simply be requesting an interview, or you may want the person to help you gain access to other officials. Notice how the sample in Figure 8.1 mentions both an interview and "suggestions on further sources of information about community corrections." In any case, you will usually want to arrange to meet or at least talk with the contact person. That leads to the third step.

Phone Call You probably already know that it can be difficult to arrange meetings with public officials (and often professors) or even to reach people by telephone. You can simplify this task by concluding your letter with a proposal for this step: arranging a phone call.

When you make the call, the executive director will have some idea of who you are and what you want. She will also have had the opportunity to contact your sponsor if she wants to verify any information in your introductory letter.

Even if you are not able to talk with the executive director personally, you will probably be able to talk to an assistant and make an appointment for a meeting (the next step). Again, this will be possible because your letter described what you eventually want—a meeting with the executive director—and established your legitimacy by naming a sponsor.

Jane Adams
Executive Director
Chaos County Community Corrections
Anxiety Falls, Colorado   1 May 2009

Dear Ms. Adams:

My colleague, Professor Marcus Nelson, suggested I contact you for assistance in my research on community corrections. I will be conducting a study of community corrections programs and wish to include the Chaos County agency in my research.

Briefly, I am interested in learning more about the different types of sentences that judges impose in jurisdictions with community corrections agencies. As you know, Colorado's community corrections statute grants considerable discretion to individual counties in arranging locally administered corrections programs. Because of this, it is generally believed that a wide variety of corrections programs and sentences have been developed throughout the state. My research seeks to learn more about these programs as a first step toward developing recommendations that may guide the development of programs in other states. I also wish to learn more about the routine administration of a community corrections program such as yours.

I would like to meet with you to discuss what programs Chaos County has developed, including current programs and those that were considered but not implemented. In addition, any information about different types of community corrections sentences that Chaos County judges impose would be very useful. Finally, I would appreciate your suggestions on further sources of information about community corrections programs in Chaos County and other areas.

I will call your office at about 10:00 a.m. on Monday, May 8, to arrange a meeting. If that time will not be convenient, or if you have any questions about my research, please contact me at the number below.

Thanks in advance for your help.

Sincerely,

Alfred Nobel
Research Assistant
Institute for Advanced Studies
(201) 555-1212

FIGURE 8.1 Sample Letter of Introduction

Meeting The final step is meeting with or interviewing the contact person. Because you have used the letter–phone call–meeting procedure, the contact person may have already taken preliminary steps to help you. For example, because the letter in Figure 8.1 indicates that you wish to interview the executive director about different types of community corrections sentences, she may have assembled some procedures manuals or reports in preparation for your meeting.

This procedure generally works well in gaining initial access to public officials or other people who work in formal organizations. Once initial access is gained, it is up to the researcher to use interviewing skills and other techniques to elicit the desired information. This is not as difficult as it might seem to novice (or apprentice) researchers for a couple of reasons.

First, most people are at least a bit flattered that their work, ideas, and knowledge are of interest to a researcher. And researchers can take advantage of this with the right words of encouragement. Second, criminal justice professionals are often happy to talk about their work with a knowledgeable outsider. Police, probation officers, and corrections workers usually encounter only their colleagues and their clients on the job. Interactions with colleagues become routine and suffused with office politics, and interactions with clients are common sources of stress. Talking with an interested and knowledgeable researcher is often seen as a pleasant diversion.

By the same token, Richard Wright and Scott Decker (1994) report that most members of their sample of active burglars were both happy and flattered to discuss the craft of burglary. Because they were engaged in illegal activities, burglars had to be more circumspect about sharing their experiences, unlike the way many people talk about events at work. As a result, burglars enjoyed the chance to describe their work to interested researchers who both promised confidentiality and treated them "as having expert knowledge normally unavailable to outsiders" (1994, 26).

Access to Informal Organizations and Subcultures

Research by Wright and Decker illustrates how gaining access to subcultures in criminal justice—such as active offenders or juvenile gangs—requires tactics that differ in many respects from those used to meet with public officials. Letters, phone calls, and formal meetings are usually not appropriate for initiating field research among active offenders. However, the basic principle of using a sponsor to gain initial access operates in much the same way.

Sponsors in this case may be people whose job involves working with offenders—such as police, juvenile caseworkers, probation officers, attorneys, and counselors at drug clinics. Lawyers who specialize in criminal defense work can be especially useful sources of information about potential subjects. Frances Gant and Peter Grabosky (2001) contacted a private investigator to help locate car thieves and people working in auto-related businesses who were reputed to deal in stolen parts. Wright and Decker (1994) were fortunate to encounter a former offender who was well connected with active criminals. The ex-offender helped researchers in two related ways. First, he referred them to other people, who in turn found active burglars willing to participate in the study. Second, he was well known and respected among

burglars, and his sponsorship of the researchers made it possible for them to study a group of naturally suspicious subjects.

A different approach for gaining access to subcultures is to hang around places where criminals hang out. Wright and Decker rejected that strategy as a time-consuming and uncertain way to find burglars, in part because they were not sure where burglars hung out. In contrast, Bruce Jacobs (1999) initiated contact with street-level drug dealers by hanging around and being noticed in locations known for crack availability. Consider how this tactic might make sense for finding drug dealers, whose illegal work requires customers. In contrast, the offense of burglary is more secretive, and it's more difficult to imagine how one would find an area known for the presence of burglars.

Reviewing field research in several cities, Scott Jacques and Richard Wright (2008) offer general advice on recruiting active offenders. First, more informal social interaction between researchers, criminals, and informants increases the likelihood that offenders will participate. Second, it often helps to pay a small fee in gaining cooperation from offenders who are recruited through a chain of referrals. Third, they maintain that:

> … criminals who are closest in relational distance to the researcher, especially those who have done previous interviews, are the ones most likely to produce the greatest amount of valid data and are thus the most appropriate persons with whom to discuss the most serious crimes. (Jacques and Wright 2008, 35)

As another example, review the description of gaining access to pimps in the opening vignette for this chapter.

Encouraging Participation

Compensation for access and participation is often required in studies where the researcher is an outsider. At the most basic level, you might compensate participants with payments, goods, or services. Another approach to compensation is to give your contact other stakes in the project. An example is co-authorship of a paper you might write. If your sponsor has more stakes in the project, then you may get richer data. Such arrangements are best established at the outset. Some researchers feel that, on principle, participants should always have a voice in the final product (Denzin 1997). Member checks, where insiders can review your final product, are the best way to get this input. Participants read your work for incorrect interpretations of meanings and sometimes ask you to eliminate certain information. I have more to say about member checks later in this chapter.

Another important question stems from social roles of participants. Is your group advantaged, such as white-collar offenders, or disadvantaged, such as pimps? Both advantaged and disadvantaged groups tend to be more secretive, albeit for different reasons, and can be hard to reach as a result.

Reluctance to participate usually occurs when participants feel that the study can be a legal, economic, physical, or psychological threat (Adler and Adler 2001). Participants who engage in illegal behavior, who are currently victims of violence, or who have powerful roles in the community may worry about some combination of these problems. Many qualitative interviews involve sensitive issues; in a sense, any questions about one's personal life are sensitive. It is often possible to allay participants' fears by being informal, carefully explaining confidentiality, and not rushing or pressuring participants into the interview.

Conducting Qualitative Interviews

By their nature, qualitative interviews are conducted in a variety of settings.

As in doing surveys, qualitative interviews can occur face-to-face, over the phone, or online. Face-to-face interviews are generally the norm. You may meet participants in public parks, restaurants, drug clinics, strip clubs, prison, or any number of settings. The quality of interaction between phone and face-to-face interviews differs because the former lacks the important social element of physicality. Think about the difference between talking to a friend on the phone versus meeting that friend in person. You may miss a lot of rich information over the phone, such as noticing that your friend may be visibly upset when you bring up a certain topic. You might be able to hear this in her voice, but it's usually more evident through a dynamic social exchange that includes nonverbal cues. Phone interviews may be useful for certain types of participants, such as if they live far away or if they are members of a group that is notably dangerous. Online or mail surveys can usually have only a few open-ended questions. More importantly, self-administered questionnaires lack the interaction and flexibility of a conversation. Overall, interview formats are largely guided by overall research objectives and how you are able gain access to the group.

Reflexivity

Reflexivity refers generally to your subjectivity in the research process. Recall that reality is constructed from multiple meanings. In qualitative interviewing, you are the instrument of data collection, which means that you are also involved in constructing meaning. Because you construct meaning based on communication with others, you essentially represent them through your interpretation of their stories. As a result, it's important to understand how to engage in reflexivity before and throughout the research process.

The process of self-reflexivity requires you to be critically conscious of who you are and your feelings. Wanda Pillow (2003) suggests that you should begin by asking yourself a few questions: "Who am I?" "How do my feelings affect my research?" The first question includes your self-location across gender, race, class, sexuality, and ethnicity. Situating yourself within the larger social structure and being aware of your feelings influence how you relate to participants.

In the example of interviewing female sex workers in Los Angeles, your interviews will likely be influenced by your gender. If you are female, you may be able to identify with your participants about safety issues on a deeper level than if you are male. Even if you have never engaged in sex work, as a female you probably have more experience thinking about safety. However, overidentification can backfire because sex workers may have very different conceptions of safety. You can think about how your position intersects with and is different from your participants. Your self-location, whether it involves difference, intersection, or insider status, can influence rapport with participants. If you choose to forego self-reflexivity, your interpretations can suffer from unchecked biases.

On the other hand, reflexivity may be overdone and can be viewed as indulgent or narcissistic if overused in the narrative interpretation. Even if reflexivity is not present in your final product, it is still important to be self-aware and keep track of how your feelings influence your research. You may opt for transparency about the process and decide to include how your assumptions shifted in the course of research. I discuss how parts of this process emerged in my research with pimps in the box, "Pimps: Stereotypes, Biases, and Self-Reflexivity."

Rapport

Once you have established access, you must think about your **rapport**, or how you connect with participants. The interaction between the interviewer and the participant is initially influenced by insider/outsider status. Initial rapport may be established through nonthreatening conversation such as talking about the weather, current events, or anything that allows for informal banter. You can strengthen rapport by finding things that you have in common with participants. Some researchers share personal information about themselves as a way to connect with participants.

Some participants feel more comfortable talking about personal issues with strangers because they do not have shared social networks and will probably never see each other again. People sometimes feel better about revealing information when there is an element of detachment (Adler and Adler 2001). Other researchers feel it is important to establish genuine relationships with participants. It is sometimes the case that having multiple conversations with participants yields the richest answers because a deeper level of rapport can be obtained.

PIMPS: STEREOTYPES, BIASES, AND SELF-REFLEXIVITY

You may begin your research project with preexisting ideas or biases about your group of interest. When I decided to interview pimps, I read as much literature as I could find and also watched a number of films. Although I was not expecting to meet Super Fly, I expected some sort of stereotypical "pimp identity." Media and academic portrayals of pimps shaped some of my preconceptions about pimps until I started interviews. This is where an acute awareness of my subjectivity had to be kept in check and self-reflexivity throughout the study was crucial to understanding my biases.

Stereotypes about pimps were elevated in the media in 1970s blaxploitation films such as *The Mack*, *Super Fly*, and *Willie Dynamite*, as well as more current movies such as *Hustle and Flow*. These renditions parody the pimp and portray him as flamboyant and comical, yet coldhearted. A few books around this time period—such as Iceburg Slim's semiautobiographical

book *Pimp, The Story of My Life* and Susan Hall's book about the life of Silky titled *Gentleman of Leisure*—also confirmed a lot of these media portrayals. Today, an Internet search for the keyword *pimp* shows that the meaning of the word has broadened. A search will yield quite an array of books and other items centered, for example, on how to coerce women, trick people, and make your car look outlandish.

Very few studies explore pimping from the perspective of a pimp. Many of the articles published focus on the role of the pimp as someone who is coercive, abusive, violent, and even psychopathic (Benoit and Millar, 2001; Greaves et al., 2004; Kennedy et al., 2007; Sanders, 2001; Silbert and Pines, 1981). Most of these inferences were gleaned from interviews with prostitutes or law enforcement and included very few conversations with pimps. The dearth of research and information on actual pimps is surprising and perpetuates our imaginings about pimps.

Once an interview is under way, you can do a number of things to maintain the rapport necessary for a quality interview. In an article entitled, "The Great Interview: 25 Strategies for Studying People in Bed," Hermanowicz (2002) used a sexual metaphor to establish characteristics of a great interview. Some key advice about rapport included the following:

- *Converse* as opposed to engaging in a mechanistic verbal exchange.

- *Listen* or hear the data in the moment.

- *Find all that your date finds important* or pay attention to meaning.

- *Probe* or make sure that you get specifics.

- Sometimes *remain quiet* when your date is quiet.

- *Persist* with probes or other inquiries.

- *Play innocent* sometimes because they may want to help you (don't overdo this because it may seem disingenuous).

- *Don't stay out all night; don't come home too early*, meaning pay attention to the length of the interview.

- *Word questions clearly*.

- *Sequence your moves* so that conversation has a good flow.

- *Be candid*.

- *Show respect*.

- *End on a positive note*.

Great interactions in an interview can be similar to great social exchanges in regular life. Of course, you do not need to take home your participants or become overly intimate with them. Instead, think about the basics of good conversations. Use your existing social abilities to help establish rapport and maintain it throughout the interview, something that can be a great benefit to your research.

Active Interviewing

By this point, you should recognize that qualitative interviewing cannot be objective. A corollary is that dynamic social exchange should not be artificially limited. Active interviewing is a dynamic two-sided social exchange that serves as a meaning-making context (Holstein and Gubrium 1995). The social exchange that is the dialogue between you and the participant is what enables the creation of meaning.

It's helpful to think of an active interview as a collaboration between you and the participant. The boundaries of how you see things become visible through the collaborative interaction. This process is sometimes referred to as *horizons of meaning* because during active interviewing, the interpretive boundaries of you and your participants are discovered (Holstein and Gubrium 1995). You and the participant may unwittingly push one another's boundaries, and the conflict between boundaries can also generate meaning.

For example, in her study on the narratives of alcoholics, Margaretha Järvinen (2000) analyzed three interviews where the interviewer's and the participant's horizons of meaning were in conflict. The aim of the overall project was to talk to alcoholics about their experiences of treatment. A few participants, despite their willingness to be in a study of long-term alcohol abusers, were in varying states of denial. For instance, Eric admitted to drinking over 30 beers a day, but the interviewer's interpretation of him as a long-term alcohol abuser clashed with his own self-image. Instead of viewing this as an unsuccessful interview, Järvinen realized that such narratives showed how people with alcohol problems have to negotiate their identities.

The active interview allows for natural conversation that enables spontaneity. You may have an interview guide, but how you use the guide will vary from one interview to the next, and on some occasions, it may be abandoned. I try not to look at my interview schedule while conversing with participants. On my first field outing with pimps in Harlem, I interviewed a higher-level pimp near the end of the day. As the interview was coming to a close, I glanced down at my interview schedule to make sure that I didn't miss any questions. The participant stated, "Why you need to look at that? You have been interviewing pimps all day. You know what questions you want to ask me." This was an important moment because I realized that some participants are offended when they realize that the conversation has been guided and, in fact, value the naturalness of a typical conversation.

In active interviews, the participant's responses determine which question comes next. They determine if you are going to shift topic or probe about the same topic. This approach lends itself to a natural conversation where meaning is produced through dialogue, but the interview remains focused. Instead of forcing questions that are unnatural to the dialogue by switching topics, you are flexible.

In my study of New York City pimps, I asked participants to describe a typical workday early on in the interview. In the first example below, the participant brought up money. Instead of ignoring this, I asked some questions about prices, which were actually at the end of the interview guide. In the second example, the participant discussed getting his sex workers ready for work. I had to use some unscheduled probes to ask more about this. Both examples show that conversation with participants should flow as naturally as possible.

Example 1

Interviewer: Tell me about a typical day at work.

Participant: A typical day at work is um we get the clients set up with the girls and um they have to bring home the money to us and at the end of the day, we give them a certain percentage.

Interviewer: What percentage do you give them?

Participant: 10%

Interviewer: 10%?

Participant: Yeah.

Interviewer: Ok. And what were you charging for stuff?

Participant: 50 dollars for sex.

Interviewer: For anything?

Participant: Yeah.

Example 2

Interviewer: And tell me about a typical day that you would have.

Participant: Well a typical day is getting up in the morning, getting them bitches out to

get ready. That was a typical day. If you got a few of them, you gotta get their hair done. They gotta get their nails done. Cause you don't want to put a girl out there that's not attractive. So you gotta take them here to get their hair done.

Interviewer: So that happens early in the morning?

Participant: You try to get there at like 10 o'clock in the morning cause the beauty parlors be jammed if you taking in like 4 to 5 hoes, bitches. You gotta wait for all 4, 5 of them to get done.

Interviewer: So you get them all ready.

Participant: You get 'em all ready. Then you probably go out for breakfast. You know what I mean? Just try to soften the mood cause what you going into at night is very, it's very dangerous. It's exhilarating. It's dangerous. And you can get locked up for it too. So you try to … after they get theyselves together, you try to soften the mood cause they know what's coming. I mean you might like soften the mood, so you may take them to breakfast. Then we might just go into the car. Go riding some place. Just to get them out. Get it off their mind. Then you bring 'em back and put them on the track.

Interviewer: So it's like an all day preparation kind of thing.

Participant: All day preparation and not just for them, for yourself too. Cause you gotta get into that frame of mind before you put them out there at night because there's no telling what might happen to them. And whatever happens to them you got to be there.

The Interactive Interview

The active interview can be taken to another level where you are more purposefully interactive. The interactive or dramaturgical interview uses elements and language of theater akin to what Erving

Goffman (1959) termed a *social performance*. Consider the idea that everyday social encounters involve some kind of performance where people are social actors who take on certain roles. The interviewer and participant send and receive messages through nonverbal and verbal communication. Some of these messages are intentional while others are unconscious. With the interactive interview, you must be highly attuned to social cues and your own reflections during the interview.

In an interactive interview, you are simultaneously *the actor*, *the director*, and *the choreographer* (Berg 1998). As the actor, you must be attune to your own lines but be respectful of the participant. As the director, you must be conscious of your performance and the participant's performance. Finally, as the choreographer, you must be insightful and constantly evaluating each move. Berg called for a highly self-conscious social performance, but this should not be confused with an entirely staged interaction. Instead of following a stilted soap opera script that is overly dramatized, your performance will be similar to improvisational theater where you are attentive to the moves of participants and yourself to draw out the richest performance.

Conducting Focus Group Interviews

If you are moderating a focus group, you have to combine all the skills of a good interviewer while navigating interactions among participants and generally monitoring the group. Among other things, you are in a balancing act where you must guide the group without being overly directive. In most focus groups, we are interested in spontaneity and the emergence of themes, but this can become difficult because conversations may more easily veer off topic. You must realize when to rein in the group and when to be silent and allow the conversation among group members to flow.

Planning and Design Considerations A number of design considerations are important in planning focus groups. The first is whether to have a homogenous (natural) or a heterogeneous (artificial) group. A group with existing connections among participants can yield richer information. They already have shared experience and perhaps shared cultural meaning. Second, you have to decide about the physical arrangement of the group. For example, you can put the group in a circle. This is not only more intimate, but also can reduce implied power differentials because no one is in a clear leadership position.

The next consideration is the length of time the focus group lasts, usually ranging between 90 minutes and 2 hours. Here's some rough guidance for a 2-hour interview: you have 15 minutes for introductions and late arrivals, 15 minutes for questions and summary, and 90 minutes of actual questioning time and closure (V. Rajah, personal communication, October 20, 2011). A final consideration is whether to have a natural, less structured question route or a more formal interview schedule. The natural question route allows for unscheduled probes, which work very well in focus group settings.

Groupthink and Dominant Group Members There are a few things to keep track of with respect to group dynamics. Two common examples are *groupthink* and *dominant group members*. Irving Janis (1972) coined the term "groupthink" to describe the need of groups for harmony to minimize conflict and reach consensus. If a focus group is exhibiting groupthink, you may not hear opposing opinions, thereby missing alternative viewpoints. To tease out other group members' opinions, you may try probes and questions that are more provocative. A different problem is a dominant group member who takes over the group, perhaps silencing participants who are more reticent. If this is happening, you may direct your questions to people who have not spoken to see if you can change the dynamic. Groupthink and dominant group members occur naturally in any group.

Generating Data on Stigmatized Topics Collecting data from a focus group about sensitive or stigmatized topics such as sexual behaviors, drug use, or criminal activity requires a few special considerations. First, you must realize that your participants are being asked to disclose private information that can result in social censure or disapproval, something that can be upsetting to participants. The focus group format cannot ensure confidentiality, and participants should be aware of this. On the other hand, awareness about the lack of privacy may produce biased responses. Kaye Wellings, Patrick Branigan, and Kirsti Mitchell (2000, 256) advocate using the focus group format "to reveal conflicts and contradictions between what is personal and private and what is public and open." In the case of sensitive topics, the focus group may be used to show how the collective verbally traverses personal and potentially stigmatizing information about themselves in conversation with others.

Recording Data

Several things must be considered in recording data from qualitative interviews.

Qualitative interviews may be captured via audio or video recording, photographs, and mapping, supplemented by note taking. After completing interviews, researchers transcribe the dialogue verbatim or summarize it for analysis. Even though technology provides you with tools to capture interactions with participants in context, recording or "logging" data is much more involved. A logging record includes transcribed interviews, notes during interviews (you should take some notes even if you are audio recording), field notes, and memoing. As described by John Lofland and Lyn Lofland (1995, 67), "the logging record is, in a very real sense, the data." Although creating logging records can be tedious, the kinds of in-depth insights that can be gained from qualitative interviewing depend on the quality of the interview log.

After you return from interviewing, your next task is to write up your field notes. Field notes can include observations and descriptions of interview context as well as the interview itself. Field notes should be written promptly as the experience is fresh in your mind and you can record as much detail as possible. Lofland and Lofland (1995) recommend that notes be written up no later than the morning after an interview. Your perceptions and

emotions about interviewing experiences may seem so intense that you think that you will not forget anything. Inevitably, your impressions will change as you have more interactions with participants. If you write up a few days work of fieldwork at the same time, you will lose nuances of your earlier experiences. So it's important to write up field notes as soon as possible.

Even if other people transcribe interviews verbatim for you, you still have to study each transcript. In any event, it is a good idea to transcribe a few interviews yourself because you may benefit from closely listening to the interview. You find ways to improve your interview style and have the chance to hear the data closely. As a general rule of thumb, you should spend as much time studying the transcript as you did conducting the interview (Lofland and Lofland 1995).

Memoing is a technique that involves writing about your research process from beginning to end. Memos allow you to explore decisions that you made as you conducted your research and serve as a window into your own subjectivity in the interview process. These documents are part of what's called an *audit trail* or record (Birks, Chapman, and Francis 2008; Bowen 2008).

Melanie Birks, Ysane Chapman, and Karen Francis (2008) describe three types of memos: *operational, coding*, and *analytic*. In operational memos, you write about the steps that you took at each stage in your research. Recalling the earlier discussion on reflexivity, memos are a great way to be self-reflexive and keep track of changes in your perception as your research progresses. Coding memos allow you to document the process of coding your data, and analytic memos provide a way for you to explore relationships in the data. These memos become part of your data log and enable you to make sense of your data more easily.

Qualitative projects can produce large data logs, and you may be wondering how you are going to keep track of all of this stuff. Specialized computer applications help organize and make sense of the data you gather. *Atlas.ti* and *NVivo* are examples that allow you to create memos and link related documents, which contribute to easier coding and analysis. It's also possible to create your own system to organize data and notes with a variety of word processing and other standard applications. Besides being compulsive about field notes, listening to interviews, and memoing, you should create a system to organize and back up all of your data on separate disks or in the cloud.

Data Analysis and Making Claims

Analyzing nonnumerical data from qualitative interviews allows researchers to make and support claims about what they have found.

Now you have arrived at the point where you are going to analyze your data. The word *analyze* literally means to separate something into parts (Kvale 1996). You engaged in a meaning-making process with participants and you must attempt to capture this in your interpretations of the data. Your interviews are conversations that took place between two people and therefore cannot be reduced to single meanings or a bunch of words. Your mode of description, analysis, and interpretation depend on your research objectives, but you should strive to retain richness in the data and uncover meaning in context.

Data Management and Reduction

Analysis usually begins with *data management* and *reduction*. You manage data through visual displays using tables, charts, and other visual displays. Data are also managed through various nonvisual techniques. Data reduction involves putting aside information that seems irrelevant (Miles and Huberman 1994).

Managing and reducing your data can feel daunting. Novice and seasoned researchers alike recall various forms of procrastination such as cleaning their entire bathroom, ironing all of their shirts, and actually returning to the field for another go around (Ely et al. 1991). Luckily, there are a few techniques during and after data collection that can help you focus in order to move deeper into your data.

Making Sense of Data: Thinking Units

Lofland and Lofland (1995) describe how you can use **thinking units** to sort out stories. Thinking units are a simple framework for making sense of all of the stories that emerge from qualitative interviews. You may already have solid categories because you started with a well-structured interpretive framework. On the other hand, if your study is less structured or if you who want to check over your data from a different perspective, then you may really benefit by using thinking units. Here are examples of common thinking units that Lofland and Lofland suggest as points of departure:

Meanings	Groups
Practices	Organizations
Episodes	Settlements
Encounters	Social Worlds
Roles	Lifestyles
Relationships	

Although these may seem unstructured and vague, they are created this way so that they may apply to different kinds of studies. Your initial thinking units can be adapted to your own study, or these examples can be changed or scrapped altogether for a list more appropriate to your study. You can add a thinking unit entitled *Open* for surprises or confusion that may arise when sifting through the data (Ely et al. 1991). For instance, in your study on sex workers in Los Angeles, you could have thinking units as shown in Table 8.2.

Your thinking units will depend largely on the framework of your study. If you began with a narrow framework, then you will probably create your own thinking units as you go along. But if your study is largely exploratory, then you may use the thinking units suggested Lofland and Lofland (1995) or some modification of them.

Another way to consider thinking units is as their role as **sensitizing concepts**. Sensitizing concepts are general references and guides about what you are looking for (Blumer 1954). To illustrate, Glenn Bowen (2008) conducted an exploratory study on antipoverty projects in Jamaica that

TABLE 8.2 Thinking Units

Topic: Sex Workers and Safety

Thinking Units	Topical Areas for Coding Based on Thinking Units
Meanings	How is safety conceptualized by sex workers?
Practices	What practices did they use to ensure safety?
Episodes	Describe periods where they felt things were particularly safe or unsafe (dangerous).
Encounters	What were specific encounters where they felt safe or unsafe (in danger)?
Roles	What were the roles of the players during safe or unsafe situations?
Relationships	What were their relationships to the people involved in safe or unsafe situations?
Groups	What roles did groups or social networks play in these safe or unsafe situations?
Settlements	How did the community negotiate safe or unsafe situations?
Social Worlds	How did their social world or the larger commercial sex market play a role in safety?
Lifestyles	In what ways does this lifestyle increase or decrease safety?
Open	

were created to improve social services and community-based organizations. After reviewing the literature, he decided to apply the sensitizing concepts of *citizen participation, social capital,* and *empowerment,* which served as the seeds for theory formulation. It is beneficial to approach your study with some kind of framework for theory generation either through thinking units or sensitizing concepts. It's even better if these predetermined thinking units or sensitizing concepts may already be evident in your interview guide.

Grounded Theory

Grounded theory stems from an analysis of patterns, themes, and common categories discovered in data. Often developed through qualitative interviewing, grounded theory combines a naturalist approach with a positivist concern for a systematic set of procedures.

According to Strauss and Corbin (1994), grounded theory evolves during research, through continuous interplay between analysis and data collection. Grounded theory is a comparative method produced by constant comparison that looks for similarities and differences to establish themes. The process is iterative and requires that you collect, code, and analyze your data. This process reveals themes that may ultimately generate theory.

Theoretical sampling is part of this theory-generating process. Suppose that in your study on sex workers in Los Angeles you realize that young sex workers are more apt to use technology, such as texting and geographic tracking devices, to ensure their safety on the job. As a result, you may decide to interview young sex workers in the hopes of fleshing out the theme of technology as it relates to safety.

Another dimension of generating grounded theory is *theoretical saturation*, the point where you feel that further interviewing will not yield new themes. As a result, you can conclude your qualitative interviewing (Strauss and Corbin 1990). Unfortunately, little guidance is available to establish when theoretical saturation is achieved (Bowen 2008). At its most basic form, saturation may be evident when you start to hear repeated or similar stories from the people you interview. You may reach a point where you can almost predict where the conversation is going. Theoretical saturation and theoretical sampling operate in tandem in the research process. For instance, you may begin to hear young sex workers describe the same techniques repeatedly, and you determine that you have reached theoretical saturation. You are not striving for representativeness, but rather adequacy in your development of themes (Bowen 2008).

Identifying Codes and Themes

Coding information from your interviews assigns units of meaning to data. In a slightly different sense, coding creates categories for the variables that you will analyze. Coding thus involves the organization of raw data into conceptual categories, a process that should be familiar to you from our earlier examination of measurement. Each code is effectively a category into which a piece of data is placed. However, we need to consider a few important dimensions of coding.

First is a type of *open coding*, or brainstorming, where you explore all possible meanings before you add conceptual labels to the data (Corbin and Straus 2007, 160). For example, research on sex workers might begin with open coding of respondent comments about safety and then later classify those comments into domains of safety—from johns, police, or predators. Open coding often begins by "chunking" small units of data in an exploratory fashion. You then look at each chunk and try to identify its *properties* and *dimensions*. What you learn from these chunks or small units will help direct your next stages in coding.

An alternative to open coding is *microanalysis* (Corbin and Strauss 2007). For example, in the study on Muslim students who are monitored by law enforcement, your frame of reference was Howard Becker's labeling theory. But after taking a deeper look at the data, you may see that the effects of labels have many different meanings. You may uncover other important concepts. By going deeper into the data and being open to challenging your original frame of reference, you generate new ideas.

The next step is to use the codes that you developed during the initial open coding or microanalysis to form categories. These codes are more abstract or conceptual. In grounded theory, this is referred to as *axial coding*. After these stages are complete, you engage in *selective coding* to look for patterns in the codes (Corbin and Strauss 2007). You may begin to ask questions such as whether certain codes can be aggregated under a more general code or whether you can organize codes

sequentially. In addition, you may look for any causal relationships. Once you find yourself in this mode, you are not only becoming more analytical, but also starting to develop themes.

Coding often involves lower-level concepts and higher-level concepts. The higher-level concepts are referred to as **themes**, which include a group of lower level concepts that are usually produced from open coding (Corbin and Strauss 2007). Alternatively, you can apply a conceptual name to a group of lower-level concepts that defines a higher-level theme. It's important to begin looking for lower-level concepts after your first interview. For example, a new theme that you term "solidarity" may emerge from your discussions with Muslim students who have been monitored by police. You may notice that many students began to develop a stronger sense of identity, and this contributes to a theory about the process.

There are many ways to find concepts that become higher-level themes. Finding these concepts requires thinking about the mechanics of coding. The following six techniques for identifying themes will be discussed: *similarities and differences, linguistic connectors, repetitions, indigenous typologies, transitions,* and *missing data* (see Ryan and Bernard 2003, for the full list of techniques).

Identifying *similarities* and *differences* is by far the most popular approach, especially for grounded theory. This is generally associated with the constant comparison method of Barney Glaser and Anselm Strauss (1967). The constant comparison method can be used in a couple of different ways. One approach is to engage in a line-by-line analysis where you compare each line of text in an interview to the previous sentence for similarities/differences. Alternatively, pairs of expressions or longer chunks from the same or different participants are compared. This method allows you to find themes within the data through various forms of comparison.

Next is *linguistic connectors*, in which interviews are examined for sentences that suggest causal or conditional relations. Examples of linguistic connectors signaling possible casual relations are words or phrases like *because, as a result,* and *since*

(Ryan and Bernard 2003). For example, "I started sex work 'cause I needed to pay the rent." A similar type of connector reveals possible time-oriented relations or events where you look for words such as *before, after, then*, and *next*. For example, "After my first guy where nothing bad happened, I started to worry less about safety." Conditional relations connectors involve if–then pairs—"If I go out working with my pimp, then I feel more protected."

It's common to recognize the emergence of a theme in your interviews because you keep hearing something over and over. Even if you hear a concept repeating within a single interview, you can create a code and see if it emerges in other interviews. *Repetitions* are when your participant(s) circles around the same kinds of ideas (Ryan and Bernard 2003). Through coding the interview, you can understand when and how this theme arises in conversation and then see how important the theme is across interviews. The more often that you see this concept, the more likely it is a theme.

Another way concepts are identified is by looking for unfamiliar, specialized words, referred to as *indigenous typologies* by Patton (2002, 454). In your project about sex workers in Los Angeles, you might notice the word *stroll*, a term used to describe an outdoor place or set of street blocks where sex workers find customers. Maybe you recognize through noting the discourse around the word *stroll* that sex workers use this to define physical territory. In terms of safety, you recognize that sex workers describe feeling the safest from clients on the stroll because they are in their comfort zone. For some sex workers, their pimps monitor interactions on the stroll. Perhaps it is only when they go off of the stroll, such as getting into a car, that their insecurities about safety are heightened.

Transitions, or shifts in content, may signal a change in themes. These two connectors are more useful in unstructured interviews because transitions are less subject to control (Ryan and Bernard, 2003).

Missing data is a different type of connector where you are alert for what participants are failing to mention. In your study on sex workers in Los Angeles, maybe most of your sex workers never mention having pimps. This would be unexpected and may prompt you to look for descriptions of relationships with friends or boyfriends. You then realize that although these people are playing the role of a pimp, sex workers think of them as close friends. By recognizing this missing information, you learned about how sex workers construct their interpersonal relationships with sex-market facilitators within this informal economy.

This list is not exhaustive, but you may have noticed that the examples center on the *hows* of a situation or the processes, which are usually the source of generated theoretical models. You may notice that a common theme is that sex workers view local residents who are fixtures in the neighborhood around the stroll as a form of protection. Informal social control occurs because others who inhabit the same urban space actively reduce public acts of aggression or violence against sex workers. You may realize that your findings are consistent with Lawrence Cohen and Marcus Felson's (1979) routine activities theory because local residents act as capable guardians. Social disorganization theory may also be evident because this process demonstrates how neighborhood networks can reduce crime. As a result, you develop a deeper understanding of how these semi-permanent networks monitor and protect those engaged in illicit work within urban space.

You may further expand these theories to explore more generally how capable guardians or networks offer crime prevention for those involved in illegal work. For an example of this process, see the article by Scott Jacques and Danielle Reynald (2012), "The Offenders' Perspective on Prevention," summarized in the box, "Theory and Qualitative Research."

Tools for Analysis and Interpretation

In qualitative interviewing, we are engaged in different levels of analysis throughout the research process as we discover themes in our data. Eventually, we reach a stage where all of this must be transformed into an authoritative written account. Three different levels of presenting qualitative data are: description, letting the data speak for

---

 THEORY AND QUALITATIVE RESEARCH

Qualitative research frequently aims to inductively build grounded theory: theory that is grounded in observations and interviews obtained though fieldwork. Elijah Anderson's (1999) qualitative fieldwork that produced *The Code of the Street* is a well-known example. Several other examples of research on active offenders have contributed to the development of theories of offending in recent years.

Qualitative field research also draws on existing theory. In an interesting example that applies situational crime prevention theory to active offenders, Scott Jacques and Danielle Reynald (2012) examine how offenders seek to avoid victimization by other criminals and arrest by police. In the same way, individuals can prevent victimization by not carrying large sums of cash or carelessly displaying valuables. Drug dealers, for example, are careful to protect cash and drugs that may be targets of theft by others. Offenders take similar precautions to avoid arrests.

Citing Clarke's typology (1997b) of techniques for crime prevention, Jacques and Reynald describe the following ways in which offenders avoid arrest and "rip-offs" by others:

- Increasing the effort required by police and offenders
- Increasing the risks by threatening retaliation against potential thieves
- Reducing the rewards by concealing cash and other targets of theft
- Reducing provocations through behavior to avoid undue attention from police
- Removing excuses that adversaries or police might exploit

Jacques and Reynald draw on qualitative interviews with active offenders to illustrate examples of these preventive actions.

---

themselves with minimal commentary; analysis, in which we expand beyond a purely descriptive account; and interpretation, or moving beyond what can be explained with a degree of certainty (Wolcott 1994, 10). You may have noticed that as you move further away from merely using the raw data as an account that you move toward a more interpretive approach.

Some researchers produce a purely descriptive account, while others begin with description and move on to analysis and interpretation. Description, analysis, and interpretation are not mutually exclusive. They can all be used in your final authoritative account, but it is important to understand how they differ. We must be aware of which mode or modes we are using and understand the options for each.

In description, participants present their accounts pretty much in their own words; some researchers feel this reduces bias. However, researchers do choose which descriptions to present and which to exclude, which adds an element of researcher selectivity. When descriptions are chosen, it's often best to strive for thick descriptions to avoid losing meaning.

A number of techniques are available to present your description. One example is a *day-in-the-life* approach, where you take your reader through a day of fieldwork. A variation on this is to show a day in the life of some participants. Understanding the everyday life of participants is an approachable type of analysis because one thing that we all have in common is the 24-hour day. Another technique is to identify a *critical* or *key point* to describe activities of participants regarding pivotal events such as how they started sex work. You may have heard of something called the *Rashoman Effect*, named after the 1950 film by Akira Kurosawa, where a violent event is described from the perspective of four witnesses. This technique centers on telling different sides of a story and is useful if you have interviewed participants from different groups. If you interviewed sex workers, pimps, clients, and police to understand the complexities of the commercial sex market, then this technique can yield insights. Lastly, you can follow an *analytic framework*, which adds structure, but in this case, you have to be careful not to force your descriptive material to fit the framework.

Interpretation is distinguished from analysis because analysis is more systematic and deliberate, while interpretation is more speculative and casual (Wolcott 1994, 23). Interpretation is trickier because it is important to be careful about how far to go in terms of speculation. Nonetheless, interpretations can be a notably refreshing portion of an authoritative account. This is where researchers connect their findings to the larger theoretical body of knowledge and discuss the *coulds, maybes*, and *possibilities* that stem from descriptions and analysis.

Several techniques are available for interpretation; Wolcott (1994, 40–45) presents an extensive list. The first is to move away from simplistic explanations and perhaps leave the reader with something to think about, or to *extend the analysis*. To illustrate, let's say you find that sex workers seem to feel safer when they have pimps and you suggest the possibility that pimps are necessary to ensure sex workers' feelings of well-being. This deeper analysis may be somewhat surprising to readers who are accustomed to popular images of pimps as violent scoundrels. Second, we can link our study to relevant theory. See the example by Jacques and Reynald (2012) in the box "Theory and Qualitative Research." Third, we can tell readers what pieces of the puzzle we think are missing, or offer alternative possible interpretations. Lastly, we can discuss our own feelings and beliefs or explore alternative formats. It's best to use several of these techniques for a more comprehensive interpretation.

Quality and Rigor in Analyzing Qualitative Interviewing

It is important to consider the reliability and validity of data from qualitative interviews.

There are a number of ways to enhance the quality and rigor in interpretations of qualitative interviews. You already have an extensive log of data, including field notes and memos, and these make up your **audit trail**. The audit trail is not only a document of decisions, but also important to enhance our confidence in the research (Bowen 2008). This record is also a sign that your research is of a higher caliber. For situations that involve multiple interviewers, it's important to include some standardized questions to assure a level of consistency across the interviews. In situations where multiple coders are used, we can examine interrater reliability, as discussed in Chapter 4.

An important check used in grounded theory and in qualitative analysis involves looking for *negative cases*. These are cases that contradict emerging themes we have coded and ultimately our theory. It's common for statistical analysis to eliminate outliers, but in qualitative research, these cases are helpful to check the viability of our emerging theory or reveal unexpected aspects of the theory.

Another technique for checking our interpretations is the use of *member checks*. In this case, we would ask some of our participants to read draft descriptions to verify the accuracy of our work. This gives participants the chance to analyze interpretation of their lived reality and make it possible to correct some of these misinterpretations. Member checks are the best way to establish *truth-value*, or confidence in the truth of the findings in a particular context (Guba 1981). By incorporating member checks into a design, we may boost the credibility or validity of our findings.

How we interpret consistency in stories or *stability of results* is different in qualitative studies because we accept the presence of multiple realities. Instead of interpreting inconsistency in stories as error, qualitative researchers view this as a shift in participant insight. This does not mean we assume all participants are telling the unvarnished truth. Instead, we expect that how participants construct and reconstruct their stories is consistent with multiple interpretations.

Transferability occurs when working hypotheses can be transferred from one context to another (Guba 1981). Thick description in both contexts is necessary to establish transferability. Qualitative studies are difficult to replicate, and claims about generalizability are tempered because we rarely use representative samples of sufficient size. However, it is common for findings to translate from one setting to another. For instance, you may find that the safety issues discussed by sex workers in

Los Angeles, California, are also present among sex workers in Rio de Janeiro, Brazil.

All of these techniques can be used to ensure that your study is trustworthy and you can discuss your techniques in detail and depth. The more transparent that you are about the research process, including your audit trail, the more your readers will trust and believe in your final product. The techniques that you use to ensure *trustworthiness* of the data and analysis should be known from the moment that you decide to start your project. Think about some of the many steps that you take to deliver the best rendition of other people's lived experience.

Qualitative Interviewing Summarized

Qualitative interviewing is an interactive data-gathering process that requires thoughtfulness and attentiveness. The researcher is the instrument of data collection, yet in this role, the researcher is also engaged in human interaction. Although this chapter has provided you with tools to become a skilled qualitative interviewer, practice is the best way to perfect your ability to enable great interviews.

Qualitative studies retain richness, recognize meanings and shared meanings, do not lose track of the context, and abide by rigorous standards of data collection and analysis. A range of activities bring you to your final authoritative written account:

- Formulating questions
- Accessing participants
- Determining your role as an interviewer
- Interacting with participants
- Coding the data for themes
- Retaining the context of data you have collected
- Taking steps to enhance the quality of data

Although your data log will include numerous documents, such as interview transcripts, field notes, and memos, you should be clear and precise in your decisions about how to organize and decipher your data. Many approaches to coding qualitative data are available, with grounded theory being the most popular. As you become more experienced, you may think about trying other approaches. You may use some combination of description, analysis, and interpretation in your final write-up. Lastly, you may experiment with different techniques in order to tell the most accurate and compelling rendition of your participants' lived experiences.

SUMMARY

- When you find yourself wondering about the "hows" involving human perspectives, emotions, or lifestyles, you are probably better off using qualitative interviews.

- The critical realist perspective assumes that multiple perspectives about reality exist, rather than a single tangible reality.

- Semi-structured interviews have standardized questions but include unscheduled probes and spontaneous questions that allow us to explore emerging themes. More like a natural conversation, unstructured interviews are best for exploratory studies.

- Focus groups involve interviewing groups of people and are best for examining the dynamics between group members. The focus group moderator must guide the conversation and be aware of dominant group members and groupthink.

- We must think carefully about how questions are phrased and how they occur in our conversations.

- When conducting qualitative interviewing, it is important to think about whether you are an insider or outsider and about how closely you are connected to your group of interest. This will shape how you gain access and how you establish rapport with participants.

- Active interviewing is a two-sided exchange that is dynamic and a meaning-making context. In the interactive interview, you are also involved in meaning-making context.

- Recording data involves field notes, transcripts, memos, and written records of the research process. Research using qualitative interviews typically produces a large data log.

- Analysis of or transforming data happens during and after data collection. Thinking units are important tools for guiding data collection.

- The three types of coding in grounded theory are open, axial, and selective. You start with open coding in order to find concepts in the data and may move on to selective coding, which involves combining multiple open codes and/or themes.

- Themes are higher-level concepts usually derived from the coding process. The most common way to find themes is through constant comparison of similarities and differences in the data to establish themes.

- Qualitative data can be analyzed through description, analysis, and interpretation. Description is closest to raw data, whereas interpretation moves farthest away.

- The best way to ensure that you have quality data is to create an audit trail of all coding decisions.

KEY TERMS

audit trail, p. 223

critical realist perspective, p. 201

focus group, p. 204

grounded theory, p. 219

insider/outsider status, p. 208

interview schedule, p. 202

memoing, p. 217

qualitative interview, p. 196

rapport, p. 213

reflexivity, p. 212

semi-structured interview, p. 203

sensitizing concepts, p. 218

structured interview, p. 202

themes, p. 220

thinking units, p. 218

unstructured interview, p. 203

REVIEW QUESTIONS AND EXERCISES

1. Watch one of the following movie clips: http://www.youtube.com/watch?v=TQ4y7GPeFBY or http://www.youtube.com/watch?v=ymsHLkB8u3s. Write down the main points that you think are conveyed. Compare your interpretation to those of two or three other people in your class.

2. Select a research topic of interest to you and write an interview schedule. First use an interview guide and then semi-structured questions. Be sure to include a few scheduled probes in your semi-structured interview schedule.

3. Interview one person using the two interview schedules created in question 2. Write a few paragraphs comparing the two approaches (unstructured and semi-structured). What were the advantages and disadvantages of each approach?

CHAPTER 9

Field Observation

The techniques described in this chapter focus on observing life in its natural habitat—going where the action is and watching. We'll consider how to prepare for the field, how to observe, how to make records of what is observed, and how to recognize the relative strengths and weaknesses of field research.

Seaport Operations and Stolen Vehicles

Together with graduate students from Rutgers University, Ronald Clarke and Mike Maxfield conducted a study to examine the effect of parts-marking on auto theft. This research used data from a variety of sources, including fieldwork on the export of stolen vehicles through large seaports.

Clarke and Maxfield had learned that over 380,000 vehicles were shipped abroad from Newark and Elizabeth, New Jersey, in 2008. According to vehicle theft records, just under 1 percent of those vehicles, about 3,750, had been reported as stolen. For an additional 104,800 vehicles, some irregularity was found with vehicle identification numbers (VINs). So the researchers arranged to visit a large shipping terminal at Port Newark in New Jersey, one of the busiest seaports in the United States. Their general objective was to understand port and shipping operations in an effort to learn more about the export of stolen vehicles. Their role was as complete observers.

They toured the huge facility, a modern port that is exclusively engaged in container handling. A shipping container is basically a semi-truck trailer without its wheels. Thousands of containers move in and out of Port Newark each day, coming by train or truck. Observations began at a portal where all container trucks were weighed and documents were presented. Port and shipping company security staff explained how containers were processed. Incoming containers passed through the portal on their way to being loaded on a ship. Outgoing containers had arrived by ship and were leaving the port by truck or train destined to other parts of the United States. In addition to weighing and checking documents, the process for containers coming into the country included inspection to screen for contraband and dangerous materials.

Maxfield and Clarke were most interested in containers to be shipped outside of the United States. Cars to be exported were in containers when they arrived at the port; each container was large enough to hold up to three autos. Containers were shuttled around several acres of the port, where they were stacked five containers high. Small trucks fetched the containers for loading on an outbound container ship. At one point, Maxfield and Clarke boarded a 950-foot ship from China to observe loading and unloading operations from the ship's bridge. Three crane towers worked the ship's length, simultaneously moving containers on and off the ship. This was quite a sight. The "round trip"—pick up → load on ship → pick up → place on dock—took only about 90 seconds.

From one morning at the shipping terminal, coupled with qualitative interviews of security and other port staff, the researchers learned several things that appeared to facilitate the export of stolen vehicles through the port:

- An enormous number of containers moved in and out of the port.

- From 800 to 1,000 autos were shipped out each day. Some containers included a car with other types of goods; other containers included only two or three cars.

- Some stolen vehicles mixed with other cargo were not listed as contents of a container.

(continued)

- Documents for outbound autos were inspected but rarely compared to VINs identifying individual cars, because:

  - Containers with cars were mixed with other containers and were difficult to access.

  - Adding to their large number, containers were frequently moved around the shipping yard.

  - Cars and other goods presented for outbound shipment were available for inspection for 72 hours before being loaded on a ship. But constraints on Immigration and Customs Enforcement staff meant that only a small fraction of containers could be inspected during this period.

  - New technology has been developed to "see" inside containers, much like the widely despised full-body scan technology at airports, but only one such machine was available and rarely used.

- Since the September 11 attacks on the United States, security officials have devoted extensive resources to screening cargo shipped *into* the country, which undermines the capacity to screen exports.

These are not conclusive findings. Instead, the observations helped Clarke and Maxfield develop tentative explanations for factors that contribute to the export of stolen vehicles. Without these observations, they could not have understood how the enormous scale of operations at the port offers cover for stolen cars commingled among the thousands of other containers handled each day at Port Newark.

You can get a feel for what a modern port is like by typing "Port Newark" into Google Earth or a mapping program. Scroll around and zoom in to see a forest of shipping containers. You might also be interested in Marc Levinson's book (2007) on the history of the shipping container. Among other things, Levinson points out how containerized cargo reduces many forms of cargo theft.

Introduction

Field observation includes qualitative techniques for observation and interviewing together with structured observations.

We turn now to what may seem like the most obvious method of making observations: field research. If researchers want to know about something, why not simply go where it's happening and watch it happen?

Field research encompasses two different methods of obtaining data: (1) making direct observation and (2) asking questions. This chapter concentrates on observation, although you should keep in mind the discussion in Chapter 8 on qualitative interviewing, which often accompanies field observation.

Most of the observation methods discussed in this book are designed to produce data appropriate for *quantitative* analysis. Surveys provide data to calculate things like the percentage of crime victims in a population or the mean value of property lost in burglaries. Field observation may yield *qualitative* data—observations not easily reduced to numbers—in addition to quantitative data. For example, a field researcher who is studying burglars may note how many times subjects have been arrested (quantitative), as well as whether individual burglars tend to select certain types of targets (qualitative).

Qualitative field research is often a theory- or hypothesis-generating activity, as well. In many types of field studies, researchers do not have precisely defined hypotheses to be tested. Field observation may be used to make sense out of an ongoing process that cannot be predicted in advance. This process involves making initial observations, developing tentative general conclusions that suggest further observations, making those observations, revising the prior conclusions, and so forth.

For example, Ross Homel and associates (Homel, Tomsen, and Thommeny 1992) conducted a field study of violence in bars in Sydney, Australia, and found that certain situations tended to trigger violent incidents. Subsequent studies tested a series of hypotheses about the links between certain situations and violence (Homel and Clark 1994) and how interior design was related to aggression in dance clubs (Macintyre and Homel 1996). Later research by James Roberts (2002) expanded these findings by examining management and serving practices in New Jersey bars and clubs. These examples offer another illustration of grounded theory, something that is commonly produced from field observations. We will consider these examples more closely later in this chapter.

By now, especially if you have experience as a criminal justice professional, you may be thinking that field research is not much different from what police officers and many other people do every day—make observations in the field and ask people questions. Police may also collect data about particular crime problems, take action, and monitor results. So what's new here?

Compared with criminal justice professionals, researchers tend to be more concerned with making generalizations and then using systematic field research techniques to support those generalizations. Consider the different goals and approaches used by two people who might observe shoplifters: a retail store security guard and a criminal justice researcher. The security guard wishes to capture a thief and prevent the loss of shop merchandise. Toward those ends, he or she adapts surveillance techniques to the behavior of a particular suspected shoplifter. The researcher's interests are different; perhaps she or he estimates the frequency of shoplifting, describes characteristics of shoplifters, or evaluates some specific measure to prevent shoplifting. In all likelihood, researchers use more standardized methods of observation aimed toward a generalized understanding.

This chapter examines methods of field observation in some detail, providing a logical overview and suggesting some specific skills and techniques that make scientific field research more useful than the casual observation we all engage in. As we cover the various applications and techniques of field research, it's useful to recall the distinction we made, way back in Chapter 1, between ordinary human inquiry and social scientific research. Field methods illustrate how the common techniques of observation that we all use in ordinary inquiry can be deployed in systematic ways. Also recall our discussion, from Chapter 3, of how qualitative and quantitative approaches can often be combined.

Topics Appropriate to Field Observation

When conditions or behavior must be studied in natural settings, field research is usually the best approach.

One of the key strengths of field research is the comprehensive perspective it gives the researcher. This aspect of field observation enhances its validity. By going directly to the phenomenon under study and observing it as completely as possible, we can develop a deeper and fuller understanding of it. This mode of observation, then, is especially (though not exclusively) appropriate to research topics that appear to defy simple quantification. The field researcher may recognize nuances of attitude, behavior, and setting that escape researchers using other methods.

For example, Clifford Shearing and Phillip Stenning (1992, 251) describe how Disney World employs subtle but pervasive mechanisms of informal social control that are largely invisible to millions of theme park visitors. It is difficult to imagine any technique other than direct observation that could produce these insights:

> Control strategies are embedded in both environmental features and structural relations. In both cases control structures and activities have other functions which are highlighted so that the control function is overshadowed. For example, virtually every pool, fountain, and flower garden serves both as an aesthetic object and to direct visitors away from, or towards, particular locations. Similarly, every Disney employee, while visibly and primarily engaged in other functions, is also engaged in the maintenance of order.

Another, grittier, example of direct observations used to understand conditions in field conditions is described in the opening vignette, "Seaport Operations and Stolen Vehicles."

Many of the different uses of field observation in criminal justice research are nicely summarized by George McCall. Comparing the three principal ways of collecting data—observing, asking questions, and consulting written records—McCall (1978, 8–9) states that observation is most appropriate for obtaining information about physical or social settings, behaviors, and events.

Field research is especially appropriate for topics that can best be understood within their natural settings. Surveys may be able to measure behaviors and attitudes in somewhat artificial settings, but not all behavior is best measured this way. For example, field research is a superior method for studying how street-level drug dealers interpret behavioral and situational cues to distinguish potential customers, normal street traffic, and undercover police officers. It would be difficult to study these skills through a survey.

Field research on actual crimes involves obtaining information about events. McCall (1978) points out that observational studies of vice—such as prostitution and drug use—are much more common than observational studies of other crimes, largely because these behaviors depend at least in part on being visible and attracting customers. One notable exception is research on shoplifting. A classic study by

Terry Baumer and Dennis Rosenbaum (1982) had two goals: (1) to estimate the incidence of shoplifting in a large department store, and (2) to assess the effectiveness of different store security measures. Each objective required devising some measure of shoplifting, which Baumer and Rosenbaum obtained through direct observation. Samples of persons were followed by research staff from the time they entered the store until they left. Observers, posing as fellow shoppers, watched for any theft by the person they had been assigned to follow.

Many aspects of physical settings are probably best studied through direct observation. The prevalence and patterns of gang graffiti in public places could not be reliably measured through surveys, unless the goal was to measure perceptions of graffiti. The work of Oscar Newman (1972, 1996), Ray Jeffery (1977), and Patricia and Paul Brantingham (Brantingham and Brantingham 1991) on the relationship between crime and environmental design depends crucially on field observation of settings. If opportunities for crime vary by physical setting, then observation of the physical characteristics of a setting is required.

An evaluation of street lighting as a crime prevention tool in two areas of London illustrates how observation can be used to measure both physical settings and behavior. Kate Painter (1996) was interested in the relationships between street lighting, certain crime rates (measured by victim surveys), fear of crime, and nighttime mobility. Improvements in street lighting were made in selected streets; surveys of pedestrians and households in the affected areas were conducted before and after the lighting improvements. Survey questions included items about victimization, perceptions of crime problems and lighting quality, and reports about routine nighttime behavior in areas affected by the lighting.

Although the pretest and posttest survey items could have been used to assess changes in attitudes and behavior associated with improved lighting, field observations provided better measures of behavior. Painter observed pedestrians in areas both before and after street lighting was enhanced. Observations like these are better measures of such behavior than are survey items because people often have difficulty recalling actions, such as how often they walk through some area after dark.

The Various Roles of the Observer

Field observer roles range from full participation to fully detached observation.

The term *field research* is broader and more inclusive than the common term **ethnography**, which focuses on detailed and accurate description rather than explanation. Field researchers need not always participate in what they are studying, although they usually will study it directly at the scene of the action. As Catherine Marshall and Gretchen Rossman (2006, 72) point out:

> The researcher may plan a role that entails varying degrees of "participantness"—that is, the degree of actual participation in daily life. At one extreme is the full participant, who goes about ordinary life in a role or set of roles constructed in the setting. At the other extreme is the complete observer, who engages not at all in social interaction and may even shun involvement in the world being studied. And, of course, all possible complementary mixes along the continuum are available to the researcher.

The full participant, in this sense, may be a genuine participant in what he or she is studying (for example, a participant in a demonstration against capital punishment)—or at least pretend to be a genuine participant. In any event, if you are acting as a full participant, you let people see you only as a participant, not as a researcher.

That raises an ethical question: is it ethical to deceive the people we are studying in the hope that they will confide in us as they would not confide in an identified researcher? Do the interests of science—the scientific values of the research—offset any ethical concerns?

Related to this ethical consideration is a scientific one. No researcher deceives his or her subjects solely for the purpose of deception. Rather, it is done in the belief that the data will be more valid and reliable, that the subjects will be more natural and honest if they do not know the researcher is doing a research project. If the people being studied know they are being studied, they might reject the researcher or modify their speech and behavior to appear more respectable than they otherwise would. In either case, the process being observed might radically change.

On the other side of the coin, if we assume the role of complete participant, we may affect what we are studying. To play the role of participant, we must participate, yet our participation may affect the social process we are studying. Additional problems may emerge in any participant observation study of active criminals. Legal and physical risks, mentioned in Chapter 2, present obstacles to the complete participant in field research among active offenders or delinquents.

Finally, complete participation in field studies of criminal justice institutions is seldom possible. Although it is common for police officers to become criminal justice researchers, practical constraints on the official duties of police present major obstacles to simultaneously acting as researcher and police officer. Similarly, the responsibilities of judges, prosecutors, probation officers, and corrections workers are not normally compatible with collecting data for research. For a notable exception to this general rule, see the book *Cop in the Hood*, in which Peter Moskos describes how he became a sworn police officer in Baltimore in order to conduct field research for his dissertation (Moskos 2009).

Because of these considerations—ethical, scientific, practical, and safety—field researchers most often choose a different role. The researcher taking the role *participant-as-observer* participates with the group under study but makes it clear that he or she is also undertaking research. If someone has been convicted of some offense and has been placed on probation, for example, that might present an opportunity to launch a study of probation officers.

McCall (1978) suggests that field researchers who study active offenders may comfortably occupy positions around the periphery of criminal activity. Acting as a participant in certain types of leisure activities, such as frequenting selected bars or dance clubs, may be appropriate roles. As Amber Horning mentioned in Chapter 8, this approach was used by Dina Perrone (2009) in her research on drug use in New York dance clubs. Furthermore, McCall describes how making one's role as a researcher known to criminals and becoming known as a "right square" is more acceptable to subjects than an unsuccessful attempt to masquerade as a colleague. There are dangers in this role also, however. The people being studied may shift their attention to the research project, and the process being observed may no longer be typical. Conversely, a researcher may come to identify too much with the interests and viewpoints of the participants. This is referred to as *going native* and results in loss of the detachment necessary for social science.

The *observer-as-participant* identifies himself or herself as a researcher and interacts with the participants in the course of their routine activities but makes no pretense of actually being a participant. Many observational studies of police patrol are examples of this approach. Researchers typically accompany police officers on patrol, observing routine activities and interactions between police and citizens. Spending several hours in the company of a police officer also affords opportunities for unstructured interviewing.

The *complete observer*, at the other extreme, observes a location or process without becoming a part of it in any way. The subjects of study might not even realize they are being studied because of the researcher's unobtrusiveness. An individual making observations while sitting in a courtroom is an example. Although the complete observer is less likely to affect what is being studied and less likely to go native than the complete participant, he or she may also be less able to develop a full appreciation of what is being studied. A courtroom observer, for example, witnesses only the public acts that take place in the courtroom, not private conferences between judges and attorneys.

McCall (1978, 45) points out an interesting and often unnoticed trade-off between the role observers adopt and their ability to learn from what they see. If their role is *covert* (complete participation) or

detached (complete observation), they are less able to ask questions to clarify what they observe. As complete participants, they take pains to conceal their observations and must exercise care in querying subjects. Similarly, complete observation means that it is generally not possible to interact with the persons or things being observed.

Researchers have to think carefully about the trade-off. If it is most important that subjects not be affected by their role as observer, known as **reactivity**, then complete participation or observation is preferred. If being able to ask questions about what they observe is important, then some role that combines participation and observation is better.

More generally, the appropriate role for observers hinges on what they want to learn and how their inquiry is affected by opportunities and constraints. Different situations require different roles for researchers. Unfortunately, there are no clear guidelines for making this choice; field researchers rely on their understanding of the situation, their judgment, and their experience. In making a decision, researchers must be guided by both methodological and ethical considerations. Because these often conflict, deciding on the appropriate role may be difficult. Often, researchers find that their role limits the scope of their study.

Selecting Cases for Observation

Different types of sampling techniques are adapted to selecting observation targets.

This brings us to the more general question of how to select cases for observation in field research. One common selection is snowball sampling. As we mentioned in Chapter 6, with snowball sampling, initial research subjects (or informants) identify other persons who might also become subjects, who in turn suggest more potential subjects, and so on. In this way, a group of subjects is accumulated through a series of referrals.

There are, of course, other ways of selecting subjects for observation. Chapter 6 discussed the more   conventional   techniques   involved   in probability sampling and the accompanying logic. Although the general principles of representativeness should be remembered in field research, controlled sampling techniques are often not possible.

As an illustration, consider the potential selection biases involved in a field study of deviants. Let's say we want to study a small number of drug dealers. We have a friend who works in the probation department of a large city and is willing to introduce us to people convicted of drug dealing and sentenced to probation. What selection problems might result from studying subjects identified in this way? How might our subjects not be representative of the general population of drug dealers? If we work our way backward from the chain of events that begins with a crime and ends with a criminal sentence, the answers should become clear.

First, drug dealers sentenced to probation may be first-time offenders or persons convicted of dealing small amounts of "softer" drugs. Repeat offenders and kingpin cocaine dealers will not be in this group. Second, it is possible that people initially charged with drug dealing were convicted of simple possession through a plea bargain; because of our focus on people convicted of dealing, our selection procedure will miss this group as well. Finally, by selecting dealers who have been arrested and convicted, we may be gaining access only to those less skilled dealers who were caught. More skilled or experienced dealers may be less likely to be arrested in the first place; they may be different in important ways from the dealers we wish to study. Also, if dealers in street drug markets are more likely to be arrested than dealers who work

through social networks of friends and acquaintances, a sample based on arrested dealers could be biased in more subtle ways.

To see why this raises an important issue in selecting cases for field research, let's return again to the sample of burglars studied by Wright and Decker (1994), described in Chapter 6. Their snowball sample began with an ex-offender and they sought out *active* burglars. An alternative approach would be to select a probability or other sample of convicted burglars, perhaps in prison or on probation. But Wright and Decker rejected this strategy for sampling because of the possibility that they would overlook burglars who had not been caught. After accumulating their sample, the researchers were in a position to test this assumption by examining arrest records for their subjects. Only about one-fourth of the active burglars had ever been convicted of burglary; an additional one-third had been arrested for burglary but not convicted. More than 40 percent had no burglary arrests, and 8 percent had never been arrested for any offense (1994, 12).

Putting all this together, Wright and Decker concluded that about three-fourths of their subjects would not have been eligible for inclusion if the researchers had based their sample on persons convicted of burglary. Thus, little overlap exists between the population of active burglars and the population of convicted burglars.

It's also possible to use probability sampling methods to select cases or places for observation. For an example, see the box by Shuryo Fujita, "Sampling Streets in Newark, New Jersey."

SAMPLING STREETS IN NEWARK, NEW JERSEY

by Shuryo Fujita, PhD
Farmingdale State College

My research on auto theft in Newark, New Jersey, used data from a variety of sources to study what sorts of environmental features of the city were related to the risk of car theft. The most useful data came from observations made on a sample of city streets.

I decided to use Google Street View to assess three measures of neighborhoods: litter, graffiti, and housing condition. Google Street View was also used to count the number of cars parked on sampled streets. After coding car make and approximate model year, I obtained a rough estimate of the number of cars at risk of theft because they were parked on city streets.

(continued)

Because it was neither practical nor necessary to observe all streets in Newark, I developed a procedure to randomly sample street segments. The first step was to obtain a digital map of the city. Next, I created a grid of 300-foot by 300-foot cells, or squares, as an overlay to the digital map. That is, the grid of cells was digitally placed on top of the map. The cell size of 300 feet was chosen because the average block length in Newark is about 300 feet. Over one-fourth of Newark's land area includes unpopulated places, such as an international airport, seaport, warehouse/industrial facilities, and city parks. I excluded these areas, ending up with a total of 4,291 cells.

Next, I selected a random probability sample of 200 cells using a statistical procedure in geographic information system software. The figure below shows the cell grid overlaid on Newark, and the 200 randomly selected cells. The white areas are the unpopulated excluded parts of the city. You can see that the selected cells are distributed all over the city. This was important to my research to reduce possible bias from using too many places next to each other. I also wanted to include high-theft and low-theft areas. The random procedure made it possible to avoid both potential sources of bias, in which cells selected had a known, equal probability of being included in the sample.

■ 200 Cells Randomly Selected
▦ Cells with Streets
☐ Excluded Areas

N
W E
S

0 0.5 1   2 Miles

Purposive Sampling in Field Research

Sampling in field research tends to be more complicated than in other kinds of research. In many types of field studies, researchers attempt to observe everything within their field of study; thus, in a sense, they do not sample at all. In reality, of course, it is impossible to observe everything. To the extent that field researchers observe only a portion of what happens, what they do observe is a de facto sample of all the possible observations that might have been made. We can seldom select a controlled sample of such observations. But we can keep in mind the general principles of representativeness and interpret our observations accordingly.

The ability to systematically sample cases for observation depends on the degree of structure and predictability of the phenomenon being observed. This is more of a general guideline than a hard-and-fast rule. The actions of youth gangs, burglars, and auto thieves are less structured and predictable than those of police officers. It is possible to select a probability sample of police officers for observation because the behavior of police officers in a given city is structured and predictable in many dimensions. Because the population of active criminals is unknown, it is not possible to select a probability sample for observation.

This example should call to mind our discussion of sampling frames in Chapter 6. A roster of police officers and their assignments to patrol sectors and shifts could serve as a sampling frame for selecting subjects to observe. No such roster of gang members, burglars, and auto thieves is available.

Now consider the case in which a sampling frame is less important than the regularity of a process. The regular, predictable passage of people on city sidewalks makes it possible to systematically select a sample of cases for observation. There is no sampling frame of pedestrians, but studies such as Painter's research (1996) on the effects of street lighting can depend on the reliable flow of passersby who may be observed.

In an observational study such as Painter's, we might also make observations at a number of different locations on different streets. We could pick the sample of locations through standard probability methods, or more likely, we could use a rough quota system, observing wide streets and narrow ones, busy streets and quiet ones, or samples from different times of day. In a study of pedestrian traffic, we might also observe people in different types of urban neighborhoods—comparing residential and commercial areas, for example. Because she was interested specifically in drug use among patrons of rave dance clubs, sampling dance clubs was a natural strategy for Dina Perrone.

Table 9.1 summarizes different sampling dimensions that might be considered in planning field research. The behavior of people, together with the characteristics of people and places, can vary by population group, location, time, and weather. We touched on the first two in this chapter and in the example of New York City homeless people described in Chapter 6. Now we will briefly discuss how sampling plans might consider time and weather dimensions.

TABLE 9.1 Sampling Dimensions in Field Research

Sampling Dimension	Variation in
Population	Behavior and characteristics
Space	Behavior
	Physical features of locations
Time, micro	Behavior by time of day, day of week
	Lighting by time of day
	Business, store, entertainment activities by time of day, day of week
Time, macro	Behavior by season, holiday
	Entertainment by season, holiday
Weather	Behavior by weather

People tend to engage in more outdoor activities in fair weather than in wet or snowy conditions. In northern cities, people are outside more when the weather is warm. Any study of outdoor activity should therefore consider the potential effects of variation in the weather. For example, in Painter's study of pedestrian traffic before and after improvements in street lighting, it was important to consider weather conditions during the times observations were made.

Behavior also varies by time, presented as micro and macro dimensions in Table 9.1. City streets in a central business district are busiest during working hours, whereas more people are in residential areas at other times. And, of course, people do different things on weekends than during the workweek.

Seasonal variation, the macro time dimension, may also be important in criminal justice research. Daylight lasts longer in summer months, which affects the amount of time people spend outdoors. Shopping peaks from Thanksgiving to Christmas, increasing the number of shoppers, who along with their automobiles may become targets for thieves.

In practice, controlled probability sampling is seldom used in field research. Different types of purposive samples are much more common. Patton (2002, 230; emphasis in original) describes a broad range of approaches to purposive sampling and offers a useful comparison of probability and purposive samples:

> The logic and power of probability sampling derive from statistical probability theory. A random and statistically representative sample permits confident generalization from a sample to a larger population. The logic and power of purposeful sampling lies in selecting *information rich cases* for study in depth.

Nonetheless, if researchers understand the principles and logic of more formal sampling methods, they are likely to produce more effective purposive sampling in field research.

Recording Observations

Many different methods are available for collecting and recording field observations.

Just as there is great variety in the types of field studies we might conduct, we have many options for making records of field observations. Researchers almost certainly write notes of some kind, but they might also make sound recordings of interviews. Photographs or videotapes can be used to make records of visual images such as a block of apartment buildings before and after some physical design change or to serve as a pretest for an experimental neighborhood cleanup campaign. This technique was used by Robert Sampson and Stephen Raudenbush (1999) in connection with probability samples of city blocks in Chicago. Videotapes were made of sampled blocks, and the recordings were then viewed to assess physical and social conditions in those areas.

We can think of a continuum of methods for recording observations. At one extreme is traditional field observation and note taking with pen and paper, such as we might use in field interviews. The opposite extreme includes various types of automated and remote measurement, such as video recordings, devices that count automobile traffic, computer tabulations of mass transit users, or photographs. In between is a host of methods that have many potential applications in criminal justice research.

Of course, the methods selected for recording observations are directly related to issues of measurement—especially how key concepts are operationalized. Thinking back to our discussion of measurement in Chapter 4, you should recognize why this is so. If we are interested in policies to increase nighttime pedestrian traffic in some city, we might want to know why people do or do not go out at night and how many people stroll around different neighborhoods. Interviews—perhaps in connection with a survey—can determine people's reasons for going out or not, whereas video recordings of passersby can provide simple counts. By the same token, a traffic-counting device can produce information about the number of automobiles that pass a particular point on the road, but it cannot measure what the blood alcohol levels of drivers are, whether riders are wearing seat belts, or how fast a vehicle is traveling.

Martin Kurti and associates (Kurti, von Lampe, and Thompkins 2013) were interested in learning about black-market cigarettes in the South Bronx, a low-income area in New York City. They could have conducted interviews with samples of smokers or cigarette dealers. Their novel approach used observations—they collected discarded cigarette packages from a sample of streets in the area and examined tax stamps. They found that only 19 percent of the 497 collected packages bore stamps from New York, concluding that the illegal cigarette market was extensive.

Cameras and Voice Recorders

Video cameras may be used in public places to record relatively simple phenomena, such as the passage of people or automobiles, or more complex social processes. For several years, London police have monitored traffic conditions at dozens of key intersections using video cameras mounted on building rooftops. In fact, the *2013 Road Atlas for Britain* includes the locations of stationary video cameras on its maps. Since 2003, video cameras have monitored all traffic entering central London as part of an effort to reduce traffic. The license plates of vehicles that do not register paying a toll are recorded, and violation notices are sent to owners.

Still photographs may be appropriate to record some types of observations, such as graffiti or litter. Photos have the added benefit of preserving visual images that can later be viewed and coded by more than one person, thus facilitating interrater reliability checks. If we are interested in studying pedestrian traffic on city streets, we might gather data about what types of people we see and how many there are. As the number and complexity of our observations increase, it becomes more difficult to reliably record how many males and females we see, how many adults and juveniles, and so on. Taking photographs of sampled areas will enable us to be more confident in our measurements and will also make it possible for another person to check on our interpretation of the photographs.

This approach was used by James Lange and associates (Lange, Johnson, and Voas 2005) in their study of speeding on the New Jersey Turnpike. The researchers deployed radar devices and digital cameras to measure the speed of vehicles and to take photos of drivers. Equipment was housed in an unmarked van parked at sample locations on the turnpike. The race of drivers was later coded by teams of researchers who studied the digital images. Agreement by at least two of three coders was required to accept the photos for further analysis.

In addition to their use in interviews, audio recording is useful for dictating observations. For example, a researcher interested in patterns of activity on urban streets can dictate observations while riding through selected areas in an automobile. It is possible to dictate observations in an unstructured manner, describing each street scene as it unfolds. Or a voice recorder can be used more like an audio checklist, with observers noting specified items seen in preselected areas.

Field Notes

Even audio recorders and cameras cannot capture all the relevant aspects of social processes. Most field researchers make some records of observations as written notes, perhaps in a field journal. Field notes should include both empirical observations and interpretations of them. They should record what we "know" we have observed and what we "think" we have observed. It is important, however, that these different kinds of notes be identified for what they are. For example, we might note that person X approached and handed something to person Y—a known drug dealer—that we think this was a drug transaction, and that we think person X was a new customer.

Every student is familiar with the process of taking notes. Good note taking in field research requires more careful and deliberate attention and involves some specific skills. Three guidelines are particularly important.

First, don't trust your memory any more than you have to; it's untrustworthy. Even if you pride yourself on having a photographic memory, it's a good idea to take notes, either during the observation or as soon afterward as possible. If you are taking notes during the observation, do it unobtrusively because people are likely to behave differently if they see you writing down everything they say or do.

Second, it's usually a good idea to take notes in stages. In the first stage, you may need to take sketchy notes (words and phrases) to keep abreast of what's happening. Then remove yourself and rewrite your notes in more detail. If you do this soon after the events you've observed, the sketchy notes will help you recall most of the details. The longer you delay, the less likely you are to recall things accurately and fully. James Roberts (2007), in his study of aggression in New Jersey nightclubs, was reluctant to take any notes while inside clubs, so he retired to his car to make sketchy notes about observations, then wrote them up in more detail later. Dina Perrone (2009) wrote up preliminary notes from her study of dance clubs while riding home, then fleshed them out no later than three days after completing her field observations.

Third, you will inevitably wonder how much you should record. Is it really worth the effort to write out all the details you can recall right after the observation session? The basic answer is yes. In field research, you can't really be sure what's important and unimportant until you've had a chance to review and analyze a great volume of information, so you should record even things that don't seem important at the time. They may turn out to be significant after all. In addition, the act of recording the details of something unimportant may jog your memory on something that is important.

Also review Amber Horning's description in Chapter 8 of recording qualitative interviews.

Structured Observations

Field notes may be recorded on highly structured forms in which observers mark items in much the same way a survey interviewer marks a closed-ended questionnaire. For example, Stephen Mastrofski and associates (1998, 11) describe how police performance can be recorded on field observation questionnaires:

> Unlike ethnographic research, which relies heavily on the field researcher to make choices about what to observe and how to interpret it, the observer using [structured observation] is guided by … instruments designed by presumably experienced and knowledgeable police researchers.

Training for such efforts is extensive and time consuming. But Mastrofski and associates compared structured observation to closed-ended questions on a questionnaire. If researchers can anticipate in advance that observers will encounter a limited number of situations in the field, those situations can be recorded on structured observation forms. And, like closed-ended survey questions, structured observations have higher reliability.

In a long-term study, Ralph Taylor (2001) developed forms to code a range of physical characteristics in a sample of Baltimore neighborhoods. Observers recorded information on closed-ended items about housing layout, street length and width, traffic volume, type of nonresidential land use, graffiti, persons hanging out, and so forth. Observations were completed in the same neighborhoods in 1981 and 1994.

Because structured field observation forms often resemble survey questionnaires, the use of such forms has the benefit of enabling researchers to generate numeric measures of conditions observed in the field. The Bureau of Justice Assistance has produced a handbook containing guidelines for conducting structured field observations, called **environmental surveys**. The name is significant because observers record information about the conditions of a specified environment:

> [Environmental] surveys seek to assess, as systematically and objectively as possible, the overall physical environment of an area. That physical environment comprises the buildings, parks, streets, transportation facilities, and overall landscaping of an area as well as the functions and conditions of those entities (Bureau of Justice Assistance 1993, 43).

Environmental surveys have come to be an important component of problem-oriented policing and situational crime prevention. Figure 9.1 is adapted from an environmental survey form used by the Philadelphia Police Department in drug enforcement initiatives. Environmental surveys are conducted to plan police strategy in drug enforcement in small areas and to assess changes in conditions following targeted enforcement. Notice that the form can be used to record both information about physical conditions (street width, traffic volume, streetlights) and counts of people and their activities.

Like interview surveys, environmental surveys require that observers be carefully trained in what to observe and how to interpret it. For example, the instructions that accompany the environmental survey excerpted in Figure 9.1 include guidance on coding abandoned automobiles:

> Count as abandoned if it appears nondrivable (i.e., has shattered windows, dismantled body parts, missing tires, missing license plates). Consider it abandoned if it appears that it has not been driven for some time and that it is not going to be for some time to come.

Other instructions provide details on how to count drivable lanes, what sorts of activities constitute "playing" and "working," how to estimate the ages of people observed, and so on.

Date:_____ Day of week:_____ Time:_____

Observer:_____

Street name:_____

Cross streets:_____

1. Street width

    Number of drivable lanes   ____

    Number of parking lanes   ____

    Median present? (yes = 1, no = 2)   ____

2. Volume of traffic flow: (check one)

    a. very light   ____

    b. light   ____

    c. moderate   ____

    d. heavy   ____

    e. very heavy   ____

3. Number of street lights   ____

4. Number of broken street lights   ____

5. Number of abandoned automobiles   ____

6. List all the people on the block and their activities:

Males	Hanging out	Playing	Working	Walking	Other
Young (up to age 12)	____	____	____	____	____
Teens (13–19)	____	____	____	____	____
Adult (20–60)	____	____	____	____	____
Seniors (61+)	____	____	____	____	____
Females					
Young (up to age 12)	____	____	____	____	____
Teens (13–19)	____	____	____	____	____
Adult (20–60)	____	____	____	____	____
Seniors (61+)	____	____	____	____	____

FIGURE 9.1 Example of Environmental Survey

Source: Adapted from Bureau of Justice Assistance (1993, Appendix B).

Linking Field Observations and Other Data

Criminal justice research sometimes combines field research with surveys or data from official records.

Although criminal justice research may use field methods or sample surveys exclusively, a given project will often collect data from several sources. This is consistent with general advice about using appropriate measures and data collection methods. Simply saying, "I am going to conduct an observational study of youth gangs" restricts the research focus at the outset to the kinds of information that can be gathered through observation. Such a study may be useful and interesting, but a researcher is better advised to consider what data collection methods are necessary in any particular study.

Recognizing the role of disorder and antisocial behavior as law enforcement problems, Sally Harradine and associates (2004) developed a guide for collecting data that combines surveys, field observations, and official records. Surveys provide measures of how people perceive problems of disorder, while official records (which we examine in Chapter 10) document problems that have been reported to police and others. More standard measures of disorder can be produced by observational "audits" of behavior and physical conditions. Harradine and associates provide a detailed guide to completing such audits and to comparing the data produced with measures obtained through surveys and official records.

A long-term research project on community policing in Chicago draws on data from surveys, field observation, and police records (Chicago Community Policing Evaluation Consortium 2003). As just one example, researchers studied what sorts of activities and discussions emerged at community meetings in 130 of the city's 270 police beats that covered residential areas. Observers attended meetings, making detailed notes and completing structured observation forms. One section of the form, shown in Figure 9.2, instructed observers to make notes of specific types of neighborhood problems that were discussed at the meeting (Bennis, Skogan, and Steiner 2003). Here is an excerpt from the narrative notes that supplemented this section of the form:

> They … had very serious concerns in regard to a dilapidated building in their block that was being used for drug sales. The drug seller's people were also squatting in the basement of the building. The main concern was that the four adults who were squatting also had three children under the age of four with them. (Chicago Community Policing Evaluation Consortium 2003, 37)

In addition, observers distributed questionnaires to community residents and police officers attending each meeting. Items asked how often people attended beat meetings, what sorts of other civic activities they pursued, and whether they thought various other issues were problems in their neighborhood. As an example, the combination of field observation data and survey questionnaires enabled researchers to assess the degree of general social activism among those who attended beat meetings.

Field research can also be conducted after a survey. For example, a survey intended to measure fear of crime and related concepts might ask respondents to specify any area near their residence that they believe is particularly dangerous. Follow-up field visits to the named areas could then be conducted, during which observers record information about physical characteristics, land use, numbers of people present, and so forth.

The type of environmental survey that focuses on security and safety of places is often called a **safety audit**. The box titled "Conducting a Safety Audit" describes how structured field observations were combined with a focus group discussion to assess the scope of environmental design changes in Toronto, Canada. Safety audits, coupled with surveys or focus groups, are becoming more widely used to assess women's security in public places (Whitzman et al. 2009). Mangai Natarajan (2012) describes her research on sexual harassment of college women in India, known as "eve teasing." Interviews with college students and police were followed by safety audits of specific areas around students' campuses.

5. Location code (circle one)

1. Police station   7. Hospital

2. Park building   8. Public housing facility

3. Library   9. Private facility

4. Church   10. Restaurant

5. Bank   11. Other not-for-profit

6. Other government

Count the house 30 minutes after the meeting. Exclude police in street clothes ... and others that you can identify as non-residents.

8. _____ Total number residents attending

Note Problems Discussed

1. Drugs (include possibles)

____   ____   Street sales or use

big   small   Building used for drugs

                Drug-related violence

9. Physical decay

____   ____   Abandoned buildings

big   small   Run-down buildings

                Abandoned cars

                Graffiti and vandalism

                Illegal dumping

FIGURE 9.2 Excerpts from Chicago Beat Meeting Observation Form

Source: Adapted from Bennis, Skogan, and Steiner (2003, Appendix 1).

The flexibility of field methods is one reason observation and field interviews can readily be incorporated into many research projects. And field observation often provides a much richer understanding of a phenomenon that is imperfectly revealed through a survey questionnaire.

 CONDUCTING A SAFETY AUDIT

by Gisela Bichler-Robertson
California State University, San Bernardino

A safety audit involves a careful inventory of specific environmental and situational factors that may contribute to feelings of discomfort, fear of victimization, or crime itself. The goal of a safety audit is to devise recommendations that will improve a specific area by reducing fear and crime.

Safety audits combine features of focus groups and structured field observations. To begin, the researcher assembles a small group of individuals (10 or fewer) considered to be vulnerable. Examples

(continued)

include: senior citizens, physically challenged individuals, young women who travel alone, students, youth, and parents with young children. Assembling diverse groups helps to identify a greater variety of environmental and situational factors for the particular area.

After explaining safety audit procedures, an audit leader then takes the group on a tour of the audit site. Since perceptions differ by time of day, at least two audits are conducted for each site—one during daylight and one after dark.

When touring audit sites, individuals do not speak to one another. The audit leader instructs group members to imagine that they are walking through the area alone. Each person is equipped with a structured form for documenting their observations and perceptions. Forms vary, depending on the group and site. In general, however, safety audit participants are instructed to document the following items:

1. Before walking through the area, briefly describe the type of space you are reviewing (e.g., a parking deck, park, shopping district). Record the number of entrances, general volume of users, design of structures, materials used in design, and type of lighting.
2. Complete the following while walking through the area.

General feelings of safety:

- Identify the places in which you feel unsafe and uncomfortable.
- What is it about each place that makes you feel this way?
- Identify the places in which you feel safe.
- What is it about each place that makes you feel this way?

General visibility:

- Can you see very far in front of you?
- Can you see behind you?
- Are there any structures or vegetation that restrict your sightlines?
- How dense are the trees/bushes?
- Are there any hiding spots or entrapment zones?
- Is the lighting adequate? Can you see the face of someone 15 meters in front of you?
- Are the paths/hallways open or are they very narrow?
- Are there any sharp corners (90° angles)?

Perceived control over the space:

- Could you see danger approaching with enough time to choose an alternative route?

- Are you visible to others on the street or in other buildings?
- Can you see any evidence of a security system?

Presence of others:

- Does the area seem to be deserted?
- Are there many women around?
- Are you alone in the presence of men?
- What do the other people seem to be doing?
- Are there any undesirables—vagrants (homeless or beggars), drunks, etc.?
- Do you see people you know?
- Are there any police or security officers present?

General safety:

- Do you have access to a phone or other way of summoning help?
- What is your general perception of criminal behavior?
- Are there any places where you feel you could be attacked or confronted in an uncomfortable way?

Past experience in this space:

- Have you been harassed in this space?
- Have you heard of anyone who had a bad experience in this place (any legends or real experiences)?
- Is it likely that you may be harassed here (e.g., drunk young men coming out of the pub)?
- Have you noticed any social incivilities (minor deviant behavior—i.e., public drinking, vandalism, roughhousing, or skateboarding)?
- Is there much in the way of physical incivilities (broken windows, litter, broken bottles, vandalism)?

Following the site visit, the group finds a secure setting for a focused discussion of the various elements they identified. Harvesting observations about good and bad spaces helps to develop recommendations for physical improvement. Group members may also share perceptions and ideas about personal safety. This process should begin with a brainstorming discussion and finish with identifying the key issues of concern and most reasonable recommendations for addressing those issues.

This method of structured observation has proven to be invaluable. Much of the public space in Toronto, including university campuses, public parks, transportation centers, and garages, has been improved through such endeavors.

Source: Adapted from materials developed by the Metro Action Committee on Public Violence Against Women and Children (METRAC) (Toronto, Canada: METRAC, 1987, http://www.metrac.org/programs/safety/safety.htm#training). Used by permission.

Illustrations of Field Observation

Examples illustrate different applications of field research to study speeding, traffic enforcement, and violence in bars.

Let's now examine some illustrations of field research in action. These descriptions will provide a clearer sense of how researchers use field observations and interviews in criminal justice research.

Field Research on Racial Profiling, Speeding, and Traffic Enforcement

Field research has been an important element in studies of racial profiling for two reasons. First, field research has provided measures of driver behavior that are not dependent on police records. As we have seen in earlier chapters, it is important to compare police records of stops to some other source of information. Second, field research has provided insights into traffic enforcement, an area of policing not much studied by researchers. Field research has also covered the wide range of applications from highly structured counting to less structured field observation and interviews.

Field Measures of Speed Studies of racial profiling in three states used highly structured techniques to measure the speed of vehicles. The most sophisticated equipment was used by Lange and associates (Lange, Johnson, and Voas 2005) in New Jersey. Here's how the authors described their setup:

> The digital photographs were captured by a TC-2000 camera system, integrated with an AutoPatrol PR-100 radar system, provided by Transcore, Inc. The equipment, other than two large strobe lights, was mounted inside an unmarked van, parked behind preexisting guide rails along the turnpike. The camera and radar sensor pointed out of the van's back window toward oncoming traffic. The two strobe lights were mounted on tripods behind the van and directed toward oncoming traffic. Transcore's employees operated the equipment. (2005, 202)

Equipment was programmed to photograph every vehicle exceeding the speed limit by 15 or more miles per hour. Operators also photographed and timed samples of 25 to 50 other vehicles per hour. Elsewhere we have described the other element of observation—coding the appearance of driver race from photographs.

Pennsylvania researchers also used radar to measure the speed of vehicles in selected locations throughout the state. Their procedures were less automated, relying on teams of two observers in a car parked on the side of sampled roadways. Undergraduate students at Pennsylvania State University served as observers. They were trained by Pennsylvania state police in the use of radar equipment, completing the same classroom training that was required of troopers. Additional training for observers was conducted on samples of roadways by the project director. State police were trained to operate radar equipment, but not to combine it with systematic field observation of driver characteristics. That was an important research task, however. Engel and associates describe training and field procedures in detail. Their simple field observation form is included in an appendix to their report (2005, 229).

William Smith and associates (Smith et al. 2003) tried but rejected stationary observation as a technique for recording speed and observing drivers, citing the high speed of passing vehicles and glare from windows as problems. Instead, a research team used mobile observation techniques—observing drivers and timing cars that passed them. Radar was also considered and rejected because it was feared that vehicles with radar detectors, said to be common in North Carolina, would slow down when nearing the research vehicle. Worse, Smith and associates report that truck drivers quickly broadcasted word of detected radar, thus eroding the planned unobtrusive measure.

As you can see, the observational component of research in these three states varied quite a lot. Reading the detailed reports from each study offers valuable insights into the kinds of things field researchers must consider.

Observing New Jersey State Police Other research in New Jersey used less structured field observation techniques because the research purpose was less structured—learning about the general nature of traffic enforcement on New Jersey highways. In a series of studies, researchers from Rutgers University (Maxfield and Kelling 2005; Maxfield and Andresen 2002; Andresen 2005) were interested in the mechanics of making traffic stops and what kinds of things troopers considered in deciding which vehicles to stop. Researchers have long accompanied municipal police on patrol, and a number of studies have documented their efforts. But, as Andresen points out, only a handful of studies have examined traffic enforcement, and even fewer considered state police.

To study video recording cameras in state police cars, Maxfield and Andresen (2002) rode with state police and watched the equipment in use. They learned that sound quality of recordings was often poor, for a variety of reasons associated with microphones and wireless transmittal. It was initially hoped that video records might make it possible to classify the race of drivers, but after watching in-car video monitors, the researchers confirmed that poor image quality undermined the potential reliability of that approach. Moreover, although the Rutgers researchers expected that troopers would be on their best behavior, on a few occasions troopers avoided recording sound and/or images. Even though people behave differently when accompanied by researchers, it's not uncommon for police to let their guard down a little.

Andresen accompanied troopers on 57 patrols overall, conducting unstructured interviews during the several hours he spent with individual troopers. He adopted the common practice of using an interview guide, a list of simple questions he planned to ask in the field. He took extensive notes while riding and repeatedly told troopers they could examine his notes. Andresen observed more than 150 traffic stops, writing field notes to document who was involved, reasons for the stop, what actions troopers took, and what comments they made after the stops. He reports that most troopers seemed to enjoy describing their work. And, as you might imagine, troopers' commentary about traffic enforcement was very interesting.

Bars and Violence

Researchers in the first example conducted systematic observations for specific purposes and produced quantitative estimates of speeding traffic stops. Field research is commonly used in more qualitative studies as well, in which precise quantitative estimates are neither available nor needed. A fascinating series of studies of violence in Australian bars by Ross Homel and associates provides an example (Homel, Tomsen, and Thommeny 1992; Homel and Clark 1994; Graham and Homel 2008).

Homel and associates set out to learn how various situational factors related to public drinking might promote or inhibit violence in Australian bars and nightclubs. Think for a moment about how you might approach their research question: "whether alcohol consumption itself contributes in some way to the likelihood of violence, or whether aspects of the drinkers or of the drinking settings are the critical factors" (1992, 681). Examining police records might reveal that assault reports are more likely to come from bars than from, say, public libraries. Or a survey might find that self-reported bar patrons were more likely to have witnessed or participated in violence than respondents who did not frequent bars or nightclubs. But neither of these approaches will yield measures of the setting or situational factors that might provoke violence. Field research can produce direct observation of barroom settings and is well suited to addressing the question framed by Homel and associates.

Researchers began by selecting 4 high-risk and 2 low-risk sites on the basis of Sydney police records and preliminary scouting visits. These 6 sites were visited five or more times, and an additional 16 sites were visited once in the course of scouting.

Visits to bars were conducted by pairs of observers who stayed two to six hours at each site. Their role is best described as complete participant because they were permitted one alcoholic drink per hour and otherwise played the role of bar patron. Observers made no notes while onsite. As soon as possible after leaving a bar, they wrote up separate narrative accounts. Later, at group meetings of observers and research staff, the narrative accounts were discussed and any discrepancies resolved. Narratives were later coded by research staff to identify categories of situations, people, and activities that seemed to be associated with the likelihood of violence. These eventually included physical and social atmosphere, drinking patterns, characteristics of patrons, and characteristics of staff.

The researchers began their study by assuming that some thing or things distinguished bars in which violence was common from those in which it was less common. After beginning their fieldwork, however, Homel and associates (1992, 684) realized that circumstances and situations were the more important factors:

> During field research it soon became apparent that the violent premises are for most of the time not violent. Violent occasions in these places seemed to have characteristics that clearly marked them out from nonviolent times.... This unexpectedly helped us refine our ideas about the relevant situational variables, and to some extent reduced the importance of comparisons with the premises selected as controls.

In other words, the research question was partly restated. What began as a study to determine why some bars in Sydney were violent was revised to determine what situations seemed to contribute to violence.

This illustrates one of the strengths of field research—the ability to make adjustments while in the field. You may recognize this as an example of inductive reasoning. Learning that even violent clubs were peaceful most of the time, Homel and associates were able to focus observers' attention on looking for more specific features of the bar environment and staff and patron characteristics. Such adjustments on the fly would be difficult, if not impossible, if you were doing a survey.

Altogether, field observers made 55 visits to 23 sites for a total of about 300 hours of field observation. During these visits, observers witnessed 32 incidents of physical violence. Examining detailed field notes, researchers attributed violent incidents to a variety of interrelated factors.

With respect to patrons, violence was most likely to break out in bars frequented by young, working-class males. However, these personal characteristics were deemed less important than the flow of people in and out of bars. Violent incidents were often triggered when groups of males entered a club and encountered other groups of males they did not know.

Physical features mattered little unless they contributed to crowding or other adverse characteristics of the social atmosphere. Chief among social features associated with violence were discomfort and boredom. A crowded, uncomfortable bar with no entertainment spelled trouble.

Drinking patterns made a difference; violent incidents were most common when bar patrons were very drunk. More importantly, certain management practices seemed to produce more drunk patrons. Fewer customers were drunk in bars that had either a restaurant or a snack table. Bars with high cover charges and cheap drinks produced a high density of drunk patrons and violence. The economics of this situation are clear: if you must pay to enter a bar that serves cheap drinks, you'll get more for your money by drinking a lot.

The final ingredient found to contribute to violence was aggressive bouncers. "Many bouncers seem poorly trained, obsessed with their own machismo (relating badly to groups of male strangers), and some of them appear to regard their employment as a license to assault people" (1992, 688). Rather than reducing violence by rejecting unruly patrons, bouncers sometimes escalated violence by starting fights.

Field observation was necessary to identify what situations produce violence in bars. No other way of collecting data could have yielded the rich and detailed information that enabled Homel and associates to diagnose the complex relationships that produce violence in bars:

> Violent incidents in public drinking locations do not occur simply because of the presence of young or rough patrons or because of rock bands, or any other single variable. Violent occasions are characterized by subtle interactions of several variables. Chief among these are groups of male strangers, low comfort, high boredom, high drunkenness, as well as aggressive and unreasonable bouncers and floor staff. (1992, 688)

Strengths and Weaknesses of Field Observation

Validity is usually a strength of field observation, but reliability and generalizability are sometimes weaknesses.

As we have seen, field research is especially effective for studying the subtle nuances of behavior and for examining processes over time. For these reasons, the chief strength of this method is the depth of understanding it permits.

Flexibility is another advantage of field research. Researchers can modify their research design at any time. Dina Perrone stated, "I consistently reevaluated my methodology to ensure the highest level of credibility, dependability, and transferability of the data. Coding methods, sampling, observational techniques and [my] interview guide evolved with the research" (2009, 37).

Most significantly, field research is a superior method for studying active offenders in field settings. Qualitative interviews and observations combine offenders' perspectives and systematic measures collected by researchers. A growing body of research has provided rich detail on the motives of offenders, how they select targets, and what sorts of things they are attentive to as incidents unfold. Researchers have studied drug dealers, robbers, burglars, gang members, carjackers, sex workers, and individuals engaged in a variety of other offenses. Although it's possible to study arrested or convicted offenders in other settings, field research offers many advantages for learning about criminal activity that is untainted by official intervention.

By the same token, field research offers advantages for studying justice officials in natural settings. Scholars have long recognized that the view of police work through a car's windshield offers much richer information about police work than the statistical analysis of arrests or crime reports. Similarly, researchers have interviewed corrections officers for many studies. Ted Conover tried that approach but was denied access to interview corrections workers in New York state prisons. So he became a corrections officer in New York and wrote up his experiences after working for two years in Sing Sing.

His book, *Newjack: Guarding Sing Sing*, provides insights into life on the job that are unobtainable through any other research method (Conover 2000).

Field research has its weaknesses, too. First, qualitative studies seldom yield precise descriptive statements about a large population. Observing casual discussions among corrections officers in a cafeteria, for example, does not yield trustworthy estimates about prison conditions. Nevertheless, it could provide important insights into some of the problems facing staff and inmates in a specific institution.

Second, field observation can produce systematic counts of behaviors and reasonable estimates for a large population of behaviors beyond those actually observed. However, because it is difficult to know the total population of given phenomena—homeless people or drivers, for example—precise probability samples cannot normally be drawn. In designing a quantitative field study or assessing the representativeness of some other study, researchers must think carefully about the density and predictability of what will be observed. Then they must decide whether sampling procedures are likely to tap representative instances of cases they will observe.

More generally, the advantages and disadvantages of different types of field studies can be considered in terms of their validity, reliability, and generalizability. As we have seen, validity and reliability are both qualities of measurements. *Validity* concerns whether measurements actually measure what they are supposed to, not something else. *Reliability* is a matter of dependability: if researchers make the same measurement again and again, will they get the same result? Note that some examples we described in this chapter included special steps to improve reliability. Finally, *generalizability* refers to whether specific research findings apply to people, places, and things not actually observed. Let's see how field research stacks up in these respects.

Validity

Recall our discussion in Chapter 7 of some of the limitations of using survey methods to study domestic violence. An alternative is a field study in which the researcher interacts at length with victims of domestic violence. The relative strengths of each approach are nicely illustrated in a pair of articles that examine domestic violence in England. Chapter 7 quoted from Catriona Mirrlees-Black's (1995) article on domestic violence as measured in the British Crime Survey. John Hood-Williams and Tracey Bush (1995) provide a different perspective through their study published in the same issue of the *Home Office Research Bulletin*.

Tracey Bush lived in a London public housing project (termed *housing estate* in England) for about five years. This enabled her to study domestic violence in a natural setting: "The views of men and women on the estate about relationships and domestic violence have been gathered through the researcher's network of friends, neighbours, acquaintances, and contacts" (Hood-Williams and Bush 1995, 11). Through long and patient fieldwork, Bush learned that women sometimes normalize low levels of violence, seeing it as an unfortunate but unavoidable consequence of their relationship with a male partner. When violence escalates, victims may blame themselves. Victims may also remain in an abusive relationship in hopes that things will get better:

> She reported that she wanted the companionship and respect that she had received at the beginning of the relationship. It was the earlier, nonviolent man, whom she had met and fallen in love with, that she wanted back. (1995, 13)

Mirrlees-Black (1995) notes that measuring domestic violence is "difficult territory" in part because women may not recognize assault by a partner as a crime. Field research such as that by Hood-Williams and Bush offers an example of this phenomenon and helps us understand why it exists.

In field research, validity often refers to whether the intended meaning of the things observed or people interviewed has been accurately captured. In the case of interviews, Joseph Maxwell (2013) suggests getting feedback on the measures from the people being studied. For example, Wright and Decker (1994) conducted lengthy semistructured interviews with their sample of burglars. The researchers recognized that their limited understanding of the social context of burglary may have produced some errors in interpreting what they learned from subjects. To guard against this, Wright and Decker had some of their subjects review what they thought they had learned:

> As the writing proceeded, we read various parts of the manuscript to selected members of our sample. This allowed us to check our interpretations against those of insiders and to enlist their help in reformulating passages they regarded as misleading or inaccurate. The result of using this procedure, we believe, is a book that faithfully conveys the offender's perspective on the process of committing residential burglaries. (1994, 33–34)

This approach is possible only if subjects are aware of the researcher's role as a researcher. In that case, having informants review draft field notes or interview transcripts can be an excellent strategy for improving validity.

Reliability

Qualitative field research can have a potential problem with reliability. Suppose you characterize your best friend's political orientations based on everything you know about him or her. There's certainly no question that your assessment of that person's politics is at least somewhat idiosyncratic. The measurement you arrive at will appear to have considerable validity. We can't be sure, however, that someone else will characterize your friend's politics the same way you do, even with the same amount of observation.

Field research measurements—even in-depth ones—are also often very personal. If, for example, you wished to conduct a field study of bars and honky-tonks near your campus, you might judge levels of disorder on a Friday night to be low or moderate. In contrast, older adults might observe the same levels of noise and commotion and rate levels of disorder as intolerably high. How we interpret the phenomena we observe depends very much on our own experiences and preferences. Dina Perrone (2009) describes how the intense sexual atmosphere in dance clubs and concomitant behavior by male patrons partly constrained her field research.

The reliability of quantitative field studies can be enhanced by careful attention to the details of observation. Environmental surveys in particular can promote reliable observations by including detailed instructions on how to classify what is observed. Reliability can be strengthened by reviewing the products of field observations. Homel and associates sought to increase the reliability of observers' narrative descriptions by having group discussions about discrepancies in reports by different observers.

Shuryo Fujita took clever steps to enhance the reliability of his measures of street conditions in Newark, New Jersey. The box earlier in this chapter describes how he selected streets to code. He then used images from Google Street View to code variables measuring litter, graffiti, and housing conditions of selected streets. Adapting a technique used for decades to measure street cleanliness in New York City (Mayor's Office of Operations 2006), Fujita selected sample photographs that showed varying degrees of litter, graffiti, and run-down housing to illustrate the attributes of his scale. These photos served as visual anchors to increase consistency of recording values for each observed measure (Fujita 2011).

The annual count of homeless people in New York City is another good example of how to enhance the reliability of field observations. During one overnight period of about 10 hours in January each year, field researchers are deployed throughout areas of New York where people who appear to be homeless are commonly seen (Silberman School of Social Work 2013). The count is done at night under the assumption that people sleeping outdoors in January are likely to be homeless. Observers approach people who meet screening criteria and use a protocol to ask questions about their living arrangements. In an effort to measure how well observers are at finding and approaching subjects, other research staff are hired as decoys to dress and act like homeless people. Decoys are trained, paid $75 (in 2014) for their work, and deployed to the same areas where observers are assigned. Decoys are known targets, so assessing the number of decoys who are approached and questioned provides an estimate of observer reliability. Check the Shadow Count website for more information (http://www.hunter.cuny.edu/socwork/shadow_count/Flyer_SC_14.pdf). Consider signing up if you live near New York City and want some (modestly) paid experience in doing field observation!

In a more general sense, reliability will increase as the degree of interpretation required in making actual observations decreases. Participant observation or unstructured interviews may require a considerable degree of interpretation on the part of the observer, and most of us draw on our own experiences and backgrounds in interpreting what we observe. At another extreme, electronic devices and machines can produce very reliable counts of persons who enter a store or of cars that pass some particular point. Somewhere in the middle are fieldworkers who observe motorists or pedestrians and tabulate a specific behavior.

Generalizability

One of the chief goals of social science is generalization. We study particular situations and events to learn about life in general. Generalizability can be a problem for qualitative field research. It crops up in two forms.

First, the personal nature of the observations and measurements made by the researcher can produce results that will not necessarily be replicated by another independent researcher. If the observation depends in part on the individual observers, it is more valuable as a source of particular insight than as a general truth. You may recognize the similarity between this and the more general issue of reliability.

Second, because field researchers get a full and in-depth view of their subject matter, they can reach an unusually comprehensive understanding. By its very comprehensiveness, however, this understanding is less generalizable than results based on rigorous sampling and standardized measurements.

For example, Maxfield's observational research with the New Jersey State Police took several forms. One experience involved learning about radar speed enforcement on a 50-mile segment of the New Jersey Turnpike. Maxfield accompanied troopers on a thorough tour of this segment, identifying where radar units were routinely stationed (termed *fishing holes* by troopers). In his fieldwork, he also examined physical characteristics of the roadway; patterns of in-state and out-of-state travel; and areas where entrance ramps, slight upward grades, and other features affected vehicle speed. Finally, he gained extensive information on priorities and patterns in speed enforcement—learning what affects troopers' decisions to stop certain vehicles.

As a result, Maxfield has detailed knowledge about that 50-mile segment of the New Jersey Turnpike. How generalizable is that knowledge? In one sense, learning about fishing holes in very specific terms can help identify such sites on other roads. And learning how slight upward grades can slow traffic in one situation may help us understand traffic on other upward grades. But a detailed, idiosyncratic understanding of 50 miles of highway is just that—idiosyncratic. Knowing all there is to know about a straight, largely level stretch of limited-access toll road with few exits is not generalizable to other roadways—winding roads in mountainous areas with many exits, for example.

At the same time, some field studies are less rooted in the local context of the subject under study. Wright and Decker (1994) studied burglars in St. Louis, and it's certainly reasonable to wonder whether their findings apply to residential burglars in St. Petersburg, Florida. The actions and routines of burglars might be affected by local police strategies, differences in the age or style of dwelling units, or even the type and amount of vegetation screening buildings from the street. However, Wright and Decker draw general conclusions about how burglars search for targets, what features of dwellings signal vulnerability, how opportunistic knowledge can trigger an offense, and what strategies exist for fencing stolen goods. It's likely that their findings about the technology and incentives that affect St. Louis burglars apply generally to residential burglars in other cities.

Perrone (2009) describes the generalizability of her field research in terms of *transferability*—whether she might obtain similar findings if she had studied different dance clubs in different settings. She conducted 45 field observations in New York City, Miami, and beach resort towns in New York and New Jersey. She argues that observing similar behavior in different settings enhanced the transferability of her research.

In reviewing reports of field research projects, it's important to determine where and to what extent the researcher is generalizing beyond her or his specific observations to other settings. Such generalizations may be in order, but it is necessary to judge that. Nothing in this research method guarantees it.

As we've seen, field research is a potentially powerful tool for criminal justice research, one that provides a useful balance to surveys. We conclude with one final example. The box, "Assessing Gun Violence Reduction Strategies in New York City" describes a study that uses field observation, interviews with innovative recording techniques, and a sophisticated type of purposive sampling that targets people exposed to street violence. The research described by Sheyla Delgado and Jeffrey Butts also illustrates evaluation research, the subject of our final chapter.

 ASSESSING GUN VIOLENCE REDUCTION STRATEGIES IN NEW YORK CITY

by Sheyla A. Delgado and Jeffrey A. Butts
Research and Evaluation Center, John Jay College of Criminal Justice, CUNY

The Research and Evaluation Center at John Jay College developed a project to evaluate gun violence reduction strategies in New York City neighborhoods. Sponsored by the New York City Council, the project tracked the deployment of gun violence reduction strategies in four areas of the city: South Bronx, Harlem, Jamaica (Queens), and East New York (Brooklyn).

Each pilot program implements Cure Violence, a public health oriented violence-reduction strategy developed at the University of Illinois-Chicago. In addition to Cure Violence, each site provides support services for at-risk youth, their families, and communities. These include mental health services, school-based conflict mediation, job training and placement, and legal services.

In 2014, the research team began field research in selected areas, conducting interviews with local residents. John Jay researchers (operating under the street brand "NYC-Cure") interviewed young men (ages 18-30) in several city neighborhoods. Interviews were designed to measure each respondent's actual

(continued)

experience of violence as well as his attitudes about violent behavior in varying situations. The project used an innovative sampling method called respondent-driven sampling (RDS). RDS makes it possible to gather data quickly and efficiently from traditionally hard-to-reach populations. The system is based on chains of referrals and field contacts, supported by a visible presence of the research team.

Each data-collection period lasted about 10 continuous days, an important feature to maintain the chain of referrals that sprouted at each interview site. When study participants saw the research at the same time and location for several days, they were more likely to encourage friends to participate in the study. The combination of RDS and a stable field presence made it possible to interview about 200 young men at each site.

Field researchers used tablet devices and a data-collection application to administer the interview protocol. Interview data was collected offline while in the field. The application used to collect the data allowed us to create different types of questions and use skip logic patterns. Back in the research office tablets were connected to the Internet, data was quickly uploaded to a password-protected site, and became readily available for analysis and review. Using tablet-based interview protocols eliminated the need for paper forms and data entry. This helped avoid many of the usual systematic data errors, made coding and cleaning of data much easier for the research team, and generally increased the reliability of data collected in the field.

Overall, automating the data collection process was cost-effective and ran much more smoothly than the paper-based interviews and observation forms traditionally used in field research. What follows are examples of screens from the tablet data collection app, and preliminary results for some of the questions in four areas of New York City.

NY**C**ure

Which social media platforms do you use to keep in touch with your friends and associates in the neighborhood? Please select all that apply.

   None

For this section of the survey we will over a list of hypothetical scenarios and we'd like to know how far you'd be willing to take each situation.

On a scale from 1-10, 1 being "Ignore" and 10 "the furthest you'd be willing to take it", we'd like to like to how far are you willing to go.

Answer choices: Ignore, react verbally, get physical, pull a weapon, use a weapon, not sure/decline

NY**C**ure

A guy takes a swing at you at a party in another neighborhood.

3 (React verbally)

1 (Ignore)   11 (Not sure/Decline)

NY**C**ure

You see a guy on the street who beat up your brother last week.

6

1 (Ignore)   11 (Not sure/Decline)

(continued)

		Harlem	East New York	South Jamaica	South Bronx
		n=182	n=198	n=191	n=200
My current age	Ages 18–20	46%	41%	54%	48%
	Ages 21 or older	54%	59%	46%	52%
My current employment status	Full-time	19%	16%	19%	18%
	Part-time	21%	25%	33%	21%
	Unemployed	60%	59%	48%	58%
Time I'm out of the neighborhood on an average day	Fewer than 5 hours	18%	37%	20%	28%
	5 or more hours	82%	63%	80%	72%
I helped a neighbor within the last week	Yes	80%	71%	71%	76%
	No	20%	29%	29%	24%
I was helped by a neighbor within the last week	Yes	36%	39%	44%	44%
	No	64%	61%	56%	56%
Feel safe in my neighborhood during the daytime	Yes	93%	95%	85%	92%
	No	7%	5%	15%	8%
Feel safe in my neighborhood at night	Yes	81%	79%	72%	76%
	No	19%	21%	28%	24%
I've been "stopped & frisked"	Yes	81%	79%	72%	78%
	No	19%	21%	28%	22%
I've been shot at before	Yes	29%	41%	30%	45%
	No	71%	59%	70%	55%
I've been stabbed before	Yes	18%	17%	17%	19%
	No	82%	83%	83%	81%
I've seen at least one gun on my block in the past year	Yes	43%	45%	32%	50%
	No	57%	55%	68%	50%
I've heard gun shots in my neighborhood	Yes	83%	83%	77%	87%
	No	17%	17%	33%	23%

Source: Preliminary data from surveys of 18– to 30–year–old men in four New York City neighborhoods. N=771. Surveys conducted in March, April, and May 2014 by the Research & Evaluation Center at John Jay College as part of a project funded by the City Council of New York City.

Note: Survey samples were created using "respondent driven sampling" (RDS) techniques. For additional information about RDS, see Heckathorn, D.D. (2011). Comment: Snowball versus Respondent-Driven Sampling. Sociological Methodology, 41(1):355–366; and Goel, S. and M.J. Salganik (2010). Assessing Respondent-Driven Sampling. Proceedings of the National Academy of Sciences of the United States, Vol. 107(15): 6743–6747.

Percentages are calculated using valid responses only. For some questions, a small number of responses (usually fewer than 5%) may have been missing or the survey subject may not have been able to answer.

SUMMARY

- Field research is a data collection method that involves the direct observation of phenomena in their natural settings.

- Field observation is usually the preferred data collection method for obtaining information about physical or social settings, behavior, and events.

- Field research in criminal justice may produce either qualitative or quantitative data. Grounded theory is typically built from qualitative field observations. Or observations that can be quantified may produce measures for hypothesis testing.

- Observations made through field research can often be integrated with data collected from other sources. In this way, field observations can help researchers interpret other data.

- Field researchers may or may not identify themselves as researchers to the people they are observing. Being identified as a researcher may have some effect on what is observed.

- Controlled probability sampling techniques are not usually possible in field research. But in some circumstances, researchers can combine probability and nonprobability sampling.

- Alternatives for recording field observations range from video, audio, and other equipment to unstructured field notes. In between are observations recorded on structured forms; environmental surveys are examples.

- Field notes should be planned in advance to the greatest extent possible. However, note taking should be flexible enough to make records of unexpected observations.

- Compared with surveys, field research measurements generally have more validity but less reliability, and field research results cannot be generalized as safely as those based on rigorous sampling and standardized questionnaires.

KEY TERMS

environmental surveys, p. 238
ethnography, p. 231

reactivity, p. 232
safety audit, p. 240

REVIEW QUESTIONS AND EXERCISES

1. We briefly described how Shuryo Fujita sampled street segments and conducted systematic observations using Google Street View. In a paragraph or so, summarize another way images from Google Street View can be used as a source of field observation data. What are some advantages and disadvantages of this

data source? Describe one example of a concept that can be readily measured with Goggle Street View and one example of a concept that cannot.

2. Review the box titled "Conducting a Safety Audit" by Gisela Bichler-Robertson on page 241. Try conducting a safety audit on your campus or in an area near your campus.

3. The Center for Urban Pedagogy (CUP) sponsors a variety of activities to educate New York City students about urban policy and to involve students in field research projects. One group of students produced a booklet, titled *Field Guide to Federalism: Bushwick, Brooklyn, NY.* In describing their research, students wrote: "We started small and began by looking for signs of federalism in our wallets. Then we took to the streets looking for some evidence of what federal, state, and city government looks like in Bushwick" (Center for Urban Pedagogy 2011, 1). Download the booklet at the CUP website. Briefly describe how the students' research involves techniques of field observation described in this chapter. By the way, CUP projects address a variety of issues in criminal and juvenile justice. For example, see the poster by Danica Navgorodoff, "I got arrested! Now what?" (Navgorodoff 2010) at the following website: http://www.courtinnovation.org/research/i-got-arrested-now-what.

/>
CHAPTER **10**

Agency Records, Content Analysis, and Secondary Data

We will examine three sources of existing data: agency records, content analysis, and data collected by other researchers. Data from these sources have many applications in criminal justice research.

Terrorist Recruitment

Dr. Niyazi Ekici used agency records and content analysis in his research on recruitment by two terrorist organizations in Turkey (Ekici 2008). A high-ranking officer in the Turkish National Police, Ekici had access to official records during his graduate study at Rutgers University. His interests centered on how terrorist organizations initiated contact with potential members, together with what sorts of factors entered into the selection process.

Several organizations that employ terrorist tactics have been active in Turkey. Ekici selected two groups with very different ideologies, expecting that the groups would seek recruits with different qualities. The Revolutionary People's Liberation Party/Front (DHKP/C) is fueled by a Marxist ideology, while Turkish Hezbollah is a religious extremist group.

Two sources were used to gather data about active terrorists and those who aspired to join the two groups. Data on active terrorists were obtained from police records of 70 individuals in each of the two organizations who had been arrested and convicted of terroristic offenses. The second source was unique—documents written by individuals who sought to join the organizations, something similar to a letter of application. These documents, seized in police raids of terrorist cells over a 10-year period, provided information on an individual's family, political and religious beliefs, and reasons for wishing to join the organization. In earlier chapters, we discussed the validity and reliability of self-reports.

Ekici writes that these documents are likely to be accurate because "the terrorist organization will not hesitate to kill members who are found to be lying" (2008, 92).

Ekici used content analysis to systematically extract information from both police records of active terrorists and seized documents of recruits. He then compared a variety of measures for recruits and active members in Turkish Hezbollah and DHKP/C.

Compared to convicted terrorists, candidate terrorists in both organizations were more likely

- to have criminal records;
- to have family members with criminal records; and
- to have associated with other terrorist organizations.

Ekici interprets these findings as some measure of selectivity, showing that loyalty and not being known to police are valued by these two terrorist groups and affect the kinds of people who become members.

This is an unusual example of research based on agency records. However, it applies many of the principles of research using agency records and content analysis discussed in this chapter. A police officer as well as a researcher, Dr. Niyazi Ekici used the tools of social science research to systematically analyze documents maintained by the Turkish National Police and to add to knowledge about terrorist recruitment.

Introduction

Agency records, secondary data, and content analysis do not require direct interaction with research subjects.

Except for the complete observer role in field research, the modes of observation discussed so far require the researcher to intrude to some degree into whatever he or she is studying. This is most obvious with survey research and some types of qualitative interviewing. Even the field researcher, as we've seen, can change things in the process of studying them.

Other ways of collecting data do not involve intrusion by observers. In this chapter, we'll consider three different approaches to using information that has been collected by others, often as a routine practice.

First, a great deal of criminal justice research uses data collected by state and local agencies such as police, criminal courts, probation offices, juvenile authorities, and corrections departments. Government agencies gather a vast amount of crime and criminal justice data, probably rivaled only by efforts to produce economic and public health indicators. We refer to such information as "data from agency records." In this chapter, we will describe different types of such data that are available for criminal justice research, together with the promise and potential pitfalls of using information from agency records.

Second, in content analysis, researchers examine a class of social artifacts—written documents or other types of messages. Suppose you want to contrast the importance of criminal justice policy and health care policy for Americans in 2004 and 2014. One option is to examine public-opinion polls from these years. Another method is to analyze articles from newspapers published in each year. The latter is an example of content analysis: the analysis of communications.

Finally, information collected by others is frequently used in criminal justice research, which in this case involves **secondary analysis** of existing data. Investigators who conduct research funded by federal agencies such as the National Institute of Justice are usually obliged to release their data for public use. Thus, if you were interested in developing sentence reform proposals for your state, you might analyze data collected by Nancy Merritt, Terry Fain, and Susan Turner in the study of Oregon's efforts to increase sentence length for certain types of offenders (Merritt, Fain, and Turner 2006).

In a general sense, then, most data we might obtain from agency records or research projects conducted by others are secondary data. Someone else gathered the original data, usually for purposes that differ from ours. That is certainly the case for research described in the vignette "Terrorist Recruitment" at the opening of this chapter. This vignette briefly describes how Niyazi Ekici used content analysis and agency records collected by the Turkish National Police.

Topics Appropriate for Agency Records and Content Analysis

Agency records support a wide variety of research applications.

Data from agency records or archives may have originally been gathered in any number of ways, from sample surveys to direct observation. Because of this, such data may, in principle, be appropriate for just about any criminal justice research topic.

Published statistics and agency records are most commonly used in descriptive or exploratory studies. This is consistent with the fact that many of the criminal justice data published by government agencies are intended to describe something. For instance, the Bureau of Justice Statistics (BJS) publishes annual figures on prison populations. If we are interested in describing differences in prison populations between states or changes in prison populations from 1990 through 2015, a good place to begin is with the annual data published by BJS. Or, if we wish to learn more about cases of identity theft, we could consult the annual *Consumer Network Data Book*, which summarizes known cases of identity theft and related frauds (Federal Trade

Commission 2014). Similarly, published figures on crimes reported to police, criminal victimization, felony court caseloads, drug use by high school seniors, and a host of other measures are available over time—for 30 years or longer in many cases.

Agency records may also be used in explanatory studies. Nancy Sinauer and colleagues (1999) examined medical examiner records for more than 1,000 female homicide victims in North Carolina to understand the relationship between female homicide and residence in urban versus rural counties. They found that counties on the outskirts of cities had higher female homicide rates than either urban or rural counties.

Agency records are frequently used in applied studies as well. Evaluations of new policies that seek to reduce recidivism might draw on arrest or conviction data for measures of recidivism. For example, a study of drug courts as an alternative way to process defendants with substance abuse problems traced arrest records for experimental and control subjects (Gottfredson et al. 2006). In another study, researchers used data from public sex offender registries in New York to examine the impact of laws restricting where sex offenders could live (Berenson and Appelbaum 2011). Sometimes, records obtained from private firms can be used in applied studies; Gisela Bichler and Ronald Clarke (1996) examined records of international telephone calls in their evaluation of efforts to reduce telephone fraud in New York City.

In a different type of applied study, James Austin, Wendy Naro, and Tony Fabelo (2007) combined data on prison releases and capacities, reincarcerations, and general-population forecasts to develop a mathematical model that predicts future prison populations. This is an example of forecasting, in which past relationships among arrest rates and prison sentences for different age groups are compared with estimates of future population by age group. Assuming that past associations between age, arrest, and prison sentence will remain constant in future years, demographic models of future population can be used to predict future admissions to prison.

Topics appropriate to research using content analysis center on the important links between communication, perceptions of crime problems, individual behavior, and criminal justice policy. The prevalence of violence on fictional television dramas has long been a concern of researchers and public officials (Anderson and Bushman 2002). Niyazi Ekici (2008) used content analysis to learn about how terrorists were recruited in Turkey. Mass media also play an important role in affecting policy action by public officials. Many studies have examined the influence of media in setting the agenda for criminal justice policy (see, for example, Chermak and Weiss 1997).

Research data collected by other investigators, through surveys or field observation, may be used for a broad variety of later studies. National Crime Victimization Survey (NCVS) data have been used by a large number of researchers in countless descriptive and explanatory studies since the 1970s. In a notably ambitious use of secondary data, Robert Sampson and John Laub (1993) recovered life history data on 500 delinquents and 500 nondelinquents originally collected by Sheldon and Eleanor Glueck in the 1940s. Taking advantage of theoretical and empirical advances in criminological research over the ensuing 40 years, Sampson and Laub produced a major contribution to knowledge of criminal career development in childhood.

Existing data may also be considered as a supplemental source of data. For example, a researcher planning to survey correctional facility administrators about their views on the need for drug treatment programs will do well to examine existing data on the number of drug users sentenced to prison terms. Or, if we are evaluating an experimental morale-building program in a probation services department, statistics on absenteeism will be useful in connection with the data our own research will generate.

This is not to say that agency records and secondary data can always provide answers to research questions. If this were true, much of this book would be unnecessary. The key to distinguishing appropriate and inappropriate uses of agency records, content analysis, and secondary data is understanding how these written records are produced. We cannot emphasize this point too strongly. Much of this chapter will underscore the importance of learning where data come from and how they are gathered.

Types of Agency Records

Researchers use a variety of published statistics and nonpublic agency records.

Information collected by or for public agencies usually falls into one of three general categories: (1) published statistics, (2) nonpublic agency records routinely collected for internal use, and (3) new data collected by agency staff for specific research purposes. Each category varies in the extent to which data are readily available to the researcher and in the researcher's degree of control over the data collection process.

Published Statistics

Most government organizations routinely collect and publish compilations of data, which we refer to collectively as **published statistics**. Examples are the Census Bureau, the FBI, the Administrative Office of U.S. Courts, the Federal Bureau of Pris-

ons, and the BJS. Two of these organizations merit special mention. First, the Census Bureau conducts enumerations and sample surveys for several other federal organizations. Notable examples are the NCVS, Census of Children in Residential Placement, Correctional Populations in the United States, and Survey of Justice Expenditure and Employment.

Second, the BJS compiles data from several sources and publishes annual and special reports on most data series. For example, the publication *Criminal Victimization in the United States* reports summary data from the NCVS each year. Table 10.1 presents a sample breakdown of domestic violence victimization rates compiled over the years 2003–2012. The BJS also issues reports on people under correctional supervision. These are based on sample surveys and enumerations of jail, prison, and juvenile facility populations. Sample tabulations of people serving sentences in state and federal prison in 2012 are shown in Table 10.2. And the series *Federal Criminal Case Processing* reports detailed data on federal court activity.

The most comprehensive compilation of published statistics on criminal justice data is the annual

TABLE 10.1   Domestic Violence Victimization: Averages 2003–2012

Victim-Offender Relationship	Average Annual Number of Victims	Rate of Violent Victimization per 1,000 Persons		
		Serious Assault	Simple Assault	Total Violent Crime
Known				
Intimate partner	967,710	1.4	2.5	3.9
Spouse	314,430	0.5	0.8	1.3
Ex-spouse	134,690	0.1	0.4	0.05
Boy/girlfriend	518,700	0.8	1.3	2.1
Other family	284,670	0.4	0.7	1.1
Parent	80,900	0.1	0.2	0.3
Child	97,490	0.1	0.3	0.4
Sibling	106,290	0.1	0.3	0.4
Other family	158,950	0.2	0.4	0.6
Acquaintance	2,103,240	2.3	6.1	8.4
Stranger	2,548,860	3.7	6.5	10.2

Source: Adapted from Truman and Morgan (2014, Tables 1 and 2).

TABLE 10.2   Prisoners in Selected States, 2012

	Number		Percent Female	Percent in Private Prisons
	Males	**Females**	**Percent Female**	**Percent in Private Prisons**
Alabama	29,782	2,649	8.2%	1.7%
Arizona	36,447	3,633	9.1%	16.1%
California	128,436	6,098	4.5%	0.5%
Florida	94,945	6,985	6.9%	11.5%
New Mexico	6,096	631	9.4%	44.6%
New York	51,963	2,247	4.1%	0%
Texas	152,823	13,549	8.1%	11.2%
Vermont	1,907	127	6.2%	24.8%

Source: Adapted from Carson and Golinelli (2013, Appendix Tables 6 and 7).

Sourcebook of Criminal Justice Statistics (http://www.albany.edu/sourcebook). Since 1972, this report has summarized hundreds of criminal justice data series, ranging from public perceptions about crime to characteristics of criminal justice agencies, to tables on how states execute capital offenders. Data from private sources such as the Gallup Poll are included with statistics collected by government agencies. The *Sourcebook* also includes notes on data sources and data collection procedures for major series and the addresses of organizations that either collect or archive original data.

Compilations of published data on crime and criminal justice are readily available from many sources. The BJS website includes summary reports on a number of data series. See the *Statistical Briefing Book* compiled by the Office of Juvenile Justice and Delinquency Protection (http://www.ojjdp.gov/ojstatbb/) for information on juvenile justice. And of course, the FBI Uniform Crime Reports series is an important source of published reports on crimes known to police (http://www.fbi.gov/about-us/cjis/ucr/ucr).

At this point, however, we want to suggest some possible uses, and limits, of what Herbert Jacob (1984, 9) refers to as being "like the apple in the Garden of Eden: tempting but full of danger ... [for] the unwary researcher."

Referring to Tables 10.1 and 10.2, you may recognize that published data from series such as the NCVS or *Correctional Populations in the United States* are summary data, as discussed in Chapter 4. This means that data are presented in highly aggregated form and cannot be used to analyze the individuals from or about whom information was originally collected. For example, Table 10.2 shows that in 2012 a total of 13,549 women were serving sentences of one year or more in state correctional institutions in Texas. By comparing that figure with figures from other states, we can make some descriptive statements about prison populations in different states. We can also consult earlier editions of *Correctional Populations* to examine trends in prison populations over time or to compare rates of growth from state to state.

Summary data cannot, however, be used to reveal anything about individual correctional facilities, let alone facility inmates. Individual-level data about inmates and institutions are available from the Census Bureau in electronic form, but published tabulations present only summaries.

This is not to say that published data are useless to criminal justice researchers. Highly aggregated summary data from published statistical series are frequently used in descriptive, explanatory, and applied studies. For example, Eric Baumer and colleagues (Baumer et al. 1998) examined Uniform Crime Report (UCR), Drug Abuse Warning Network (DAWN), and Drug Use Forecasting (DUF) data for 142 U.S. cities from 1984 to 1992. Interested in the relationship between crack cocaine use and robbery, burglary, and homicide rates, the researchers found that high levels of crack cocaine use in the population were found in cities that also had high rates of robbery. In contrast, burglary rates were lower in cities with high levels of crack cocaine use.

Ted Robert Gurr used published statistics on violent crime dating back to thirteenth-century England to examine how social and political events affected patterns of homicide through 1984. A long-term decline in homicide rates has been punctuated by spikes during periods of social dislocation, when:

> significant segments of a population have been separated from the regulating institutions that instill and reinforce the basic Western injunctions against interpersonal violence. They may be migrants, demobilized veterans, a growing population of resentful young people for whom there is no social or economic niche, or badly educated young black men trapped in the decaying ghettos of an affluent society. (1989, 48–49)

Published data can therefore address questions about highly aggregated patterns or trends—drug use and crime, the covariation in two estimates of crime, or epochal change in fatal violence. Published data also have the distinct advantage of being readily available; a web search or a trip to the library can quickly place several data series at your disposal. Most publications by the BJS and other Justice Department offices are now available only on the Internet. Selected printed copies have been scanned or otherwise archived.

Many basic crime data can be downloaded from the BJS website in spreadsheet formats or read directly into presentation software. More importantly, complete data series are available in electronic formats. Although printed reports of the NCVS limit you to summary tabulations such as those in Table 10.1, the original survey data from 60,000 or more respondents is available online. Online analysis tools from the BJS enable researchers to produce custom tabulations from all major data series (http://www.bjs.gov/index.cfm?ty=daa). We will return to these resources later in the chapter.

Of course, before using either original data or tabulations from published sources, researchers must consider the issues of validity and reliability and the more general question of how well these data meet specific research purposes. It would make little sense to use only FBI data on homicides in a descriptive study of domestic violence because murder records measure only incidents of fatal violence. Or data from an annual prison census would not be appropriate for research on changes in sentences to community corrections programs.

Nonpublic Agency Records

Despite the large volume of published statistics in criminal justice, those data represent only the tip of the proverbial iceberg. The FBI publishes the summary UCR, but each of the nation's several thousand law enforcement agencies produces an incredible volume of data not routinely released for public distribution. The BJS series *Correctional Populations in the United States* presents statistics on prison inmates collected from annual surveys of correctional facilities, but any given facility also maintains detailed case files on individual inmates. *Court Caseload Statistics*, published by the National Center for State Courts, contains summary data on cases filed and disposed in state courts, but any courthouse in any large city houses files on thousands of individual defendants.

Although we have labeled this data source *nonpublic agency records*, criminal justice organizations quite often make such data available to criminal justice researchers. But obtaining agency records is not as simple as scrolling through a list of publications on the BJS website, or clicking a download button to get data from the Census Bureau. Obtaining access to nonpublic records involves many of the same steps we outlined in Chapter 8 for gaining access to participants and organizations.

At the outset, we want to emphasize that the potential promise of agency records is not without cost. Jacob's caution about the hidden perils to unwary researchers who uncritically accept published data applies to nonpublic agency records as well. On the one hand, we could devote an entire book to describing the potential applications of agency records in criminal justice research, together with advice on how to use and interpret such data. On the other hand, we can summarize that unwritten book with one piece of advice: understand how agency records are produced. Restated slightly, researchers can find the road to happiness in using agency records by following the paper trail.

By way of illustrating this humble maxim, we present two types of examples. First, we describe a study in which nonpublic agency records were used to reveal important findings about the etiology of crime. Second, we briefly review two studies in which the authors recognized validity and reliability problems but still were able to draw conclusions about the behavior of criminal justice organizations. At the end of this section, we summarize the promise of agency records for research and note cautions that must be exercised if such records are to be used effectively.

Child Abuse, Delinquency, and Adult Arrests In earlier chapters, we described Cathy Spatz Widom's research (Widom 1989) on child abuse as an example of a quasi-experimental design. For present purposes, her research illustrates the use of several different types of agency records.

Widom identified cases of child abuse and neglect by consulting records from juvenile and adult criminal courts in a large midwestern city. Unlike adult courts, juvenile court proceedings are not open to the public, and juvenile records may not be released. However, after obtaining institutional review board approval, Widom was granted access to these files for research purposes by court authorities. From juvenile court records, she selected 774 cases of neglect, physical abuse, or sexual abuse. Cases of extreme abuse were processed in adult criminal court, where charges were filed against the offender. Criminal court records yielded an additional 134 cases.

As described in Chapter 5, Widom constructed a comparison group of nonabused children through individual matching. Comparison subjects were found from two different sources of agency records. First, abused children who were age 6 to 11 at the time of the abuse were matched to comparison subjects by consulting public school records.

An abused child was matched with a comparison child of the same sex, race, and age (within six months) who attended the same school. Second, children who were younger than 6 years old at the time of abuse were matched on similar criteria by consulting birth records and selecting a comparison subject born in the same hospital.

These two types of public records and matching criteria—attending the same public school and being born in the same hospital—were used in an attempt to control for socioeconomic status. Although such criteria may be viewed with skepticism today, Widom (1989, 360) points out that during this time period (1967 to 1971) school busing was not used in the area where her study was conducted, and "elementary schools represented very homogeneous neighborhoods." Similarly, in the late 1960s, hospitals tended to serve local communities, unlike contemporary medical-industrial complexes that advertise their services far and wide. Widom assumed that children born in the same hospital were more likely to be from similar socioeconomic backgrounds than children born in different hospitals.

Though far from perfect, school and birth records enabled Widom to construct approximate matches on socioeconomic status, which illustrates our earlier advice to be creative while being careful.

Widom's research purpose was explanatory—to examine the link between early child abuse and later delinquency or adult criminal behavior. These two dependent variables were measured by consulting additional agency records for information on arrests of abused subjects and comparison subjects for the years 1971 through 1986. Juvenile court files yielded information on delinquency. Adult arrests were measured from criminal history files maintained by local, state, and national law enforcement agencies. In an effort to locate as many subjects as possible, Widom searched state Department of Motor Vehicles files for current addresses and Social Security numbers. Finally, "marriage license bureau records were searched to find married names for the females" (Widom 1989, 361).

Findings revealed modest but statistically significant differences between abused and comparison subjects. As a group, abused subjects were more likely to have records of delinquency or adult arrests (Maxfield and Widom 1996). However, Widom (1992) also found differences in these dependent variables by race and gender.

Now let's consider two potential validity and reliability issues that might be raised by Widom's use of nonpublic agency records. First, data from juvenile and adult criminal courts reveal only cases of abuse that come to the attention of public officials. Unreported and unsubstantiated cases of abuse or neglect are excluded, and this raises a question about the validity of Widom's measure of the independent variable. Second, dependent variable measures are similarly flawed because juvenile and adult arrests do not reflect all delinquent or criminal behavior.

Recognizing these problems, Widom is careful to point out that her measure of abuse probably reflects only the most severe cases, those that were brought to the attention of public officials. She also notes that cases in her study were processed before officials and the general public had become more aware of the problem of child abuse. Widom understood the limits of official records and qualified her conclusions accordingly: "These findings, then, are not generalizable to unreported cases of abuse or neglect. Ours are also the cases in which agencies have intervened, and in which there is little doubt of abuse or neglect. Thus, these findings are confounded with the processing factor" (1989, 365–366).

Agency Records as Measures of Decision Making
Research by Richard McCleary and associates (McCleary, Nienstedt, and Erven 1982) illustrates why it's essential to learn about agency record-keeping practices when using official data. McCleary and associates discovered that an apparent reduction in burglary rates was, in fact, due to changes in record-keeping practices. When a police department assigned officers from a special unit to investigate burglaries, it was learned that earlier investigative procedures sometimes resulted in double counts of a single incident; the special unit also reduced misclassification of larcenies as burglaries.

McCleary and colleagues became suspicious of police records when they detected an immediate decline in burglary rates following the introduction of the special unit, a pattern that was not reasonable given the technology of burglary. Following the paper trail, they were able to discover how changes in procedures affected these measures. In the same article, they describe additional examples—how replacement of a police chief and changes in patrol dispatch procedures produced apparent increases in crime and calls for service. However, after carefully investigating how these records were produced, they were able to link changes in the indicators to changes in agency behavior rather than changes in the frequency of crime.

In a similar type of study, Hugh Whitt (2006) examined mortality data for New York City over 16 years. While deaths by homicide and accidents varied little from year to year between 1976 and 1992, the number of suicides dropped dramatically from 1984 through 1988, then rose sharply in 1989 to match the numbers in earlier years. Reasoning that such sharp changes in a short period are unlikely to reflect natural variation in suicide, Whitt traced the deviation to a series of personnel and policy changes in the city medical examiner's office. So the sharp, short-term variation was due to changes in how deaths were recorded, not changes in the manner of death.

New Data Collected by Agency Staff

Thus far, we have concentrated on the research uses of information routinely collected by or for public agencies. Such data are readily available, but researchers have little control over the actual data collection process. Furthermore, agency procedures and definitions may not correspond with the needs of researchers.

It is sometimes possible to use a hybrid source of data in which criminal justice agency staff collect information for specific research purposes. We refer to this as a "hybrid" source because it combines the collection of new data—through observation or interviews—with day-to-day criminal justice agency activities. Virtually all criminal justice organizations routinely document their actions, from investigating crime reports to housing convicted felons. By slightly modifying forms normally used for recording information, researchers may be able to have agency staff collect original data for them.

For example, in their study of traffic enforcement in Pennsylvania, Robin Shepard Engel and associates (Engel et al. 2005) worked with troopers from the state police to develop special forms to collect data on traffic stops. The research team first worked with agency command staff to gain approval. They then included line officers and union representatives in a collaborative effort to design new data collection forms and procedures. One of the chief concerns was whether individual troopers would be identified on the stop records. All confidentiality procedures were approved by troopers—the people who prepared the traffic stop records. Researchers believed this was an important component of their efforts to enhance the accuracy of the data they collected.

Incorporating new data collection procedures into agency routine has two major advantages. First, and most obvious, having agency staff collect data for us is much less costly than fielding a team of research assistants. It is difficult to imagine how

original data on all traffic stops made by Pennsylvania State Police could be collected in any other way.

Second, we have more control over the measurement process than we would by relying on agency definitions. Instead of adapting existing measures on traffic stops, Engel and associates were able to tailor data collection to meet their specific research needs.

The box by Marie Mele, "Improving Police Records of Domestic Violence," gives another example of this approach to gathering new data from agency records. You should recognize the importance of collaboration in this example. Less obvious, but equally important, is a lesson we will return to later in this chapter: agency records are not usually intended for research purposes and, as a consequence, are not always well suited to researchers' needs. Sometimes, as was the case for Marie Mele, some subtle tweaking can transform unusable mounds of paper files into computer-based record systems. In any event, researchers are well advised to be careful, not to assume that existing data will meet their needs, but to also be creative in seeking ways to improve the quality of agency data.

 IMPROVING POLICE RECORDS OF DOMESTIC VIOLENCE

by Marie Mele

An interest in domestic violence led me to learn more about repeat victimization. Research conducted in England has indicated that repeated domestic violence involving the same victim and offender is quite common (Hanmer, Griffiths, and Jerwood 1999; Farrell et al. 2000). For example, combining data from four British Crime Surveys, Pease (1998, 3) reports that about 1 percent of respondents had four or more personal victimizations and that these victims accounted for 59 percent of all personal victimization incidents disclosed to British Crime Survey interviewers. Other studies in England have shown that many other types of offenses are disproportionately concentrated among small groups of victims. Identifying repeat victims and directing prevention and enforcement resources to them have the potential to produce a large decrease in crime rates.

My interest centered on determining the distributions of incidents, victims, and offenders in cases of domestic violence reported to police in a large city in the northeastern United States. Partly this was exploratory research, but I also wished to make policy recommendations to reduce repeat victimization. Working with Michael Maxfield, my initial inquiries found that, although data on assaults and other offenses were available in paper files, it was not possible to efficiently count the number of repeat incidents for victims and offenders. However, seeing the potential value of gathering more systematic information on repeat offenders and victims, senior department staff collaborated with Maxfield and me to produce a database that reorganized existing data on domestic violence incidents. A pilot data system was developed in November 2001. Plans called for the database to be maintained by the department's

(continued)

domestic violence and sexual assault unit (DVSAU); staff would begin entering new incidents in January 2002. In the meantime, I proposed to test the database and its entry procedures by personally entering incidents from August through December 2001. After ironing out a few kinks, the final system was established, and I continued entering new incident reports for a period of time.

This is an admittedly brief description of a process that unfolded over several months. The process began as an attempt to obtain what we thought were existing data. Finding that suitable data were not available, Maxfield had sufficient access to the department to begin discussions of how to supplement existing record-keeping practices to tabulate repeat victimization. Many public agencies will accommodate researchers if such accommodation does not unduly burden the agency. Collecting new data for researchers does qualify as unduly burdensome for most public organizations. The key here was collaboration in a way that helped both the researchers and the host organization.

It's obvious that my research benefited from having the department design and ultimately assume responsibility for tabulating repeat victimization. The department benefited in three ways. First, DVSAU staff recognized how a data file that identified repeat offenders and victims could produce information that would aid their investigations of incidents. I emphasize offenders here because, all other things being equal, police are more interested in offenders than they are in victims. So the database was designed to track people (offenders) of special interest to police and people (victims) of special interest to my research. Second, recognizing that setting up a new data system is especially difficult in a tradition-bound organization, I was able to ease the transition somewhat by initially entering data myself. One intentional by-product of this was to establish quality-control procedures during a shakedown period. As a criminal justice researcher, I knew that the reliability of data-gathering procedures was important, and I was able to establish reliable data-entry routines for the department.

The DVSAU staff benefited in yet another way that was probably most important of all. This department had incorporated its version of Compstat for about three years. Two important components of Compstat are timely data and accountability. Each week, the DVSAU commander was required to present a summary of the unit's activity and was held accountable for the performance of unit staff. Before the database was developed, the DVSAU commander spent several hours compiling data to prepare for each week's Compstat meeting. After the database was operational, preparation time was reduced to minutes. In addition, the DVSAU commander was able to introduce new performance measures—repeat offenders and victims—that came to be valued by the department's chief.

This approach to data collection has many potential applications. Probation officers or other court staff in many jurisdictions complete some type of presentence investigation on convicted offenders. A researcher might be able to supplement standard interview forms with additional items appropriate for some specific research interest.

At the same time, having agencies collect original research data has some disadvantages. An obvious one is the need to obtain the cooperation of organizations and staff. The difficulty of this varies in direct proportion to the intrusiveness of data collection. Cooperation is less likely if some major additional effort is required of agency personnel or if data collection activities disrupt routine operations. The potential benefit to participating agencies is a related point. If a research project or an experimental program is likely to economize agency operations or improve staff performance, as was the case for Marie Mele's research, it will be easier to enlist their assistance.

Researchers have less control over the data collection process when they rely on agency staff. Staff in criminal justice agencies have competing demands on their time and naturally place a lower priority on data collection than on their primary duties. If you were a probation officer serving a heavy caseload and were asked to complete detailed 6- and 12-month reports on services provided to individual clients, would you devote more attention to keeping up with your clients or filling out data collection forms?

Reliability and Validity

Understanding the details of how agency records are produced is the best guard against reliability and validity problems.

The key to evaluating the reliability and validity of agency records, as well as the general suitability of those data for a research project, is to understand as completely as possible how the data were originally collected. Doing so can help researchers identify potential new uses of data and be better able to detect potential reliability or validity problems in agency records.

Any researcher who considers using agency records will benefit from a careful reading of Herbert Jacob's invaluable little guide *Using Published Data: Errors and Remedies* (1984). In addition to warning readers about general problems with reliability and validity, such as those we discussed in Chapter 4, Jacob cautions users of these data to be aware of other potential errors that can be revealed by scrutinizing source notes. Clerical errors, for example, are unavoidable in such large-scale reporting systems as the UCR. These errors may be detected and reported in correction notices appended to later reports.

Users of data series collected over time must be especially attentive to changes in data collection procedures or changes in the operational definitions of key indicators. As you might expect, such changes are more likely to occur in data series that extend over several years. David Cantor and James Lynch (2005) describe how changes in the NCVS, especially the redesign elements introduced in 1992, should be kept in mind for any long-term analysis of NCVS data. In earlier chapters, we described the NCVS redesign that was completed in 1994. If we plan to conduct research on victimization over time, we will have to consider how changes in sample size and design, increased use of telephone interviews, and questionnaire revisions might affect our findings.

Longitudinal researchers must therefore diligently search for modifications of procedures or definitions over time to avoid attributing some substantive meaning to a change in a particular measure. Furthermore, as the time interval under investigation increases, so does the potential for change in measurement. Roger Lane (1989, 24) cites a good example:

> In the first two decades of the 20th century many American police forces treated the fatalities of the auto age as homicides. The sharp increase in "homicide" rates that followed has led to some dubious conclusions. Careful study of the sources and their historical and institutional context is necessary to identify and screen out the potentially misleading effects of these factors on long-term trends.

The central point is that researchers who analyze criminal justice data produced by different cities or states or other jurisdictions must be alert to variations in the definitions and measurement of key variables. Even when definitions and measurement seem straightforward, they may run into problems. For example, Craig Perkins and Darrell Gilliard (1992, 4)—statisticians at the BJS—caution potential users of corrections data:

> Care should be exercised when comparing groups of inmates on sentence length and time served. Differences may be the result of factors not described in the tables, including variations in the criminal histories of each group, variations in the offense composition of each group, and variations among participating jurisdictions in their sentencing and correctional practices.

Descriptions of most regular data series present basic information on definitions and collection procedures. The BJS website includes copies of questionnaires used in surveys and enumerations. Researchers should, however, view summary descriptions in printed reports as no more than a starting point in their search for information on how data were collected.

Sources of Reliability and Validity Problems

We conclude this section on agency records by discussing some general characteristics of record keeping by public agencies. Think carefully about each of the features we mention, considering how each might apply to specific types of criminal justice research. It will also be extremely useful for you to think of some examples in addition to those we mention, perhaps discussing them with your instructor or others in your class.

Social Production of Data Virtually all criminal justice record keeping is a social process. By this we mean that indicators of, say, arrests, juvenile probation violations, court convictions, or rule infractions by prison inmates reflect decisions made by criminal justice officials in addition to the actual behavior of juvenile or adult offenders. As Baumer and associates state, "Researchers must realize that performance measures are *composites* of offenders' behavior, organizational capacity to detect behavior, and decisions about how to respond to offenders' misbehavior" (Baumer, Maxfield, and Mendelsohn 1993, 139; emphasis added). For example, Richard McCleary (1992) describes the social production of data by parole officers. A small number of classic articles have described the **social production of data** in the form of crime records by police (Black 1970; Kitsuse and Cicourel 1963; Seidman and Couzens 1974), showing that police may fail to record minor infractions to avoid paperwork or, alternatively, may keep careful records of such incidents in an effort to punish troublesome parolees by returning them to prison.

Discretionary actions by criminal justice officials and others affect the production of virtually all agency records. Police neither learn about all crimes nor arrest all offenders who come to their attention. Similarly, prosecutors, probation officers, and corrections staff are selectively attentive to charges filed or to rule violations by probationers and inmates. At a more general level, the degree of attention state legislatures and criminal justice officials devote to various crime problems varies over time. Levels of tolerance of such behaviors as child abuse, drug use, acquaintance rape, and even alcohol consumption have changed over the years.

Agency Data Are Not Designed for Research In many cases, criminal justice officials collect data because the law requires them to do so. More generally, agencies tend to collect data for their own use, not for the use of researchers. Court disposition records are maintained in part because of legal mandates, and such records are designed for the use of judges, prosecutors, and other officials. Record-keeping procedures reflect internal needs and directives from higher authorities. As a consequence, researchers sometimes find it difficult to adapt agency records for a specific research purpose.

For example, Michael Maxfield once wished to trace court dispositions for arrests made by individual police officers in Louisville, Kentucky. "No problem," he was assured by a deputy prosecutor, "we keep all disposition records on the computer." Following this electronic version of a paper trail to the county data-processing facility, Maxfield discovered that only the previous year's cases were maintained on computer tape, the most common bulk storage medium in the 1970s. Such tapes were said to be expensive (about $17), and nobody had authorized the data-processing staff to buy new tapes for each year's files. Instead, voluminous computer printouts from the previous year were microfilmed and saved, whereas the "costly" computer tape was erased for the new year. Maxfield abandoned the project after realizing that data collection would involve viewing literally hundreds of thousands of microfilmed case files, instead of running a quick-and-easy computer search.

Keep in mind that research needs may not be congruent with agency record-keeping practices. Courts or police departments commonly use idiosyncratic definitions or methods of classifying information that make such records difficult to use. Also recognize that conceptual and operational definitions of key concepts, however thoughtful and precise, will seldom be identical to actual measures maintained by criminal justice agencies.

For another example of how definitional differences can be traced to different agency needs, see the box titled "How Many Parole Violators Were There Last Month?"

HOW MANY PAROLE VIOLATORS WERE THERE LAST MONTH?

by John J. Poklemba
New York State Division of Criminal Justice Services

Question: How many parole violators were there last month? Answer: It depends. More accurately, it depends on which agency is asked. Each of the three answers below is right in its own way:

New York State Commission of Correction   611

New York Department of Correctional Services   670

New York Division of Parole   356

The State Commission of Correction (SCOC) maintains daily aggregate information on the local under-custody population. Data are gathered from local sheriffs, using a set of common definitions. The SCOC defines a parole violator as follows: an alleged parole violator being held as a result of allegedly having violated a condition of parole—for example, a new arrest. This makes sense for local jails; a special category is devoted to counting alleged parole violators with new arrests. However, New York City does not distinguish between parole violators with and without new arrests, so the SCOC figure includes violators from upstate New York only.

The Department of Correctional Services (DOCS) is less interested in why people are in jail; its concern centers on the backlog of inmates whom it will soon need to accommodate. Furthermore, as far as DOCS is concerned, the only true parole violator is a technical parole violator. This makes sense for DOCS, because a parole violator convicted of a new crime will enter DOCS as a new admission, who—from an administrative standpoint—will be treated differently than a parolee returned to prison for a technical violation.

The Division of Parole classifies parole violators into one of four categories: (1) those who have violated a condition of parole, (2) those who have absconded, (3) those who have been arrested for a new crime, and (4) those who have been convicted of

a new crime. Once again, this makes sense, because the Division of Parole is responsible for monitoring parolee performance and wishes to distinguish different types of parole violations. The Division also classifies a parole violation as either alleged (yet to be confirmed by a parole board) or actual (the violation has been confirmed and entered into the parolee's file). Further differences in the fluid status of parolees and their violations, together with differences between New York City and other areas, add to the confusion.

Taking the varying perspectives and roles of these three organizations into account, answers to the "how many" question can be made more specific:

SCOC: Last month, there were 611 alleged parole violators who were believed to have violated a condition of their parole by being arrested for a new offense and are being held in upstate New York jails.

DOCS: Last month, there were 670 actual parole violators who were judged to have violated a condition of their parole and are counted among the backlog of persons ready for admission to state correctional facilities.

Parole Division: Last month, 356 parolees from the Division's aggregate population were actually removed from the Division's caseload and were en route to DOCS.

One of the major reasons that agency counts do not match is that agency information systems have been developed to meet internal operational needs. A systemwide perspective is lacking. Questions that depend on data from more than one agency are often impossible to answer with confidence. Recognize also that the availability and quality of state data depend on data from local agencies.

As stated above, the best answer to the question is: it depends.

Source: Adapted from Poklemba (1988, 11–13).

Tracking People, Not Patterns At the operational level, officials in criminal justice organizations are generally more interested in keeping track of individual cases than in examining patterns. Police patrol officers and investigators deal with individual calls for service, arrests, or case files. Prosecutors and judges are most attentive to court dockets and

the clearing of individual cases, and corrections officials maintain records on individual inmates. Although each organization produces summary reports on weekly, monthly, or annual activity, officials tend to be much more interested in individual cases. Michael Geerken (1994) makes this point clearly in his discussion of problems that researchers are likely to encounter in analyzing police arrest records. Few rap-sheet databases are regularly reviewed for accuracy; rather, they simply accumulate arrest records submitted by individual officers. Joel Best (2008) offers additional examples of how small errors in case-by-case record keeping can accumulate to produce compound errors in summary data.

Criminal justice agencies are increasingly developing the capability to analyze data in addition to tracing individual cases. Crime analysis by police tracks spatial patterns of recent incidents; prosecutors are attentive to their scorecards; state correctional intake facilities consider prison capacity, security classification, and program availability in deciding where to send new admissions.

As problem-oriented and community approaches to policing become more widely adopted, many law enforcement agencies have improved their record-keeping and crime analysis practices. New York City's reduction in reported crime has been attributed to police managers' use of timely, accurate crime data to plan and evaluate specific anticrime tactics (Bratton 1999). This illustrates an important general principle about the accuracy of agency-produced data: when agency managers routinely use data to make decisions, they will be more attentive to data quality. The box describing Marie Mele's research offers another example: when domestic violence detectives realized how a database would help them prepare for weekly command staff meetings, they endorsed the effort to improve their record-keeping procedures.

However, record-keeping systems used in most cities today are still designed more to track individual cases for individual departments than to produce data for management or research purposes. Individual agencies maintain what are sometimes called *silo databases*, a colorful label that refers to stacks of data that are isolated from each other. Similar problems have been linked to the failure of intelligence agencies to share information about suspicious activities leading up to the 9/11 attacks (Farmer 2009; National Commission on Terrorist Attacks upon the United States 2004).

This does not mean that computerized criminal history, court disposition, or prison intake records are of little use to researchers. However, researchers must be aware that even state-of-the-art systems may not be readily adaptable for research purposes.

Error Increases with Volume The potential for clerical errors increases as the number of clerical entries increases. This seemingly obvious point is nonetheless important to keep in mind when analyzing criminal justice records. Lawrence Sherman and Ellen Cohn (1989, 34) describe the "mirror effect" of duplicate calls-for-service (CFS) records. Handling a large volume of CFS, phone operators in Minneapolis, or any large city for that matter, are not always able to distinguish duplicate reports of the same incident. An updated report about a CFS may be treated as a new incident. In either case, duplicate data result.

The relationship between the volume of data entry and the potential for error can be especially troublesome for studies of relatively rare crimes or incidents. Although murder is rare compared with other crimes, information about individual homicides might be keyed into a computer by the same clerk who inputs data on parking violations. If a murder record is just one case among hundreds of parking tickets and petty thefts awaiting a clerk, there is no guarantee that the rare event will be treated any differently than the everyday ones.

While preparing a briefing for an Indianapolis commission on violence, Maxfield discovered that a single incident in which four people had been murdered in a rural area appeared twice in computerized FBI homicide records. This was traced to the fact that officers from two agencies—sheriff's deputies and state police—investigated the crime, and each agency filed a report with the FBI. But the thousands of murders entered into FBI computer files for that year obscured the fact that duplicate records had been keyed in for one multiple murder in a rural area of Indiana.

In concluding our discussion of agency records, we do not mean to leave you with the impression that data produced by and for criminal justice organizations are fatally flawed. Thousands of studies making appropriate use of such data are produced each year. It is, however, essential that researchers understand potential sources of reliability and validity problems, as well as ways they can be overcome. Public agencies do not normally collect information for research purposes. The data they do collect often reflect discretionary decisions by numerous individuals. And, like any large-scale human activity, making observations on large numbers of people and processes inevitably produces some error.

Content Analysis

Content analysis involves the systematic study of messages.

The Office of Community Oriented Policing Services (COPS) was established by the 1994 Crime Bill to promote community policing by providing funds to local law enforcement agencies. In addition to being concerned about the effectiveness of these efforts, COPS staff wanted to know something about the public image of community policing as presented in local newspapers. Stephen Mastrofski and Richard Ritti conducted a content analysis of stories about community policing in newspapers serving 26 cities. The researchers found more than 7,500 stories from 1993 through 1997, with most focusing on a small number of themes: "community, resources, and producing real results for the community. Stories that offer a viewpoint on community policing are nearly always overwhelmingly positive" (1999, 10–11).

This is an example of **content analysis**, the systematic study of messages and the meaning those messages convey. For the COPS office, the study by Mastrofski and Ritti was satisfying—many stories about community policing were published in urban newspapers, and most stories presented positive images.

Content analysis methods may be applied to virtually any form of communication. Among the possible artifacts for study are books, magazines, films, songs, speeches, television programs, letters, laws, and constitutions, as well as any components or collections of these. Content analysis is particularly well suited to answering the classic questions of communications research: who says what, to whom, why, how, and with what effect? As a mode of observation, content analysis requires a considered handling of the *what*, and the analysis of data collected in this mode, as in others, addresses the *why* and *with what effect*.

Coding in Content Analysis

Content analysis is essentially a coding operation, and of course, coding represents the measurement process in content analysis. Communications—oral, written, or other—are coded or classified according to some conceptual framework. Thus, for example, newspaper editorials might be coded as liberal or conservative. Radio talk shows might be coded as bombastic or not. Novels might be coded as detective fiction or not. Political speeches might be coded as containing unsupported rhetoric about crime or not. Recall that terms such as these are subject to many interpretations, and the researcher must specify definitions clearly.

Coding in content analysis involves the logic of conceptualization and operationalization we considered in Chapter 4. In content analysis, as in other research methods, researchers must refine their conceptual framework and develop specific methods for observing in relation to that framework.

For all research methods, conceptualization and operationalization typically involve the interaction of theoretical concerns and empirical observations. If, for example, you believe some newspaper editorials support liberal crime policies and others support conservative ones, ask yourself why you think so. Read some editorials, asking which ones are liberal and which ones are conservative. Is the political orientation of a particular editorial most clearly indicated by its manifest content or by its overall tone? Is your decision based on the use of certain terms (such as *moral decay* or *need for rehabilitation*) or on the support or opposition given to a particular issue, such as mandatory prison sentences versus treatment programs for drug users?

As in other decisions relating to measurement, the researcher faces a fundamental choice between depth and specificity of understanding. The survey researcher must decide whether specific closed-ended questions or more general open-ended questions will better suit her or his needs. By the same token, the content analyst has a choice between searching for manifest or for latent content. Coding the **manifest content**—the visible, surface content—of a communication more closely approximates the use of closed-ended items in a survey questionnaire. Alternatively, coding the **latent content** of the communication—its underlying meaning—is an option. In the most general sense, manifest and latent content can be distinguished by the degree of inter-pretation required in measurement.

Throughout the process of conceptualizing manifest- and latent-content coding procedures, remember that the operational definition of any variable is composed of the attributes included in it. Such attributes, moreover, should be mutually exclusive and exhaustive. A newspaper editorial, for example, should not be described as both liberal and conservative, although we should probably allow for some to be middle-of-the-road. It may be sufficient to code TV programs as being violent or not violent, but it is also possible that some pro-grams could be antiviolence.

No coding scheme should be used in content analysis unless it has been carefully pretested. We must decide what manifest or latent contents of communications will be regarded as indicators of the different attributes that make up our research variables, write down these operational definitions, and use them in the actual coding of several units of observation. If we plan to use more than one coder in the final project, each of them should in-dependently code the same set of observations so that we can determine the extent of agreement. In any event, we'll want to take special note of any difficult cases—observations that were not easily classified using the operational definition. Finally, we should review the overall results of the pretest to ensure that they are appropriate to our analytic concerns. If, for example, all of the pretest newspa-per editorials have been coded as liberal, we should certainly reconsider our definition of that attribute.

Before beginning to code newspapers, crime dramas on television, or detective fiction, we need to make plans to assess the reliability of coding.

Fortunately, reliability in content analysis can read-ily be tested, if not guaranteed, in two related ways. First, interrater reliability can be determined by having two different people code the same message and then computing the proportion of items coded the same. If 20 attributes of newspaper stories about crime are being coded and two coders score 18 attributes identically, their reliability is 90 percent.

The second way to assess coding reliability is the test–retest method, in which one person codes the same message twice. Of course, some time should elapse between the two coding operations. Test–retest procedures can be used when only one person is doing the coding; reliability can be com-puted in the same way as if the interrater method were being used.

Illustrations of Content Analysis

We now turn to examples of content analysis in action. The first illustration describes content analy-sis of violence in video games. The second demon-strates how extracting information from police records is a form of content analysis.

Violence in Video Games It seems that whenever some new technology or musical idiom becomes popular, someone becomes interested in linking it to behavior. Examples include television and vio-lence, pornography and sexual assault, and sugges-tive lyrics in popular music and sexual behavior. It is always difficult to establish causality in such cases, and we will say nothing more about that. But content analysis is the appropriate research tool for classifying content as violent or sexually explicit.

Kimberly Thompson and Kevin Haninger examined the contents of video games rated in cat-egories "E" (suitable for everyone) and "T" (teens, age 13 and up) by the Entertainment Software Rat-ing Board (ESRC). Their first study (Thompson and Haninger 2001) sampled 55 of more than 600 E-rated games available at the time. An undergrad-uate college student "with considerable video gam-ing experience" was assigned to play all games for 90 minutes or until the game reached a natural conclusion. Videotapes of the game-player formed the basis for content analysis. One researcher (also described as being an experienced player) and the game-player reviewed the video, coding several dimensions of what was depicted.

Coders counted the number of violent incidents depicted while the game was being played and also timed the duration of each violent incident. Violence was defined as "acts in which the aggressor causes or attempts to cause physical injury or death to another character." This is an example of latent content. The duration of violent acts was manifest content, though researchers had to distinguish short pauses between violent acts. Additional variables coded included the number of deaths; the presence of drugs, alcohol, or tobacco; profanity and sexual behavior; weapon use; and whether any music was included that itself was rated as explicit. Comparing the duration of violent acts and the number of deaths to how long each game was played yielded two standardized measures: violent minutes as a percentage of all minutes, and the number of deaths per minute.

Results showed quite a lot of violence. Action games ranged from 3.3 percent (*Sonic Adventure*) to 91 percent (*Nuclear Strike*) violence as a portion of total time. *Paperboy* depicted no deaths, but *Rat Attack* averaged 8.4 deaths per minute. Games classified as "sports" rarely showed violence.

Later research used similar methods to examine violence in a larger number of games rated as suitable for teens (Haninger and Thompson 2004). These games displayed a wider variety of behaviors in the general domains of violence, obscenity, substance use, and sexual behavior. Again, the authors did not attempt to link such content with behavior. Their content analysis centered on systematically classifying what sorts of things were depicted in video games, thus providing information independent of industry ratings. Of their findings, the authors highlight that ESRC ratings did not mention several examples of violence in almost half of the games reviewed.

Classifying Gang-Related Homicides When is a homicide gang-related? Are there different types of gang-related homicides? These two questions guided research by 30Rosenfeld and associates (Rosenfeld, Bray, and Egley 1999) to understand how gang membership might facilitate homicide in

different ways. To address these questions, the researchers conducted a content analysis of police case files for homicides in St. Louis over a 10-year period.

By now, you should recognize the importance of conceptualization in most criminal justice research. Rosenfeld and associates began by further specifying the ambiguous term *gang-related*. They distinguished *gang-motivated* and *gang-affiliated* homicides. Gang-motivated killings "resulted from gang behavior or relationships, such as an initiation ritual, the 'throwing' of gang signs, or a gang fight" (1999, 500). Gang-affiliated homicides involved a gang member as victim or offender, but with no indication of specific gang activity; a gang member killing a nongang person during a robbery is an example. A third category, nongang youth homicide, included all other murders in which no evidence of gang activity was available and the suspected offender was between ages 10 and 24.

Because St. Louis police did not apply the labels *gang-affiliated* or *gang-motivated*, it was necessary for researchers to code each case into one of the three categories using information from case files. This was a form of content analysis—systematically classifying the messages contained in homicide case files. Homicide case files are good examples of police records that are not maintained for research purposes. Recognizing this, Rosenfeld and associates coded the files in a two-stage process, building reliability checks into each stage.

First, one person coded each case as either gang-related or not gang-related. This might seem like a step backward, but it focused researchers' measurement on the separate dimensions of homicide that were of interest to them by simplifying the coding process. It was relatively easy to determine whether any evidence of gang activity or membership was present; if not, the case was classified as a nongang youth killing and set aside. Cases that had some evidence of gang involvement were retained for the second coding stage. During this stage, a second researcher randomly selected a 10 percent sample of cases and coded them again, without knowing how the first coder had classified the sampled cases. You will recognize this as an example of interrater reliability.

The second coding stage involved the finer and more difficult classification of cases as either gang-motivated or gang-affiliated. Interrater reliability checks were again conducted, this time on a 25 percent sample of cases. More cases were selected because reliability was lower in this stage—the two coders exhibited less agreement on how to classify gang homicides. Cases in which independent coding produced discrepancies were reviewed and discussed by the two coders until they agreed on how the homicide should be classified.

From these very different examples, we expect that you can think of many additional applications of content analysis in criminal justice research. You might wish to consult Ray Surette's (2006) excellent book *Media, Crime, and Justice: Images, Realities, and Policies* to learn more about the scope of topics for which content analysis can be used. The Government Accountability Office (formerly the General Accounting Office) has an excellent guide to content analysis generally (General Accounting Office 1996).

Secondary Analysis

Data collected by other researchers are often used to address new research questions.

Our final topic encompasses all sources of criminal justice data we have described in this and preceding chapters: content analysis, agency records, field observation, and surveys. We begin with an example of an unusually ambitious use of secondary data by a prolific criminal justice scholar.

For almost three decades, Wesley Skogan has examined the influence of crime on the lives of urban residents. In most cases, his research has relied on sample surveys to investigate questions about fear of crime (Skogan and Maxfield 1981) and the relationships between urban residents and police (Skogan 1990b), among others. He has long recognized the importance of incivilities—symbols of social disorder—as indicators of neighborhood crime problems and as sources of fear for urban residents.

THEORY AND DATA COLLECTION FROM AGENCY RECORDS

Jacqueline Berenson and Paul Appelbaum (2011) frame their study of sex offender residency restrictions on spatially based theories that include the principle of *distance decay*, meaning that offenders tend to commit crime near where they work or live. As the distance from an offender residence increases, the likelihood that the offender will commit a crime decreases. An example is research by George Rengert and associates on distance decay and burglary (Rengert, Piquero, and Jones 1999).

Distance decay underlies laws restricting where sex offenders can live. For example, New York state law prohibits sex offenders from living within 1,000 to 2,000 feet of locations such as parks, schools, playgrounds, and child-care facilities. The assumption is that if sex offenders lived close to such places, children would be at greater risk of victimization.

Distance decay led Berenson and Appelbaum to publicly available data from sex offender registries. State laws in recent years have required that information

about where sex offenders live be made available to the public. For example, if you do an Internet search on the phrase "sex offender residence [state]" and input any specific state, with only a few clicks on links that show up you'll be able to do a place-based search for registered sex offenders.

Berenson and Appelbaum compiled a geographically coded data file of registered sex offender home addresses for two counties in New York State. They then obtained publicly available data on the locations of schools, licensed child-care providers, and other facilities that were named in residency restrictions for sex offenders in New York. Computing the distances between where sex offenders lived and sites named in residency restrictions, the researchers found that 89 percent of sex offenders in Erie County and 90 percent in Schenectady County lived within a restricted zone. In other words, for these two counties in New York, only about 10 percent of registered sex offenders were in compliance with residential restrictions.

In 1990, Skogan published a comprehensive study of incivilities, drawing on his own research as well as studies by others (Skogan 1990a). However, instead of conducting new surveys to collect original data, Skogan's findings were based on secondary analysis of 40 surveys conducted in six cities from 1977 through 1983. He aggregated responses from about 13,000 individuals and examined questions about the sources of disorder, its impact, and the scope of action by individuals and police.

Secondary analysis of data collected by other researchers has become an increasingly important tool. Like Skogan, numerous criminal justice researchers have reanalyzed data collected by others. Several factors contribute to this practice, including the high cost of collecting original data through surveys or other means. More important, however, is that data for secondary analysis are readily available. We describe two important sources below.

Suppose you are interested in the relationship between delinquency, drug use, and school performance among adolescents. The National Youth Survey (NYS), which includes responses from 1,725 youths interviewed nine times from 1975 through 2004, might suit your needs nicely. NYS data were originally collected by Delbert Elliott and associates (for example, Elliott, Huizinga, and Ageton 1985). However, like Cesar Rebellon and Karen Van Gundy (2005), who used the NYS to examine links between child maltreatment and delinquency, you may be able to reanalyze the survey data to address your own research questions.

Original NYS data were collected by Elliott and associates (1985, 91) for three related research purposes: (1) to estimate the prevalence and incidence of delinquency and drug use among U.S. adolescents, (2) to assess causal relationships between drug use and delinquency, and (3) to test a comprehensive theory of delinquency. The NYS was designed as a panel survey, in which a nationally representative sample of youths age 11 to 17 in 1976 was interviewed once each year from 1976 through 1989. As we described in Chapter 3, this is an example of a longitudinal study, and it is especially well suited to disentangling the time ordering of such behaviors as drug use and delinquency.

Rebellon and Van Gundy (2005) were interested in the time order of somewhat different behaviors—physical abuse in childhood and delinquency—that were not directly addressed by the original researchers. A longitudinal design was equally important in this secondary analysis. Given this research interest, they faced two choices: collect original data by conducting a new panel survey, or reanalyze existing data from a panel survey that included questions on victimization and self-reported delinquency. Because the NYS included questions appropriate for their research purpose, Rebellon and Van Gundy were spared the need and (considerable) expense of conducting a new panel study.

Sources of Secondary Data

As a college student, you probably would not be able to launch a nine-wave panel study of a national sample of adolescents or even gather records from some 2,600 felony cases in Michigan. You do, however, have access to the same data used in those studies, together with data from thousands of other research projects, through the **Interuniversity Consortium for Political and Social Research (ICPSR)** at the University of Michigan.

Since 1962, the ICPSR has served as a central repository of machine-readable data collected by social science researchers. In the early 1960s, "machine-readable" meant punch cards and magnetic tape. Current online holdings include data from thousands of studies conducted by researchers all over the world.

Of particular interest to criminal justice researchers is the **National Archive of Criminal Justice Data (NACJD)**, established by the BJS in cooperation with the ICPSR (http://www.icpsr. umich.edu/icpsrweb/NACJD/). Here you will find the NYS, the NCVS, and each of the 40 surveys analyzed by Skogan for the book we mentioned earlier. There's more, including surveys on criminal justice topics by national polling firms, periodic censuses of juvenile detention and correctional facilities, a study of thefts from commercial trucks in

New York City, and data from the classic study of a Philadelphia birth cohort by Marvin Wolfgang and colleagues (Wolfgang, Figlio, and Sellin 1972). Data from the growing National Incident-Based Reporting System (NIBRS) are now available, with an expanding number of participating agencies dating from 1996. Data from selected studies are even available for online data analysis. The possibilities are almost endless and grow each year as new data are added to the archives.

Two special features of the NACJD website are important. First, NACJD has developed a number of data resource guides to help researchers understand how data were collected and how data files are organized. For example, the National Juvenile Corrections Data Resource Guide summarizes important information about a data series formerly known as "Children in Custody" (http://www.icpsr.umich.edu/icpsrweb/content/NACJD/guides/ncjd.html). Links are included to data series files that have been formatted for analysis. Also included are summary descriptions of samples, data collection procedures, and questionnaires. NACJD offers comprehensive guides to may other data sources, including the Terrorism and Preparedness Data Resource Center.

Second, working with other universities, the NACJD has formatted a variety of data series for online analysis. Among other things, this means that researchers do not have to download data, format data files, or even have access to any statistical analysis software. Basic, descriptive analysis can be executed online. Available data include a wide range of series collected by government agencies, as well as selected research studies. See the complete list at: http://www.icpsr.umich.edu/icpsrweb/NACJD/studies?sdaAvailable=true.

The BJS has also developed data analysis tools for selected series, such as the NCVS, UCR trends since 1960, and tools to examine arrests and prisoner recidivism risk. These tools are especially useful for obtaining baselines, trends, or current descriptive data. For example, using the arrest analysis tool reveals that in the year 2011, the Ferguson, Missouri, Police Department reported the following arrests for aggravated assault:

Number of arrests for aggravated assault, 2011
Ferguson, Missouri

Race	Juvenile	Adult	Total
Black	6	18	24
White	0	0	0

Source: http://www.bjs.gov/index.cfm?ty=datool&surl=/arrests/index.cfm#. Accessed August 25, 2014.

You can use this data analysis tool to find out more about crime and arrests in Ferguson, Missouri, or any other jurisdiction that reports data to the UCR system.

Advantages and Disadvantages of Secondary Data

The advantages of secondary analysis are obvious and enormous: it is cheaper and faster than collecting original data, and depending on who did the original study, you may benefit from the work of topflight professionals and esteemed academics. Considering some of the secondary data that have become available in recent years, it's easy to understand why many criminal justice researchers spend their entire careers analyzing secondary data.

The National Longitudinal Study of Adolescent Health, known as Add Health, began in 1994 with a nationally representative sample of people in grades 7 to 12. Data are available for four waves of follow-up interviews through 2008. Data include survey questions, self-report, a variety of physiological measures, and many other items (Harris and Udry 2014). Criminologists have used Add Health to address a variety of questions on offending and substance use. For example, Marie Skubak Tillyer and Emily Wright (2014) examined the co-occurrence of victimization and offending in domestic violence. J.C. Barnes and associates took advantage of some key features of the Add Health sample to explore whether genetic factors might be associated with patterns of offending over time (Barnes, Beaver, and Boutwell 2011).

Comparative or international research is possible by using data collected by researchers in other countries or by accessing international data sources. Marcelo Aebi and Antonia Linde (2012) examined long-term trends of police-recorded crime in eight European countries and found declines for some offenses but a substantial and steady increase in drug offenses. Aebi and Linde used data compiled in the

European Sourcebook of Crime and Criminal Justice Statistics. Graham Farrell and associates combined crime data from the United States, England, and Wales to assess the effects of different requirements for vehicle security on auto theft rates (Farrell et al. 2011). As expected, researchers found that the introduction of laws requiring electronic immobilizers in England and Wales produced sharp drops in auto theft compared to theft rates in the United States.

These examples illustrate important advantages of conducting research with secondary data. Researchers can gain access to information from large-scale studies conducted over an extended period of time and using complex measures. Additionally, web-based compilations of secondary data have made it easier to conduct research for populations and sites outside the United States. Finally, Skogan's 1990 analysis is an example of combining data from a large number of independent studies.

Potential disadvantages must be kept in mind, however. The key problem involves the recurrent question of validity. When one researcher collects data for one particular purpose, you have no assurance that those data will be appropriate to your research interests. Typically you'll find that the original researcher collected data that come close to measuring what you are interested in, but you may wish key variables had been operationalized just a little differently. The question, then, is whether secondary data provide valid measures of the variables you want to analyze.

This closely resembles one of the key problems in the use of agency records. Perhaps a particular set of data does not provide a totally satisfactory measure of what interests you, but other sets of data are available.

Even if no one set of data provides totally valid measures, you can build up a weight of evidence by analyzing all the possibilities. If each of the imperfect measures points to the same research conclusion, you will have developed considerable support for its accuracy. The use of replication lessens the problem.

In general, secondary data are least useful for evaluation studies. This is because evaluations are designed to answer specific questions about specific programs. It is always possible to reanalyze data from evaluation studies, but secondary data cannot be used to evaluate an entirely different program. Thus, for example, a number of researchers have reexamined data collected for a series of domestic violence experiments conducted by Lawrence Sherman and others in several cities (see Sherman 1992b for a summary). In most cases, these secondary researchers (such as Maxwell, Garner, and Fagan 2001) wished to verify or reassess findings from the original studies. But it is not possible to use those data to answer questions about domestic violence interventions other than arrest or to evaluate arrest policies in new cities where the experiments did not take place.

In this book, the discussion of secondary analysis has a special purpose. As we conclude our examination of modes of observation in criminal justice research, you should have developed a full appreciation for the range of possibilities available in finding the answers to questions about crime and criminal justice policy. No single method of getting information unlocks all puzzles, yet there is no limit to the ways you can find out about things. And, more powerfully, you can zero in on an issue from several independent directions, gaining an even greater mastery of it.

SUMMARY

- Data and records produced by formal organizations may be the most common source of data in criminal justice research.

- Many public organizations produce statistics and data for the public record, and these data are often useful for criminal justice researchers.

- All organizations keep nonpublic records for internal operational purposes, and these records

are valuable sources of data for criminal justice research.

- Public organizations can sometimes be enlisted to collect new data—through observation or interviews—for use by researchers.

- Although agency records have many potential research uses, because they are produced for

- purposes other than research, they may be unsuitable for a specific study.

- Researchers must be especially attentive to possible reliability and validity problems when they use data from agency records.

- "Follow the paper trail" and "expect the expected" are two general maxims for researchers to keep in mind when using agency records in their research.

- Content analysis is a research method appropriate for studying human communications. Because communication takes many forms, content analysis can study many other aspects of behavior.

- Units of communication, such as words, paragraphs, and books, are the usual units of analysis in content analysis.

- Coding is the process of transforming raw data—either manifest or latent content—into a standardized, quantitative form.

- Secondary analysis refers to the analysis of data collected earlier by another researcher for some purpose other than the topic of the current study.

- Archives of criminal justice and other social data are maintained by the ICPSR and the NACJD for use by other researchers.

- Online data analysis tools are available for many sources of secondary data.

- Secondary data offer many advantages to criminal justice researchers. The disadvantages of using secondary data are similar to those for agency records—data previously collected by a researcher may not match our own needs.

KEY TERMS

content analysis, p. 269

Interuniversity Consortium for Political and Social Research (ICPSR), p. 273

latent content, p. 270

manifest content, p. 270

National Archive of Criminal Justice Data (NACJD), p. 273

published statistics, p. 258

secondary analysis, p. 256

social production of data, p. 266

REVIEW QUESTIONS AND EXERCISES

1. The NACJD includes a variety of data resource guides on its home page (http://www.icpsr. umich.edu/icpsrweb/NACJD/). Each resource guide describes how a data series is collected, along with key features of measures and other information. Choose two data resource guides, then (a) summarize in a paragraph or so how data were collected, and what are units of analysis; and (b) formulate at least one research question that you think can be addressed by data in the series.

2. Visit the FBI UCR website (http://www.bjs. gov/ucrdata/). Use the table-building tool to find violent crime rates and property crime rates for 10 states. Or examine trends in reported crime for a 20-year period. Briefly write up a summary of results.

3. In New York City, police officers assigned to a specialized gang squad pay special attention to graffiti, or tagging. In doing so, they conduct a type of content analysis to study actions, threats, and other messages presented in this form of communication. Describe how you would plan a formal content analysis of graffiti. Be sure to distinguish manifest and latent content, units of analysis, and coding rules for your study.

PART 4

Application and Analysis

This final section of the book draws on concepts and ideas from earlier chapters to consider applied research in criminal justice. Having examined the role of theory, cause and effect, measurement, experiments, and different ways of collecting data, we are now ready to see how these pieces come together in an especially important area.

Criminal justice research can be conducted in many ways to answer many different types of questions. We have touched on various research purposes throughout the text, and the chapter in this section examines a specific research purpose more closely. Because crime is an important social problem, applied research is of great interest to researchers and public officials alike. Chapter 11 describes evaluation research and problem analysis. As we will see, carefully specifying concepts and being attentive to measures are as important for applied research as they are for other research purposes.

CHAPTER **11**

Evaluation Research and Problem Analysis

In this chapter, our attention centers on applied criminal justice research. Evaluation studies are conducted to learn whether (and why) programs have succeeded or failed. Problem analysis helps officials plan their actions and anticipate the possible effects of new programs.

Evaluating Vehicle Security

Graham Farrell and associates (2011) investigated vehicle theft trends for Australia, Canada, England and Wales, and the United States. This was part of a research project undertaken by Maxfield and Ronald Clarke on the effectiveness of auto parts marking in the United States.

Vehicle theft had been persistently high in Australia for many years, prompting officials to take a variety of measures to reduce the problem (Carroll 2004). Farrell and associates took advantage of the staged introduction of security measures in different parts of Australia to conduct an evaluation of the effectiveness of electronic engine immobilizers. These devices prevent a vehicle's engine from being started unless an electronic key code matches the code installed in the vehicle.

The figure below shows trends in motor vehicle theft for Western Australia, one of the country's states and territories, and for the other seven states and territories. Data points are an index set at 100 for the year 1997. Thefts in subsequent years are expressed as change in that base. For example, the value for Western Australia in 1998 was 118, which means vehicle theft had increased 18 percent in 1998 compared to the previous year. By the year 2008, the index for Western Australia had decline to about 40, which means vehicle theft had dropped by about 60 percent from 1997 through 2008.

The figure also shows vertical lines that correspond to government action regarding electronic immobilizers:

- In 1999, immobilizers were required for *all cars* less than 12 years old registered in Western Australia.

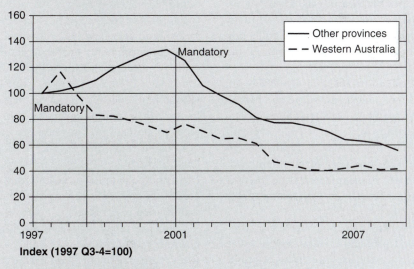

Trends in Australian Vehicle Theft 1997–2007
Source: Adapted from Farrell et al. (2011).

(continued)

- In 2001, immobilizers were required for *all new cars* sold throughout Australia.

You can see a clear trend downward in the two series after immobilizer requirements were introduced in different places at different times. The declines correspond roughly with requirements, and the requirements were introduced in different years.

This figure presents an example of an interrupted time series, a type of evaluation often used to assess whether change follows some new law. We describe this and other approaches to evaluation in this chapter. Keep this example in mind as you read our discussion of different types of applied research.

Introduction

Evaluation research and problem analysis are increasingly important activities for researchers and public officials alike.

Evaluation research—sometimes called *program evaluation*—refers to a research purpose rather than a specific research method. Its special purpose is to evaluate the effects of policies such as mandatory arrest for domestic violence, innovations in probation, and new sentencing laws. Another type of evaluation study, **problem analysis**, helps public officials plan and select alternative actions. Virtually all types of designs, measures, and data collection techniques can be used in evaluation research and problem analysis.

Growth of evaluation research over the last several years no doubt reflects desire on the part of criminal justice researchers to actually make a difference in the world. At the same time, we cannot discount the influence of two additional factors: (1) increased federal requirements for program evaluations to accompany the implementation of new programs, and (2) the availability of research funds to meet that requirement.

By the same token, increased interest in program evaluation and problem analysis has followed heightened concern for the accountability of public officials and public policy. Criminal justice agencies are expected to justify the effectiveness and cost of their actions. If traditional approaches to probation

supervision, for example, do not deter future law-breaking, new approaches should be developed and their effectiveness assessed. Or if using temporary detention facilities fabricated from recycled semi-trailers is less costly than constructing new jails, public officials should consider whether the lower-cost alternative will meet their needs for pretrial detention and short-term incarceration.

Justice agencies have come to rely more on **evidence-based policy**, in which the actions of justice agencies are linked to evidence used for planning and evaluation. Traditional practices are being reevaluated against evidence provided by social science research. The *Problem-Oriented Guides* series summarizes evidence concerning responses by police and others to problems ranging from abandoned buildings and lots (Shane 2012) to witness intimidation (Johnson 2006). CompStat and its variations base police actions on evidence about the location and circumstances of crime problems. Corrections policies are increasingly evaluated to sort out those that do in fact reduce reoffending (Aos and Drake 2013). This trend represents an expansion of applied research that moves beyond collaborations between justice professionals and professional researchers.

Finally, researchers at the John Jay College of Criminal Justice Research and Evaluation Center (REC) have launched an initiative for **evidence generation**. Prompted partly by New York State policies to reform juvenile justice, nonprofit organizations in New York City have developed innovative programs tailored to the needs of local youths involved in juvenile or criminal justice courts. Researchers at the REC help affiliated organizations evaluate and document their programming, thus generating evidence that can be shared with others. For more information and examples of this collaborative work, see the website evidencegeneration.org.

Topics Appropriate for Evaluation Research and Problem Analysis

Problem analysis and evaluation are used to develop justice policy and determine its impact.

Evaluation research is appropriate whenever some policy intervention occurs or is planned. A policy intervention is an action taken for the purpose of producing some intended result. In its simplest sense, evaluation research is a process of determining whether the intended result was produced. Problem analysis focuses more on deciding what intervention should be pursued. Given alternative courses of action, which is likely to be least costly, most effective, or least difficult to implement? Our focus, of course, is on the analysis and evaluation of criminal justice policy and criminal justice agencies. However, it will be useful to first consider a simple general model of the policy-making process in order to understand various topics appropriate to evaluation and problem analysis.

The Policy Process

Figure 11.1 presents our model, adapted from Robert Lineberry's (1977, 42–43) classic summary of a policy system. A similar type of input–output model is described in a National Institute of Justice publication on evaluation guidelines (McDonald and Smith 1989). Although we will examine each step in turn, it is important to recognize that the

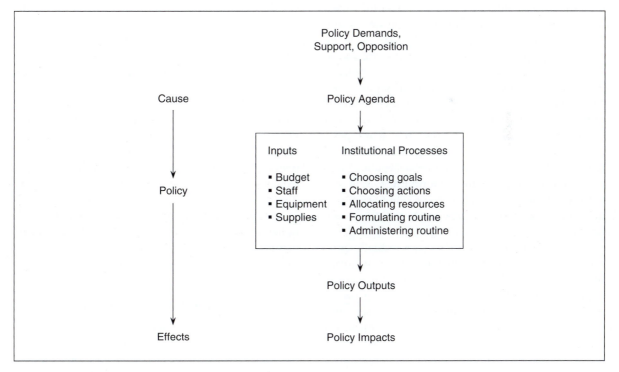

FIGURE 11.1 The Policy Process
Source: Adapted from Lineberry (1977, 24–43).

policy process, like the research process generally (see Chapter 1), is fluid and does not always start at the beginning and conclude at the end.

The policy process begins with a demand that normally appears as support for a new course of action or opposition to existing policy. Such demands can emerge from within a public organization or from outside sources. For example, widely publicized cases of racial discrimination in drug sentencing eventually led to the revision of federal sentencing guidelines for drug offenses (United States Sentencing Commission 2014). Or a local prosecutor may independently decide to review all sentence recommendations made by deputies who prosecute drug cases. In any case, before action can be taken, demands must find a place on the policy agenda.

The next step, as shown in Figure 11.1, actually encompasses several steps. Policy makers consider ultimate goals they wish to accomplish and different means of achieving those goals. Does a local prosecutor seek absolute equality in sentences recommended for all white and African American drug defendants, or should there be ranges of permissible variation based on criminal history, severity of charges, and so on? Resources must be allocated from available inputs, including personnel, equipment, supplies, and even time. Who will review sentence recommendations? How much time will that take, and will additional staff be required? Because the word *policy* implies some standard course of action about how to respond to a recurring problem or issue, routine practices and decision rules must be formulated. Will sentence recommendations for each case be reviewed as they are prepared, or is it sufficient to review all cases on a weekly basis?

Policy outputs refer to what is actually produced, in much the same manner that a manufacturer of office supplies produces paper clips and staples. In our hypothetical example, the prosecutor's policy produces the routine review of sentence recommendations in drug cases. Or, to consider a different example, a selective traffic enforcement program intended to reduce auto accidents on a particular roadway may produce a visible police presence together with traffic citations for speeding.

In the final stage, we consider the impact of policy outputs. Does the prosecutor's review process actually eliminate disparities in sentences? Are auto accidents reduced in the targeted enforcement area?

The distinction between policy outputs and their impacts is important for understanding applications of evaluation to different stages of the policy process. Unfortunately, this difference is often confusing to both public officials and researchers. *Impacts* are fundamentally related to policy goals; they refer to the basic question of what a policy action is trying to achieve. *Outputs* embody the means to achieve desired policy goals. The prosecutor seeks to achieve equality in sentence recommendations (impact), so a review process is produced as a means to achieve that goal (output). Or a police executive allocates officers, patrol cars, and overtime pay to produce traffic citations (outputs) in the expectation that citations will achieve the goal of reducing auto accidents (impact).

Now consider the left side of Figure 11.1. Our policy model can be expressed as a simple cause-and-effect process, as we considered in earlier chapters. A cause has produced the variation in sentences for African American and white defendants, or a cause has produced a concentration of auto accidents. Policies are formulated to produce an effect or impact. In this sense, a policy can be viewed as a hypothesis in which an independent variable is expected to produce change in a dependent variable. Sentence review procedures are expected to produce a reduction in sentence disparities; targeted enforcement is expected to produce a reduction in auto accidents. Goal-directed public policies may therefore be viewed as if–then statements: if some policy action is taken, then we expect some result to be produced.

Linking the Process to Evaluation

If we compare this simple model with a general definition of program evaluation given in one of the most widely used texts on the subject (Rossi, Freeman, and Lipsey 1999), the topics appropriate to applied research will become clearer.

Peter Rossi and associates (1999, 4; emphasis in original) define program evaluation as:

the use of social science research procedures to systematically assess the effectiveness of social intervention programs. More specifically, evaluation researchers (evaluators) use social research methods to study, appraise, and help improve social programs in all their aspects, including the diagnosis of the social problems they address, their conceptualization and design, their implementation and administration, their outcomes, and their efficiency.

We have been discussing systematic social scientific research procedures throughout this book. Now let's substitute criminal justice for social programs and see how this definition and Figure 11.1 help us understand program evaluation applications.

Problem Analysis Activities listed under "Institutional Processes" in Figure 11.1 refer to conceptualization and design. For example, faced with a court order to maintain prison populations within established capacity, corrections officials might begin by conceiving and designing different ways to achieve this demand. Problem analysis is an example of a social scientific research procedure that can help corrections officials evaluate alternative actions, choose among them, and formulate routine practices for implementing policy to comply with a court order.

One approach might be to increase rated capacity through new construction or conversion of existing facilities. Another might be to devise a program to immediately reduce the existing population. Still another might be to cut back on the admission of newly sentenced offenders. A more general goal that would certainly be considered is the need to protect public safety. Each goal implies different types of actions, together with different types and levels of resources, that would be considered within constraints implied by the need to protect public safety. If officials from other organizations—prosecutors, judges, or state legislators—were involved in conceptualization and design, then additional goals, constraints, and policies might be considered.

Increasing capacity by building more prisons would be the most costly approach in financial terms, but it might also be viewed as the most certain way to protect public safety. Early release of current inmates would be cheaper and faster than building new facilities, but this goal implies other decisions, such as how persons would be selected and whether they would be released to parole or to halfway houses. Each of these alternatives requires some organizational capacity to choose inmates for release, place them in halfway houses, or supervise compliance with parole. Refusing new admissions would be least costly. Political support must be considered for each possible approach. Each alternative—spending money on new construction, accepting responsibility for early release, or tacitly passing the problem on to jails that must house inmates refused admission to state facilities—requires different types of political influence or courage.

Many other topics in criminal justice research are appropriate for problem analysis. Police departments use such techniques to help determine the boundaries of patrol beats and the allocation of other resources. In most large cities, analysts examine the concentration of calls for service in terms of space and time and consider how street layout and obstacles might facilitate or impede patrol car mobility.

A growing number of law enforcement agencies are using computerized crime maps to detect emerging patterns in crime and develop appropriate responses. Producing computer-generated maps that display reported crimes within days after they have occurred is one of the most important policy planning tools for the New York City Police Department (Silverman 1999). Other departments have taken advantage of funding and technical assistance made available by federal funding to enhance mapping and other crime analysis capabilities (Santos 2012).

Program Evaluation Problem analysis takes place in the earlier stages of the policy process. In contrast, program evaluation studies are conducted in later stages and seek answers to two types of questions: (1) Are policies being implemented as planned? and (2) Are policies achieving their intended goals? Evaluation, therefore, seeks to link the intended actions and goals of criminal justice policy to empirical evidence that policies are being carried out as planned and are having the desired effects. These two types of questions correspond to two related types of program evaluations: process evaluation and impact assessment. Returning to our example of policies to reduce prison population, we will first consider impact assessment and then process evaluation.

Let's assume that corrections department policy analysts select an early-release program to reduce the population of one large institution. Inmates who have less than 120 days remaining on their sentence and who were committed for nonviolent offenses will be considered for early release. Further assume that of those inmates selected for early release, some will be assigned to parole officers, and some will serve their remaining sentence in halfway houses—working at jobs during the week but spending evenings and weekends in a community-based facility.

The program has two general goals: (1) to reduce prison population to the court-imposed ceiling and (2) to protect public safety. Whereas the first goal is fairly straightforward, the second is uncomfortably vague. What do we mean by "protecting public safety"? For now, let's say we will conclude that the program is successful in this regard if, after six months, persons in the two early-release conditions have aggregate rates of arrest for new offenses equal to or less than a comparison group of inmates released after completing their sentences.

Our **impact assessment** would examine data on the prison population before and after the new program was implemented, together with arrest records for the two types of early releases and a comparison group. We might obtain something like the hypothetical results shown in Table 11.1.

Did the program meet its two goals? Your initial reaction might be that it did not, but Table 11.1 presents some interesting findings. The prison population certainly was reduced, but it did not reach the court-imposed cap of 1,350. Those released to halfway houses had lower arrest rates

TABLE 11.1   Hypothetical Results of Early-Prison-Release Impact Assessment

	New Arrests After 6 Months	Number of Inmates Released
Normal release	26%	142
Early release	27%	71
Early release to halfway houses	17%	25
Early parole	33%	46
Total	26%	213

Note: Preprogram population = 1,578; actual population after implementation = 1,402; court-imposed population cap = 1,650.

than others, but persons placed on early parole had higher arrest rates. Averaging arrest rates for all three groups shows that the total figure is about the same as that for persons released early. Notice also that almost twice as many people were released to early parole as were placed in halfway houses.

The impact assessment results in Table 11.1 would have been easier to interpret if we had conducted a **process evaluation**. A process evaluation focuses on program outputs, as represented in Figure 11.1, seeking answers to the question of whether the program was implemented as intended. If we had conducted a process evaluation of this early-release program, we might have discovered that something was amiss in the selection process. Two pieces of evidence in Table 11.1 suggest that one of the selection biases we considered in Chapter 5 might be at work in this program. Recall the natural tendency of public officials to choose experimental subjects least likely to fail. In this case, selectivity is indicated by the failure of the early-release program to meet its target number, the relatively small number of persons placed in halfway houses, and the lower re-arrest rates for these persons. A process evaluation would have monitored selection procedures and probably revealed evidence of excessive caution on the part of corrections officials in releasing offenders to halfway houses.

Ideally, impact assessments and process evaluations are conducted together. To paraphrase Peter Drucker's (1973) famous comment about efficiency and effectiveness, the different types of evaluations address similar questions:

- *Process evaluation*: Are we doing things right?
- *Impact evaluation*: Are we doing the right things?

Our example illustrates the important general point that process evaluations make impact assessments more interpretable. In other cases, process evaluations may be conducted when an impact assessment is not possible. To better understand how process evaluations and impact assessments complement each other, let's now look more closely at how evaluations are conducted.

Getting Started

Learning policy goals is a key first step in doing evaluation research.

Several steps are involved in planning any type of research project. This is especially true in applied studies, for which even more planning may be required. In evaluating a prison early release program, we need to think about design, measurement, sampling, data collection procedures, analysis, and so on. We also have to address such practical problems as obtaining access to people, information, and data needed in an evaluation.

In one sense, however, evaluation research differs slightly in the way research questions are developed and specified. Recall that we equated program evaluation with hypothesis testing; policies are equivalent to if–then statements postulating that an intervention will have the desired impact. Preliminary versions of research questions, therefore, will already have been formulated for many types of evaluations. Problem analysis usually considers a limited range of alternative choices; process evaluations focus on whether programs are carried out according to plans; and impact assessments evaluate whether specified goals are attained.

This is not to say that evaluation research is a straightforward business of using social scientific methods to answer specific questions that are clearly stated by criminal justice officials. It is often difficult to express policy goals in the form of if–then statements that are empirically testable. Another problem is the presence of conflicting goals. Many issues in criminal justice are complex, involving different organizations and people. And different organizations and people may have different goals that make it difficult to define specific evaluation questions. Perhaps most common and problematic are vague goals. Language describing criminal justice programs may optimistically state goals of enhancing public safety by reducing recidivism without clearly specifying what is meant by that objective.

In most cases, researchers have to help criminal justice officials formulate testable goals, something that is not always possible. Other obstacles may interfere with researchers' access to important information. Because of these and similar problems, evaluation researchers must first address the question of whether to evaluate at all.

Evaluability Assessment

An evaluability assessment is described by Rossi and associates (1999, 157) as sort of a "preevaluation," in which a researcher determines whether conditions necessary for conducting an evaluation are present. One obvious condition is support for the study from organizations delivering program components that will be evaluated. The word *evaluation* may be threatening to public officials, who fear that their own job performance is being rated. Even if officials do not feel personally threatened by an impact assessment or other applied study, evaluation research can disrupt routine agency operations. Ensuring agency cooperation and support is therefore an important part of evaluability assessment. Even if no overt opposition exists, officials may be ambivalent about evaluation.

This might be the case, for example, if an evaluation is required as a condition of launching a new program. This and other steps in evaluability assessment may be accomplished by scouting a program and interviewing key personnel (Rossi, Freeman, and Lipsey 1999, 135). The focus in scouting and interviewing should be on obtaining preliminary answers to questions that eventually will have to be answered in more detail as part of an evaluation. What are general program goals and more specific objectives? How are these goals translated into program components? What kinds of records and data are readily available? Who will be the primary consumers of evaluation results? Do other persons or organizations have a direct or indirect stake in the program? Figure 11.2 presents a partial menu of questions that can guide information

gathering for the evaluability assessment and later stages.

The answers to these and similar questions should be used to prepare a program description. Although official program descriptions may be available, evaluation researchers should always prepare their own description, one that reflects their own understanding of program goals, elements, and operations. Official documents may present incomplete descriptions or ones intended for use by program staff, not evaluators. Even more importantly, official program documents often do not contain usable statements about program goals. As we will see, formulating goal statements that are empirically testable is one of the most important components of evaluation research.

Douglas McDonald and Christine Smith (1989, 1) describe slightly different types of questions to be addressed by criminal justice officials and evaluators in deciding whether to evaluate state-level drug control programs:

- How central is the project to the state's strategy?

- How costly is it relative to others?

- Are the project's objectives such that progress toward meeting them is difficult to estimate accurately with existing monitoring procedures?

Such questions are related to setting both program and evaluation priorities. On the one hand, if a project is not central to drug control strategies or if existing information can help determine project effectiveness, then an evaluation should probably not be conducted. On the other hand, costly projects that are key elements in antidrug efforts should be evaluated so that resources can be devoted to new programs if existing approaches are found to be ineffective.

Problem Formulation

We mentioned that evaluation research questions may be defined for you. This is true in a general sense, but formulating applied research problems that can be empirically evaluated is an important and often difficult step. Evaluation research is a matter of finding out whether something is or is not there, whether something did or did not happen. To conduct evaluation research, we must be

---

1. Goals
   a. What is the program intended to accomplish?
   b. How do staff determine how well they have attained their goals?
   c. What formal goals and objectives have been identified?
   d. Which goals or objectives are most important?
   e. What measures of performance are currently used?
   f. Are adequate measures available, or must they be developed as part of the evaluation?

2. Clients
   a. Who is served by the program?
   b. How do they come to participate?
   c. Do they differ in systematic ways from non-participants?

3. Organization and operation
   a. Where are the services provided?
   b. Are there important differences among sites?
   c. Who provides the services?
   d. What individuals or groups oppose the program or have been critical of it in the past?

4. History
   a. How long has the program been operating?
   b. How did the program come about?
   c. Has the program grown or diminished in size and influence?
   d. Have any significant changes occurred in the program recently?

FIGURE 11.2 Evaluation Questions
Source: Adapted from Stecher and Davis (1987, 58–59).

able to operationalize, observe, and recognize the presence or absence of what is under study.

This process normally begins by identifying and specifying program goals. The difficulty of this task, according to Rossi and associates (1999, 167), revolves around the fact that formal statements of goals are often abstract statements about ideal outcomes. Here are some examples of goal statements paraphrased from actual program descriptions:

- Equip individuals with life skills to succeed (a state-level shock incarceration program; MacKenzie, Shaw, and Gowdy 1993).

- Provide a safe school environment conducive to learning (a school resource officer program; Johnson 1999).

- Encourage participants to accept the philosophy and principles of drug-free living (an urban drug court; Finn and Newlyn 1993).

- Provide a mechanism that engages local citizens and community resources in the problem-solving process (a probation-police community corrections program; Wooten and Hoelter 1998).

Each statement expresses a general program objective that must be clarified before we can formulate research questions to be tested empirically. We can get some idea of what the first example means, but this goal statement raises several questions. The objective is for individuals to succeed, but succeed at what? What is meant by "life skills"—literacy, job training, time management, self-discipline? We might also ask whether the program focuses on outputs (equipping people with skills) or on impacts (promoting success among people who are equipped with the skills). On the one hand, an evaluation of program outputs might assess individual learning of skills, without considering whether the skills enhance chances for success. On the other hand, an evaluation of program impacts might obtain measures of success such as stable employment or not being arrested within some specified time period.

In all fairness, these goal statements are taken somewhat out of context; source documents expand on program goals in more detail. They are,

however, typical of stated goals or initial responses we might get to the question "What are the goals of this program?" Researchers require more specific statements of program objectives.

Wesley Skogan (1985) cautions that official goal statements frequently oversell what a program might realistically be expected to accomplish. It's natural for public officials to be positive or optimistic in stating goals, and overselling may be evident in goal statements. Another reason officials and researchers embrace overly optimistic goals is that they fail to develop a micromodel of the program production process (Weiss 1995). That is, they do not adequately consider just how some specified intervention will work. Referring to Figure 11.1, we can see that developing a micromodel can be an important tool for laying out program goals and understanding how institutional processes are structured to achieve those goals. Skogan (1985, 38; emphasis in original) describes a micromodel as:

> part of what is meant by a "theory-driven" evaluation. Researchers and program personnel should together consider just how each element of a program should affect its targets. If there is not a good reason why "X" *should* cause "Y" the evaluation is probably not going to find that it did! Micromodeling is another good reason for monitoring the actual implementation of programs.

A micromodel can also reveal another problem that sometimes emerges in applied studies: inconsistent goals.

For example, Michael Maxfield and Terry Baumer (1992) evaluated a pretrial home detention program in which persons awaiting trial for certain types of offenses were released from jail and placed on home detention with electronic monitoring. Five different criminal justice organizations played roles in implementation or had stakes in the program. The county sheriff's department (1) faced pressure to reduce its jail population. Under encouragement from the county prosecutor (2), the pretrial release program was established. Criminal court judges (3) had the ultimate authority to release defendants to home detention, following recommendations by bail commissioners in a county criminal justice services agency (4). Finally, a community corrections department (5) was responsible for actually monitoring persons released to home detention.

Maxfield and Baumer interviewed persons in each of these organizations and discovered that different agencies had different goals. The sheriff's department was eager to release as many people as possible to free up jail space for convicted offenders and pretrial defendants who faced more serious charges. Community corrections staff, charged with the task of monitoring pretrial clients, were more cautious and sought only persons who presented a lower risk of absconding or committing more offenses while on home detention. The county prosecutor viewed home detention as a way to exercise more control over some individuals who would otherwise be released under less restrictive conditions. Some judges refused to release people on home detention, whereas others followed prosecutors' recommendations. Finally, bail commissioners viewed pretrial home detention as a form of jail resource management, adding to the menu of existing pretrial dispositions (jail, bail, or release on recognizance).

The different organizations involved in the pretrial release program comprised multiple **stakeholders**—persons and organizations with a direct interest in the program. Each stakeholder had different goals for and different views on how the program should actually operate—who should be considered for pretrial home detention, how they should be monitored, and what actions should be taken against those who violated various program rules. After laying out these goals and considering different measures of program performance, Maxfield and Baumer (1992, 331) developed a micromodel of home detention indicating that electronic monitoring is suitable for only a small fraction of defendants awaiting trial.

Clearly specifying program goals, then, is a fundamental first step in conducting evaluation studies. If officials are not certain about what a program is expected to achieve, it is not possible to determine whether goals are reached. If multiple stakeholders embrace different goals, evaluators must specify different ways to assess those goals. Michael Maxfield (2001) describes a number of different approaches to specifying clear goals, a crucial first step in the evaluation process.

Measurement

After we identify program goals, our attention turns to measurement, considering first how to measure a program's success in meeting goals. Obtaining evaluable statements of program goals is conceptually similar to the measurement process, in which program objectives represent conceptual definitions of what a program is trying to accomplish.

Specifying Outcomes If a criminal justice program is intended to accomplish something, we must be able to measure that something. If we want to reduce fear of crime, we need to be able to measure fear of crime. If we want to increase consistency in sentences for drug offenses, we need to be able to measure that. Notice, however, that although outcome measures are derived from goals, they are not the same as goals. Program goals represent desired outcomes, whereas outcome measures are empirical indicators of whether those desired outcomes are achieved. Furthermore, if a program pursues multiple goals, then researchers may have to either devise multiple outcome measures or select a subset of possible measures to correspond with a subset of goals.

Keeping in mind our program-as-hypothesis simile, outcome measures correspond to dependent variables—the Y in a simple $X \rightarrow Y$ causal hypothesis. Because we have already considered what's involved in developing measures for dependent variables, we can describe how to formulate outcome measures. Pinning down program goals and objectives results in a conceptual definition. We then specify an operational definition by describing empirical indicators of program outcomes.

In our earlier example, Maxfield and Baumer (1992) translated the disparate interests of organizations involved in pretrial home detention into three more specific objectives: (1) ensure appearance at trial, (2) protect public safety, and (3) relieve jail crowding. These objectives led to corresponding outcome measures: (1) failure-to-appear rates for persons released to pretrial home detention, (2) arrests while on home detention, and (3) estimates of the number of jail beds made available, computed by multiplying the number of persons on pretrial home detention by the number of days each person served on the program. Table 11.2 summarizes the goals, objectives, and measures defined by Maxfield and Baumer.

Measuring Program Contexts Measuring the dependent variables directly involved in an impact assessment is only a beginning. As Ray Pawson and Nick Tilley (1997, 69) point out, it is usually necessary to measure the context within which the program is conducted. These variables may appear to be external to the experiment itself, yet they still affect it.

Consider, for example, an evaluation of a job-skills training program coupled with early prison release to a halfway house. The primary outcome measure might be the participants' success at gaining employment after completing the program. We will, of course, observe and calculate the subjects' employment rates. We should also be attentive to

TABLE 11.2 Pretrial Home Detention with Electronic Monitoring: Goals, Objectives, and Measures

Actor/Organization	Goals
Sheriff	Release jail inmates
Prosecutor	Increase supervision of pretrial defendants
Judges	Protect public safety
Bail commission	Provide better jail resource management
Community corrections	Monitor defendant compliance
	Return violators to jail

Objectives	Measures
Ensure court appearance	Failure-to-appear counts
Protect public safety	Arrests while on program
Relieve jail crowding	N defendants X days served

Source: Adapted from Maxfield and Baumer (1992, 321).

what has happened to the employment and unemployment rates of the community and state where the program is located. A general slump in the job market should be taken into account in assessing what might otherwise seem to be a low employment rate for subjects. Or if all the experimental subjects get jobs following the program, that might result more from a general increase in available jobs than from the value of the program itself.

There is no magic formula or set of guidelines for selecting measures of program context, any more than there is for choosing control variables in some other type of research. Just as we read what other researchers have found with respect to some topic we are interested in—say, explanatory research—we should also learn about the production process for some criminal justice program before conducting an evaluation.

Measuring Program Delivery In addition to making measurements relevant to the outcomes of a program, it is necessary to measure the program intervention—the experimental stimulus or independent variable. In some cases, this measurement will be handled by assigning subjects to experimental and control groups, if that's the research design. Assigning a person to the experimental group is the same as scoring that person "yes" on the intervention, and assignment to the control group represents a score of "no." In practice, however, it's seldom that simple.

Let's continue with the job-training example. Some inmates will participate in the program through early release; others will not. But imagine for a moment what job-training programs are actually like. Some subjects will participate fully; others might miss sessions or fool around when they are present. So we may need measures of the extent or quality of participation in the program. And if the program is effective, we should find that those who participated fully have higher employment rates than those who participated less.

Other factors may further confound the administration of the experimental stimulus. Suppose we are evaluating a new form of counseling designed to cure drug addiction. Several counselors administer it to subjects composing an experimental group. We can compare the recovery rate of the experimental group with that of a control group (a group that received some other type of counseling or none at all). It might be useful to include the names of the counselors who treat specific subjects in the experimental group, because some may be more effective than others. If that turns out to be the case, we must find out why the treatment works better for some counselors than for others. What we learn will further elaborate our understanding of the therapy itself.

Obtaining measures that reflect actual delivery of the experimental intervention is very important for many types of evaluation designs. Variation in the levels of treatment delivered by a program can be a major threat to the validity of even randomized evaluation studies. Put another way, uncontrolled variation in treatment is equivalent to unreliable measurement of the independent variable.

Specifying Other Variables It is usually necessary to measure the population of subjects involved in the program being evaluated. In particular, it is important to define those for whom the program is appropriate. In evaluation studies, such persons are referred to as the program's *target population*. If we are evaluating a program that combines more intensive probation supervision with periodic urine testing for drug use, it's probably appropriate for convicted persons who are chronic users of illegal drugs, but how should we define and measure chronic drug use more specifically? The job-skills training program mentioned previously is probably appropriate for inmates who have poor employment histories, but a more specific definition of employment history is needed.

This process of definition and measurement has two aspects. First, the program target population must be specified. This is usually done in a manner similar to the process of defining program goals. Drawing on questions like those in Figure 11.2, evaluators consult program officials to identify the intended targets or beneficiaries of a particular program. Because the hypothetical urine-testing program is combined with probation, its target

population will include persons who might receive suspended sentences with probation. However, offenders convicted of crimes that carry nonsuspendable sentences will not be in the target population. Prosecutors and other participants may specify additional limits to the target population—employment or no previous record of probation violations, for example.

Most evaluation studies that use individual people as units of analysis also measure such background variables as age, gender, educational attainment, employment history, and prior criminal record. Such measures are made to determine whether experimental programs work best for males, those older than 25, high school graduates, persons with fewer prior arrests, and so forth.

Second, in providing for the measurement of these different kinds of variables, we need to choose whether to create new measures or use ones already collected in the course of normal program operation. If our study addresses something that's not routinely measured, the choice is easy. More commonly, at least some of the measures we are interested in will be represented in agency records in some form or other. We then have to decide whether agency measures are adequate for our evaluation purposes.

Because we are talking about measurement here, our decision to use our own measures or those produced by agencies should, of course, be based on an assessment of measurement reliability and validity. If we are evaluating the program that combined intensive probation with urinalysis, we will have more confidence in the reliability and validity of basic demographic information recorded by court personnel than in court records of drug use. In this case, we might want to obtain self-report measures of drug use and crime commission from subjects themselves, rather than relying on official records.

By now, it should be abundantly clear that measurement must be taken very seriously in evaluation research. Evaluation researchers must carefully determine all the variables to be measured and obtain appropriate measures for each. However, such decisions are typically not purely scientific ones. Evaluation researchers often must work out their measurement strategy with the people responsible for the program being evaluated.

Designs for Program Evaluation

Designs used in basic research are readily adapted for use in evaluation research.

Chapter 5 introduced a variety of experimental and other designs that researchers use in studying criminal justice. Recall that randomly assigning research subjects to experimental or control groups controls for many threats to internal validity. Here our attention turns specifically to the use of different designs in program evaluation.

Randomized Evaluation Designs

To illustrate the advantages of random assignment, consider this dialogue from Lawrence Sherman's book *Policing Domestic Violence: Experiments and Dilemmas* (1992b, 67):

> When the Minneapolis domestic violence experiment was in its final planning stage, some police officers asked: "Why does it have to be a randomized experiment? Why can't you just follow up the people we arrest anyway, and compare their future violence risks to the people we don't arrest?"
>
> Since this question reveals the heart of the logic of controlled experiments, I said, "I'm glad you asked. What kind of people do you arrest now?" "Assholes," they replied. "People who commit aggravated POPO."
>
> "What is aggravated POPO?" I asked.
>
> "Pissing off a police officer," they answered. "Contempt of cop. But we also arrest people who look like they're going to be violent, or who have caused more serious injuries."
>
> "What kind of people do you not arrest for misdemeanor domestic assault?" I continued.
>
> "People who act calm and polite, who lost their temper but managed to get control of themselves," came the answer.

> "And which kinds of people do you think would have higher risks of repeat violence in the future?" I returned.
>
> "The ones we arrest," they said, the light dawning.
>
> "But does that mean arrest caused them to become more violent?" I pressed.
>
> "Of course not—we arrested them because they were more trouble in the first place," they agreed.
>
> "So just following up the ones you arrest anyway wouldn't tell us anything about the effects of arrest, would it?" was my final question.
>
> "Guess not," they agreed. And they went on to perform the experiment.

Sherman's dialogue portrays the obvious problems of selection bias in routine police procedures for handling domestic violence. In fact, one of the most important benefits of randomization is to avoid the selectivity that is such a fundamental part of criminal justice decision making. Police selectively arrest people, prosecutors selectively file charges, judges and juries selectively convict defendants, and offenders are selectively punished. In a more general sense, randomization is the great equalizer: through probability theory, we can assume that groups created by random assignment will be statistically equivalent.

Randomized designs are not suitable for evaluating all experimental criminal justice programs. Certain requirements of randomized studies mean that this design cannot be used in many situations. A review of those requirements illustrates many of the limits of randomized designs for applied studies.

Program and Agency Acceptance Random assignment of people to receive some especially desirable or punitive treatment may not be possible for legal, ethical, and practical reasons. We discussed ethics and legal issues in Chapter 2. Sometimes practical obstacles may also be traced to a misunderstanding of the meaning of random assignment. It is crucial that public officials understand why randomization is desirable and that they fully endorse the procedure.

Richard Berk and associates (2003) describe how researchers obtained cooperation for an evaluation of a new inmate classification system in the California Department of Corrections (CDC) by appealing to the needs of agency managers. Preliminary research suggested that the experimental classification system would increase inmate and staff safety at lower cost than classification procedures then in use. In addition:

> Plans for the study were thoroughly reviewed by stakeholders, including CDC administrators, representatives of prison employee bargaining unions, … California State legislative offices, and a wide variety of other interested parties. There was widespread agreement that the study was worth doing. (Berk et al. 2003, 211)

At the same time, justice agencies have expanding needs for evaluations of smaller-scale programs. John Eck (2002) explains how designs that are less elaborate are more likely to be accepted by public agencies.

Minimization of Exceptions to Random Assignment In any real-world delivery of alternative programs or treatments to victims, offenders, or criminal justice agency staff, exceptions to random assignment are all but inevitable. In a series of experiments on police responses to domestic violence, officers responded to incidents in one of three ways, according to a random assignment procedure (Sherman et al. 1992). The experimental treatment was arrest; control treatments included simply separating parties to the dispute or attempting to advise and mediate. Although patrol officers and police administrators accepted the random procedure, exceptions were made as warranted in individual cases, subject to an officer's discretionary judgment.

As the number of exceptions to random assignment increases, however, the statistical equivalence of experimental and control groups is threatened. When police (or others) make exceptions to random assignment, they are introducing bias into the selection of experimental and control groups. Randomized experiments are best suited for programs in which such exceptions can be minimized.

The prison classification study by Berk and associates (2003, 224–225) offers a good example. Random assignment was automatic—inmates having odd identification numbers at intake were assigned to the treatment group, while those having even numbers were in the control group. This procedure produced treatment and control groups that were virtually identical in size: 9,662 in treatment and 9,656 controls.

Adequate Case Flow for Sample Size In Chapter 6, we examined the relationship between sample size and accuracy in estimating population characteristics. As sample size increases (up to a point), estimates of population means and standard errors become more precise. By the same token, the number of subjects in groups created through random assignment is related to the researcher's ability to detect significant differences in outcome measures between groups. If each group has only a small number of subjects, statistical tests can detect only very large program effects or differences in outcome measures between the two groups. This is a problem with statistical conclusion validity and sample size, as we discussed in Chapters 5 and 6.

Case flow represents the process through which subjects are accumulated in experimental and control groups. In Sherman's domestic violence evaluations, cases flowed into experimental and control groups as domestic violence incidents were reported to police. Evaluations of other types of programs will generate cases through other processes—for example, offenders sentenced by a court or inmates entering a correctional facility. In a drug court evaluation by Denise Gottfredson and associates (2006), it took 18 months to accumulate 235 cases for the treatment group (drug court). Berk and associates (2003) accumulated their 9,662 treatment subjects in six months.

If relatively few cases flow through some process and thereby become eligible for random assignment, it will take longer to obtain sufficient numbers of cases. The longer it takes to accumulate cases, the longer it will take to conduct an experiment and the longer experimental conditions must be maintained. Imagine filling the gas tank of your car with a small cup: it would take a long time, it would test your patience, and you would probably tarnish the paint with spilled gasoline as the ordeal dragged on. In a similar fashion, an inadequate flow of cases into experimental groups risks contaminating the experiment through other problems. Getting information about case flow in the planning stages of an evaluation is a good way to diagnose possible problems with numbers of subjects.

Maintaining Treatment Integrity Treatment integrity refers to whether an experimental intervention is delivered as intended. Sometimes called *treatment consistency*, treatment integrity is therefore roughly equivalent to measurement reliability. Experimental designs in applied studies often suffer from problems related to treatment inconsistencies. If serving time in jail is the experimental treatment in a program designed to test different approaches to sentencing drunk drivers, treatment integrity will be threatened if some defendants are sentenced to a weekend in jail while others serve 30 days or longer.

Criminal justice programs can vary considerably in the amount of treatment applied to different subjects in experimental groups. For example, Gottfredson and associates (2006) acknowledge that the drug-court treatment in Baltimore County was unevenly implemented. Only about half of those assigned to the experimental group received certified drug treatment. In contrast, the classification system tested by Berk and associates (2003) was a relatively simple treatment that was readily standardized. There was no danger of treatment dilution as in the drug-court experiment.

Midstream changes in experimental programs can also threaten treatment integrity. Rossi and associates (1999, 297) point out that the possibility of midstream changes means that randomized designs are usually not appropriate for evaluating programs in early stages of development, when such changes are more likely. For example, assume we are evaluating an intensive supervision probation program with randomized experimental and control groups. Midway through the experiment, program staff decide to require weekly urinalysis for everyone in the experimental group (those

assigned to intensive supervision). If we detect differences in outcome measures between the experimental and control groups (say, arrests within a year after release), we will not know how much of the difference is due to intensive supervision and how much might be due to the midstream change of adding urine tests.

Summing Up the Limits of Randomized Designs Randomized experiments therefore require that certain conditions be met. Staff responsible for program delivery must accept random assignment and further agree to minimize exceptions to randomization. Case flow must be adequate to produce enough subjects in each group so that statistical tests will be able to detect significant differences in outcome measures. Finally, experimental interventions must be consistently applied to treatment groups and withheld from control groups.

These conditions, and the problems that may result if they are not met, can be summarized as two overriding concerns in field experiments: (1) equivalence between experimental and control groups before an intervention, and (2) the ability to detect differences in outcome measures after an intervention is introduced. If there are too many exceptions to random assignment, experimental and control groups may not be equivalent. If there are too few cases, or inconsistencies in administering a treatment, or treatment spillovers to control subjects, outcome measures may be affected in such a way that researchers cannot detect the effects of an intervention.

Let's now look at an example that illustrates both the strengths of random experiments and constraints on their use in criminal justice program evaluations.

Home Detention: Two Randomized Studies

Terry Baumer and Robert Mendelsohn conducted two random experiments to evaluate programs that combine home detention with electronic monitoring (ELMO). In earlier chapters, we examined how different features of these studies illustrated measurement principles; here our focus is on the mechanics of random assignment and program delivery.

In their first study, Baumer and Mendelsohn evaluated a program that targeted adult offenders convicted of nonviolent misdemeanor and minor felony offenses (Baumer and Mendelsohn 1990; also summarized in Baumer, Maxfield, and Mendelsohn 1993). The goal of the program was to provide supervision of offenders that was more enhanced than traditional probation but less restrictive and less costly than incarceration. Several measures of outcomes and program delivery were examined, as we have described in earlier chapters.

Baumer and Mendelsohn selected a randomized posttest-only design, in which the target population was offenders sentenced to probation. Subjects were randomly assigned to an experimental group in which the treatment was electronically monitored home detention or to a control group sentenced to home detention without electronic monitoring. Figure 11.3 summarizes case flow into the evaluation experiment. After a guilty plea or trial conviction, probation office staff reviewed offenders' backgrounds and criminal records for the purpose of recommending an appropriate sentence. The next step was a hearing, at which sentences were imposed by a criminal court judge.

Persons sentenced to probation were eligible for inclusion in the experiment. Their case files were forwarded to staff in the community corrections agency responsible for administering the home detention programs. On receiving an eligible case file, community corrections staff telephoned the evaluation researchers, who, having prepared a random list of case numbers, assigned subjects to either the treatment or control group. Subject to two constraints, this process produced 78 treatment subjects and 76 control subjects.

Thinking back on our consideration of ethics in Chapter 2, you should be able to think of one constraint: informed consent. Researchers and program staff explained the evaluation project to subjects and obtained their consent to participate in the experiment. Those who declined to participate

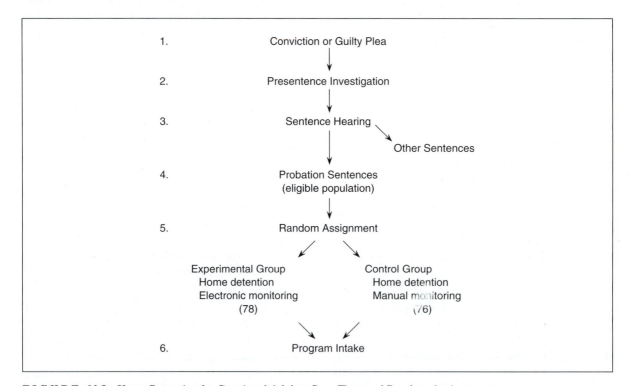

FIGURE 11.3   Home Detention for Convicted Adults: Case Flow and Random Assignment

in the evaluation study could nevertheless be assigned to home detention as a condition of their probation. The second constraint was made necessary by the technology of ELMO: subjects could not be kept in the treatment group if they did not have a telephone that could be connected to the ELMO equipment.

Notice that random assignment was made after sentencing. Baumer and Mendelsohn began their evaluation by randomizing subjects between stages 2 and 3 in Figure 11.3. This produced problems because judges occasionally overruled presentence investigation recommendations to probation, thus overriding random assignment. After detecting this problem, Baumer and Mendelsohn (1990, 27–29) moved randomization downstream, so that judicial decisions could not contaminate the selection process.

Baumer and Mendelsohn (1990, 26) obtained agreement from community corrections staff, prosecutors, and judges to use random assignment by getting all parties to accept an assumption of "no difference":

> That is, in the absence of convincing evidence to the contrary, they were willing to assume that there was no difference between the … methods of monitoring. This allowed the prosecutor to negotiate and judges to assign home detention as a condition of probation only, while permitting the community corrections agency to make the monitoring decision.

Convinced of the importance of random assignment, the community corrections agency delegated to researchers the responsibility for making the monitoring decision, a "decision" that was randomized.

In this example, the experimental condition—ELMO—was readily distinguished from the control condition, home detention without ELMO. There was no possibility of treatment spillover; control subjects could not unintentionally receive ELMO because they had neither the bracelet nor the home-base unit that embodied the treatment. ELMO could therefore be readily delivered to subjects in the experimental group and withheld from control subjects.

The second ELMO evaluation conducted by Baumer and Mendelsohn reveals how program delivery problems can undermine the strengths of random assignment (Baumer, Maxfield, and Mendelsohn 1993). In their study of juvenile burglars, they used similar procedures for randomization, but eligible subjects were placed in one of four groups, as illustrated in this table:

	Electronic Monitoring?	
Police Visits?	**No**	**Yes**
No	C	E1
Yes	E2	E3

Juvenile burglars could be randomly assigned to three possible treatments: ELMO only (E1), police visits to their home after school only (E2), or ELMO and police visits (E3). Subjects in the control group (C) were sentenced to home detention only. As in the adult study, outcome measures included arrests after release.

Although there were no problems with random assignment, inconsistencies in the delivery of each of the two experimental treatments produced uninterpretable results (Maxfield and Baumer 1991, 5):

> Observations of day-to-day program operations revealed that, compared with the adult program, the juvenile court and cooperating agencies paid less attention to delivering program elements and using information from … the electronic monitoring equipment. Staff were less well trained in operating the electronic monitoring equipment, and police visits were inconsistent.

The box titled "Home Detention" in Chapter 1 elaborates on differences in the operation of these two programs and a third ELMO program for pretrial defendants. However, the lesson from these studies bears repeating here: *randomization does not control for variation in treatment integrity and program delivery.*

Randomized experiments can be powerful tools in criminal justice program evaluations. However, it is often impossible to maintain the desired level of control over experimental conditions. This is especially true for complex interventions that may change while an evaluation is under way. Experimental conditions are also difficult to maintain when different organizations work together in delivering some service—a community-based drug treatment provider coupled with intensive probation, for example.

Largely because of such problems, evaluation researchers are increasingly turning to other types of designs that are less fragile—less subject to problems if rigorous experimental conditions cannot be maintained.

Quasi-Experimental Designs

Quasi-experiments are distinguished from true experiments by the lack of random assignment of subjects to an experimental and a control group. Random assignment of subjects is often impossible in criminal justice evaluations. Rather than forgo evaluation altogether in such instances, it is usually possible to create and execute research designs that will permit evaluation of the program in question.

Quasi-experiments may also be nested into experimental designs as backups should one or more of the requisites for a true experiment break down. For example, William Shadish, Thomas Cook, and Donald Campbell (2002) describe how time-series designs can be nested into a series of random experiments. In the event that case flow is inadequate or random assignment to enhanced or standard counseling regimens breaks down, the nested time-series design will salvage a quasi-experiment.

We considered different classes of quasi-experimental designs—nonequivalent groups, cohorts, and time series—in Chapter 5, together with examples of each type. Each of these designs has been used extensively in criminal justice evaluation research.

Nonequivalent-Groups Designs As we saw in Chapter 5, quasi-experimental designs lack the built-in controls for selection bias and other threats to internal validity. Nonequivalent-groups designs, by definition, cannot be assumed to include treatment and comparison subjects who are statistically equivalent. For this reason, quasi-experimental program evaluations must be carefully designed and analyzed to rule out possible validity problems.

For evaluation designs that use nonequivalent groups, attention should be devoted to constructing experimental and comparison groups that are as similar as possible on important variables that might account for differences in outcome measures. Rossi and associates (1999) caution that procedures for constructing such groups should be grounded in a theoretical understanding of what individual and group characteristics might confound evaluation results. In a study of recidivism by participants in shock incarceration programs, we certainly want to ensure that equal numbers of men and women are included in groups assigned to shock incarceration and groups that received another sentence. Alternatively, we can restrict our analysis of program effects to only men or only women.

One common reason for using nonequivalent-groups designs is that some experimental interventions are intended to affect all persons in a larger unit—a neighborhood crime prevention program, for example. It may not be possible to randomly assign some neighborhoods to receive the intervention while withholding it from others. And we are usually unable to control which individuals in a neighborhood are exposed to the intervention.

Different types of quasi-experimental designs can be used in such cases. In a Kansas City program to reduce gun violence, police targeted extra patrols at gun crime hot spots (Sherman, Shaw, and Rogan 1995). Some beats were assigned to receive the extra patrols, while comparison beats—selected for their similar frequency of gun crimes—did not get the special patrols. Several outcome measures were compared for the two types of areas. After 29 weeks, gun seizures in the target area increased by more than 65 percent and gun crimes dropped by 49 percent. There were no significant changes in either gun crimes or gun seizures in the comparison beat. Drive-by shootings dropped from 7 to 1 in the target area and increased from 6 to 12 in the comparison area. Homicides declined in the target area but not in the comparison area. Citizen surveys showed less fear of crime and more positive feelings about the neighborhood in the target area than in the comparison area.

Time-Series Designs Interrupted time-series designs require attention to certain validity threats because researchers cannot normally control how reliably the experimental treatment is implemented. Foremost among these issues are instrumentation, history, and construct validity. In many interrupted time-series designs, conclusions about whether an intervention produced change in an outcome measure rely on simple indicators that represent complex causal processes.

In their evaluation of legislation to provide for mandatory minimum sentences in Oregon, Nancy Merritt and associates (Merritt, Fain, and Turner 2006) examined changes in sentences for different types of offenses. They found that sentences for offenses clearly covered by the law did in fact increase in the first five years after its passage. However, they also found declines in the number of cases filed that were clearly included in the mandatory provisions. Meanwhile, more charges were filed for offenses covered by discretionary provisions. Of course, criminal case prosecution and sentencing are complex processes. The authors could not directly control for different circumstances surrounding cases processed before and after the law took effect. However, their time-series analysis does clearly show changes in case filings, suggesting that prosecutors exercised discretion to evade the mandatory provisions of Oregon's legislation.

Understanding the causal process that produces measures used in time-series analysis is crucial for interpreting results. Such understanding can come in two related ways. First, we should have a sound conceptual grasp of the underlying causal forces at work in the process we are interested in. Second, we should understand how the indicators used in any time-series analysis are produced.

Patricia Mayhew and associates (Mayhew, Clarke, and Elliott 1989) concluded that laws requiring motorcycle riders to wear helmets produced a reduction in motorcycle theft. This might seem puzzling until we consider the causal constructs involved in stealing motorcycles. Assuming that most motorcycle thefts are crimes of opportunity, Mayhew and associates argue that few impulsive thieves stroll about carrying helmets.

Even thieves are sufficiently rational to recognize that a helmetless motorcycle rider will be unacceptably conspicuous—an insight that deters them from stealing motorcycles. Mayhew and colleagues considered displacement as an alternative explanation for the decline in motorcycle theft, but they found no evidence that declines in motorcycle theft were accompanied by increases in either stolen cars or bicycles. By systematically thinking through the causal process of motorcycle theft, Mayhew and associates were able to conclude that helmet laws were unintentionally effective in reducing theft. For another study of vehicle theft, see the opening vignette for this chapter, "Evaluating Vehicle Security."

Other Types of Evaluation Studies

Earlier in this chapter, we noted how process evaluations are distinct from impact assessments. Whereas the latter seek answers to questions about program effects, process evaluations monitor program implementation, asking whether programs are being delivered as intended.

Process evaluations can be invaluable aids in interpreting results from an impact assessment. We described how Baumer and Mendelsohn were better able to understand outcome measures in their evaluation of ELMO for juvenile burglars because they had monitored program delivery. Similarly, process evaluations were key elements of closed-circuit television (CCTV) evaluations reported by Martin Gill and Angela Spriggs (2005), discussed in Chapter 5. They were able to describe whether cameras were placed and monitored as intended. In many cases, camera placement was modified, something the authors suggest was related to the relative success of different CCTV installations. Without a process evaluation, information about program implementation cannot be linked to outcome measures.

Process evaluations can also be useful for criminal justice officials whose responsibility centers more on the performance of particular tasks than on the overall success of some program. For example, police patrol officers are collectively responsible for public safety in their beat, but their routine actions focus more on performing specific tasks such as responding to a call for service or, in community policing, diagnosing the concerns of neighborhood residents. Police supervisors are attentive to traffic tickets written, arrests made, and complaints against individual officers. Probation and parole officers are, of course, interested in the ultimate performance of their clients, but they are also task-oriented in their use of records to keep track of client contacts, attendance at substance abuse sessions, or job performance. Process evaluations center on measures of task performance—on the assumption that tasks are linked to program outcomes. So process evaluations can be valuable in their own right, as well as important for diagnosing measures of program effects.

Problem Analysis and Scientific Realism

Problem analysis, coupled with scientific realism, helps public officials use research to select and assess alternative courses of action.

Program evaluation differs from problem analysis with respect to the time dimension and where each activity takes place in the policy process. Problem analysis is used to help design alternative courses of action and to choose among them.

In reality, there is not much of a difference between these two types of applied research. Similar types of research methods are used to address problem analysis questions (What would happen? What should we do?) as are brought to bear on program evaluation questions (What did happen? What have we done?). Consider, for example, a definition of a similar approach, policy analysis, from a prominent text: "Attempting to bring modern science and technology to bear on society's problems, policy analysis searches for feasible courses of action, generating information and marshalling evidence of the benefits and other consequences that would follow their adoption and implementation" (Quade 1989, 4). Except for the form of the verb ("would follow"), this is not too different from the way we defined program evaluation.

Results from program evaluations are frequently considered in choosing among future courses of

action. Problem analysis and policy analysis depend just as much on clearly specifying goals and objectives as does program evaluation. And the achievement of goals and objectives worked out through problem analysis can be tested through program evaluation. Measurement is also a fundamental concern in both types of applied studies.

Problem-Oriented Policing

More than an alternative approach to law enforcement, the core of problem-oriented policing is applying problem analysis methods to public safety problems. Problem-oriented policing depends on identifying problems, planning and taking appropriate action, and then assessing whether those actions achieved intended results.

This approach centers on problems, not individual incidents. For example, traditional policing responds to reports of auto thefts, writing up details about the incident to support an insurance claim, then moving on to the next incident. Let's consider this *incident-oriented policing*. In contrast, **problem-oriented policing** would begin by analyzing a number of auto theft reports. Reports would be examined for similarities, such as where and when they occurred, types of autos stolen, whether stolen cars were eventually recovered, and if so in what condition. Such analysis would define a more general problem of auto theft. Subsequent steps would consider what kinds of actions might be taken to address the problem.

A fundamental tool in problem-oriented policing is **problem solving**. As initially defined by Ronald Clarke and John Eck, problem solving involves four analytic steps:

(1) carefully define specific problems …; (2) conduct in-depth analysis to understand their causes; (3) undertake broad searches for solutions to remove these causes and bring about lasting reductions in problems; (4) evaluate how successful these activities have been. (2005, step 7–1)

You can easily see how problem solving merges the application of problem analysis and evaluation (assessment) of the effects of interventions.

Problem-oriented policing is an especially useful example of applied research because a large number of resources are available. We'll briefly describe three types of such resources: how-to-do-it guides, problem and response guides, and case studies. Most of the first two categories have been prepared with support from the Community Oriented Policing Services (COPS) office in the U.S. Department of Justice. Resources are available at the Center for Problem-Oriented Policing website (www.popcenter.org).

How-to-Do-It Guides Ronald Clarke and John Eck (2005) have prepared a general guide to crime analysis to support problem-oriented policing. Adapted from a document originally prepared for the Jill Dando Institute of Crime Science in London, this publication offers succinct guidance on analysis and reporting results. The COPS office has also sponsored guides that provide more detail on different problem analysis tools. Examples include assessment and evaluation (Eck 2003a); applying environmental design principles to prevention (Zahm 2007); interviewing offenders (Decker 2005); and analyzing crime displacement (Guerette 2009).

Crime mapping and other methods of space-based analysis are important tools in problem-oriented policing. *GIS and Crime Mapping* by Spencer Chainey and Jerry Ratcliffe (2005) is an excellent general guide. John Eck and associates (2005) focus on the use of mapping to identify crime hot spots.

Problem and Response Guides In an earlier chapter, we mentioned that justice agencies frequently adopt programs that appear to have been successful in other jurisdictions. While this can sometimes be advisable, a key principle of problem-oriented policing is to base local actions on an understanding of local problems. Instead of trying an off-the-shelf program or so-called "best practice," appropriate interventions should be considered only after analyzing the data.

This principle is evident in two series of guides that describe what is known about effective responses based on past experience. *Problem guides* describe how to analyze very specific types of problems (for example, "Exploitation of Trafficked

Women") and what are known to be effective or ineffective responses to each problem. *Response guides* describe very general kinds of actions that might be undertaken to address different types of problems (for example, "Sting Operations").

Case Studies and Other Research One of the hallmarks of applied research is to use research to change practice. The two groups of guides discussed so far were prepared for use by criminal justice professionals, but they were developed following many years of research. Many examples of research that contributed to changes in justice policy have been published in the series *Crime Prevention Studies*. We now turn to an example that illustrates the application of problem analysis, as well as other research principles presented in this and earlier chapters.

Auto Theft in Chula Vista

Chula Vista is a medium-sized city of just under 200,000 residents, bordered by the Pacific Ocean on the west and sandwiched by San Diego on the north and southwest; the city is about seven miles north of the U.S.–Mexico border. Nanci Plouffe and Rana Sampson (2004) began their analysis of vehicle theft by comparing Chula Vista to other southern California cities. After noting that theft rates tended to increase for cities closer to the border, they began to disaggregate the problem by searching for areas where vehicle thefts and break-ins were concentrated. Deborah Weisel (2003) refers to this as "parsing," or breaking down a large-area measure to examine smaller areas.

Plouffe and Sampson first determined that 10 parking lots accounted for 25 percent of thefts and 20 percent of break-ins in the city. Furthermore, 6 of those 10 lots were also among the top 10 calls-for-service locations in Chula Vista. This meant that auto-theft hot spots also tended to be hot spots for other kinds of incidents. Continuing their analysis, the analysts found some notable patterns:

- Recovery rates for stolen cars and trucks were lower in Chula Vista than in areas to the north.
- Recovery rates in 4 of the 10 hot parking lots were especially low, under 40 percent.

- Smaller pick-up trucks and older Toyota Camrys had even lower recovery rates.
- High-risk lots were close to roads that led to the Mexico border.

Together these findings suggested that many cars stolen from the high-risk areas were being driven into Mexico.

Plouffe and Sampson next moved beyond using existing data from police records. This is again consistent with the methods of problem analysis: use existing data to identify problems and their general features, then collect additional data to better understand the mechanisms of problems. For Plouffe and Sampson that meant conducting environmental surveys of high-risk parking lots, observing operations and interviewing officials at U.S.–Mexico border crossings, and interviewing a small number of individuals arrested for auto theft from target lots. They sought to understand why particular lots were targeted and whether stolen cars could be easily driven into Mexico.

We described environmental surveys in Chapter 9. In conducting theirs, Plouffe and Sampson discovered that the highest-risk lot was a two-minute drive from vehicle entry points into Mexico. The lot served a midrange general shopping mall with typical open parking. Access was easy and thieves could expect that vehicles would be unguarded for some time. Information gathered from the border crossing confirmed that few cars entering Mexico were stopped and vehicle identification documents were rarely requested.

In-person interviews with auto thieves used a 93-item questionnaire, asking about target selection, techniques, and other routines. Thieves preferred older cars because they could be easily stolen—steering column locks wear out and can be broken with simple tools. They watched people entering stores, judged that their vehicle would be unguarded for a time, and then drove the few minutes into Mexico. Cars were rarely stolen from parking garages because thieves would have to produce a ticket in order to exit.

With this and other information, Plouffe and Sampson discussed strategies with Chula Vista police and security staff at parking lots and shopping malls. More diligent screening at the border was rejected, largely because most vehicles had been driven into Mexico before the theft was even discovered. They recommended that high-risk shopping malls install gates at entrance and exit points for parking lots. Drivers would take a ticket upon entering and would have to produce it when leaving. This, it was argued, would substantially increase the effort required to steal vehicles from parking lots near the border.

Other Applications of Problem Analysis

Partly because it has proved helpful in law enforcement applications, problem analysis is being adopted by other criminal justice agencies. Veronica Coleman and associates describe how local and federal prosecutors in several U.S. cities have formed planning teams to identify crime problems and develop appropriate interventions. Teams include U.S. attorneys, researchers, and other criminal justice professionals who pursue a form of problem analysis labeled Strategic Approaches to Community Safety Initiatives (SACSI). SACSI involves five steps, four of which should look familiar (Coleman et al. 1999, 18):

1. Form an interagency working group.
2. Gather information and data about a local crime problem.
3. Design a strategic intervention to tackle the problem.
4. Implement the intervention.
5. Assess and modify the strategy as the data reveal effects.

We have only scratched the surface of problem analysis applications in criminal justice. This is an area of applied research that is growing daily. Other examples draw on methods of systems analysis, operations research, and economics for such purposes as cost-benefit studies, police patrol allocation, and decisions about hiring probation officers. Cost-benefit analysis, in particular, is used to assess the relative value and expense of alternative policies. Although the mathematical tools that form the basis of problem analysis can be sophisticated, the underlying logic is relatively simple. For example, police departments traditionally used pin maps to represent the spatial and temporal concentrations of reported crime.

Space- and Time-Based Analysis

Pin maps are examples of "low-tech" problem analysis that are nonetheless conceptually identical to computer models of hot spots used in many departments to plan police deployment. Growing numbers of justice agencies, especially police and sheriff's departments, have taken advantage of rapid advances in computing and telecommunications. Computerized mapping systems now permit police to monitor changes in crime patterns on a daily or hourly basis and to develop responses accordingly. Furthermore, simultaneous advances in computing power and declines in the cost of that power make it possible for even small agencies to use mapping tools (Santos 2012). The ongoing technological advances in mapping have fueled the application of statistical models to geographic clusters of crime problems. Thomas Rich (1999) describes this as *analytic mapping*, whereby statistical tools supplement the "eyeballing" approach to locating concentrations of crime.

Crime maps usually represent at least four different things: (1) one or more crime types, (2) a space or area, (3) some time period, and (4) some dimension of land use, usually streets. The most useful crime maps will show patterns that can help analysts and police decide what sort of action to take. That's part of applied research. An example will illustrate some basic features of crime maps.

Figure 11.4 shows four crime maps prepared by Shuryo Fujita (2011), for a midsized city in the northeast United States. All four maps show completed auto theft, but for different areas and time periods. The map in panel A shows auto thefts for the year 2005 in one of four police precincts in the city. About 1,750 completed thefts are represented, about 33 percent of all thefts in the city. You will probably notice two things about panel A. First, car theft seems to be everywhere in this area, except

for blank spots in the center and on the right side of the map—a large park and a river, respectively. Second, because car theft seems to be everywhere, the map is not especially useful. Much of the district appears to be a hot spot. Panel B changes the time reference, showing the 30 car thefts that occurred in the first week of August 2005. You might think this is somewhat more useful, showing more theft in the southern part of the district. But while panel A shows too much, panel B shows smaller numbers that don't seem to cluster very much.

Panel C shifts the geographic focus to one sector within the district, to the left of the park. This sector happens to have the highest volume of car theft, 464 completed thefts in 2005; it's the hottest sector in the hottest precinct in the city. Again, car theft seems to be all over the sector. A closer look shows more dots on the longer north-south streets than on cross streets. This is more clear in panel D, which shows a crime density map of the sector. Crime density is a numerical value showing how close some dots are to each other and how distant those clusters are from outlying dots. These values are mapped, showing patterns much more clearly than simple dots. The darker areas of panel D represent more dense concentrations of car theft. There seem to be two corridors of car theft, running north-south below the diagonal street that bisects the map. These corridors are sort of connected in the middle, showing a rough H-shape. This shape happens to correspond with some major thoroughfares in the area. You might be able to imagine cruising up, across, and down, looking for cars to steal. That's useful information a crime analyst can provide for police managers. During the summer months of 2006, police in this city deployed special patrols on the streets within the H-shaped area depicted in panel D.

Tools for mapping crime and other problems are similar to the tools of statistical analysis, a topic we consider in the final chapter. Maps and statistics are most useful when we seek to understand patterns in a large number of observations. Very small police departments that report very few incidents need neither statistical nor geographic analysis to

A. District 2, 2005

B. District 2, 1-7 August 2005

C. Sector 212, 2005

D. Sector 212, 2005 Density

FIGURE 11.4   Mapping Auto Theft

Source: Maps prepared by Shuryo Fujita.

understand crime problems. But departments serving cities like the one in Figure 11.4 can really benefit from space-based analytic tools, such as crime mapping and density analysis.

Computerized crime mapping has been used for many years in a small number of departments and is spreading to many large and midsized cities. Software is more powerful, and web-based mapping programs have been used to make crime maps generally available. More published guides are appearing that describe how to combine maps with other analysis programs and sources of data. Jerry

Ratcliffe (2004) describes how to classify crime concentrations across space and time dimensions to produce a hot spot matrix.

Crime mapping and other types of problem analysis illustrate another advantage of incident-based data—the potential for use in the kind of problem analysis we have described. Most crime mapping and similar tools are developed and used by individual departments, reflecting the fact that crime analysis is based on locally generated data. With incident-based reporting, crime analysis can be conducted on larger units. For example, Steven

Haas and associates (2007) use National Incident-Based Reporting System (NIBRS) data to show that clusters of violent crime in West Virginia are associated with incidents in which illegal guns were seized.

Scientific Realism and Applied Research

Traditional research and evaluation are based on the model of cause and effect we considered in Chapters 3 and 5. An independent variable (cause) produces some change in a dependent variable (effect). Experimental and quasi-experimental designs seek to isolate this causal process from the possible effects of intervening variables. Designs thus try to control for the possible effects of intervening variables.

Problem analysis as we have described it represents a bridge between traditional research approaches and applied research that is the foundation of scientific realism. Ray Pawson and Nick Tilley (1997) propose that, instead of trying to explain cause in a traditional sense, evaluators should search for mechanisms acting in context to explain outcomes. As we have seen, experiments do this by producing pretest statistical equivalence between groups of subjects who receive an intervention and groups of subjects who do not. Quasi-experiments using nonequivalent groups might seek to control intervening variables by holding possible intervening variables constant. So, for example, if we believe that employment status might be an intervening variable in the relationship between arrest and subsequent domestic violence, we will try to structure an evaluation to hold employment status constant between treatment and control groups.

Scientific realism treats employment status as the *context* in which an arrest *mechanism* operates on the *outcome* of repeat domestic violence. Rather than try to control for employment status, a scientific realist will study the mechanism in context and conclude, for example, that arrest is effective in reducing subsequent violence in situations in which an offender is employed but is not effective when the offender is unemployed. This finding will be no different from what Sherman and associates (1992) conclude in their assessment of a series of randomized experiments.

What is different is that the scientific realist approach is rooted in the principle that similar interventions can naturally be expected to have different outcomes in different contexts. Most notably, this approach is more compatible with the realities of evaluation than is the experimental approach. Pawson and Tilley (1997, 81) put it this way: "Ultimately, realist evaluation would be *mechanism-* and *context-driven* rather than program-led" (emphasis in original). This means that interventions should not be designed as comprehensive programs that apply equally in all situations. Instead, interventions should be developed for specific contexts, and evaluations of those interventions must consider context as a key factor in whether the intervention achieves the desired outcome.

Situational crime prevention (Clarke 1997c) is an example of the scientific realist approach that bridges problem analysis and evaluation because it focuses on what mechanisms operate for highly specific types of crime in specific situations. So, for example, rather than develop and evaluate large-scale programs intended to reduce auto theft generally, situational crime prevention seeks specific interventions that will be effective in reducing particular types of auto theft. Ronald Clarke and Patricia Harris (1992) distinguish several types of auto theft by their purposes: joyriding, temporary transportation, resale or stripping, or insurance fraud. Theft of certain models for joyriding may be reduced by modest increases in security, while theft of expensive cars for resale or export requires different approaches. Many types of auto theft can be reduced by placing attendants at the exits of parking garages, but car break-ins may not be affected by that intervention.

As we mentioned in Chapter 5, the realist approach resembles a case-study approach. Both are *variable-oriented* strategies for research—they depend on measures of many variables to understand and assess a small number of cases. Detailed data and information are gathered about specific interventions, often in very small areas. Whereas an experimental evaluation uses probability theory to control for intervening variables, the case-study approach depends on detailed knowledge to understand the context in which mechanisms operate.

In his discussion of applied research tools for problem solving, Eck (2002, 2003b) makes the case even more strongly. Public officials, he argues, are more interested in solving local problems than in identifying robust cause-and-effect relationships. Both problem solving and evaluation are concerned with answering the question "Did the problem decline?" But eliminating alternative explanations for a decline, which is the central concern of internal validity and the rationale for stronger evaluation designs, is important only if officials wish to use the same intervention elsewhere.

In what Eck terms "small-claim, small-area problem solving," analysts develop appropriate interventions for problems in context. This is the essence of the problem-solving process. Like Eck, we emphasize *process*—systematically studying a problem, developing appropriate interventions, and seeing if those interventions have the intended effect. This is quite different from what Eck terms "large-claim interventions"—such as Drug Abuse Resistance Education (DARE) or corrections boot camps—that are developed to apply in a wide variety of settings. Because small-claim, small-scale interventions are tailored to highly specific settings, they cannot easily be transferred intact to different settings. However, the *process* of diagnosing local problems, selecting appropriate interventions, and then assessing the effects of those interventions can

be generally applied. Anthony Braga (2008a) offers more examples of this reasoning. Gloria Laycock presents an even stronger case for scientific realism in applied criminal justice research generally (2002) and in making specific plans for crime prevention (Tilley and Laycock 2002).

Randomized or quasi-experimental evaluations should be conducted when such designs are appropriate. But it is important to recognize the formidable requirements for deploying these designs. The scientific realist approach to evaluation is flexible and may be appropriate in many situations. A scientific realist evaluation or case study can be especially useful in smaller-scale evaluations in which interest centers on solving some particular problem in a specific context more than on finding generalizable scientific truths. In any case, a variety of approaches can satisfy the definition of program evaluation that we discussed earlier in this chapter by systematically applying social science research procedures to an individual program or agency.

Tinus Kruger offers a good example of the strengths of scientific realism in the box, "Participatory Crime Analysis." Kruger and colleagues work with community residents in South African urban townships to learn about crime mechanisms in specific context. Each project produces small-claim interventions to reduce threats to public safety. Reading through this example, you should be reminded of our description of safety audits in Chapter 9. Consider also Amber Horning's discussion of qualitative interviewing in Chapter 8. Finally, consider how Kruger and colleagues combine low-tech community-based data collection with more sophisticated analytic techniques.

 PARTICIPATORY CRIME ANALYSIS

by Tinus Kruger
Council for Scientific and Industrial Research,
Pretoria, South Africa

Participatory crime analysis uses community-based mapping and other tools to identify crime hot spots in

some of South Africa's townships. Large numbers of people live in these low-income communities, often in cramped, substandard housing typically located on the outskirts of large cites. They do not always have access to adequate police services. And in many cases

(continued)

lack adequate water, electricity, and other basic resources found in more affluent communities. Dwellings and streets, particularly in informal settlements, are not always mapped. Violence and other types of crime are serious problems that many community residents face on a daily basis.

In an effort to reduce crime and increase safety, the Council for Scientific and Industrial Research (CSIR) works with partners to systematically analyze problems and develop crime prevention initiatives tailored to community needs. Our approach is grounded in the belief that people know best the places where they live. The CSIR uses a collaborative process, adding analytic skills to local knowledge of problems.

The analysis involves the mapping of crime-related problems, providing a perspective of local spatial dynamics through the eyes of residents. An important objective is to improve relations between residents and local policing structures.

The process is begun in a one-day workshop that involves the following steps.

1. **Crime prevention concepts**. Workshop participants are introduced to the concept of crime prevention, in particular, crime prevention through environmental design (CPTED). Many of the resident community participants have never heard of crime prevention, so this introduction is an import step.
2. **Individual maps**. Community participants draw pictures of areas where they live, indicating the places where they feel unsafe or where they know crime problems are routinely found. The mapping process helps people think about the locations of trouble spots in the community.
3. **Group maps**. Places identified in the drawing, as well as other problem areas, are superimposed on aerial photos or detailed maps.
4. **Site visits**. Workshop participants—community residents and CSIR staff—visit selected areas from these maps, and take photos or videos of the areas. During visits to each place, the problems are described by individual(s) who identified the place.
5. **Analysis**. The photos are reviewed, and photo maps are created. Information about a particular problem spot is organized according to the crimes that occur there, the victims, the offenders, and the characteristics of the place. The area's spatial relationship to the surrounding environment is also considered. For example, how might a particular feature act as a link (or a barrier) between the houses and their surroundings?
6. **Developing responses**. The problem places are prioritized according to certain criteria, such as the types of crime that occur there, whether these crimes constitute priority crimes, whether other role-players, such as the local authority, are required to alleviate the problem. The three or four most critical problem areas are then selected and possible responses are developed. Some responses might involve the community in cutting grass and cleaning up a dangerous open field. Another type of response engages community residents in lobbying the municipality to provide streetlights or to close an illegal liquor outlet.

The development of a possible intervention is a joint exercise for the whole group. It is important for everybody to realize that the solution is often more complex than just identifying someone, usually the police, to blame for not doing their job. Community residents have a stronger sense of empowerment as a result of the process. Police are better able to address crime problems with the information produced by participatory crime analysis.

Source: Adapted from http://www.saferspaces.org.za/be-inspired/entry/mapping-and-spatial-design-for-community-crime-prevention. Accessed August 28, 2014.

Our general advice in planning evaluation and problem analysis is simple: do the best you can. This requires two things: (1) understanding the strengths and limits of social science research procedures, and (2) carefully diagnosing what is needed and what is possible in a particular application. Only by understanding possible methods and program constraints can we properly judge whether any kind of evaluation study is worth undertaking with an experimental, quasi-experimental, or non-experimental design, or whether an evaluation should not be undertaken at all.

THEORY AND APPLIED RESEARCH

Although it may seem that theory has little to contribute to applied research, the opposite is true. Routine activity theory (Cohen and Felson 1979) and crime pattern theory (Brantingham and Brantingham 2009) are frequently cited in problem analysis and evaluation research. Routine activity theory describes a crime triangle in which suitable victims and motivated offenders come together in the absence of capable guardians. Crime pattern theory predicts where crimes will occur by studying where offenders and victims are active, the travel routes that connect them, and the types of facilities where they may come in contact.

Each has played a major role in problem-oriented policing, as illustrated by the large collection of problem guides produced by the Center for Problem-Oriented Policing. By way of illustration, we describe selected features of the guide *Spectator Violence in Stadiums* by Tamara Madensen and John Eck (2008).

Madensen and Eck first consider how three different clusters of characteristics might contribute to spectator violence. Here are examples:

Venue	Staff	Event
Performance proximity	Training	Performer behavior
Noise level	Experience	Alcohol availability
Seating arrangements	Communication	Crowding

Drawing on routine activity theory, the role of each factor in potentially contributing to spectator violence is considered.

Next is a consideration of stakeholders—the people and organizations that have some interest in spectator violence or the things that might contribute to it. This list of stakeholders includes stadium owners, event planners and managers, emergency medical service providers, insurance companies, police, and the community near a stadium.

Problem analysis requires collecting data, so Madensen and Eck describe what kind of information should be collected about victims, locations, and circumstances of violent incidents. After getting a detailed understanding of local problems and settings, appropriate responses are considered and selected. Finally, data are collected to assess the effectiveness of responses.

The guide by Madensen and Eck lays out each of these steps in detail, ending with a summary table that lists responses, how they work, and things to be considered in applying responses to specific stadiums and events. Reviewing this guide, it's easy to see how routine activity theory plays a major role in applied research.

The Political Context of Applied Research

Public policy involves making choices, and that involves politics.

Applied researchers bridge the gap between the body of research knowledge about crime and the practical needs of criminal justice professionals—a process that has potential political, ideological, and ethical problems. In the final section of this chapter, we turn our attention to the context of applied research, describing some of the special problems that can emerge in such studies.

Some similarities are evident between this material and our discussion of ethics in Chapter 2. Although ethics and politics are often closely intertwined, the ethics of criminal justice research focuses on the methods used, whereas political issues are more concerned with the substance and use of research findings. Ethical and political aspects of applied research also differ in that there are no formal codes of accepted political conduct comparable to the codes of ethical conduct we examined earlier. Although some ethical norms have political aspects—for example, not harming subjects relates to protection of civil liberties—no one has developed a set of political norms that can be agreed on by all criminal justice researchers.

Evaluation and Stakeholders

Most applied studies involve multiple stakeholders—people who have a direct or indirect interest in the program or evaluation results (Rossi, Freeman, and Lipsey 1999, 204–205). Some stakeholders may be enthusiastic supporters of an experimental program, others may oppose it, and still others may be neutral. Different stakeholder interests in programs can produce conflicting perspectives on evaluations of those programs.

Emil Posavec and Raymond Carey (2002) describe such problems as dysfunctional attitudes toward program evaluation. Program supporters may have unrealistic expectations that evaluation results will document dramatic success. Conversely, they may worry that negative results will lead to program termination. Agency staff may feel that day-to-day experience in delivering a program imparts a qualitative understanding of its success that cannot be documented by a controlled experiment. Staff and other stakeholders may object that an evaluation consumes scarce resources better spent on actually delivering a program.

We have two bits of advice in dealing with such problems. First, identify program stakeholders, their perspectives on the program, and their likely perspectives on the evaluation. In addition to agency decision makers and staff, stakeholders include program beneficiaries and competitors. For example, store owners in a downtown shopping district might benefit from an experimental program to deploy additional police on foot patrol, whereas people who live in a nearby residential area might argue that additional police should be assigned to their neighborhood.

Second, educate stakeholders about why an evaluation should be conducted. This is best done by explaining that applied research is conducted to determine what works and what does not. The National Institute of Justice (NIJ) and the Office of Community Oriented Policing Services (COPS) have issued brief documents that describe how evaluation can benefit criminal justice agencies by rationalizing their actions (Eck 2003a; Maxfield 2001). Such publications, together with examples of completed evaluations, can be valuable tools for winning the support of stakeholders.

Also keep in mind that applied research is very much a cooperative venture. Accordingly, researchers and program staff are mutual stakeholders in designing and executing evaluations. Evaluators' interest in a strong design that will meet scientific standards must be balanced against the main concern of program sponsors—obtaining information that is useful for developing public policy.

The flip side of being cautious about getting caught in stakeholder conflict is the benefit of applied research in influencing public policy. Evaluation studies can provide support for continuing or expanding successful criminal justice programs or evidence that ineffective programs should be modified or terminated. And problem analysis results can sometimes be used to influence actions by public officials. For an example, see the box titled "When Politics Accommodates Facts," in which Tony Fabelo describes how problem analysis dissuaded Texas legislators from costly, ineffective lawmaking.

WHEN POLITICS ACCOMMODATES FACTS

by Tony Fabelo

The 1994 federal anticrime bill, and related politics emanating from this initiative, put pressure on the states to adopt certain sentencing policies as a condition for receiving federal funds. Among these policies is the adoption of a "three strikes and you're out" provision establishing a no-parole sentence for repeat violent offenders. Facts have prevented a criminal justice operational gridlock in Texas by delineating to policy makers the operational and fiscal impact of

(continued)

broadly drafted policies in this area. Facts established through policy analysis by the Criminal Justice Policy Council (CJPC) have clearly stated that a broad application of the "three strikes and you're out" policy will have a tremendous fiscal impact.

Therefore, state policy makers have carefully drafted policies in this area. For example, during the last legislative session, the adoption of life with no parole for repeat sex offenders was considered. State policy makers, after considering facts presented by the CJPC, adopted a policy that narrowly defined the group of offenders for whom the law is to apply. They also adopted a 35-year minimum sentence that must be served before parole eligibility, rather than a life sentence with no parole. The careful drafting of this policy limited its fiscal impact while still accomplishing the goal of severely punishing the selected group of sex offenders.

Unlike Texas, politics did not accommodate facts in California, where lawmakers adopted a fiscally unsustainable "three strikes and you're out" policy.

For my part, I need to maintain personal integrity and the integrity of the CJPC in defining the facts for policy makers. I have to be judged not only by "objectivity," which is an elusive concept, but by my judgment in synthesizing complex information for policy makers. To do this, I follow and ask my staff to follow these rules:

1. Consider as many perspectives as possible in synthesizing the meaning of information, including the perspectives of those stakeholders who will be affected.
2. State the limits of the facts and identify areas where drawing conclusions is clearly not possible.
3. Consult with your peers to verify methodological assumptions and meet accepted criteria to pass the scrutiny of the scientific community.
4. Provide potential alternative assumptions behind the facts.
5. Set clear expectations for reviewing reports and releasing information so that facts are not perceived as giving advantage to any particular interest group.
6. Judge the bottom-line meaning of the information for policy action based on a frame of reference broader than that of any particular party or constituency.
7. Finally, if the above are followed, never succumb to political pressure to change your judgment. Integrity cannot be compromised even once. In the modern crowded marketplace of information, your audience will judge you first for your motives and then for your technical expertise.

Source: Adapted from Fabelo (1997, 2, 4).

Politics and Objectivity

Politics and ideology can color research in ways even more subtle than those described by Fabelo. You may consider yourself an open-minded and unbiased person who aspires to be an objective criminal justice researcher. However, you may have strong views about different sentencing policies, believing that probation and restitution are to be preferred over long prison sentences. Because there is no conclusive evidence to favor one approach over the other, your beliefs would be perfectly reasonable.

Now, assume that one of the requirements for the course you are taking is to write a proposal for an evaluation project on corrections policy. In all likelihood, you will prepare a proposal to study a probation program rather than, say, a program on the use of portable jails to provide increased detention capacity. That is natural, and certainly legiti-mate, but your own policy preferences will affect the topic you choose.

Ronald Clarke (1997b: 28) describes political objections to applied studies of situational crime prevention: "Conservative politicians regard it as an irrelevant response to the breakdown in morality that has fueled the postwar rise in crime. Those on the left criticize it for neglecting issues of social justice and for being too accepting of the definitions of crime of those in power." By the same token, ELMO is distrusted for being simultaneously too lenient by allowing offenders to do time at home and too close to a technological nightmare by enabling the government to spy on individuals. Evaluations of situational crime prevention or ELMO programs may be criticized for tacitly supporting either soft-on-crime or heavy-handed police state ideologies (Lilly 2006; Nellis 2006).

It is difficult to claim that criminal justice research, either applied or basic, is value-free. Our own beliefs and preferences affect the topics we choose to investigate. Political preferences and ideology may also influence criminal justice research agendas by making funds available for some projects but not others. For example, in 2013, the National Institute of Justice awarded money for projects to study these topics: "Testing Geospatial Predictive Policing Strategies," and "The Impact of Probation/Parole Officer Home Visits on Offender Outcomes." No funds were awarded, however, for such projects as "The Scope of Institutionalized Racism in Drug Arrests" or "Exploratory Research on Torture in Immigrant Detention Camps." It is, of course, possible for researchers—consciously or unconsciously—to become instruments for achieving political or policy objectives in applied research.

It may sometimes seem difficult to maintain an acceptable level of objectivity about or distance from evaluation results in criminal justice research. This task can be further complicated if you have strong views one way or another about a particular program or policy. Researchers who evaluate, say, an experimental program to prevent offenders from repeating probably sincerely hope that the program will work. However, substantially less consensus exists about other criminal justice problems and policies. For example, how do you feel about a project to test the effects of restrictive handgun laws or mandatory jail sentences for abortion protesters?

SUMMARY

- Evaluation research and problem analysis are examples of applied research in criminal justice.

- Different types of evaluation activities correspond to different stages in the policy process—policy planning, process evaluation, and impact evaluation.

- An evaluability assessment may be undertaken as a scouting operation or a preevaluation to determine whether it is possible to evaluate a particular program.

- A careful formulation of the problem, including relevant measurements and criteria of success or failure, is essential in evaluation research.

- Organizations may not have clear statements or ideas about program goals. In such cases, researchers must work with agency staff to formulate mutually acceptable statements of goals before proceeding.

- Evaluation research may use experimental, quasi-experimental, or nonexperimental designs. As in studies with other research purposes, designs that offer the greatest control over experimental conditions are usually preferred.

- The use of randomized field experiments requires careful attention to random assignment, case flow, and treatment integrity.

- Randomized designs cannot be used for evaluations that begin after a new program has been implemented or for full-coverage programs in which it is not possible to withhold an experimental treatment from a control group.

- Process evaluations can be undertaken independently or in connection with an impact assessment. Process evaluations are all but essential for interpreting results from an impact assessment.

- Problem analysis is more of a planning technique. However, problem analysis draws on the same social science research methods used in program evaluation. Many variations on problem analysis are used in applied criminal justice research.

- The scientific realist approach to applied research focuses on mechanisms in context, rather than generalizable causal processes.

- Criminal justice agencies are increasingly using problem analysis tools for tactical and strategic planning. Crime mapping and other space-based procedures are especially useful applied techniques.

- Problem solving, evaluation, and scientific realism have many common elements.

- Evaluation research entails special logistical, ethical, and political problems because it is embedded in the day-to-day events of public policy and real life.

KEY TERMS

evaluation research, p. 280

evidence-based policy, p. 280

evidence generation, p. 280

impact assessment, p. 284

problem analysis, p. 280

problem-oriented policing, p. 298

problem solving, p. 298

process evaluation, p. 284

stakeholders, p. 288

REVIEW QUESTIONS AND EXERCISES

1. In presentations to justice practitioners, Michael Maxfield describes evaluation as answering two questions: "Did you get what you expected?" and "Compared to what?" Discuss how particular sections of this chapter relate to those two questions.

2. When programs do not achieve their expected results, it's due to one of two things: the program was not a good idea to begin with, or it was a good idea but was not implemented properly. Discuss why it is necessary to conduct both a process and an impact evaluation to learn why a program failed.

3. What are the principal advantages and disadvantages of randomized designs for field experiments? Are such designs used in problem analysis? Explain your answer.

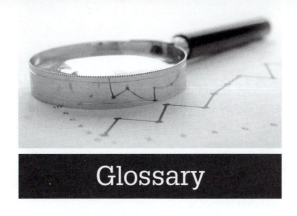

Glossary

aggregates Groups of units—people, prisons, courtrooms, or stolen autos, for example. Although criminal justice professionals are usually most concerned with individual units, social science searches for patterns that are reflected in aggregations of units. For example, a probation officer focuses on probation clients as individuals, whereas a social scientist focuses on groups of probation clients, or aggregates. See Chapter 3.

anonymity The identity of a research subject is not known, and it is therefore impossible to link data about a subject to an individual's name. Anonymity is one tool for addressing the ethical issue of privacy. Compare with *confidentiality*. See Chapter 2.

applied research A type of *explanatory research* purpose (see *explanatory research*) to determine links between justice policy and crime or other problems. Examples include estimating whether prison populations will be reduced from changes in parole standards, or whether requiring steering column locks reduces car theft. See Chapter 1.

attributes Characteristics of persons or things. See Chapter 3. See also *variables*.

audit trail An all-inclusive document of the research process that can include field notes, memos, etc. This record enhances the trustworthiness of research. See Chapter 8.

Belmont Report A publication that proposed three ethical principles to guide the protection of human subjects: respect for persons, beneficence, and justice. Federal regulations for the protection of human subjects are based on this report. See Chapter 2.

bias That quality of a measurement device that tends to result in a misrepresentation of what is being measured in a particular direction. For example, the questionnaire item "Don't you agree that the president is doing a good job?" would be biased in that it would generally encourage more favorable responses. See Chapter 7.

binomial variable A variable that has only two attributes is binomial. *Gender* is an example; it has the attributes *male* and *female*. See Chapter 6.

case-oriented research A research strategy in which many cases are examined to understand a comparatively small number of variables. Examples include experiments (Chapter 5) and surveys (Chapter 7).

case studies A research strategy in which the researcher's attention centers on an in-depth examination of one or a few cases on many dimensions. Case studies can be exploratory, descriptive, or explanatory. Case studies can also be used in evaluation research. See Chapter 5.

classical experiment A research design well suited to inferring cause, the classical experiment involves three major pairs of components: (1) independent and dependent variables, (2) pretesting and posttesting, and (3) experimental and control groups, with subjects randomly assigned to one group or the other. See Chapter 5.

closed-ended question Survey question in which the respondent is asked to select an answer from a list provided by the researcher. Closed-ended questions are especially popular in surveys because they provide a greater uniformity of responses and are more easily analyzed than open-ended questions. See Chapter 7.

cluster samples Multistage samples in which natural groups (clusters) are sampled initially, with the members of each selected group being subsampled afterward. For example, you might select a sample of municipal police departments from a directory, get lists of the police officers at all the selected departments, and then draw samples of officers from each. See Chapter 6.

computer-assisted interviewing (CAI) Survey research by computer in which questionnaires are presented on computer screens instead of paper. In computer-assisted personal interviewing, an interviewer reads items from the computer screen and keys in responses. In computer-assisted self-interviewing, respondents read items (silently) on the screen of a laptop computer and key in their answers. Another variation is audio-assisted self-interviewing, whereby respondents hear questions through headphones, then key in their answers. Both types of self-interviewing are especially useful for sensitive questions, such as those in self-reports. See Chapter 7.

concepts The words or symbols in language that we use to represent mental images. *Crime*, for example, is a concept that represents our mental images of violence and other acts that are prohibited and punished by government. We use conceptual definitions to specify the meaning of concepts. Compare with *conception*. See Chapter 4.

conception The mental images we have that represent our thoughts about things we routinely encounter. We use the word *speeding* (a concept) to represent our mental image (conception) of traveling above the posted speed limit. See Chapter 4.

conceptual definition Defining concepts by using other concepts. Concepts are abstract—the words and symbols that are used to represent mental images of things and ideas. This means that a conceptual definition uses words and symbols to define concepts. In practice, conceptual definitions serve as working definitions of what a researcher means by a concept. A conceptual definition of prior record might be "recorded evidence of one or more convictions for a criminal offense." See Chapter 4. See also *operational definition*.

conceptualization The mental process whereby fuzzy and imprecise notions (concepts) are made more specific and precise. So you want to study fear of crime? What do you mean by fear of crime? Are there different kinds of fear? What are they? See Chapters 1 and 4.

confidence interval The range of values within which a population parameter is estimated to lie. A survey, for instance, may show that 40 percent of a sample favor a ban on handguns. Although the best estimate of the support that exists among all people is also 40 percent, we do not expect it to be exactly that. We might, therefore, compute a confidence interval (for example, from 35 to 45 percent) within which the actual percentage of the population probably lies. Note that it is necessary to specify a confidence level in connection with every confidence interval. See Chapter 6.

confidence levels The estimated probability that a population parameter lies within a given confidence interval. Thus, we might be 95 percent confident that between 35 and 45 percent of all residents of California favor an absolute ban on handguns. See Chapter 6.

confidentiality Researchers know the identity of a research subject but promise not to reveal any information that can be attributed to an individual subject. Anonymity is similar, but sometimes researchers need to know subjects' names to link information from different sources. Assuring confidentiality is one way of meeting our ethical obligation to not harm subjects. See Chapter 2.

construct validity (1) The degree to which a measure relates to other variables as expected within a system of theoretical relationships. See Chapter 4. (2) How well an observed cause-and-effect relationship represents the underlying causal process a researcher is interested in. See Chapters 4 and 5. See also *validity threats*.

content analysis The systematic study of messages and their meaning. Researchers use content analysis to study all forms of communication, including text, pictures, and video recordings. See Chapter 10.

control group In experimentation, a group of subjects to whom no experimental stimulus is administered and who should resemble the experimental group in all other respects. The comparison of the control group and the experimental group at the end of the experiment indicates the effect of the experimental stimulus. See Chapter 5.

criterion-related validity The degree to which a measure relates to some external criterion. For example, the validity of self-report surveys of drug use can be shown by comparing survey responses to laboratory tests for drug use. See Chapter 4.

critical realist perspective A philosophical view that reality exists but knowledge is constructed through multiple meanings. See Chapter 8.

cross-sectional studies Studies based on observations that represent a single point in time. Compare with *longitudinal studies*. See Chapter 3.

deductive reasoning A mode of inquiry using the logical model in which specific expectations of hypotheses are developed on the basis of general principles. Starting from the general principle that all deans are meanies, you might anticipate that your current one won't let you change courses. That anticipation would be the result of deduction. See Chapter 3. See also *inductive reasoning*.

dependent variable The variable assumed to depend on or be caused by another variable (called the independent variable). If you find that sentence length is partly a function of the number of prior arrests, then sentence length is being treated as a dependent variable. See Chapters 3 and 5.

descriptive research A type of research purpose to systematically describe the scope of a subject under study. Annual reports of the number of people under correctional supervision would be an example. See Chapter 1.

dimension A specifiable aspect, or feature, of a concept. See Chapter 4.

disproportionate stratified sampling Deliberately drawing a sample that overrepresents or underrepresents some characteristic of a population. We may do this to ensure that we obtain a sufficient number of uncommon cases in our sample. For example, believing violent crime to be more common in large cities, we might oversample urban residents to obtain a specific number of crime victims. See Chapter 6.

ecological fallacy Erroneously drawing conclusions about individuals based solely on the observation of groups. See Chapter 3.

empirical From experience. Social science is said to be empirical when knowledge is based on what we experience. See Chapter 1.

environmental surveys Structured observations undertaken in the field and recorded on specially designed forms. Note that interview surveys record a respondent's answers to questions, whereas environmental surveys record what an observer sees in the field. For example, a community organization may conduct periodic environmental surveys to monitor neighborhood parks—whether facilities are in good condition, how much litter is present, and what kinds of people use the park. See Chapter 9.

equal probability of selection method (EPSEM) A sample design in which each member of a population has the same chance of being selected in the sample. See Chapter 6.

ethical Conforming to norms and standards embraced by a group or profession. Norms regarding ethical behavior for research on human subjects are often described by professional associations of researchers. See Chapter 2.

ethnography A report on social life that focuses on detailed and accurate description rather than explanation. See Chapters 8 and 9.

evaluation research An example of applied research, evaluation involves assessing the effects of some program or policy action, usually in connection with the goals of that action. Determining whether a sex offender treatment program attained its goal of reducing recidivism by participants would be an example. Compare with *problem analysis*. See Chapter 11.

evidence-based policy Using data and other sources of information to formulate and evaluate justice policy. This usually means planning justice actions based on evidence of need, such as deploying police patrols to crime hot spots. It also includes assessing the results of justice policy, such as measuring any change in recidivism among a group of offenders processed through drug court. See Chapter 11.

evidence generation Collaborative applied research where evaluators and justice professionals build evidence on the effectiveness of community-based interventions. Evidence is then used to manage accountability. See Chapter 11.

experimental group In experimentation, a group of subjects who are exposed to an experimental stimulus. Subjects in the experimental group are normally compared with subjects in a control group to test the effects of the experimental stimulus. See Chapter 5.

explanatory research A type of research purpose that seeks to explain why things happen. This is sometimes referred to as causal research. An example would be research to determine whether increased rates of mortgage foreclosures appear to cause increases in property crime. See Chapter 1.

exploratory research A type of research purpose to learn about the basic nature of a research problem or question about which little is known. For example, a researcher might learn how auto body shops screen out parts removed from stolen cars. See Chapter 1.

external validity Whether a relationship observed in a specific population, at a specific time, and in a specific place would also be observed in other populations, at other times, and in other places. External validity is concerned with generalizability from a relationship observed in one setting to the same relationship in other settings. Replication enhances external validity. See Chapter 5.

face validity The quality of an indicator that makes it seem a reasonable measure of some variable. That sentence length prescribed by law is some indication of crime seriousness seems to make sense without a lot of explanation; it has face validity. See Chapter 4.

focus group Interviews with a group of participants. This format is best for uncovering the perspective of a particular group where group dynamics between group members generate data. See Chapter 8.

generalizability That quality of a research finding that justifies the inference that it represents something more than the specific observations on which it was based. Sometimes this involves the generalization of findings from a sample to a population. Other times it is a matter of concepts: if you are able to discover why people commit burglaries, can you generalize that discovery to other crimes as well? See Chapter 5.

grounded theory A type of inductive theory that is based on (grounded in) field observation. The researcher makes observations in natural settings, then formulates a tentative theory that explains those observations. See Chapter 8.

hypothesis An expectation about the nature of things derived from a theory. It is a statement of something that will be observed in the real world if the theory is correct. See Chapter 3. See also *deductive reasoning*.

hypothesis testing The determination of whether the expectations that a hypothesis represents are indeed found in the real world. See Chapter 3.

idiographic A mode of causal reasoning that seeks detailed understanding of all factors that contribute to a particular phenomenon. Police detectives trying to solve a particular case use the idiographic mode of explanation. Compare with *nomothetic*. See Chapter 3.

impact assessment A type of applied research that seeks to answer the question: "Did a public program have the intended effect on the problem it was meant to address?" If, for example, a new burglary prevention program has the goal of reducing burglary in a particular neighborhood, an impact assessment would try to determine whether burglary was, in fact, reduced as a result

of the new program. Compare with *process evaluation*. See Chapter 11.

incident-based measures Refers to crime measures that express characteristics of individual crime incidents. The FBI Supplementary Homicide Reports are well-known examples, reporting details on each homicide incident. Compare with *summary-based measure*. See Chapter 4.

independent variable An independent variable is presumed to cause or determine a dependent variable. If we discover that police cynicism is partly a function of years of experience, then experience is the independent variable and cynicism is the dependent variable. Note that any given variable might be treated as independent in one part of an analysis and dependent in another part of the analysis. Cynicism might become an independent variable in the explanation of job satisfaction. See Chapters 3 and 5.

inductive reasoning Uses the logical model in which general principles are developed from specific observations. Having noted that teenagers and crime victims are less supportive of police than older people and nonvictims are, you might conclude that people with more direct police contact are less supportive of police and explain why. That would be an example of induction. See Chapter 3. See also *deductive reasoning*.

informed consent Telling research subjects about research goals, procedures, and potential risks before asking them to participate. This standard procedure addresses the norm of voluntary participation, a basic tenet of research ethics. See Chapter 2.

insider/outsider status The researcher's level of closeness to the group of interest, with outsiders having little or no affiliation/relationship to the group. "Insiderness" may be through membership, connection, or similarity to location in the social structure. See Chapter 8.

internal validity Whether observed associations between two (or more) variables are, in fact, causal associations or are due to the effects of some other variable. The internal validity of causal statements may be threatened by an inability to control experimental conditions. See Chapter 5. See also *validity threats*.

Interuniversity Consortium for Political and Social Research (ICPSR) Based at the University of Michigan, ICPSR is an organization that archives and distributes major social science data collections. Most universities and many smaller colleges are member institutions, which gives students and faculty access to vast sources of secondary data. See also the *National Archive of Criminal Justice Data*. See Chapter 10.

interval measures A level of measurement that describes a variable whose attributes are rank ordered and have equal distances between adjacent attributes. The Fahrenheit temperature scale is an example because the distance between 17 and 18 is the same as that between 89 and 90. See Chapter 4. See also *nominal measure, ordinal measure*, and *ratio measure*.

interview schedule The structure of the interview that may have predetermined questions or topical areas to be discussed with participants. It determines how in depth and interactive an interviewer will be during an interview. See Chapter 8.

interview survey Interview surveys use a questionnaire in a systematic way to interview a large number of people. The National Crime Victimization Survey (NCVS) is an example. Interview surveys can be face-to-face, over the telephone, or a mix of these two together with computer-assisted interviewing. See Chapter 7. See also *environmental survey*.

latent content As used in connection with content analysis, this term describes the underlying meaning of communications as distinguished from their manifest content. See Chapter 10.

longitudinal studies A study design that involves the collection of data at different points in time, as contrasted to a cross-sectional study. See Chapter 3.

manifest content In connection with content analysis, the concrete terms contained in a communication, as distinguished from latent content. See Chapter 10.

memoing The act of writing documents about research decisions made, such as adding a question or creating a code, as well as personal feelings about the process. See Chapter 8.

methodology The study of methods used to understand something; the science of finding out. See Chapter 1.

National Archive of Criminal Justice Data (NACJD) A special collection within the Interuniversity Consortium of Political and Social Research, the NACJD includes data series of special interest to criminal justice researchers and practitioners. The NCVS, Uniform Crime Reports (UCR), and data series on correctional populations are included, as are hundreds of other examples of published statistics. The data collection also includes data from most research studies

funded by the National Institute of Justice, something that makes the NACJD an excellent source of secondary data. See also the *Interuniversity Consortium of Political and Social Research*. See Chapter 10.

nominal measures A variable whose attributes have only the characteristics of exhaustiveness and mutual exclusiveness. In other words, a level of measurement describing a variable that has attributes that are merely different, as distinguished from ordinal, interval, or ratio measures. Gender is an example of a nominal measure. See Chapter 4.

nomothetic A mode of causal reasoning that tries to explain a number of similar phenomena or situations. Police crime analysts trying to explain patterns of auto thefts, burglaries, or some other offense use nomothetic reasoning. Compare with *idiographic*. See Chapter 3.

nonprobability sampling A sample selected in some fashion other than those suggested by probability theory. Examples are *purposive, quota*, and *snowball samples*. See Chapter 6.

open-ended question A question for which the respondent is asked to provide his or her own answer. See Chapter 7.

operational definition Specifying what operations should be performed to measure a concept. The operational definition of prior record might be "Consult the county (or state or FBI) criminal history records information system. Count the number of times a person has been convicted of committing a crime." See Chapter 4.

operationalization One step beyond conceptualization. Operationalization is the process of developing operational definitions by describing how actual measurements will be made. See Chapter 1.

ordinal measures A level of measurement that describes a variable whose attributes may be rank ordered along some dimension. An example is socioeconomic status as composed of the attributes high, medium, and low. See Chapter 4. See also *nominal measure, interval measure*, and *ratio measure*.

population All people, things, or other elements we wish to represent. Researchers often study only a subset or sample of a population, then generalize from the people, things, or other elements actually observed to the larger population of all people, things, or elements. See Chapter 6.

population parameter The summary description of a particular variable in the population. For example, if the mean age of all professors at your college is 43.7, then 43.7 is the population parameter for professors' mean age. Compare with *sample statistic* and *sampling distribution*. See Chapter 6.

probabilistic A type of causal reasoning that certain factors make outcomes more or less likely to happen. Having been arrested as a juvenile makes it more likely that someone will be arrested as an adult. See Chapter 3.

probability sampling The general term for a sample selected in accord with probability theory, typically involving some random selection mechanism. Specific types of probability samples include *simple probability sample*, *equal probability of selection method (EPSEM)*, *simple random sample*, and *systematic sample*. See Chapter 6.

problem analysis Using social science research methods to assess the scope and nature of a problem so that one can plan and select actions to address the problem. For example, examining patterns of auto theft to decide what preventive and enforcement strategies should be pursued is an example of problem analysis. Compare with *evaluation research*. See Chapter 11.

problem-oriented policing An approach to policing that depends on analysis to understand patterns of incidents and conditions that police are expected to handle, and then developing responses based on that analysis. It differs from traditional approaches in its focus on patterns rather than individual incidents. See Chapter 11.

problem solving An example of applied research that combines elements of evaluation and policy analysis. Problem-oriented policing makes extensive use of problem solving. See Chapter 11.

process evaluation A type of applied research that seeks to determine whether a public program was implemented as intended. For example, a burglary prevention program might seek to reduce burglaries by having crime prevention officers meet with all residents of some target neighborhood. A process evaluation would determine whether meetings with neighborhood residents were taking place as planned. Compare with *impact assessment*. See Chapter 11.

published statistics Summary data collected by public agencies and routinely made available to the public; sometimes referred to as "administrative data." Agencies are often required to keep and publish such measures. See Chapter 10.

purposive sample A type of nonprobability sample in which you select the units to be observed on the basis of your own judgment about which ones will be best suited to your research purpose. For example, if you were interested in studying community crime prevention groups affiliated with public schools and groups affiliated with religious organizations, you would probably want to select a purposive sample of school- and church-affiliated groups. Most television networks use purposive samples of voting precincts to project winners on election night; precincts that always vote for winners are sampled. See Chapter 6.

qualitative interview Contrasted with survey interviewing, the qualitative interview is based on a set of topics to be discussed in depth rather than based on the use of standardized questions. It's more of a verbal interaction between an interviewer and a participant where the interviewer has a general plan of inquiry. See Chapter 8.

quasi-experiment A research design that includes most, but not all, elements of an experimental design. *Quasi* means "sort of," and a quasi-experiment is sort of an experiment. Two general classes of quasi-experiments are nonequivalent groups and time-series designs. Compare with *classical experiment*. See Chapter 5.

questionnaire A document that contains questions and other types of items designed to solicit information appropriate to analysis. Questionnaires are used primarily in survey research and also in field research. See Chapter 7.

quota sampling A type of nonprobability sample in which units are selected in the sample on the basis of prespecified characteristics, so that the total sample will have the same distribution of characteristics as are assumed to exist in the population being studied. See Chapter 6.

randomization A technique for randomly assigning experimental subjects to experimental groups and control groups. See Chapter 5.

rapport The connection between researchers and participants usually formed through informal conversation. See Chapter 8.

ratio measures A level of measurement that describes a variable whose attributes have all the qualities of nominal, ordinal, and interval measures and in addition are based on a true zero point. Length of prison sentence is an example of a ratio measure. See Chapter 4.

reactivity The problem that the subjects of social research may react to the fact of being studied, thus altering their behavior from what it would have been normally. See Chapters 8 and 9.

reflexivity The researcher's awareness of his or her perspectives (i.e., subjectivity), including his or her personal biases. See Chapter 8.

reliability Consistency of measurement. Measures are reliable if researchers obtain the same results when measuring something more than once. This is not to be confused with validity. See Chapter 4.

replication Repeating a research study to test the findings of an earlier study, often under slightly different conditions or for a different group of subjects. Replication results either support earlier findings or cause us to question the accuracy of an earlier study. See Chapter 1.

respondent A person who provides data for analysis by responding to a survey questionnaire that is self-completed or administered as an interview. See Chapter 7.

response rate The number of people participating in a survey divided by the number selected in the sample, in the form of a percentage. This is also called the completion rate or, in self-administered surveys, the return rate—the percentage of questionnaires sent out that are returned. See Chapter 7.

safety audit A type of environmental survey that focuses on security and safety of places. Safety audits are often combined with interviews or focus groups to measure *perceptions* of safety among people who regularly use specific places. See Chapter 9.

sample element The unit about which information is collected and that provides the basis of analysis. Typically, in survey research, elements are people. Other kinds of units can be the elements for criminal justice research—correctional facilities, gangs, police beats, or court cases. See Chapter 6.

sample statistic The summary description of a particular variable in a sample. For example, if the mean age of a sample of 100 professors on your campus is 41.1, then 41.1 is the sample statistic for professor age. We usually use sample statistics to estimate population parameters. Compare with *sampling distribution*. See Chapter 6.

samples Subsets of a population selected according to one or more criteria. Two general types are probability and nonprobability samples. See Chapter 6.

sampling distribution The range, or array, of sample statistics we would obtain if we drew a very large number of samples from a single population. With random sampling, we expect that the sampling distribution for a particular statistic (mean age, for example) will cluster around the population parameter for mean age.

Furthermore, sampling distributions for larger sample sizes will cluster more tightly around the population parameter. See Chapter 6.

sampling frame The list or quasi-list of units composing a population from which a sample is selected. If the sample is to be representative of the population, it is essential that the sampling frame include all (or nearly all) members of the population. See Chapter 6.

sampling units Like sampling elements, these are things that may be selected in the process of sampling; often, sampling units are people. In some types of sampling, however, we often begin by selecting large groupings of the eventual elements we will analyze. *Sampling units* is a generic term for things that are selected in some stage of sampling but are not necessarily the objects of our ultimate interest. See Chapter 6.

scientific realism An approach to evaluation that studies what's called "local causality." Interest focuses more on how interventions and measures of effect are related in a specific situation. This is different from a more traditional social science interest in finding causal relationships that apply generally to a variety of situations. As explained by Ray Pawson and Nick Tilley (1997), scientific realism is especially useful for evaluating justice programs because it centers on analyzing interventions in local contexts. See Chapters 3 and 11.

secondary analysis A form of research in which the data collected and processed by one researcher are reanalyzed—often for a different purpose—by another. This is especially appropriate in the case of survey data. Data archives are repositories, or libraries, for the storage and distribution of data for secondary analysis. See Chapter 10.

self-report surveys Self-report surveys ask people to tell about crimes they have committed. This method is best for measuring drug use and other so-called victimless crimes. Confidentiality is especially important in self-report surveys. See Chapters 4 and 7.

semi-structured interview An interview that may have standardized questions but allows for unscheduled probes or spontaneous questions. See Chapter 8.

sensitizing concepts A term coined by Herbert Blumer (1954), sensitizing concepts are general references and guides about what to look for in data. They are derived from themes or existing theories. See Chapter 8.

simple random sample A type of probability sample in which the units composing a population are assigned numbers, a set of random numbers is then generated, and the units that have those numbers are included in the sample. Although probability theory and the calculations it provides assume this basic sampling method, it is seldom used for practical reasons. An alternative is the systematic sample (with a random start). See Chapter 6.

snowball sampling A method for drawing a nonprobability sample. Snowball samples are often used in field research. Each person interviewed is asked to suggest additional people for interviewing. See Chapters 6 and 8.

social production of data Referring mostly to agency records, data that reflect organization processes and decision rules in addition to the condition measured. Crime reports and probation records are examples. See Chapter 10.

special populations Regulations concerning human subjects specify juveniles and prisoners as populations that require special protections. Juveniles are considered unable to grant informed consent, just as juveniles are treated differently in most areas of the law. Special rules apply to prisoners because they may feel compelled to participate in research or because participation may be especially desirable. See Chapter 2.

stakeholders Individuals with some interest, or stake, in a specific program. Any particular program may have multiple stakeholders with different interests and goals. See Chapter 11.

standard error A measure of sampling error, the standard error gives us a statistical estimate of how much a member of a sample might differ from the population we are studying, solely by chance. Larger samples usually result in smaller standard errors. See Chapter 6.

statistical conclusion validity Whether we can find covariation among two variables. This is the first of three requirements for causal inference (see Chapter 3 for the other two). If two variables do not vary together (covariation), there cannot be a causal relationship between them. See Chapter 5 for more on statistical conclusion validity.

stratification The grouping of the units composing a population into homogeneous groups (or strata) before sampling. This procedure, which may be used in conjunction with simple random, systematic, or cluster sampling, improves the representativeness of a sample, at least in terms of the stratification variables. See Chapter 6.

structured interview An interview with a set of specific questions and answer choices. See Chapters 7 and 8.

summary-based measure Crime measures that report only total crimes for a jurisdiction or other small area are summary-based measures of crime. The FBI Uniform Crime Reports is one well-known summary measure. Compare with *incident-based measure*. See Chapter 4.

survey A method for collecting data by applying a standard instrument in a systematic way to take measures from a large number of units. See Chapter 7. See also *interview survey* and *environmental survey*.

systematic sampling A method of probability sampling in which units occurring in some specified interval in a list are selected for inclusion in the sample—for example, every 25th student in the college directory of students. Within certain constraints, systematic sampling is a functional equivalent of simple random sampling and is usually easier to do. Typically the first unit is selected at random. See Chapter 6.

themes In grounded theory, themes are higher-level concepts (usually derived from selective codes) that include a group of lower-level concepts (usually from open coding). See Chapter 8.

theory A systematic explanation for the observed facts and laws that relate to a particular aspect of life. For example, routine activities theory (see Cohen and Felson 1979) explains crime as the result of three key elements coming together: a suitable victim, a motivated offender, and the absence of capable guardians. See Chapter 3.

thinking units A term coined by John Lofland and Lyn Lofland (1995) to indicate a simple framework or loose coding device used to make sense of narratives. See Chapter 8.

typology Classifying observations in terms of their attributes. Sometimes referred to as taxonomies, typologies are typically created with nominal variables. For example, a typology of thieves might group them according to the types of cars they steal and the types of locations they search to find targets. See Chapter 4.

units of analysis The "what" or "who" being studied. Units of analysis may be individual people, groupings of people (a juvenile gang), formal organizations (a probation department), or social artifacts (crime reports). See Chapter 3.

unstructured interview An open style of interviewing that is more akin to a conversation, but there may be a list of topical areas for discussion. Compare to *structured interview* and *semi-structured interview*. See Chapters 8.

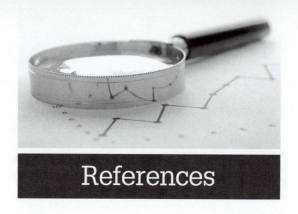

References

Academy of Criminal Justice Sciences. 2000. "Code of Ethics." Greenbelt, MD: Academy of Criminal Justice Sciences. Accessed 19 January 2003. http://www.acjs.org/new_page_13.htm

Adler, Patricia A., and Peter Adler. 2001. "The Reluctant Respondent." In *The Handbook of Interview Research*, eds. J. F. Gubrium and J. Holstein. Thousand Oaks, CA: Sage Publications.

Aebi, Marcelo F., and Antonia Linde. 2012. "Crime Trends in Western Europe According to Official Statistics from 1990 to 2007." In *The International Crime Drop: New Directions in Research*, eds. Jan van Dijk, Andromachi Tslenoi, and Graham Farrell. *Crime Prevention Studies*, vol. 17. London: Palgrave.

American Association of University Professors. 2006. *Protecting Human Beings: Institutional Review Boards and Social Science Research*. AAUP Redbook. Washington, DC: American Association of University Professors. Accessed 18 November 2009. http://www.aaup.org/AAUP/comm/rep/A/humansubs.htm

American Psychological Association. 2010. *Ethical Principles of Psychologists and Code of Conduct*. 2002 Code as amended. Washington, DC: American Psychological Association. Accessed 6 January 2011. http://www.apa.org/ethics/index.aspx

American Society of Criminology. 2014. "Code of Ethics." Columbus, OH: American Society of Criminology. Accessed 1 November 2014. http://asc41.com/ethicspg.html

American Sociological Association. 1999. "Code of Ethics." Washington, DC: American Sociological Association. http://www.asanet.org/galleries/default-file/Code%20of%20Ethics.pdf

Anderson, Craig A., and Brad Bushman. 2002. "The Effects of Media Violence on Society." *Science* 295 (29 March): 2377–79.

Anderson, Elijah. 1999. *Code of the Street: Decency, Violence, and the Moral Life of the City*. New York: Norton.

Andresen, W. Carsten. 2005. *State Police: Discretion and Traffic Enforcement*. Unpublished Ph.D., dissertation. Newark, NJ: School of Criminal Justice, Rutgers University.

Aos, Steve, and Elizabeth Drake. 2013. *Prison, Police, and Programs: Evidence-Based Options That Reduce Crime and Save Money*. (Document No. 13-11-1901.) Olympia, WA: Washington State Institute for Public Policy. http://www.wsipp.wa.gov/

Austin, James, Wendy Naro, and Tony Fabelo. 2007. *Public Safety, Public Spending: Forecasting America's Prison Population 2007-2011*. Philadelphia: Pew Charitable Trusts.

Baker, Al, and Kate Taylor. 2012. "Bloomberg Defends Police's Monitoring of Muslim Students on the Web." *New York Times*, 21 February.

Barnes, J. C., Kevin M. Beaver, and Brian B. Boutwell. 2011. "Examining the Genetic Underpinnings to Moffitt's Developmental Taxonomy: A Behavioral Genetic Analysis." *Criminology* 49(4): 923–54.

Baron, Stephen W., and Timothy F. Hartnagel. 1998. "Street Youth and Criminal Violence." *Journal of Research in Crime and Delinquency* 35(2): 166–92.

Barth, Fredrick. 2002. "Toward a Richer Description and Analysis of Cultural Description." In *Anthropology Beyond Culture*, eds. R. G. Fox and B. J. King. Oxford: Berg.

Baumer, Eric, Janet L. Lauritsen, Richard Rosenfeld, and Richard Wright. 1998. "The Influence of Crack Cocaine on Robbery, Burglary, and Homicide Rates: A Cross-City Longitudinal Analysis." *Journal of Research in Crime and Delinquency* 35(3): 316–40.

Baumer, Terry L., Michael G. Maxfield, and Robert I. Mendelsohn. 1993. "A Comparative Analysis of Three Electronically Monitored Home Detention Programs." *Justice Quarterly* 10(1): 121–42.

Baumer, Terry L., and Robert I. Mendelsohn. 1990. *The Electronic Monitoring on Non-Violent Convicted Felons: An Experiment in Home Detention*. Final report to the National Institute of Justice. Indianapolis, IN: Indiana University, School of Public and Environmental Affairs.

Baumer, Terry L., and Dennis Rosenbaum. 1982. *Combatting Retail Theft: Programs and Strategies*. Boston: Butterworth.

Beauregard, Eric, D. Kim Rossmo, and Jean Proulx. 2007. "A Descriptive Model of the Hunting Process of Serial Sex Offenders: A Rational Choice Perspective." *Journal of Family Violence* 22(6): 449–63.

Beck, Allen J., Marcus Berzofsky, Rachel Caspar, and Christopher Krebs. 2013. *Sexual Victimization in Prisons and Jails Reported by Inmates, 2011-2012*. Washington, DC: U.S. Department of Justice, Office of Justice Programs, Bureau of Justice Statistics.

Becker, Howard. 1963. *Outsiders*. New York: Free Press.

Bench, Lawrence L., and Terry D. Allen. 2003. "Investigating the Stigma of Prison Classification: An Experimental Design." *The Prison Journal* 83(4): 367–82.

Bennett, Trevor, and Katy Holloway. 2005. "Association Between Multiple Drug Use and Crime." *International Journal of Offender Therapy and Comparative Criminology* 49(1): 63–81.

Bennett, Trevor, Katy Holloway, and David Farrington. 2008. "The Statistical Association Between Drug Misuse and Crime: A Meta-Analysis." *Aggression and Violent Behavior* 13(2): 107–18.

Bennis, Jason, Wesley G. Skogan, and Lynn Steiner. 2003. "The 2002 Beat Meeting Observation Study." Community Policing Working Paper No. 26. Evanston, IL: Center for Policy Research, Northwestern University. Accessed 27 April 2003. http://www.northwestern.edu/ipr/publications/policing.html

Benoit, C., and A. Millar. 2001. *Dispelling Myths and Understanding Realities: Working Conditions, Health Status, and Exiting Experiences of Sex Workers* [Short Report]. 2nd ed. Victoria, BC: Prostitutes Empowerment, Education, and Resource Society.

Berenson, Jacqueline A., and Paul S. Appelbaum. 2011. "A Geospatial Analysis of the Impact of Sex Offender Residency Restrictions in Two New York Counties." *Law and Human Behavior* 35(3): 235–46.

Berg, Bruce L. 1998. "A Dramaturgical Look at Interviewing." In *Qualitative Research Methods for the Social Sciences*, ed. Bruce L. Berg. Needham Heights, MA: Allyn and Bacon.

Berk, Richard A., Heather Ladd, Heidi Graziano, and Jong-ho Baek. 2003. "A Randomized Experiment Testing Inmate Classification Systems." *Criminology and Public Policy* 2(2, March): 215–42.

Bernstein, Margaret. 2012. "Signs of Human Trafficking Can Stay Hidden in Plain Sight." *Cleveland Plain Dealer*, 12 February.

Best, Joel. 2008. *Stat-Spotting: A Field Guide to Identifying Dubious Data*. Berkeley, CA: University of California Press.

Best, Samuel L., and Benjamin Radcliff. 2005. *Polling America: An Encyclopedia of Public Opinion, Volume II, P-Z*. Westport, CT: Greenwood Press.

Bichler, Gisela, and Ronald V. Clarke. 1996. "Eliminating Pay Phone Toll Fraud at the Port Authority Bus Terminal in Manhattan." In *Preventing Mass Transit Crime*, ed. Ronald V. Clarke. *Crime Prevention Studies*, vol. 6. Monsey, NY: Criminal Justice Press.

Birks, Melanie, Ysanne Chapman, and Karen Francis. 2008. "Memoing in Qualitative Research." *Journal of Research in Nursing* 12(4): 68–75.

Black, Donald. 1970. "The Production of Crime Rates." *American Sociological Review* 35(4): 733–48.

Black, Michele C., et al. 2011. *The National Intimate Partner and Sexual Violence Survey (NISVS): 2010 Summary Report.* Atlanta, GA: National Center for Injury Prevention and Control, Centers for Disease Control, 21 December.

Blumberg, Stephen J., and Julian V. Luke. 2012. *Wireless Substitution: Early Release Estimates from the National Health Interview Survey, July-December 2011.* Atlanta, GA: Centers for Disease Control and Prevention. http://www.cdc.gov/nchs/data/nhis/earlyrelease/wireless201206.htm

Blumer, Herbert. 1954. "What Is Wrong with Social Theory?" *Journal of the American Sociological Society* 19(1): 3–10.

Blumstein, Alfred, and Richard Rosenfeld. 1998. "Explaining Recent Trends in U.S. Homicide Rates." *Journal of Criminal Law and Criminology* 88(4, summer): 1175–216.

Bolling, Keith, Catherine Grant, and Jeri-Lee Donovan. 2009. *2008-9 British Crime Survey (England and Wales) Technical Report.* Volume I, 2d ed. London: Home Office RDS.

Bouchard, Martin. 2007. "A Capture-Recapture Method to Estimate the Size of Criminal Populations and the Risks of Detection in a Marijuana Cultivation Industry." *Journal of Quantitative Criminology* 23(3): 221–41.

Bourgois, Philippe. 2002. *In Search of Respect: Selling Crack in El Barrio.* Cambridge: Cambridge University Press.

Bowen, Glenn. 2008. "Supporting a Grounded Theory with an Audit Trail." *International Journal of Social Research Methodology* 12(4): 305–16.

Braga, Anthony A. 2008a. *Problem-Oriented Policing and Crime Prevention.* 2d ed. Monsey, NY: Criminal Justice Press.

Braga, Anthony A. 2008b. "Pulling Levers Focused Deterrence Strategies and the Prevention of Gun Homicide." *Journal of Criminal Justice* 36(4): 332–43.

Braga, Anthony A., David M. Kennedy, Elin J. Waring, and Anne Morrison Piehl. 2001. "Problem-Oriented Policing and Youth Violence: An Evaluation of Boston's Operation Ceasefire." *Journal of Research in Crime and Delinquency* 38(3, August): 195–225.

Brantingham, Paul J., and Patricia L. Brantingham. 1984. *Patterns in Crime.* New York: Macmillan.

Brantingham, Paul J., and Patricia L. Brantingham, eds. 1991. *Environmental Criminology.* 2d ed. Prospect Heights, IL: Waveland.

Brantingham, Paul J., and Patricia L. Brantingham. 2009. "Crime Pattern Theory." In *Evaluating Crime Reduction Initiatives,* eds. Johannes Knutsson and Nick Tilley. *Crime Prevention Studies,* vol. 24. Monsey, NY: Criminal Justice Press.

Bratton, William J. 1999. "Great Expectations: How Higher Expectations for Police Departments Can Lead to a Decrease in Crime." In *Measuring What Matters.* Proceedings from the Policing Research Institute Meetings, ed. Robert Langworthy. Washington, DC: U.S. Department of Justice, Office of Justice Programs, National Institute of Justice.

Brotherton, David, and Luis Barrios. 2004. *The Almighty Latin King and Queen Nation.* New York: Columbia University Press.

Brown, Rick, and Ronald V. Clarke. 2004. "Police Intelligence and Theft of Vehicles for Export: Recent U.K. Experience." In *Understanding and Preventing Car Theft,* eds. Michael G. Maxfield and Ronald V. Clarke. *Crime Prevention Studies,* vol. 17. Monsey, NY: Criminal Justice Press.

Burch, Andrea M. 2011. *Arrest-Related Deaths, 2003-2009—Statistical Tables.* Washington, DC: U.S. Department of Justice, Office of Justice Programs, Bureau of Justice Statistics.

Bureau of Justice Assistance. 1993. *A Police Guide to Surveying Citizens and Their Environment.* Washington, DC: U.S. Department of Justice, Office of Justice Programs, Bureau of Justice Assistance. NCJ-143711.

Campbell, Donald T. 2003. "Introduction." In *Case Study Research: Design and Methods.* 3d ed., ed. Robert K. Yin. Thousand Oaks, CA: Sage Publications.

Campbell, Donald T., and Julian Stanley. 1966. *Experimental and Quasi-Experimental Designs for Research.* Chicago: Rand McNally.

Canter, David, and Samantha Hodge. 2000. "Criminals' Mental Maps." In *Atlas of Crime: Mapping the Criminal Landscape,* eds. Linda S. Turnbull and Elaine Halsey Hendrix. Phoenix, AZ: Oryx Press.

Cantor, David, and James P. Lynch. 2005. "Exploring the Effects of Changes in Design on the Analytical Uses of the NCVS Data." *Journal of Quantitative Criminology* 21(3): 293–319.

Cantor, David, and James P. Lynch. 2007. "Addressing the Challenge of Cost and Error in Victimization Surveys: The Potential of New Technologies and New Methods." In *Surveying Crime in the 21st Century*, eds. Mike Hough and Mike Maxfield. *Crime Prevention Studies*, vol. 22. Monsey, NY: Criminal Justice Press.

Cantor, David, et al. 2010. *NCVS Task 4 Report: Summary of Options Relating to Local Area Estimations*. Rockville, MD: Westat. http://bjs.ojp.usdoj.gov/content/pub/pdf/westat_lae_5-19-10.pdf

Carroll, Ray. 2004. "Preventing Vehicle Crime in Australia Through Partnerships and National Collaboration." In *Understanding and Preventing Car Theft*, eds. Michael G. Maxfield and Ronald V. Clarke. *Crime Prevention Studies*, vol. 17. Monsey, NY: Criminal Justice Press.

Carson, E. Ann, and Daniela Golinelli. 2013. *Prisoners in 2012*. BJS Bulletin. Washington, DC: U.S. Department of Justice, Office of Justice Programs, Bureau of Justice Statistics, October.

Center for Urban Pedagogy. 2011. *Field Guide to Federalism: Bushwick, Brooklyn, NY*. Comic book. Brooklyn, NY: Center for Urban Pedagogy, Making Public Policy. http://welcometocup.org/Store?product_id=29

Centers for Disease Control and Prevention. 2014. *Preventing Sexual Violence on College Campuses: Lessons from Research and Practice*. Atlanta, GA: Division of Violence Prevention, Centers for Disease Control and Prevention.

Chaiken, Jan M., and Marcia R. Chaiken. 1982. *Varieties of Criminal Behavior*. Santa Monica, CA: Rand.

Chaiken, Jan M., and Marcia R. Chaiken. 1990. "Drugs and Predatory Crime." In *Crime and Justice: A Review of Research: Vol. 13. Drugs and Crime*, eds. Michael Tonry and James Q. Wilson. Chicago: University of Chicago Press.

Chainey, Spencer, and Jerry Ratcliffe. 2005. *GIS and Crime Mapping*. New York: Wiley.

Chaplin, Rupert, John Flatley, and Kevin Smith. 2011. *Crime in England and Wales 2010/11*. Home Office Statistical Bulletin. London: Research, Development and Statistics Directorate, Home Office.

Chermak, Steven M., and Alexander Weiss. 1997. "The Effects of the Media on Federal Criminal Justice Policy." *Criminal Justice Policy Review* 8(4): 323–41.

Chicago Community Policing Evaluation Consortium. 2003. *Community Policing in Chicago, Years Eight and Nine*. Chicago: Illinois Criminal Justice Information Authority.

Chicago Community Policing Evaluation Consortium. 2004. *Community Policing in Chicago, Year Ten*. Chicago: Illinois Criminal Justice Information Authority.

Chin, Ko-Lin, and James O. Finckenauer. 2012. *Selling Sex Overseas: Chinese Women and the Realities of Prostitution and Global Sex Trafficking*. New York: New York University Press.

Choi, Bernard C. K., and Anita W. P. Pak. 2005. "A Catalog of Biases in Questionnaires." *Preventing Chronic Disease: Public Health Research, Policy, and Practice* 2(1, January): 1–13.

Church, Wesley T., et al. 2008. "The Community Attitudes Toward Sex Offenders Scale: The Development of a Psychometric Assessment Instrument." *Research on Social Work Practice* 18(3): 251–59.

Clarke, Ronald V. 1997a. "Deterring Obscene Phone Callers: The New Jersey Experience." In *Situational Crime Prevention: Successful Case Studies*. 2d ed., ed. Ronald V. Clarke. New York: Harrow and Heston.

Clarke, Ronald V. 1997b. "Introduction." In *Situational Crime Prevention: Successful Case Studies*. 2d ed., ed. Ronald V. Clarke. New York: Harrow and Heston.

Clarke, Ronald V., ed. 1997c. *Situational Crime Prevention: Successful Case Studies*. 2d ed. New York: Harrow and Heston.

Clarke, Ronald V., Stephanie Contre, and Gohar Petrossian. 2010. "Deterrence and Fare Evasion: Results of a Natural Experiment." *Security Journal* 23(1): 5–17.

Clarke, Ronald V., and John Eck. 2005. *Crime Analysis for Problem Solvers in 60 Small Steps*. Washington, DC: U.S. Department of Justice, Office of Community Oriented Policing. http://www.popcenter.org

Clarke, Ronald V., and Patricia M. Harris. 1992. "Auto Theft and Its Prevention." In *Crime and Justice: An Annual Review of Research*, vol. 16, ed. Michael Tonry. Chicago: University of Chicago Press.

Clarke, Ronald V., and Graeme R. Newman. 2006. *Outsmarting the Terrorists*. Westport, CT: Praeger Security International.

Clarke, Ronald V., and Phyllis A. Schultze. 2005. *Researching a Problem*. Tool Guide. Washington, DC: U.S. Department of Justice, Office of Community Oriented Policing Services. http://popcenter.org/Tools/tool-researchingProblem.htm

Cohen, Lawrence E., and Marcus Felson. 1979. "Social Change and Crime Rate Trends: A Routine Activity Approach." *American Sociological Review* 44(4): 588–608.

Coleman, Veronica, et al. 1999. "Using Knowledge and Teamwork to Reduce Crime." *National Institute of Justice Journal*, October, 16–23.

Committee on Science, Engineering, and Public Policy. 2009. *On Being a Scientist: Responsible Conduct in Research*. 3d ed. Washington, DC: National Academy Press.

Conover, Ted. 2000. *Newjack: Guarding Sing Sing*. New York: Random House.

Copes, Heith, Andy Hochstetler, and Michael Cherbonneau. 2012. "Getting the Upper Hand: Scripts for Managing Victim Resistance in Carjackings." *Journal of Research in Crime and Delinquency* 49(May): 249–68.

Corbin, Juliet, and Anselm Strauss. 2007. *Basics of Qualitative Research*. 3d ed. Thousand Oaks, CA: Sage Publications.

Cornish, D. B., and Ronald V. Clarke, eds. 1986. *The Reasoning Criminal: Rational Choice Perspectives on Offending*. New York: Springer-Verlag.

Cullen, Francis T., and Paul Gendreau. 2000. "Assessing Correctional Rehabilitation: Policy, Practice, and Prospects." In *Policies, Processes, and Decisions of the Criminal Justice System*, ed. Julie Horney. *Criminal Justice 2000*, vol. 3. Washington, DC: U.S. Department of Justice, Office of Justice Programs, National Institute of Justice.

Curtis, Ric, and Travis Wendel. 2007. "You're Always Training the Dog: Strategic Interventions to Reconfigure Drug Markets." *Journal of Drug Issues* 37(4): 867–90.

D'Alessio, Stewart J., Lisa Stolzenberg, and W. Clinton Terry. 1999. "'Eyes on the Street': The Impact of Tennessee's Emergency Cellular Telephone Program on Alcohol Related Crashes." *Crime and Delinquency* 45(4): 453–66.

Decker, Scott H. 2005. *Using Offender Interviews to Inform Police Problem Solving*. Problem Solving Tools series.

Washington, DC: U.S. Department of Justice, Office of Community Oriented Policing Services.

Decker, Scott H., and Barrik Van Winkle. 1996. *Life in the Gang: Family, Friends, and Violence*. New York: Cambridge University Press.

Dennis, Michael L. 1990. "Assessing the Validity of Randomized Field Experiments: An Example from Drug Abuse Treatment Research." *Evaluation Review* 14(4): 347–73.

Denzin, Norman K. 1997. *Interpretive Ethnography: Ethnographic Practices for the 21st Century*. Thousand Oaks, CA: Sage Publications.

Devine, Joel A., and James D. Wright. 1993. *The Greatest of Evils: Urban Poverty and the American Underclass*. Hawthorne, NY: Aldine de Gruyter.

Dillman, Don A., Jolene D. Smyth, and Leah Melani Christian. 2014. *Internet, Mail, and Mixed-Mode Surveys: The Tailored Design Method*. 4th ed. New York: Wiley.

Dinkes, Rachel, Emily Forrest Cataldi, Wendy Lin-Kelly, and Thomas D. Snyder. 2007. *Indicators of School Crime and Safety: 2007*. Washington, DC: National Center for Education Statistics, Institute of Education Sciences, U.S. Department of Education, and Bureau of Justice Statistics, Office of Justice Programs, U.S. Department of Justice, December.

Ditton, Jason, and Stephen Farrall. 2007. "The British Crime Survey and the Fear of Crime." In *Surveying Crime in the 21st Century*, eds. Mike Hough and Mike Maxfield. *Crime Prevention Studies*, vol. 22. Monsey, NY: Criminal Justice Press.

Drucker, Peter F. 1973. *Management: Tasks, Responsibilities, Practices*. New York: Harper & Row.

Duneier, Mitchell. 2000. *Sidewalk*. New York: Macmillan.

Eck, John E. 2002. "Learning from Experience in Problem-Oriented Policing and Situational Prevention: The Positive Functions of Weak Evaluations and the Negative Functions of Strong Ones." In *Evaluation for Crime Prevention*, ed. Nick Tilley. *Crime Prevention Studies*, vol. 14. Monsey, NY: Criminal Justice Press.

Eck, John E. 2003a. *Assessing Responses to Problems: An Introductory Guide for Police Problem-Solvers*. Problem-Oriented Guides for Police. Washington, DC: U.S. Department of Justice, Office of Community Oriented Policing Services.

Eck, John E. 2003b. "Police Problems: The Complexity of Problem Theory, Research and Evaluation." In *Problem-Oriented Policing: From Innovation to Mainstream*, ed. Johannes Knutsson. *Crime Prevention Studies*, vol. 15. Monsey, NY: Criminal Justice Press.

Eck, John, et al. 2005. *Mapping Crime: Understanding Hot Spots*. NIJ Special Report. Washington, DC: U.S. Department of Justice, Office of Justice Programs, National Institute of Justice.

Eisenberg, Michael. 1999. *Three Year Recidivism Tracking of Offenders Participating in Substance Abuse Treatment Programs*. Austin, TX: Criminal Justice Policy Council.

Ekici, Niyazi. 2008. *The Dynamics of Terrorist Recruitment: The Case of the Revolutionary People's Liberation Party/Front (DHKP/C) and the Turkish Hezbollah*. Unpublished Ph.D. dissertation. Newark, NJ: School of Criminal Justice, Rutgers University.

Elliott, Delbert S., David Huizinga, and Suzanne S. Ageton. 1985. *Explaining Delinquency and Drug Use*. Thousand Oaks, CA: Sage.

Ely, Margot, et al. 1991. *Doing Qualitative Research: Circles Within Circles*. Philadelphia: Falmer.

Engel, Robin Shepard, et al. 2005. *Project on Police-Citizen Contacts: Year 2 Final Report*. Cincinnati, OH: Criminal Justice Research Center, University of Cincinnati.

Fabelo, Tony. 1995. "What Is Recidivism? How Do You Measure It? What Can It Tell Policy Makers?" *Bulletin from the Executive Director*, number 19. Austin, TX: Criminal Justice Policy Council, November.

Fabelo, Tony. 1997. "The Critical Role of Policy Research in Developing Effective Correctional Policies." *Corrections Management Quarterly* 1(1): 25–31.

Fagan, Jeffrey, Franklin E. Zimring, and June Kim. 1998. "Declining Homicide in New York City: A Tale of Two Trends." *Journal of Criminal Law and Criminology* 88(4, summer): 1277–323.

Farmer, John J. 2009. *The Ground Truth: The Untold Story of America Under Attack on 9/11*. New York: Riverhead Books.

Farrell, Graham, Alan Edmunds, Louise Hobbs, and Gloria Laycock. 2000. *RV Snapshot: UK Policing and Repeat Victimisation*. Crime Reduction Research Series. Policing and Reducing Crime Unit, Paper 5. London: Home Office.

Farrell, Graham, Andromachi Tseloni, Jen Mailley, and Nick Tilley. 2011. "The Crime Drop and the Security Hypothesis." *Journal of Research in Crime and Delinquency* 48(2): 147–75.

Farrington, David P., Trevor H. Bennett, and Brandon C. Welsh. 2007. "The Cambridge Evaluation of the Effects of CCTV on Crime." In *Imagination for Crime Prevention: Essays in Honour of Ken Pease*, eds. Graham Farrell, Kate J. Bowers, Shane D. Johnson, and Michael Townsley. *Crime Prevention Studies*, vol. 21. Monsey, NY: Criminal Justice Press.

Farrington, David P., Patrick A. Langan, Michael Tonry, and Darrick Jolliffe. 2004. "Introduction." In *Cross-National Studies in Crime and Justice*, eds. David P. Farrington, Patrick A. Langan, and Michael Tonry. Washington, DC: U.S. Department of Justice, Office of Justice Programs, Bureau of Justice Statistics.

Farrington, David P., Lloyd E. Ohlin, and James Q. Wilson. 1986. *Understanding and Controlling Crime: Toward a New Research Strategy*. New York: Springer-Verlag.

Federal Bureau of Investigation. 2000. *National Incident-Based Reporting System. Vol. 1: Data Collection Guidelines*. Washington, DC: U.S. Department of Justice, Federal Bureau of Investigation, August.

Federal Bureau of Investigation. 2012. *About Crime in the United States 2012*. Washington, DC: U.S. Department of Justice, Federal Bureau of Investigation. http://www.fbi.gov/about-us/ucr/crime-in-the-u.s/2012

Federal Bureau of Investigation. 2013a. *Crime in the United States 2012*. Washington, DC: U.S. Department of Justice, Federal Bureau of Investigation. http://www.fbi.gov

Federal Bureau of Investigation. 2013b. *National Incident-Based Reporting System (NIBRS) User Manual*. Washington, DC: U.S. Department of Justice, Federal Bureau of Investigation, Crime Statistics Management Unit, Law Enforcement Support Section, August.

Federal Trade Commission. 2014. *Consumer Sentinel Network Data Book for January-December 2013*. Washington, DC: Federal Trade Commission, February. http://www.ftc.gov/system/files/documents/reports/consumer-sentinel-network-data-book-january-december-2013/sentinel-cy2013.pdf

Felson, Marcus, et al. 1996. "Redesigning Hell: Preventing Crime and Disorder at the Port Authority Bus Terminal." In *Preventing Mass Transit Crime*, ed. Ronald V. Clarke. *Crime Prevention Studies*, vol. 6. Monsey, NY: Criminal Justice Press.

Felson, Richard B., Steven F. Messner, Anthony W. Hoskin, and Glenn Deane. 2002. "Reasons for Reporting and Not Reporting Domestic Violence to the Police." *Criminology* 40(3, August): 617–47.

Ferrell, Jeff. 2002. *Tearing Down the Streets: Adventures in Urban Anarchy*. London: Palgrave/MacMillan.

Finn, Peter, and Andrea K. Newlyn. 1993. *Miami's Drug Court: A Different Approach*. Program Focus. Washington, DC: U.S. Department of Justice, Office of Justice Programs, National Institute of Justice.

Flick, Uwe. 2009. *An Introduction to Qualitative Research*. 4th ed. Thousand Oaks, CA: Sage Publications.

Forster, Emma, and Alison McCleery. 1999. "Computer Assisted Personal Interviewing: A Method of Capturing Sensitive Information." *IASSIST Quarterly* 23(2): 26–38. http://iassistdata.org/iq/issue/23/2

Fox, James Alan. 2000. "Demographics and U.S. Homicide." In *The Crime Drop in America*, eds. Alfred Blumstein and Joel Wallman. New York: Cambridge University Press.

Fujita, Shuryo. 2011. *Why Are Older Cars Stolen? Examining Motive, Availability, Location, and Security*. Unpublished Ph.D. dissertation. Newark, NJ: Rutgers University.

Gant, Frances, and Peter Grabosky. 2001. *The Stolen Vehicle Parts Market*. Trends and Issues, no. 215. Canberra, Australia: Australian Institute of Criminology, October.

Geerken, Michael R. 1994. "Rap Sheets in Criminological Research: Considerations and Caveats." *Journal of Quantitative Criminology* 10(1): 3–21.

Geertz, Clifford. 1973. *The Interpretation of Cultures*. New York: Basic Books.

General Accounting Office. 1996. *Content Analysis: A Methodology for Structuring and Analyzing Written Material*. Transfer paper 10.3.1. Washington, DC: U.S. General Accounting Office.

Gill, Martin, and Angela Spriggs. 2005. *Assessing the Impact of CCTV*. Home Office Research Study, 292. London: Her Majesty's Stationery Office.

Gill, Martin, et al. 2005. *Technical Annex: Methods Used in Assessing the Impact of CCTV*. Online Report 17/05. London: Research, Development and Statistics Directorate, Home Office. http://www.homeoffice.gov.uk/rds/onlinepubs1.html

Glaser, Barney G., and Anselm Strauss. 1967. *The Discovery of Grounded Theory*. Chicago: University of Chicago Press.

Goffman, Erving. 1959. *The Presentation of Self in Everyday Life*. New York: Random House.

Gottfredson, Denise C., Stacy S. Najaka, Brook W. Kearly, and Carlos M. Rocha. 2006. "Long-Term Effects of Participation in the Baltimore City Drug Treatment Court: Results from an Experimental Study." *Journal of Experimental Criminology* 2(1): 67–98.

Gottfredson, Michael R., and Travis Hirschi. 1990. *A General Theory of Crime*. Stanford, CA: Stanford University Press.

Graham, Kathryn, and Ross Homel. 2008. *Raising the Bar: Preventing Aggression in and Around Bars and Clubs*. Portland, OR: Willan Publishing.

Greaves, C., A. Spidel, K. Kendrick, B. S. Cooper, and H. F. Herve. "Pimping and Psychopathy." Paper presented at the Annual Meeting of the American Psychology-Law Society, Scottsdale, AZ, March 2004.

Greenwood, Peter. 1975. *The Criminal Investigation Process*. Santa Monica, CA: RAND Corporation.

Guba, Egon G. 1981. "Criteria for Assessing the Trustworthiness of Naturalistic Inquiries." *Educational Communication and Technology* 29(2): 75–91.

Guerette, Rob T. 2009. *Analyzing Crime Displacement and Diffusion*. Problem Solving Tools series. Washington, DC: U.S. Department of Justice, Office of Community Oriented Policing Services.

Guerette, Rob T., and Kate J. Bowers. 2009. "Assessing the Extent of Crime Displacement and Diffusion of Benefits." *Criminology* 47(4): 1331–68.

Gurr, Ted Robert. 1989. "Historical Trends in Violent Crime: Europe and the United States." In *Violence in America: The History of Crime*, ed. Ted Robert Gurr. Thousand Oaks, CA: Sage.

Haas, Stephen M., John P. Jarvis, Eric Jefferis, and Erica Turley. 2007. "Gun Availability and Crime in West Virginia." *Justice Research and Policy* 9(2): 139–60.

Haney, Craig, Curtis Banks, and Philip Zimbardo. 1973. "Interpersonal Dynamics in a Simulated Prison." *International Journal of Criminology and Penology* 1(1): 69–97.

Haninger, Kevin, and Kimberly M. Thompson. 2004. "Content and Ratings of Teen-Rated Video Games." *Journal of the American Medical Association* 291(7, 18 February): 856–65.

Hanmer, Jalna, Sue Griffiths, and David Jerwood. 1999. *Arresting Evidence: Domestic Violence and Repeat Victimisation*. Police Research Series, Paper 104. London: Home Office.

Harocopos, Alex, and Mike Hough. 2005. *Drug Dealing in Open-Air Markets*. Problem-Oriented Guides for Police, no. 31. Washington, DC: U.S. Department of Justice, Office of Community Oriented Policing Services.

Harradine, Sally, Jenny Kodz, Francesca Lemetti, and Bethan Jones. 2004. *Defining and Measuring Anti-Social Behaviour*. Home Office Development and Practice Report 26. London: Home Office Research, Development and Statistics Directorate. http://www.homeoffice.gov.uk/rds/pdfs04/dpr26.pdf

Harris, Kathleen Mullan, and J. Richard Udry. 2014. *National Longitudinal Study of Adolescent Health (Add Health)*. Chapel Hill, NC, and Ann Arbor, MI: Carolina Population Research Center, University of North Carolina-Chapel Hill, Interuniversity Consortium for Political and Social Research. http://doi.org/10.3886/ICPSR21600.v15

Hempel, Carl G. 1952. "Fundamentals of Concept Formation in Empirical Science." In *International Encyclopedia of Unified Science: Foundations of the Unity of Science*. Vol. 2. Chicago: University of Chicago Press.

Hermanowicz, Joseph C. 2002. "The Great Interview: 25 Strategies for Studying People in Bed." *Qualitative Sociology* 25(4): 479–99.

Hesseling, René B. P. 1994. "Displacement: A Review of the Empirical Literature." In *Crime Prevention Studies*, vol. 3, ed. Ronald V. Clarke. Monsey, NY: Criminal Justice Press.

Hirschfield, Alex. 2005. "Analysis for Intervention." In *Handbook of Crime Prevention and Community Safety*, ed. Nick Tilley. Cullompton, Devon: Willan Publishing.

Holstein, Jaber A., and James F. Gubrium. 1995. *The Active Interview*. Thousand Oaks, CA: Sage Publications.

Homel, Ross, and Jeff Clark. 1994. "The Prediction and Prevention of Violence in Pubs and Clubs." In *Crime Prevention Studies*, vol. 3, ed. Ronald V. Clarke. Monsey, NY: Criminal Justice Press.

Homel, Ross, Steve Tomsen, and Jennifer Thommeny. 1992. "Public Drinking and Violence: Not Just an Alcohol Problem." *Journal of Drug Issues* 22(3): 679–97.

Hood-Williams, John, and Tracey Bush. 1995. "Domestic Violence on a London Housing Estate." *Research Bulletin* 37: 11–18.

Hunter, Rosemary S., and Nancy Kilstrom. 1979. "Breaking the Cycle in Abusive Families." *American Journal of Psychiatry* 136(10): 1318–22.

Idaho State Police. 2013. *Crime in Idaho 2012*. Meridian, ID: Idaho State Police, Bureau of Criminal Identification, Uniform Crime Reporting Unit. http://www.isp.idaho.gov/BCI/CrimeInIdaho/CrimeInIdaho2012/Complete%202012%20Crime%20in%20Idaho%20Publication.pdf

Inciardi, James A. 1993. "Some Considerations on the Methods, Dangers, and Ethics of Crack-House Research." Appendix A. In *Women and Crack Cocaine*, eds. James A. Inciardi, Dorothy Lockwood, and Anne E. Pettieger. New York: Macmillan.

Jackson, Peter. 1989. *Maps of Meaning: An Introduction to Cultural Geography*. New York: Routledge.

Jacob, Herbert. 1984. *Using Published Data: Errors and Remedies*. Thousand Oaks, CA: Sage.

Jacobs, Bruce A. 1996. "Crack Dealers' Apprehension Avoidance Techniques: A Case of Restrictive Deterrence." *Justice Quarterly* 13(3): 359–81.

Jacobs, Bruce A. 1999. *Dealing Crack: The Social World of Streetcorner Selling*. Boston: Northeastern University Press.

Jacobs, Bruce A. 2012. "Carjacking and Copresence." *Journal of Research in Crime and Delinquency* 49(May): 471–78.

Jacobs, Bruce A., Volkan Topalli, and Richard Wright. 2003. "Carjacking, Streetlife and Offender Motivation." *British Journal of Criminology* 43(4): 673–88.

Jacques, Scott, and Danielle Reynald. 2012. "The Offenders' Perspective on Prevention: Guarding Against Victimization and Law Enforcement." *Journal of Research in Crime and Delinquency* 49(2): 269–94.

Jacques, Scott, and Richard Wright. 2008. "Intimacy with Outlaws: The Role of Relational Distance in Recruiting, Paying, and Interviewing Underworld Research Participants." *Journal of Research in Crime and Delinquency* 45(February): 22–38.

Jagatic, Tom N., Nathaniel A. Johnson, Markus Jakobsson, and Filippo Menczer. 2007. "Social Phishing." *Communications of the ACM* 50(10): 94–100.

Janis, Irving. 1972. *Victims of Groupthink*. New York: Houghton Mifflin.

Järvinen, Margaretha. 2000. "The Biological Illusion: Constructing Meaning in Qualitative Interviews." *Qualitative Inquiry* 6(3): 370–91.

Jeffery, C. Ray. 1977. *Crime Prevention Through Environmental Design*. 2d ed. Thousand Oaks, CA: Sage.

Johansen, Helle Krogh, and Peter C. Gotzsche. 1999. "Problems in the Design and Reporting of Trials of Antifungal Agents Encountered During Meta-Analysis." *Journal of the American Medical Association* 282(18, 10 November): 1752–59.

Johnson, Bruce, Andrew Golub, and Eloise Dunlap. 2000. "The Rise and Decline of Hard Drugs, Drug Markets, and Violence in Inner-City New York." In *The Crime Drop in America*, eds. Alfred Blumstein and Joel Wallman. New York: Cambridge University Press.

Johnson, Ida M. 1999. "School Violence: The Effectiveness of a School Resource Officer Program in a Southern City." *Journal of Criminal Justice* 27(2): 173–92.

Johnson, Kelly Dedel. 2006. *Witness Intimidation*. Problem-Oriented Guides for Police, no. 42. Washington, DC: U.S. Department of Justice, Office of Community Oriented Policing Services.

Johnson, Shane D., Aiden Sidebottom, and Adam Thorpe. 2008. *Bicycle Theft*. Problem-Oriented Guides for Police, no. 52. Washington, DC: U.S. Department of Justice, Office of Community Oriented Policing Services.

Johnston, Lloyd D., et al. 2014. *Monitoring the Future National Results on Drug Use 1975-2013: Overview, Key Findings on Adolescent Drug Use*. Ann Arbor, MI: Institute for Social Research, University of Michigan.

Jones-Brown, Delores, Jaspreet Gill, and Jennifer Trone. 2010. *Stop, Question & Frisk Practices in New York City: A Primer*. New York: Center on Race, Crime, and Justice, John Jay College of Criminal Justice.

Karmen, Andrew. 2000. *New York Murder Mystery: The True Story Behind the Crime Crash of the 1990s*. New York: New York University Press.

Katz, Jack. 1988. *Seductions of Crime: Moral and Sensual Attractions in Doing Evil*. New York: Basic Books.

Kelling, George L., and William J. Bratton. 1998. "Declining Crime Rates: Insiders' Views of the New York City Story." *Journal of Criminal Law and Criminology* 88(4): 1217–31.

Kelling, George L., Tony Pate, Duane Dieckman, and Charles E. Brown. 1974. *The Kansas City Preventive Patrol Experiment: A Technical Report*. Washington, DC: Police Foundation.

Kennedy, David M. 1998. "Pulling Levers: Getting Deterrence Right." *National Institute of Justice Journal* 236(July): 2–8.

Kennedy, M. A., et al. 2007. "Routes of Recruitment: Pimps' Techniques and Other Circumstances That Lead to Street Prostitution." *Journal of Aggression, Maltreatment, and Trauma* 15(2): 1–19.

Kennet, Joel, and Joseph Gfroerer, eds. 2005. *Evaluating and Improving Methods Used in the National Survey on Drug Use and Health*. Publication no. SMA 03-3768. DHHS Publication No. SMA 05-4044, Methodology Series M-5. Rockville, MD: Office of Applied Studies, Substance Abuse and Mental Health Services Administration. http://oas.samhsa.gov/nsduh/methods.cfm

Kessler, David A. 1999. "The Effects of Community Policing on Complaints Against Officers." *Journal of Quantitative Criminology* 15(3): 333–72.

Killias, Martin. 1993. "Gun Ownership, Suicide and Homicide: An International Perspective." *Canadian Medical Association Journal* 148(10): 1721–25.

Killias, Martin, Marcelo F. Aebi, and Denis Ribeaud. 2000. "Learning Through Controlled Experiments: Community Service and Heroin Prescription in Switzerland." *Crime and Delinquency* 46(2): 233–51.

Kitsuse, John I., and Aaron V. Cicourel. 1963. "A Note on the Uses of Official Statistics." *Social Problems* 11: 131–138.

Kounadi, Ourania, Kate Bowers, and Michael Leitner. 2014. "Crime Mapping On-line: Public Perception of Privacy Issues." *European Journal on Criminal Policy and Research* 5 June. http://link.springer.com/article/10.1007%2Fs10610-014-9248-4

Kreuter, Frauke, Stanley Presser, and Roger Tourangeua. 2008. "Social Desirability Bias in CATI, IVR, and Web Surveys: The Effects of Mode and Question Sensitivity." *Public Opinion Quarterly* 72(5): 847–65.

Krueger, Richard A., and Mary Anne Casey. 2000. *Focus Groups: A Practical Guide for Applied Research*. 3d ed. Thousand Oaks, CA: Sage.

Kubrin, Charis E., and Ronald Weitzer. 2003. "Retaliatory Homicide: Concentrated Disadvantage and Neighborhood Culture." *Social Problems* 50(2): 157–80.

Kurti, Marin K., Klaus von Lampe, and Douglas E. Thompkins. 2013. "The Illegal Cigarette Market in a Socioeconomically Deprived Inner-City Area: The Case of the South Bronx." *Tobacco Control* 22(2): 138–40.

Kvale, Steinar. 1996. *Interviews: An Introduction to Qualitative Research Interviewing*. Thousand Oaks, CA: SAGE Publications.

Lane, Roger. 1989. "On the Social Meaning of Homicide Trends in America." In *Violence in America: The History of Crime*, ed. Ted Robert Gurr. Thousand Oaks, CA: Sage.

Lange, James E., Mark B. Johnson, and Robert B. Voas. 2005. "Testing the Racial Profiling Hypothesis for Seemingly Disparate Traffic Stops on the New Jersey Turnpike." *Justice Quarterly* 22(2): 193–223.

Langton, Lynn, and Matthew Durose. 2013. *Police Behavior During Traffic and Street Stops, 2011*. Special Report. Washington, DC: U.S. Department of Justice, Office of Justice Programs, Bureau of Justice Statistics, April.

Langton, Lynn, and Michael Planty. 2010. *Victims of Identity Theft, 2008*. BJS Special Report. Washington, DC: U.S. Department of Justice, Office of Justice Programs, Bureau of Justice Statistics, November.

Lauritsen, Janet L., and Robin J. Schaum. 2005. *Crime and Victimization in the Three Largest Metropolitan Areas, 1980-98*. Bureau of Justice Statistics Technical Report. Washington, DC: U.S. Department of Justice, Office of Justice Programs, Bureau of Justice Statistics.

La Vigne, Nancy G., Sara Debus-Sherrill, Diana Brazzell, and P. Mitchell Downey. 2011. *Preventing Violence and Sexual Assault in Jail: A Situational Crime Prevention Approach*. Washington, DC: Urban Institute, Justice Policy Center.

Laycock, Gloria. 2002. "Methodological Issues in Working with Policy Advisers and Practitioners." In *Analysis for Crime Prevention*, ed. Nick Tilley. *Crime Prevention Studies*, vol. 13. Monsey, NY: Criminal Justice Press.

Leclerc, Benoit, Richard Wortley, and Stephen Smallbone. 2011. "Getting into the Script of Adult Child Sex Offenders and Mapping Out Situational Prevention Measures." *Journal of Research in Crime and Delinquency* 48(2): 209–37.

Leiber, Michael J., and Jayne M. Stairs. 1999. "Race, Contexts, and the Use of Intake Diversion." *Journal of Research in Crime and Delinquency* 36(1): 56–86.

Lempert, Richard O. 1984. "From the Editor." *Law and Society Review* 18 (2): 505–13.

Levinson, Marc. 2007. *The Box: How the Shipping Container Made the World Smaller and the World Economy Bigger*. Princeton, NJ: Princeton University Press.

Lilly, J. Robert. 2006. "Issues Beyond Empirical EM Reports." *Criminology and Public Policy* 5(1, February): 93–102.

Lineberry, Robert L. 1977. *American Public Policy*. New York: Harper and Row.

Loeber, Rolf, Magda Stouthamer-Loeber, Welmoet van Kammen, and David P. Farrington. 1991. "Initiation, Escalation and Desistance in Juvenile Offending and Their Correlates." *Journal of Criminal Law and Criminology* 82(1): 36–82.

Lofland, John, and Lyn H. Lofland, eds. 1995. *Analyzing Social Settings: A Guide to Qualitative Observation and Analysis, Part 2*. 3d ed. Belmont, CA: Wadsworth.

Lopez, Natalie, and Chris Lukinbeal. 2010. "Comparing Police and Residents' Perceptions of Crime in a Phoenix Neighborhood Using Mental Maps in GIS." *Yearbook of the Association of Pacific Coast Geographers* 72: 33–55.

Lum, Cynthia, et al. 2013. "Discretion and Fairness in Airport Security Screening." *Security Journal* 7 January. http://www.palgrave-journals.com/sj/journal/vaop/ncurrent/full/sj201251a.html

Maass, Dave. 2012. "County Misreports Data About Sexual Violence in Juvenile Jails." *San Diego City Beat*, 25 January.

Macintyre, Stuart, and Ross Homel. 1996. "Danger on the Dance Floor: A Study of the Interior Design, Crowding and Aggression in Nightclubs." In *Policing for Prevention: Reducing Crime, Public Intoxication, and Injury. Crime Prevention Studies*, vol. 7, ed. Ross Homel. Monsey, NY: Criminal Justice Press.

MacKenzie, Doris Layton, Katherine Browning, Stacy B. Skroban, and Douglas A. Smith. 1999. "The Impact of Probation on the Criminal Activities of Offenders." *Journal of Research in Crime and Delinquency* 36(4): 423–53.

MacKenzie, Doris Layton, James W. Shaw, and Voncile B. Gowdy. 1993. *An Evaluation of Shock Incarceration in Louisiana*. Research in Brief. Washington, DC: U.S. Department of Justice, Office of Justice Programs, National Institute of Justice, June.

Madaleno, Isabel Maria. 2010. "How Do Remote Southern Hemisphere Residents Perceive the World? Mental Maps Drawn by East Timorese and Mozambican Islanders." *Scottish Geographical Journal* 126(2): 112–36.

Madensen, Tamara D., and John E. Eck. 2008. *Spectator Violence in Stadiums*. Problem-Oriented Guides for Police, no. 54. Washington, DC: U.S. Department of Justice, Office of Community Oriented Policing Services.

Maher, Lisa. 1997. *Sexed Work: Gender, Race, and Resistance in a Brooklyn Drug Market*. Oxford: Clarendon Press.

Marcus, Anthony, et al. "Is Child to Adult as Victim is to Criminal? Social Policy and Street-Based Sex Work in the USA." *Sexuality Research and Social Policy* 9.2(2012): 153–66.

Marshall, Catherine, and Gretchen B. Rossman. 2006. *Designing Qualitative Research*. 4th ed. Thousand Oaks, CA: Sage.

Marteache, Nerea. 2012. "Deliberative Processes and Attitudes Toward Sex Offenders in Spain." *European Journal of Criminology* 9(2): 159–75.

Martin, Elizabeth. 1999. "Who Knows Who Lives Here? Within-Household Disagreements as a Source of Survey Coverage Error." *Public Opinion Quarterly* 63(2): 220–36.

Marx, Karl. 1880. "Revue Socialist." Reprinted. In *Karl Marx: Selected Writings in Sociology and Social Philosophy*, eds. T. N. Bottomore and Maximilien Rubel. New York: McGraw-Hill.

Mastrofski, Stephen D., and R. Richard Ritti. 1999. "Patterns of Community Policing: A View from Newspapers in the United States." COPS Working Paper no. 2. Washington, DC: U.S. Department of Justice, Office of Community Oriented Policing Services.

Mastrofski, Stephen D., et al. 1998. *Systematic Observation of Public Police: Applying Field Research Methods to Policy Issues*. Research Report. Washington, DC: U.S. Department of Justice, Office of Justice Programs, National Institute of Justice, December.

Matz, David. 2007. "Development and Key Results from the First Two Waves of the Offending Crime and Justice Survey." In *Surveying Crime in the 21st Century*, eds. Mike Hough and Mike Maxfield. *Crime Prevention Studies*, vol. 22. Monsey, NY: Criminal Justice Press.

Maxfield, Michael G. 1999. "The National Incident-Based Reporting System: Research and Policy Applications." *Journal of Quantitative Criminology* 15(2, June): 119–49.

Maxfield, Michael G. 2001. *Guide to Frugal Evaluation for Criminal Justice*. Final report to the National Institute of Justice. Washington, DC: U.S. Department of Justice, Office of Justice Programs, National Institute of Justice. www.ncjrs.org/pdffiles1/nij/187350.pdf

Maxfield, Michael G., and W. Carsten Andresen. 2002. *Evaluation of New Jersey State Police In-Car Mobile Video Recording System*. Final report to the Office of the Attorney General. Newark, NJ: School of Criminal Justice, Rutgers University.

Maxfield, Michael G., and Terry L. Baumer. 1991. "Electronic Monitoring in Marion County Indiana." *Overcrowded Times* 2: 5, 17.

Maxfield, Michael G., and Terry L. Baumer. 1992. "Home Detention with Electronic Monitoring: A Nonexperimental Salvage Evaluation." *Evaluation Review* 16(3): 315–32.

Maxfield, Michael G., and George L. Kelling. 2005. *New Jersey State Police and Stop Data: What Do We Know, What Should We Know, and What Should We Do?* Newark, NJ: Police Institute at Rutgers-Newark, March.

Maxfield, Michael G., and Cathy Spatz Widom. 1996. "The Cycle of Violence: Revisited Six Years Later." *Archives of Pediatrics and Adolescent Medicine* 150(4): 390–95.

Maxfield, Mike, Mike Hough, and Pat Mayhew. 2007. "Surveying Crime in the 21st Century: Summary and Recommendations." In *Surveying Crime in the 21st Century*, eds. Mike Hough and Mike Maxfield. *Crime Prevention Studies*, vol. 22. Monsey, NY: Criminal Justice Press.

Maxwell, Christopher D., Joel H. Garner, and Jeffrey A. Fagan. 2001. *The Effects of Arrest on Intimate Partner Violence: New Evidence from the Spouse Assault Replication Program.* Research in Brief. Washington, DC: U.S. Department of Justice, Office of Justice Programs, National Institute of Justice, July.

Maxwell, Joseph A. 2005. *Qualitative Research Design: An Interactive Approach.* 2d ed. Thousand Oaks, CA: Sage Publications.

Maxwell, Joseph A. 2012. *A Realist Approach for Qualitative Research.* Thousand Oaks, CA: Sage Publications.

Maxwell, Joseph A. 2013. *Qualitative Research Design: An Interactive Approach.* 3d ed. Thousand Oaks, CA: Sage Publications.

Mayhew, Patricia, Ronald V. Clarke, and David Elliott. 1989. "Motorcycle Theft, Helmet Legislation, and Displacement." *Howard Journal* 28(1): 1–8.

Mayor's Office of Operations. 2006. *Evaluating Municipal Services: Scorecard Cleanliness Program.* New York: Mayor's Office of Operations, November.

McCahill, Michael, and Clive Norris. 2003. "Estimating the Extent, Sophistication and Legality of CCTV in London." In *CCTV*, ed. Martin Gill. Leicester: Perpetuity Press.

McCall, George J. 1978. *Observing the Law: Field Methods in the Study of Crime and the Criminal Justice System.* New York: Free Press.

McCleary, Richard. 1992. *Dangerous Men: The Sociology of Parole.* 2d ed. New York: Harrow and Heston.

McCleary, Richard, Barbara C. Nienstedt, and James M. Erven. 1982. "Uniform Crime Reports as Organizational Outcomes: Three Time Series Experiments." *Social Problems* 29(4): 361–72.

McDonald, Douglas C., and Christine Smith. 1989. *Evaluating Drug Control and System Improvement Projects.* Washington, DC: U.S. Department of Justice, Office of Justice Programs, National Institute of Justice.

McKenna, Laura, and Antoinette Pole. 2008. "What Do Bloggers Do: An Average Day on an Average Political Blog." *Public Choice* 134(1–2): 97–108.

Meriam Library. 2010. "Evaluating Information: Applying the CRAAP Test." Chico, CA: California State University. Accessed 13 March 2014. http://www.csuchico.edu/lins/handouts/eval_websites.pdf

Merritt, Nancy, Terry Fain, and Susan Turner. 2006. "Oregon's Get Tough Sentencing Reform: A Lesson in Justice System Adaptation." *Criminology and Public Policy* 5(1, February–March): 5–36.

Messerschmidt, James W. 1993. *Masculinities and Crime.* Baltimore, MD: Rowman and Littlefield.

Miles, Matthew B., and A. Michael Huberman. 1994. *Qualitative Data Analysis.* 2d ed. Thousand Oaks, CA: Sage Publications.

Milgram, Lester. 1965. "Some Conditions of Obedience to Authority." *Human Relations* 18: 57–76.

Mirrlees-Black, Catriona. 1995. "Estimating the Extent of Domestic Violence: Findings from the 1992 BCS." *Research Bulletin* 37: 1–9.

Mirrlees-Black, Catriona. 1999. *Domestic Violence: Findings from a New British Crime Survey Self-Completion Questionnaire.* Home Office Research Study. London: Home Office Research, Development, and Statistics Directorate.

Mitford, Jessica. 1973. *Kind and Usual Punishment: The Prison Business.* New York: Random House.

Monahan, John, et al. 1993. "Ethical and Legal Duties in Conducting Research on Violence: Lessons from the MacArthur Risk Assessment Study." *Violence and Victims* 8(4): 387–96.

Moskos, Peter. 2009. *Cop in the Hood.* Princeton, NJ: Princeton University Press.

Mott, Joy, and Catriona Mirrlees-Black. 1995. *Self-Reported Drug Misuse in England and Wales: Findings from the 1992 British Crime Survey*. Research and Planning Unit Paper 89. London: Home Office.

Murphy, Dean E. 2005. "Arrests Follow Searches in Medical Marijuana Raid." *New York Times*, 23 June.

Natarajan, Mangai. 2012. *Women Police in a Changing Society: Back Door to Equality*. 5th ed. Burlington, VT: Ashgate Publishing.

National Commission for the Protection of Human Subjects of Biomedical and Behavioral Research. 1979. *The Belmont Report: Ethical Principles and Guidelines for the Protection of Human Subjects of Research*. Washington, DC: U.S. Department of Health, Education, and Welfare.

National Commission on Terrorist Attacks upon the United States. 2004. *The 9/11 Commission Report*. Final Report of the National Commission on Terrorist Attacks upon the United States. New York: Norton.

National Institute of Justice. 2014. *Solicitation: Methodological Research to Support NIJs Program of Research Examining Violence and Victimization of American Indian and Alaska Native Youth Eligibility*. Washington, DC: U.S. Department of Justice, Office of Justice Programs, National Institute of Justice. https://ncjrs.gov/pdffiles1/nij/sl001100.pdf

National Research Council. 1996. *The Evaluation of Forensic DNA Evidence*. Washington, DC: National Academy Press.

National Research Council. 2001. *Informing America's Policy on Illegal Drugs: What We Don't Know Keeps Hurting Us*. Committee on Data and Research for Policy on Illegal Drugs, eds. Charles F. Manski, John V. Pepper, and Carol V. Petrie. Washington, DC: National Academy Press.

National Research Council. 2004. *Fairness and Effectiveness in Policing: The Evidence*. Committee to Review Research on Police Policy and Practices. Committee on Law and Justice, Division of Behavioral and Social Sciences, eds. Wesley G. Skogan and Kathleen Frydl. Washington, DC: National Academy Press.

National Research Council. 2009. *Ensuring the Quality, Credibility, and Relevance of U.S. Justice Statistics*. Panel to Review the Programs of the Bureau of Justice Statistics. Committee on National Statistics and Committee on Law and Justice, Division of

Behavioral and Social Sciences, eds. Robert M. Groves and David L. Cork. Washington, DC: National Academy Press.

National Research Council. 2013. *Estimating the Incidence of Rape and Sexual Assault*. Panel on Measuring Rape and Sexual Assault in Bureau of Justice Statistics Household Surveys, eds. Candace Kruttschnitt, William D. Kalsbeek, and Carol C. House. Washington, DC: National Academy Press.

National Security Agency. 2007. *Untangling the Web: A Guide to Internet Research*. Approved for release by NSA 19 April 2013. Redacted. Fort Meade, MD: Center for Digital Content, U.S. National Security Agency. http://www.nsa.gov/public_info/_files/Untangling_the_Web.pdf

National Youth Gang Center. 1999. *1997 Youth Gang Survey*. Washington, DC: U.S. Department of Justice, Office of Justice Programs, Office of Juvenile Justice and Delinquency Prevention, December.

Navgorodoff, Danica. 2010. *I Got Arrested! Now What?* Comic book. Youth Justice Board Center for Court Innovation. Brooklyn, NY: Center for Urban Pedagogy, Making Public Policy. http://welcometocup.org/Store?product_id=14

Nellis, Mike. 2006. "Surveillance, Rehabilitation, and Electronic Monitoring: Getting the Issues Clear." *Criminology and Public Policy* 5(1, February): 103–108.

Newman, Oscar. 1972. *Defensible Space*. New York: Macmillan.

Newman, Oscar. 1996. *Creating Defensible Space*. Washington, DC: U.S. Department of Housing and Urban Development, Office of Policy Development and Research.

Nolan, James J., and Yoshio Akiyama. 1999. "An Analysis of Factors That Affect Law Enforcement Participation in Hate Crime Reporting." *Journal of Contemporary Criminal Justice* 15(1): 111–27.

NOP Market Research Limited. 1985. *1984 British Crime Survey Technical Report*. London: NOP Market Research Limited.

Overall, Chris, Shalendra Singh, and Bhekekhya Gcina. 2008. "Crime Mapping and Analysis: Filling the Gaps." *PositionIT*, May–June.

Painter, Kate. 1996. "The Influence of Street Lighting Improvements on Crime, Fear and Pedestrian Street Use After Dark." *Landscape and Urban Planning* 35(2–3): 193–201.

Paternoster, Raymond, Jean Marie McGloin, Holly Nguyen, and Kyle J. Thomas. 2013. "The Causal Impact of Exposure to Deviant Peers: An Experimental Investigation." *Journal of Research in Crime and Delinquency* 50(4): 476–503.

Paterson, Barbara L., David Gregory, and Sally Thorne. 1999. "A Protocol for Researcher Safety." *Qualitative Health Research* 9(2): 259–69.

Patton, Michael Quinn. 2002. *Qualitative Research and Evaluation Methods.* 3d ed. Thousand Oaks, CA: Sage Publications.

Pawson, Ray, and Nick Tilley. 1997. *Realistic Evaluation.* Thousand Oaks, CA: Sage.

Pease, Ken. 1998. *Repeat Victimisation: Taking Stock.* Crime Prevention and Detection Series, Paper 90. London: Home Office.

Perkins, Craig, and Darrell K. Gilliard. 1992. *National Corrections Reporting Program, 1988.* Washington, DC: U.S. Department of Justice, Office of Justice Programs, Bureau of Justice Statistics.

Perrone, Dina. 2009. *The High Life: Club Kids, Harm and Drug Policy.* Qualitative Studies in Crime and Justice. Monsey, NY: Criminal Justice Press.

Pillow, Wanda S. 2003. "Confession, Catharsis or Cure? Rethinking the Uses of Reflexivity as Methodological Power in Qualitative Research." *The International Journal of Qualitative Research in Education* 16(2): 175–96.

Pires, Stephen, and Ronald V. Clarke. 2011. "Are Parrots Craved? An Analysis of Parrot Poaching in Mexico." *Journal of Research in Crime and Delinquency* 49(1): 122–46.

Plouffe, Nanci, and Rana Sampson. 2004. "Auto Theft and Theft from Autos in Parking Lots in Chula Vista, CA: Crime Analysis for Local and Regional Action." In *Understanding and Preventing Car Theft*, eds. Michael G. Maxfield and Ronald V. Clarke. *Crime Prevention Studies*, vol. 17. Monsey, NY: Criminal Justice Press.

Poklemba, John J. 1988. *Measurement Issues in Prison and Jail Overcrowding.* Albany, NY: New York Division of Criminal Justice Services, Criminal Justice Information Systems Improvement Program.

Pollock, Jocelyn M. 2012. *Ethics in Crime and Justice: Dilemmas and Decisions.* 7th ed. Belmont, CA: Cengage Learning.

Posavec, Emil J., and Raymond G. Carey. 2002. *Program Evaluation: Methods and Case Studies.* 6th ed. Englewood Cliffs, NJ: Prentice Hall.

Pösö, Tarja, Päivi Honkatukia, and Leo Nyqvist. 2008. "Focus Groups and the Study of Violence." *Qualitative Research* 8(1): 73–89.

President's Commission on Law Enforcement and Administration of Justice. 1967. *The Challenge of Crime in a Free Society.* Washington, DC: U.S. Government Printing Office.

Pudney, Stephen. 2002. *The Road to Ruin? Sequences of Initiation into Drug Use and Offending by Young People in Britain.* Home Office Research Study, 253. London: Her Majesty's Stationery Office. http://www.crimereduction.gov.uk/drugsalcohol62.htm

Quade, Edward S. 1989. *Policy Analysis for Public Decisions.* 3d ed. Rev. Grace M. Carter. New York: North-Holland.

Ragin, Charles C. 2000. *Fuzzy-Set Social Science.* Chicago: University of Chicago Press.

Rajah, Valli. 2010. "Intimacy, Time, and Scarcity: Drug-Involved Women Account for Secretly Withholding Financial Capital in Violent Intimate Relationships." *Journal of Contemporary Ethnography* 39(2): 131–58.

Ramsay, Malcolm, and Sarah Partridge. 1999. *Drug Misuse Declared in 1998: Results from the British Crime Survey.* Home Office Research Study, 197. London: Her Majesty's Stationery Office.

Ramsay, Malcolm, et al. 2001. *Drug Misuse Declared in 2000: Results from the British Crime Survey.* Home Office Research Study, 224. London: Her Majesty's Stationery Office.

Rand, Michael R., and Callie M. Rennison. 2005. "Bigger Is Not Necessarily Better: An Analysis of Violence Against Women Estimates from the National Crime Victimization Survey and the National Violence Against Women Survey." *Journal of Quantitative Criminology* 21(3): 267–91.

Rasinski, Kenneth A. 1989. "The Effect of Question Wording on Public Support for Government Spending." *Public Opinion Quarterly* 53(3): 388–94.

Ratcliffe, Jerry H. 2004. "The Hotspot Matrix: A Framework for the Spatio-Temporal Targeting of Crime Reduction." *Police Practice and Research* 5(1): 5–23.

Ratcliffe, Jerry H., et al. 2011. "The Philadelphia Foot Patrol Experiment: A Randomized Controlled Trial of Police Patrol Effectiveness in Violent Crime Hotspots." *Criminology* 49(3): 795–831.

Rebellon, Cesar J., and Karen Van Gundy. 2005. "Can Control Theory Explain the Link Between Parental Physical Abuse and Delinquency? A Longitudinal Analysis." *Journal of Research in Crime and Delinquency* 42(3): 247–74.

Rengert, George F., Alex R. Piquero, and Peter R. Jones. 1999. "Distance Decay Reexamined." *Criminology* 37(2): 427–45.

Reuter, Peter, Robert MacCoun, and Patrick Murphy. 1990. *Money from Crime: A Study of the Economics of Drug Dealing in Washington, D.C.* Santa Monica, CA: Rand.

Reynolds, Paul D. 1979. *Ethical Dilemmas and Social Research.* San Francisco, CA: Jossey-Bass.

Rich, Thomas F. 1999. "Mapping the Path to Problem Solving." *National Institute of Justice Journal*, October.

Roberts, James C. 2002. *Serving up Trouble in the Barroom Environment.* Unpublished Ph.D. dissertation, Rutgers University School of Criminal Justice. Newark, NJ: School of Criminal Justice, Rutgers University.

Roberts, James C. 2007. "Barroom Aggression in Hoboken, New Jersey: Don't Blame the Bouncers." *Journal of Drug Education* 37(4): 429–45.

Roberts, Jennifer, et al. 2005. "A Test of Two Models of Recall for Violent Events." *Journal of Quantitative Criminology* 21(2): 175–93.

Rosenfeld, Richard. 2000. "Patterns in Adult Homicide: 1980-1995." In *The Crime Drop in America*, eds. Alfred Blumstein and Joel Wallman. New York: Cambridge University Press.

Rosenfeld, Richard, Timothy M. Bray, and Arlen Egley. 1999. "Facilitating Violence: A Comparison of Gang-Motivated, Gang-Affiliated, and Nongang Youth Homicides." *Journal of Quantitative Criminology* 15(4): 495–516.

Rossi, Peter H., Howard E. Freeman, and Mark W. Lipsey. 1999. *Evaluation: A Systematic Approach.* 6th ed. Thousand Oaks, CA: Sage.

Roth, Andrea. 2010. "Database-Driven Investigations: The Promise—and Peril—of Using Forensics to Solve 'No-Suspect' Cases." *Criminology and Public Policy* 9(2): 421–28.

Rubin, Herbert J., and Irene S. Rubin. 2011. *Qualitative Interviewing: The Art of Hearing.* 3d ed. Thousand Oaks, CA: Sage Publications.

Ryan, Gery W., and H. Russell Bernard. 2003. "Techniques to Identify Themes." *Field Methods* 15(1): 85–109.

Sampson, Robert J., and John H. Laub. 1993. *Crime in the Making: Pathways and Turning Points Through Life.* Cambridge, MA: Harvard University Press.

Sampson, Robert J., and John H. Laub. 2005. "A Life-Course View of the Development of Crime." *The Annals* 602(1): 12–45.

Sampson, Robert J., and Stephen W. Raudenbush. 1999. "Systematic Social Observation of Public Spaces: A New Look at Disorder in Urban Neighborhoods." *American Journal of Sociology* 105(3, November): 603–51.

Sanders, T. 2001. "Female Street Sex Workers, Sexual Violence, and Protection Strategies. " *Journal of Sexual Aggression*, 7: 5–8.

Santos, Rachel Boba. 2012. *Crime Analysis with Crime Mapping.* 3d ed. Thousand Oaks, CA: Sage.

Sauer, Carl. 1925. "The Morphology of Landscape." *University of California Publications in Geography* 2: 19–54.

Schuck, Amie M., and Cathy Spatz Widom. 2001. "Childhood Victimization and Alcohol Symptoms in Females: Causal Inferences and Hypothesized Mediators." *Child Abuse and Neglect* 25(8): 1069–92.

Seidman, David, and Michael Couzens. 1974. "Getting the Crime Rate Down: Political Pressure and Crime Reporting." *Law and Society Review* 8(3): 457–93.

Semaan, Salaam, Jennifer Lauby, and Jon Liebman. 2002. "Street and Network Sampling in Evaluation Studies of HIV Risk-Reduction Interventions." *AIDS Reviews* 4(4): 213–23.

Shadish, William R., Thomas D. Cook, and Donald T. Campbell. 2002. *Experimental and Quasi-Experimental Designs for Generalized Causal Inference.* Boston: Houghton Mifflin.

Shane, Jon. 2012. *Abandoned Buildings and Lots.* Problem-Oriented Guides for Police, no. 64. Washington, DC: U.S. Department of Justice, Office of Community Oriented Policing Services.

Shearing, Clifford D., and Phillip C. Stenning. 1992. "From the Panopticon to Disney World: The Development of Discipline." In *Situational Crime Prevention: Successful Case Studies*, ed. Ronald V. Clarke. New York: Harrow and Heston.

Shepard, Steven. 2012. "The Presidential Polls Were Right After All—but the Argument Continues." *National Journal*, 8 November.

Sherman, Lawrence W. 1992a. "The Influence of Criminology on Criminal Law: Evaluating Arrests for Misdemeanor Domestic Violence." *Journal of Criminal Law and Criminology* 83(1): 1–45.

Sherman, Lawrence W. 1992b. *Policing Domestic Violence: Experiments and Dilemmas*. New York: Free Press.

Sherman, Lawrence W. 1995. "Hot Spots of Crime and Criminal Careers of Places." In *Crime and Place*, eds. John E. Eck and David Weisburd. *Crime Prevention Studies*, vol. 4. Monsey, NY: Criminal Justice Press.

Sherman, Lawrence W., and Richard A. Berk. 1984. *The Minneapolis Domestic Violence Experiment*. Washington, DC: Police Foundation.

Sherman, Lawrence W., and Ellen G. Cohn 1989. "The Impact of Research on Legal Policy: The Minneapolis Domestic Violence Experiment." *Law and Society Review* 23(1): 117–44.

Sherman, Lawrence W., James W. Shaw, and Dennis P. Rogan. 1995. *The Kansas City Gun Experiment*. Research in Brief. Washington, DC: U.S. Department of Justice, Office of Justice Programs, National Institute of Justice, January.

Sherman, Lawrence W., et al. 1992. "The Variable Effects of Arrest on Criminal Careers: The Milwaukee Domestic Violence Experiment." *Journal of Criminal Law and Criminology* 83(1): 137–69.

Shweder, Richard A. 2006. "Protecting Human Subjects and Preserving Academic Freedom." *American Ethnologist* 33(4, November): 507–18.

Sieber, J. E. 2001. *Summary of Human Subjects Protection Issues Related to Large Sample Surveys*. Washington, DC: U.S. Department of Justice, Office of Justice Programs, Bureau of Justice Statistics, June.

Silberman School of Social Work. 2013. *Shadow Count 2014*. Flyer to recruit decoys. New York: Silberman School of Social Work, Hunter College, City University of New York, 2013. Accessed 12 June 2013. http://www.hunter.cuny.edu/socwork/shadow_count/Flyer_SC_14.pdf

Silbert, M. H., and A. M. Pines. 1981. "Occupational Hazards of Street Prostitutes." *Justice and Behavior*, 8: 395–399.

Silver, Nate. 2012. "Google or Gallup? Changes in Voters' Habits Reshape Polling World." *New York Times*, 11 November.

Silverman, Eli B. 1999. *NYPD Battles Crime: Innovative Strategies in Policing*. Boston: Northeastern University Press.

Sinauer, Nancy, et al. 1999. "Comparisons Among Female Homicides Occurring in Rural, Intermediate, and Urban Counties in North Carolina." *Homicide Studies* 3(2): 107–28.

Skogan, Wesley G. 1985. *Evaluating Neighborhood Crime Prevention Programs*. The Hague, Netherlands: Ministry of Justice, Research and Documentation Centre.

Skogan, Wesley G. 1990a. *Disorder and Decline: Crime and the Spiral of Decay in American Neighborhoods*. New York: Free Press.

Skogan, Wesley G. 1990b. *The Police and the Public in England and Wales*. Home Office Research Study, 117. London: Her Majesty's Stationery Office.

Skogan, Wesley G., Susan M. Hartnett, Natalie Bump, and Jill Dubois. 2008. Evaluation of CeaseFire-Chicago. Assisted by Ryan Hollon and Danielle Morris. Evanston, IL: Center for Policy Research, Northwestern University. http://www.ipr.northwestern.edu/publications/papers/urban-policy-and-community-development/docs/ceasefire-pdfs/executivesummary.pdf

Skogan, Wesley G., and Michael G. Maxfield. 1981. *Coping with Crime: Individual and Neighborhood Reactions*. Thousand Oaks, CA: Sage.

Smith, Kevin, and Jacqueline Hoare. 2009. *Crime in England and Wales 2008/09. Volume 2: Explanatory Notes and Classifications*. Home Office Statistical Bulletin. London: Research, Development and Statistics Directorate, Home Office.

Smith, Steven K., Greg W. Steadman, Todd D. Minton, and Meg Townsend. 1999. *Criminal Victimization and Perceptions of Community Safety in 12 Cities, 1998*. Washington, DC: U.S. Department of Justice, Office of Justice Programs, Bureau of Justice Statistics and Office of Community Oriented Police Services, June.

Smith, William R., et al. 2003. *The North Carolina Highway Traffic Study*. Final report to the National Institute of Justice. With Harvey McMurray and C. Robert Fenlon. Raleigh, NC: North Carolina State University, 21 July.

Sommers, Samuel R., et al. 2006. "Race and Media Coverage of Hurricane Katrina: Analysis, Implications, and Future Research Questions." *Analyses of Social Issues and Public Policy* 6(1): 39–55.

Spelman, William. 2000. "The Limited Importance of Prison Expansion." In *The Crime Drop in America*, eds. Alfred Blumstein and Joel Wallman. New York: Cambridge University Press.

Spriggs, Angela, Javier Argomaniz, Martin Gill, and Jane Bryan. 2005. *Public Attitudes Towards CCTV: Results from the Pre-Intervention Public Attitude Survey Carried Out in Areas Implementing CCTV*. Online Report 10/05. London: Research, Development and Statistics Directorate, Home Office. http://www.homeoffice.gov.uk/rds/onlinepubs1.html

Stecher, Brian M., and W. Alan Davis. 1987. *How to Focus an Evaluation*. Thousand Oaks, CA: Sage Publications.

Steinhauer, Jennifer. 2014. "Behind Focus on College Assaults, a Steady Drumbeat by Students." *New York Times*, 29 April.

Straus, Murray A. 1999. "The Controversy over Domestic Violence by Women: A Methodological, Theoretical, and Sociology of Science Analysis." In *Violence in Intimate Relationships*, eds. Ximena Arriaga and Stuart Oskamp. Thousand Oaks, CA: Sage Publications.

Strauss, Anselm, and Juliet Corbin. 1990. *Basics of Qualitative Research: Grounded Theory Procedures and Techniques*. London: Sage Publications.

Strauss, Anselm, and Juliet Corbin. 1994. "Grounded Theory Methodology: An Overview." In *Handbook of Qualitative Research*, eds. Norman K. Denzin and Yvonne S. Lincoln. Thousand Oaks, CA: Sage Publications.

Substance Abuse and Mental Health Services Administration. 2013. *Results from the 2012 National Survey of Drug Use and Health: Summary of National Findings*. NSDUH Series H-46, HHS Publication No. SMA 13-4795. Rockville, MD: Substance Abuse and Mental Health Services Administration. http://www.oas.samhsa.gov/

Surette, Ray. 2006. *Media, Crime, and Justice: Images, Realities and Policies*. 3d ed. Belmont, CA: Wadsworth.

Sutterlüty, Ferdinand. 2007. "The Genesis of Violent Careers." *Ethnography* 8(3): 267–96.

Sutton, Mike. 2007. "Improving National Crime Surveys with a Focus on Fraud, High-Tech Crimes, and Stolen Goods." In *Surveying Crime in the 21st Century*, eds. Mike Hough and Mike Maxfield. *Crime Prevention Studies*, vol. 22. Monsey, NY: Criminal Justice Press.

Taxman, Faye S., and Lori Elis. 1999. "Expediting Court Dispositions: Quick Results, Uncertain Outcomes." *Journal of Research in Crime and Delinquency* 36(1): 30–55.

Taylor, Ralph B. 2001. *Breaking Away from Broken Windows: Baltimore Neighborhoods and the Nationwide Fight Against Crime, Grime, Fear, and Decline*. Boulder, CO: Westview Press.

Thompson, Kimberly M., and Kevin Haninger. 2001. "Violence in E-Rated Video Games." *Journal of the American Medical Association* 286(5, 1 August): 591–98.

Thompson, Steven K. 1997. *Adaptive Sampling in Behavioral Surveys*. NIDA Monograph no. 167. Bethesda, MD: U.S. Department of Health and Human Services, National Institute of Drug Abuse.

Tilley, Nick, and Gloria Laycock. 2002. *Working out What to Do: Evidence-Based Crime Reduction*. Crime Reduction Research Series, paper 11. London: Home Office, Policing and Reducing Crime Unit, Research, Development and Statistics Directorate.

Tillyer, Marie Skubak, and Emily M. Wright. 2014. "Intimate Partner Violence and the Victim-Offender Overlap." *Journal of Research in Crime and Delinquency* 51(1): 29–55.

Tjaden, Patricia, and Nancy Thoennes. 2000. *Full Report of the Prevalence, Incidence, and Consequences of Violence Against Women*. Findings from the National Violence Against Women Survey. Research Report. Washington, DC: U.S. Department of Justice, Office of Justice Programs, National Institute of Justice, November.

Tourangeau, Roger. 2004. "Survey Research and Societal Change." *Annual Review of Psychology* 55(2): 775–801.

Townsley, Michael, Ross Homel, and Janet Chaseling. 2003. "Infectious Burglaries: A Test of the Near Repeat Hypothesis." *British Journal of Criminology* 43(3): 615–33.

Tremblay, Pierre, Bernard Talon, and Doug Hurley. 2001. "Body Switching and Related Adaptations in the Resale of Stolen Vehicles." *British Journal of Criminology* 41(4): 561–79.

Truman, Jennifer L., and Rachel E. Morgan. 2014. *Nonfatal Domestic Violence, 2003-2012.* BJS Special Report. Washington, DC: U.S. Department of Justice, Office of Justice Programs, Bureau of Justice Statistics, May.

Truman, Jennifer L., and Michael Planty. 2012. *Criminal Victimization, 2011.* Washington, DC: U.S. Department of Justice, Office of Justice Programs, Bureau of Justice Statistics. http://www.bjs.ojp.usdoj.gov/content/pub/cv11.pdf

United States Sentencing Commission. 2014. *Amendments to the Sentencing Guidelines.* Washington, DC: United States Sentencing Commission.

University of California Berkeley Library. 2014. *Evaluating Web Pages: Techniques to Apply and Questions to Ask.* Online tutorial. Berkeley, CA: UC Berkeley Teaching Library. http://www.lib.berkeley.edu/TeachingLib/Guides/Internet/FindInfo.html

van Dijk, Jan. 2007. "The International Crime Victims Survey and Complementary Measures of Corruption and Organised Crime." In *Surveying Crime in the 21st Century*, eds. Mike Hough and Mike Maxfield. *Crime Prevention Studies*, vol. 22. Monsey, NY: Criminal Justice Press.

Venkatesh, Sudhir. 2006. *Off the Books: The Underground Economy of the Urban Poor.* Cambridge, MA: Harvard University Press.

Venkatesh, Sudhir. 2011. "How Tech Tools Transformed New York's Sex Trade." *Wired* 19.02 (January).

Van Kirk, Marvin. 1977. *Response Time Analysis.* Washington, DC: U.S. Department of Justice, National Institute of Law Enforcement and Administration of Justice.

Voas, Robert B., Eduardo Romano, and Raymond Peck. 2009. "Validity of Surrogate Measures of Alcohol Involvement when Applied to Nonfatal Crashes." *Accident Analysis and Prevention* 41(3): 522–30.

Walker, Samuel. 1994. *Sense and Nonsense About Crime and Drugs: A Policy Guide.* 3d ed. Belmont, CA: Wadsworth.

Wallace, Aurora. 2009. "Mapping City Crime and the New Aesthetic of Danger." *Journal of Visual Culture* 8(1): 5–24.

Walsh, Christine A., et al. 2008. "Measurement of Victimization in Adolescence: Development and Validation of the Childhood Experiences of Violence Questionnaire." *Child Abuse and Neglect* 32(11): 1037–57.

Weisburd, David, Anthony Petrosino, and Gail Mason. 1993. "Design Sensitivity in Criminal Justice Experiments." In *Crime and Justice: An Annual Review of Research*, ed. Michael Tonry. Chicago: University of Chicago Press.

Weisel, Deborah. 1999. *Conducting Community Surveys: A Practical Guide for Law Enforcement Agencies.* Washington, DC: U.S. Department of Justice, Office of Justice Programs, Bureau of Justice Statistics and Office of Community Oriented Police Services, October.

Weisel, Deborah Lamm. 2003. "The Sequence of Analysis in Solving Problems." In *Problem-Oriented Policing: From Innovation to Mainstream*, ed. Johannes Knutsson. *Crime Prevention Studies*, vol. 15. Monsey, NY: Criminal Justice Press.

Weiss, Carol H. 1995. "Nothing as Practical as Good Theory: Exploring Theory-Based Evaluation for Comprehensive Community Initiatives for Children and Families." In *New Approaches to Evaluating Community Initiatives: Concepts, Methods, and Contexts*, eds. James P. Connell, Anne C. Kubisch, Lisbeth B. Schorr, and Carol H. Weiss. Washington, DC: Aspen Institute.

Weiss, Robert S. 1994. *Learning from Strangers: The Art and Method of Qualitative Interview Studies.* New York: The Free Press.

Wellings, Kaye, Patrick Branigan, and Kirsti Mitchell. 2000. "Discomfort, Discord, and Discontinuity as Data: Using Focus Groups to Research Sensitive Topics." *Culture, Health, & Sexuality* 2(3): 255–67.

West, Donald J., and David P. Farrington. 1977. *The Delinquent Way of Life.* London: Heinemann.

White, Norman A., and Rolf Loeber. 2008. "Bullying and Special Education as Predictors of Serious

Delinquency." *Journal of Research in Crime and Delinquency* 45(4): 380–97.

Whitt, Hugh P. 2006. "Where Did the Bodies Go? The Social Construction of Suicide Data, New York City, 1976-1992." *Sociological Inquiry* 76(2): 166–87.

Whitzman, Carolyn, Margaret Shaw, Caroline Andrew, and Kathryn Travers. 2009. "The Effectiveness of Women's Safety Audits." *Security Journal* 22(3): 205–18.

Whyte, William Foote. 1993. *Street Corner Society: The Social Structure of an Italian Slum.* 4th ed. Chicago: University of Chicago Press.

Widom, Cathy Spatz. 1989. "Child Abuse, Neglect, and Adult Behavior: Research Design and Findings on Criminality, Violence, and Child Abuse." *American Journal of Orthopsychiatry* 59(3): 355–67.

Widom, Cathy Spatz. 1992. *The Cycle of Violence.* Research in Brief. Washington, DC: U.S. Department of Justice, Office of Justice Programs, National Institute of Justice, October.

Widom, Cathy Spatz, Barbara Luntz Weiler, and Linda B. Cotler. 1999. "Childhood Victimization and Drug Abuse: A Comparison of Prospective and Retrospective Findings." *Journal of Consulting and Clinical Psychology* 67(6): 867–80.

Williams, Terry, Eloise Dunlap, Bruce D. Johnson, and Ansley Hamid. 1992. "Personal Safety in Dangerous Places." *Journal of Contemporary Ethnography* 21(3): 343–74.

Wilson, James Q., and Richard J. Herrnstein. 1985. *Crime and Human Nature.* New York: Simon and Schuster.

Wilson, James Q., and George Kelling. 1982. "Broken Windows: The Police and Neighborhood Safety." *Atlantic Monthly* March: 29–38.

Wilson, Meagan Meuchel. 2014. *Hate Crime Victimization, 2004-2012—Statistical Tables.* BJS Statistical Tables. Washington, DC: U.S. Department of Justice, Office of Justice Programs, Bureau of Justice Statistics, July.

Wilson, William Julius. 1996. *When Work Disappears: The World of the New Urban Poor.* New York: Knopf.

Wolcott, Harry. 1994. *Transforming Qualitative Data: Description, Analysis and Interpretation.* Thousand Oaks, CA: Sage Publications.

Wolfgang, Marvin E., Robert M. Figlio, and Thorsten Sellin. 1972. *Delinquency in a Birth Cohort.* Chicago: University of Chicago Press.

Wolfgang, Marvin E., Robert M. Figlio, Paul E. Tracy, and Simon I. Singer. 1985. *The National Survey of Crime Severity.* Washington, DC: U.S. Department of Justice, Office of Justice Programs, Bureau of Justice Statistics, NCJ-96017.

Wooten, Harold B., and Herbert J. Hoelter. 1998. "Operation Spotlight: The Community Probation-Community Police Team Process." *Federal Probation* 62(2): 30–35.

World Health Organization. 2003. *WHO Ethical and Safety Recommendations for Interviewing Trafficked Women.* Geneva: World Health Organization.

Wright, Doug, Peggy Barker, Joseph Gfroerer, and Lanny Piper. 2002. "Summary of NHSDA Design Changes in 1999." Chapter 2. In *Redesigning an Ongoing National Household Survey: Methodological Issues.* Publication no. SMA 03-3768, eds. Joseph Gfroerer, Joe Eyerman, and James Chromy. Rockville, MD: Office of Applied Studies, Substance Abuse and Mental Health Services Administration. Accessed 14 December 2006. http://www.oas.samhsa.gov/redesigningNHSDA.pdf

Wright, Richard T., and Scott H. Decker. 1994. *Burglars on the Job: Streetlife and Residential Break-Ins.* Boston: Northeastern University Press.

Wright, Richard T., and Scott H. Decker. 1997. *Armed Robbers in Action: Stickups and Street Culture.* Boston: Northeastern University Press.

Yin, Robert K. 2008. *Case Study Research: Design and Methods.* 4th ed. Thousand Oaks, CA: Sage Publications.

Zahm, Diana. 2007. *Using Crime Prevention Through Environmental Design in Problem-Solving.* Problem-Oriented Guides for Police. Problem Solving Tools series, no. 8. Washington, DC: U.S. Department of Justice, Office of Community Oriented Policing Services.

Zanin, Nicholas, Jon M. Shane, and Ronald V. Clarke. 2004. *Reducing Drug Dealing in Private Apartment Complexes in Newark, New Jersey.* Final report to the Office of Community Oriented Police Services. Washington, DC: U.S. Department of Justice, Office of Community Oriented Police Services. http://www.popcenter.org/Library/researcherprojects/DrugsApartment.pdf

Author Index

Academy of Criminal Justice Sciences, 38
Adler, Patricia A., 212, 213
Adler, Peter, 212, 213
Aebi, Marcelo F., 37, 72, 274
Ageton, Suzanne S., 273
Akiyama, Yoshio, 200
Allen, Terry D., 114
American Association of University Professors, 41
American Psychological Association, 37
American Sociological Association, 37
Anderson, Craig A., 257
Anderson, Elijah, 222
Andresen, W. Carsten, 244
Andrew, Caroline, 240
Aos, Steve, 280
Appelbaum, Paul S., 18, 257, 272
Argomaniz, Javier, 123–125, 161, 297
Austin, James, 257

Baek, Jong-ho, 119, 292–293
Baker, Al, 202
Banks, Curtis, 43, 44
Barker, Peggy, 188
Barnes, J. C., 274
Baron, Stephen W., 163
Barrios, Luis, 196
Barth, Fredrick, 201

Baumer, Eric, 259
Baumer, Terry, 5, 40, 230, 266, 287–289, 293–295
Beauregard, Eric, 49, 67
Beaver, Kevin M., 274
Beck, Allen, 3
Becker, Howard, 203
Bench, Lawrence L., 114
Bennett, Trevor, 63, 64, 162
Bennis, Jason, 240
Benoit, C., 213
Berenson, Jacqueline A., 18, 257, 272
Berg, Bruce L., 206, 216
Berk, Richard A., 119, 292–293
Bernard, H. Russell, 221
Bernstein, Margaret, 26
Berzofsky, Marcus, 3
Best, Joel, 268
Best, Samuel L., 141
Bichler, Gisela, 241–242, 257
Birks, Melanie, 217
Black, Donald, 266
Black, Michele C., 29, 173
Blumberg, Stephen J., 152
Blumer, Herbert, 218
Blumstein, Alfred, 64–65
Bolling, Keith, 185
Bouchard, Martin, 163
Bourgois, Philippe, 198, 200
Boutwell, Brian B., 274
Bowen, Glenn, 217, 218–219, 223

Bowers, Kate, 29, 36
Braga, Anthony, 131–132, 133, 304
Branigan, Patrick, 217
Brantingham, Patricia L., 198, 230, 306
Brantingham, Paul J., 198, 230, 306
Bratton, William J., 64–65, 268
Bray, Timothy M., 271
Brazell, Diana, 3
Brotherton, David, 196
Brown, Charles E., 6
Brown, Rick, 58
Browning, Katherine, 71
Bryan, Jane, 123–125, 161, 297
Bump, Natalie, 130, 131
Burch, Andrea M., 77
Bureau of Justice Assistance, 238–239
Bureau of Justice Statistics, 159, 256
Bush, Tracey, 247
Bushman, Brad, 257
Butts, Jeffrey A., 249–251

Campbell, Donald T., 62, 63, 116, 120, 121, 126, 130, 131, 132, 296
Canter, David, 198
Cantor, David, 101, 190, 265
Carey, Raymond G., 307
Carroll, Ray, 279
Carson, E. Ann, 259
Casey, Mary Anne, 204

Subject Index

Note: Page numbers followed by f indicate figures; those followed by t indicate tables.